Helping People:
Karen Horney's
Psychoanalytic Approach

Karen Horney

HELPING
PEOPLE:

KAREN HORNEY'S
PSYCHOANALYTIC APPROACH

HAROLD KELMAN, M.D.

Science House
New York
1971

Library of Congress Catalog Card Number: 75-140098
Standard Book Number: 87668-039-2

Designed by Jennifer Mellen

Manufactured by Haddon Craftsmen, Inc.
Scranton, Pennsylvania

To Karen Horney

A pioneer in finding newer ways
for understanding human suffering

Acknowledgments

Acknowledgment is first due to Horney who made this book possible and to Freud on whose pioneering work she built. A debt is owed to the many contributors to psychoanalysis, to my colleagues, and to the many psychiatrists who have critically questioned my ideas.

I am especially indebted to Marianne Horney Eckardt, M.D., for the many helpful suggestions she made regarding her mother's biography. In her letter of November 21, 1969, she wrote, "Your own valuable personal experience with the group or groups, your own personal experience in the travails of her creative work are part of the history and should be included. No one was closer to her over the years than you were." Data about Dr. Horney's brother Bernt was supplied by his son, Dr. Berndt Gramberg-Danielsen of Hamburg, Germany, and to him I give thanks. Of course, the final responsibility for the contents of Dr. Horney's biography is mine.

Particular appreciation is expressed to Dr. Joseph W. Vollmerhausen, co-author of "On Horney's Psychoanalytic Techniques: Developments and Perspectives" which appeared in *Psychoanalytic Tech-*

niques: A Handbook for the Practicing Psychoanalyst, edited by B. B. Wolman and published by Basic Books. Dr. Vollmerhausen made valuable suggestions throughout the writing of this book and contributed a number of illuminating instances from his analytic practice. Acknowledgment is also made to Basic Books for the frequent references to "Classical Psychoanalysis Since 1939" by M. Kanzer and H. P. Blum, also contained in the above volume.

To George P. Brockway, President of W. W. Norton & Co., who gave permission for quotations from Dr. Horney's works, all published by them, my indebtedness is great. I would like to thank the David McKay Company, Inc. and Tavistock Publications Ltd. for permission to quote from, respectively, *Cure for Chaos* by Simon Ramo and *The Basic Fault: Therapeutic Aspects of Regression* by Michael Balint. I wish also to acknowledge frequent reference to the *American Journal of Psychoanalysis* of which I was editor for many years.

Gordon Lander's valuable editorial sugestions significantly added to the book's readability. Hadassah Gold did all things an excellent secretary can do and more. For the cooperation I experienced in the arduous work of an editor and a secretary I am pleased to acknowledge a special debt.

H. K.

Contents

Author's Note

My debt to the many people with whom I have worked is immeasurable. They brought me their pains and their problems and patiently worked with me as I struggled to give meaning to what they told me. An inner wisdom often protected them from the effects of my errors and a deep humanity responded to the occasional glimpse of a truth that I conveyed to them. I believe they would want others — helpers as well as those seeking help — to benefit from what we have learned together. Their identities have, of course, been preserved through the use of fictitious names.

H.K.

Karen Horney, M.D.
1885–1952

Hamburg

Karen Clementine Theodore Horney was born in Hamburg, Germany, on September 16, 1885.

Her father, Bernt Henrik Wackels Danielssen (1835-1910), was a Norwegian sea captain from Bergen who became a German citizen and rose to Commodore of the Hansa Shipping Lines. His influence on Horney's development was limited because of his long absences. A stern and deeply religious man, he was respected by his crews and superiors. Franz Alexander reported Horney as saying: "I can still recall the frightening gaze of my father's blue eyes." *(64)* Horney's eyes were blue, flecked with light green and certainly not frightening.

In her early teens Horney went through an intense religious period, but since this was common among adolescent girls of her time the experience was probably not directly attributable to her father's influence. In her middle teens, she made sea voyages with her father, one around Cape Horn to Peru. These trips stimulated the young girl's interest in travel, in foreign customs, and in wider horizons.

1

Horney's mother, Clothilde Marie van Ronzelen (1852-1911), was Dutch. She was seventeen years younger than her husband, who had four grown children by a previous marriage. A dynamic, intelligent, and imperious beauty, she was the major influence in Horney's life. Humorously deprecating of her husband, particularly of his silences and his Bible-reading, Horney's mother was a free thinker. Dominated by her mother, Horney accepted this evaluation of her father.

Horney's brother, Bernt (1882-1923), older by about four years, was her favorite. Horney accepted her mother's evaluation of him also. In his late teens, as he began going out with girls, Bernt spent less time with his sister. Horney felt rejected and suffered deeply. In later years, Bernt played a limited role in her life. He became a lawyer and died of pneumonia at forty-one.

During her early years, as did many German children of her era, Horney played out in games the lives and exploits of American Indians as portrayed by Karl May, Germany's James Fenimore Cooper. Around eight she vowed blood brotherhood with her friend "Tutti." This ceremony was performed with much solemnity and little blood as they gave each other Indian chieftain names which they used in their lifelong friendship. Horney told me this story with much humor, love, and a certain poignancy.

By the end of the nineteenth century, the feminist movement had broken down some of the barriers against women entering the professions. Still, it was unusual for a woman to become a physician. "According to my own early wishes, I studied medicine."(95) In this pursuit she had the encouragement of her mother. She was always an excellent student, often first in her class, very much liked by her colleagues and highly regarded by her professors. Horney graduated from the Hamburg Johanneum Realgymnasium as a medical student on March 31, 1906. Because her conversational English was superior she received a good grade despite only average composition, — a stimulus, perhaps, which encouraged Horney to become an outstanding stylist.

Berlin

According to the continental custom she spent varying numbers of semesters at the Universities of Freiburg, Göttingen and Berlin, graduating from the latter on December 28, 1911.

"After having finished the state examination I worked for three years in a psychiatric clinic [Berlin-Lankwitz Sanitarium] and for one year at the neurological institute of Herman Oppenheimer, who was then the most famous German neurologist. During the war I had charge of a military neurological hospital."(95) Berlin University awarded her a medical degree on January 15, 1915 for her dissertation, *"Ein Kasuisticher Beitrag zur Frage Der Traumatischen Psychosen."(1)* On October 30, 1909, "in the midst of my medical studies, I married" Dr. Heinrich Wilhelm Oscar Horney (1882-1948).

Brigitte, their first child, was born in 1911. She became a famous actress in the theater and in films. In addition to her deft talent for satirical humor, she is admired for her ability to portray complete naturalness. A dominating personality, Horney saw much of her own mother in Brigitte and was greatly influenced by her. Marianne, two years younger, temperamentally quieter and more introverted, followed a scholarly path and became a physician and a psychoanalyst. Renate, four years younger, impressed Horney as the most vivacious and social of her daughters. A mischievous tomboy in her youth, she married early and emigrated to Mexico. There she adapted with delight the Mexican way of life.

Horney loved Berlin and the Berliners, with their deep ties to their city and their special brand of humor which mocks life's absurdities even in the midst of great adversities. The jokes about the Kaiser, about the astronomically inflated paper money during the '20s, about Hitler and Goebbels during the '30s and the happenings during the war were myriad. Horney related many of them to me. After a particularly devastating night air raid, one Berliner laughed uproariously on meeting his friend the following morning: "That will fix them. The next time they come they will have to bring their own buildings."

Horney's humor had some of the qualities of the Berliner. Although she was not a good raconteur, her enjoyment of these stories while relating them was infectious.

Horney had a deep understanding of the human drama and of human foibles. She retained, however, a childlike wonder about life, which accounted, in part, for the freshness with which she approached problems and the abundance and originality of what she produced.

Although I often asked Dr. Horney why she has studied medicine and become interested in psychoanalysis, I can recall no illuminating replies. In 1946, in reply to a request for biographical material, her daughter Marianne wrote: "My mother's early personal life was difficult and complex. School and the theater were her early territories of pleasure and passion. Always an intense student, she pursued her professional development with remarkable sureness of aim. She knew early in her medical studies that she would study psychoanalysis. What influence led her to such a decision I do not know. Her keen sense of the drama of human existence provided the material for her ever ongoing pursuit of a theoretical system for neurotic development."*(64, p. 451)*

Indeed, although music did not hold her interest, often she sat enthralled in the top stall of a theater rather than being at school.

Horney's own account of her early interest in psychoanalysis is briefly factual: "In the midst of my [medical] studies I became interested in psychoanalysis, had my training analysis with Karl Abraham and have been, since 1911, a member of the Berlin Psychoanalytic Society . . . . After the war I started my analytic practice."*(95a)* Sometime after 1920, when Hanns Sachs came to Berlin, she did further analytic work with him. From both analyses she felt she had derived only limited benefit.

In 1917, six years before Freud's *The Ego and the Id,* Horney's "The Technique of Psychoanalytic Therapy"*(2)* appeared. "Psychoanalysis can free a human being who has been tied hand and foot. It cannot give him new arms and legs." She added: "Psychoanalysis, however, has shown us that much that we have regarded as constitutional merely represents a blockage of growth which can be lifted." Here are the first outlines of her growth-oriented, life-affirming, freedom-seeking philosophy. For Horney, constitution was not something fixed at birth and unchanging throughout life, but a dynamic process which presented plastic possibilities to be shaped by interaction with the environment. This was four years before Kretschmer's *Physique and Character (98)* appeared, which presented constitution as a fixed quantity. His position subsequently evolved to regard constitution as a source of dynamic possibilities and a force for their unfolding. This theoretical evolution suggests why, in 1950, he invited Horney to join the editorial board of the *Zeitschrift für Psychotherapie.*

In the 1917 paper Horney defined her holistic concept of blockages, which contrasts with Freud's mechanistic notion of resistance. Also evident is her emphasis on the basic unity of theory and therapy: "The analytical theories have grown out of observations and experiences which were made in applying this method. The theories, in turn, later exerted their influence on the practice." Horney always began with and returned to clinical observation. In his 1933 discussion of Horney's "Maternal Conflicts," Zilboorg said this is "clinical psychoanalysis" which emphasizes the need for "clinical observation, of clinical phenomena, in clinical circumstances" so essential to counteract "the unusually strong and undeservedly popular trend toward technical problems and theoretical considerations."*(24)*

What Horney wrote in 1917 questioned the foundations of Freud's theories already extant and would apply equally to much of what was still to be formulated. Maybe because she was still so young in the field, because her ideas were still in their formative stages, because she was a woman, and because Freud had stimulated an interest in feminine psychology, her interests became focused in that direction.

"My scientific interest concentrated more and more on female psychology and connected fields such as the differentiation between masculine and feminine psychology, general disturbances in the relation between the two sexes, marriage problems. As psychology has been until now mostly worked at from the side of men, it seems to me to be the given task for a woman psychologist — or at least I think it to be mine — to work out a fuller understanding for specifically female trends and attitudes in life."*(95)* If she had first to confront the problems of so-called feminine psychology to transcend them, she also had to come to terms with a so-called male psychology to arrive at a whole person philosophy and psychology.

"Since 1920, when the Berlin Analytical Institute was founded by Max Eitingon, I have participated in the work there — partly in organizing all that had to do with training young analysts such as working out the *Richtlinien zur Zulassung für die Ausbildung* [Guidelines for Admission to Analytic Training], or in judging the candidates, as to whether or not they seemed to be suitable for our training. On the other hand I gave lectures and seminars, particularly on analytical technique, also trying to outline the value of psychoanalysis for the general practice of medicine and for the gynecologist. Now and then I was asked to read papers outside the Institute, such as in the Society of Sexual Knowledge, in the Institute for the History of Medicine, in the Sociological branch of the Medical Society to Combat Venereal Disease, in the *Arztliche Gesellschaft für Psycho-Therapie* [Medical Society for Psycho-therapy] and others."*(95)*

There was great vitality and competence among the many gifted men and women of the Berlin Psychoanalytic Society and Institute from its founding in 1910 by Abraham. A new era began in 1920 with the founding of the Berlin Polyclinic by Eitingon, assisted by Abraham and Simmel. The first low-cost psychoanalytic clinic, it contributed to Berlin becoming a center for psychoanalytic education and training analysis. Those who were trained and taught there had a feeling of living in a great time. Many of them became prime movers — the theoreticians, the teachers, the therapists, and the organizers of what was to be psychoanalysis for the next half century.

In Berlin at this time was Harald Schultz-Henke, whose publications influenced Horney's thinking (in 1945 his influence and theoretical ideas culminated with the founding of the very vital and still expanding neo-Freudian *Deutsche Analytische Gesellschaft*).

Alexander was the "first student" at the Berlin Institute. In 1921 Freud awarded him "a prize for the best clinical essay."*(64, p. 386)* To Rado, Alexander's old friend from Budapest, Freud privately remarked: "You will see — this man will do a great deal for psychoanalysis." And so did Rado, who came first to Berlin in 1922, and then to New York in 1931 where he organized "a psychoanalytic institute on the Berlin Psychoanalytic model."*(64, p. 243)* At Columbia University in 1944 he helped found the first psychoanalytic institute in a university.

To Berlin in 1920 came Hanns Sachs, author of *Freud, Master and Friend* and to Boston in 1932 where he became the senior analyst. In 1921 Melanie Klein arrived in Berlin. Five years later she went to London where she founded her own school of thought. Siegfried Bernfeld was in Berlin from 1926 to 1932. After many vicissitudes, he arrived in San Francisco in 1937, a respected scholar and senior analyst.

Among those trained in Berlin were Edward and James Glover, Ella Freeman Sharpe, and Theodor Reik.

At the Berlin Institute Horney analyzed a number, supervised more and many more were in her classes. I have met many in the United States who knew Horney in Berlin, Weigert, for example. *(85)* In Europe I've met others — Gustav Bally of Zurich; Harald Schjelderup of Oslo; and Stefan Betlheim of Zagreb. I have met many others in out of the way places during the course of lecture tours around the world. Horney's personal influence has been both numerically great and geographically widespread. The impact of her books has been global. They have been translated into thirteen languages including Yugoslav, Persian, Greek, and Japanese.

Horney saw and had brief contacts with Freud at the annual Psychoanalytic Congresses. When she spoke of him I sensed a feeling of respect and awe. More than once I asked her why she had never visited him in Vienna, but I sensed her discomfort when I did so. Her reply, "Maybe I should have," while conveying her unhappiness that she had not visited Freud also suggested that the thought of such a visit stirred up an uneasy mixture of feelings. I believe some of these stemmed from her unresolved problems with authority — male authority in particular.

What Freud felt about Horney we may infer from his responses to her papers on feminine psychology. They occurred in the face of his refusal to become involved in polemics, or to allow discussion of papers following their presentation. With the passing years Freud's comments became sharper, possibly because her ideas grew increasingly challenging, while he advanced in years and his health declined.

Feminine Psychology

In "Some Psychological Consequences of the Anatomical Distinction Between the Sexes" Freud said: "In the valuable and com-

6

prehensive studies upon the masculinity and castration complex in women by Abraham (1921), Horney (1923), and Helene Deutsch (1925), there is much that touches closely upon what I have written but nothing that coincides completely, so that here again I feel justified in publishing this paper."*(100, p. 197)*

In "Female Sexuality" he wrote: "Some authors are inclined to disparage the importance of the child's first, most primal libidinal impulses, laying stress rather on later developmental processes, so that — putting this view in its extreme form — all that the former can be said to do is to indicate certain trends, while amounts of energy [*Intensitäten*] with which these trends are pursued are drawn from later regressions and reaction-formations. Thus, for example, K. Horney (1926) is of the opinion that we greatly overestimate the girl's primary penis-envy and that the strength of her subsequent striving towards masculinity is to be attributed to a *secondary* penis-envy, which is used to ward off her feminine impulses, especially those connected with her attachment to her father. This does not agree with the impression that I myself have formed."*(101, p. 271)*

Freud was consistent in his opinion. Jones stated: "There is a healthy suspicion growing that men analysts have been led to adopt an unduly phallo-centric view of the problems in question, the importance of the female organs being correspondingly underestimated." *(102, p. 459)* Freud responded: "A similar objection applies to Jones' view (1927) that the phallic phase in girls represents a secondary, protective reaction rather than a genuine stage of development. This does not correspond to either the dynamic or the chronological conditions."*(101, p. 272)*

The following, in *An Outline of Psychoanalysis,* may have been a response to Horney's paper, "The Denial of the Vagina."*(22)* "The occurrence of early vaginal excitations is often asserted. But it is most probably a question of excitation in the clitoris, that is, in an organ analogous to the penis, so that this fact would not preclude us from describing the phase as phallic."*(103, p. 29)*

Embryonic research has contradicted the primacy Freud gave to the penis and to the clitoris being "analogous to" it. Initial anatomical bisexuality does not occur. All mammalian embryos, male and female, are morphologically female during early fetal life. Human male genitals appear as a differentiation from the female in the sixth week of embryonic life. *(104)*

"Referring to the pre-Oedipus phase in the little girl's development," Freud wrote that "everything connected with this first mother attachment has in analysis seemed to me so elusive . . . . It would in fact appear that women-analysts — for instance, Jeanne Lampl de Groot and Helene Deutsch — had been able to apprehend the facts with greater ease and clearness because they had the advantage of being suitable mother-substitutes in the transference situation."*(101, p. 254)* But what Karen Horney found, as a mother-substitute, "in the transference situation" Freud did not find "suitable."

Regarding "the lack of agreement among analysts," Freud maintained that "We shall not be so very greatly surprised if a woman analyst who has not been sufficiently convinced of the intensity of her own desire for a penis also fails to assign an adequate importance to that factor in her patients."*(103, p. 107)* Here Freud seemed to have disregarded his own admonition: "The use of analysis as a weapon of controversy obviously leads to no decision."*(101, p. 258)*

But history does add a clarifying perspective. Freud felt Ferenczi was asking for too much when he expected that in a successful analysis penis envy and the struggle against passivity would be resolved. "When we have reached the wish for a penis and the masculine protest, we have penetrated all the psychological strata and reached 'bedrock' . . . . Our task is accomplished . . . . The repudiation of femininity must surely be a biological fact, part of the great riddle of sex." *(105, pp. 356-7)*

Many of the biological "bedrock" facts and sexual riddles have since been resolved by Freud's own disciples, and they confirm many of the positions that Horney had taken years earlier. To mention one more: Comparing the male ideas about girls and the theory of feminine development, Horney was struck by a "remarkable parallelism." Quoting Georg Simmel, philosopher of culture, on the "essentially masculine" orientation of our society, Horney stated that having assumed a primary penis envy by "a-posteriori reasoning" the logic for its "enormous dynamic power" was arrived at. *(5, pp. 325-33)*

Freud's male oriented theory led Horney "as a woman" to "ask, in amazement, and what about motherhood? and the blissful consciousness of bearing a new life within oneself? and the ineffable happiness of the increasing expectation of the appearance of this new being? and the joy when it finally makes its appearance and one holds it for the first time in one's arms? and the deep pleasurable feeling of satisfaction in suckling it and the happiness of the whole period when the infant needs her care? . . . When one begins, as I did," said Horney, "to analyze men only after a fairly long experience of analyzing women, one receives a most surprising impression of the intensity of this envy of pregnancy, childbirth, and motherhood as well as of breasts and of the act of suckling."*(5, p. 329)*

Zilboorg spoke of the "woman envy on the part of man, that is psychogenetically older and therefore more fundamental." He added that "deeper studies of man's psyche will" lead to a discounting of "the androcentric veil which . . . has covered . . . important psychological data."*(106)* Anthropologists are familiar with these various forms of envy by men of female anatomical characteristics and functions.

K. Van Leewen wrote in 1966, that "comparatively little attention has been focused in psychoanalysis on man's envy of the female sex and childbearing functions, in contrast to woman's envy of man's penis, which has long held a central position in the understanding of female psychology." What Van Leewen discovered in the analysis of a young man undertaken while she was pregnant, *(107)* Horney had discussed in 1924.

The most significant of Horney's papers on feminine psychology are in *Feminine Psychology. (63)* It received unanimously favorable reviews, including one from a Freudian analyst: "The publication of this beautifully written volume of papers is most timely. Although dating from 1922 to 1936 they have a surprisingly modern ring and a stimulating pertinence to current problems and interests .... Altogether this is a stimulating and important book."*(108)* Within the year it was reprinted by Allen & Unwin for the British Empire and in the year thereafter was translated into Swedish, French and Spanish. It had an immediate large sale and was a selection of several book clubs.

Chicago

On May 13, 1932, Alfred K. Stern, President of the Board of Trustees of the Chicago Institute for Psychoanalysis and an officer of the Julius Rosenwald Fund, wrote the American Consul in Berlin: "I am very much interested in the development of a Chicago Institute for Psychoanalysis. The particular reason for going ahead with this Institute now is the fact that it is possible to secure the services as associate director of an eminent European scientist, Dr. Karen Horney."

Alexander had come to Chicago in 1930 to fill the first university chair of psychoanalysis. After a trial there and a short period in Boston he returned to Chicago to form an independent Institute until such time as universities would fully accept psychoanalysis.

"Franz Alexander knew Horney well in Berlin. He was deeply impressed by the outstanding clarity of her thought and by her characteristic way of always beginning her theoretical approach from her clinical observations. She was, he has said, one of the most independent, skeptical, and questioning thinkers in the Berlin group, yet she was at the same time a 'full-fledged Freudian.' "

Alexander "needed a senior analyst as associate director of the Chicago Institute for Psychoanalysis."*(64, p. 453)* Recalling the early winter events of 1931, Horney told me: "One night I got a transatlantic call from Alexander to come to Chicago. I was surprised and decided to go in a few days." Her interest in the United States

9

and her regard for Alexander may have influenced her decision. To my knowledge the political situation in Germany was not a significant influencing factor.

Horney came to Chicago in the summer of 1932, with her fifteen-year-old daughter Renate. Marianne, who was in the midst of her pre-medical training, followed a year later. Immediately on arrival Horney started training and supervisory analyses and teaching. She also began lecturing, in English, before a variety of organizations. Among them were the American Orthopsychiatric Association and the American Psychoanalytic Association, as well as numerous surgical, gynecological, neurological, and social worker societies.

The association between Horney and Alexander was "neither productive nor congenial," and she came to New York in the summer of 1934.

In 1964, Alexander was invited to give the Twelfth Karen Horney Lecture. In it Alexander said: "Both Horney and I believed that psychoanalytic theory and practice required revision and clarification of many obscure, never fully-tested assumptions. However, I felt at that time (the early '30s) just as I feel today, that these revisions do not require discarding the basic concepts of Freud, and particularly that the observational foundation of psychoanalysis represents a solid body of knowledge on which further advancements can safely rest. Horney opposed this evolutionary orientation and tried to rebuild the whole theory. Hers was a revolutionary approach which implied the repudiation of many of Freud's fundamental conceptions."

Although her publications "had a definite influence on psychoanalytic thought and practice . . . in my opinion, they did not replace successfully the Freudian foundation of our discipline. Many of Horney's contributions, however, appear to me of definite value, and I feel it a distinction to honor her memory with this presentation."*(88)*

"Alexander found three major contributions in Horney's work: (1) her emphasis that general needs lead to the importance of the erogenous zones, rather than the reverse; (2) that ego development does not stop at the sixth year of age; and (3) her emphasis on the present situation."*(64, pp. 453-4)* This evaluation was most likely made in the early '60s.

The Neurotic Personality of Our Time
New Ways in Psychoanalysis

In New York, Horney continued with training and supervisory analyses, teaching and writing. The New School for Social Research, an experiment in education founded in 1919, rapidly made its mark under the guidance of Alvin Johnson. His "University in Exile" (opened in 1933) became the home of many of Europe's greatest minds, driven to our shores by Hitler. Johnson encouraged Horney to come to the New School. He introduced her to W. W. Norton, another man of vision, who created the publishing house which produced all of Horney's books. Out of her New School lectures came *The Neurotic Personality of Our Time, (33)* translated into ten languages and now in its twenty-seventh printing. All of Horney's subsequent books were evolved through sequences of lectures given at the New School, at the New York Psychoanalytic Institute, at the American Institute for Psychoanalysis and, for a short period, at the New York Medical College.

From the solid ground of her basic philosophy, outlined in 1917, always adhering to clinical data, Horney worked at what confronted her. Individuals — their problems, the consequences of environmental impingements on them, whether family, culture, or cosmos — held the center of her interest.

Feminine psychology was her main concern almost from the beginning of her analytic training. By working in this area and through her reading in social philosophy and anthropology, she became more sharply aware of societal influences on all people and how they differently influence the lives of men and women, not only determining their roles, but also the structure of their theories of psychology. Earlier there had been the impact of other countries seen on sea voyages with her father and, in childhood games, the identification with American Indians. The confrontation with life in the United States now sharpened her awareness of the influence of environmental factors. All of these experiences crucially determined the writing of *The Neurotic Personality of Our Time. (33)* "The main contention here was that neuroses are brought about by cultural factors — which more specifically meant that neuroses were generated by disturbances in human relationships."*(39, p. 12)*

In her introduction, Horney explained: "The purpose I have in mind in writing this book has been to give an accurate picture of the neurotic person who lives among us, with the conflicts which actually move him, with his anxieties, his suffering, and the many difficulties he has in his relations with others as well as with himself. I am not concerned here with any particular type or types of neurosis, but have concentrated on the character structure which recurs in nearly all neurotic persons of our time in one or another form." *(33, p. vii)*

Horney considered infantile anxiety neither the sole, sufficient, nor necessary cause of later neurotic development because cultural factors might intensify or mitigate it. In the childhood history of adult neurotics she found that there had been a lack of genuine warmth, arousing hostility in the child which had to be repressed, thereby reinforcing existing anxiety.

The resultant feeling "is an insidiously increasing, all-pervading feeling of being lonely and helpless in a hostile world. The acute individual reactions to individual provocations crystallize into a character attitude. This attitude as such does not constitute a neurosis but is the nutritive soil out of which a definite neurosis may develop at any time. Because of the fundamental role this attitude plays in neurosis I have given it a special designation: the basic anxiety; it is inseparably interwoven with a basic hostility."*(33, p. 89)* With each subsequent book the concept of basic anxiety was reformulated and developed.

The *Angst der kreatur* of German philosophical and religious thinking is similar to basic anxiety regarding the element of helplessness toward greater powers but different in that "it does not connote hostility on the part of those powers."*(33, p. 95)* The basic anxiety concept reflects existential thinking two decades before it found expression in the United States. Although Horney never regarded herself as a phenomenologist or existentialist, her use of the phenomenological approach is evident in all her work.

The existential orientation is clearly evident in "The Dread of Women"*(19)* where she describes the ontological differences between *being* and *having* — and by implication *doing* — in the sexual functioning of men and women. Her works make frequent reference to existentialist thinkers to whom she expresses her debt: Kierkegaard, Nietzsche, Scheler, Tillich, and to Zen Buddhism, particularly to D. T. Suzuki.

In his review of *The Neurotic Personality of Our Time (33)* Jones wrote: "This volume appears to be addressed to the public . . . . She constantly deprecates what she considers to be Freud's exaggerated views on biological factors" and sees "a great part of what appears as sexuality" as having "in reality very little to do with it." Jones considered her position a "dangerous half truth." Her attitude toward the "overdetermination of sexual impulses" by anxiety making them less sexual he saw as "emptying the baby with the bath." Jones closed his review by noting that "the name of no English analyst is among the numerous analytical writings referred to."*(109)*

Alexander's lead review of five pages is of a different order. "Her polemical fervor involves the author in many theoretical arguments which detract attention from her valuable contributions: the fine descriptions of emotional connections. Here her independent, scrutinizing attitude, uninfluenced by accepted abstractions shows its constructive side. She studies the material with her own clinically trained eyes and is never satisfied with mechanisms but only with well understood psychological connections. Here lies her strength and her contribution toward counteracting a current trend to substitute theoretical abstractions for psychological understanding."(82) Although their parting in 1934 had been strained, by 1937 the American Psychoanalytic Association was considering dropping Alexander for his heretical ideas, a factor which may have influenced the tenor of his review.

In *New Ways in Psychoanalysis* (1939), now in its nineteenth printing, Horney defined her position with reference to Freud. "The more I took a critical stand toward a series of psychoanalytical theories, the more I realized the constructive value of Freud's fundamental findings and the more paths opened up for the understanding of psychological problems."(35, p. 8)

Horney saw "as the most fundamental and most significant of Freud's findings his doctrines that psychic processes are strictly determined, that actions and feelings may be determined by unconscious motivations and that motivations driving us are emotional forces."(35, p. 18) She also found significant Freud's concept of repression; his elucidation of the meaningfulness of dreams; and his pointing out that neuroses are the result of conflict, that anxiety plays a central role in neuroses, and that childhood experiences have a crucial significance for neurotic development. The concepts of resistance and transference and the technique of free association she regarded among Freud's most valuable contributions. But in *New Ways* and in her later writings her formulations of these issues not only varied from Freud but also evolved in crucial ways.

Stern, chairman of the Educational Committee of the New York Psychoanalytic Institute, reviewed *New Ways*. He felt it was a "very readable though somewhat ambitious book." While recognizing many of Freud's fundamental ideas he added, "She dismisses most of his other almost equally far-reaching concepts." Stern comments on her emphasis on social factors rather than on structural ones. About her therapeutic approach he concludes that it "sounds rather more heterodox than in fact it is," and that she "does not stray very far from a reasonably analytic attitude." He concludes that Horney's book "does not always give a fair picture of the views it is attacking, and that, when the attack is over, the target does not seem greatly damaged."(111)

"On its constructive side" he saw her "psychological observations" as "undeniably true and shrewdly seen . . . . One cannot help feeling that they stay on a comparatively superficial level and do not take us very very deep into the recesses of the human mind . . . . It seems that, on the whole, Dr. Horney does not lead us so far astray from the fields of orthodox analysis as she wishes to make out. As far as her positive contributions go, there should not be much difficulty in introducing a number of them into the regular body of psychoanalytic knowledge — if they have not already found a place there — without disturbing its existing structure to any great extent." Stern's concerns are as evident as the spirit of the review.

In his six-page lead review Fenichel wrote: "Because the conceptions of Dr. Horney have little to do with psychoanalysis that is not to say they are false . . . . When Dr. Horney stresses the fact that psychoanalysis has long neglected character problems . . . she is right . . . . In Dr. Horney's books there are . . . very good and important contributions to the description of . . . unified defense systems . . . . Dr. Horney makes one criticism of psychoanalysis which is not wholly unjustified. The structure of the human being is determined constitutionally and environmentally. How much this 'environment' is culturally determined has until recently received too little attention . . . . I am convinced of the greater significance of psychoanalysis amplified by a more comprehensive sociological conception of the processes which influence the individual in human society, but I refer to *sound* psychoanalysis — the kind Dr. Horney rejects." *(112)* Greenson, Fenichel's analysand and biographer, *(64, p. 443)* wrote, "Some of his book reviews are masterpieces particularly his reviews of the works of Karen Horney and Erich Fromm." The authority and dignity of this one supports this view.

Having defined her agreements and differences with Freud, Horney was now in a position to develop her own ideas. Studying her publications from her first, in 1917, to her last, in 1952, is to participate in the creative process of an observant clinician, a dedicated therapist, and a rigorous theoretician. Always she started with the clinical data, out of which came the hypothesis to be again tested against the clinical facts. She might start with a limited clinical construct, move on to a molar hypothesis, and then on to a higher order abstraction having a unifying function. This is clearly portrayed in the movement from the concept of basic conflict in *Our Inner Conflicts, (39)* which focused on relations to others, to central inner conflict in *Neurosis and Human Growth, (49)* which unified the interpersonal and the intrapsychic, the moves toward health and the moves toward sickness. Always there was the spirit of searching, testing, revising, changing, dropping old and adding new hypotheses.

14

The Psychoanalytic Movement, 1934-1941

Horney came to New York at a crucial time in the history of the psychoanalytic movement. American psychoanalysts were receiving a more considerate hearing in the councils of the International Psycho-Analytical Association. Regulations for "admission to training were amended to suit American requirements" in 1934.

In 1935 the constitution and by-laws of the American Psychoanalytic Association were ratified. Impetus for these changes come from the increasing strictures on European analysts imposed by Hitler, the immigration of many, and the disintegration of the International Training Committee. *(64, p. 556)* In 1936 Jones suggested that the American Psychoanalytic Association be divorced from all control by that committee. The center of psychoanalysis was shifting from Europe to the United States, with the largest group in New York rapidly being augmented by refugees from Germany and Austria. By 1939 one heard more German than English at the meetings of the New York Psychoanalytic Society, a condition soon made even more obvious by the departure of American analysts into the armed forces.

"In 1939 the American Psychoanalytic Association declared its independence of the International Psycho-Analytical Association and made it very clear that actions of the American would no longer be subject to approval by the International."*(64, p. 558)* But soon the American would become as authoritarian as the authorities against which it had rebelled. The deference to the Europeans who had come earlier and to those who arrived later was a crucial factor. The authoritarian attitude of these Europeans was passed on to the American analysts they trained. These, in turn, encouraged the same tendencies in succeeding generations.

In "Psychoanalysis in the United States," Millet described the evolution and repercussions of these developments: "Teachers who felt unduly restricted by the regulations and teaching schedules of the New York Psychoanalytic Society's Educational Committee became increasingly restive."*(64, p. 559)*

Clara Thompson, M.D., was a participant in those happenings. In 1933 she returned to America from Budapest where she had been analyzed by Ferenczi, and moved from Baltimore to New York. Thompson, Sullivan, Silverberg (who had been analyzed by Alexander in Berlin), and Horney met regularly on Monday nights. Sullivan named the group the Zodiac Club. "In this zodiac, Sullivan was represented by a horse, Clara Thompson by a cat, Silverberg by a gazelle, and Karen Horney by a water buffalo."*(113, p. 358)*

Erich Fromm, who had come to the United States in 1933 to be a guest lecturer at the Chicago Institute for Psychoanalysis, moved to New York in 1934 and became the fifth member of the club. Soon he was lecturing at the New School for Social Research. Thompson "was devoted to Fromm, who later psychoanalyzed her, and she greatly admired Karen Horney for her penetrating observation and pithy style."*(113, p. 361)* In 1936 Horney persuaded Thompson to leave the Washington-Baltimore Society and join the New York Society, where she soon became a training analyst. *(114)*

Some indication of the professional reaction to Horney's published work has been given in the reviews previously quoted. The true magnitude, however, of this reaction is vividly described by Clara Thompson: "When Horney's *The Neurotic Personality of Our Time* came out it produced a landslide of anger. The first thing that happened was that her students never graduated. The next step was to take away Horney's status as a training analyst and demote her to a 'lecturer.' Kardiner's students began having troubles. Then mine began to be afraid, too. When they took away Horney's training analyst status, five of us resigned from the New York Psychoanalytic."*(114)*

The night of Horney's demotion was a most dramatic one. Psychoanalysis as a movement was never the same thereafter. Its organizational aspects, its methods of training, and its influence on psychiatry and a host of ancillary disciplines was permanently altered. At that meeting faculty and students were outraged by the blatant violation of academic freedom. Almost fifty percent of those present refrained from voting.

After the vote, Horney and the four others "marched jubilantly away from the Institute, led by Clara singing one of her favorite hymns, 'Go Down, Moses' — a hymn celebrating the liberation of the Jews from the tyranny of the Egyptian Pharaoh."*(113, p. 362)* The choice of the hymn was paradoxical and most meaningful. Thompson and Horney, the two *goyim* of the five, had many friendships with Jews and had left behind in the New York Psychoanalytic a group of which the large majority were Jews.

Horney's close friendships with Jews went back to her earliest years. While their marriage certificate stated that she and her husband were of the "Evangelical" religion, the witnesses were Mrs. Ida Behrmann and Louis Grote, two Jews. From the time she came to Berlin most of her friends were Jews. With pride, genuine pleasure, and a girlish laughter, which I heard when she was deeply moved and pleased, she told me she had been elected an Honorary Jew by her colleagues at the Institute. After coming to the United

States most of her friends were Jews. Her three daughters are married to Jews.

With the advent of Hitler, the sums of money and numbers of food and clothing parcels to Germany steadily mounted. As Horney's fame spread, more and more asked for, and received, signed affidavits from her which enabled them to emigrate to the United States. She supplied them with funds and helped them to find positions and to set up a new life. Although not directly involved in politics, in 1941 she expressed her position as "outspokenly anti-Fascist." She enunciated her belief that "democratic principles in sharp contrast to Fascist ideology . . . uphold the independence and the strength of the individual and assert his right to happiness."(96)

Horney, while politically informed, had an aversion to its forms of operation. This attitude also extended to organizations in general, administrative functioning, and the whole structure required for group activities. She was most reluctant to accept official positions, resented the role of leadership in organizations, was irked by the burden of meetings, and delegated her functions as soon as she could if she couldn't withdraw from the position. Partly because of her desire to get out of such tasks, her selection of the people to whom she delegated responsibilities was often dubious. When events confirmed their limitations she was surprised, confused, and pained.

Before that memorable night in the spring of 1941, there had been talk among the students of Horney, Thompson, Kardiner, and Rado that a split would occur and that a national organization would be formed, possibly joined by David Levy, the progressive Baltimore-Washington Society, and the Chicago Psychoanalytic Institute headed by Sullivan and Alexander.

The Association for the Advancement of Psychoanalysis

A national organization was founded in May, 1941, the Association for the Advancement of Psychoanalysis (AAP). Sullivan did not join. Kardiner, Rado, and Levy did not join either, but with eight others organized, in 1945, what became the Association for Psychoanalytic Medicine. Although Alexander participated in the programs of the AAP, he did not join.

The nucleus of the AAP was formed of the five who left the Institute: Karen Horney, Clara Thompson, Bernard S. Robbins, Harmon S. Ephron and Sarah R. Kelman (my sister). "With us went fourteen students; my students, Horney's and Kardiner's," reported Thompson on March 15, 1955. "Silverberg and Fromm joined the five, beginning the Association for the Advancement of Psychoanalysis and the American Institute for Psychoanalysis . . . . We were starting out with high hopes."*(114)*

Thompson's "high hopes" for the AAP were not to last: "Horney was the first Dean of this new group. Presently it became apparent that no new students were being sent to either Fromm or me. Fromm, Horney and I were the first training analysts. Then she made Ephron and Robbins training analysts. The next thing we knew, Fromm was deprived of his status as a training analyst. This time Fromm and I and our students left. Sullivan joined us and we formed the Washington School of Psychiatry" in 1943. It was renamed the William Alanson White Institute of Psychiatry, Psychoanalysis and Psychology in 1946 and celebrated twenty-five years of successful and productive operation in 1968. "Several of Kardiner's students went back to the New York Psychoanalytic Institute and got themselves reanalyzed for their rebellion and became good New York Psychoanalytic members."*(114)*

Judd Marmor, M.D., one of the founders of the AAP, recalled that with the resignation of Thompson some of the "original idealism seemed to have been tarnished. There was a growing concern . . . that the Association seemed to be becoming a 'Horney Group' rather than . . . an Institute and Society in which varying points of view would have free expression and would be freely taught."*(115)*

Stephen P. Jewett, Professor of Psychiatry at the New York Medical College, another founding member of the AAP, was willing to sponsor a full psychoanalytic training program within the framework of his department of psychiatry. Many favored it, according to Marmor, because it "not only would be reaffirming the roots of psychoanalysis in medical practice, but also we would be bringing it into a university setting, where academic freedom was a long-established and hallowed principle . . . . Horney, however, objected, on the grounds that the autonomy of psychoanalytic education would be jeopardized. To those of us who favored the move, this seemed to confirm our fears that what Horney wanted to do, consciously or unconsciously, was to perpetuate her own particular school of thought rather than sponsor an open system of psychoanalytic training. Although most of us admired her tremendously, we did not wish to be her 'disciples' or anyone else's. Consequently in 1944 a number withdrew and organized the first medical school-affiliated psychoanalytic training institute in America at the New York Medical College . . . . The faculty . . . represented a wide spectrum of psychoanalytic viewpoints."*(115)* In 1969 "The Comprehensive Course in Psychoanalysis" celebrated twenty-five years of highly successful operation. *(116)*

18

The people who came together in 1941 to found the AAP all had a deep commitment to the advancement of psychoanalysis. Many of them had been, and continued to be, friends before and after these breaks. By 1955, a number began to look for ways of coming back together in a national organization.

The American Academy of Psychoanalysis, founded on April 29, 1956, was the result of this search for cohesion. "There was remarkable harmony," said Janet Rioch, M.D., the first president of the American Academy of Psychoanalysis. "At the suggestion of Kardiner, I was appointed Chairman of the first organizing meeting, because I was a less controversial figure than Clara Thompson," who had been one of the moving forces in getting the organization going. "The objective was to get under way with no great fanfare or polemics." This was a group of people who had learned from their own history. "Our major interest was to write as simple a document [constitution] as possible, but one which would obviate the conditions that tend to lead to schism. The rules were designed to stymie individual power operations."(117) The growth and success of the Academy attests to its vitality and the good will of the people who came together to found and support it. In May, 1970, it held its fourteenth anniversary meeting.

Accepted as the most noted member of those who left the New York Psychoanalytic Society in 1941, Horney was placed in a leadership role she neither wanted nor found congenial. Characteristically, she tried to delegate the organizational tasks as quickly as she could.

Clara Thompson's disappointment with the Association for the Advancement of Psychoanalysis was genuine. Her description of events is, however, somewhat different from my own. Her statement that Horney made "Ephron and Robbins training analysts" does not give sufficient importance to the fact that she and Fromm were also training analysts as was Silverberg, whose opinion carried much weight. Also I and others do not recall that "no new students were being sent to" Thompson. Regarding Fromm, many besides Horney were opposed to his continuing as a training analyst. Horney herself, was simply being consistent with the position she took in the famous panel discussion on lay analysis in 1927. (6)

Her 1927 presentation exemplifies the clarity and rigor of her thinking. Her interest was not in the response of those outside the field of psychoanalysis to lay analysis but in how lay analysis would affect those within the field. Also she did not concern herself with the specific training of the therapeutic analyst but with the nature of the preliminary training which could be found in the philosophical or medical faculties. Even more important than the nature of the preliminary or psychoanalytic training were personal qualifications, namely, "suitability," which for her was "the *sine qua non*."

Both philosophical training, which included the social sciences, and medicine, had their advantages and drawbacks. The philosophical training stimulated an interest in theory which in her opinion was being overemphasized while medical training contained much that an analyst wouldn't use.

She concluded that "Medicine has the advantage that its object of study is the same as that of the analyst, i.e. the living human being and particularly the suffering human being." She agreed there was a one-sided emphasis on the organic in medicine but saw this as no disadvantage since it would be "more than compensated for by his special analytic training. Further it gives an education in dealing with sick people, and a feeling of responsibility toward them and above all a will to heal. This last factor does not rank very high with us, but I am not certain whether it really deserves to be relegated to this humble position."*(6)*

She went on to say that these attitudes can be acquired without studying medicine but medicine insures and "emphasizes" the value of wide "clinical practice for medical students." She added that medicine leads into psychiatry, emphasizing that solid psychiatric training has great value for psychoanalysis in particular. Medicine further stimulates an interest in other methods of therapy which she felt did not dilute "the pure gold of analysis." Horney concluded that "Medicine is the study which offers more to an analyst than any other." If it is a question which training "is the most desirable as a preliminary to analytic training; there we must give medicine the preference."*(6)*

When splits occurred in psychoanalytic groups, issues other than ideological ones were quite naturally involved. Power, envy, and jealousy also operated, as *Psychoanalytic Pioneers* so clearly reveals in its account of the personal lives of the founders of psychoanalysis. *(64)*

Among those who first departed from the AAP, lay analysis was not the only issue. The relationship between Fromm and Horney had changed, personally and ideologically. At the time of the break Thompson "was devoted to Fromm, who later psychoanalyzed her." Because of his wife's illness, Fromm moved to Mexico, where he spent more and more time after her death. Colleagues and students at the White Institute "felt abandoned by him." By the summer of 1957, Thompson "was resigned to the fact that she and Fromm were moving in separate directions."*(113, pp. 361-376)*

As previously quoted, Marmor suggested that the responsibility for the second split in 1944 was largely Horney's. In his "Origins of the Institute"*(115, W.A.W.)* published four years after "The Pre-History and the Founding of the Comprehensive Course in Psychoanalysis,"*(115)* his criticism becomes more moderate. The implications of Thompson, Marmor, and others was that Horney alone made all the decisions on those two occasions. Having been a participant, I know this not to have been the case.

Those who remained in the AAP were moved by a spectrum of emotions and opinions. In 1943, the opposition to lay analysis and to Fromm's remaining as a training analyst was about three to one. In 1944, the majority was about two to one against moving to the New York Medical College, primarily on the grounds that it would mean loss of autonomy. While quite disturbed with the first break, after the second, Horney was in despair. She wanted to give up the AAP and to withdraw from all organizations. It required considerable support and encouragement from those who remained to help her through this difficult period.

Personal Relationship with Horney

The notion that Horney alone made all decisions implies that those who remained were so emotionally tied to her they were incapable of having their own opinions. From the time I began my first supervision with her, in 1939, I have been involved with her and with organizations which she helped to found. My meeting with her significantly altered the rest of my life. Although I had been in analysis with Abram Kardiner from 1936 to 1941, I felt the need for more help. I had further analysis and supervisory work with Horney. I also discussed with her my ideas and publications. She was a hard taskmaster, indeed. When I showed her a paper she would often say, "Now you can begin to work it out." She was even harder on herself.

But influence, indebtedness, and regard do not equal abrogation of convictions. In my psychoanalytic career, begun in 1936 at the New York Psychoanalytic Institute, I have been involved in four separations. The first involved leaving the New York Psychoanalytic Institute in 1941 to help found the AAP. The second and third were in 1943 and 1944, when divisions within the AAP caused fellow members to leave and to found first the W.A.W. Institute and then the Comprehensive Course in Psychoanalysis. The fourth took place on June 25, 1969, when twenty-one graduates and sixteen candidates-in-training left the American Institute for Psychoanalysis to organize the Specialty Program in Psychoanalytic Medicine at the Postgraduate Center for Mental Health in New York.

The first departure was in protest against the authoritarian dogmatism of the New York Psychoanalytic Institute. The second was over the issue of lay analysis, and the third over concerns about autonomy of teaching.

In the fourth instance, strong personal feelings arose over the question of adequate standards of training. My colleagues and I were about to be totally excluded from the training and teaching of candidates and from having any representation on the Faculty Council and Board of Trustees. Prior to the completion of my elected term, I was removed on October 21, 1969 as Editor of the *American Journal of Psychoanalysis*. Two colleagues on the editorial board were also removed at the same time.

If there have been separations, there have also been periods when analysts came together. The first such coming together for me came in 1939 at the New York Psychoanalytic Institute where I helped establish the first candidates association to be formed in an institute. Later as one of those who thought it was time for post- and neo-Freudians to come together, I participated in the early discussions, was a Charter Member of the American Academy of Psychoanalysis in 1956, and became President in May 1968. In a sense, the organizing of the program at the Postgraduate Center was a coming together. Its director, Lewis R. Wolberg, M.D., was one of the first graduates of the American Institute for Psychoanalysis and on the staff were many Fellows of the Academy. They were joined by many more who had graduated from the American Institute for Psychoanalysis.

I have briefly described the overt organizational changes which affected Horney, myself, and other analysts from the late '30s onward. It is an evolution which continues to have its reverberations. But there was also an internal process with which Horney had to deal. After writing *New Ways* Horney literally burned her bridges with the Establishment. Having made a critical evaluation of psychoanalytical theories, she became "convinced that psychoanalysis should outgrow the limitations set by its being an instinctivistic and genetic psychology." Certain that "the analysis of the actual character structure" was moving into the foreground of attention, she now had to chart her own course. The work of others was there to guide her. She expressed her debt particularly to psychoanalysts Harald Schultz-Hencke, Wilhelm Reich, and Max Horkheimer for the "elucidation of certain philosophical concepts."*(35, pp. 7-12)*

Out of her efforts from 1939 to 1942 came *Self-Analysis*, now in its eighteenth printing. During this period she was excluded from training and teaching *(38)* by the Establishment and was forcibly involved in organizational matters to which she had such a marked aversion. These organizational problems were particularly painful for her because she was in the throes of self-analysis and the creative process of theory building.

Self-Analysis is based on the premise that "It has always been regarded as not only valuable but also feasible to 'know oneself,' but it is possible that the endeavor can be greatly assisted by the discoveries of psychoanalysis." In this book Horney presented an elaboration of "the framework of a theory of neuroses" based on her two earlier books. She tried to do so "as simply as possible." *(38, p. 10)* She later conceded that she was "not entirely satisfied." The individual neurotic trends "were accurately described; but I was haunted by the feeling that in a simple enumeration they appeared in a too isolated fashion . . . . What I failed to see was that . . . a neurotic need for affection, compulsive modesty, and the need for a 'partner' belonged together — " and "represented a basic attitude toward others and the self, and a particular philosophy of life. These trends are the nuclei of what I have now drawn together as a 'moving toward people.' "*(39, p. 14)*

Clare, the "protagonist" in *Self-Analysis,* was to evolve into what Horney called the compliant type in *Our Inner Conflicts. (39)* Clare would later be developed as the self-effacing solution with its end stage of morbid dependency in *Neurosis and Human Growth. (49)* Many, over the years, have wondered if Clare was Horney. Clare was a composite of many people with such problems. She did reveal many of Horney's own character problems — problems with which she was acutely and painfully struggling from the time she finished *New Ways* to the completion of *Self-Analysis.* Her later works reveal the continuation of that struggle illuminated out of her own pain and her work with people with similar problems.

What Horney wrote about the self-effacing solution makes more understandable many of her responses. People with these problems shun that which those whose neurotic solution is expansiveness need and seek. Her evaluation of such people was therefore often inaccurate. She misjudged their arrogant-vindictiveness as strength and self-confidence, and their narcissism as a certainty of their self-worth. Her misevaluation of people was understandably greater with those close to her and with those she needed for support. She was not so blind to the perfectionist because she was painfully aware of this problem in herself. She often said, "I am not a good fighter," and needed to have around her people who she thought were. Her shunning of leadership positions, organization, and parliamentary procedures fits this general picture.

Striking was Horney's lack of bitterness toward people — particularly toward those in the New York Psychoanalytic Society who had excluded her. When asked why, her response was almost one of wonderment that I had even considered it an issue. So far as she was concerned the whole situation was over. It had passed. Besides, her energies were taken up with many more important matters now holding her attention.

It was somewhat different with persons with whom she had had a close relationship because the personal touched her much more deeply. She was reluctant to realize that a relationship was coming to a close and that she may have been inaccurate in her evaluation of that person. Although she did not talk about her former friends, from occasional remarks, over the years, I learned that the pain of such breaks healed very slowly. But again, rarely did I feel that she was bitter about these personal breaks.

Because of my relation to the Candidates Association at the New York Psychoanalytic Society, I had a significant role in the prehistory of the AAP and was involved with it from its founding. Following the first break I assumed more tasks, and with the second one, I held a number of offices and taught four courses yearly. Shortly after 1945, with the avalanche of new candidates, I had in analysis, at one point, sixteen candidates and only one private patient. All of these activities brought me into continuing contact with Horney. We were a small group fighting for survival — a situation which pushes personal needs and wishes into the background. Senior candidates in training and graduates were asked to take on teaching and administrative tasks in an attempt to deal with the sudden postwar expansion which affected all institutes and created excessive burdens for all concerned.

While I only knew of the creative process of writing *Self-Analysis* and of Horney's self-analysis after the fact, I was aware of and informed about both processes in connection with *Our Inner Conflicts*. It came out in 1945 and is now in its sixteenth printing. While being affected by the creative process in a gifted person, I was aware of what I observed and its impact on me. But only later did I appreciate in depth what had been happening. It was a painful and difficult experience for me, but I realized that I had been privileged to be a limited participant in a unique happening. Then I was able to understand the process better, and in greater detail without so much bewilderment and hurt, as *Neurosis and Human Growth (49)* was being written.

In the earlier phases of the writing of *Our Inner Conflicts*, Horney would present her ideas as they evolved in small intramural association meetings at the AAP, before Institute classes, and at the New

School for Social Research. Concomitantly she would discuss them with those closest to her. She needed a sounding board very much, and she found our questions most helpful.

In the last six to nine months of the writing of a book she was a person seized by a creative passion. She was moody, restless, and, at times, intensively irritable. If your responses were close to what she was involved with, she was overly appreciative; if they were remote — after the fact or before she had reached that point — she could be unwittingly quite hurting. Later the same comments might be met with enthusiasm and no indication that you had brought them up before. In those last months, reaching to a peak, she was like a woman giving birth, more and more centered on the process and the product to be born.

Once the manuscript was delivered she was spent. Then came a period of several weeks or months of slow recuperation, after which she wanted to play. She would go to the theater and the movies, read voraciously, and invite her many friends to delightful evenings in her twenty-fourth floor apartment overlooking Central Park. She would also visit her children and grandchildren wherever they might be — in the United States, Mexico, or Europe.

Following the completion of *The Neurotic Personality of Our Time* she wanted a vacation. She went to Germany to spend the Christmas holidays with her daughters Brigitte and Renate, who had recently married. Horney also visited her lifelong friend, Tutti, and her many other friends.

While there, on December 23, 1936, she gave a paper on "The Neurotic Need for Love"*(34)* before the *Deutsche Psychoanalytische Gesellschaft*. Although it was only four years since her departure, she already was having difficulty translating into German ideas she had formulated in English. This problem became increasingly apparent to her over the years. Her experience, common to others and the bane of translators, particularly to those of existentialist writers, confirms that the fullest meanings of concepts can only be experienced in the matrix of the language in which they were created.

While in Germany Horney also visited her husband Oscar to discuss their divorce, which took place in 1939. Over the years, as Horney had become more involved in the many aspects of psychoanalysis, the divergence of their interests had become increasingly apparent. They separated in 1926. Horney's move to the United States confirmed what was emotionally evident. She never remarried, and continued an amicable relationship with her husband, helping him during the difficult postwar years until his death in 1948.

In 1939 Butchy, a jet black cocker spaniel puppy, came into Horney's life and into that of many others. He lay at her feet through many analytic sessions, supervisions, and group discussions. A source of much laughter, his sad soulful eyes looked at you accusingly with an expression of pained hurt. He could somehow make you feel deeply guilty for treating him badly, right after he had emptied, almost at one gulp, a bowl of delicious dog food or a plate of filet mignon from the dinner table.

Full grown, Butchy was ten inches high and weighed about twenty pounds. Horney said that in his "Idealized Image," he saw himself as a combination of a dignified Great Dane and a fierce and courageous police dog. When she walked him in Central Park, opposite her apartment, he got into endless scrapes, and was often mauled by bigger dogs. If, despite his "Idealized Image," it dawned on him that he was in trouble, he fled in terror.

Snoring at Horney's feet, Butchy would pant, grunt, bark, and make running movements with his feet until he finally woke himself with a surprised expression on his face. He appeared in the dreams of many patients and in those of many of Horney's colleagues.

Butchy accompanied Horney on her weekends. As he got older, he became less active and, as Horney humorously remarked, "settled down to being a dignified old gentleman who had never had a wife." About his casual liaisons, she of course could not be certain.

In the early '40s Horney became interested in painting and worked at it quite seriously, taking lessons from able teachers. It gave her great pleasure and relaxation. She was aware her competence was modest. Although she always had excellent housekeepers, she enjoyed cooking and was quite good at it, though not exceptional. Decorating her apartment and various weekend homes, which she did tastefully, was a source of great gratification.

She enjoyed buying and giving presents and did so with much thoughtfulness and discernment. What gave her particular pleasure was looking for dolls for her five granddaughters. Horney had loved dolls since she was a little girl. There is a charming picture of her in a native German costume, taken when she was about eight, sitting in a chair with three dolls on her lap, and three more on a chair beside her. In her home and country places, there were always several dolls to be seen.

Horney read widely. Her bookshelves were filled with the classics to which she often referred in her books, as she did to modern writers of stature. Her reading ranged over religion, anthropology, sociology, and philosophy. While she expressed an aversion to philosophy in the abstract — its concepts and methodology — and was often annoyed by my discussion of these issues, she had a very real grasp of them. Her own work was obviously guided by methodological principles. Her later books show increasing evidence of system thinking. She was a systemizer and a conceptualizer of rare intuitive ability. Yet when this was brought to her attention it irritated her.

She was equally wide ranging in her friendships. For years she maintained relationships with novelists, dramatists, humorists, people from the world of the theater and films, anthropologists, sociologists, philosophers, and theologians. Her friendships with Erich Fromm and Ernst Schactel extended over many years. Through Fromm she met Horkheimer. Paul Tillich was a frequent visitor in her home. Harold Lasswell she knew from her arrival in Chicago, and she met D. T. Suzuki shortly thereafter.

Our Inner Conflicts (39) came out of "a crescendo of observation . . . which opened my eyes to the significance of . . . conflicts" engendered by contradictory "attitudes toward self" with concomitant "contradictory qualities and contradictory sets of values."*(p. 15)* In an attempt to "solve," not resolve, these contradictions, the person moves "toward people" (the compliant type), "against people" (the aggressive type), "away from people" (the detached type). He tries to harmonize these contradictions in an "Idealized Image"*(ch. 6)* of himself. He moves farther away from himself by the process of externalization.*(ch. 7)* To further buttress this neurotic character structure he uses what Horney called "Auxiliary Approaches to Artificial Harmony."*(ch. 8)* She then dealt with the "Consequences of Unresolved Conflicts," *(Part II)* and the therapeutic techniques required for the "Resolution of Neurotic Conflicts."*(p. 217)*

As soon as she completed the book, she edited and wrote two chapters for *Are You Considering Psychoanalysis?(40)* in which five of her colleagues participated. The book came out of a series of lectures for the laity and was written in response to that need. Published in 1946, it still continues to be a source of income to the AAP, to which the proceeds were contributed. Editing such a joint venture was quite a contrast to producing her own book. This was simply an interim task in support of her colleagues and in the service of the group with which she was identified.

Horney was literally deluged by requests for consultations, most of which she referred to her colleagues. She elected to work almost solely with those patients whose problems held her interest. Her fees were of quite secondary consideration, often only minimal. As a result, younger colleagues soon earned almost as much as she did. Wealthy patients who might have become contributors to the AAP went elsewhere or gave up the idea of therapy if they couldn't have Horney. Her attitude toward fees was indicative of her attitude toward money. She enjoyed spending and giving it away. Her earnings were never great and she saved very little.

Neurosis and Human Growth (49) was a far more important task than *Our Inner Conflicts,* and it took much longer to produce. It was the culmination of all her earlier work. It is now in its fourteenth printing. Since 1964 all her books, with the exception of *Neurosis and Human Growth* and *Feminine Psychology,* have appeared in paperback editions.

In *Our Inner Conflicts,* Horney defined neurosis as a disturbance in relations to others and focused on basic conflict, i.e., conflicts between the various moves. In *Neurosis and Human Growth,* however, she defined neurosis as *"a disturbance in one's relation to self and to others,"* and concerned herself with "central inner conflict" — namely, between health and sickness, between the constructive urge toward self-realization and the compulsive drivenness toward self-idealization. *(p. 368)* She delineated in exquisite detail the neurotic process, and the many participant neurotic solutions in hierarchies of dimension. She also described, for the first time, what had been implicit from her first paper: the dynamic process that motors the human urge toward authenticity, the real self.

While the second split united the group through the desperateness of the situation, the rapid postwar expansion alleviated our concern about survival, gave enthusiasm and impetus to our efforts, and diminished the possibilities for interpersonal frictions. Everybody who could possibly assume teaching and administrative responsibilities was pressed into service, thus limiting feelings of being excluded. But such rapid expansion made for a group in rapid transition, and the many different rates of mobility in the structure led to increasing instability.

In her "Study of the Emotional Climate of Psychoanalytic Institutes," Thompson has written perceptively that "A psychoanalytic institute has many of the qualities — good and bad — of a close family group." What gives institutes their particular feeling and tone is "first, persecution from without . . . and, second, unresolved transferences and countertransferences — that is, problems from within."*(113, p. 54)* The feeling of being embattled and the crusading spirit were there, as well as the relationship problems and personality differences, all leading to competitiveness, jealousies, and feelings about loyalties. In her "Tenth Anniversary" address, Horney said, "Naturally with different personalities working closely together, frictions were unavoidable."*(91)*

Horney was unquestionably the leader, and rivalry for her attention and interest was inevitable, making it very difficult for her, particularly since she did not want the position in the first place. The allocation of desirable administrative functions, teaching, and training positions created intensities of feelings and frictions. Since I held more than anyone else, next to Horney, there were strong feelings toward me, intensified by my productivity, and how I was experienced personally.

In this rapidly changing, emotionally charged matrix, Horney had completed *Our Inner Conflicts,* edited *Are You Considering Psychoanalysis?* and, a year later, slowly became increasingly involved with the writing of *Neurosis and Human Growth.*

By this time, I had begun evolving my own ideas, particularly on dreams. Toward the end of 1951, Horney began to voice her criticism of them, first intramurally and then publicly. This had a particularly unsettling effect on the people with whom I was working analytically. Strong feelings became polarized about me. What my colleagues needed not to see was that Horney and I regularly sat together in the front row. She would leave the seat next to me, to make the critical comments, and return to it after she had done so. Not known was that following such public criticism we continued to have discussions in her home, by telephone and through letters.

Private Discussions

Those discussions had begun in 1941 but did not become of great depth and duration until late 1942 as she was becoming involved with the writing of *Our Inner Conflicts.* Many of our conversations are still vivid. Several stand out. When we talked about the disruptive power of conflict, and the patient's terror of experiencing it, I emphasized that the therapist had better be aware that "he is working with dynamite." This American and rather masculine expression appeared in: "Panic reactions in response to a sudden recognition of a conflict showed me I was working with dynamite."*(39, p. 15)* Our discussions regarding the moral and existential implications of self-hate leading ultimately to suicide were many and extended over a number of months.

Having been a limited participant as *Our Inner Conflicts* was being written, I was better prepared and more aware of what was happening in the production of *Neurosis and Human Growth.* In her acknowledgement she wrote, "I also want to express my appreciation for some stimulating discussions on the subject matter with Dr. Harold Kelman." My personal copy is inscribed: "Toward a good comradeship! To Harold Kelman with cordial wishes. From Karen."

Throughout the late winter, spring and early summer of 1951, Horney was in the throes of a desperate struggle, this one much more intense than that which preceded her last book. The task that confronted her had certain similarities to the situation she faced after completing *New Ways.* Only this one had far greater implications theoretically, therapeutically, and philosophically. And she was now fifteen years older. It was to involve the development of the notion of the real self. A concept as old and as elusive as human history, it touches on the definition of health and the meaning of life. Her trip to Japan with short stays in Zen monasteries after many years of conversations with Dr. Suzuki was an expression of that search.

Her last two articles, "On Feeling Abused,"*(51)* and "The Paucity of Inner Experiences,"*(52)* indicate the directions in which she was moving. Existing blocks to contacting authentic feelings had to be defined before they could be resolved and allow for the identification, support, extension, expansion, and expression of human spontaneity.

Horney often wrote to me because writing helped clarify her feelings and ideas. Her letter of February 27, 1951 reads:

Dear Harry:

. . . The whole upheaval developing now — since last fall — has, I think to do with the completion of Human Growth. Remarque to whom I intimated the troubles in work, said something to this effect: that with the last book I had, as it were, finished one road and that something new was developing, which is not yet articulate. This struck me as right. Of course, if right, it is only a background.

I am looking forward to talking with you — and I do *not expect* miracles — and I am grateful.

Cordially yours,
Karen

Horney knew Eric Maria Remarque for many years. Author of *All Quiet on the Western Front* and many other novels, he had a home on Lago Maggiore in Italian Switzerland, one of Horney's favorite vacation spots. I met him several times in her home in New York. On a card from Lago Maggiore (July 20, 1951) she wrote: "I have an arthritic condition in one knee and go to Bad Gastein for bathing. Also otherwise am old wreck like last year. Seems to be no help. About to give up." She was still deep in the throes of a struggle with her personal problems and the creative process. When she returned in the fall, this despair had diminished. She was becoming more active with the familiar, increasing irritability. Then followed the private and public criticisms. She sent me a Holiday Greetings card:

Dear Harry:

. . . I still hope for a better contact in 1952, at least for a good discussion of your scientific ideas!

Yours Karen.

The extended discussions tapered off and stopped by late spring when she began to plan her visit to Japan. She always respected my practicality and organizing ability, and therefore turned to me for help with this trip. This partly explains her card from Tokyo on August 20, 1952:

Dear Harry:
Once more many thanks for your help . . . . It is quite some experience to be in a country of such old and peculiar culture. I'll give a lecture in Tokyo . . . I think with your keen sense for subtle beauty you would be delighted by these gardens and rooms.

Greetings,
Karen

There were a few more telephone conversations up to about mid-November and none thereafter. This pained me deeply because I knew in detail of her illness.

The intensity of her criticisms steadily mounted during the spring and fall of 1952. We sat apart at meetings. This was an increasingly difficult time for me, because of the impact of such criticism from someone I still regarded so highly, and because of what it was doing to the whole group, the people I worked with, and to Horney herself. I felt she was still caught in a painful struggle and was putting up a valiant fight. All I could offer was availability and silent support. I kept what might be provocative at a minimum while maintaining my own viewpoints. Close friends who saw what was happening but who were unaware of the private aspects of our relationship were deeply concerned for me and suggested that I resign. This I would not do. What I drew strength from was the help Horney had given me in my therapeutic work with her, our friendship, and the hope that this painful situation somehow might be mitigated in time and even be resolved.

It is a regrettable oversimplification to say that Horney wanted only disciples. This was often said about Freud, most recently in a book about Victor Tausk, (118) one of the most brilliant of his early pupils, who committed suicide. My own development as a person and a contributor were experienced and seen as evidence of a moving apart and on my own. Moving apart had always been deeply painful to Horney, beginning with what she experienced as her brother's rejection. I can only conjecture that something similar may have happened with her father was never worked through, and may have accounted for her unease in response to my questions regarding her not visiting Freud in Vienna. Many colleagues aided and abetted her in this mounting opposition to me. Others were bewildered and frightened. They could not or would not take a stand, which left me in a painful and isolated position.

Obituary

In late November, Horney became ill and died within two weeks on December 4, 1952. First there was malaise and high fever, then pleuritic pain and fluid in the chest. She had carcinoma of bile ducts of the liver with generalized metastases, a diagnosis rarely made during life.

The impact of her death on the whole group was deeply shocking. I feel it significantly contributed to Dr. Muriel Ivimey's death on February 23, 1953 at age sixty-four. She had been analyzed by Horney and worked closely with her as Associate Dean of the Institute from 1941 until Horney's death. For myself, the first six months were most difficult and somewhat less so during the next year. The group, shaken as it was, went through some trying periods. From 1954 to 1967 I was Dean, holding a number of offices, including being Editor of the *American Journal of Psychoanalysis*, from 1954 to 1969. That the group still exists today, in spite of two splits, the death of Horney, and my exclusion from continuing as Dean in 1967 and Editor in 1969 shows that her personal influence, her ideas, and her psychoanalytic theories have an extraordinary vitality and a toughness.

In the Karen Horney Memorial Issue, Dr. Medard Boss of Zurich prefaced his article, "Mechanistic and Holistic Thinking in Modern Medicine," with "Perhaps it would be possible to add editorially that during the years 1931-32 I was in training at the Berlin Psychoanalytic Institute and there I did supervised analytic work with Karen Horney. From her I received my first impulses which led me to overcome mechanistic thinking and to replace it with a holistic view which since has developed into my *daseins*-analytic concept."*(57, p. 48)*

"With the death of Karen Horney," wrote Oberndorf, "there passed from the psychoanalytic scene a distinguished, vigorous and independent figure . . . . Notwithstanding her defection from the American Psychoanalytic Association, there seems little doubt that Horney retained a strong devotion to Freud's procedure of a thoroughgoing investigation of psychic conflict and did not sacrifice conscientious work with patients to rapid or superficial methods.

"Time will eventually decide the value of Horney's ideology in psychoanalytic therapeusis. But her responsive and warm personality will remain affectionately in the memories of many of her earlier colleagues, as well as her later students and followers."*(119)*

Horney was a human being with strengths and weaknesses, greatnesses and foibles, gifts and limitations. With and despite them she has made a significant contribution to psychoanalysis and to many human beings, among whom I count myself. Paul Tillich, in his funeral oration, said it all so simply and beautifully. "If I were asked to say what above all was her work I would answer: she herself, her being, her power to be, the well-founded balance of an abundance of striving and curative possibility."*(120)*

I would particularly like to thank Marianne Horney Eckardt, M.D., who made many helpful suggestions during the writing of her mother's biography. In her letter of November 21, 1969, she wrote: "Your own valuable personal experience with the group or groups, your own personal experience in the travails of her creative work are part of the history and should be included. No one was closer to her over the years than you were."

Of course, the final responsibility for the contents is mine.

H.K.

Chapter 1

History

Horney's 1917 paper *(2)* outlines some fundamentals of her views on theory, therapy, technique, and the nature of man. The focus of a subsequent paper or book might be on a particular issue, but it would also contain developments and revisions of these fundamental concerns and concepts.

While her main interest, from 1923 to 1935, was in feminine psychology, her papers on the subject *(63)* contain frequent references to culture and a host of other topics. In 1930, "The Specific Problems of Compulsion Neurosis in the Light of Psychoanalysis"*(13)* appeared — a paper which prepared the way for her comprehensive notion of compulsiveness as characteristic of all sickness in contrast to healthy spontaneity. "The Role of Aggression in Civilization" (1931) was devoted mainly to that subject, with a critique of Freud's concept of the Death Instinct. *(15)*

Horney's ideas on the influences of culture on human development found their culmination in *The Neurotic Personality of Our*

Time. (33) In it she also elaborated her concepts of basic anxiety, the neurotic character structure, and the nature and importance of the actual situation.

In *New Ways in Psychoanalysis,* a critique of Freudian theory, she formulated her reasons for rejecting an "instinctivistic and genetic psychology." She demonstrated, instead, how "disturbances in human relationships become the crucial factor in the genesis of neurosis."*(35, p. 9)*

These disturbances are of a primary nature. "Sexual difficulties are the effect rather than the cause of the neurotic character structure."*(35, p. 10)* This shift is a radical one, philosophically and methodologically. Instead of a part, or a function, no matter how broadly defined, determining the whole, it was the whole that clearly determined the meaning of the functioning of any part of the totality. This was holism made explicit. Moral problems, authentic and pseudo, became of greater importance. Discarding the notion of superego, and seeing the ego in a new perspective had additional consequences for an understanding of masochistic phenomena, guilt feelings, narcissism, transference, resistance, and therapeutic technique in general.

Beyond the concern with the feasibility, desirability, types, and limitations of self-analysis, in the book of that title *(38)* Horney amplified her ideas about neurotic trends and the concept of the neurotic character structure.

Neurotic conflicts — their sources, their functions, their consequences, and the defenses against them — are the central focus of *Our Inner Conflicts. (39)* In her use of the movements "toward," "against," and "away from" people, she evolved a loose neurotic character typology of people whose foreground neurotic solution in relation to others was compliance, aggressiveness, or detachment. With the revision and expansion of her ideas in *Neurosis and Human Growth,* she cautioned that "Perhaps it would be more nearly correct to speak of directions of development than of types."*(49, p. 191)*

This book contains the fruits of all her previous work. Neurosis is both cause and reflection of disturbances in relation to others and to oneself. There is not only basic, but also central conflict. The motive power of human authenticity — the real self-dynamism — is defined, and compulsiveness receives a more detailed characterization. The pride-system, of which neurotic pride and self-hate are aspects, and the tyranny of the *should,* receive rigorous exposition. System thinking, implicit in all of Horney's work, is made clearly explicit in the notion of the pride system. The neurotic character structure with its comprehensive and partial solutions, as well as the "General Measures To Relieve Tension," are delineated as aspects of the whole defensive system. *(49. ch. VII)* The consequences for human development, for therapy, and for technique are systematically described.

Anna Freud's "The Ego and the Mechanisms of Defense" appeared in 1936. *(121)* In 1937, Freud's "Analysis Terminable and Interminable"*(105)* and Horney's *The Neurotic Personality of Our Time (33)* were published, to be followed in 1939 by Hartmann's "Ego Psychology and the Problem of Adaptation."*(122)* This seminal literature on the ego was to influence significantly the entire direction and evolution of psychoanalysis.

In 1955, Munroe said that "Freudians, mostly under the label of ego psychology, are just beginning to give proper theoretical weight to concepts which Horney has been shouting from the housetop for twenty years."*(123)* Tarachow confirmed Horney's position in 1960 by stating that Horney had contributed to Freudian psychoanalysis by stimulating "interest in ego psychological problems."*(124)*

By 1965 Lomas stated that "passivity is not a specifically sexual phenomenon;" that "this myth" has resulted in a "faulty conception of activity, passivity and identity;" and that it has led to "an unnecessarily large divergence between the theories of male and female development."*(125)* In 1966, Apfelbaum asserted that ego analysis supersedes rather than supplements id analysis and that psychoanalytic development is blocked by the presence of two incompatible theories intertwined in one system. *(126)* In his theory of "primary love," Balint asserted in 1968 that "the aim of all human striving is to establish . . . an all-embracing harmony with one's environment, to be able to love in peace."*(127, p. 65)* He emphasized that his theory did not imply that "sadism or hate have no or only a negligible place in human life" but that they are "secondary phenomena, consequences of inevitable frustrations."*(127, p. 65)* The latter is, almost verbatim, Horney's position in 1937. *(33)*

A further expression of this development has been made by Weisman, training analyst at the Boston Psychoanalytic Institute. In 1965 he said that the existential core of the therapist determines how he organizes his data and sees his patients, and in 1968 he added that "the traumatic theory of neurosis" is "no more" and that "the notion of psychic causality has proved to be less and less tenable."*(128)*

Psychoanalysis had evolved from a position of absolute to one of relative determinism, and from closed system thinking to one more characteristic of the open system variety. What had evoked such intense responses in 1937 and 1939 *(The Neurotic Personality of Our Time* and *New Ways)* had become integrated into the thinking of many post-Freudians.

The inextricable nature of theory and therapy which Horney had enunciated in her first paper remained an undeviating idea. Every successive paper had something about the consequences for therapy of each theoretical revision or extension. Each book, which was a change and amplification of theory, had a closing chapter on therapy. In the last chapter of *New Ways in Psychoanalysis* she emphasized her point by saying: "New ways in theory necessarily condition new ways in therapy."*(35, p. 276)* In 1950, she again affirmed the unity of theory and therapy in "The Road of Psychoanalytic Therapy."*(49, ch. XIV)*

"When giving a series of lectures on the subjects presented in this book [*Neurosis and Human Growth*] I was asked after the ninth lecture when I was finally going to talk about therapy. My answer was that everything I had said pertained to therapy. All information about possible psychic involvements gives everyone a chance to find out about his own troubles. When similarly we ask here what must the patient become aware of in order to uproot his pride system and all it entails we can simply say that he must become aware of every single aspect of what we have discussed in this book: his search for glory, his claims, his shoulds, his pride, his self-hate, his alienation from self, his conflicts, his particular solution — and the effect all these factors have on his human relations and his capacity for creative work."*(49, p. 341)*

The primacy of Horney's interest in therapy is further indicated by her opening *New Ways* with the statement that her "desire to make a critical reevaluation of psychoanalytical theories had its origin in a dissatisfaction with therapeutic results."*(35, p. 7)*

The last example of Horney's lifelong concern with therapy is a poignant one. She was conducting the course, "Psychoanalytic Therapy," when she became fatally ill in November, 1952. Her synopsis read: "These lectures do not intend to teach psychoanalytic technique but rather to present and discuss viewpoints which may help those who desire to develop their own ways of conducting analysis."*(129)*

In referring to viewpoints, Horney was recognizing the necessity for principles, for guides for action, while at the same time emphasizing the individuality of their application. To her "a constantly evolving and changing theory" did not easily lend itself to formulations of technique. "Horney regarded therapy as a uniquely human cooperative venture. Anything that suggested dogma or rules, techniques or dehumanization, was contrary to the spirit of her theory, philosophy, and goals in therapy." She continually reaffirmed the notion that "holistic psychoanalysis, by its very nature, must conduct its therapy and investigations with the loosest kinds of tentative, though clearly stated, guides to make possible the emergence of the uniquely human."*(129, p. 1449)*

About the uniqueness of each analytic situation and each analyst, Freud said: "I must, however, expressly state that this technique has proved to be the only method suited to my individuality; I do not venture to deny that a physician quite differently constituted might feel impelled to adopt a different attitude to his patients and to the task before him."(130) This admonition Freud frequently repeated.

As he became aware of the uniqueness of the relationship between patient and therapist, he formulated his concepts of transference and countertransference. To diminish the adverse consequences of the latter, he recommended that "anyone who wishes to practice analysis of others should first submit to be analyzed himself by a competent person."(131, p.329) As guides for this unique human venture, he wrote his papers on technique between 1910 and 1915, with little thereafter on the subject. In one he said: "The rules which can be laid down for the practical application of psychoanalysis in treatment are subject to" limitations similar to trying to learn "the fine art of the game of chess from books." The learner "will soon discover that only the opening and closing moves of the game admit of exhaustive systematic description." The moves in between can be filled in only by "the zealous study of games fought out by master-hands."(131)

Since Freud, psychoanalysts have been attempting to refine the opening and closing moves, and to formulate guides for the moves in between. In 1914, Fenichel believed that the time was "not yet ripe" for a technique book in "the young science" first referred to as psychoanalysis in 1888. He felt that, while there was a paucity of literature on technique, it was only one among many problems still needing development. Then there were the analyst's "subjective uncertainty or restraint," as well as "the objective difficulties of the matter itself." The "decisive" factor was that "the infinite multiplicity of situations arising in analysis does not permit the formulation of general rules about how the analyst should act in every situation, because each situation is essentially unique."(132)

While Freud had compared psychoanalytic technique to "the fine art" of chess, he constantly spoke of the science of psychoanalysis: Psychoanalysis "is a part of science and can adhere to the scientific *Weltanschauung*."(133)

Many analysts would now agree in principle with Weisman's statement that "Psychoanalysis is a somewhat scientific pursuit, but it is scarcely a science."(100, p.6) Calling psychoanalysis "a merger of the aesthetic with the scientific," Weisman says that "The ideas and practices of psychoanalysis emerge from an existential attitude within the analyst." He further asserts "that this attitude influences his perceptions and his generalizations." The existential attitude "recognizes that each person's version of reality is determined by his unique way of polarizing existence."(128, p.viii)

The uniqueness of the individual that science attempts to bring under theoretical and technical generalizations continues to reassert itself. "Books on psychoanalytic technique fall short," says Weisman, adding that "No manual can account for the personal contribution . . . which an analyst brings to his work." He must investigate experience — his own and his patients' — on the "scientific, categorical, phenomenal and, existential" levels. Psychologically these levels are referred to as the "psychophysical, psychodynamic, descriptive, and existential."*(128, pp. 7-8)* Being open to and operating on all these levels is essential to effective therapy. They constitute the holistic orientation.

It is noteworthy that most existentially oriented analysts, while asserting the limitations of psychoanalytic theory, tend to agree on the values of psychoanalytic technique, though differently applied. "It is by no means unusual," said Boss, "to find *Daseins*analysts who adhere more strictly to most of Freud's practical suggestions than do those psychoanalysts whose theoretical orientation remains orthodox."*(134, p. 446)*

Because psychoanalysis is non-proselytizing and because spiritual anguish is ultimately what brings the sufferer to seek the helper, I see psychoanalysis as closer to Buddhism, Hinduism and Taoism, which are nonproselytizing, than to Christianity or Mohammedanism, which are. Ultimately, psychoanalysis is more Eastern in its technique and Eastern in its ultimate aims and aspirations than Western. It is not Eastern in its theories, however. Psychoanalysis and its theories are a product of the West and of the subject-object dualism in thought. Between theory and technique there is a built-in dichotomy. *(135)*

Freud's theory was embedded in nineteenth-century scientific, materialistic, and dualistic rationalism. It came out of a world of Newtonian mechanics and closed-system thinking. As psychoanalytic theorizing becomes more congruent with twentieth-century scientific thought, which is expressed in a language of field relationships and hierarchies of open systems, the subject-object dichotomy and its oppositional nature lessens. Horney's holistic approach, based upon, and consonant with, twentieth-century thought, is more congenial to our current needs.

From a wider perspective, which would include preliterate groups with their animistic thinking, the types of consciousness found in the East, and the forms of thought characteristic of the West, we now see that, to the extent that human beings remain in contact with their own organicity, commonality, and communality, their techniques of teaching-learning-knowing and of helping-healing continue universally applicable.

These techniques comprise a special form of human relationship, be it medicine man-ailing one, priest-penitent, master-disciple, doctor-patient, scholar-pupil, transference-countertransference, Begegnung, or I-thou relationship. There is — in attitude or fact — a lower position *vis-à-vis* the helper-healer-teacher, whether on bended knee, in the lotus position, reclining, prostrate, or on a couch. There is a special atmosphere induced by physical and/or chemical means: chanting, dancing, sound accompaniments, starvation, exhaustion, ingesting drugs, forms of frustration and renunciation, inflicting pain, silence, or isolation. There is also a mutually agreed upon code of arrangements enhanced by culturally supported myths, rituals, curricula, rules in analysis. There is striving toward total self-revelation: confession, free association, or dialogue. There is the reporting of dreams: dream books, dream interpreters, dream work, communal dream interpreting, and analysis of dreams. And, finally, there is the relating of events and the interpretation of behavior. These techniques, with variations and commentaries on them, remain universal and similar.

Theories, however, and the promulgators of them, are constantly changing. This confirms us in the necessity for recurrently "reminding"*(137)* ourselves that we are our own myth makers, and that "the image of man is no eternal thing. We must remake it generation by generation."*(138)*

Horney was very much aware of the foregoing considerations. "Her deductively brilliant formulations were framed in the twentieth-century language of field relationships. The significance of these newer formulations lay in their availability for further exploration and testing."*(139)*

Our concern is to show how Horney, building on Freud's pioneering efforts and exquisite insights, was attuned to the *Weltanschauung* of her time. With her gifts and training, plus the newer tools from anthropology and sociology which were available to her, she sensed the future directions that developments in psychoanalysis would take in a Western world moving toward the centenary of psychoanalysis (1988).

In 1941 Fenichel wrote that "Freud once said any treatment can be considered psychoanalysis that works by undoing resistances and interpreting transferences, that is, any method that makes the ego face its pathogenic conflicts in their full emotional value by undoing the opposing defensive forces, effective as 'resistances,' through the interpretation of derivatives and especially of the derivatives expressed in the transference. This alone is the criterion . . . a 'nonclassical procedure,' when the classical one is not possible, remains psychoanalysis. It is meaningless to distinguish an orthodox psychoanalysis from an 'unorthodox' one."*(140, p. 573)*

In his 1946 valedictory to the British Psycho-Analytic Association, Jones said: "Psychoanalysis is simply the study of mental processes of which we are unaware, of what for the sake of brevity we call the unconscious. The psychoanalytic method of carrying out this study is that characterized by the free associative technique of analyzing the observable phenomena of transference and resistance. As Freud himself said, anyone following this path is practicing psychoanalysis even if he comes to conclusions different from Freud's . . . and it is plain that we should be forsaking the sphere of science for that of theology were we to regard these conclusions . . . as being sacrosanct and eternal."*(141)*

The positions of Fenichel and Jones were strenuously affirmed in 1967: "It should not be forgotten that modified forms of analysis are as legitimate descendants of psychoanalytic insights as is the classical model," said Kanzer and Blum who wrote "Classical Psychoanalysis Since 1939" in *Psychoanalytic Techniques,* a book to which frequent reference will be made. "Deviant movements which now tend to show wide areas of agreement with the established school," they assert, "may find representation and mutual tolerance in official psychoanalytic organizations."*(142)*

The foregoing suggests that what Horney evolved as theory and technique fulfills the criteria of what is now defined as psychoanalysis. I have indicated my feeling regarding its appropriateness for twentieth-century Western man. It also fulfills the criterion of a fruitful theory in that it makes possible the more productive answering of old questions and the raising of new ones. One evidence of this fulfillment is the many contributions of Horney's colleagues.

In one of the lectures in the course on "Psychoanalytic Therapy" (1952) Horney said: "When we know what does what, how, then I could write the book on technique that I have been trying to write for years." Horney never did write her book on technique, a lack which this book attempts to fill. Other interests precluded her from doing so. However, she showed her deep concern with technique issues through her continuing efforts in attempting to bring clarity to the many knotty questions it raised.

To adequately present her principles of technique and their application, as well as those of her colleagues, a synoptic presentation of her final theory formulations is essential.

Chapter 2

Theory

Implicit in Horney's holistic concepts is the assumption that there is no life course in which every developmental experience has been traumatic, nor one from which all deleterious influences have been absent. As a result of harmonious constructive experiences on the one hand, and destructive traumatic experiences on the other, the personality of the child develops around two nuclei and forms two basic patterns. In the former, there is a basic feeling of confidence that one's striving for love, belonging, and autonomy may be more or less realized. In the latter, there is a basic feeling of helplessness and isolation in a potentially hostile world.

The pattern that is most deeply and extensively embedded determines how the energies, abilities, and resources of the individual will be used. These patterns change in proportion and proceed in an oscillating manner. Adverse physical and psychological environmental factors, as well as internal ones — hereditary, constitutional, and psychogenetic — propel the development of the defensive systems, restrict growing ones, extend, and embed basic anxiety and basic hostility

43

which are inextricably bound together. *(33, chs. 3-4)*

Martin's "The Body's Participation in Anxiety and Dilemma Phenomena"*(143)* increases our effectiveness in identifying and working with these processes in therapy. In Kelman's "A Unitary Theory of Anxiety"*(144)* healthy and neurotic fear and anxiety, as well as their sources, functions, and the attitudes toward them, are rigorously delineated. Portnoy *(145)* makes a detailed study of "Anxiety States" and Willner *(146)* elaborates on the role of anxiety in the genesis, history, and therapy of obsessive-compulsives and of schizophrenics.

The influence of phenomenological and existential thought is evident throughout Horney's early papers on *Feminine Psychology. (63)* Her original formulation of basic anxiety has existential roots. *(33, p. 94)* Nietzsche's *Lebensneid* — feelings of bitter, begrudging envy and of being excluded from life — and Scheler's *Ressentiment* are sources for her ideas on sadistic trends. *(39, p. 201; 49, p. 211)* References to Kierkegaard appear frequently. His *Diary of the Seducer* is quoted for its insights on sadistic trends; *(39, ch. 12)* and *Sickness unto Death* is used to improve our understanding of hopelessness, despair, and the fear of nothingness. *(39, pp. 51, 183, 185)* She relies on Kierkegaard and more particularly on William James as sources for her concept of the real self. *(49, pp. 377, 157)* Horney also valued Paul Tillich's exposition of non-being. *(54)*

In order to keep his basic anxiety at a minimum, the child's spontaneous moves toward closeness in affection, away from people to be by himself, and against others to affirm a stand become compulsive compliance, aggression, and detachment. *(39, chs. 3-5)* While spontaneous moves are freely oscillating, the compulsive ones are rigid, absolute, and indiscriminate — attributes which make for ease and intensity of conflict. Horney called them "basic conflicts" — the consequence of opposing needs and attitudes in regard to others. *(39, ch. 2)*

The earliest integration of personality tends to give full rein to one set of needs and attitudes while suppressing the other set. This predominating trend, with its system of needs, attitudes, inhibitions, fears, and values becomes more firmly embedded. Oscillations in general, and particularly foreground ones in the other direction, become constricted. *(39, chs. 3-5)*

Horney postulated the "Idealized Image" as a further attempt at the integration of the personality. *(39, ch. 6)* The most deeply embedded trend becomes idealized in all its aspects and serves as a basis for identity feelings and as a directive for living. Compulsive compliance, for example, with its concomitant needs for affection, submissiveness, suppressed aggressions, fear of hostility, and hope for satisfaction through being loved, becomes the all-loving, totally eager to please, the most gentle and kind soul whose absolute goodness remains unappreciated. This idealization is the work of imagination. The individual, however, also needs to make it an actuality.

The shifting of his energies toward actualizing the idealized self is what Horney calls "The Search for Glory."*(49, ch. 1)* In its service are the need for perfection, neurotic ambition, and the drive toward a vindictive triumph. Although a person may speak of wanting, actually in this search, he is driven. The compulsiveness in the search is revealed in its indiscriminateness and insatiability, in the person's utter disregard for himself and his best interests, and in his reactions when frustrated. Dictated by his imagination, driven as he is, he aims at the absolute and the ultimate. The major direction of his interests in life shifts from a search for constructive self-realization to an almost total involvement with proving that he is his idealized self.

To maintain the fiction that he has actualized his idealized image — for he is existing on an *as if* basis in an *as if* world — the individual needs constant proof and affirmation from others. In the service of this proof are his claims. *(49, ch. 2)* These are not simply an expression of his wants or needs, although they arise from them. They are extremely stringent demands for recognition of his very special self. He feels entitled to have them fulfilled. Reality and the needs of others take second place. His response to nonfulfillment of these claims is a mixture of anxiety and vindictive fury combined with a deepening feeling that the world is indeed a hostile place.

The individual's value system is oriented toward actualizing his idealized image. He tries to mold himself into his image of perfection by means of a constellation of *shoulds* and *should nots* — "The Tyranny of the Should."*(49, ch. 3)* These imperatives operate with a supreme disregard for their feasibility or even desirability. They operate on the premise that nothing is or should be impossible for oneself.

With all his strenuous efforts toward perfection, a person, so driven, does not gain what he so desperately needs: self-confidence and self-respect. He develops instead an inflated and unrealistic pride in himself which is based on imagined merits. Because "Neurotic Pride" is based on false premises, it is very vulnerable. *(49, ch. 4)* There are automatic defenses erected against pride being endangered or harmed, and there are automatic ways of restoring it when it is hurt. The defensive maneuvers consist largely of a system of avoidances and a rigid attitude of righteousness. The chief way of restoring hurt pride is retaliatory vindictiveness with the need to triumph over the offender in order to vindicate the self.

A therapeutic situation which illustrates some of the foregoing issues was described to me by J. W. Vollmerhausen, M.D. A thirty-five-year-old nurse had stringent needs to present an imperturbable front and to control all her feelings. In the fourth year of her analysis, she began to use the couch which had been a great source of terror for her. Her first responses were about how easy it was now that she had finally gotten there. Soon she began to twist and turn and complained of a full bladder. She ignored any connection of this symptom with her fear of the couch and attributed it to having had too much coffee. She refused the suggestion that she use the bathroom and emphatically insisted that she could control herself.

This same symptom of a painful urge to urinate recurred in the next five sessions. She could not deny the evidence to herself, but remained adamant in her refusal to relieve herself. She continued to proclaim her pride in her self-control. The appearance of a painful urge to urinate had threatened and hurt her neurotic pride in self-control. She had numerous impulses to urinate right on the couch. She also expressed fury at the analyst in many other ways during these sessions. This was understood as an expression of her vindictiveness toward him for wounding her pride in her imperturbability. After considerable struggle, she used the bathroom in the middle of the sixth session. When she returned her whole being expressed and revealed a mixture of relief, shamefacedness, and good humor. She said, "I've urinated 1,000 cc."

This was the beginning of her confronting. She began to take a stand against, and work through, her compulsive need to be unmoved, her pride in absolute self-control, and her claim that nobody could do anything to upset her. In this instance, we can see the tenacity of the pride-invested position, the claim that fortifies it, the *shoulds* that sustain it, and the vindictive retaliation in fantasy and in verbal expression which occurs when the position is damaged or undermined. Just the issues of hurt pride, the attempts to restore it, and some aspects of working it through have been dealt with here. The many other implications of this example will be elucidated through further instances cited throughout the book.

"The glorified self becomes a *phantom* to be pursued; it also becomes a measuring rod with which to measure his actual being." *(49, ch. 5)* The neurotic cannot but despise his actual being which, like reality, keeps interfering with his search for glory. Self-hate has an integrative function in the service of self-glorification. Together with *shoulds,* claims, and neurotic pride, it constitutes what Horney called *the pride system.* This system is for the most part unconscious. For a long time in therapy, the hatred for the real self which opposes the whole search for glory remains deeply buried.

Self-hate when directly experienced, appears as merciless self-accusations, relentless demands on self, self-contempt, self-frustration, self-tormenting, or self-destructive acts. Any one or more of these modes of operation may be perceptible. More often, the process of self-hate is externalized. This increases and alters basic anxiety. The neurotic now feels and becomes more helpless, one who is incapable of defending himself.

For the sake of unification and integration, the individual identifies himself *in toto* with his glorified or despised self. He experiences himself as one or the other, and may vacillate from one identity to the other. More likely, the attempt at solution will be a kind of streamlining in either the expansive or the self-effacing direction. Whatever the direction, it is sustained and supported by auxiliary defenses. While they tend to reduce tension and smooth over the disruptive conflicts caused by contradictory attempts at solution, they contribute to a person's unawareness of himself, as well as to intrinsic feelings of weakness.

Foremost among these auxiliary defenses is the process of *alienation* from self. It is both an outcome of the neurotic development as well as a defensive measure to relieve tension. *(49, ch. 6)* In its more extreme form it appears as depersonalization. All that is compulsive moves the individual away from his real self as well as from his actual or empirical self. His possessions and experiences are not felt as his. He becomes numb and remote, a stranger to himself. Camus describes him with penetrating insight in *The Stranger*. His relations to himself and others become increasingly impersonal and mechanical. He loses the capacity to feel his own feelings, and is made worse by his neurotic pride dictating what he should and should not feel. He has lost his inner self-directedness and become other- and outward-directed.

The richness of possibilities in Horney's concept was explored in a symposium on "Alienation and the Search for Identity." *(60)* In a similar direction and from a Freudian orientation, Bychowski discusses the phenomenon. *(147)*

Another of the "General Measures to Relieve Tension" and diminish conflict is the *externalization* of inner experience. *(49, ch. 7)* This is a more comprehensive phenomenon than projection which is concerned with "the shifting of blame and responsibility to someone else for subjectively rejected trends or qualities." *(39, p. 116)* Any psychic process, including aspects of the pride system and the real self, can be externalized. "Externalized Living," as a whole way of life, represents an extreme of the externalizing process. *(148)*

A further measure for tension reduction — an outcome of the preceding measures — is *psychic fragmentation* or *compartmentalization*. When these fail to do away with disruptive conflicts, *automatic self-control* sets in to check all impulses indiscriminately. This results in an increased rigidity and constriction of the personality. The last

47

auxiliary measure is the belief in the *supremacy of the mind*. It functions as a spectator of the self, gleefully and sadistically finding fault with it. It also functions as a magic ruler with beliefs in omnipotence and omniscience. For the mind "as for God, everything is possible." *(49, p. 184)*

All these tension-relieving measures are homeostatic. Something more goal-directed is still necessary for the individual. He needs something that will give form, direction, and meaning to his whole personality. The energies, drives, and values of the individual become organized and integrated around three further "directions of development" which Horney calls the three major solutions to intrapsychic conflict.

They are centrifugally and centripetally oriented, focus on the individual and his environments, and mutually influence each other in constructive and destructive ways. Because Horney's approach combines the intrapsychic and the interpersonal it is referred to as holistic. Individual and environment are seen as mutually influencing and extending into each other, only arbitrarily separable. All aspects of this unitary process are considered, from the physicochemical to the spiritual, from emotional responses to cultural patterns. Taken into account are man's physical and psychological processes in health and sickness, his social behaviors and moral values, his responses at work and in leisure. Horney is concerned with the whole human being in the totality of his living, with his relations to himself, to others, and to the cosmos of which he is an aspect.

While pointing out the holistic nature of Horney's theory, Martin has seen the task of therapy as helping the patient become aware of his total involvement in conflict. *(149)* This awareness lessens acquired inner conflicts, and healthier perceptual and conceptual awareness is expanded. My own concern has been with unitary process thinking as a way of developing holistic concepts, and with formulating a language of process concepts to describe human integrating.

Sullivan evolved "the Interpersonal Theory of Psychiatry."*(150)* Fromm-Reichmann's "Principles of Intensive Psychotherapy"*(151)* reflect the influence of Sullivan's thinking, as do Fromm's writings. *(152)* In the interpersonal approach, the focus is on what happens between people in relationship; Arieti's "The Intrapsychic Self" balances this centrifugal, outward-oriented interpersonal reference and emphasis. *(153)*

Because Horney is concerned with the moves toward self-realization and self-actualization she rigorously differentiates solution from resolution. The neurotic attempts to *solve,* that is do away with, to deny his conflicts. Only by analyzing the conditions which brought these conflicts into being can they be *resolved,* and the energy previously invested in them and in attempts to solve them become available for productive living. As a consequence of neurotic conflict resolving, the person's center of gravity which had shifted to the outside now moves back into the center of his being.

The first of these three major solutions is the expansive one in which the appeal and goal are of mastery. *(49, ch. 8)* Here the individual is identified with his pride or with his standards, which may be predominantly narcissistic, perfectionistic, or arrogantly vindictive. The second is the self-effacing solution in which the individual identifies with his subdued self. *(49, ch. 9)* He has the goals of love and surrender. The third is the solution of resignation in which the individual aims at freedom and noninvolvement. *(49, ch. 11)* He attempts to remain out of the conflict between his expansive and self-effacing drives by withdrawing from active participation in life. This solution may have the form of *persistent resignation, rebellious resignation,* and those deteriorated states which Horney called *shallow living.* The focus of such people is on having fun, on prestige and opportunistic success, and on being well-adapted automatons. These needs often combine with those in "Externalized Living." *(148)*

Each solution represents a complex interplay of drives, inhibitions, fears, sensitivities, and values. It determines the kinds of satisfaction attainable, what is to be avoided, the hierarchy of values, and how that person will experience and relate to himself and others, in work and leisure, in sex and marriage, and in confronting life's bigger questions.

Chapter 3

Neurotic Disturbances
in Human Relationships I:
Love and Sex

In *Neurosis and Human Growth,* Horney's definition of neurosis, which had been "essentially a disturbance in human relationships . . . *now became a disturbance in one's relation to self and to others."* *(49, pp. 367-8)* This shift followed from her expanded ideas on intrapsychic processes involving the central inner conflict between the pride system and the real self. She described how the pride system affects our human relations and how it removes "the neurotic from others by making him *egocentric."* By egocentricity, Horney does not mean egotism or selfishness in the sense of considering merely one's advantage, but the state of being all wrapped up in oneself. Elsewhere she said, "egocentricity is a moral problem insofar as it entails making others subservient to one's needs. Instead of their being regarded as human beings in their own right they come to be merely means to an end."*(39, p. 163)*

Because of his egocentricity, the neurotic does not see others clearly. His picture of them is not only blurred, it is positively distorted. These *"distortions"* occur *"in the light of the needs* engendered by the pride system," because of his reactions to others, and *"in the light of his externalizations."(49, p. 292)* His externalizations distort by endowing others with characteristics, neurotic and healthy, which they do not have, and in blinding himself to attributes which they do have. His neurotic problems may also make him particularly clear-sighted about some problems they do have. A person who believes he is a saint will quickly spot another hypocrite.

Because of his needs, his reactions to others and because of his externalizations, the neurotic is difficult to relate to. He may feel, however, that he is "the easiest person in the world to get along with," as one such patient put it. Another said, "If it weren't for others the world would be a pleasant place to live in." Because of his distortions and their consequences, "the *insecurity* which the neurotic feels with regard to others is considerably reinforced."*(49, p. 295)* His inner uncertainty shows in his not knowing where he stands with others and where they stand with him. He also has too much or too little confidence or trust in himself or others. All of this *"increases his fears of people."* When we review the effects the pride system has on human relationships, we see that "it *reinforces the basic anxiety,"* and makes the neurotic feel all the more isolated and helpless toward a potentially hostile world. *(49, pp. 296-97)*

All the factors disturbing relationships in general will unavoidably operate in a love relationship. Many have the fallacious notion that there must be love if sex is satisfactory. Actually, while temporarily easing the tension, sex may serve to perpetuate an essentially neurotic relationship. When a person experiences his sex and/or love as satisfactory, we must ask, satisfactory for what? The *"meaning and the functions which love and sex assume for the neurotic"* are questions we must answer. *(49, p. 299)*

Of one thing we can be sure, he has a deeply ingrained feeling he is unlovable. This feeling is too painful to confront directly so he deals with it in a vague, blurred way. Either he feels some day the right person will come along and love him or, with an equally unrealistic pessimism, accepts his unlovability as an unalterable fact. The neurotic feels he is unlovable because somewhere he is aware that his capacity to love is impaired. His feeling of unlovability is constantly reinforced by his self-hate and its externalization. He also expects more of love than it can do. Love cannot, for example, relieve him of his self-hate. He ends up feeling he is not really loved and hence has further proof that he is unlovable. Regardless of the foreground symptom picture, neurotic or psychotic, at bottom, present in all, and most difficult to loosen and lessen, is the feeling of unlovability.

51

Speaking of the neurotic functions of sex, Horney said: "It is probably as little accurate to make a too neat distinction between love and sex as it is to link them too closely (Freud). Since, however, in neuroses sexual excitment or desires more often than not are separate from a feeling of love, I want to make a few special comments on the role which *sexuality* plays in them. Sexuality retains in neurosis the function it naturally has as a means of physical satisfaction and of intimate human contact. Also sexual well-functioning adds in many ways to the feeling of self-confidence. But in neuroses all these functions are enlarged and take on a different coloring. Sexual activities become not only a release of sexual tensions but also of manifold nonsexual psychic tensions. They can be a vehicle to drain self-contempt (in masochistic drives) or a means to act out self-torment by sexual degrading or tormenting of others (sadistic practices). They form one of the most frequent forms of allaying anxiety."*(49, p. 300)*

Sex served all the above neurotic functions for a young Swiss-French career woman. She came from a rigid religious, moral, and intellectual background. She had become rebelliously resigned, morbidly dependent, and severely alienated, with intense feelings of unlovability and ugliness. These she massively externalized to her mother with whom she had been in a life and death struggle, literally from birth. Her mother had rejected her because she had been born a girl. Denial of her authentic femininity was extreme. Papa's little girl, she adored him as did her mother. He died when she was a child. Fiercely ambitious, she had to be first in her class, desperately so if her competitor was female. At the same time she behaved like a coquettish, seductive little girl.

From her late teens, she acted out sexually. Being without a partner was unbearable. When inner and outer circumstances demanded the abrupt ending of a relationship, she was literally propelled into the arms of another man. When seized by these impulses, life was a torture. Often she was driven into quite self-destructive and self-degrading behavior. The partners acquired under such circumstances were often quite unattractive. Driven by another impulse she, as opportunity arose, would drop them sadistically for someone less unacceptable.

After a year and a half of analysis, the level of her tension and anxiety gradually diminished. Now she could be aware of what happened with sudden increases in both. Such upsurges might have many sources. After her marriage, the impulse to have an affair would become almost uncontrollable. She came close to doing so, but never did. With each episode, it became clearer that she submitted to her husband sexually only to hold him. She almost never desired him, except when she was generally anxious or to placate him when he was angry at her. She never had orgasms with him.

Before her marriage, she was in love with another man with whom she said she had enjoyed sex. What she enjoyed was not sex but being held in his arms like a little girl, being protected from life's vicissitudes and from the demands of mature responsibilities. This became clear during analysis. Sex was the price and the passport. She offered her body as payment for protection from anxiety. It was immediately available to men when her anxieties became unbearable. Her use of sex to allay anxiety had an almost addictive character.

For detached people sexuality may be the only bridge they have to people. Inhibited people and those with grave self-doubts may rush into sex to overcome those inhibitions and to deny those doubts. "Lastly, the normal relation between sexuality and self-confidence shifts to one between sexuality and pride," Horney wrote. "Sexual functioning, being attractive or desirable, the choice of a partner, the quantity or variety of sexual experiences — all become a matter of pride more than of wishes and enjoyment. The more the personal factor in love relations recedes and the purely sexual ones ascend, the more does the unconscious concern about lovability shift to a conscious concern about attractiveness."(49, p. 301)

Oliver S. was almost crushed by his overpowering mother. His sweet, weak father who died tragically, feeling himself a failure, was of no support. His mother, who had undermined his father, also severely damaged Oliver's sisters and brothers. Oliver's doubts about his worth as a person and his desirability as a male were considerable.

His first analytic experience, in his teens, was imposed upon him by his mother and he resisted it. His second was in his late twenties. Of five years' duration, he terminated this analysis after limited results. His third, which had been helpful, was terminated after two years by his therapist, who moved to another city.

During his year with me, his self-doubts abated, and his periods of self-confidence became longer and more frequent. His previous practice of bringing prostitutes to his home almost ceased. More frequently now, he asked for dates from girls he met in his daily activities. At times he could feel self-confident in his business, and allow himself small increments of feeling successful without too severe repercussions.

Oliver opened his session with expressions of appreciation for the help he was getting, particularly with his fear of success and his repercussions to being successful. "What happened last night is so clear." At a party the night before, Oliver was successively approached by two beautiful girls almost as soon as he came into the room. "I felt confident of myself. I was enjoying myself and the girls. As soon as I got home, I called a prostitute. When I woke up the next morning, I realized what had happened. There it is."

In our discussion he described his usual anxiety response at being affirmed as a male. As soon as he got home he "called a prostitute" in a somewhat clouded, dissociated state. His state in the morning was like coming to after a bad dream and finding it hard to believe it wasn't real. He mentioned that soon after the girls approached him the night before, he had felt free enough to ask immediately for their telephone numbers.

The girls Oliver met the night before were a number of notches above any previous girls he had met. He had felt *too good* about the way he had conducted himself, and in their *liking* him. The repercussion was already happening at the party. He couldn't possibly have asked them for a date that same night. Under the onslaught of self-hate, anxiety, and intense feelings of loneliness, he had to call a prostitute to allay all these feelings and his temporarily intensified self-doubts. He called one of the girls several days later.

This episode was different from previous ones in the sympathy for himself, in his self-understanding, and in his expectation of further help from me. In the previous month, there had been several occasions during which he spoke of "how different it would have been if" he "had had someone like me as a father in the first place" — one who could have protected him from his mother. Clearly sex and lovability had quite different meanings during the party and immediately after.

In the six months following the evening described, Oliver became considerably surer of himself, both in his relationships and in his business, which tripled in size. He then took in a partner, which further enlarged his business. During this period, he also moved through a succession of relationships with women that increased his self-confidence and satisfactions. These relationships were part of a delayed maturational process.

As Horney points out, the "increased functions which sexuality assumes in neurosis do not necessarily lead to more extensive sexual activities than in a comparatively healthy person. They may do so, but they may also be responsible for greater inhibitions." In the healthy person sexuality assumes a harmonious, appropriate place in the psychic economy. In the neurotic "it often assumes an *undue* importance" which stems from nonsexual sources. Sexual functioning can also be easily disturbed: "There are fears, there is a whole host of inhibitions, there is the intricate problem of homosexuality, and there are perversions. Finally, because sexual activities (including masturbation and fantasies) and their particular forms are determined — or at least partly determined — by neurotic needs or taboos, they are often compulsive in nature . . . .

"The special difficulties existing toward love and sex are after all only one expression of his total neurotic disturbances. The variations in addition are so manifold because in kind they depend not only upon the individual's neurotic character structure but also on the particular partner he has had or still has."*(49, pp. 302-3)* The partner was chosen because of neurotic needs. Being so restricted in his choice by psychological factors, his neurotic problems would factually also narrow the field from whom he might "choose."

That one woman successively married and divorced five alcoholics shows how narrow this "choosing" can be. Another woman married and divorced two, the second to remarry the first. These instances are unusual only in that divorce occurred. Frequent and long separations, often with the husband barred from the house, are not infrequent when a woman marries an alcoholic. The reunions have a familiar variety of promises and protestations. The rigidity and special nature of the patterns of the partners accounts for their inability to learn from experience and for their mutual distress when the husband stops drinking.

One of my first patients, for example, was sent by his wife to help him resume drinking. Pressured by her to stop, he had become a compulsive nondrinker and the leader of a very active local chapter of Alcoholics Anonymous. His righteousness and rages now made living with him much more difficult than it was when he drank. He interrupted after a brief period in therapy, his rages and righteousness less intense, but with his anxieties increasing with the possibility of resuming his drinking.

Rather than describe the manifold variations of erotic and sexual experiences determined by the factors already mentioned, it might be better to mention certain central tendencies common to all. The neurotic *"may tend to exclude love"*; give it a *"prominent place in his imagination"*; or there may be *"an overemphasis placed on love and sex in actual life.* Love and sex then constitute the main value of life and are glorified accordingly."*(49, pp. 304-5)*

Based on long experience with the therapy of homosexuals, individually and in groups, Gershman considers this perversion a symptom based on the total character structure. *(154)* He delineated three categories of homosexuals: overt, subliminal, and symbolic. They represent a spectrum ranging from those most involved with homosexual behavior to those whose homosexuality is mainly evident in thought, fantasy, and dreams. Gershman regards homosexuality as an attempt at repairing a defective self-image through the magic ritual of fusion. Weiss saw the "magic-mirror symbiosis" as the essential aspect of the homosexual relationship. *(155)* Rubins did not find in either fetishists, transvestites, voyeurs, or exhibitionists, the extreme identity confusion and the excessive self-contempt focused on the genitals and other sexual attributes which he found in homosexuals. *(156)*

Gershman regards faulty gender identification as the basis of the major sexual perversions with maximal distortion in transsexuals. The latter perceives himself *as* female, while the homosexual sees himself only as a *defective* male or female. While manifold neurotic and psychotic problems of transsexuals were treatable, Gershman found that the therapy of the basic problem was difficult because of their lack of core, gender identity. When approached therapeutically, ego dissolution and panic resulted. *(154)*

The histories and therapies of these young men illustrate many aspects of sexuality, of love and hate in human relationships. Horney's theories, while helpful in their therapies, needed more of the guides that are implied in the holistic orientation.

Some are explicated in modern ego psychology, in Erikson's identity formation, crises, confusion and diffusion, *(157)* in Gergen's core identity, *(158)* in Stoller's sexual and gender identity, *(159)* in Schilder's ideas on body image, *(160)* and in Knapp's "Image, Symbol and Person."*(161)*

Sullivan's notion of the *self-system* and Angyal's concept of the *symbolic self*, help integrate the various identity concepts. *(199, p. 109; 162, p. 325)* They take into account the organic *substrate* as determined by heredity, endowment and life history. Many of the ideas mentioned are subsumed in my concepts of the symbolizing process, the symbolic self, and the self-system, which are discussed in chapters 5 and 6.

Arthur G., age twenty-two, entered analysis because of marital problems. Two years later he divorced his wife Betty C., and continued his affair, begun before analysis, with Wanda G., a non-Jewish divorcee who lived in his building. In the fourth year of our work, he became engaged to her, introduced her to his parents, and six months later broke off with her. Six months later, after many brief affairs, he became deeply involved with Sue R. and decided to marry her. Abruptly, a year later and toward the end of the seventh year of our work, he stopped seeing her. After a period of several months of no girls, he began having sexual relations with many different ones in the spirit of the adolescent boy he felt he never had been. He eventually became bored with these activities, and said he wanted more out of a relationship.

There was a certain maturing in experiencing himself as an adolescent having lots of girls. His relationships during this period were mainly sexual acting out with a woman who affirmed his narcissism. Earlier in this phase there was occasional cunnilingus and fellatio. Later, he practiced mainly coitus. The realization that he wanted more from his relationships was an additional maturation.

During World War II, Arthur's father had to be away often and long; but when the war was over, he used a variety of rationalizations for continuing his absences. When at home, a fun-loving, rather sensual man, Arthur and Saul, his older brother by six years, enjoyed him. Saul had been very sickly from childhood. Arthur had always been robust. His mother was an intensely masochistic woman filled with terrors of life and of the world. These fears were communicated to her sons, and they became bound to her in paralyzed terror.

Arthur was forced to make Saul a father surrogate and a protector from his mother. He smarted under the submission imposed by Saul. Saul was an intellectual who insisted emotions did not exist. Everything could be reasoned out. This sent Arthur into helpless rages.

At nine, Arthur had compared bottoms and tried anal intercourse with a boyfriend. He told his mother, and she anxiously brushed it aside. From about ten to fourteen, he had a close relationship with a boy who may have had homosexual tendencies, although nothing happened between them. While they slept in the same room, there was never anything sexual between Arthur and Saul. Their intellectual relationship, however, was highly eroticized — almost sexualized. At fifteen, he impregnated the next door neighbor's daughter, and forced his father to take care of the abortion, a pattern he repeated several times.

The first four years of analysis were involved with the fierce vendetta he carried on against his father who had not been there for him, leaving him to the mercies of his mother and, consequently, to those of Saul. This vendetta was acted out toward me with a brutal callousness, coldness, and stoniness. During the third year, he did not pay his bill for three months, while testing me out in many additional ways. He acted out similarly toward his father who was about to stop calling him. Arthur broke with his father first, and decided to refuse all financial help. This was a piece of vicious vindictiveness, but also a violent and desperate attempt to save himself.

In the fourth year, he began to experience the world of terror his mother had communicated to him. There was, concomitantly, murderous rage at her for what she had done to him. In the eighth year, these episodes of total body-shaking terror became more frequent and longer lasting.

Starting about the second year, there were brief discussions about his brother. They evoked intense repercussions, followed by long periods during which he was not mentioned. From the fifth to the seventh year, they became more frequent as his trust in me became deeper. He became able to express monumental rage at what his brother had done to him. In eight years of analysis, he only saw him twice and talked to him three times.

In the middle of the eighth year he woke from a nightmare: "A guy was sucking my cock. I was on my back. That goddamn passive position. The worst of it was I felt paralyzed and I couldn't move. I woke with a hard on. I didn't come. I woke up stiff and rigid. I told you that's the way I often woke up. Now I understand why I never had wet dreams and often woke up with an erection. I was paralyzed because I was aroused but it wasn't sexual. It was like I felt with my brother. I couldn't get away from him. I always felt bound and tied to him when he started to explain something and I had to agree to. I would scream in rage and I would get powerless and I couldn't move."

In response to my question, he answered, "Oh no, we never looked at each other naked. We actively averted looking at each other's cocks. In the past few days I have been blind with rage at my brother and mother. I couldn't think. I've had a splitting headache most of the time."

This dream and associations could fit into Freudian theory which was not what guided me in therapy. Something different and more comprehensive was necessary. In the remainder of the eighth year, the passivity diminished, his capacity to initiate increased, and his relations with women and men improved.

Arthur is very good looking, but not handsome because of a certain prettiness. Girls adore him, hence are easily available. In the second and third year of analysis, he often experienced and fantasied himself as a pretty little girl. In the seventh year of analysis, he often wondered about my genitals, and had sensations of feeling or holding them. In the eighth year, the above-mentioned nightmare occurred. He began masturbating early. It was one of his severest problems when he began analysis. There were frequent frenzies of vicious and prolonged masturbation. These assaults on his genitals continued for the first four years. Thereafter they slowly abated, occurring only rarely by the eighth year. Masturbation led to a recurrent urethritis, and on one occasion required cystoscopy. Inflammation of the urethra and spasm of the neck of the bladder were diagnosed.

Seeing his father-in-law as the father he never had, and his wife's family as the kind of family he wished he had had were crucial factors determining his marriage. In divorcing his wife he was avenging himself against a father surrogate who didn't measure up, and against mother surrogates, his mother-in-law and his wife. The latter he also degraded by refusing sex, and by having an affair with a woman in the same building. His wife he experienced as physically unattractive and his paramour the most beautiful woman he ever knew. The need for beautiful women was persistent and powerful.

He did not consult his parents about the marriage or divorce, nor about getting engaged to the second girl. The second engagement allowed him to revenge himself on both parents because the girl was not Jewish, to affirm that, by getting such a beautiful woman, he was "the preferred one." He then avenged himself further on his mother by rejecting the girl. With the third girl, he fleetingly felt some pleasure in sex and a slight suggestion of tenderness, both for the first time. He also experienced playfulness with her. As she pressed for marriage, after he had previously suggested it, he felt trapped and abruptly dropped her. A year later, in a brief accidental meeting on the subway, he realized he had out-grown her.

Arthur is very intelligent and did very well in college. He dropped out of law school with the intent to wound his parents, particularly his father. He is musically gifted, and there were battles with his mother about practicing. Only in the last year, on his own, has he again taken up serious study of the piano. He has created a business from which he supports himself. He has no real friends, only a few acquaintances and a few more people he knows superficially.

Diagnostically, Arthur manifests a borderline syndrome. He is sociopathic, sadistic, narcissistic, arrogant-vindictive and extremely alienated. Crucial in describing him are the vagueness and insubstantiality of real self and of core identity. His sexual identity originally was quite confused and diffused, at times he experienced himself as a little girl; his gender identity was behavioristically masculine but without the whole substratum of feelings, thoughts, and fantasies that would go with feelings of maleness. Uncertainty about gender identity was further shown by his interest in my genitals, and the nightmare of a young man performing fellatio on him. Although his physical identity from the viewpoint of body image was the most substantial, it was still limited because his mother had forbidden, in fact had terrorized him against, getting involved in fights or in competitive, contact sports. He was, however, an excellent swimmer.

What made it possible for him to stay in analysis, and ultimately to get as far as he did, relates to the person of the therapist as the most important instrument in therapy. My years of experience and experiences with persons with such structures were highly important to Arthur. Stringently required, also, was that I *be there* giving balance and imperturbability. He needed me to go along with almost anything he did. Going along with did not mean agreeing or condoning, but actively *being there* as he went through these behaviors. The details of how I went along with, while maintaining and building my position of leverage, is explicated in this example and elsewhere, particularly in Chapters 9 and 16, where the therapist as instrument is discussed. In the third year, when I finally said this is it, after he had not paid his bill for three months, all his rationalizations for not doing so vanished. My value to him had been steadily increasing in the process, so that he chose paying rather than leaving me. Nonpayment is one example of how he was constantly testing and palpating me for consistency, reliability, dependability, responsibility, trustworthiness, understanding, and impartiality.

During the first four years, Arthur related to me not *as if I was* his father, but as though I *in fact was* — a therapeutic situation more fully discussed in Chapter 16. No individuality and separateness was tolerated or seemed possible. If, when, and how he was going to allow this distinction was to be decided by him. It began to happen in the fifth year, when his relation to his father also began to improve. During the eighth year, they began to enjoy each other, but the father was not allowed to mention Arthur's mother or his brother.

We went through the same sequence with his mother. I was her, not reminiscent or equivalent to her. My being his brother was not as intense and did not last as long. As he felt stronger, and became able to finally look at that relationship, his rages at his brother mounted. He explicitly said, "I want to deal with that S.O.B. myself."

In the eighth year, secure in his relationship with me and his father, and with a considerable resolution of his ties to his brother, he turned to an in-depth experiencing of how it really had been with his mother. Often two to three times in a single session he would become that terrified and terrorized little kid cowering under the covers after having performed endless rituals before daring to get into bed. Simultaneously he was experiencing the lack of a father to turn to, the ominous terrorizing figure of his mother, and the inimical character of his brother — no ally because Saul and his mother Arthur always felt as united and as one. As he goes through these terrors Arthur experiences the smells, sounds and appearances of the bedroom, the house, and the town they lived in at the time.

In the eighth year, I became a person in my own right about whom he was curious. For the first time, he wanted to complete his analysis. This would be the first project in his life that he has chosen to begin that he has finished.

During the summer of the ninth year he spent a long holiday with his father. Now more substantial and with a clearer perception of himself, he could look more realistically at his father. He was quite disturbed at his awareness of his previous misperception of him. He also saw his father's "fiendish and diabolical charm" which reminded him of his own. This subject opened up for the first time, in a serious way, his own immorality.

He dared to spend some time with his mother which he had avoided up to then as a survival necessity. He experienced her engulfing and omnivorous possessiveness. He was distressed at seeing in her face the wish for and the pull toward death. He had become aware of his search for "the dream girl," and hated himself for its sentimentality and romanticism. He realized how it had crucially determined his becoming, after a period, disappointed in one girl after another. He saw its connection with his mother and wondered about its relationship to his possibly being or having been a homosexual.

"To have become a homosexual would have been a complete capitulation to my mother and a triumph for her. This summer I also became aware of the ferocity of my passivity."

I sensed without his mentioning it that for some time he was going to continue on a three times weekly schedule. He said, "This time it doesn't make any difference that you are back." Before, my return had been experienced as "Now everything will be taken care of." He continued, "Now I know it's up to me. These are my problems. Sure I want your help but I know in the final analysis it's up to me."

Leonard P. came into analysis with what he considered a specific problem: the urge to have an ejaculation by pressing against women's behinds in public places had become all consuming. He was terrified of the possibly dangerous consequences of these frenzies of mounting intensity. He loathed himself for his inability to control his behavior. He frequented prostitutes, paying them to allow him to press up against them and/or to perform fellatio.

This only intensified his self-loathing and guilt. But by degrading the prostitutes in manner and tone, he held his self-loathing somewhat in check.

At twenty-five, he had, since eighteen, seen many analysts in consultation, written to many more, and made two attempts at therapy, each of about two years' duration. There was considerable exhibitionism, narcissism, and voyeurism, with himself as object, in these activities. He wrote broadside letters, for example, to well-known analysts in the United States and abroad about his condition.

Leonard is quite good looking. With the face of a sensitive young man, many women find him attractive. He is also very intelligent, and probably an able piano player. A graduate student in history, he was failing to do many of the required papers and constantly delaying working on his Ph.D. thesis.

About his father he said: "The S.O.B. is a cipher. My mother had contempt for him. He was terrified of her." His father, a very able professional, is a detached intellectual. His mother carried on an implicit, and at times almost explicit, sexual seduction of her son in an attempt to possess and own him. This emasculated her husband in Leonard's eyes.

In contrast to Arthur G., who became paralyzed by his mother in a world of terror, and hence could never run away or appeal to anyone for help, Leonard would run away to a female neighbor or out into the street with his mother at his heels. When brought back, he was terrified of his mother's rages and was afraid she would kill him. In this childhood, he always experienced his mother as gigantic and consumed by monumental rage.

In his early teens be began fondling the breasts of a maid, and eventually had intercourse with her. With girls of his own age, he felt terrified. Between seven and nine, there may have been some exhibiting of genitals with boys of his own age. Masturbating occurred from an early age. He was concerned about getting caught, but felt no guilt. Masturbating was never excessive or a problem to him because his sexual tensions were mainly relieved in his relation with the maid.

When therapy began, with about forty hours in the first year and seventy in the second, he was under violent tension and anxiety, intensely restless, making frequent jerky movements with his torso and head. He constantly questioned the value of what I was doing. Once he went to see another analyst. He told me about it, before and after, later admitting he knew he was acting out. As he noted the pattern of the sessions which opened with agitation and closed with his being quieter, he became suspicious and mistrustful. He was somehow being tricked. My comments usually came toward the end of the session. I identified changes in old patterns and pointed out the emergence of new ones, while constantly focusing on the anxiety process.

Using the issue of finances, his parents attempted to involve themselves in the therapy. He tried to abet it. The attempts of both failed. He had to work extra, at no great sacrifice, to pay for his therapy. In the second year, he cut himself off from his parents' financial help, took on more work, and asked for another session. Now he felt freed, and freer to act out. For the first year and a half, he had been doing just that, but with quite some terror, particularly with reference to his mother against whom his rages were intense. His animosity toward his father faded. He began to let himself hope for a better relationship with him.

From the sixth month, and for the following year, the evolving pattern of dreams was most revealing. Women were seen from behind, later it included men. In time he saw them from in front, but with the whole midsection covered, to be gradually exposed. Then followed increasing sex play with women. After a year and a half, he woke with a very firm erection from a dream of being in bed with a girl. About this time he reported that for a month he had been free of the intolerable seizures of anxiety which he had had since he was about ten.

Concomitantly, the need for pressing against women fell away. He forced himself to see girls who would demand that he penetrate them. This he finally did with a surprising lessening of his fear of looking at, and entering, the vagina, an act he felt would never be possible. During this phase, the detailed structure of his mother's seductiveness emerged. It had collusive and threatening elements. It was a secret they kept from "your father" and maintained in a hot, sticky atmosphere of sexual arousal.

While Leonard's symptomatology was more dramatic than Arthur's, and the rate of change equally so, in both the acting out was of considerable proportions. Both manifested the borderline syndrome, are sociopathic, narcissistic, arrogant-vindictive, alienated, and extremely egocentric. In Arthur, the sadism, callousness, coldness, and stoniness are much greater than Leonard's. Arthur could not flee, and had to turn to stone to deal with his terrors. His father, while having positive qualities, was physically almost totally absent, which created even greater problems.

63

The qualities I mentioned about myself in regard to Arthur were also essential in the work with Leonard. Both were very intelligent, cunning, quick, and cruel, always alert to trip me up and to lead me into traps. Well into the second year, Leonard said, "You're the most unflappable guy I know. I don't know if you're really that way, and it isn't because I haven't tried to find out." After about a year, his attacks on me began to fall away, and more and more of a shy little boy emerged — a little boy who gradually took on and then abandoned some of the qualities of a coy little girl. The hippie accouterments regarding hairdo, clothes, speech, and behaviors which had previously been so much a part of Leonard, began to fall away to the point that at times he was looked at, and acted like, a square.

During the last six months, the quality of his work at school has begun to improve. He has become slightly more disciplined, and has resumed practicing the piano in a serious way. The terror of his mother has fallen away, much to his surprise.

While Leonard's relation to his younger sister had been bad up to until about six years ago, it began to improve slowly, and then rapidly when she married "a guy who is a real man." His relationship with his brother-in-law and his sister was his most important and meaningful relationship until he began, in the second year, his first meaningful and extended involvement with a woman. He has one very close male relationship, and a half dozen others of some depth. He has had a number of continuing, meaningful relationships with married couples and with single girls, of course without sex. The contrast with the paucity of human relationships in Arthur's case is obvious.

Both have had practically no experience in fighting or in competitive sports. Arthur has a powerful body, and could have become one of the "muscle boys" but didn't. Both experience their body image differently. Behavioristically, Arthur's sexual identity has been more exercised, but the experiencing of it has been limited, as it has with Leonard. Both have ill-defined, diffused, and confused gender identities. Core and real self-identity are insubstantial, even less defined than gender identity.

The therapeutic test suggests a shorter analysis for Leonard although he might return for short periods of therapy. *Life as a therapist* will be his most valuable ally.

In the first session after the summer holiday he informed me he wanted to interrupt because for months he had only an occasional anxiety attack, and his impulse to press against women's behinds had almost disappeared. In discussing his relationship with his girlfriend, he mentioned caring for her.

64

I said anxiety had been his motivation for therapy. Now the issue was how much did he care for himself. He tried to get me to make his decision for him. After several weeks of discussion, he decided to continue with the same number of sessions he had had before his vacation.

The results of therapy thus far and the life history of Arthur and Leonard clearly indicate how crucial was the person of the therapist and the relationship, in Arthur's case the only one, and for both the most meaningful relationship they had ever had.

Understandably they would turn to such a person from time to time for help and counsel.

By age seven Walter O. knew he was "different" from the other boys. Experimenting began shortly thereafter, with overt homosexual behavior soon following. When analysis began at thirty-three, he was involved in frantic, promiscuous contacts in toilets and Turkish baths, their frequency depending on the level of his anxiety.

His father was weak and petulant. Constantly bickering with his mother, Walter saw him as "no man." His mother constantly provoked these fights and threatened to leave. She was flirtatious and seductive with her darling son and only child. Although they never even separated, Walter was in constant terror that there would be a divorce. From his earliest years he was forced into the role of go-between and peacemaker. This role dominated his life. He had a horror of friction, fighting, and even mild differences of opinion. He considered himself a "nice guy" who didn't see why people "couldn't settle things amicably." Contributory was a crucial experience at age eight. Taunted into a frenzy, he went berserk and almost killed another little boy by pounding his head on the pavement. Since then he has had a horror of the violence and of the controlled murderous rage in him.

During analysis, as his anxiety lessened, his frantic, indiscriminate contacts diminished and relationships of longer duration increased. First, he went through a phase of "I should not be homosexual." This became unbearable. Next, came a phase of "I should be heterosexual," and he ultimately attempted sex with a willing woman. It was a painful failure. Then came a phase of "I'll have as many affairs as I want" which also petered out. I have seen this sequence quite frequently in the therapy of homosexuals if they remain in analysis long enough. Following the first two phases, he attacked me for suggesting the behaviors he had followed, which of course I hadn't. The third was frantic rebellious defiance. About two years before he terminated his six years of analysis, he began a continuing relationship with a somewhat older man. One reason given for interrupting therapy was that I was "trying to make him give up this relationship and turn him into a heterosexual," a statement frequently made by homosexuals in therapy.

With Arthur, Leonard and Walter we have seen intermittently physically and emotionally absent fathers. Arthur's and Leonard's mothers were dominating; and Walter's was also, but less obviously so. There is evidence that homosexuality is more common where the mother is dominating and seductive and the father absent, weak, brutal, or aloof. But all sons of such parents do not become homosexuals. These categorizations, though helpful guides, do not inform us regarding the intricacies of the relationships, nor about the impact of other children and ordinal sequence.

In Walter's case there was intense narcissism, but not of the obvious variety as with Arthur and Leonard. Likewise, there was much arrogant-vindictiveness, but subtly played out. What was very different was his pseudo-compliance, his self-effacement, his being a nice guy with a vengeance. The sociopathy was pervasive, although subtly present, except in his dreams and flagrantly so in some of his nightmares. Alienation was extreme. Some of his earliest dreams were eerie and gruesome in their remoteness, mechanicalness, and dehumanization.

Clearly there was little of real self-identity in Walter. He had no interest in sports, and his body image was undeveloped. His experience at age eight turned him away from fighting, friction, and competition. There was no healthy male or female figure to help him in his gender identity development, in fact, both opposed it. Turning away from males toward females further diffused, confused, and warped his gender identity. Early homosexual experiences had consequences for his sexual identity. Most obviously damaged was core identity. Actually, there was constant interference with the development of all forms of identity feelings. From infancy he had to be there for his parents, trying to hold them together, although he was torn himself. If we assume a moral identity, so essential to the sense of moral integrity, and of integrity in its many other senses, this is where he was most damaged, most diffused, confused, and underdeveloped.

Our understanding of identity formation may be amplified by the following observations on homosexuals, both male and female.

As far back as James A. can recall, he lived under the shadow of his brother Steve, although Steve died at nine when James was only three. At four his father, the dominant parent, lost everything in the Depression. His mother, who had elevated her position by marrying him, became the significant figure as his father shrank into silence.

Cybil W. was constantly reminded of her sister Sue, who died in infancy before Cybil was born. While the wonderfulness of Steve was only implied by James A.'s mother, Cybil's mother left no doubt about how remarkable this infant Sue was and would have become.

These two people were made to feel that they were not acceptable; in fact, they were positively rejectable because they fell so far short of an older brother or sister who had died. In these two cases the comparison was with a member of the same sex. In the case of an only male child who became a homosexual the comparison was made with what his brother would have been like if he had been conceived.

Then there are those who are constantly compared with some composite of their parents' expectations. It is something they could have been if they had really tried. Clearly such an atmosphere does not foster, but actively inhibits identity formation, destroying it where it begins to form, or distorting it by a stream of contradictory expectations.

In the homosexual relationship it would appear that the one with the big penis, the prized object, is more secure as he waits in a passive, aggressive, narcissistic, arrogant-vindictive, and withholding posture for the other to seek and gain his favors. At bottom, he feels no less alienated, empty, anxious, insecure, incomplete and defective because he just as frantically needs to be sought and taken before he can have a momentary feeling of being, of identity. It is an endless struggle of having and not having, seeking and getting and not getting, moments of having and being. The existential meanings of being, having, and doing, add dimensions to our understanding of the varieties of male homosexuality. Seeking, taking, and having the big penis can have a similar meaning for the woman who feels incomplete, defective, and unlovable.

Andrea R. was supposed to have been a boy, and when her brother came he was favored. Her father was weak, and her mother coldly dominated the household. She shocked her first boy friend by reaching for his penis inside his pants and by immediately wanting to perform fellatio. She had had no prior heterosexual experience and had never heard of or known about fellatio. She was aggressive in sex before her marriage, during it, and in extramarital affairs she initiated. She would not let her husband touch her genitals for a long time, and she was revulsed by the idea of girls masturbating. In her twenties and after marriage, she had a close relationship with a woman who may have been a lesbian. When she began to feel this might be so, she broke off the relationship.

Andrea R. has had a number of therapists and many years of analysis which originated because of recurrent depression and a suicide attempt. After some years of therapy with me, her wish to be a boy and to have a penis emerged. Then she recalled that as a little girl with a mirror, she had looked for a penis hidden in the folds of her labia. Concomitantly, much came out about the wish to have a penis through fellatio and penetration.

The night after a session in which there had been much discussion of such issues, while brushing her hair, she had a sudden realization. With a feeling of revelation, with chills and goose pimples on the back of her neck, and with a feeling of freeing it came to her that "Yes, when I have a penis in me, I have a penis. I am a man." As she related this experience and elaborated on it in the session, she felt still freer and said: "Now I can feel free to be a woman."

She now understood her compulsion to have a man. Life was not livable for her without a man. Occasions in her life when she might be without a man around were unbearable. There always was one, and often several. In addition to the compulsion to have a man, she now understood the desperate need for sex, and the need to have a penis, a big one, because without it she felt incomplete, "as if I was nothing." In that session Andrea became aware of the diminishing need for the big penis which disappeared entirely in time. Her attitudes toward sex changed radically. Sexual relations became more totally involving, with much more holding, fondling, relating, and tenderness than she had been able to achieve previously.

Dorothy S. found love in the arms of an understanding teacher in her teens. As with Andrea, there was a dominating, possessive, suffocatingly intimidating mother and a remote, subtly sadistic father who used her as a son. There was a younger sister. Following the teacher, there were a number of shorter and longer lesbian relationships.

Years of analysis with several analysts helped her out of a deep depression with feelings of alienation, meaninglessness, and self-loathing. After several short heterosexual relationships, which began as the intensity of the lesbian ones waned, she began a longer one. Her analysis with me began shortly afterward. In the sexual affair, she was used and abused, aiding and abetting such behavior because of her feelings of unlovability and her masochistic needs. With much pain and struggle she ended it.

About two years after breaking off with this man she began to enjoy living alone. For many years life without a partner had been intolerable. As she was daring to express positive feelings toward me as a person and as a man, she had the following dream. She was in bed with a man. Both were naked. He had gotten out of bed, and she noted that he had a very large penis and that it was erect. With a feeling of pleasure and admiration she thought, "What a man!" About nine months later, she dreamt she was having intercourse with her father and sadly said, "To think that at my age I had to go through this. I still haven't grown up."

Shortly after she had begun analysis with me, even urges toward women disappeared. At the time of the big penis dream, she had strong sexual urges toward a man which continued for some months thereafter. About a year after the dream about her father, all sexual urges toward me disappeared, and there was frequent expression of simple liking for me as a person.

The emphasis on the big penis has several obvious sources. The focus on bigness immediately informs us of that person's feeling of smallness, littleness, and impotence. To be simply potent is not sufficient. Omnipotence is necessary, and it is affirmed in bigness. The focus is on the sex of a person and on the organ that most obviously defines his sexuality. It is an expression of overconcreteness. The big penis is also a measure of, and is proportionate to, the motivating anxiety. It exemplifies the taking of a physically functioning part for the whole of functioning, of physicality, of being, of personhood.

In the following instances, the focus is not on the part, nor on its size, but on omnipotence in functioning. Five different men have reported attempting to perform self-fellatio. Two women, while lying supine, fantasied having a penis and penetrating themselves. In all seven there is obviously the need to be complete unto themselves. They want to be all things sexual to themselves. It was acted out concretely by the men with accompanying fantasies of being women, their mouths being vaginas. The women with a fantasied penis experienced penetrating themselves. Vaguely the penis grew out of the groin. Several other women had vague thoughts that if their tongue was long enough they could penetrate themselves with it. Another fantasied performing cunnilingus on herself in an acrobatic position. When objects were vaginally inserted, it was done in frustration, for lack of a male, and when clitoral masturbation was unsatisfying. Such behaviors were often followed by guilt and self-loathing.

Although one of the five men who tried self-fellatio was very attractive to women, and while he could and did have many sexually, in the sexual act his anxieties about himself as a man were still present. The two women who fantasied a penis were ardently desired and had affairs, but their feelings of unlovability were not mitigated. Because of their life history and the defenses they had to evolve, these sexual behaviors and fantasies gave them, if only fleetingly, a feeling of identity and wholeness.

Such needs for self-sufficiency and self-enclosure inform us of their terror of relationship. Only sick total independence was possible for them. Sick dependency or sick interdependency was too terrifying, and only slowly allowed into awareness. It was years before they could glimpse healthy dependence, independence, and interdependence.

These people reveal the basic problem of all sexually perverted people and of very sick people in general. They all need to avoid feelings of being lacking and of not being enough. Such feelings are experienced as being basically defective, incomplete, inadequate, different, odd, or peculiar. With some, possessing and being possessed of the big penis in homo- and heterosexual relationships via partnership in the sexual act is an attempt to repair the defect, complete the incompleteness, allay the feelings of being different by being like others, and replace the feelings of impotence with those of omnipotence. The attempt gives some a momentary respite from anxiety. With others, anxiety persists in the very act and becomes intensified after it.

Being lacking or not being enough may also be experienced as being empty, hollow, or of being split, or having a rift in oneself. While the latter does express the experience of conflict and the terror of it, these feelings are also expressive of feelings of being defective and damaged.

The issue of being defective, incomplete, split, and damaged bring up the concept of penis envy. At a lecture Horney was asked what she put in place of this concept. She smilingly replied, "Nothing." The questioner felt she was evading the issue. Rooted in a philosophy that premised the part as determining the whole, he could not follow one that saw the totality of functioning of the parts as determining the functioning and the meaning of the part. Horney's position was that sex did not determine character but that character determined the meaning of the sexual relating. Her criticisms of penis envy are extensively documented in *Feminine Psychology* and in *New Ways. (63; 35)*

The questioner was operating on the premises of nineteenth century notions of biology which Freud shared. It is stated that Freud's orientation was biological. His biology was, however, materialistic, derived from nineteenth century science, and based on Newtonian mechanics. Horney's thinking is rooted in twentieth century notions of biology which are organismic and holistic. Biology derives from bios, meaning life, and biology is concerned with all aspects of living. The biosphere is the area in which life occurs through a sequence of biospheric occurrences. *(162, ch. 5)* This notion of biology is consonant with that of modern evolutionary and morphological biologists. These biologists think in terms of life phenomena, manifesting themselves in moving fields.

Finally the questioner was operating from still other premises of nineteenth century philosophy. These assume absolute determinism and isolated closed systems, which focus on one variable. This variable is then made into an object and into an idealized case, be it phenomenon, part, or function. Horney's thinking is system oriented, makes use of theories of field relations, and is guided by notions of relative determinism.

The concept of penis envy would not have to be replaced because the phenomena which could be so described and understood from a Freudian viewpoint can be described and understood from quite other vantage points. This issue can be illuminated more sharply by means of the following life history, dreams, and therapeutic experiences.

At the end of the second year of her analysis with me, after two previous therapies which totaled seven years, a middle-aged married woman with two children had these two dreams:

"I saw that my mother had hung two dogs by the paws on the clothesline in the backyard of our house. It was a sunny day. One was a German police dog and one was a mutt. I could see they were male. Both dogs were squirming and wriggling, particularly the mutt, as they hung on the line. It was awful to see. I took the clothespin off the right paw of the mutt and was holding it and was about to take the clothespin off the left paw when the foot broke off. It went off walking on the three feet and the stump."

"The second dream was very funny. I put my hand in my pocket and found that I had a long erect penis. It was long and thin like this (with which she held up her thumb). It was erect and kept jumping out of the pocket and I kept trying to put it back. It was long and thin and red like a dog's erect penis. After I tried a number of times to hide it in my pocket, I finally decided why not let it stick out where it can be seen."

Although she couldn't say what the first dream might be saying, she was certain that "The mutt in the dream is me." There were no associations to being crippled and defective. She immediately associated the second dream with smiles and laughing: "That stands for strength, virility, and self-confidence. Yes, I thought, why not show it, but my mother always said I was hard."

The dreams occurred after a series of nightmares which she couldn't recall, and after she had expressed herself toward her parents in a way she never had dared to do before. In fact, it was only in the three previous months that she had become aware of feelings of resentment and rage buried since childhood. She had always been terrified of how they would respond if she criticized them. She now dealt with their responses very effectively, and went on to even further progress in analysis.

Realizing its oral implications, she decided to give up smoking. What had made taking a stand against her parents possible was a steady letting go of the need to be loved, and an increasing ability to allow herself to be happy by herself. Most of her life she had needed to surround herself with people who she now realized meant little to her.

Her identification with "the mutt" to whose anguish she responded, revealed the beginning of being able to feel compassion for herself and of being strong enough to come to her own aid. The loss of the foot fits with the consequences of her mother's destructive behavior toward her since birth. It also could represent her failure to endow her with a penis. The police dog could have stood for her brother, five years younger, toward whom she acted as a mother to gain her parents' favor because he was the favorite. For almost a year, she had stopped being a surrogate mother to her brother.

In the second dream, she restores the defect and gives herself a penis which she finally dares to reveal with pride because of its size and power. At the time of the dream, she was feeling sexually aroused and quite unsatisfied and resentful because of her husband's impotence. The evidence could be read as a corroboration of the penis envy concept, except that it did not function as a guiding principle in the therapy. There was much to support her expressed feelings of increasing strength and self-confidence, as well as her new ability to lovingly care for herself and to help herself heal the wounds inflicted on her by her parents in childhood. While for years her anger had been mostly at her mother, in recent months it had become deep-felt organic rage which also included her father.

What we have been discussing regarding love, sex, and human relationships has crucial relevance for the analytic relationship which concerns itself not only with interpersonal but equally with intrapsychic factors. Just as the neurotic has put excessive expectations on love and sex, on changing his partner, and on his environment, so does he place unrealistic expectations on the analytic relationship. Changes in all of these may help, but they cannot "cure" any more than can an analyst's "love" (verbal, emotional, social, or sexual) make up for what was lacking in that patient's childhood and adolescence. In the first place, "making up for" is impossible; in the second, the person is no longer a child or adolescent; in the third, "cure" is not solely determined by one person; and finally, "we cannot 'cure' the wrong course which the development of a person has taken."*(49, p. 333)*

"The error involved in all these expectations does not lie in over-rating the importance of human relations but in underrating the power of intrapsychic factors. Although human relations are of signal importance, they do not have the power to uproot a firmly planted pride system in a person who keeps his real self out of communication . . . . Self-realization does not exclusively, or even primarily, aim at developing one's special gifts. The center of the process is the evolution of one's potentialities as a human being; hence it involves — in a central place — the development of one's capacities for good human relations."*(49, p. 308)* And that takes time, effort, pain, disillusionment, and work — working with, working through, and working continuously on one's own after regular analytic work has been completed.

Rose B., forty-seven years old and married, began analysis after opposing it for ten years. She had increasingly severe migraine since age nine. Five feet four inches tall, she weighed eighty-eight pounds. She was confronted with dying in her darkened bedroom of anorexia, inanition, dehydration, anemia, and drug intoxication due to codein, barbiturates, and a variety of drugs taken for her asthma and hay fever, or from progressive ergotism due to increasing doses of Gynergen (ergotamine tartrate).

Entering analysis meant a stand against powerful pulls toward dying and death, and an adamant family taboo against ever revealing the truth of your feelings or thoughts. It would mean the exposure of family myths pervaded with pretenses, hypocrisy, and cynicism. These clashing oppositions led, after six months of analysis, to an exacerbation of her symptoms, and she required two weeks hospitalization to stabilize her physical condition.

After eighteen months of therapy, she had her gall bladder removed. Though she bled on the eighth day post operative, as she had following a hemorrhoidectomy, a hysterectomy, and the birth of her two children, this was the first time she had felt: "I don't want to drown in my own blood" and "I didn't want to die under the anesthesia." Hematologists could find no basis for this bleeding or for her easy bruising.

Two years after analysis began, she went through a suicidal phase and made a serious attempt with barbiturates. Thereafter, a definite and progressive turning toward living and life was evident, not without repercussions. A year later, she had to be hospitalized for an intestinal obstruction. Three years prior to analysis, she was hospitalized for a small bowel intusussception not present with the recent obstruction. On both occasions medical treatment alleviated the condition.

She began analysis in the *vis-à-vis* position. Successively, she experimented first with turning her head away from me and then her back to me. Next she used the couch, sitting, then lying down. Finally she moved to the floor next to my chair which is behind the couch. After three months in this position, and toward the end of the fourth year of analysis, she had a dream in which I was vaguely there in bed with her. She had an orgasm and woke in a panic with intense feelings of shame. She experienced this dream as evidence of disloyalty to her husband, an idea which was most upsetting to her.

The dream opened up the tabooed subject of sex, present and past, attitudes toward being a woman, toward her body, and toward her physiological functions, and their lifelong disturbances through illness. What resulted was a steadily increasing interest in sex. Ultimately she had orgasms with her husband after having been frigid for almost fifteen years. About a year after the orgasm dream, she came to her session directly from a concert, having recently shown an increased interest in the functioning of the conductor. In the session, as she related the crescendo of her feelings, during the concert, they reached a peak, and she had an orgasm, after which she became silent, relaxed, and sleepy. When questioned about this therapeutic experience she described the picture of a total orgastic response. When asked whether she had experienced anything like it before, she said: "Yes, in a sexual orgasm."

For the next year and a half, she had orgasms during sessions with increasing intensity and frequency, with less fear of them and more pleasure. This also obtained in occasional, concurrent dreams with orgasms. Concomitantly, her dreams, previously always in black and white, began to be replete with color, first in pastels, and then in very rich hues.

As her sex interest increased, her husband became increasingly impotent, until finally he could be only partially aroused by her supportive assertiveness. The orgasms during sessions and in dreams diminished, almost abruptly, with the emergence of a sequence of vindictive dreams in which she physically assaulted her mother and a hated daughter-in-law. She derived pleasure from those dreams and from the relating of them to me. Thereafter, her orgasms were mild and enjoyable, followed by feelings of quiet contentment.

About a year and a half after the original orgasm dream, associations to it again came up. In the interim, some of the roots of her lifelong feeling of being "stupid," and of her intense fear of "saying something silly," which had kept her silent in situations where she would have to express herself, had become clearer. She became aware of a compulsive, passionate need to know everything and to know it perfectly, to control feelings with her mind and to have appropriate feelings by simply ordering them.

She unconsciously had equated her move from the couch, a position at a distance, to the floor, a position closer to me and at a lower level, with the below, intimate sexual position. Her anxiety on waking from the orgasm dream came mainly from letting go of and hurting her neurotic pride in controlling feelings through intellect. The shame was mainly a hurt-pride reaction to being disloyal, not to her husband, but to her old neurotic patterns. In short, anxiety and shame were her responses to an unpredicted breakthrough of spontaneous, unpremeditated, uncontrollable feelings toward me which were translated into sexual symbols and sexual bodily responses.

That the sexual orgasm dream, which presaged the orgasms during sessions, and the changed attitudes to sex in general, was a prototype of total organismal responses is evident from the following sequence. About three years after the orgasm dream, she dreamt she had moved her bowels in bed. It was so real that on awakening, even with the lights on and after careful examination, she still could not believe it had not happened. A detailed discussion of her lifelong problems with her bowels, involving constipation requiring frequent enemas since infancy, was followed by further alleviation, already in progress, of these difficulties.

One year later she dreamt she was seated at a table eating with gusto her favorite foods which she had cooked for herself. They included steak and celery, the crunching sound of which she clearly recalled. She always had been a poor eater and often was put on bland diets, because of easy intestinal irritation leading to spasms and transient obstructions. After this dream and a discussion of her eating habits, her appetite improved. About six months later, the dreams of aggressive violence began.

A year after that, there were three episodes of intense and painful clitoral spasm, and a dimly experienced impulse, with associated back spasm, to kick me, as residual patterns of clutching and clinging were increasingly frustrated and undermined. She had had some outbursts of anger of mounting intensity toward her husband and other members of the family during the previous few years. About a year after the clitoral spasms, I increasingly pressed her to examine why there had been enjoyable sexual orgasms, orgastic pleasure from emptying a full bladder and a full bowel, with eating, at a concert, and in a number of other situations but, as yet, no orgasms of fury. She finally erupted in a fury with: "I want to make you suffer the way you have made me suffer!" Following this outburst, she rushed to the bathroom to vomit. She had violent palpitations which gradually became quieter. She then went home and slept for nine hours. Thereafter, she had a changed viewpoint on herself, life, and the analysis.

Prior to the orgasm dream and particularly since her suicide attempt, she had become aware of how she had clung to and admired her mother through fear. She realized how her mother had used her from her earliest years to keep her father out of her mother's bed. Her mother's "sinister tenderness" was experienced in depth and worked through.

She recalled how at age nine, when a little boy tried to kiss her, she fled in terror. Her mother had instilled in her a fear and hatred of men, particularly of her father, which resulted in an almost complete ignorance regarding sex. When she married, sex was a frightening and painful experience which she avoided on any pretext. Only after one year of marriage was there penetration. Her husband was also a virgin. All of these awarenesses of what her mother had done to her brought out much resentment toward her, toward mothers in general and toward the kind of mother she herself had been.

Four months after she used the reclining position in the fourth year of the analysis, I moved from my chair behind the desk facing her to another behind her on the couch. It was a full six months before she could mention the panic she experienced at seeing my empty chair. The panic had lasted for four months. My empty chair opened the subject of the emptiness in her life.

Several months after I moved to the chair behind her, she moved to the floor beside my chair and began to talk of having something solid under her. At this point and several months before the orgasm dream, came a recollection of a bicycle her father had bought for her in her early teens and a particular experience with it. Riding on the beach, she received a strong impact when she saw that the tires left an imprint in the sand. She was now discovering in analysis that she also carried weight, had substance, and could leave an imprint.

This experience opened the subject of walking, swimming,

bicycle riding, and roller skating; breathing, talking and singing, laughing and crying, screaming, and her diminishing attacks of asthma and hay fever. Breasts which, in her teens, she had flattened with brassieres and hidden by stooped shoulders, she now enjoyed as she walked erectly and men noticed her.

Following the bicycle recollection came many positive memories connected with her father. She also recalled that during her early teens, she had exciting genital sensations when close to athletic young men. She fled in terror the moment she had these feelings, and they ceased at age sixteen. Before and after puberty she held her thighs tightly together or put a pillow between them to generate pleasurable genital sensations.

For years she had cystitis, which would flare up during analysis in periods of sexual tensions as on the occasion of the clitoral spasms in the tenth year. While in the eighth year, she thought of having an affair because of her husband's impotence. In the twelfth year she was becoming enraged at it. She now has a quiet acceptance of her husband's impotence. Not long after, only powerful self-blinding kept her from seeing the obviousness of her seductive maneuvers toward me. In the fourth year of analysis, she had experienced her omnivorous possessiveness and wanted to tear my penis off so that other women couldn't have it.

During the tenth and eleventh years, much material emerged which could be interpreted as body-as-phallus. Her early wishes to be a boy also emerged. An unwanted child, her parents had wished very much for her to be a boy, having had only girls so far. Not long after these early wishes emerged, she had a dream of vaginal bleeding so real that even with the lights on she could not believe it was not so.

At sixty-eight, she is a very vital woman. She is now the strongest member of her extended family where before she had been the weakest. Her counsel is constantly sought. She gives it as she wishes, and will not allow herself to be used. Her sessions, which had, until the fifteenth year, been three times weekly, have now diminished to about twenty yearly.

By the eighth year of analysis, she no longer needed Gynergen and rarely had any kind of headache. She used no sedatives or codein and had no need for medication for her asthma and hay fever which had considerably diminished. Her blood picture was normal, and she could with care keep her weight at 110. On a rare occasion it went up to 115.

From the tenth year on, in the United States and abroad, I presented my work with this woman to groups of post-Freudians (including a Kleinian one), neo-Freudians, and a group with a strong existential leaning. Each tried to reformulate the presented findings within their own frames of reference. All were impressed with the therapeutic results, even when they were quite antagonistic to my theoretical orientation.

The sequence of dreams of a sexual orgasm, defecating in bed and eating a delicious meal with gusto would seem to validate the concept of regression and stages of libido development except that the therapy was not guided by Freudian theory. Because of the focus on orgastic responses, the guidance of Reich's theories is suggested. Much regarding the most developed concepts of ego psychology can be seen. One group felt I had been much influenced by Fairburn's *(163)* theories on object relationships. I believe what made the results possible was the holistic or organismic approach I used.

Rose B.'s therapy confirms research findings regarding the similarity in the results achieved by experienced, innovative, and mature, therapists for whom rigid theories are only the loosest kinds of guides. This is not to say that theory is irrelevant. It must, however, be expressive of the times, of the place, the person, and the patient.

How important all these considerations are was sharply brought to my attention when I presented my work with this woman in Holland before a slightly post-Freudian group, in Switzerland before an existentially oriented group, and in Italy before a moderately post-Freudian group. Since the presentations were given within a ten-day period the national and theoretical juxtapositions were sharp. I had the very strong feeling that national and cultural values were equally if not more important in determining response than theoretical persuasions. They were more Dutch, Swiss-German, and Roman-Italian than analysts of a particular orientation. The importance of historical, national, and cultural factors must not be overlooked.

Chapter 4

Neurotic Disturbances
in Human Relationships II:
Work and Leisure

Horney investigated the influence of intrapsychic factors upon the process of work and the individual's attitude toward it. She was aware that disturbances in work can arise from external conditions such as economic problems, or a lack of time, or cultural factors such as the pressure of public opinion forcing a man to drive himself toward success. In studying the influence of attitudes toward others — superiors, inferiors, and peers in the work situation — Horney limited her focus to work requiring "personal initiative, vision, responsibility, self-reliance, ingenuity . . . creative work in the broadest sense of the word." This means creative work not only in the arts and sciences, but also in running a house or a business, being a mother or a union organizer.

Problems in work may affect the quality or the quantity of it. The presence of these problems is indicated by "inordinate strain, fatigue, exhaustion," or by "fears, panic, irritability, or conscious suffering under inhibitions."*(49, p. 310)* Whether he is conscious of it or not in the working situation, the neurotic's self-confidence is shaky. His appraisal of what is entailed is unrealistically measured. He works under conditions which are usually too rigid or odd. Because of his egocentricity, his relatedness to the work is tenuous, and the joy and satisfaction he might get from his work is impaired.

The differences in work disturbances, found in various kinds of neurosis are greater than their commonalities. *Expansive types* will overrate their capacities and the quality of their work while underrating its difficulties. Each of the *expansive types* varies in his responses. The *narcissistic* one, in spite of good capacities, does comparatively poor work because he is swayed by his imagination, scatters his energies in too many directions, and has a violent aversion to consistent efforts and to involvement with details. The *perfectionist*, plagued by his standards, is too meticulous, works too slowly, cramps his originality, and quickly ends up exhausted.

The *arrogant-vindictive type* is the most prodigious worker of all neurotics. He is relentlessly driven by ambition and a cold passion. The results of his efforts are often sterile. "His concern seems to be *to master the particular subject matter rather than to enrich it.*"(49, p. 315) Because of his arrogance, he cannot give credit to others or delegate responsibility. While he can organize, make long-range plans, and deal with temporary setbacks, serious test situations panic him, as does the possibility of failure, which he must deny.

The *self-effacing type* looks like the opposite of the expansive type in every detail. He sets his sights too low and underrates himself. He is almost always under the stress of anxiety, except for the moment when he first conceives an idea and before he gets caught up in his demands on himself and his self-berating. Because he must not be aware of his resources, and because he has a taboo against advantage for himself, he works under intense restrictions. To initiate is torture for him, and once the work starts to go well, he begins to destroy it by attempting to "improve" it. He therefore works slowly, wastefully, toward exhaustion and despair.

I spent a summer close to a colony of painters, and I often watched one in particular. He could outline and complete a first draft very quickly. It would have color, aliveness, freshness, and that incompleteness which adds so many possibilities. Then he would start to improve it, a process which took hours. The picture would end dull, drab, lifeless, and overpainted, with the painter exhausted, disgusted, irritable, and somewhat depressed. He would generally then get mildly drunk.

Having seen this a number of times, a group decided to distract him when he finished the first draft and take it away from him so he couldn't "improve" it. On a pretext they took him off for a drink. When he came back and could not find his painting, he became angry and quite disturbed. He then went off on a frightening drunk. No one dared to interfere with his improvements thereafter. I heard some years later that he had gradually lost the capacity for that first draft and deteriorated into alcoholism.

The *resigned type's* problems are distinctly different from those of the other two. In his work he settles for less as an expression of his life orientation. He works better alone and can't stand coercion, whether from others or from himself. He checks both expansive and self-effacing movements, as well as any spontaneous moves he feels in himself. His greatest problem is inertia. Either he rebels against conforming to others and his own expectations, or he restricts himself even further, feeling work a necessary evil and, in the case of *shallow livers*, an interference with his having "fun."

"Freud saw the frequency of neurotic disturbances in work and recognized their importance by making the capacity to work one of his aims in therapy."*(49, p. 327)* Horney felt he saw the problem too narrowly and formalistically. He was not aware that such disturbances could only be "an expression of the total personality," — that they had to be worked out in detail because of given individual differences and because of the varieties of neurotic solutions.

The consequences of neurotic disturbances in work are great. The amount of suffering and waste engendered by these disturbances is incalculable because it has its basis in unawareness. The waste results from the *not daring* in the working process; from not tapping one's resources; and from the consequently lesser quality of the work produced. The accumulated individual losses amount to a vast loss to mankind. It is regrettable how little concern there is about losses from a human viewpoint, in contrast to the great emphasis business and industry place on tangible losses.

Arthur G. had failed to complete many major tasks in college and graduate school. There had been a fair number of special projects he sought and received because of his intelligence and originality. He could sell his ideas and get the necessary support from his professors for his projects. Often he would work productively until it came time to gather the material together and put it into final form. Then something happened. The work never got done, thus disappointing those who had placed high hopes on him. He could do prodigious amounts of work in bursts, be outstanding in class, and then, suddenly, he would stop studying. His grades remained good only because he was extremely intelligent, very verbal, and a good listener.

After two years of analysis he dropped out of graduate school. Because of a special aptitude for computer technology he could earn significant sums rapidly as a systems analyst. In the earlier years of analysis he was quite irresponsible about deadlines. His exceptional ability made it possible for him to get away with it. He got no satisfaction from the work. His earning capacity was a factor in his daring to have a blow-up with his father and cut himself off from any funds from him.

While continuing with his computer work, he became interested in social action and politics, at which he worked prodigiously though sporadically. Because of his organizing and writing ability he assumed a leadership role, but his arrogance and insensitivity got him into many difficulties. This occurred from the fourth through the sixth years of analysis. Unrealistically, he thought he could easily find someone to take over an organization he had created and then lost interest in. With effort and ingenuity he did find personnel. He then devoted himself to political action, only to lose interest after two years of it.

In the seventh and eighth years of analysis he developed his knowledge of data processing techniques in a more organized way. In the ninth year he created his own consulting business. He has become more dependable and reliable, has better relations with people, and wants to make this venture succeed because he wants to prove to himself that he can be a responsible person.

Always in the background Arthur has the feeling that his work is only interim until he becomes clearer about what he wants to do with his life. This most likely will involve returning to a graduate school.

The change in Arthur's attitude toward work and effort was related to the steady diminution of his rebellious resignation, particularly against real or imagined authorities. The lessening of his sociopathy, his narcissism, and his arrogant-vindictiveness led to a lessening of his contempt for what he was doing and the people for whom he produced it. The fact that he was supporting himself and paying for his analysis increased his own self-respect and removed a source of tension and friction with his father.

About the fourth year of analysis, Arthur had begun to have some pride in his competence, in doing the work, and in being able to teach it to others, but the lack of belief in the product diminished his satisfaction and motivation. When he began to feel he could create a business of his own and succeed, the challenge became meaningful. He showed originality and inventiveness in improving on his skill. He rarely complained about difficulties in working *per se*. His difficulties were caused by his attitudes toward what he produced, toward people, and toward life.

Arthur speaks and writes with facility. He has attempted various forms of writing, and he gets great satisfaction from the challenge, as well as from the frustration. He experiences this as fun — something he does for himself. He feels that in the future he may produce something which might be salable. He is also artistically gifted. In the last four years he applied himself in energetic bursts to drawing and sketching. He enjoyed it, but does not pursue it.

Arthur's work capacity has not yet really been tested. I believe that will come when he finds what will be meaningful to him. My feeling is that work as such will not be a problem, nor the frustration which accompanies the creative process. Arthur's problems will come from how he and his work relate to the people with whom he will become meaningfully involved.

Leonard P., at the beginning of analysis, had many required assignments unwritten and had done almost nothing on his thesis. His rebellious defiance was outstanding. His anxieties were also so intense he couldn't sit still for more than a few minutes at a time. After a year of analysis he could begin to sit for longer periods and study. He misused his verbal facility and his capacity for argument to avoid really applying himself to his studies. Although he felt his main problem was sexual perversion, after only a few months it clicked with him that there was a more crucial difficulty with accepting responsibility "like a mature individual," as he later described it.

After a year there were the beginnings of a sense of responsibility to himself. His studies improved. Because of his verbal facility and his other abilities, he was given an opportunity to teach. Here he felt he was being tested in his own eyes. He began to work at preparing his lectures, though with quite some difficulty at first.

After a year and a half, I noted an absence of comment about his work. He did mention that he had begun to practice the piano in a disciplined way. When asked how his studying and paper writing were going, he became flushed and anxious. He brushed it off with a quick "All right." Pressed a bit, he said he didn't like to talk about it because it made him anxious. "Maybe sometime later."

Contributory to Leonard's changed attitudes toward work have been his diminishing preoccupation with his sexual problem; the

83

lowered level of his tension and anxiety; the lessening of his rebellious defiance, narcissism, and arrogant-vindictiveness; his lessening alienation; and his feeling that he was beginning to function sexually like a mature male.

It is too early to conjecture how he will function when it comes to his thesis. Native ability and intelligence are there. I discern evidences of originality. The fact that he has begun disciplined piano practice suggests that this discipline may carry over to his academic work. He believes he has special ability in his field. The spirit in which he makes this statement and further evidence suggest that this may well be.

Even at the beginning of analysis, Walter O. had a facility for rapidly producing short bits of writing for a variety of needs. He was very good at synopsizing and summarizing. During the analysis this ability improved. He also could dare longer projects which were collations of impressions with some slight originality. The amount and speed of his producing such material increased, but the depth and originality did not, which caused him to suffer greatly.

What blocked him was his intolerance to tension, friction, and conflict. With these feelings he would have to become involved if he were to become committed and responsible in depth. He would also have to recognize dilemma and struggle and realize the necessity for decisiveness and discipline. This remained impossible for him, hence the lack of originality which requires chance-taking — daring with oneself, with others, and with their criticisms. His intense need to be liked by everyone made this practically impossible.

James A., who had lived under the shadow of his dead brother Steve, had been active homosexually by the time he was eight or nine, although he didn't know this was what was happening. There had been a number of short affairs and some longer ones. One with Porter B. started that way. After a year the sexual aspect ended. The relationship continued as a very real and enduring friendship. This is a sequence I have often seen, as is the mutual exclusivity of sex and friendship between homosexuals. Prior to his relationship with Porter, he was caught in one with devastating consequences. "I froze and became numb." In the succeeding three years this depressive state became progressively worse, and finally unbearable, which is what brought him into analysis.

During his middle teens, on several occasions, James had what for him were violent explosions against his father in his mother's presence. Although such experiences were therefore not entirely alien to him, he had a terror of getting close to a situation remotely involving friction and tension. He avoided self-assertion at all costs. Bit by bit this terror diminished, and by the end of our first year he was able to oppose being pushed around. By the middle of the second year he was becoming a bit assertive. At the close of the second year he was enjoying standing up for himself, fighting for a raise, and taking over the leadership of a project where he had been second in command. He also began to be quite expansive about bigger jobs of which he felt himself capable.

While he always could work hard and fast for others, he could never initiate anything for himself. In the last six months, as project head, he found he could turn out quantities of work. On one occasion, he confronted a challenge and took a large project out of another man's hands. He proudly commented on the increasing originality of his writing. He also began to think of writing short stories and maybe a novel. After writing the first page of one, however, he became anxious. Nine months later he still had not returned to it. He realized it would be autobiographical, and therefore would function as a catharsis and a process of self-creation.

Martin distinguishes between active and reactive effort. In therapy patients attempt to avoid active effort, conceal such efforts when they make them, and try to maintain the illusion of effortless superiority and magical omnipotence. The contrast is striking when patients start making efforts actively and openly in therapy. Martin concludes that "throughout our culture, there seems to be a preference for reactive effort and resistance to active effort" as well as a "search for easy, effortless ways to success."(164)

Martin's study of effort aids our understanding of procrastination. The work problems of the procrastinator are very intriguing, although frustrating to the analyst. It is furthermore distressing to see the procrastinator's bewildered panic when he has trapped himself. Now he must be aware that he has procrastinated and take the consequences of the problems he has created for himself and others. Most procrastinators, however, remain adamantly and stonily unaware of the problem even when forcibly and repetitively confronted with the facts. When chance puts a procrastinator at the head of an organization, the destructive consequences can be considerable.

At one extreme are those procrastinators who will escape work in every possible way, find ways to hide when tasks are being handed out, avoid accepting work, or make a vague promise to do it which they later assert they never gave. At the other extreme are those who rush to make offers of help, and are irritated or hurt when reminded of their many past derelictions. When they are finally given a task, they do nothing while constantly promising to do something with each reminder.

When the rationalizations have run out, and they are pressed to get on with the work and fulfill their promises, they usually respond with cold and defiant silence. Since procrastinators are persistently resigned and also rebellious, they feel enraged at what they experience as being unfairly pressured.

Finally forced to act, the procrastinator is blind to the previous consequences of his promises and delays. He is unaware of other procrastinators. Because of his intense egocentricity, he expects everyone to be immediately cooperative and delighted to fit in with his plans. When these responses are not forthcoming, he looks bewildered, confused, even panicked, but his rage usually is not overt. More often it shows as abused feelings, withdrawal, and more procrastinating.

The procrastinator's participation is active, reactive, and compulsive. Things do not get done because the procrastinator is blocked from doing. He is blocked by contradictory shoulds and should nots, which leave him in an impasse situation. He is blocked by having to defend so many contradictory positions against so much conflict, anxiety, and hostility. He is blocked by his compulsive contradictory needs which leave him indecisive, undecided, and, consequently, inert. He is paralyzed and can't move except in his imagination. The paralysis is increased by feelings of hopelessness, futility, and despair.

Finally, even if there were enough of the spontaneous left viable and available to make clear for himself what he did want, he would not have the energy available to make a choice and carry it out. His choices are choices by default, made in spite of and under duress.

The procrastinator's attitude toward time has addictive qualities. When he is pressed for time and he is given more, there is an enormous feeling not only of relief but even of elation.

I had one patient who vividly described this addictive experience to me. He had gotten fired from several jobs because of his procrastination and had already aroused the ire of one of the senior members of his new job. He was for the first time becoming quite depressed and hopeless about his procrastinating. I was pleased that finally something about this problem was beginning to touch him, and that he was responding.

At this point the subject of more time came up. He looked

depressed and fearful, and was making promises to himself that he must get back at the task. He suddenly had the thought of having more time. This was quite unrealistic because he already was beyond the deadline. With the thought of having more time his face became transformed. He began to smile and giggle and even laugh as he said, "That would be great to have more time." He knew it would be more time to procrastinate still further with. He continued, "Oh, when I can have time, that's great, I feel wonderful." His reaction was similar to an alcoholic who finally makes it to a bar and sits there twirling his Martini glass by the stem without touching the drink. You can see the smile on his face, the sense of power, and the fantasying going on because he has the magic answer to all his problems right in hand.

But with this man the picture was even more extreme. I had the picture of someone who had just "mainlined" amphetamine. There was the agitated, restless, euphoric high. There would be a comedown later, a descent into depression, apathy, and restlessness. But what also made me think of amphetamines and hard drugs is the low moral level to which such patients sink and the extent of their unreality.

When they take on a task it is often in an unconnected, dissociated way. You feel they are not listening. You feel they have already completed the task in their imagination. They simply cannot look at a task realistically. The task understandably always takes far more work and time than they thought because they have already done it effortlessly in fantasy. This unreality also accounts for the difficulties they get into when they have a task which involves others.

When they finally are forced to act, they expect the whole world to be waiting with bated breath. The bewilderment when this does not happen is quite intense. They can't understand, become anxious, and start to beg and plead. They block out the realities of the other person's needs. The result of course is that the task takes even longer because they did not plan in terms of the realities of others' lives and needs.

When the therapy is effective and they realize that their procrastinating is a problem, that those close to them are suffering from it, and that they are bringing havoc into their lives, they may finally get depressed. This is a hopeful sign. Up to then, the responses have been fearfulness, bewilderment, and confusion, which indicate that they do not feel connected with what they have done and its consequences. With the feeling of depression, resignation, and often hopelessness, they can be helped to connect with some of the intent of their procrastinating. They begin to see that it not only expresses defiance and rebelliousness, but also arrogance — a need not only to frustrate and torture, but also to provoke.

When procrastinators do have bursts of productivity, the results vary in quantity, quality, and originality. Some seem to procrastinate in order to create an unbearable crisis situation, which is the only condition that can force them through their blocks. Others maintain a chronic crisis state for fear that if it terminates, they will lapse into procrastination.

Few obvious, severe procrastinators come into analysis because they procrastinate about that decision too. They may arrive with complaints expressive of the problem. Among them are inertia, difficulties in getting started, indecisiveness, and hopelessness. They may be driven into analysis because of the consequences of their procrastination: losing jobs, failure to be promoted, threat of a divorce, or the breaking up of a business partnership. They may be forced to seek help by symptoms such as despair, depression, various forms of self-hate, panic states, and increasing irritability.

Usually degrees of procrastination are discovered during analysis, having been masked by other problems. Arthur G. provides a good example of this process. Procrastination can be one of the most severe blockages *(ch. 12)* to analytic progress. Both the procrastination and the blocking can be so severe, and so covered by other problems and defenses that, as such, the problem is never defined and hence, never confronted.

To avoid tension, friction, and conflict, procrastinators become resigned. Among the forms which severe procrastination takes, the most obvious is persistent resignation. Next comes the overt rebellious form. The covert forms of rebellious defiance are the most flagrant. Hardest to see are those who escape their problems in the less obvious forms of *shallow living*.

When the determined procrastination is breached, what comes to the fore is painful and maddening indecisiveness. To decide would mean getting into conflict, against which the resignation was the overall defense. Indecisiveness is self-perpetuating. One man first put off dictating a letter. Having started, he stopped short of completion. Completed and typed, he delayed checking it over. This done, he put off signing it. Then, after signing it, he did not tell his secretary that he had finished it and put it where she couldn't find it, which occasioned still further delays.

Once the resignation is undermined, what emerges is a wild, bewildered feeling of being unjustifiably trapped — trapped with unbearable anxiety, self-hate, conflict, and rage. There are intense hurt pride reactions because in their *idealized image*, procrastinators are good, willing workers.

In time, some of the expansive aspects of the problem become visible. The procrastinator's arrogance can be colossal, at times quite obvious, and at others covered by the facade of a sweet, dear person. Because of his arrogance he feels the task is beneath him. Nobody is going to tell him what to do. If it's the boss who gave him the job, that just makes it worse. Coerced by the tyranny of his own contradictory *shoulds*, this added pressure from authority is more than he can bear. It triggers his inner tyranny which he externalizes.

One man was fired from two jobs. He did almost everything quickly and well, at times better than the second-in-command asked of him. However, two tasks that the boss had assigned he delayed. When the boss asked a second and a third time, he still did not complete the tasks. He was not promoted and was ultimately fired. He repeated the same pattern in a second job.

With procrastinators there is a vindictive, frustrating intent and a refined and subtle torturing of those they experience as their torturers. One man would smile and giggle at the helpless frustration and suffering of someone attempting to get him to do something. Another's voice would become lower than usual, sweeter, and ever so reasonable as he remained deaf to complaints about the consequences of his procrastination.

With the arrogance, arbitrary rightness is often present. Things have to be done *their way,* even though they rarely get anything done. They often defensively argue, "I want to do it right," but also state or imply, "I know what's right and you don't." This attitude persists in the face of their not having acted or acted in error repeatedly and despite the clear evidence that the other is more experienced and most likely right.

Usually present are inordinate standards and perfectionism. They endlessly correct for fear of making a mistake, and they can't let go. Even the simplest mistake was unbearable to one man. He would go to fantastic lengths and resort to the most tortured reasoning to make it come out that it was not a mistake, even if it meant describing a mistake as a stroke of genius.

The narcissistic component is usually hidden, but it is there. He is God's gift to whatever organization he is connected with, or whoever has him or her as a spouse. He is wonderful, and he wonderfulizes everything about himself, about what he does, or imagines he does. Others should adore him for what he would do if he did it.

The severe procrastinators I have been discussing all have superior intelligence. In all procrastinators the neurotic solution of the *supremacy of the mind* is intense. They misuse and pervert their intelligence in the service of maintaining their neurotic defenses. Understandably, they were virtuoso rationalizers — argumentative, literal-minded, insistent, querulous, quarrelsome, stubborn, and combative. They used their intelligence in fiendishly clever ways.

When asked if they have fulfilled a promise that they haven't, they will cover up endlessly if they know the truth can't be verified. When asked a question, they distort or cut off part in their minds and decide what you are asking by recreating the question. If they can't imagine what you say in a way to fit their needs, they misunderstand you. Their ways of evading and avoiding questions and hiding the fact that they have done nothing can be most sly and cunning. It takes years of analysis to uncover them.

The procrastinator's evasiveness, elusiveness, and capacity to confuse and obfuscate are at the least frustrating, and at times maddening. In addition the solution of compartmentalization and psychic fragmentation makes confronting them almost impossible. All these defenses are complicated and intensified by the fact that they are massive externalizers usually of the passive variety. They are always being done to, hence their righteous retaliations are justified. At times they "rise above" their petty tormentors. After having driven his wife to despair by his procrastinating, with contemptuous benignity one husband would sweetly offer to discuss her problem of "overreacting."

As the mind reigns supreme, reason, imagination, and magic hold sway. The procrastinator lives on the premises of the total solution of magic — a solution which is more fully discussed in chapter 16. The impossible has already been accomplished by effortless superiority. His omnipotence has been affirmed. Others are not simply connected with, or extensions, of him, not *as if*, or identical with him, but *are* him. He is the universe; hence the notion of vicarious living is not quite accurate.

All the categories of neurotic solutions are used by the procrastinator; both the comprehensive and the partial solutions, as well as what Horney named the general measures to relieve tension. *(49)* One of them is alienation. It is increased by moving away from and against the real-self. Alienation is then a process and a consequence of all the other neurotic solutions. Understandably, the procrastinator is severely alienated, and his whole neurotic structure is also a determined attempt to maintain the alienation and the procrastination while increasing both.

Because all these solutions are abundantly present, making the psychic structure rigid and brittle, change is painfully slow. Even at the slowest pace, intense repercussions of anxiety, self-hate, conflict, and rage occur. Each procrastinator I have worked with has been in analysis for many years and usually with several previous analysts who gave up exhausted. As their structure is gradually shaken, frequent episodes of sullenness, silence, and violent, vindictive withdrawal occur. As these prove insufficient, momentary (or longer) disorganizing panic states may supervene.

It is many years before the self-effacing aspects of the problem come to the fore in analysis. In procrastinating they are forcing you to be an unwilling partner taking care of them. You, as the analyst, are giving to them patience, interest, understanding, effort, and they are giving back as little as possible. They have a genius for seducing you with hope and apparent little gifts of change which are immediately wiped out. One of the most tenacious functions of procrastinating is to put off the analysis of dependency needs as long as possible. These needs are deeply embedded and intense.

To come to grips with them would also bring the procrastinator into conflict with his residual expansive needs and with the whole structure of the resigned solution which functions to avoid all conflict. The procrastinator must control himself inwardly by an automatic control on feelings. The environment he must control to forestall being trapped into facing what for him is unbearable. He can neither let go inwardly nor outwardly and uses the supremacy of the mind in the service of these controls. He cannot *give*, in all its dimensions. He cannot give out, give in, give way, simply give, because that is experienced as submitting, yielding, bending, surrendering — all of which are essential to freer associating and movement in the analytic process. To do so in the slightest would, as he experiences it, lead to dissolution of this fragile, yet stony structure. In short, the whole defensive system is adamantly opposed to commitment, involvement, and depth.

The procrastinator has a truly limited sense of core-identity and his sense of body identity is frequently very vague. He often carries himself very stiffly and awkwardly. Several have expressed the feeling of having an armor around them, as if to hold their bodies together. All have varying intensities of gender- and sexual-identity problems. Real self-identity is the least substantial of all.

The inertia, paralysis, and numbness are both process and consequence. Procrastinators actively paralyze and benumb themselves to keep everything permanent and fixed.

When forced into facing the consequences of procrastinating and the frustrated rage of those for whom he had created great difficulties, one man whimpered like a little child, "Somebody help me! Help me! Help me! All I want to do is to please people and do the right thing." A woman, when trapped into facing that she was still procrastinating, after endless promises to deliver, and into seeing the consequences of her behavior, would immediately have a helpless, frightened little girl look in her eyes, a look that demanded pity while trying to make the other person feel guilty for having put her on the spot. When this mechanism was forcibly brought to her awareness her face was suffused with rage.

Not only must feelings of anxiety, self-hate, conflict and rage be experienced, but also the horrible feelings of emptiness and nothingness which accompany intense feelings of despair. The picture thus far described accounts for why they are unable to forgive themselves or others. I use forgive in the sense of *being for giving*, to be on the side of giving. In this root sense only can we forgive ourselves. Procrastinators cannot forgive because they do not feel they have anything to give.

The degree of pathology in procrastinators is usually severe. In my experience, they manifested severe neurosis to the extreme of possible compensated schizophrenia in one instance. Many procrastinators manifest the borderline syndrome. The anal sadistic character and the obsessive personality also identifies them. Existentially they are determinedly trying to maintain the status quo, to hold back, and to stop life and living.

All, at periods in their life, had shown originality or brief bursts of productivity and then had closed down until coming to analysis. While there can be no significant change in their symptomatology, much alleviation of suffering, and improvement in many areas of their living, the best results so far as the procrastination is concerned are shorter and longer periods of varying degrees of productivity. Usually this lasts only as long as someone is stimulating and pressing them. When this is absent, they fall back into inertia, paralysis, and procrastination. A significant resolution of the procrastination occurs rarely; occasionally it happens to a moderate degree.

From his holistic orientation Martin examines "The Fear of Relaxation and Leisure" in therapy, in the creative process, and in life. *(165)* Resistance to active effort and the fear of relaxation are involved in "The Dynamics of Insight." "Insight," Martin believes, "should be reserved for the phenomenon that accompanies some greater and richer awareness, some revelation of the self, some growth in consciousness."*(166)*

Because of self-alienation there is a loss of leisure integral to *"free association"* which *"is in every respect and in essence a leisure process,"* to the creative flash which can happen *"only during the leisure phase,"* to the creative process, to opening up to "the problems of the human heart *in conflict with itself,"* namely, to becoming involved in healthy friction. *(167)* Martin adds that self-alienation is reinforced by social alienation characterized by the demand for the frictionless, the fear of the unconscious, the compulsive in all its patterns, and the need to overintellectualize. Because of increasing leisure — more real free time on their hands for which people have not been prepared — the normally existing terrors of freedom and play have become accentuated.

What seems to evoke the greatest interest in disturbances in work — though not necessarily concern — is the relation between art and neurosis or, more precisely, between "the creative ability of an artist and his neurosis." The prevalent attitudes are that artists are neurotic, that their suffering is an "indispensable condition for their artistic creativity"; and that it would "curtail or even destroy his creativity if an artist were analyzed?"*(49, p. 328)*

Gifts exist independent of neurosis, and neurosis blocks rather than facilitates their expression. As with all expressions of the creative process in working, the artist also suffers because of his neurotic problems. The *self-effacing type* knows most clearly how his neurosis interferes. It is mostly the *expansive* and *rebellious-resigned types* who fear analysis will adversely affect their creative work. Their fears are actually concerned with threats to their neurotic solutions and are expressed in the fear that analysis will destroy their "personality" and take away their "individuality." They fear it will dull their "sensitivity," which in fact is their neurotic hypersensitivity.

The idea of sensitivity brings up a common misconception. On the basis of his experience with homosexuals Gershman concludes that the percentage or degree of creativity among them is no greater than among heterosexuals. There is a greater concentration of homosexuals in certain art fields due to sociocultural factors. Just as with others, their personality problems interfere with their creativity and to a certain extent and in some ways favor it. Fear of success, severe work inhibitions, and fear of competition with male heterosexuals for jobs are common. *(174)*

Because of his greater sensitivity to "beauty and harmony" as well as to "discords and suffering,"*(49, p. 330)* and because of his capacity for greater emotional experience, the artist will always experience greater distress and tension than others. As he is relieved of the suffering from neurotic sources he will become that much more effective. An artist's neurotic conflicts may stimulate him to try to work them through, and he may do so through his art medium. If he doesn't succeed, he becomes sterile; and if he does, he is that much less neurotically motivated. Horney concludes that *"An artist then creates not because of his neurosis but in spite of it."(49, p. 332)*

Personal experience with people in the arts has confirmed

Horney's position. Some came into analysis because they were blocked. They felt they had run dry. Psychological problems were interfering with their work directly, or were causing the artists difficulties in their human relations with those with whom they had to work or live. On occasion, the major complaints did not at first pertain to their work, but it soon became obvious how their problems interfered with it. Not infrequently artists felt they were failing while others saw them advancing. Sometimes they felt their best work was unappreciated. What often engendered panic was a success, particularly of a first novel, and the terror that they could never again do as well.

Speaking generally, therapy can bring the artist increased comfort, better internal conditions for working, and greater productivity.

Rollin S., a middle-aged writer for the performing arts, said his problem was drinking. He tried unsuccessfully to involve me with its details. With his wife he succeeded, turning her into a watchdog which he then resented. Months later, in telling me how highly he regarded his internist, who would not allow himself to be pushed into the same role, he expressed his appreciation for my not having fallen into the trap. As a result, he was always quite honest about his drinking with both of us.

How depressed he was came through in the second week. He was in despair because he was totally blocked in his work. Going into his life history brought out more about his work problem. In the third month, he visited his birthplace, an experience which revived much about his childhood. Quite upsetting was his realization that his mother had bound him to her in an intimidating dependency relationship and had further undermined, in his eyes, his weak and often absent father.

In the fifth month, following a severe binge, his wife's serious threat of divorce got through to him. This intensified his already upset state and led to several nights of severe insomnia. A week from the beginning of the insomnia he woke one morning with a breakthrough.

That day, in a few hours, he completed a play, and went for a holiday with his wife. This meant, as an old lover of New York, a walk up Fifth Avenue looking in the shops, a stop in Hicks for hot chocolate, and a visit to a museum to see a showing of a famous impressionist. He said, "If he can begin again at sixty, why can't I at my age?"

What had helped free this man for this breakthrough was my evading the trap of being made into a watchdog; exploring the structure of his depression and later his despair; bringing the blockage of his creative efforts into clear focus; reviewing the history of his work habits and his creative writing; throwing light on his relationship with his mother; and elucidating how his drinking began, and the functions it served. Crucial was his respect for me, an attitude absent toward two previous analysts with whom he stayed only a short time.

His therapy extended over eight years with actual work amounting to two years on a three times a week basis. There were many rationalized interruptions and some legitimate ones. Over the years, with many setbacks, his drinking gradually lessened. To stop drinking altogether, which he did on his own for longer and longer periods, he experienced as a humiliation because that meant to him he was weak and no man, a lush who could not control himself. The wisdom of the necessity for doing so he came to by himself, most painfully and reluctantly.

The drinking was intimately connected with his depression and despair, which resulted from his onslaughts of self-hate, his unrealistic demands on himself, and the usual anguish inherent in the creative process. As the depressions and despair become less intense and less frequent, as his *idealized image* of himself as "The Artist" was undermined, he became more realistic.

This was a big breakthrough, because he had felt degraded and humiliated to have to work for bread and butter. To do so he experienced as an admission of creative failure and as a degrading prostitution of his abilities. Once he could experience these discriminations he could work and free himself from the pressure of finances. Then he was able to work with more pleasure and freedom. In those eight years he did two pieces of work in which he felt pride, although they were not successful commercially.

Having worked with a number of people, male and female, in the performing arts, some crucial distinctions are essential. There is what the individual feels is creative and original, what people whose ability and integrity he values feel is original, and what the public responds to positively. Creative people can often accept commercial failure if they pride themselves on their work, and if others whom they respect also highly value it.

How the public responds has much to do with the climate of the times. Although the product may be of high order it may not catch on. The creative person produces out of a certain phase of his development. Always growing and changing, he may no longer be producing what made him successful in the past. His present product might also be of high order but out of tune with what the public is ready for.

Some people found, in the course of analysis, that they had

overestimated their gifts and were able to drop the notion of a vocation in the arts and retain a satisfying and fulfilling avocation. Others dropped their interest altogether and felt relieved at being unburdened.

In view of the human resources which are being tapped, the discovery or rediscovery of an interest, ability, and even gift is not uncommon in the course of analysis.

At the beginning of analysis, Rose B. was mostly mute. When she did speak, her voice was almost inaudible. She brought in scraps of paper with topics to discuss, a practice I implicitly supported. I suggested she write up her life history during our first summer interruption. This she did. Additions were suggested because of large omissions. The material was the source of our discussions for many months.

In the second year, quite disturbed because of current difficulties with her family, she wrote a poem on the back of her program at a concert. During a suicidal period two months later, she looked for, but could not find it. When she accidentally did, she mentioned that at six, when taught words and numbers, she began to create jingles and rhymes in her head, about which she told no one, and that between nine and twelve she wrote poetry, also kept secret.

In the sixth year of analysis, after several years of indecisiveness, she began taking poetry courses, as well as a course in which biographies of friends were written and discussed. With trepidation she finally offered to present one herself. In the eighth year, I suggested she rewrite her life history. This took two years and again was the basis for much analytic work because of further recollections; because of what had transpired since she had begun; and because of changed perceptions of herself, of others, and of happenings in her life.

From the fourth year she had been writing children's jingles and poems. Pressured by close relatives, she visited some poets and finally submitted her work for publication. The first rejection was most painful, but she got enough courage to try several times more. The result was still rejection. She read these jingles and poems to her grandchildren. Both the writing and the reading gave her great pleasure. After the rejections, she continued to write them until the nephews were too old for them. After completing the second rewrite of her life history which involved the saga of her unusual family, she got the idea of novelizing it. She worked at this for four years until she realized it was beyond her competence.

A variety of parameters were used which aided the progress of this long and difficult analysis. At the first summer break I suggested she could write to me if she was so moved. This possibility, which she used sparingly, was of great support and dropped away about the sixth year. The recall of the forgotten rhymes and jingles, and the writing of more serious poems later brought her into painful but productive contact with poets and the publishing world. The written word on pieces of paper, originally as topics for discussion, and later as prose and poetry, was a crucial parameter in the therapy. It almost became a vocation. Accepted as a productive avocation, it became a source of pleasure and of communication and relationship for herself and many others.

In addition to all that she had created out of her writing, she created a life for herself and her husband, at home, in business affairs, and in leisure activities. An accomplished musician, concert-going became a more leisurely and enjoyable part of her life as was going to movies, the theater, and to restaurants.

I first saw Marvin W. when he was twenty-seven years old, tormented by thoughts that God would strike him dead for having convinced a girl to have an abortion. I could not be certain whether he in fact had visual and auditory hallucinations. Even as early as age eight Marvin had severe phobias and obsessions. I worked with him for ten years, a colleague for seven years intensively and with diminishing frequency for twelve more, and a second colleague for four years thereafter. About the fourteenth year of his analysis, for a period of some months, during a stressful period in his personal life and in his analysis, he experienced hallucinatory phenomena which were of hostile delusional character. They served the unifying and integrating functions that a paranoid system does.

During his work with me, Marvin resumed and completed his education, receiving his degree while working with my colleague. He also progressed through several jobs. He has had his present job for many years, having advanced to a senior creative and executive position. At about forty he married. Through mutual choice, conscious and unconscious, there are no children. He designed and furnished his own home, and has created a fulfilling life for himself which includes a very constructive use of his leisure time.

From the beginning of our work Marvin frequently reported that his superiors complained about his slowness and limited productivity, although he considered himself overworked. About the fifth year of analysis, he began to show me his paintings.

97

His perfectionism and obsessiveness were obvious. It was meticulous, with endless details and no open spaces. It seemed tight to the point of strangulation. Originality was almost completely choked off.

He was pleased when promoted and given more responsibility for original work. It also terrified him. By the time I interrupted our work — necessitated by my own personal circumstances — and he accepted my referral, he had again advanced in his organization. Through my colleague I learned of his progress. The patient himself gave me reports from time to time — at least once yearly to the present. Some excellent color photos of his home show it to be open, light, free, and furnished colorfully. Pets and gardens add that much more to evidences of increased creative living. Analysis helps us become "artists of life." According to the Zen Masters, the creation of a good life, a full life, is the greatest human artistic creation, a truism which cannot be repeated too often.

Marvin W.'s story reveals how analysis helped him improve the quality and quantity of his work while deriving greater comfort and satisfaction while doing so. He became able to tap his resources and do the work necessary to receive his degree. His increased productivity in his work was reflected in advancements with greater responsibility for original work in projects of increasing magnitude. He also became creative in his living — marrying, building his own home, and creating a life of enjoyable and productive leisure.

It is thirty-three years since I first saw him. The evidence of severe illness already present in childhood, the possibility of hallucinatory phenomena when I first saw him, could have suggested the diagnosis of schizophrenia, particularly in view of the recurrence of such symptomatology in his later analytic work. The life course to date contradicts such a diagnosis and we must conclude that analytic therapy and the therapy of an increasingly fulfilling life can considerably mitigate a process which could well have gone on in a progressively deteriorating process until the schizophrenic diagnosis would have been definitely confirmed.

Finally, Marvin's total history reveals the intimate relation of Horney's holistic approach — her notion of the urge toward self-realization and its relation to constructive growth possibilities. It seems to confirm her basic thesis. "My own belief is that man has the capacity as well as the desire to develop his potentialities and become a decent human being, and that these deteriorate if his relationship to others and hence to himself is, and continues to be, disturbed. I believe that man can change and go on changing as long as he lives, and this belief has grown with deeper understanding."(39, p. 19)

Horney's holistic approach expands our possibilities for understanding and enhancing the creative process. In a symposium devoted to "Psychoanalysis as Creative Process," I discussed how creative talent and creative passion participate in therapy. (168) Prerequisite is a therapist who has some endowment — talent, maybe even gift — for being an "artist of life"; who has had some experience of it; who is aware that passions participate in creative living; and who can contain and transform those passions toward that end. This means he neither screams them out nor chokes them down, and is open also to the quiet passions and to the poignant sounds of silence. He is someone who is aware that the ultimate of the impersonal is the ultimate of personal; that theories are provisional conveniences whose validation is their own invalidation; and that his theory of creative living must be congruent with theories of the creative process expressive of the *zeitgeist* of which he is participant and manifestation.

Also essential, as a minimum, are a capacity and aptitude for the art of therapy. With his endowment the therapist should have had some experience in self-creating and in helping creating in others. Rigorous training in theory and technique can help a therapist make the most of his endowment, but it cannot give him what he does not have.

There are also prerequisites for the patient. He must have the capacity for what Huxley calls "animal grace," which "comes when we are living in full accord with our nature on the biological level"; for "human grace" which comes from persons; and for "spiritual grace," which "cannot be received continuously or in its fullness except by those who have willed away their self-will to the point of being able to say, 'Not I, but God in me.' "(169, pp. 166-67)

Like Aldous Huxley, Sorokin emphasizes "the powerful grace of man's constructive creativity" and sees "maximal cultivation and development of this creative grace as man's paramount task of the present and the future."(170)

Dreams are a vital creative element in psychoanalysis. Weiss notes that self-alienation is lessened in dreaming — perception and particularly self-perception are widened. "Strivings, conflicts and attempts at solution are crystallized" in the creative act of symbolizing. Because of these attributes, dreaming becomes "a creative force in therapy." "An active creative process," dreaming reflects "the striving for self-realization."(171)

Hulbeck distinguished between the creativity related to Horney's concept of self-realization, creativity as a part of human nature, and the creating of objects or activities. There are three different aspects to the creative process in psychoanalysis: the encounter or collision between the distorted reality of the patient and that of the analyst; the dialogue or use of verbal means to evaluate the inner world, to discover the relativism of facts and hindrances, and to provide confidence in the possibility of redefining; and the articulation, or actual ongoing redefinitions of the patient's views of himself and his environment. (172)

The self-creating in analysis is both similar yet different from artistic creativity according to Wenkart. (173) In artistic creation there is a direct perception, an "intuition," followed by a formulated version of the phenomenon in consciousness. Something new is brought into existence, something not directly explainable or logically accountable. In analysis, the self-creating results from an unconditional, unreserved openness to stimuli, an acceptance of one's own being that allows for fresh spontaneous responses. The main source for analytic self-creation is freedom from inhibitions and fears. One expression of this open free attitude is visible in relating to others, which can be a highly creative endeavor.

Chapter 5

The Symbolizing Process I:
Formal, Phenomenological,
and Metaphorical Free Association

As Horney's theoretical formulations became more systematic, while remaining open-ended, her ideas on technique continued to be loosely organized. What emerged, particularly in her later courses on technique, was an increasing emphasis on the person of the analyst as his most important instrument in therapy. For giving structure to this and other topics, a brief summary of the symbolizing process is essential.

A universal forming process is postulated *(137)* of which the symbolizing process is an aspect. *(175)* In much of my thinking on form and process I follow Whyte. *(176)* The moment there is aware-ness of being and any of its attributes it has emerged into form. They have taken form through the forming process itself. Form may become organized as a sequential hierarchy of forms, which are denotable and capable of being organized into concepts. The forms may be vague, inchoate, and variously named. No attribute of being can be captured in a single, even in a whole series or matrix of forms. This impossibility can stimulate the continuing attempt to do so. Paul Klee's genius was directed, for example, not to static form, but to the forming process, as a means of communicating his intuitions of art and living.

The symbolizing process, an aspect of human integrating, may be described metaphorically as a spiral or as a sequence of interconnected levels starting from the ground of all forms, phenomena, and appearances, variously named through time as *chit* (Hinduism), *hsing* (in Chinese philosophy), *tathata* (Zen), *pure fact (177)* and *dasein* (Existentialism). At the metaphorical bottom of the spiral is *pure fact*, from which all forms emerge and back into which they are resorbed. It is the all embracing continuum, undifferentiated, aesthetic, ineffable, and immediately apprehendable. *(177)*

The lowest levels of the spiral are pre-rationative, which means they are prior to, and essential to, human intellection. It is at these levels that human communing takes place. The communing of mother and infant is a fact, a prototype, and a paradigm. Human communing is "the basis of all communication, hence also of the communication that makes psychotherapy possible."*(178)* It is "the strifeless phase of awareness . . . the preconscious mode" of Burrow *(179)* which is analogous to the "prototaxic mode" of Sullivan. *(180)* Burrow states: "Basic to all else in the development of the mind is a current of physiological continuity of child and mother, person and world." *(179, p. ix)*

The forms expressive of this continuity have been called *preverbal, subverbal, subliminal*. It is from the prerationative levels that the forms we name *empathy, intuition, insight, hunch, psi-phenomena, mystic participation*, and *satori* emerge. These levels participate in flash feelings, thoughtless imagery, metaphors, fantasies and dreams. When intellection takes over to structure these emerging processes dualistically and logically order them, the rationative levels of the spiral emerge manifested as forms evolved to the highest order of abstraction.

We can see how vast is the realm of "Prelogical Experience." *(181)* It is the world of the immediately experienceable, the ineffable, the impressionistic, the purely factual and empirical, the positivistic component which is the mystical factor in knowledge. *(177)* It is that realm in which new paradoxes take shape and old ones are resolved, where creative tensions are maximal and most available. This is life's growing edge where logical associative connections are loosest — where living is most open-ended. It is where life's greatest potentialities can be realized. *(76, 182)*.

The values of being open, attuned to, and able to work with prelogical experiences — in analyst and patient — is exemplified in the following abstraction related to me by J. W. Vollmerhausen, M.D.

A thirty-year-old mother of two children places great emphasis on will power and is a compulsive intellectualizer, feeling little. For several hours the theme of feeling herself to be a worm had been emerging, a worm which has a blind, senseless existence. Near the end of an hour in which this theme had occurred, I felt a very strong urge to smoke a cigar. It so happened that the cigars had been lying there for a week and I hadn't smoked one. The urge continued, and I finally lighted one. At that moment the patient expressed a very warm feeling which she didn't understand. The recollection suddenly came to her that her father had always been very fond of cigars. Even though I told her of my underlying feeling about smoking the cigar, she completely resisted the idea that there had been any communication between us and insisted it was entirely an accident.

The subsequent hour she was in severe conflict. The conflict first took the form of a fight she had with her husband about buying party shoes for her little girls. As she was relating the conflict she added, "Well, it's the same old garbage. He's so stingy. He won't give them anything." As she was talking about his stinginess towards the children and herself, I suddenly thought of an incident she had related a long time back about going to several parties in boy scout shoes. I wondered why this wasn't coming up. About three or four minutes later — and on her own — she recalled the incident, but this time with a different feeling than before. Instead of an interesting anecdote, she now felt a mixture of anger and sadness at the neglectful and uncaring attitude of her mother. The vague feeling of "uncared for" became stronger and stronger until suddenly she felt herself to be a sad, neglected little girl. The moment she had this experience she began to fight it off, and kept repeating, "It's ridiculous. It's silly. It's un-grownup."

These two aspects — the emerging feeling as well as her fighting against it — continued the rest of the hour with some increase of feeling to the point of tearfulness at the end. She was still in the phase, at the end of the hour, of actively struggling against the feeling. The old paradox with her mother came up in terms of "mother was too busy working to take care of me;" "it shouldn't bother me but it did." The new paradox was in terms of "I feel this but I'm too grownup to feel this." I feel very definitely that my own mobility, both up and down, in the symbolic spiral made it possible for her to move in her spiral. My own relaxation of consciousness helped her to relax hers.

Subsequent hours were taken up with her pride-invested defense — "They can't hurt — Ha! Ha!" She realized more and more that not only did they hurt her in the past, but that she was feeling more hurt than ever, here and now. This was the beginning breakthrough of other feelings which had been choked off for many years.

This example is illustrative of several other points in technique. No explicit attempt was made to help her see that she was externalizing her feelings of deprivation to her daughters. If I had done so, she would have understood intellectually but she would not have gone on to become open to her feelings. The fuller emergence of her feelings followed some alteration in underlying processes. Her awareness (insight — see chapter 23) is an outcome of her struggle for and against letting herself go with the consequent relaxation in the constrictedness of her consciousness. This instance also describes aspects of the patterning of associations as they become freer and freer.

In being attuned to and working with prelogical experiences, we are *being there,* for the patient. As we are, we become attuned to, and responsive to, the comprehensive complaint of every patient, in fact of every human being who seeks succor. They are all saying that "Nobody was there for me." It may be verbalized as a statement, as a question, as a criticism, as an accusation, or as wondering: "What was there about me that was so bad, so different?" "Nobody was there for me where I was;" "Nobody was there when I wanted them;" or "When I needed them."

Some of the detailed expressions of the encompassing feeling and statement, *nobody-was-there-for-me-are:* Nobody listened to me and if they did listen to me, they didn't hear me. Nobody looked at me and if anybody looked at me they didn't see me. Nobody was interested in me. In these and more statements to follow are expressed the root meanings of the Latin *interesse,* to be between, to make a difference, to be of importance.

Nobody who was important made a difference and was between me and others, was interested in what I felt, in what I wanted, and in what I thought. Nobody was interested enough to explain anything. The German *erklären* also carries the meaning to clarify from *klar,* clear. This means that even basic information was not imparted. That person was left ignorant. No more poignant example can there be than of the young female adolescent who was not informed about or prepared for her menses.

Nobody understood me. To understand means literally and figuratively to stand under, to support, to stand with, to stand where the other is standing. The German *verstehen* as word and philosophy covers all these meanings. When someone says nobody understood me, they not only imply nobody was interested, but also that nobody cared.

Caring has a long history and deep roots in all religious, ethical, and philosophical systems. In the Western world we know it in the Greek *Eros;* St. Augustine's *Caritas;* modern Protestantism's *Agape;* in the Jewish Mitzvah; and in Existentialism's emphasis on *Sorge.* What that person is saying is nobody was on my side.

In saying nobody was there for me, that person is also saying I didn't exist for anybody. They acted as if I didn't exist. What is implied is that since I didn't exist for anybody, how was I to feel I had an existence, that I existed for myself and that existence had a meaning for me?

All of these aspects of nobody-was-there-for-me also express the statement, nobody was present for me. This could mean factually and physically in space and time, or being present emotionally, responsive to that other one present. Nobody was present as a presence present for me. Nobody was present who had substance, who carried weight, who was an identity, a person, who had personhood.

All these formulations of nobody-was-there-for-me are what all people say to one another — to a friend, a spouse, a relative, a teacher, a counselor, or anybody who participates as a helping agency, as a non-professional, paraprofessional, or a professional.

To be a presence, present to another, means to have touched and been touched by the dimension of the spiritual. The dimension of the spiritual is prerequisite to being a presence present to another person who is looking, groping, and struggling toward understanding and clarification of the big questions regarding existence. And this dimension I feel is essential to effective helping and healing.

As the helper is sensitive and responsive to these many ways of saying, no one was there for me, he will be aware that that person is asking, and will you be? Although the helper's response as presence may be affirmative, the patient is confronted by the ancient paradox. He must have faith that what he has heard, seen, and felt is there and is true before he is able to have faith. Before he can trust, he must have faith; and he is asked to trust and have faith while still incapable of both. As one patient put it, "I know I have got to make a commitment. It is a matter of trust. I have never trusted anybody. I feel I can trust you. This is more painful than anything I've ever done, but I must make that leap of faith."

If someone comes for help it means some of the foregoing complaints are there and have a basis, however sick and exaggerated they may be. For fulfilling these unmet needs the notion of the symbolic spiral can be a most helpful guide. How we respond to these needs tells us much about our relationship with the patient, the depth of communion obtaining, and the state of the analytic process.

How in tune patient and therapist are may be determined in a variety of ways. You may, in a most tentative way, ask a patient what he feels about a hypothesis you have, or an intuitive feeling that has arisen in you. This same process may be initiated from the side of the patient.

Other confirmations of the close communion between patient and therapist are situations that could unwisely be taken as instances of extrasensory perception. What they indicate is that you and your patient have been concerned with similar problems, been working on similar aspects of them, have been discussing them off and on, and have arrived in the same area of concern at about the same time.

> In one analysis, with increasing frequency, either my patient or I would be about to discuss the same subject or ask a similar question. One or the other would mention the topic first to have the other report that almost simultaneously it had been on his mind. On one occasion, seemingly out of nowhere, I had the flash thought, "When is he going to talk about his father?" Recently we had not been discussing him. I had no idea what I was telling myself with that thought.
>
> Almost immediately thereafter my patient said, "I don't know where it came from but the other night I dreamt my father came to visit me." His father was a symbol to him of inertia and hopelessness. He interpreted the dream as meaning that he now felt capable of facing these problems in nimself and that is what happened in the succeeding weeks. What I was saying in my flash thought was, "He should soon be strong enough to face his own inertia and hopelessness." It was not clairvoyance but something arrived at from the data in the areas in which we both had been working.

Such happenings are to be distinguished from "doctrinal compliance," which involves the patient's compliance with the therapist's unconscious and intentional wishes and expectations as determined by his doctrines. (183) This is a circular feedback situation in which the therapist's interpretation and theories always turn out to be right. Doctrinal compliance is something other than the therapist's conscious, intentional suggestion. It does not refer to the fact that each therapist will understandably see the data through the lens of his theoretical persuasion. The dreams of Freudian, Jungian, and Adlerian therapists seem, for example, to contain patterns congenial to their respective theories. Finally, doctrinal compliance is still different from authentic instances of extrasensory happenings.

To help students learn to work analytically, we guide them into experiencing increasing dimensions of the ongoing continuum, the bipolar unitary process which we call the analytic process. In becoming increasingly attuned to that moving matrix, they can be in wider contact with that substrate from which nonverbal and verbal cues and clues emerge. This material is idiosyncratic to that context, that patient, and that therapist. Emerging as idioms, they can be further abstracted and serve as ordering principles when they become concepts.

Through these idiosyncratic idioms the therapist learns the variety of theories the patient has of himself, his world, and the world, and also his ways of formulating and communicating them. The therapist can now more effectively fulfill the task of being there where the patient is and thereby be able to learn his many private languages, verbal and nonverbal. When we give the patient the feeling of our knowing them in their depths, they will trust us in our helping them to unlearn what they have mislearned and to learn new ways of learning with new and more appropriate idioms.

The emerging forms expressive of and manifesting the various levels — prerationative and rationative — of the symbolic spiral become images. They do so by a process of imaging of which perceiving and imagining are abstractions. From them evolve perceptual and conceptual symbols. Imagining differs from perceiving in that it does not require an immediate or present object. An imagining person can form conceptual symbols of the past and future and what is not spatially or temporally present to the senses. Feelings as such cannot be had directly in imagination, nor can sensations, autonomic responses, or urges; but we can have sensory, perceptual, conative, and emotive images of them.

Shortly after discussing the symbolic spiral with E. Papowitz, M.D., a younger colleague, he made effective use of his knowledge.

Describing his experiencing of analysis, and some improvements he had made socially, the patient paused for a moment, and said that he wondered what remained to be seen. "It goes like this," he said, and inscribed in the air with his finger the shape of a spiral with the base upward and the apex pointing down. "It gets deeper and deeper till it gets to a point where you no longer can communicate with anyone except your psychiatrist." The patient was silent for a while, and my colleague asked him to tell him more about the spiral figure he had drawn.

The patient continued: "It goes around in deeper and deeper circles. You don't plummet. You go down by orderly levels. It's not a mixed-up unpredictable movement. Even though it's free it's not unpredictable. You finish one thing in a predictable way and another thing comes up. Gradually you come to it all. This memory of my younger days can come up right away like when you're hypnotized.

"When the teacher says, 'Bernstein will give us the answer now,' the burden is like when my mother said, 'You ate the spinach yesterday (so you must like it today),' the burden when the sun rises and sets on your backside. Look at all the forces that can act on me. My mother who walked around naked and lavished all this affection on me. She picked up my underwear after me. All my life my father said, 'You're killing him with kindness.' It's not easy what I'm doing but it's not difficult. *You can come home when you want* [italics supplied]. You can manage your own life. *When you live on your own, there's more to you* [italics supplied]. I don't think I would have been able to do that if not for coming here. If it's done in conjunction with a psychiatrist, it's not bad."

Our notion of the symbolizing process of which imaging is an aspect is crucial to our ideas on freer associating. *(182)* Through freer and freer associating, the patient contacts deeper levels of the symbolic spiral, which are communicated to the therapist who, through his reacting, responding, and resonating, supports, extends, and expands his own freer associating and that of his patient. He does so by his *presence,* communicated nonverbally and verbally. The following instance, related to me by A. E. Koblentz, M.D., illustrates not only the ways the therapist supports freer associating, but also the use of questions, particularly of the what variety.

A single middle-aged woman, while carrying on in a routine editorial capacity, was gradually able to free herself of blocks to her creative writing. This became evident in the freer use of the poetry of her language as she more freely associated and described the emergence of her feelings. She had opened her session discussing a move from her old apartment, where she had resided for many years, to another, in a new, unfinished building. She was concerned about the move, and particularly about the traffic problems and the transportation difficulties there might be in going from her new home to her place of business, an old, established organization where she had worked for many years.

"It's interesting and strange how my mind works. I find myself saying things here that never occurred to me, and it's odd that it's so. Not only do I say them, but I believe they are true and it's only an illustration of how important it is to give out. I can't think of a better expression. I know my trouble has been that I haven't talked of things that were important to me, or written about them."

"What more on giving out?" asked the therapist.

"It seems to work as a device for marshalling my ideas and my feelings. The opposite of it is a kind of atrophy."

"What more on giving out as a way of marshalling your feelings?"

"In formulating my comments as I do here, I get hold of otherwise unrealized and unrecognized feelings among other things."

"Tell me about unrealized and unrecognized feelings among other things."

"It's a process like mining," she said. "They lie deep and have to be hacked at, dredged out. Since I no longer write, there is no other way or occasion to get at them."

"What more on getting hold of your unrealized feelings?"

After a long pause, she replied, "I have a feeling I'm reaching down and pulling up something. It's somewhat of an unknown quantity to me. Whatever kind of feelings I come up with — that's what I find so strange and so interesting."

"What about reaching down and pulling up?"

"The unexpected, not frightening, but I suppose it has the capacity for astonishment. I find myself owning to feelings that are unexpected because they are unrealized. I find myself unprepared for what I realize or what I recognize. My mind isn't prepared. As an idea it's something startling to me. Apparently we feel first and then we think. I've always thought it was the other way around. It seems to me now that feelings take primacy, and I can understand it. There are difficulties that I run into because if I carry out what my mind tells me, then it's what I should think, do, or act."

"What more on owning to feelings?"

"There are feelings that are apparently dormant, and it's only in naming that I recognize them, and since they exist it's well to have them named. If someone were to ask me if I possessed such feelings, I would probably deny it and honestly so, because I would not know that I possessed them. It's only when I have named them that I acknowledge them."

This example and the previous one were from supervisory sessions. They indicate that these ways of working with patients can be taught and learned. The second session is an example of showing while telling. It is experiencing while implicitly talking about, both of which are aspects of a continuum, of the symbolic spiral, of the unitary process — feeling-thinking, thinking-feeling — which we artificially dichotomize into separate abstractions.

The notion of the symbolic spiral also aids in a phenomenological description of the evolving patternings of freer associating which become a valuable guide for evaluating change (see chapter 24). Freer associations are participants in working through and are expressive of it. They reveal the results of our conduct of the analysis and of our interpretation as seen immediately and in the long run.

The patternings of freer associating will be manifestations of prelogical experiences and logical phenomena, of aspects of the symbolic self, of the formed and forming aspects of the self-system. They will also reflect what was formed, apparently permanent, known, familiar, tried and maybe not so true, and compulsive, as well as what is forming, dynamic, actually impermanent, unknown, new, untried and maybe truer, and spontaneous. They will further reflect what was tension-producing and tension-reducing, as well as conflict- and co-operation-forming and resolving.

There will be patternings reflecting a reversal of a sequence inherent in the nature of intellection — the subject-predicate-object structure of our language, and the dualistic nature of our Western mind structure.

Eastern language and mind structure is quite different. Prof. Moses Berg, Director of the Orient-Occident Research Center in Tokyo, explained to me that "In Japanese, the term for objective is pronounced *kyakkan,* while the term for subjective, is pronounced *shukan.* The character *shu* has the basic meaning of *host* or *master* while the character of *kyaku* has the basic meaning of *guest.* The second character *kan* has the basic meaning of perception. Subjective phenomena are phenomena perceived in the subjective mode and objective phenomena are phenomena perceived in the objective mode. Experiencing is polarized into a subjective mode, symbolized by *the host,* and an objective mode symbolized by *the guest.* Thus, formerly, when Orientals sought to establish the concept of objective reality, they still approached it not as something out there, independent of our psychological processes, but rather as a mode of experiencing."

Because the Japanese approached objective reality as a mode of experiencing, movement in the direction of greater depths and extents of experiencing to the point of oneness or cosmic feelings was more accessible to them while the conceptualization of objective reality, essential to scientific thinking, had not occurred. Before Perry arrived in Japan in 1853, the Japanese had no words for the Western notions of "abstract" and "philosophy." This does not mean that the Japanese or Easterners in general are more feeling and Westerners more intelligent, but that the feeling function is more developed in one, while the thinking function is greater in the other. This also does not mean that one is generally healthier or sicker than the other because each can distort and pervert the forms of their particular mind structure.

Formalistically, in moments of communing (see chapter 12) there is neither experiencing nor awareness of subject or object, no I-watching-a-me doing the experiencing. Formalistically, there is only continuity and no contiguity expressive of the forms we name subject and object. The emergence of these contiguous forms is by the processes of subjectifying and objectifying.

As the movement is away from pure continuity there occurs through subjectifying, step by step, introjection, internalization, and, ultimately, *being the objective processes* with the real objective world extinguished. By a process of objectifying, there occurs, step by step, projection and externalization to the point of *being emptied of subjective processes* with the total self exhausted and extinguished.

At this point, we have another kind of continuity. Having originally been totally in ratio with reality and his reality, the individual has moved to the other extreme of being, totally out of ratio with his reality and the reality of the cosmos. He has become totally irrational in the mathematical meaning of rational, namely, to be in and out of ratio in a two term relationship.

Concomitantly, psychodynamically defined, he has become increasingly alienated from his real self. He has been actualizing his Idealized Image. Horney said that "If we regard the degree of removal from reality as making the difference between psychosis and neurosis we may consider the idealized image as a bit of psychosis woven into the texture of neurosis."*(39, p. 97)* The more irrational, the further removed from reality, the more alienated, the greater the possibilities there are for the operation of the total solution of magic (see chapter 16).

This detailed formalistic and psychodynamic pattern of movement from pure continuity, total rationality, and complete health to pure continuity of another order characterized by total irrationality, alienation, and sickness, in which state the operation of the total solution of magic can hold sway, can function as a guide for what obtains when the process and direction is reversed in therapy from greater sickness toward greater health. As this occurs, the pattern in the patient's productions will reflect freer and freer associating. Gradually the individual will experience himself, perceptually and conceptually, in decreasingly irrational and increasingly rational proportions. As this occurs, he will be approaching that degree of health in which many more moments of rational oneness, of genuine cosmic feelings, prerequisite to, and expressive of, moments of communing, will be obtaining.

As the analysis proceeds, patternings reflecting *centrifugal living* will become less, and associations reflecting *centripetal living* will become more manifest until there are moments of experiencing being and becoming, in and out, as one. With centrifugal living, implicitly and explicitly, associations manifest concern with the where, the when, and the why questions, focusing on the past and the future, on the there, the then, and on the reasons. Participating who's are turned into things, and things are anthropomorphized and personalized. Freer associating is happening when the content manifests more non-teleological experiencing of what and how, the here and now, which means more centripetal living is obtaining.

Initially, then, associations are expressions of thoughts about two-ness, separateness, difference, and conflict which gradually become manifestations of feelings of oneness, similarity, and cooperation. This happens through sequences initially reflecting thoughts about struggle to ultimately being evidence of experiencing struggling. As therapy proceeds, there will be more struggling against struggling. One crucial form of struggling is rejecting-accepting. What the patient initially found unacceptable takes the form of an entity. It functions like a foreign body with which he must struggle until it becomes acceptable and accepted. The struggling continues to exhaustion and despair. Then there is a letting go, a surrendering, submitting, giving way, giving in, and in time there is genuine giving.

With the letting go there will be *breakdowns* in the higher levels of the symbolic spiral of irrational sick processes, just as there were *break-ups* while the person was becoming sicker. *(184)* With the letting go, the patternings will reflect whatever theoretical construct one has of how a therapy proceeds to a successful conclusion. And finally, with the letting go there will be intense feelings of conflict, anxiety, dread, despair, meaningless, emptiness, and nothingness, which, as formulated awareness of man's present condition, is existential philosophy.

Ultimately, there will be feelings of fullness for which the feelings of emptiness are prerequisite. In its patternings, freer associating will reflect more of courage, which is choicefully entering painful situations that have possible future gain. There will be more leaps into the unknown, into formlessness, which is spontaneity. The patient will no longer have to be asked to "let himself go" or be admonished not to "push aside." Paradoxically, he will have become the unbiased approach, the "basic rule," without *having chosen* to let go. It will have happened to him and through him and in him.

It will then be accepted as self-evident that "being alive has always been dangerous" and "that it is not man's hostility and man's guilt that are the most obstructive dynamisms but that the fear of knowing oneself and the other person and the fear of loving and being loved are man's greatest threats."*(181, p. 65)*

Chapter 6

The Symbolizing Process II:
Symbols, the Symbolic Self,
and the Self-System

Further aspects of the symbolizing process, of symbol attributes, functions, and categories can be delineated through a discussion of the dreaming process. The many aspects of symbolizing play a crucial role in dreaming and in associations. A knowledge of symbolizing can serve as a most valuable tool and guide for identifying the many dimensions of the ongoing therapeutic process so essential to working effectively with dreams as an aspect of the working-through process.

"In dreams we are closer to the reality of ourselves,"*(49, p. 349)* Horney said; hence, symbols which constitute dreams have the attribute of realism. To say we are closer to the truth of ourselves in dreams defines another attribute of these symbols. Symbols present the truth of our truths, and the truth of our falsehoods. When closer to the truth of ourselves, we deal with what is essentially concerning us. It is not in the nature of the organism to concern itself with non-essentials, nor to expend itself on what is not relevant to the urge toward self-realization.

Symbols are a product of the creative process of symbolizing.

While dreaming, man reveals his genius in memory and in art. His recall is staggering, and he uses many more symbol forms in dreams than in any of the arts. While dreaming, man is creating his greatest creation, a living life. Symbols are artistic because they are abstractions from pure fact, a continuum of ineffable, aesthetic, undifferentiated processes. As an expression of the urge toward self-realization, symbols formulate and favor the process we call cure.

Symbols have then these attributes: they are realistic, truthful, deal with essentials, relevant, adequate, condensed, artistic, and curative. Whatever processes are portrayed in dreams, from the sickest to the healthiest, these symbol attributes will be present and participating.

There are four restrictions on symbol choice. First, although there is a world of experience from which to choose symbols, only those symbols can be selected which can transform internal or external energy. In that transforming process, man alters himself and the world around him in the direction of creation and/or miscreation.

Secondly, man can only select symbols built from responses which the organism has experienced and hence is capable of. He cannot form symbols of what he has not experienced. It is unlikely, for example, that an Eskimo would dream of camels or a Bedouin of igloos. Life circumstances imposed by parents, economics, culture, and the rational and irrational conditions under which each person grows up, make symbol selection a unique and highly individual process.

Thirdly, energy selects suitable forms for its expression. Man can only choose from those forms which will serve his self-realization. Also, forms do not select meaning. The meaning to be conveyed will select the form suitable to convey it.

The fourth restriction on symbol choice is the rigidity of a person's neurotic character structure. It narrows his external vistas and constricts what he can do with what he takes in. As a consequence, he can neither freely abstract nor freely choose his symbols. In the main, what happens is forced upon him. The classic example is the obsessive compulsive. An even more extreme instance is the mute, immobile catatonic.

Symbols may be discursive or nondiscursive. Verbal symbolism is discursive. The structure, particularly of Indo-European languages, which are subject/predicate in form, phonetic and alphabetical, involves the hypostatizing of processes. From these processes an aspect is abstracted and hypothesized into an "I" who is an actor. He or it acts on another aspect of these hypostatized processes, created by our dichotomizing intellection. "I push the lawn mower." "Gasoline drives the car."

These distorting processes require that we string out our ideas even though what they refer to rests one within the other. It is as if we were asked to wear our clothes spread out separately on a clothsline rather than on top of one another, the way we actually wear them. This tendency is less marked in verb-oriented languages like Burmese and Eskimo. Chinese, Japanese, and Korean are ideographic — at once picture, process, and ideation — and convey a whole moving matrix of ideas in one complex of symbols. They are really not written language but painted ideas. To say that ideographs are both picture and idea is to say that they unify the emotive, the aesthetic, the moral, and the theoretic. This process characterizes unitary man.

By contrast with the verbal ones, visual symbols are nondiscursive or presentational. They do not present their constituents successively, like words, but simultaneously, so that a painting, for example, is grasped in one act of vision. This also obtains for tonal symbols which are nondiscursive and participate in verbalizing, in poetry and in music, vocal or instrumental. Then there are such nondiscursive symbols as the kinaesthetic and emotive ones, the former expressed in the dance and in the religious rituals.

Creative reality bursts forth and expresses itself in a variety of symbols. But in none will it be imprisoned totally. That very impossibility is a constant stimulus, prod, and challenge which leads to the production of ever new forms in response to novel, emerging circumstances. Even a dream, which is man's greatest creation, is still but an aspect of the creative reality of that person at the moment he dreamed it.

It is unproductive to ask what a symbol is. The more fruitful question is what aspects of symbol functioning can we identify? Because of the nature of mind and discursive thought, we have to go through a process of abstracting to delineate its four aspects. These four aspects of symbol functioning are subject, symbol, conception, and object. Symbols are not proxies, substitutes for objects or events, but vehicles for the conception of objects and events. The lumping together of symbol and conception and of substituting symbols for the objects they stand for have created all manner of human havoc.

To put into discursive thought an instance of nondiscursive symbol functioning, such as the perception, to-look-at-a-mother, we have to separate the four aspects and string them out, one next to the other. First, there is the *subject* me — the actual person, not the pronoun me. Then, there is the *object*, a mother, an actual mother, not the noun mother. Then, there is the *symbol*, a whole composed of visual, olfactory, gustatory, kinaesthetic, emotive, conative, and cognitive images phenomenally present to me. Fourthly, we have the

116

conception — the denotation and connotation of the symbol mother, the meaning the symbol has for me.

This denotation-connotation, this organic conception, has been built up from past experiences, or organismic-environmental sequences, into which my mother, mothers, motherly, motherlike, and mothering persons entered. My conception of mothering, as an experienced process, is a residue of all maternal contexts.

For that organically embedded symbol to have meaning, there must not only be a somebody capable of forming images of an object, but also a somebody capable of being an interpretant, of forming a conception of that object. This implies the ability of a meaning function, of mentation. There always has to be a someone to whom the object means something, and that somebody else is man.

The process of perceiving a mother differs from imagining a mother. The crucial difference is that for imagining an actual mother need not be present to the senses. The stimulus for elaborating a conceptual symbol of a mother could originate in me and from any outside source except from an actual mother present to my senses. The conceptual symbol I form of a mother will be appropriate and adequate to convey what is going on in me, here and now, whether the symbol I form has a time reference of past, present, or future and a place reference of here or any location other than here, called there.

Just as all varieties of human receptors participate in forming the symbols of mothers and mothering, so do they participate in forming the symbols of fathering, brothering, sistering, and personing across time. This includes all symbol forms and dimensions of them that participate in the relating of all of these people which makes up the experience of a family, of being of a family, and of being of the family of man. All stages of an individual's development take place in this moving matrix of relationships which is called the *familying* process, extended to that total matrix of persons called the family of man. This means that man by nature and through nature is a social, socialized, and socializing animal.

In this moving matrix of relating processes, involving persons with varying intensities and extensities of relevance for the developing infant, the physiological functions of eating, defecating, sleeping, being touched, fondled, and talked to, are taking place. With such experiences go feelings of joy, sorrow, anger, fear, and anxiety. These experiences form the ground out of which symbols are formed, as they are from the natural biological rhythms of sleeping and waking, fatigue and rest, locomotion and quiescence, heat and cold, and hunger and satiation. These are some of the basic universal human experiences from which symbols forms are created. But universal human experiences should not be confused to mean universal symbols because symbols pointing at these universal human experiences will have different individual meanings, at different times and in different places. The meaning of each symbol is unique to that individual, at the time and place he uses it, no matter how many similarities of meaning it may have to others in his group.

An actual mother is integral to the fact and to the paradigm of the infant-mother unity, and to its analogue happening in the therapeutic process. To the extent the patient is able to manifest the anaclitic (dependent) attitude of the child, to the extent that the analyst can fulfill the diatrophic functions of mothering, of fathering, of the total possible humaning process, to that extent it is possible to help that person have experiences which resolve ego dystonic (neurotic character structure) patterns and transform them into ego syntonic (real self) ones. The patient also gains the opportunity to have experiences equivalent to, but not identical with, those he did not have at various stages of his development because of disturbances in the mothering process and in all other personing processes which should have contributed to his having become a healthy, wholesome human.

The analyst is not making up for what the patient did not get as a child because that is an impossibility. The patient is now an adult with a fully developed nervous system. He is not capable of the biosocial responses of a child going through the normal maturational phases, nor is he capable of responding with the symbol forms available and appropriate to those phases. Also, because of his life experience, he will be able to respond in the variety of ways not available to a child.

For the working through of ego dystonic patterns, or faults in development, work with dreams can be crucial. By identifying, in dreams, the patient's symbols of his actual mother and mothering ones and exploring them — by helping the patient contact and experience their organic embeddedness as they appear in sequences of dreams and associations, by explicitly and implicitly relating such symbols to symbols in other dreams, fantasies, and associations — the distortions of the meaning of mother and of mothering ones can be resolved. The patient can become better able to contact and to accept the child in him and accept the therapist's mothering *as if* he were his actual mother. This would mean, having experienced basic assurance, he will develop basic trust, and, ultimately, the primordial basic trust of the child as experienced by an adult. As he has such experiences, he will have become more the adult he could have become and at the same time be taking over his mothering of the child in him. As he does so, he will also be able to become more mothering to others.

Although I have used mothering to exemplify how we work with such symbols as they appear, as associations, in the analytic relationship and in dreams, I realize that healthy growing of the infant is not possible without fathering, brothering, sistering, and personing. It remains a debated issue whether familying as we have known it in the Western world is crucial to healthy development. Some countries still continue the rearing of children in collectives, as does Israel on some *kibbutzim,* although many Iron Curtain countries have discontinued the experiment. That the children who grow up under such circumstances differ from adolescents and adults raised in the typical Western pattern is unquestionable.

Yet, so far as the West and the rest of the world becoming Westernized are concerned, our patterns of child rearing and family structure still predominate, with their consequences.

From the moment of impregnation, the unitary process organism-environment begins. *(185)* The organism, as an autonomous agent, cooperates and conflicts with its environment. In the sense of memory as aftereffects, as traces in the present, we can speak of the organism remembering before, during, and after birth up to the time a feeling of identity begins to develop. This feeling of identity has its first vague beginnings as early as ten days and becomes fairly well-defined by twelve to eighteen months. From then on, through various maturational phases, more aspects of the symbolizing process come into being and are developed.

The development of identity is inferred from the way the infant follows shiny objects, turns toward sounds, smiles, gestures, cries, makes sounds, some wordlike, and by the natural rhythmicity of his development. *(186)* These experiences, by inference, participate in core identity and identity feelings, vague, amorphous, and inchoate as they may be at this early stage of growth.

An infant's feeling of selfness becomes more apparent when there are some expressions of self-identifying, such as looking at himself in the mirror, kissing his mirror image, and, ultimately, through his uttering such words as "me," "I," "baby," "Johnny," "Ruthie." His feeling of self increases as he discriminates himself from mommy, daddy, teddy, dolly.

The feeling of self must, however, be distinguished from the concept of self, or the symbolic self, from its vaguest indications, to its more complex and constant evolution. The formation of the symbolic self begins with the first instances of awareness, in the sense I will later define it. The symbolic self is continuously being formed through sequences of dysforming and reforming, concomitant with, and expressive of, organismal-environmental sequences. The symbolic self is built up out of symbol forms from all receptors and from all modalities of them. My symbolic self contains my conception of myself as an identity, as a self, my conception of my body and a body of a certain sex, my conception of my feelings, willing, thinking, acting, my conception of my relations to myself and to others, and my conception of my philosophy of life, of my world, the world, and me in it.

The symbolic self is a subwhole of the organism. Being a formal construction, the symbolic self is therefore not identical with the psychodynamic structural notion of ego with its adaptive functions. Formalistically, the notion of ego is an aspect of the symbolic self. Likewise, the symbolic self is not identical with Horney's notion of the idealized image which is also a psychodynamic construct. The notion of the symbolic self concerns and is derivative of the formal realm of cognition. The symbolic self is an outcome based upon the interactions of the organic substrate with its successive environments.

Although the symbolic self is always there, neither the individual nor the analyst can have the totality of it in awareness at any one moment. All that patient and therapist can do is to focus on aspects of it which are present in awareness, vaguely or sharply. It is also impossible to have many aspects in awareness at one time. Many aspects can only be identified over an extended period of analysis. They would also have changed during that time. Even though such changing might be at a very slow rate and give the impression of being static, it is always in flux. Patient and therapist, in being and becoming aware of aspects of the symbolic self, are active agents in effecting changes in it.

The individual's integrating is predominantly rational when and as his symbolic self is closer to what he realistically is. I use rational to refer to a vertical two-term relationship — the mathematical meaning of the word — specifically, to be in ratio. An individual's integrating is predominantly irrational, or out of ratio, when it is a consequence of varying degrees of remoteness from that person's reality, when his reality has become increasingly blurred to him, and as his reality more and more becomes for him what he imagines it to be rather than what it actually is. As his integrating moves in that direction, the predominance of patternings shifts from the neurotic, to the psychopathic, to the psychotic.

The symbolic self must be distinguished from the actual self which is represented in the symbolic self, more and less rationally and irrationally. The actual self is the total self at any given moment. The aim of self-knowledge is the approximation toward total knowledge of the actual self, "Intelligence being the total awareness of our processes."*(187)* As we approach that ideal — attainable only by a rare few — more moments of communing arise, the essential dualism between the formed and forming aspects of the self-system is at a minimum, and for moments becomes non-existent. Then we are identical with the "all in the all," as the so-called primitive is with "the society of life."

To be distinguished from the symbolic and the actual self is the empirical self — that part of the actual self which is immediately apprehendable and observable at any given moment. By empirically observing the actual self at any moment and in an extended contact, as in the therapeutic process, we attempt to help the patient toward increasing depths and extensities of awareness of his actual self so that his picture of himself becomes more congruent with it. This happens as the contrasts between the imagined irrational and the experienced actual are integrated and corrections are made in the symbolic self.

The organism integrates as a whole. The whole or actual self is a hierarchy of systems which are either apparently rigid and permanent or dynamic, plastic, impermanent, and forming. An oscillating equilibrium obtains between the formed and forming aspects of the self-system. The contrast between the formed and forming aspects of the self-system reflects a polarity of aspects, a duality, not to be confused with a dichotomy which has an irreconcilable opposition of parts.

Between the formed and forming aspects of the self-system there is tension, friction, and conflict because of their different rates of change. I call this the essential conflict, universally present between the known and static and the unknown and plastic. The universal conflict between being and becoming when formulated formalistically has a different meaning when formulated existentially. Actually becoming is being to which we attach a future tense. In moments of communing the formed and the forming aspects of the symbolizing process are experienced as identical. In such moments, being and becoming are experienced as identical and identical with all of being.

In the mind of the magic world of the so-called primitive, each individual is at the same time the collectivity. In Eastern thought, the juxtaposition of the subject and all otherness disappears, and all is identity. Put formally, all contiguity ceases and there is only experiencing continuity. Not formlessness as chaos, but formlessness as lucidity results. Then "there can be awareness without anything of which awareness is aware — hence a state of pure lucidity."*(188)*

The essential conflict exists whether that person is moving toward greater sickness or greater health, while still being moved by the urge toward self-realization. The essential conflict is derivative of the formal aspects of cognition and is based on my formulation of the universal forming process of which the symbolizing process is an aspect. The essential conflict is to be differentiated from Horney's psychodynamic concepts of central inner conflict and basic conflict, and from the psychodynamic conflicts within the typographical structure of id, ego, and superego.

Angyal, many of whose ideas on symbolizing have influenced mine, said with regard to the symbolic self that "there is a strong tendency in the symbolic or conscious self to establish its own autonomy within the total organism: a state within a state. This creates a split in the personality organization which is greatly aggravated by the fact that the symbolic self tends to take over the government of the total personality; a task for which it is not qualified . . . . The relative autonomy of the symbolic realm within the total organism is the most vulnerable point in human personality organization." *(162, p. 123)* Sullivan describes the evolution "of the self system or self dynamism" through learning from life experiences. "Not only does the self become the custodian of awareness, but when anything spectacular happens that is not welcome to the self, not sympathetic to the self dynamism, anxiety appears, almost as if anxiety finally became the instrument by which the self maintained its isolation within the personality."*(189)*

Because the forming aspect of the self-system is dynamic, flexible, and impermanent, it contains the greatest opportunities for change and the greatest possibilities for effecting it. For these reasons and more, anxiety in varying intensities and extensities is constantly triggered. This is the paradox of all therapy.

We ask the patient to relinquish his demand for immediate relief, to accept accessions of anxiety for shorter and longer periods, and to let go of his need to solve his conflicts in order that he may resolve them. Prerequisite to his being able to do so is a relationship in which there is basic trust. The patient is implicitly promised a diminution in the level of that kind of anxiety from which he demands immediate relief, while acquiring an increasing ability to enter foreknown anxiety situations of his own choosing. The implication is made that instead of being driven to solve his conflicts, he will increasingly be able to resolve them. Out of such occurrences he will develop moral compassion and moral toughness, which together constitute moral courage.

This conception of symbolizing is congruent with Vico's (1668-1744) conceptions in *Scienza Nuova* (1725), which are recurrently discovered and forgotten as is Heraclitus' flux and change. Vico theorized that the living force in humanity creates itself. *(190)* Man can create mathematical systems which he can know because he created them. Man can use them to formulate laws about nature which he cannot know because he did not create it. Man can know other men because they are like himself, although he did not create them. The physical sciences are abstract and circumscribed to aspects of external reality. The human sciences are more profound and difficult because they have to take the world as they find it with its continuing unpredictable novelty.

Kant (1724-1804) continued Vico's criticism of Francis Bacon (1561-1626) and Descartes (1596-1650). Kant said that we do not know objects but the objects conform to our ways of knowing them. "The mind is *constitutive* of its objects. It creates them in knowing them."*(191)* Kuhn argued in 1962 that "paradigms" are not only "constitutive of science" but they are "constitutive of nature as well."*(192)* Caws asserts that "scientific discovery is no less logical than deduction," and offers the hypothesis that hypotheses which constitute scientific discovery "strictly speaking . . . arise *naturally.*" *(193)* Heraclitus and Vico are alive and well in the modern scientific universe.

In discovering ourselves we create ourselves. Such creation and miscreation is a natural expression of our humanity. Nature is profligate in its forms. Children welcome and play with the wealth and welter of forms expressive of their spontaneity. In understanding the universal forming process, of which the symbolizing process is one aspect, we are being natural and naturally acquiring knowledge of our living humanity, of our biology.

"Biological knowledge is continued creative activity, by which the idea of the organism comes increasingly within reach of our experience," wrote Goldstein. *"The symbols which biology requires for the coherent representation of the empirical facts are of a kind other than those in physics . . . .* In practice we usually proceed in such a way that, from the facts gained by analysis, we sketch a picture of the whole organism, which in turn instigates further questions and investigations so long as we encounter discrepancies between this picture and factual experience . . . . The material is essentially supposed to demonstrate over and over again that *method* as well as theory must originate from nothing but the most concrete evidence." *(186, pp. 143, 403, 507)*

What Goldstein describes is a picture of psychoanalysis as investigation, theory, therapy, and creative process, which all could well emulate. His organismic approach is also consonant with the most modern concepts in biology.

Biology is used by Angyal in the widest sense and in the root meaning of bios, namely, life. The biosphere refers to all aspects of living processes whether the reference is to physical or psychological processes in the individual or in the environment. On this basis, biology means all disciplines concerned with living processes from human history and human ecology, to human physiology and human psy-

123

chology. Life proceeds through sequences of events in the biosphere. They are therefore referred to as biospheric occurrences having a subject and an object pole. *(162, ch. 4)*

This idea of biology is evident in modern evolutionary, morphologic, and human biology. A modern "textbook of medicine" states King, in his critique of Harrison (1966) and Cecil-Loeb (1967), *"is a study of human biology, and not a strict categorization and analysis of specific entities which we call disease.* In biology we become aware of the extraordinary interpenetration of all factors, which we sometimes call ecology where everything has to do with everything else, to a greater or less extent, and boundaries seem to get more and more artificial."*(194)* This description could well apply to textbooks of psychoanalysis.

In the totality of biospheric occurrences which constitute the world as it is lived by us, segmental sciences can be derived, but not by isolation, which would lead to a disregard of *"certain features of the biological reality."* It can be done, says Angyal, by a procedure "called *Einklammerung* — 'placing in parenthesis' — a term used by Husserl with a somewhat different meaning."*(162, p. 103)* It avoids the distorting consequences of focusing on a problem out of context rather than focusing on it in context. We now need general scientists to integrate the micro findings of specialists into the macro fields of biology.

For effecting this integration the systems approach gains wider use as it is refined. Its emergence is consonant with the awareness that with each context and its contingencies a new image of man must be created as well as methods to understand that image. The systems approach, which can deal with multiple variables operative in moving fields constituted of hierarchies of systems in dominance relationships, seems most appropriate for our current context.

"In the systems approach, the concentration is on the analysis and design of the whole, as distinct from analysis and design of the components or the parts. It is an approach that insists upon looking at a problem in its entirety, taking into account all the facets, all the intertwined parameters. It is a process for understanding how they interact with one another and how these factors can be brought in proper relationship for the optimum solution of the problem. The systems approach relates the technology to the need, the social to the technological aspects; indeed, it starts by insisting on a clear understanding of exactly what the problem is, and of the goals that should dominate the solution and lead to the criteria for evaluating alternative systems. As the end result, the approach seeks to work out a detailed description of a specified combination of men and machines — with such concomitant assignment of function, designated use of material, and pattern of information flow that the whole system represents a compatible, optimum, interconnected ensemble for achieving the end desired."*(195)*

The systems approach and system thinking can integrate the findings of the segmental sciences of biology we call the behavioral sciences. For studying the systems and subsystems of these various sciences, a variety of models applicable to each can be used. Among them are the homeostatic, medical, and epidemiological models. The latter combined with deviance models have a wide range of utility in social and cultural studies.

Stochastic models are essential for studying the stochastic systems in "The Uncertain Nervous System."*(196)* Utilizing the systems approach, the nervous system, seen as a general purpose computer, becomes more understandable. Such models make it possible to see that spontaneous firing of neurons occurs; that nerve nets are better thought of as floating points; that within the unpredictable nervous system, certain activities are more predictable than others; that different types of learning lead to different types of nerve nets; and that different types of development may result in different types of nerve net combination. The nervous system has many characteristics of the analytic process.

The systems approach can integrate the conceptual aspects of self: as real self and core identity, as physical, sexual, and gender identity, as identity diffusion, confusion, and formation through the processes in developmental crises; as symbolic self; and as the self system. It can integrate Horney's psychodynamic formulations, because they are congruent with the methodologies of modern biology and the acquisition of biological knowledge as defined by Goldstein.

Chapter 7

Unconscious Processes

In *New Ways* Horney said, "I regard as the most fundamental and most significant of Freud's findings his doctrines that psychic processes are strictly determined, that actions and feelings may be determined by unconscious motivations, and that the motivations driving us are emotional forces."*(35, p. 18)* As her theories evolved, determinism became more relative through the inclusion of human spontaneity. Her notion of unconscious motivation was expanded by the concept of the real self and her definition of sickness was extended. Concomitantly, the emotional forces functioning as motivations were enhanced through the enlarged meaning of unconscious processes.

Central to Horney's understanding of unconscious processes is her concept of the real self — a concept which is integral to her growth oriented philosophy that regards man's essential nature and his spontaneous morality as inseparable. In "A Morality of Evolution," she says:

Broadly speaking, there are three major concepts of the goal of morality which rest upon these different interpretations of essential human nature. Superimposed checks and controls cannot be relinquished by anyone who believes — in whatever terms — that man is by nature sinful or ridden by primitive instincts (Freud). The goal of morality must then be the taming or overcoming of the *status naturae* and not its development.

The goal must be different for those who believe that there is inherent in human nature both something essentially "good" and something "bad," sinful or destructive . . . . Here the emphasis is not exclusively upon combatting and suppressing evil . . . . The positive program rests either upon supernatural aids of some sort or upon a strenuous ideal of reason and will, which in itself suggests the use of prohibitive and checking inner dictates.

Lastly, the problem of morality is again different when we believe that inherent in man are evolutionary constructive forces, which urge him to realize his given potentialities. This belief does not mean that man is essentially good . . . . It means that man, by his very nature and of his own accord, strives toward self-realization, and that his set of values evolves from such striving . . . . He can grow, in the true sense, only if he assumes responsibility for himself.

We arrive thus at a *morality of evolution,* in which the criterion for what we cultivate or reject in ourselves lies in the question: is a particular attitude or drive inducive or obstructive to my human growth? . . . The way toward this goal is an ever increasing awareness and understanding of ourselves . . . . In this sense, to work at ourselves becomes not only the prime moral obligation, but at the same time, in a very real sense, the prime moral *privilege* . . . . The ideal is the liberation and cultivation of the forces which lead to self-realization. *(49, pp. 14-16)*

Consistent with this ideal is Horney's belief that "The human individual, given a chance, tends to develop his particular human potentialities" and in doing so "will grow, substantially undeviated, *toward self-realization.* And that is why I speak . . . of the *real self* as that central inner force, common to all human beings and unique to each, which is the deep source of growth."*(49, p. 17)*

To present more fully its propensities in the terms of William James: it provides the "palpitating inward life;" it engenders the spontaneity of feelings, whether these be joy, yearning, love, anger, fear, despair. It also is the source of spontaneous interest and energies, "the source of effort and attention from which emanate the fiats of will;" the capacity to wish and to will; it is the part of ourselves that wants to expand and grow and to fulfill itself. It produces the "reactions of spontaneity" to our feelings or thoughts, "welcoming or opposing, appropriating or disowning, striving with or against, saying yes or no." All this indicates that our real self, when strong and active, enables us to make decisions and assume responsibility for them. It therefore leads to genuine integration and a sound sense of wholeness, oneness. Not merely are body and mind, deed and thought or feeling, consonant and harmonious, but they function without serious inner conflict. In contrast to those artificial means of holding ourselves together, which gain in importance as the real self is weakened, there is little or no attendant strain. *(49, p. 157)*

The real self is that dynamic principle which guides and gives constructive impetus to the individual in his struggle toward self-realization. To grow means "free, healthy development in accordance with the potentials of one's generic and individual nature."*(49, p. 17)* Under adverse conditions, another process is set in motion: "The neurotic process is a special form of human development, and — because of the constructive energies which it involves — is a particularly unfortunate one. It is not only different in quality from healthy human growth but, to a greater extent than we have realized, antithetical to it in many ways."*(49, p. 13)*

The concept of the real self has appeared under various names, in ancient and modern philosophies, as has the notion of the urge toward self-realization. After defining self-realization, central to her thinking, Fromm-Reichmann added, "Goldstein's 'self-actualization,' Fromm's 'productive character,' Whitehorn's 'mature personality,' and 'the self-affirmation' of the existentialists are formulations of the same concept."*(198, p. 311)* Had Horney lived, I believe, as her later publications showed, *(49, 51, 54)* her work would have been in the area of the real self, its clearer definition, the impediments to its growth, and better ways of freeing its operations in therapy.

Freud's 1937 statement that "id and ego are originally one;" that id is not our sole "archaic heritage;" and that "even before ego exists, its subsequent lines of development, tendencies and reactions are already determined" reflected a significant shift in his thinking. *(105, p. 344)* Freud's last formulations depicted the ego "as equipped with an inborn (primary autonomous) apparatus possessing functions ... which form a basis for the 'non-conflictual sphere' of psychic activity .... Personality development normally occurs through interactions of the conflictual and the nonconflictual .... Mental health, or successful psychic adaptation, depends on a proper balance among the structures of the personality (id, ego, superego)."*(142, p. 95)* Anna Freud's *The Ego and the Mechanisms of Defense* and Hartmann's *Ego Psychology and the Problem of Adaptation* evidenced still more of such developments. *(121, 122)* Through Anna Freud's contributions from child analysis "The real world of the child — not only his sex phantasies in later years — thus became the basis for concepts of mental health and illness;" and through Hartmann's "broad orientation in the natural and social sciences and the humanities" came his ideas on the adaptive functions of ego that "impressed positive aims on all behavior."*(142, p. 94-95)*

Apfelbaum's views on ego psychology, Munroe's position regarding Horney's contribution, Tarachow's confirmation, and Balint's notion of primary love and its similarity to Horney's concept of the real self have been mentioned in Chapter 1. "Deviant movements," wrote Kanzer and Blum in 1967, "now tend to show wide areas of agreement with the established school." *(142, p. 139)*

The evolution of Freudian theory suggests that Freud and the post-Freudians have been moving toward positions the neo-Freudians had been evolving for many years. From id as primary in early Freudian theory, to id and ego as congruent, to ego superseding id, represents almost a complete turnabout. How far this evolution has gone is evident in Balint's concept of "primary love."*(127, p. 65)*

While one may speak of the newest ideas regarding the ego as analogous to Horney's position that human spontaneity, the real self, and the urge toward straighter growing are primary, Balint's concept of "primary love" is close to being identical with it. Horney, as did Balint, regarded sadism and hate as "secondary phenomena," consequences of "frustrations" and blockages to growth. These sick processes can be analogized to the id.

This evolution regarding the place in theory of id and ego, of primary love and real self, influences the meaning of primary and secondary process thinking, of sublimation, and of our concepts regarding creativity. This evolution also determines how unconscious processes are defined.

"What we regard as healthy striving toward self-realization for Freud was . . . only an expression of narcissistic libido," Horney said. *(49, p. 378)* Balint was also critical of Freud's theory of primary narcissism. He called it a "suitcase theory" because it contains three theories "about the individual's primitive relationship to his environment" which "apparently contradict each other." They are the theories of "primary-object love, primary auto-erotism, and primary narcissism." Balint offered his alternative theory of primary love. In his opinion, "all narcissism is secondary" to interferences with the most primitive relationships based on primary love. *(127)* In Horney's terms, this means that what Freud subsumed under narcissism was a consequence of blockages of the urge toward self-realization. It leads to disturbances in healthy self-love and self-esteem in one's relation to self, to others, and to the cosmos of which one is an aspect. What for Freud was secondary process thinking, namely, creativity through sublimation, Horney regarded as primary, and Freud's primary process thinking, Horney saw as a secondary consequence of blockages to straighter growing.

Unconscious processes are not directly observable but inferred and while the patient, in Freud's phrase, "does not know that he knows," he can be helped to know his knowing. Although they may be analogous at times, unconscious processes are not identical with the prerationative levels of the postulated symbolic spiral. The notion of the symbolic spiral, which participates in defining the actual situation, communing and communicating, and the doctor-patient relationship, widens the concept of unconscious processes and gives a much more comprehensive basis for mutual contacting of therapist and patient.

The structure and content of the prerationative levels define the therapist's task as aiding, and maintaining a situation of creative tension through "Freer Associating."*(182)* This attitude will be communicated to the patient so that there may be less fear of unconscious processes which are usually regarded as chaotic, unpredictable, and destructive. This focus on the prelogical, on the so-called latent, is no de-emphasizing of the logical, the so-called manifest, but a proportionate enlarging of the basis for understanding and explaining the logical and the directly observable.

My interest in the surface and in the manifest, as an aspect of exploring and experiencing all levels of the symbolic spiral has also been reflected in Freudian literature. Hartmann attempts to reconcile "neglected general (or surface) psychology" with depth psychology. *(142, p. 95)* In his concept of "reconstruction upwards," Lowenstein recognizes the need for the analyst to move not only from surface to depth but also from depth to surface. *(142, p. 112)*

"The libido theory in all its contentions is unsubstantiated," Horney said. *(35, p. 68)* This was her reason for discarding it. Her growth-oriented, holistic, process patterned, system thinking is a rejection of the concept of the repetition compulsion. "Freud's mechanistic, evolutionistic thinking . . . implies that present manifestations not only are conditioned by the past, but contain nothing but the past; nothing really new is created in the process of development; what we see today is only the old in a changed form."*(35, p. 42)*

Hartmann also questioned Freud's position. He felt that a later neurosis need not be modeled on an earlier one but could develop out of current interactions between the individual and his environment: "Simple genetic continuities and repetition compulsions should not be postulated; the genetic construction must include a functional appraisal of each stage of development in its own context."*(142, p. 121)* Influenced by Hartmann's thinking, Kanzer and Blum suggested that implying direct continuity between infantile smearing impulses and the sublimations was not sufficient. The complex processes of development and regression must be traced. While a child might become interested in painting during the smearing phase, this painting interest may serve as an outlet briefly or be longer lasting. Painting may also emerge in later years quite independent of the influence of early impulses. *(142, p. 96)*

Horney discarded the notion of the Oedipus complex, but retained "the highly constructive finding that early relationships *in their totality* mold the character to an extent which can be scarcely overestimated."*(35, p. 87)*

Anna Freud's researches in child analysis reflect Horney's concern with the "totality" of relationships and emphasize that limiting past reconstructions to libidinal phases of development is inadequate. Postulating a primal scene or an Oedipus Complex is also insufficient. "The exact relations between the individual and the persons in his environment, their behavior as well as his own, the identifications he made, and his handling of aggression, anxiety, and object relationships must and can be reconstituted with the key provided by the transference neurosis."*(142, p. 105)* I believe further that these objectives can be accomplished without recourse to the concept of the transference neurosis which requires the dubious concept of regression.

The doctrine of regression is "inextricably interwoven with the libido theory," and Horney rejected it as but "a special form of repetition."*(35, pp. 147-49)* Menninger regarded regression as "one of the more ambiguous" psychoanalytic concepts and felt that the "metaphorical language" used to grasp it, while helpful, "will be confusing if one pushes it too far."*(200, p. 49)* Just how "regression suddenly turns around" at a certain point, "and becomes a progression . . . remains something of a mystery . . . . An existential concept, *kairos,* may apply here," said Menninger. "It means crisis, in the special sense of a dramatic moment, full of emotional charge, particularly 'right time' with various possibilities."*(200, pp. 75-76)* Menninger's concept and definition of kairos is developed in chapter 25.

The regression-progression duality is derivative of the myth of progress which has concerned existentialists. Since pagan times, Western theories of history have reflected variations of two "shapes" according to Manuel, one cyclical and the other progressive. *(201)* The cyclical one derives from daily experience, is morally neutral; hence, depressive and pessimistic to Westerners. The myth of progress is a product of reflection. It involves a moral order, and optimistically offers, in the form of the Christian and scientific myths, an escape from eternal human suffering. History has made a blasphemy of the myth of progress. The concept of regression, with its Christian and scientific underpinnings and overtones, is derivative of the myth of progress. Regression has the same limitations as the myth of progress and the same negative consequences follow from it.

In his *Basic Fault,* Balint tried to diminish the unclarities and develop what might be of value in regression. He delineated two "clusters" or forms of regression, "benign and malignant." He tried to show that regression "is not only an intrapsychic phenomenon, but also an interpersonal one; for its therapeutic usefulness, its interpersonal aspects are decisive." Regression "depends only partly on the patient, his personality and his illness, but partly also on the object; in consequence it must be considered as *one* symptom of the interaction between the patient and his analyst. This interaction has at least three aspects : the way (a) in which the regression is recognized by the object, (b) in which it is accepted by the object, (c) in which it is responded to by the object."*(127, pp. 146, 148)*

Balint is describing a holistic process having intrapsychic and interpersonal reference. He clearly sees the analyst as a "co-actor" in the transference and countertransference and finds the "therapeutic usefulness" of the "interpersonal aspects . . . decisive." These issues will be elaborated in my discussion of the transference neurosis.

In commenting on the therapeutic efficacy of his and a patient's prolonged silence, Balint asks, "But can this episode be called a regression or a repetition? My answer is . . . that logically it cannot. One can repeat something only if the something existed at least once before; and on the whole the same holds true for regression. Instead of these two misleading terms, I suggest calling this episode a 'new beginning' or a new discovery, leading to a different, more satisfactory relationship to an important object." Balint has not only identified one "cluster" of forms of regression as benign, he has substituted for the "misleading" terms regression and repetition the more felicitous one of "new beginning or new discovery" and he has questioned the notion of repetition compulsion. *(127, p. 143)*

Theorists of human nature such as Goldstein and Angyal who are guided by the organismic and holistic approach describe so-called regressive phenomena. They do so without recourse to the concept of regression, but use holistic concepts such as the adequacy of the individual and the environment for each other, or notions of organismic trends toward autonomy and homonomy in an environment moved by forces heteronomous to it. *(186, 162)*

A holistic orientation gives us a different perspective on phenomena described as regressive. Their emergence is made possible by movement and change in the analytic process. They seemingly reproduce earlier phases of development retrogressively. What they represent might more accurately be described by the paradoxes of regressing forward, advancing toward childhood, or becoming childish and childlike. In the classical model, with regression and the development of the transference neurosis, there is a drive toward archaic object relationship, toward fusion (symbiosis), toward the undifferentiated state characteristic of the basic unity of mother and infant. Because of the Freudian concept of the unconscious, this is viewed as having predominantly negative connotations and is avoided by interpretation which supports the drive toward separation.

The positive values in contacting the undifferentiated state cannot be so clearly seen, nor so effectively used, when the therapist is guided by the classical model. The holistic view of the undifferentiated state is, however, integral to, and expressive of, the primary notions of autonomy and spontaneity and my view that there is human integrating on the basis of being in the world of the primitive, of the East as well as of the West. From this viewpoint, effective conduct of the analysis has as its aim analyzing irrational relating, so that more of rational relating, to the point of communing, becomes possible. This means that there are more moments of basic unity when self-system boundaries, such as self (ego), are loose, vague, or dissolved, moments which are expressive of that paradigm, the mother-child unity, as a fact and manifestation.

Developments in ego psychology have brought fundamental changes in psychoanalytic theory. Unconscious processes are now seen quite differently by psychoanalysts. The libido theory has been revised out of existence by some. Fixation, regression and repetition compulsion now have radically altered meanings as does the concept of sexuality and narcissism.

To repeat Kanzer and Blum: "Deviant movements . . . now tend to show wide areas of agreement with the established school." Balint, however, is careful to add that though a number of analysts are in agreement with his viewpoints they are not members of "the classical massive center."*(127, p. 155)* A spokesman from this "massive center" asserts that "the future of psychoanalysis depends, in my opinion, on Freud's original conceptions being first of all *preserved* (italics mine), and then built upon."*(202)*

Freudians, who reflect the "classical massive center," and post-Freudians, have had many more years than did Horney to test Freud's evolving hypotheses. They have had many more opportunities to refine and correct, in minor and major ways, the productions of a steadily expanding group of trained analysts. Understandably, many more areas of human personality have been explored, and many more hypotheses have been exposed to extensive trial than was possible for one person. That Horney did not significantly touch on a number of areas of psychoanalytic theory and technique is evident. The gaps, however, are not as great as some would have it. Her use of a different language and other methodologies accounts for some of these apparent lacks.

The above described evolution of psychoanalytic theory currently reveals a range of viewpoints. The "classical massive center" preserves Freud, and the revisions of others reflect a spectrum from the slight to the radical. In the evolution of Freudian theory we nevertheless see a shift from closed system to open system thinking, from absolute to relative determinism, from an exclusive focus on the individual to a consideration of patient and therapist as whole persons interacting with and upon each other. Not only do deviant movements, as Kanzer and Blum have stated, show areas of agreement with the established school; the latter have also integrated many earlier positions of deviant theorists, once considered heretical.

Chapter 8

The Actual Situation

The discussion of unconscious processes gave essential background for understanding Horney's concept of the actual situation. "Emphasis is put on the actually existing conflicts and the neurotic's attempts to solve them, on his actually existing anxieties, and the defenses he has built up against them."*(33, p. vii)* In "Culture and Neurosis," she further elaborated on the actual situation. *(35)*

With Horney's concept of the actual situation a multidimensional genetics emerged. The meaning of development and the influence of hereditary and constitutional factors interacting with environmental influences is delineated in a language of process and character structure. Of these, Horney's description of the evolution of morbid dependency is a detailed illustration. *(49, ch. 10)*

An ontogeny of being became evident in her concept of basic anxiety and in her phenomenological analysis of the being of the therapist. Her ontology, of the actual situation included all dimensions of the present, extending back into the past and forward into the future. The latter is evident in the dynamics of the real self as having acted in the past, as acting in the present, and as pointing toward action in the future. The genetics of the future are implied in her immediate and ultimate goals for therapy.

Fromm-Reichmann felt that "it is not only helpful but indispensable for psychotherapeutic success to study the patient's and psychiatrist's mutual relationships in terms of their repetitional characteristics. But we keenly feel that this should not be done to the point of neglecting to scrutinize the reality of the actual experience between therapist and patient in its own right."*(151, p. 4)*

I have developed some of Horney's meanings of the actual situation and added some of my own. According to my notion of the symbolizing process, what we start and end with, and are always in and of, is the actual, total, immediate, present situation. *(137, 175)* Organismal-environmental happenings becoming manifest as feelings, sensations, perceptions and thoughts, signs, gestures, and sounds. These happenings may be clothed in symbols having the time form of past, present, or future, and the place form of here and there. We have two modes of knowing these phenomena, inferentially through rationality, and directly through numinous awareness. The aim of such knowing is the widening and deepening of here-now experiencing of those symbol forms and what they point at, preformed. *(136)*

Those symbol forms having the time form of past and the place attribute of there, can be read as information, about back there then, and as having later confirmed degrees of accuracy and/or distortion. They can be seen as a defense, such as an externalization, or as an aspect of more extensive blocking. They can be understood as aspects of the doctor-patient relationship in which the analyst is seen and experienced in a distorted manner *as if* he were identical with someone. But identical with is radically different from *similar, like, reminiscent of, analogous,* or *equivalent* to a person in that patient's life. The analyst also might be experienced as he is in reality, and also might be *reminiscent of* someone other than himself in that patient's life who is also seen *realistically.* All of these symbol forms may be read as changing perceptions of persons and events. This means we can change our past as memory, as after-effects, and as perceptions of it in much the same way as we can change our enduring present and our anticipated futures. *(136, 137, 204)*

The symbol forms and arrangements of them, happening into awareness, will be pointing at what brought them into being and what is perpetuating, embedding, and resolving them. These symbol forms will reflect what is formed and in awareness; what is vague, being formed, and at "life's growing edge;" and what may be inferred, unconscious, and helped into awareness. The analysis is conducted so as

136

to favor a shift of energy investments in the patterns of process in that four-dimensional moving matrix, the actual situation, so that the balance increasingly favors self-realizing and opposes the actualizing of the Idealized Image.

As this is happening, new symbol forms in new arrangements will be constantly emerging, illuminating these shifts and their connections. Meaning is the experiencing of the connectedness, interrelationship, and coherence of patterns, the awareness of the how and what, in the here and now. Meaning is the experiencing of the fitting and not-fitting in that moving gestalt, the analytic process. From such experiencing emerge feelings of understanding and of knowledge. This means we conduct the analysis of the ongoing and changing actual situation so that the patient is searching for and finding his own interpretations, his own meanings. This means we are helping him toward conducting his own analysis, for in the final analysis who knows his wilderness better than the patient? As guides we know terrains in general, and many in specific, but we do not know his, about which he must be telling us, and usually is, if we can but look and see, listen and hear.

The suggested model of the symbolizing process can also give structure to what has come into the field of the analyst's "evenly hovering attention" during his own analysis, course in training, and general experience with patients. As forms, expressive of and pointing at aspects of his being, they are manifestations of reactions, responses, and resonations to his confronting (*Begegnung*); contacting (empathy, intuition, intersubjectivity); relating (transference, transaction, the interpersonal relationship, the doctor-patient relationship, being with); and being in communion with his patient (being, being there, being at his patient's core of being while concomitantly being at his own). These forms are indicators showing him what he should see and hear as information and acquire as knowledge regarding the immediacies transpiring.

As I have said elsewhere, the actual therapeutic situation can be viewed "as a bipolar unitary process. Doctor and patient are the two aspects of this therapeutic process, this single integral reality, having a subject and an object pole. Object means that which objects, which is temporarily, and to a degree, under the influence of an environment governed by laws heteronomous to the object's nature. From moment to moment doctor and patient function, now as subject and now as object, for the other.

"From such a concept of the therapeutic situation it follows that the notion of an uninfluenced or an uninfluencing therapist or patient is not tenable."*(205)* The influences can range from the most felicitous to the most adverse, each on the other. The issue then becomes how to identify and effectively forestall what could block the resolution of what is destructive while enhancing what is constructive and growth promoting.

"The notion of passivity is also not tenable. Passivity in therapist and/or patient can be a very active and stubborn problem. The passivity is only apparently so, for in nature, and hence in human nature, all processes are active."*(205)* Being is action, is being active. Being and action are in the nature of all persons, male and female,

Lomas sharply confronts the passivity-activity issue in classical theory, particularly as it relates activity to being masculine and superior and passivity to being feminine and inferior. "Passivity is not a specifically sexual phenomenon." He adds that "This myth has led to errors in psychoanalytic theory." It has resulted in a "faulty conception of activity, passivity, and identity, and of the distinction between real and false identity" and to "an unnecessarily large divergence between the theories of male and female development"*(125)* to which Horney made such significant contributions. *(63)*

Horney's concept of the real self in the context of her ideas on unconscious processes and the actual situation significantly influence my perspectives on "Diagnosing and Prognosing in Psychoanalysis." *(204)* Diagnosing is a process of evaluating growing possibilities by analysts while working with patients. Prognosing is a process of predicting immediate and future growing possibilities by analysts while working with patients. Both of these are operational definitions because they describe "operations to be performed so that the thing defined (or its effects) will be observed."*(206)* The present participle form of a verb is used to indicate that we are dealing with an active process which is ongoing. We do so to show that we are not only concerned with being but also with becoming. In short, we are concerned with growing, self-realizing, being, and becoming, spontaneous. For these processes to expand and extend, the diagnosing and prognosing by the therapist of himself and his patient must be an ongoing process from the first contact to the interruption of regular sessions.

The data essential for diagnosing and prognosing emerge into awareness as forms, as patternings carrying values as to fact, aesthetics, morality, and spirituality. Displayed in these patternings are energy investments pointing at possibilities for straighter growing. These patternings can be described as manifesting ill-being and well-being, ugliness and beauty, sin and innocence, physical and emotional sickness and health — all of which are aspects of the holistic model of human being.

These patternings can be described as rational and irrational. The closer the patternings approximate the ultimate of rationality, the more they are in ratio, the more of the energy investments will be in patterns of process reflecting greater health. The more they will approximate the ultimate of irrationality, the more they are out of ratio, the more the energy investment will be in processes reflecting increasing sickness. Perfect health and the perfectly rational person does not exist; and the perfectly sick or perfectly irrational person would die.

Human beings living and existing in environments are always moving, more and less, toward greater rationality and greater irrationality. The patterns of rationality are explicit. They may be described as constructive forces or resources, ego strength, growth possibilities, and actualities, or simply as *assets*. The patterns of irrationality are also explicit. The physical form of these processes are medically described as symptoms, syndromes, disease entities, and disease processes. The psychological patterns we refer to as neurosis, psychopathy, and psychosis. They are also described in terms of symptoms, syndromes, entities, or processes.

Using the holistic concept of irrational patternings, we can obtain a more comprehensive understanding of psychological sickness as an interconnected continuum of neurotic, psychopathic, and psychotic processes. These may be named obstructive or destructive forces, ego weakness or fragility, developmental failures, arrests, fixations, and regressions, in short, *liabilities*. Even those who disagreed with Horney's viewpoints admired the rigor, clarity, and precision of her delineation of the neurotic process. Many are now attempting to do likewise with the psychotic process. A few have been attempting to describe the formal and psychological patterns of the psychopathic process. *(153, 208)* Recently Grinker has delineated the "Borderline Syndrome."*(209)*

What determines whether a person is predominantly sick or healthy, and the direction in which he is moving, is the balance of energy investments in the totality of processes. The foreground patterns of the processes are helpful guides, however they may be classified. But they are only part of the totality of available information. The shifts, therefore, which we observe in foreground pictures of the various types of neurosis, psychopathic phases of illness, and the various types of psychosis, need not be disconcerting. Everyone has some of health, neurosis, psychopathy, and psychosis in him. "If we regard the degree of removal from reality as marking the difference between psychosis and neurosis," said Horney, "we may consider the idealized image as a bit of psychosis woven into the texture of neurosis."*(39, p. 97)* The limitations of our diagnostic and prognostic abilities, must be recognized, and the crucial import of the natural history approach and the necessity for long term follow-up studies must be realized. More of the latter are now being done both in the

United States and Europe with humbling and cautioning impact on notions regarding mental illness and mental health.

In diagnosing and prognosing our task thus becomes identifying and describing, as an ongoing process, the assets and liabilities of the patient and the therapist in their immediate, intermediate, and ultimate environments, past, present and future. The data, the values expressed through them and their arrangement as forms in patternings which carry energy investments, are all manifested as assets and liabilities and organized in a variety of models that give us many more details regarding the form, structure, and content of processes in the total actual situation.

Among what we have defined as assets are a favorable heredity and a tendency to good physical and psychic health and to longevity. A patient who has a history of good health, rapid, uncomplicated recoveries from sickness, few serious illnesses — a person, in short, with good physical and psychic vitality and resilience has considerable assets. A requirement for, and an expression of, assets is the availability and ultilization of good food, clothes, adequate housing, medical care, and contact with nature. Other assets are aptitudes, skills, and talents. Advantageous also are education, training, or experience in a specialized field or profession.

It is also an asset if a person has been able to learn and to grow through and from his life experience. All of us have the capacity to feel, think, will, and act. The maintenance of genuine feelings, the ability to have small pleasures even in the midst of adversity, and a sense of humor with regard to oneself and life are indeed assets. A person who has had the experience of having taken healthy stands in personal matters or in broader human affairs has maintained some contact with his convictions and his will to fight for what he believes. If he can recall incidents where he felt his judgment regarding himself and others was sound and that the actions based on such reasoning were warranted, he has had some experience in self-reliance in human affairs. If in addition, he can honestly say that here or there his judgment was poor and his actions impulsive or compulsive, he is indeed a wiser person. Add to these the learning that has come from suffering through critical participation in life, and we have some of the elements of wisdom. Closely connected are the capacity to tolerate psychic pain, with which often goes a degree of integrity and a capacity to face the truth squarely. When a patient has also a capacity for psychological thinking, his assets have been measurably added to.

Crucial among environmental assets is continuity in a family structure where the emotional climate was in a measure harmonious or at least consistent. Continuity and consistency are essential requirements for developing human relatedness through actual experiencing.

140

This becomes more possible when the family has lived for longer periods, particularly in the patient's earlier years, in the same house, the same neighborhood, or in the same town. Such continuity makes for greater opportunities for developing friendships in the pre-school and grammar school periods. The parents' participation in community affairs, as in parent-teacher groups, aids in developing this feeling of belonging. Living in smaller communities or close to a park and taking even short summer vacations provide chances for those important contacts with nature. A person with such experiences in relatedness is more available to further possibilities in school, in college, in employment situations, and in the armed forces. We know how essential it is to develop these feelings of human relatedness, prerequisite for genuine self-reliance, and yet how difficult it is in a tension-filled world threatened by the breakdown of those institutions which have been the main source of healthy values — the family, religion, and decent societal values.

If the constructive effects of having productively experienced assets is not fairly visible, the analyst might wonder if he is not dealing with a more recent increase of neurotic problems due to an accession of environmental stresses not particularly of the individual's making.

Regarding liabilities in the individual, one could say they amount to decreasing degrees of the assets listed above. But that would not be entirely accurate because it is not merely an absence of assets that we see but the positive presence of deleterious factors. It is not simply a matter of addition and subtraction but one of geometric progression in the direction of sickness that concerns us. An increasing occurrence of, or tendency toward, heredo-familial disorders, lowered physical and psychic vitality, frequent and prolonged illness, and early deaths — from, say, heart disease or cancer — are what the patient starts with at birth in his genes. A person born with a club foot or a scoliosis of the spine grows up with distorted notions of locomotion, as a congenital visual defect affects another's perspective and his ways of looking and seeing. Frequent or prolonged physical illness with complicated recoveries leaves not only the factual, irreversible pathology, but also a tendency to lowered resistance and a *locus minoris resistentia*.

With all of these go sick attitudes toward being sick; the tendency to make a career of illness, or to deny self-destructively the flagrant evidence of physical disease; intolerance to physical pain, or extreme, stoic enduring and self-benumbing. The latter may also be evident in the psychic sphere.

Although malnutrition is infrequent, there are many whose diets were barely adequate because of personal problems or indifference on

141

the part of their parents. Inadequate dental and medical care is not rare, even among financially secure families. Children who have had little contact with nature because of overprotective mothers who would not allow them to go to camp or to play with the rough children in the park are not infrequent.

It is evident how physical liabilities create sick psychological attitudes which in turn prolong the physical problems and create others. Reciprocally reinforcing each other, these problems have their effect on a person's educational pattern and what he does about using available opportunities to develop a profession or a particular skill.

Poorly off in a different way is a person who, although fairly healthy physically and psychologically to start with, has to fight against great odds for almost everything he gets. These people are often left with feelings of bitterness toward the world and an inability to enjoy what their finances and time now allow them. Physical and psychological handicaps in early life, as well as in later years, blunt and distort the ends to which skills, talents, and gifts may be put. Some are never discovered and, if they come to light, they are not developed, even as a source of neurotic pride, let alone for genuine pleasure.

These liabilities further tend to create certain attitudes which can be most serious blocks in therapy. The factual existence of heredo-familial disorders prompts deep feelings of hopelessness, as do factual congenital disorders. There can be many sources for an acquired feeling of hopelessness, but when a patient barricades himself behind obvious facts, the task becomes all the more difficult. Initially, and for a long time, he cannot know he is using heredity and constitution for externalizing. With this hopelessness often goes bitterness, cynicism, and diatribes against fate, God, society. An attitude of "what's the use," "don't care," or numb indifference is supported by the fact that "everyone in my family dies early." An aversion to changing and daring also may occur for fear of, or because of, even the slightest pain in, for example, the cardiac area if early death from heart disease has been familial. Hopelessness, cynicism, bitterness, and indifference can be used as overt justification for obvious and concealed vindictiveness toward the analyst. These attitudes, coupled with the numbing and deadening of feelings, create most difficult problems in analysis, particularly when they are covered by pseudo-feelings.

Patients in whom acting out is prominent often act themselves out of analysis. They find it difficult to give even lip service to the idea that they have been impulsive and compulsive. Their capacity for self-discipline is very limited. Although they freely use the word *want,* it is really a compulsive *have to.* And what they want, they must have immediately. Where this is not possible they become desperate and frantic. When there is such great egocentricity that rational self-evaluation or evaluation of others is limited, learning from experiences seems impaired. They suffer greatly, genuinely as well as neurotically, but through this suffering they do not gain wisdom, for they have participated too little in the experiences which caused them pain. Understandably, pain avoidance is a dominant drive in their lives.

Where there is great intolerance to psychic pain the analyst is confronted with a most serious block to therapy. The claim, hidden or overt, that life should be easy, painless, frictionless, smooth and effortless, is tenacious and deeply embedded. The theme of relief is constantly in the foreground. The analyst is accused of being "hurting," "hard," and "cruel" if he does not immediately produce relief. Such a person has a much weakened integrity and an intense terror at the painful prospect of looking squarely at the truth of himself. Frequently concomitant, as defenses, are tenacious literal mindedness, argumentativeness, and needling assaultiveness for failing to dot your i's and cross your t's. The creating of confusion is a further defense. Often associated, and even more serious, are elusiveness and evasiveness to others. When there is elusiveness to self, the problem becomes formidable.

An environment that does not offer or, in fact, frustrates opportunities for developing human relatedness is a liability of mounting importance the earlier it occurs. Rather than continuity and consistency, some people, from earliest childhood, know mainly fragmentation, inconsistency, a familial atmosphere of violent mood swings, apathy, and indifference. These are overtly manifested in divorces and in being cared for by a succession of nurses, relatives, stepparents, housekeepers, maids, baby-sitters, and at times no one at all. Frequent changes of abode, fragmented schooling, and opportunities for forming relationships with children their own age or with a teacher here or there also do not occur. A consequence may be the development of the psychopathic process, as I have defined it, to the point of the so-called psychopathic personality. *(208)*

From identical twin studies we know that the hereditary factor may at times not be as important as the atmosphere created in a family where there is a history or the factual presence, for longer or shorter periods, of severely disturbed, psychotic, or mentally defective members. With the above, so often go limited chances of gain from educational opportunities; from relationships in school, in play, in work; from recreation in playgrounds and on vacations; and from adequate medical and dental care. This impairment of assets can occur in so-called normal families in covert forms which can be most destructively active.

Assets in the present are understandably different in persons of twenty and sixty. The wisdom gained from a long and productive life is a future possibility for a younger person with his vitality in his world-to-be. Both may have areas of productive interest in work and leisure, and the time and the money to work in analysis. In their environment are constructive relationships with their family, their friends, and their work. An important expression of these is an encouraging and supporting attitude toward the patient in his decision to work in analysis. One of the more important assets a patient can have in his environment is an analyst with whom he feels he can work and who, in turn, not only feels similarly but who is capable of carrying on the work with him. This environmental asset is crucial because the analyst will be a focal figure in helping to resolve existing problems and to open up new vistas of growing possibilities in his life.

Individual liabilities in the present are largely the progressive effects of those in the past, hopefully mitigated and ameliorated by periods of less stressful living. A person's physical and psychic vitality may be at such a low ebb that the additional energy necessary to carry on analytic work is not available. Even at a much slower pace, the analyses of such patients are frequently interrupted by minor or major physical illnesses. Because their psychic tolerance is so low, great flexibility in the frequency of visits is necessary. So often, just those people who need so much more help can avail themselves of it that much less. In addition, they often have problems of too little time and limited finances.

Among the environmental liabilities in the present are the expected consequences of past accumulations. A man who has few or no friends, or who lost those he had through being unable to maintain them or through having antagonized them, is in a pretty isolated, helpless, and often hostile position. It is unlikely he will find support from others for his analytic venture. More likely, the attitude will be one of accusatory blaming or destructive interference. In such a spirit, a family was "all for" a daughter's analysis. Once she began to rebel more healthily against their demands for conformity, the analysis had to be interrupted, in spite of her valiant efforts and mine. In a number of instances, attempts — some successful — are made to interrupt the analytic work when the victim seems to be slipping out of the grip of his or her master. A record of one or a few jobs with few promotions, or a succession of jobs lost due to personal problems, adds to feelings of failure and pessimism. A history of one or more divorces, the responsibility of a present family and alimony to a previous one adds special difficulties imposed for a long time to come. So often these patients have not only exhausted their own reserves, but also all possible sources of financial help in the environment.

In some cases, mounting environmental liabilities which put the person's back to the wall seem to be an essential prerequisite for coming into analysis and for remaining in it. In other instances, such environmental pressures are an expression of great liabilities. The threats of parents toward children, — the threat of a divorce, the cutting off of income, a possible fine, or a prison sentence — are among the poorest incentives for analytic work.

I have observed that those patients with mounting liabilities in themselves and in their environment are decreasingly likely to find an analyst they want or with whom they feel they can work. This is understandable because they require far greater competence, experience, and maturity of their therapist and analysts who can fulfill their real requirements are few. Because of their problems, their judgment in making a choice is also poor. Their claims also are so great that their demand that something magical be done immediately is bound to be frustrated. Finally, they start work with a defeatist attitude, for this might be, not their second, but their tenth attempt to get some help. The possibility of such a patient finding or believing he has an environmental asset in his analyst is not great, but I know of instances where such tenacity on the part of a patient has been ultimately rewarded.

How does the analyst discover the assets and liabilities in the patient, in his environment, in his past, and in his present? Actually, most of this information could come from an extensive life history questionnaire, which is one method of research with particular boundaries of usefulness. Although I have classified the information as relating to the past and the present, it is all past the moment after we have received it verbally or in writing.

Our only actual source of information is the continuing, immediate present and that is multidimensional. The present is a gestalt which extends into the past and into the future, in depth and sideways. In the continuing, immediate present we obtain narrative information which has intrapsychic and interpersonal reference. There is also all that we can obtain by observation and intuition. Information and the sources for it are abundant.

I believe one can rarely say he lacks information. I make this point because some tend to overemphasize the value of information as such, and collect more and more of it. The tendency leads some beginners to overfocus on history or to talk to members of the patient's family. I felt I was becoming a more effective therapist in general when, during the simultaneous analysis of husband and wife, I found I could be with the patient with whom I was working without being distracted, for example, by the fact that the patient made no mention of having walked out on his wife, an event which had filled his wife's hour the day before (see chapter 22).

How can the therapist make more effective use of the continuing, immediate present? Practically, he can extend a consultation for one

145

or several sessions in an attempt to arrive at whatever decisions are necessary. If it is a question of depth therapy, he can extend it for several months and call it a trial analysis. Ultimately, he can extend a consultation into a continuing analysis for more effective diagnosing and prognosing and for arriving at a mutual decision regarding the interrupting of regular work.

The continuing, immediate present is not only used to gather information at the narrative level, but also to observe all that can be obtained in the *vis-à-vis* and in the couch positions. *(79)* Briefly, this information concerns bodily movements, posture, bodily configurations, clothes, and manner and tone of speech. From what a patient says with reference to himself and to me while he is giving narrative information, I can gather what his attitudes are toward analysis and toward me as his analyst.

The analyst must always be asking the ever-present question, why is this coming up at this time? Which also implies, how come a lot of other things are not? The first dream is often an important source of information regarding the patient's attitudes toward himself, others, analysis, and his analyst. A test interpretation of the dream may be made to note from the response how accurate evaluations have been. This continuing, immediate present is our opportunity to feel and immediately intuit our patient as a whole human being. As this information is becoming available to us, we are formulating it as assets and liabilities, as rational and irrational patterns of integrating, in terms of our theory and experience.

Chapter 9

The Analyst as Instrument

The more an analyst is attuned to his person as instrument, the more he can approach "the method of no method," which Leopold Auer taught his pupils so that they played brilliant violin with "effortless effort." Then the analyst discovers that, as Freud said, "the most successful cases are those in which one proceeds, as it were, aimlessly, and allows oneself to be overtaken by surprises, always presenting to them an open mind, free from expectations."*(130, p. 327)*

Toward these ends, becoming experienced with those forms which point at operations of the analyst's sensory and autonomic systems, as well as at his emotive, conative, and cognitive processes, is essential. As the analyst is open to and can live with these emerging forms, through experiencing their connectedness in the actual situation, their meanings will emerge and appropriate weight will be given to them. These emerging forms are more likely to appear, with freshness and vividness, in an initial interview. Often they are not sufficiently respected or relied on, an experience ruefully confirmed months and years later.

These forms may emerge as vague indefinable sensings or as ungraspable feelings and thoughts. They may appear as images, tunes, metaphors, and analogies; as flash feelings and thoughts; as a character in, or a plot of, a play or book; or as a panoramic vision of something in the past, present, or anticipated future. They may come in response to the first telephone call, letter, impression in the waiting room, or at some point during the initial interview. The forms may be in sensory categories, as aesthetic pleasures or aversions, or as an emotional uplifting or recoil. People have a real and metaphorical smell and taste about them, pleasant or malodorous, sweet or bitter. Patients speak with the endless tonal variations of their voices, as well as with gestures and facial expressions.

An analyst's response to the symphony or cacophony of stimuli from a spectrum of sensory modalities may be expressed in a feeling of being pressed in on, grated upon, and clawed at; or he might have the uncomfortable feeling of confronting an insubstantial wraith, an absence being present. Autonomic responses are most telling: inner shivers, goose pimples, blushing, perspiring, changes in pulse rate, heart action, breathing patterns, genital, scrotal and sexual sensations, borborygmi, belching, and intestinal tightening and relaxing. Then there are the general feelings of warmth and well being, with an urge to some expression of lightheartedness; or of a feeling of chill, of being depressed, or of irritation. When kinaesthetic, joint, and stereognostic responses combine with autonomic ones, the analyst can have the telling experience of being unbalanced and internally dizzy.

For total responding there must be openness to feeling, the greatest degree of awareness without prejudgment, condemnation, embellishment or intellectualization. (74) Such feeling leads to wisdom; to a greater discrimination of what is spontaneous or compulsive; and to knowledge of the types of feeling and their nuances, their intensity and extensity of imbeddedness. Feelings of liberation, self-acceptance, and a stronger feeling of self follow. (210, 211) Constructive forces are thereby identified, supported, extended, and expanded. They soon develop their own momentum, becoming more effective in opposing all that obstructs straighter growing.

Having had such experiences, the therapist becomes attuned to their happening, becomes much more sensitive in his timing, and is better able to help move the feeling process in his patient. He becomes more alert in directing his patient to his feelings, their absence, vagueness, dullness, or deadness. He becomes able to expose his patient's compulsive feelings and draw his attention to the self-deception of his pseudo feelings. He is able to help the patient contact his feelings, stay with them, and become attuned to their rhythmicity. Ultimately the patient is able to enter and rest in foreknown painprovoking situations which brings an additional accrual of feelings of being able, of confidence, and of courage.

Only through having experienced, in his own personal analysis, the discriminations in being open and opening, in being closed and closing, in compulsive and spontaneous ways, will the analyst be attuned to them in his patient. Only after similar personal experiences will he be able to help his patient discriminate among compulsive willing, having to will, wanting, spontaneous willing, willing not to will, motivationless motivation, and the "will-power of desirelessness." *(200, p. 11)* These processes are premised on the urge toward self-realization.

Essential to the analyst's becoming aware of the operation of his person as instrument is his detailed acquaintance with his experiencing process as he changes in the course of his own analysis and thereafter. Gendlin presented "A Theory of Personality Change" evolved from his "Experiencing and the Creation of Meaning." This theory can account for change because "It employs concepts that apply to the experiencing process, and to the relationships between that process and content aspects of personality." *(212, p. 100)* Gendlin's theory deals with the problems of becoming aware of the changing of personality content. It asserts that in personality change, an intense affective or feeling process is involved, and that change nearly always occurs in the context of an ongoing personal relationship.

Gendlin's theory is concerned with experiencing as an ongoing process which involves concrete psychological events and which refers to a felt process. In experiencing there are not only external events and thoughts about them, but also "an inward bodily feeling or sensing." "Experiencing, in the mode of being directly referred to," is termed the "direct referent." Through the process of "continuous focusing" on the "direct referent," the patient begins to experience "the self-propelled feeling process." Gendlin then delineates how personal relationships affect an individual's experiencing, how personality contents are changed, and the process through which it happens. *(212, pp. 111-23)*

In analysis, as patients contact their "direct referents" and "the self-propelled feeling process," they say: "I feel it arising in me." "I feel it comes from me." "It seems to or feels like it belongs to me." "I feel like it moves me." "It carries me." "I feel I want to go along with it." In contrast are feelings which they had previously experienced as coming from outside, as imposed, alien, forbidding, and cold: "I wanted to get away from them." "I felt threatened and I felt frightened." "I wanted to run away." "I felt helpless and bewildered." "I felt confused by them."

As they begin to experience these inner movements as "mine," patients describe an inner feeling which supports the movement. This happens whether the feelings are pleasant or unpleasant, whether they be joy, sadness, fear, anxiety, conflict, hostility, or self-hate. Once they have had and contained such experiences, patients become aware of the consequent liberating effects. They paradoxically become able to "rest in anxiety" and "rest in panic." Patients then report feeling more, feeling more of themselves, and feeling themselves as being more. They begin to enter, live in, and live through experiences of greater depth and intensity. This may happen after experiencing quite some intensities of central conflict. Then they may say, "I never felt so good in my life and I never felt so awful." They respond and feel liberated by the therapist's interpretation: "You have never been able to feel so good and never been able to feel so awful because you have never been able to feel so much."

In time, a shift from a predominance of overfocusing on the painful aspects of emerging feelings takes place, and, with it, the anxious concern about pain falls away. Patients recognize, retrospectively, how fear of, and fighting against, pain had made it worse and how, paradoxically, openness to and accepting pain made it less, after the immediate intensity of pain passed. Pain is then not desired or sought but accepted, borne, borne with, as part of the living, growing process. This is healthy suffering in contrast to neurotic suffering, which involves enduring for the sake of enduring, masochism, and martyrdom. As healthy pain is owned, "the self-propelled feeling process" takes on an increasing momentum which patients open themselves to.

Patients struggle to describe the feel of the inner processes by which they attempt to move themselves to the side of this "self-propelled feeling process." Facial changes, movements of the trunk, extremities, and other parts of the body expressive of such inner efforts, can be observed. A patient might also say, for example, "I feel an inner movement, a moving over, a moving toward, a moving to the side of. It's hard to locate but I feel it clearly and it feels like it is in the center of me, all through my insides. I know I can do something about moving over to that side. I have done it before and am getting more of the feel of doing it and how to do it. I'm clearer about it and know how not to press too hard and how far I can go. I have a good feeling when I can do it — when I'm able to — a feeling of well-being, of warmth inside me. It's hard work, and I know I must rest and give it time."

Concomitant with palpating and supporting this "self-propelled feeling process," there is a clearer feel of the processes that oppose it and a learning of inner ways to oppose the opposing, to dilute its impact, and even to push back its borders. "I feel a process in my chest," said one patient. "It's opposed to something and is pushing it

150

back. I want free space in myself to move around. Now I feel feelings of feelings coming up in me."

Through such happenings a patient is learning self-analysis in preparation for continuing on his own. At this phase of the therapy the patient is taking over a greater share of the work. This is a crucial criterion for a decision to interrupt regular, scheduled appointments.

As an analyst becomes more attuned to the various modalities of his person as instrument during his own analysis and with his increasing therapeutic experience, he will increasingly manifest those attitudes which maximize his productive conduct of the analysis. Martin described six attitudes required of the holistic therapist. *(149)* His ideas are here elaborated and modified. A seventh attitude is added, and nine therapeutic modes of being are identified.

The first of the seven attitudes is (1) the *nonteleologic* attitude — a focus on what, not why. The therapist by his what questions directs the patient to sequences of his whatness and thereby to his howness, opening him to deeper and wider contact with his "direct referents" and his "self-propelled feeling process."*(212)* Guided by the *universal forming process* and Whyte's notion of the "formative tendency,"*(176, p. 19)* we might more accurately name this attitude teleonomic. In functional biology, Mayr adds, teleonomy simply describes the fact that systems are end-directed, that is, they are operating on the basis of a program, a code of information. *(213)*

Guided by the attitude of (2) *unconventionality,* the analyst does not become involved in the manifest content, the patient's questions, or in social amenities. Utilizing his patient's distress in response to this attitude, the therapist helps him experience how compulsively attached he has been to conventional patterns, and how blocking they have been to spontaneous communing. Kanzer and Blum describe this attitude in the "basically self-effacing position" of the analyst which eliminates the conventional and fosters in the patient freer development and expression of his innermost thoughts. *(142, p. 104)*

By his (3) *unobtrusiveness,* that is, by not intruding himself into the life of his patient, the therapist allows free rein for his patient's projections and externalizations onto him. In time the patient sees how compulsive, contradictory, and unreal they have been. Kanzer and Blum call this "passive neutrality" and emphasize that the analyst is not passively neutral to the illness, which it is his task to treat. "He is a detached scientific observer" only so far as it contributes to the therapeutic tasks at hand. *(142, p. 105)*

By his (4) *incorruptibility,* the therapist avoids involvement in destructive relating which the patient attempts to use in order to preserve his defenses as they begin to crumble. While maintaining this attitude, the therapist cannot be drawn into the patient's systems of claims and counterclaims, rewards and punishments, or his submission-defiance patterns.

In being (5) *respectfully vigilant,* the therapist respectfully listens to the whole patient and helps him, by his questions, to open himself to what is hidden and denied. "Respectful vigilance," Martin says, "goes along with wondering, marveling, and contemplating, and only occurs during periods of leisure and relaxation. In time, episodes of emotional insight occur with its concomitants. With each step toward feeling this total involvement in conflict, he acquires a greater sense of extensity, integration, uniqueness, and strength, and thus a positive spiral develops."*(149)*

Regarding being (6) *threshold conscious,* Martin adds, "Growth both in the outer and inner world involves a progression of threshold experiences with natural feelings of uneasiness, anticipation, something impending . . . followed by startling revelations."*(149)*

To Martin's six attitudes I add Krishnamurti's (7) *choiceless awareness:* "What is important, surely, is to be aware without choice, because choice brings about conflict. The chooser is in confusion, therefore he chooses . . . . The man who is clear and simple does not choose; what is, is . . . . The important thing . . . is to be aware from moment to moment without accumulating the experience which awareness brings; because, the moment you accumulate, you are aware only according to that accumulation . . . . There must be awareness which is pliable, an awareness which is alertly passive, not aggressively active . . . . Thus we open the door into the hidden, which becomes the known . . . . Reality is not a thing which is knowable by the mind, because the mind is the result of the known, of the past; therefore the mind must understand itself and its functioning, its truth, and only then is it possible for the unknown to be."*(187, pp. 97-98)*

Identifying, experiencing, and being these seven attitudes, the therapist adds further dimensions to the functioning of his person as instrument. Thereby he can become and be more open, be more directly in tune with and more immediately responsive with enhanced ingenuity and originality.

The nine modes of being can best be described in paradoxes.

As the therapist is being and becoming more of the ideal instrument of therapy, his mode of being can be further characterized by (1) passionate objectivity concomitant with dispassionate subjectivity. He moves (2) toward the ultimate of the impersonal which is the ultimate of the personal. He becomes attuned to (3) action in nonaction simultaneously present with nonaction in action. Concomitantly he is able (4) to contain and respond to dualistic and non-dualistic theories and techniques simultaneously and harmoniously. Likewise, he is (5) open to tension producing and tension reducing as natural oscillations in himself, as an aspect of the system of the whole. This means (6) being and having in awareness conflicting and cooperating dominant and subordinate hierarchies of systems in process.

Then he is moved (7) by "The will power of desirelessness." Menninger further mentions that "Freud was so little driven by the *furor sanandi* that he was able to restrain himself from the compulsion to do (or even to say) something to the patient struggling through the various steps of self-discovery."*(200, p. 11)* Some have characterized this attitude as being unambitious for one's patients as well as for oneself. This form of description only points up how often we must resort to the negative metaphysic of the Orient, that is, to constantly assert what something is not in order to become open to and arrive at what it is.

Also characteristic of the analyst's mode of being is (8) moral toughness which requires moral compassion as moral compassion requires moral toughness. When both are present we have moral courage, which is love. As St. Augustine said, "Love, and do what you will."

The final attribute of his mode of being is (9) his seemingly paradoxical ability to be simultaneously at the core of his own being while being at the core of his patient's. Kant did not believe that such was possible for human beings. He asserted that "We can know *phenomena* but we are forever barred from having knowledge of *noumena* (things in themselves). Thus, though the mind is distinct from nature as it is in itself, it is intimately and essentially related to nature as humanly known and experienced."*(191)* Husserl, in his pure phenomenology, went beyond Kant's *a prioris*. He insisted we can have contact with reality and knowledge of it. "According to him, objects of understanding or thought can be *intuited;*" hence, his concept of "categorical intuition."*(191, p. 24)* Husserl's notion of the *epoche* is reflected in Freud's *fundamental rule* (free association). Such experimentations with, on, and through the mind result in "pure lucidity," which, in terms of "The Zen Doctrine of No-Mind," is the state where the mind is wiped clean. Then contiguity and continuity become identical.

These seven attitudes and nine attributes of the analyst's mode of being were required in depth in my work with the analyses I have cited, particularly in the first three years of my work with Arthur G. Even more so were they necessary and tested in my work with a middle-aged married man, a corporate research specialist in a large agglomerate.

Irving W. had consulted eight different analysts. With the first he worked one year and with two more three years each. His contact with analysts extended over twenty-three years. He felt he had been helped by none, although I did not and do not agree. His constant search for help was a positive manifestation of aid received. I feel the help he had received was supportive and protected him from going into a deeper and possibly paralyzing depression.

He was a big man, at times weighing 260 pounds, due to compulsive gorging on chocolate after being on rigid diets that had brought him down to 210. He felt as though he weighed a ton. As he walked that weight seemed to bend the floor in. More serious was the weight of his depression. It felt ponderous, depressive, and depressing. He felt massively hopeless, and he would sit in a drooping, weighed-down posture looking at me with a blank stare until his eyes got red and began to tear. He called it "My poor Irving look." He complained bitterly of his hopelessness, helplessness, self-loathing, and self-destructiveness.

He brutally and defiantly demanded help while blocking almost all attempts to give it to him. He also was subtly and overtly sadistic in a host of ways. Later in our work he spontaneously admitted with a smile: "I know I have been fencing with you." There were long silences, particularly at the beginning of the session when he just sat and stared at me. He would say repeatedly that he had nothing to say. Nothing had happened. He couldn't recall his dreams and would add, "What's the use of saying the same thing over and over?" while proceeding to do just that. He demanded that I guide him and make specific suggestions. When I did so, he would, with a hostile denigrating smile, imply or say, "Is that supposed to help?" Later, there was often evidence that what I said had had an impact and effect.

He was violently opposed to any medication. He was horrified at the possibility of being out of control. Also he was terrified that he "might get addicted." Time and again he raised the question of medication, thinking "maybe it would help." As soon as I started to explore it, he would back away in fear and cut off discussion. Because of his compulsive, almost addictive, chocolate gorging he may have accurately sensed that the same pattern might develop with drugs.

Constantly I had to keep in the forefront of my awareness the fact that this man had come to me and seemed willing to continue to do so. He desperately needed his massive depression and opposition. I had to assume that somewhere in him he also wanted help. I realized I must not become invaded and pervaded by this depression and hopelessness. Otherwise I would be crushed under it. Also I must not be caught in his defiant, oppositional, sadistic maneuvers. On several occasions he explicitly mentioned suicide. Although I did not feel the likelihood of an attempt was great, I had to be constantly alert to the possibility, particularly should there be a sudden lifting of his lifelong massive depression.

My hope was that by using what Irving brought to me as symptomatology, his life history, daily events, and relations with his wife and children — all of which were bad — I could begin to find pattern and meaning and identify subtle nuances of change, making use of new facts as they emerged. Whatever of these came up, I attempted to explore. He would often retort with a sneering smile that he had "been over that so many times with the others." On a rare occasion, I noted responsiveness to some new perspective I had given to what was "no use going over again."

To gain time, while using this information, and to communicate my firm, identifiable, and supportive presence, I adopted an attitude of ease, of slight lightheartedness, and of humor verging on banter. The latter had to be only subtly present because too much would have evoked reactive rage and self-destructiveness. In time, he began to ask, "What are you so happy about?" He finally began to laugh, saying, "I don't know why I'm laughing. There is nothing to laugh about."

Besides the above, I would underline, by asking further questions, the slightest shift in his patterns, and explore any new facts that had come up. This had to be done most cautiously because there were usually immediate repercussions and intensifications of his symptoms illustrated by statements to the effect that "I keep getting worse. My wife won't put up with me any longer. I'm destroying my children. I don't know how long they will take it from me at the office. My human relations are terrible. I can't say a civil word to anyone. I'm viciously critical and I'm hypersensitive. I can't take any criticism." He *was* being avoided and circumvented at the office. As was later confirmed, part of this was an expression of his superior's personality. Irving's responses, however, were excessive and somewhat paranoid.

One of the main aids in therapy were his dreams. While I focused mainly on the details of the patternings, their contents, and on the slightest shifts, my focus was also on the underlying process and change, although I never explicity said there was anything constructive in it.

At first I could sense only a slight lifting of the depression between sessions. After six months, there was a sudden significant lightening of it between sessions. Irving remarked on it but

155

immediately added, "It won't last. Why should I be feeling better?" He did have a violent repercussion after a few days. Its duration was shorter than before and subsequent periods of feeling lighter were longer. The viciousness of his self-loathing abated, and he began to open himself to his inner processes in greater detail.

He became aware of how his tension would rise, how he would click off, wouldn't be hearing me, and would feel far away. Against quite some opposition we explored the processes involved in this blocking which was alienating to the point of depersonalization. We also began to explore what triggered his chocolate binges. He gradually could open himself to the violence of the anxiety, the upsurge of vicious self-hate and self-loathing, the despair, as well as to other aspects of the inner structure of this process.

In the first six months, the brutality of his defiance and opposition lessened, and during the next six months his dreams showed obvious evidences of change. They became looser and more open. There was more evidence of initiative and activity which previously had been almost completely blocked. I could sense he was pleased, although he made no mention of these feelings. I felt I had a more solid basis for hope when he dreamt of a scrawny little kitten. There was a pool of some yellow stuff in front of it, not urine. He was feeding it milk with an eye dropper. This dream occurred at the end of the first year. The beginning of compassion, it was a picture of how he saw himself and of being able to mother himself with the milk, perhaps of human kindness.

Working with a sequence of dreams replete with rather extreme grandiosity helped to undermine that aspect of his pride system, thus mitigating a crucial source of his self-hate and his tyrannical shoulds.

In the month before the second summer holiday, he showed more initiative and expressed some of his ideas on a project. These were appreciated and led to his being asked to take on a few more. Greedily he took over some additional ones. His immediate superior, a very rigid man who had been blocking him and with whom he was in a continuing battle, had alienated his own superiors, as a result of which Irving was asked to report directly to those above him. He did a good job, but because it was not startlingly wonderful he felt his results were insignificant.

During the summer he made a combined holiday and business trip with his family. Upon his return, he opened his first session with the usual hostile defensiveness and an attack of

156

hopelessness, which I very firmly cut through. I then explored the inner structure of his repercussions to some very enjoyable days during his summer holiday. The repercussions were manifested as violent hostile withdrawal, defiance, and a refusal to complete and submit his reports. As usual, I had to read his responses to my comments by the expressions on his face and in his subsequent associations. I could see that he got what I was saying, and that it was meaningful to him. He had been quite anxious about resuming our work after a three months break. With his defensive hostility he was holding himself together and testing me. My having stood the test made him feel more secure. He began to relax a bit and tell me more about his summer and what was going on with him.

What soon became evident was that the depression had lifted so much and his alienation diminished to such a degree that the anxiety and self-hate previously held in check and benumbed were now being more acutely experienced. He was also more sharply aware of his hostility and his constant need for approval. He was having severe insomnia. During sessions he was restless and often left his chair opposite me to pace the floor. His mood was slightly elevated, evident in more rapid joking and a heightened alertness.

Within two weeks this slight hypomania began to abate and approach a state of well being. If he goes into a depression I feel it will hardly be to the depth that originally obtained.

From the beginning of our work he spoke with certainty of his being finished so far as advancement in his present company was concerned. He measured psychological improvement in terms of being able to go out and get another job. A month after we resumed our sessions, he received a significant promotion and was looking forward to the challenge with less fear. There will be repercussions when he actually is functioning in his new role, but I feel he will be able to deal with them better than heretofore.

In the two years since we began, I have seen him about ninety times because of many legitimate interruptions, both from his side and because of my own absences. What has been done and what has happened also indicate that which remains to be worked through. Without the attributes and modes being described in this chapter, without the experience in using them, and without a knowledge of such depressive sadomasochistic patients, Irving and I could not have gotten as far as we have.

Chapter 10

The Analyst's Understanding

The more experience an analyst has with the various ways of being — the *nine modes* and the *seven attitudes* — the more they will function in unison, quickly and without reflection. His responding will be inventive and ingenius, appropriate and adequate to the requirements of the moment. Though all levels of the symbolic spiral participate, it is the prerationative ones that contribute to the comprehensive form of being which we call understanding (*verstehen*) as contrasted with explaining (*erklären*).

Horney regarded "Understanding the Patient As the Basis of All Technique."*(66)* About this comprehensive understanding she said: "Understanding is a social and specific human process, a moving with one aspect of our being toward the stand which another person maintains, but while so moving still maintaining our own stand. Therefore, we can never be completely where the other person stands. We stand *under* the person's stand: we understand his position, and it is this which enables us to compare his stand with ours . . . . Understanding is therefore a movement of emotional and intellectual energies . . . . Real understanding is a wholehearted and receptive observing and 'feeling into' the other person with all of one's own self."

Horney detailed the process by which an analyst came to such understanding, how he defended himself against it, and how gradually he let go of his defending with concomitant experiencing of anxiety, conflict, hate, and self-hate. This is the *disillusioning process* through which all patients must go. This means there are no didactic or training analyses but only therapeutic ones. *(215)* During his therapy the analyst is integrating what he gains from courses, reading, work with patients, supervision — the totality, in fact, of his experiences. As this happens, he sees how his patient's associations and behaviors fit into larger wholes. In this understanding process, the analyst's feelings are crucial. With it come feelings of change, in the patient, the therapist, and the doctor-patient relationship. In short he is being and becoming more aware.

In being aware, we are more open to the "pure fact"*(177)* of ourselves and the world of which we are an aspect. This is saying that when we start with pure fact we are starting with the moment, the here and now. The pure fact of ourselves and the world are what Krishnamurti calls "inspired spontaneity."*(187)* For Watts, these pure facts are the "creative reality."*(216)* They are unspeakable in words because words are about reality, are described reality, but are not *reality*. Pure facts can be shown and pointed at through words and gestures, but nobody can feel your feelings, your reality. In therapy we show the patient aspects of his reality and ways toward experiencing more of it. To be the moment, to be reality, we must be silent. I have emphasized the constructive value of silence, of "creative quietism" (Laotse) in therapy, particularly when on the couch. After years of regarding silence as something negative, Freudian analysts *(217)* now find that "silence may be a mode of self-expression or relatedness that is not necessarily resistant."*(142, p. 121)*

In speaking of awareness, we must not fall into the error of ascribing a directing, controlling role to consciousness. "Unitary thought rejects the dualistic implication of the conception of consciousness," says Whyte. "The valuable element in" the concept "is the reference to a relation of attention between the organism and a particular external or internal stimulus . . . . Attention to it [a stimulus] is always transient. Nothing ever remains continuously in consciousness. It is therefore wrong to isolate those transient moments of attention to particular forms, to endow them with a special metaphysical status as a 'state of consciousness' and then to ascribe to consciousness the supreme directing role in behavior."*(176, p. 49)* Attention, for Whyte, is a transitory focusing process of the entire integrative capacity of the organism. It has no directive capacity. Paying attention to something is so fixed in our minds as connected with altering behavior, that we can hardly conceive of a kind of attention which is not so intended. However, we can have attending without intending as in Gendlin's "continuous focusing" on a "direct referent," with change occurring through having influenced "the self-propelled feeling process."*(212, p. 123)*

Krishnamurti speaks of the altering-intending attention as introspection and the nonaltering-intending attention as awareness. "Where there is introspection, which is the desire to modify or change the responses, the reactions of the self, there is always an end in view . . . . Awareness is entirely different . . . . There is no end in view but awareness of everything as it arises . . . . Introspection is self-improvement and therefore introspection is self-centeredness. Awareness is not self-improvement. On the contrary, it is the ending of the self, of the 'I', with all its peculiar idiosyncracies, memories, demands and pursuits." *(187, pp. 172-3)* These statements recall Freud's remark that "The most successful cases are those in which one proceeds, as it were, aimlessly, and allows oneself to be overtaken by surprise, always bringing to them an open mind, free from expectations."*(130, p. 327)*

Krishnamurti continues, "The man who wants to improve himself can never be aware because improvement implies condemnation and the achievement of a result. Whereas in awareness there is observation without condemnation, without denial or acceptance." This concept is reminiscent of Freud's "evenly hovering attention." "This awareness," Krishnamurti continues, this "being sensitive to things, to nature, to people, to ideas, is not made up of separate processes, but is one unitary process. It is a constant observation of everything, of every thought and feeling and action as they arise within oneself . . . . Awareness is from moment to moment."*(187, pp. 173-4)*

It becomes then more understandable why in the process of introspection there is an introspector and someone introspected. Included in this process are subtle and covert forms of fault finding. In addition there is the inevitable drive to improve oneself, with the concomitant needs to prove one's improvement, and to disprove evidence to the contrary. Such tendencies interfere with being aware, with here and now experiencing. The focus is shifted to the past deed or to the promise of a changed future.

A further perspective on the difficulties created by the concept of there being a conscious self with a controlling and directing role is voiced by Watts: "I can only think seriously of trying to live up to an idea to improve myself, if I am split in two pieces. There must be a good 'I' who is going to improve the bad 'me.' "*(216, p. 78)* Here we recognize Horney's second category of theories of human nature which has the premise that man is both good and bad. In the struggle between the good and bad "me," the differences are stressed, the distance between the two increases, the cooperation between the two decreases, and the conflict increases, as well as the feelings of being cut off and isolated from one another. This is a picture of Western man, dissociated from himself, from his feelings, from his organicity, and from the society of which he is an aspect. It is a picture of the consequences of intellection which dualizes processes and leads to oppositions.

"The principal thing is to understand that there *is* no safety or security," says Watts. "To understand insecurity it is not enough to face it but to be it. The notion of security is based on the feeling that there is something continuous and permanent in us which we struggle to preserve for the sake of safety. Actually not until we realize there is no center, soul or 'I' to struggle, to preserve, do we begin to feel secure. There can never be a separate I, who is watching you think present thoughts, feel present feelings or be 'aware of being aware.' " The illusion of an 'I' separate from experience comes from our ideas of memory and because of the rapidity of thought. "If you imagine that memory is a direct knowledge of the past rather than a present experience, you get the illusion of knowing the past and the present at the same time." There is no *something* that remembers. "Memory is a form of present experience . . . . There are no feelings but present feelings, and whatever feeling is present is 'I' . . . .

"Sanity, wholeness, and integration lie in the realization that we are not divided, that man and his present experiences are one, and that no separate 'I' or mind can be found . . . . To understand this moment I must not try to be divided from it; I must be aware of it with my whole being."*(216, pp. 79-87)*

The realization that the patient and his present experience are one enables the therapist to more quickly identify the manifold ways he tries to separate himself from his experience, such as in attempting to treat his history as something discrete back there then, or the ongoing therapeutic process as a something separate and unconnected with him. And this similarly holds true for the therapist. He should not separate himself from his experiences, nor from that single integral reality, that unitary moving matrix, the actual, ongoing therapeutic process. Of that process, he and his patients are aspects, from which the reflecting process only momentarily abstracts them while still being of it, in it, it.

Such views of being aware make Horney's concept of the actual situation that much more productive. The therapist is aware that while the patient is relating to him with the totality of himself he is for a long time identified predominantly with his neurotic character structure. These ideas on being aware point up the values of Horney's multidimensional concept of the actual situation, all of which can emerge into the purview of our "evenly hovering attention" (Freud) in the forms of "freer and freer associating."*(182)* These notions of being aware also underline the rigor and comprehensiveness of the demands made on the holistic therapist, and hence on his understanding.

These ideas on being aware expand and clarify the meaning of attention and the attending process. To repeat Whyte's definition: "Attention is only a transitory focusing of the extended system of processes which guide behavior."*(176, p. 49)* Schachtel expands the meaning of the attending process in "The Development of Focal Attention and the Emergence of Reality."*(218)* The attending process can be focused now inwardly and now outwardly, as it is moved to do so, by emerging processes.

In "The Quality of the Analyst's Attention"*(72)* Horney lists as attributes, "wholeheartedness, comprehensiveness, and productiveness." In "The Analyst's Personal Equation"*(69)* she gives a picture of what favors and obstructs the qualities that should be present in the analyst's attention. Among the "Desirable Qualities of a Good Analyst" are: (1) "maturity, directness, discernment and objectivity;" (2) "a real interest in and for the patients, and for their practical as well as psychological problems;" (3) "a prevalent striving toward self-realization, an honest wish to help patients toward their self-realization;" (4) "a capacity for healthy emotional involvement with the patient;" (5) "a searching mind with an untiring curiosity about challenging problems."

The analyst's residual neurotic problems interfere with his attention. They will interfere with what is positively required. He may try to come to an understanding too rapidly or tend to avoid anxiety, conflict, and hostility in his patient. His egocentricity and preconceived notions will cause him to have a distorted picture. In short, his continuing difficulties will interfere with his comprehensively being aware, in his freely attending, with the depths of his understanding.

As the analyst becomes more able, in discriminating the processes of his person as instrument, the more effective he becomes in self-diagnosing, an essential ongoing process in each therapy. He must function both as subject and object of his own investigations. This is an impossibility with his head. He can only do it intuitively. As he can, the spurious dualisms of subject and object will diminish. As we move toward that ultimate of real selfness, while still being caught in our subject-predicate language, we can only do as well as we can. The first step in that direction gradually becomes more possible for many of us, namely, the act of directing our attention more inwardly instead of predominantly outwardly toward the patient. But the ultimate of this inward-directedness does not come easily. I refer to that state of being in which we are not longer distracted by the noise of our own mind

162

and, better still, when it is silent; when we are no longer distracted by our patient's words or, better still, both hear and do not hear what our patient is saying; and when we are open to the depths of our being. Then we will also be directly intuiting our patient. Then there will no longer be an *I* watching a *me* doing all this. It will simply all be happening. This condition of being will be discussed further in chapter 12, "Communing and Relating."

There is nonetheless quite some valuable information to be obtained by *I* watching *me* introspecting for self-diagnosing with reference to a particular patient. This diagnosing is a process of evaluating growing possibilities. It is done by a particular analyst of himself with a particular patient. No two situations are identical. "The more complete definition of diagnosing would then be: 'Diagnosing is a process of evaluating growing possibilities in themselves and their patients by analysts while working with patients.' "*(204)*

One important thing to learn about self-diagnosing is that there is such a task in analysis. This fact has far-reaching implications. It means that in a therapy based on human communing and relating, the human factor of the therapist is crucial. It is quite different from physical medicine in which techniques are easily communicated and tested for application to a wide variety of patients. In analysis, the therapist simply does not apply techniques; he must be theory and technique, the vehicle of them and more. He is an integral aspect of that therapeutic endeavor in which he not only treats but is treated, in which he not only helps growing possibilities in his patient and in himself, but is helped in that effort by his patient. Self-diagnosing also implies that much as we wish to become more scientific, there is still much of art in our work. After he has collected quite some data about his patient and himself, the therapist must rely on his intuition to unify all this material, which only a human being can do. We are confronted with the fact that our intuition, our most valuable diagnostic and therapeutic tool, is the one least describable and communicable.

In self-diagnosing, the therapist is asking himself, am I the right therapist for this particular patient? As he does so, he will become more proficient in answering his questions. These questions and answers will become an embedded part of him through having been experienced. They will be operating unconsciously while he consciously goes on with other aspects of his questing. While becoming acquainted with the variables that are known, he will realize how many more variables in himself and his patient are still unknown, so many of which are subsumed under the human factor. He will come to know and accept that all therapists cannot treat all patients. Such a developing attitude will lead to greater caution and care in deciding with whom to work and what patient he will refer to what analyst. As a consequence, his effectiveness in therapy with the patients with whom he does work will increase, and more patients will receive better therapy.

A therapist in self-diagnosing is really asking, "What have I to call on in myself and my environment for more effective working with this particular patient? What liabilities in myself must I keep in mind?" As human beings we all have had experience with helping and with growing. In some measure, those experiences may have stimulated some of us to become physicians, in which profession the philosophy of healing and the maintaining of physical health are so integral. These experiences, plus a searching for answers to our emotional problems, may have led some of us into psychiatry. A feeling of limited competence in therapy, with our patients and with ourselves, has led many into seeking psychoanalytic training. In fact, when all these feelings were not present to a significant degree, I have found that person did not turn out to be a good therapist or a significant contributor to psychoanalysis. Bluntly put, I feel that an essential prerequisite to being a good therapist is not suffering for its own sake, but human suffering that leads to some measure of maturing and wisdom.

All analysts, by the time they begin treating patients, have had some personal experience in analysis which they can apply in their therapeutic work. Yet not infrequently in supervisory work, analysts are startled when I ask, in an attempt to confront them with their analytic expectations of their patients, "What has been your experience in your own analysis?" By the time an analyst begins treating patients analytically, he has had two experiences as a novice — as a physician and as a psychiatrist. He has known feelings of confusion, incompetence, and awkwardness, as well as the experience of slowly finding more solid ground in himself through his successes and failures. He has known through friends, acquaintances, and predecessors in training that growing is possible. Through contact with his analyst and teachers, and through a knowledge of psychoanalytic history, he knows that a wide range of people have been helped, that the boundaries of therapeutic effectiveness have deepened and extended, and that psychoanalytic theory and therapy have been steadily and constructively expanding and evolving. Finally, there is all that is known and has been tested still open to him for the effort, the help of more experienced therapists, and the support of his own analyst as he works through personal problems brought to his attention while working with patients. All of this is available, but often overlooked or taken for granted. Even a novice has a whole lot in himself to count on — the assets in himself, in his personal analysis and self-analysis, and in the field of analysis. They have a constructive momentum which should be more often tapped.

These general considerations can give an analyst with limited experience a feeling of some solid ground to stand on. They can help him more accurately diagnose himself while he is going through the upsets which are a normal part of his new venture. They might in some measure protect him from the tendency to take every patient who comes to him, which can result in extremes of overoptimism or over-pessimism.

While there is a legitimate desire to accept the challenges that a wide variety of patients present, and to expand one's practice, the analyst must not let these urges persuade him to overburden himself by taking on too many patients too fast. He must allow himself time for other aspects of his life, and for the emergencies that are bound to occur. If he does not take these precautions, he will end up with too many very sick patients, some of whom may be beyond his competence. It is a common observation that less-experienced therapists have too many very sick patients. Their practice becomes too taxing psychologically and physically, the number of patients dropping out of therapy is greater, and the results achieved are usually limited or poor. All this can have a disheartening effect on a therapist and lead to a spirit of over-cautiousness, as well as other adverse effects upon his therapeutic growth and development.

Naturally, into each therapeutic venture he will bring all that I have defined as assets and liabilities in a patient. As he proceeds in his analysis and self-analysis, his knowledge of them will extend and deepen. He will grow as a person and a therapist. In working with patients, there is no substitute for experience. Knowledge of theory and technique are not sufficient. But working with many patients without learning and growing, without suffering and satisfaction, without failures and successes, is a reflection to me of a pretty limited therapist. There is an erroneous notion, particularly among beginners, that "holding onto" patients means being a good therapist, and "losing" many patients, a poor one. Factually, beginning therapists who "hold" and "lose" patients may have about equal competence. Both will be growing when they can ask themselves squarely, "How come I lose so few (or so many) patients?" When this has happened, I have observed that the disproportion in both directions begins to recede.

Another fallacious notion is that a smooth or painless analysis means a good therapist, and that a turbulent or painful course, a poor one. Again, consistent and repetitive occurrence of either of these extremes indicates that something is amiss. The therapies of one analyst were smooth because he terminated his work when the analyses became too threatening to his persistent resignation. Another dropped his patients when the analyses became smooth. This he interpreted as their having become healthy. Because he still felt so turbulent in himself, he considered his patient healthier than himself, and felt unable to give further help. These examples may help correct the common error of making point-for-point correlations, using simple cause-and-effect thinking, and giving oversimplified answers to quite intricate problems.

Through therapeutic experiences that lead to increasing growing, wisdom, and competence, an analyst can learn some of the following for self-diagnosing. By this time it is hoped he will have enough patients to choose from, his finances will be much less pressing, his working schedule will approximate the number of hours he wants to devote to practice, and he will be feeling free enough in himself to be able to make choices. What choices he then makes will depend upon what he has learned of his assets and how available they are to him, what his residual liabilities are and their extent. He will have the experience of having worked with a wide variety of patients and have some estimate of how poor and how good his results were. Because his results were poor with certain patients will not necessarily mean he will choose not to work with similar patients in the future. Through those very errors he may find what in himself had contributed. He may feel he can be, or already is becoming, quite effective with just those very problems. He may also feel that working again with such patients is a challenge. Likewise, good results in certain directions need not mean a selection of such patients. With a broadening or shift of his interests, he may have been stimulated to work in quite other areas.

Concomitantly in his self-diagnosing, an analyst should be asking himself, "What are my liabilities which indicate it would be wiser for me not to work with this man?" There might be predominant feelings of "I can't" and "I don't want to." Such feelings might be prompted by limited interest in the problem the patient presents, predominant dislikes over likes, not enough of a challenge or too much, not enough of a response of compassion or sympathy, too little hope of satisfactions to be expected from the work to be put in, limited results in working with such patients, and a voice that keeps saying "no" while the analyst is wavering or even thinking his decision is weighted more on the "yes" side. Other special factors might be the questions of time and fee, and the drain on the analyst that such a patient will be, and the concomitant adverse effect on his work with other patients.

"As far as the awareness and the conscious understanding of transference and countertransference are concerned, the whole psychoanalytic literature is full of papers which treat this subject." Fromm-Reichmann adds, regarding the crucial import of the analyst's person. "Balint has most aptly emphasized the problem when he says that the doctor must learn, as best he can, to know 'the pharmacology of his most important drug — himself.' "*(198, p. 35)*

"The reactions of the prospective patient and the analyst to each other are of fundamental importance; these are not limited to factors of transference and countertransference but include the impact of two real personalities upon each other."*(142, pp. 99-100)* Not only is the analyst's person of central significance, but his unique personality as a special kind of medicine, to be curative, also must be congenial to his patient's unique personality and his special kind of illness. The person making a referral must always consider who might work better with whom? The analyst considering working with a patient must seriously ask, "Am I the person for this particular patient?"

Kanzer and Blum also emphasize that the "ability to relate to people in the past and at present," and that the existence of "positive personality resources (talents, capacity to sublimate, courage, patience, etc.)" are important in evaluating prognosis so far as patients are concerned. *(142, p. 99)* These criteria also apply to therapists. Their position moves in a holistic direction and is close to what I have described in evaluating assets and liabilities for diagnosing and prognosing of patient and therapist.

We are in need of greater rigor and precision in defining the what and the how of the analyst's person as instrument. This definition becomes more possible as our theories of personality change, improve, and more sharply delineate the processes of change. Freud touched on a theory of personality change when he discussed the variability in analytic results. He noted that when formulating generalizations to bring order in chaos, while we simplify we also falsify, "especially when we are dealing with processes of development and change." While trying to define the qualitative aspects of change, we often overlook the quantitative attributes. Freud added that we lose sight of the fact that most changes and developments are intermediate, incomplete and "really only partial."*(165, p. 330)*

Theories of personality change have become more refined as, for example, the one suggested by Gendlin. *(212)*

Kanzer and Blum state that "the standardization of an analytic case history must involve endless intricacies" and presents many unsolved problems, "recent developments in psychoanalysis" concerned with "the quantitative and systematic recording of data and comparative studies of the methods of different analysts suggest that the era of 'scientific validation' is drawing closer . . . . The need for a more precise approach to the problems of estimating analyzability" is recognized as is "the need to 'standardize' the analyst himself as a judge of analyzability." With these might come the "standardization of the training of that ultimate instrument of psychoanalytic therapy, the analyst himself," an objective shadowed by the dangers of dogma and dehumanization. *(142)*

That there have been significant strides in the direction of scientific rigor in clinical medicine regarding standardizing the therapist's person is suggested in Feinstein's *Clinical Judgment*. He "demonstrates the clinician to be a uniquely discriminating, adaptable, and portable scientific apparatus that can also be calibrated" and who "requires *self-standardization* of bedside performance to match . . . the assumed precision of non-clinical colleagues."*(219)*

Discipline, rigor, precision, consistency, reliability, specification, and self-standardization enhance the effectiveness of the investigator as researcher and therapist. They help him become more scientific and do not dehumanize him.

Absolute objectivity is an impossibility because no observation is free of impurities. The forms and functions of the observer's operations, their contents and objectives, must therefore be refined. This has been attempted here and in chapter 9 with the identification and description of the categories of being of the therapist as instrument, as well as his experiencing process, his attitudes, his modes of being, his understanding, and the assets and liabilities essential to his self-diagnosing. The human calibration of this "uniquely discriminating, adaptable, and portable scientific apparatus" for humane purposes hopefully now appears more possible.

Chapter 11

The Doctor-Patient Relationship I:
The Transference-Countertransference
and the Transference Neurosis

The view of the person of the analyst as his most important instrument in therapy organically determines how transference is seen. "Of Freud's discoveries, I value most highly . . . his finding that one can utilize for therapy the patient's emotional reactions to the analyst and to the analytical situation." Horney adds: "Disentangled from the theoretical bias of the repetition compulsion . . . my viewpoint concerning the phenomenon is this: . . . the analytical relationship is one special form of human relationships and existing disturbances are bound to appear here as they appear elsewhere. The particular conditions under which an analysis is conducted render it possible to study these disturbances here more accurately than elsewhere and to convince the patient of their existence and the role they play . . . . The principle that the analyst's emotional reactions should be understood as a 'counter-transference' may be objected to on the same grounds as the concept of transference."*(35, pp. 154, 167)*

As Horney's ideas on theory and technique evolved, the concept of the doctor-patient relationship emerged. *(205)* This concept considers the whole person of the therapist in relationship with the whole person of the patient. All that is neurotic and healthy in each participates.

The therapist's experience in utilizing his person as means and ends in the relating process will make communing more possible. A quicker realization of what is happening results in more effective utilization of the varieties of imagery and symbolizations in the patient's associations and dreams.

The therapist, the more whole he is, will be better able to discern when a patient is seeing him as a magician; when the patient is externalizing his own attributes in a glorified or despised way; when he is truly touching on some of the analyst's own neurotic residuals; and when he is seeing him more *realistically*. That the patient will see him *as if* he were all kinds of people in his past, present, and future will become evident in the relationship, in his behaviors, associations, and in his dreams. In the service of working through some of these *as if* persons, in response to overt and implied assertions, as they come up in associations and dreams, the analyst may ask such questions as "Who do you have me being?" "Who do I feel like today?" "Who do I remind you of?" "What if you experience me in the dream as your father?" "What if your mother in the dream stands for me?" "What would you have me saying in answer to your question if I were your brother?"

I do not agree with the theoretical premises for the transference neurosis, its inevitability, and the requirement that it, as such, be worked through. The phenomena which these assumptions attempt to explain are directly observable. I have indicated, based on the model of the symbolizing process, that the symbols chosen and the arrangements of them will appropriately and adequately point at and communicate what that patient is experiencing in the here-now, unconsciously and in awareness. He may feel the persons, relationships, and situations conveyed in those symbol forms *as if* they were identical with those back there-then.

The emergence of such symbol forms and arrangements is an expression of a mounting threat from, involvement with, and openness to the analytic process and relationship. As the analysis proceeds and more peripheral defenses are relinquished, the patient is opening himself to experiencing threats to major defenses having greater subjective value, such as dependency needs to the point of masochism, and neurotic expansiveness with its arrogant-vindictive components. At such points, when conflict, basic and central, with intensities of self-hate and onslaughts of anxiety and hostility, are being experienced and flight is not available as a solution, a resurgence of intensified dependency needs, and/or with assaultiveness with reference to the analyst, often occur. With the latter, "the so-called negative thera-peutic reaction may become manifest."*(220)*

Crucial for working through such difficult periods is the depth and strength of the doctor-patient relationship. Basic trust must be present. Basic trust makes possible a patient's willingness to go along with the therapy and stick through trying and painful periods. It allows the therapist to take chances. Basic trust must be built slowly and carefully on the clearest kind of evidence. This cannot be done by giving what Martin calls "false reassurance."

This "occurs where there is a complete disregard of the un-conscious determinants of behavior and a failure to see the value and functions of symptoms. Opportunities are missed to give patients a broader perspective and a more meaningful orientation toward their symptoms and their whole way of life."*(221)* One of the most common instances of "false reassurance" is when a physician gives physical tests to prove there is no physical basis for an objectified somatic symptom, and reaps the consequences when the patient responds with a return of non-objectified anxiety to the point of panic.

The therapist is using "superficial or defense reassurance," says Martin, when a neurotic defense is breaking down and the therapist focuses entirely on restoring it. *(221)* Earlier he may have done just that, before the patient was strong enough to integrate its dissolution. Later on it is essential to support the patient in this happening and prepare him to experience the conflicts that are on the point of emerging.

Martin's notion of "basic reassurance" is integral to his holistic orientation as well as to his emphasis on assisting the "patient con-sciously to accept his total involvement in conflicts." He underscores that it is the "conflicts in childhood" rather than the "memories of conflicts" that are "repressed and dissociated . . . . Because the child lives mainly at a perceptual level, more . . . conflicts at the earthy, sensuous level must be made conscious . . . . This phase . . . must be brought out and linked with the present, with the dream life, with the relationships with the analyst, and with the experiences in extra-analytic relationships."*(221)*

"Basic reassurance" also comes from accepting the child within us, "the crude, unrefined, inchoate elements" in ourselves. This is all repressed in the repression of childhood conflicts. "There is something about getting down to earth, literally and figuratively, that is a means toward basic reassurance . . . . We can return to the earth, return to sleep, to the past, and to darkness, not as an escape, but as a means of going into the darker reaches of ourselves, to extend our aware-ness, to get closer to ourselves."*(221)*

How Martin brings about these awarenesses in the service of "basic reassurance" he indicated in connection with a case citation: "I had to get it over to him, not in so many words, but by (1) moving the analysis in various directions to bring out in the past, in the present, and in dreams how intensive and extensive had been his conflicts over control, restriction, and confinement; and (2) by showing him the literal and figurative implications of what he was saying and really wishing."*(221)*

Reassurance has its special meanings in the context of the classical model. Tarachow defines his while elaborating on "The Limitations of Technique." The paradoxes and antitheses which make perfect technique impossible supply the motivation for therapy. "The imperfections of the analyst make analysis possible." Tarachow's thesis is that the psychoanalytic situation drives toward fusion, that is, patient and therapist each move toward each other as objects, to the point of the regressive, archaic, object relationship of symbiosis. The function of the analytic technique, the analytic work of interpretation, is to frustrate that movement, manifested as the transference neurosis, in which the neutrality of the analyst also serves. "Psychoanalytic work, i.e., interpretation, drives toward separation, better ego boundaries, improved sense of reality, improved object relations, victory over narcissism, and movement from primary to secondary process and from unconscious to preconscious."

In the light of these viewpoints, Tarachow sees reassurance as interfering "with the patient's sense of reality because the therapist, in the act, agrees with the patient's infantile fantasies about himself and does not give the patient the task of confronting his own fantasies. Instead, the therapist acts these fantasies out in collusion with the patient. This is an acting out on the part of the therapist, in which he assumes all the responsibilities of the mother."*(222, pp. 208-11)*

The foregoing comments are Tarachow's response to the dangers he sees in the use of parameters (Eissler) which "may have done more harm than good" and to Strachey's notion that reassurance is the "attempt on the part of the analyst to behave like a 'good' fantasy object rather than as he is in reality. This is the corrective emotional experience which Alexander proposed." It, Tarachow feels, has the "fatal flaw" of robbing the patient "of the chance to make a distinction between his own archaic fantasy and reality." He regards Stone's "plea" for more "humanity and humanness to enter the aseptic analytic relationship" as unnecessary because it is something "we really cannot avoid doing in the first place." The real issue is to clearly understand the "extent to which we are human in the first place and are incapable of establishing the ideal psychoanalytic situation."

Tarachow's comments may give an erroneous impression regarding reassurance which his definition corrects: "Reassurance in its best sense would be simply offering oneself to the patient as an object in his (to him) *real world* without interpretation, neither as good or bad, or as either good or bad, it really makes no difference. It might be an act of kindness, a comment about the weather, an act of joining in a discussion, or a scolding or caution or reproach. It might be any action designed to enter the *real life* of the patient. You have joined the patient, broken his isolation, but have not interpreted anything. You have joined the fantasy systems of the patient. The patient appreciates this as entering his *real world*. [Italics added.] This is reassurance in the best sense."*(222, pp. 205-08)*

I have italicized *real life* and *real world* to connect it with my notion of rational, as being in ratio with reality; to connect it with the recent emphasis on the *real* aspect of the relationship as distinct from the transference aspect; and to connect it with the new dimensions of meaning and effectivness added to the therapeutic alliance.

Tarachow's definition of reassurance in the "best sense" closely approximates what Horney called human help. Tarachow's reassurance and Horney's human help would be included in Martin's basic reassurance. The term reassurance, however, creates confusion. I believe it would be better to speak of assurance because to assure means "to confirm, to give confidence to." Because reassure means "to assure anew," its value is limited without operative and effective primary basic assurance. Better assurance leads to better analysis, and better analysis is better assurance.

"When I speak of general human help," said Horney, "I mean the way the analyst helps the patient — not through his interpretations but through his attitude toward the patient. This includes his willingness to understand, his unflagging interest in the patient's growth, his faith in the patient's existing potentialities, his firmness that permits him to view the patient's suffering with concern without letting himself be crushed by them, to remain unswayed by the patient's admiration and undaunted by the patient's attacks . . . .

"You may wonder . . . whether the relationship between patient and analyst is not a kind of friendship. In a sense, it is friendship at its very best," though it lacks "the measure of spontaneity and mutuality essential to a friendship." Following MacMurray, who distinguishes functional and personal relationships, Horney adds, though "Your analyst and you may like and respect each other . . . the relationship is for a definite purpose . . . it is essentially a functional one."*(40, pp. 202-04)*

In *Therapeutic Communication,* Ruesch asserts that "At times, this process is referred to as therapy; at other times as education;

some call it counseling; others simply friendship."*(223)* All of these are aspects of the doctor-patient relationship. The comprehensive knowing process to be discussed in chapter 12 subsumes educating which can be therapeutic, as well as aspects of counseling which include "general human help" and "friendship." According to Kanzer and Blum "Freud did not hesitate to suggest the appropriateness of advice, support and parental guidance, subordinated, however, to the attainment of ultimate analytic goals."*(142, p. 106)* Freud also frequently made reference to the educative aspects of psychoanalysis.

The classical response, in the late '30s and early '40s, to Horney's and Alexander's ideas regarding transference and the transference neurosis was quite negative. It was revolutionary of Alexander to say that "The concept of the inevitability of a complete transference neurosis has been abandoned by most psychiatrists. It is realized that frequently such a transference neurosis is not merely unnecessary or undesirable, it is sometimes almost impossible." Alexander added, "Our flexible approach has brought us to recognize the tremendous importance not only of external happenings in a patient's life, but also of giving active direction and help. This automatically alters the transference relationship, making the development of an unwieldy transference neurosis less probable because of the emphasis on the reality situation of the present."*(224, pp. 43, 54)*

Some of what Alexander had suggested under "The Principle of Flexibility"*(224, p. 25)* and what Horney had developed in her holistic approach began to appear in Freudian literature as "parameters," and was referred to as the "Widening Scope," "Variations," as "Similarities and Differences with the Traditional Psychoanalytic Techniques," and as "Modified Psychoanalysis."*(142, p. 99)* Anna Freud cautioned that the various techniques are "mere tools of treatment," and should be "periodically inspected, reviewed, sharpened perfected, and if necessary altered."*(225)*

The meaning of transference has widened and deepened. Many aspects now include what Horney had mentioned, as have I, concerning the relating process. *(204)* They touch on the importance of the healthy aspects of the therapist and patient and of their respective environments. The constructive aspects of patient and therapist manifested in the total relationship are now being stressed by Freudian analysts. The healthy, the *real*, aspects of the transference in the transference alliance, are differentiated from the resistance aspects which perpetuate the transference neurosis.

Freud emphasized the helping function of the positive transference and noted that it was also a source of resistance. Distinguishing what within the positive transference "is actually the *realistic* therapeutic alliance, should clarify a source of theoretical and practical confusion." [Italics added.] Likewise, "the 'negative transference' may include protests on the part of the normal ego for failure to accord due recognition to the mature portion of the personality. Transference manifestations can be recognised and tested only in the context of total behavior."*(142, p. 109)*

Freud further stated that "Every happy relation between an analyst and the subject of his analysis, during and after analysis, was not to be regarded as transference; there were friendly relations with a *real basis* [emphasis supplied] which were capable of persisting."*(105, p. 323)* Freud's admonition regarding "a real basis" for "happy" and "friendly relations" between "patient" and "therapist" gave impetus to new directions in thinking regarding transference.

How far this evolution has gone is evident in Karush. In discussing the working-through-process, he sees the therapeutic alliance as mainly evolving from the transference. The functions of the analyst that he underscores are noteworthy: teacher, definer of *reality*, nonjudgmental object of drive-motivated behavior, and superego representative influenced by suggestion and even by authority. Most important is the analyst's functioning as idealized object for the patient, thus giving a basis for the expansion and reconstruction of his ego ideal, ultimately a source of *realistic* self-esteem. *(226)*

Greenson and Wexler, writing in 1969, have quite definite ideas about the transference-free, *"real* part" of the analytic relationship. They state that total anonymity is impossible, that obstinate silence may produce irreversible negative transference, and that even the most full-blown transference neurosis does not submerge the *"real"* relationship. They suggest not only recognizing, but even nurturing the *"real"* relationship, and assert that this is not being anti-analytic or destructive to the analytic work. The *"real"* relationship and not the positive transference is the core of the working or therapeutic alliance. The *"real"* relationship can be misused, but, significantly, they feel that a persistent neglect is the greater danger. *(227)*

Kanzer and Blum present another aspect of the Freudian position: "The transference is the underlying system of fantasies and associated effects, attitudes, and motor dispositions which tend to cluster about current figures and situations and utilize them to revive the past. As such, transference is an aspect of memory . . . . Memory is not used as an aid in adapting to present needs; rather, the present must be fitted into the past and appear as a repetition of it . . . . The substitution of the analyst for the original figures in these traumatic episodes and the current revival of old conflicts, which now center about his person, constitute the transference phenomena . . . . The

175

analytic setting and procedure are specifically designed to draw into the open, and in sheltered surroundings the underlying fantasy." *(142, pp. 104-07)*

These quotes, though brief, and representative of only a segment of Freudian opinion, do point up some essentials and give a basis for comparison. In his "Interactional Psychoanalysis," Wolman presents many views close to my own. "The patient's attitude toward the analyst is a transference phenomenon, but at the same time it is a 'here-and-now' relationship. Apparently, from the inception of Freud's work, the analyst's reaction to the patient was the ever important clue." Wolman asserts that technique kept changing in response to the analyst's response to widening categories of patients being treated psychoanalytically. In his discussion of "Transference as Interaction," he asserts that *"transference is always manipulated by the analyst,"* and that he had better be aware that this is so, do it *"wittingly"* and *"be aware of what he is and what he is doing."* And finally, he advocated "the rule of getting *involved* with the patient's cause *without getting involved* with the patient in a personal way (avoidance of countertransference)."*(142, pp. 242, 261-62)*

The following statement by Kanzer and Blum sounds unequivocal: "No theory of the neuroses that fails to explain the role of infantile sexuality in symptom formation can be seriously considered by analysts." But when read with the following, its arbitrariness is leavened: "Therapeutic results that bypass the sexual factors are, of course, possible." When is added, "Simple genetic continuities and repetition compulsions should not be postulated; the genetic construction must include a functional appraisal of each stage of development in its own context," the meaning of the original very emphatic statement has been radically altered. *(142, pp. 108, 121)* Due to the work of Anna Freud and others, "The *real* world [italics added] of the child — not only his sex fantasies in later years — thus become the basis for concepts of mental health and illness."*(142, p. 95)*

In reply to the Freudian position that "Transference is an aspect of memory" whose contents tend to "cluster about current figures and situations and utilize them to revive the past" and that "the present must be fitted into the past and appear as a repetition of it," it is necessary to reiterate that the only place we can be is here, the only time we can be is now, and the only feelings we can be, not have, are here-now feelings. Repetition of the past is logically and factually impossible. What appears as past is only *as if* it were past in time and location.

Schachtel's studies "On Memory and Childhood Amnesia" illuminate the contrast between a child's recall of its experiences which are genuine and have freshness, spontaneity, and originality and the memories of an adult which are "schematized" and "conventionalized." Schachtel hypothesizes that *"The categories (or schemata) of adult memory are not suitable receptacles for early childhood experiences and therefore not fit to preserve these experiences and enable their recall. The functional capacity of the conscious, adult memory is usually limited to those types of experience which the adult consciously is aware of and is capable of having."(218, p. 284)* The symbol forms, moreover, available to children and adults differ considerably.

Consonant with his holistic approach, Goldstein states that "Remembrance . . . presupposes a similarity between the situation of the organism at the time of the experience and a later condition" emphasizing the necessity for learning each patient's unique idioms which can best guide the therapist in contacting the "modality in which it [the event] first appeared." But similarity is not identity and the similarity of a past event, as memory, as "after-effect," simply may not be available not because it was *"forgotten* through repression" but rather, it *"cannot be remembered,"* because it is "no longer part of the attitudes of later life, and therefore cannot be effective." Voluntary repression is less important and less present in childhood. More important is "the building up of new and adequate habits. Their development makes for the passive disappearance of the older inadequate reactions and leads to their fading away into the background."*(228, pp. 158-59)* This partially explains why life is also a therapist, and why the notions of the repetition compulsion as well as of regression are not tenable.

Stating the Freudian position, Kanzer and Blum say, "The present must be fitted into the past and appear as a repetition of it."*(142, p. 106)* But the present cannot be fitted into the past. The past, real and apparent, and the adumbrated future can only be seen as expressions of the present.

The transference neurosis implies the concept of regression, logically and factually also an impossibility. The notion of the symbolizing process, of emerging and resorbing patternings, protects us from, and undercuts, the fallacies in the notions of regression.

Also prerequisite to the development of the transference neurosis is the experiencing of frustration. Menninger noted that "The sense of frustration experienced by the patient in the analytic situation is partially a reflection of the reality situation, but it can and must be regulated by the analyst." Menninger also mentioned that some of his colleagues questioned his use of the word *"induction"* regarding the regression. He wanted it understood that "the regression occurs; it develops; it is induced by the total situation."*(200, pp. 49, 53)*

Horney would agree that the frustration is built into the situation, does not have to be induced, and is not due to a re-enactment. It would happen because of the patient's psychology, as it became manifest in, through, and because of the structure of the actual situation of which the analytic relationship is a crucial aspect. These frustrations are felt "all the time," "easily," and "disproportionately" by the neurotic because "many of his expectations and demands are prompted by anxiety, whereby they become imperative and thus make frustration a threat to security. His expectations, furthermore, are often not only excessive, but also contradictory, thus rendering their fulfillment in reality impossible. Finally, his wishes are often prompted by unconscious impulses to triumph maliciously over others by imposing his will upon them, so that if frustration is felt as a humiliating defeat, the ensuing hostile reactions are a response not to the frustration of wishes but to the humiliation which the person subjectively experiences."*(35, pp. 66-67)* The issues of frustration, pain and suffering and their place in therapy will be further elaborated in chapter 13.

The Freudian concept of transference neurosis implies a genetic reconstruction, a theory of history, and a theory of etiology which contrasts with my own. I feel that history is information about the lived past, the living present, and the to-be-lived future, whether obtained in response to questions or whether it arises spontaneously, whether verbally or non-verbally communicated. History is a changing gestalt of perceptions, conceptions, and relations in sequences of organismal-environmental happenings, extending backward into the receding past, forward into the upcoming future.

The concept of regression has no place in such a concept which precludes the notion of reliving past events in the present except on an *as if* basis. This multidimensional, open-ended definition of history is a more comprehensive operational tool in therapy, and lays the basis for an equally encompassing definition of etiology.

"Etiology is the study of transformations in organismal-environmental happenings, from conception to the continuing present, in which genetic, constitutional and environmental factors participate to produce irrational neurotic, "psychopathic, and psychotic" processes. *(229)*

In the light of what has been developed, particularly in this chapter, the following classical statement takes on new and different meanings and possible interpretations. "There are many clusters of 'transferences' operating in, and emerging from, such a fantasy [in the present, pointing to the past]. The unraveling of the intricacies becomes more and more associated with the art of inducing, translating, and resolving the transference neurosis."*(142, pp. 108-09)* There is no necessity for induction because the emergence of the so-

178

called transference neurosis is said to be built into the analytic setting when guided by the classical model. "Translating" is what every analyst does from the vantage point of his theoretical and technical orientation. "Resolving" irrational configurations is consonant with my own viewpoint.

Some current perspectives in Freudian thinking seem to move in directions similar to what has been presented under basic reassurance, basic trust, the functioning of the therapist, and what will be developed regarding communing and relating in chapter 12. These newer viewpoints are particularly pertinent to working with adolescents as well as with such conditions as pernicious vomiting, mucous and ulcerative colitis, and anoxia nervosa in which so-called fixation at the oral and anal phases seems so obvious.

Anna Freud feels that where an arrest at a preverbal phase has occurred there does not exist "the background against which these early phases can be analyzed." She believes that where dependence has not been outgrown, and independence achieved and then lost, it is impossible "to cure in analysis" the original state of dependency. *(230)*

Gitelson's position is that "the reoccurrence of those 'primitive mechanisms' of introjection-projection which phenomenologically we call 'rapport,' and which eventuate in transference" are what we have to depend on. He believes that the transference alliance cannot even be established without arousing and including stray residues of infantile object relationships. *(231)* This is indeed a far reaching and encompassing statement, because it pertains to all analyses and is consonant with my view of the place of communing in therapy based on the paradigm and fact of the mother-child unity.

According to Spitz, the anaclitic attitude with which the patient presents himself for treatment finds a complementary disposition in the diatrophic function of the analyst; that is, his healing intentions which reproduce "fostering influences of the kind which emanate from the effective mother during the child's early development."*(232)* "Gitelson sees therapeutic agencies such as suggestion, manipulation, and confrontation as potential expressions of the diatrophic attitude, which may be 'directed toward increasing the patient's autonomy and preparing the way for analysis proper.' "*(142, p. 125)* There are echoes here of Alexander's viewpoints of the '30s which were so vigorously criticized, and of Ferenczi's first attempts in these directions which were frowned on by Freud in the '20s.

Zetzel underlines and complements Gitelson's position. She believes that there should be maximal mobilization of ego attributes which resulted from successes achieved in the earliest stages of psychic developments, namely, as a form of assets. "Such mobilization will be fostered by intuitive adaptive responses on the part of the analyst which may well be compared with the successful parent."*(233)*

Both Zetzel and Gitelson believe that the diatrophic function is within the possibilities of a flexibly used classical technique. Kanzer and Blum add: "Although the analyst must retain an objective and dispassionate role, which insures against uncontrollable regression, his areas of sympathetic alliance with the patient in his sufferings and reliving activities inherently expand his functions beyond that of the object and interpreter of the transference neurosis and make him a participant in reliving experiences that revise the personality." *(142, p. 125)*

While Anna Freud's point was that "it becomes impossible to cure in analysis the state of dependency" where a state of independence had not been once reached and lost, Gitelson and Zetzel felt that in spite of this lack it could be done by the analyst's reliance on his "intuitive adaptive responses" and his "diatrophic functions." What is subsumed under the therapeutic alliance under the "real relationship" keeps expanding and its importance increasing.

Sources of theoretical and practical confusion could be clarified according to Kanzer and Blum if an element in the positive transference could be clearly identified as the *"realistic* therapeutic alliance." *(142, p. 109)* Part of this confusion reflects differences of opinion, of emphasis, attempts at increasing rigor, maybe a tendency to purism, and much is due to a lack of precision in the use of terms. And always there is the difficulty of putting into words what is wordless. The following exemplify some of these issues. They are presented to define my own position in contrast to a spectrum of them by Freudian analysts.

In discussing changes in the superego "effected by purely analytical means" Bibring stated in 1937 that "the patient's relationship to the analyst from which a sense of security emanates is not only a precondition of the procedure but also effects an immediate (apart from an analytical) consolidation of his sense of security which he has not successfully acquired or consolidated in childhood. Such an immediate consolidation — which, in itself, lies outside of the field of analytic therapy — is, of course, only of permanent value if it goes along with the coordinated operation of analytic treatment."*(234)*

The expression "by purely analytical means" implies a purity which Tarachow says is unattainable. Tarachow refers to the analytic work as interpretation which drives toward separation and the analytic situation, of which the real therapeutic alliance is an aspect, which drives toward fusion. He asserts ideal psychoanalysis is impossible and there is always some psychotherapy in psychotherapy. *(222)* As I understand Tarachow the purity is impossible and the analytic therapy, to which Bibring refers, is the analytic work of interpretation, one aspect of the analytic situation leading to the therapeutic results.

In commenting in 1950 on the distinction between psychological influence in psychoanalysis and suggestion in hypnosis, MacAlpine is even more uncompromising. "The analyst . . . is never a co-actor . . . . The analytic transference relationship ought strictly speaking, not to be referred to as a relationship between analysand and analyst, but more precisely as the analysand's relation to his analyst." While she does not deny analysis is "team-work," she insists that "the essential difference between psychoanalysis and all other psychotherapies is" that the former is "the only psychotherapeutic method in which a one-sided, infantile regression — analytic transference — is induced in a patient (analysand), analyzed, worked through, and generally resolved."*(235)*.

While not denying that analysis is "teamwork," in stating that "the analyst is never a co-actor" MacAlpine makes her position rigorously clear. Her statements "never a co-actor" and "a one-sided, infantile regression" are presented as absolutes, as if they are realized actualities, both describable and necessary. Her position is an aspiration toward an ideal. Its actualization Tarachow and others see as impossible.

Commenting on the position of Bibring, MacAlpine, and others, Strupp failed "to see how its [an "objective relationship" between patient and therapist] hypothesized existence defiles the purity of analytic therapy. Yet analysts have strained to postulate the absence of an interpersonal relationship as a defining characteristic of psychoanalysis in the 'orthodox' sense. That interpretations also play an important, though probably secondary, part is not denied, but their curative effect has been greatly overestimated."*(236)* I feel Strupp's criticisms are occasioned by the confusions mentioned above. They will be discussed further in chapter 27.

These are issues that have bedeviled psychoanalysis from its founding. The more "purely" it can be an investigative tool, the more rigor and purity its theoretical terms and technical maneuvers can have. As therapeutic aims intrude, this rigor and purity blurs, and the "science" of psychoanalysis becomes more art. "It is indeed one of the distinctions of psychoanalysis that research and treatment proceed hand in hand," said Freud. "But still the technique required for the one begins at a certain point to diverge from that of the other," and he adds the "most successful cases" occur when we proceed "as it were, aimlessly."*(130)*

The positions of Anna Freud, Gitelson, and Zetzel have definitely expanded the "*real* therapeutic alliance" in what they have subsumed under the "diatrophic functions" of "the effective mother," "the successful parent," and what they phenomenologically describe as "intuitive adaptive responses" and "rapport." Equivalent concepts are Horney's notion of human help and Sullivan's *mothering one* and *the participant-observer*.

The ultimate criterion as to whether it is possible to treat someone fixated at the so-called oral, anal, and pregenital phases who has not attained some measure of independence is actual therapeutic experience. It of course would require the most detailed presentation of the history of the person and his therapy to satisfy those who legitimately question this possibility, as does Anna Freud. I believe I and others have been successful with such people after long years of analysis. To obtain that maturity and independence which should be the result of a successful analysis with such patients, a unique set of circumstances to support them and me through these many years of effort and struggle were required. I also had to avail myself of all that Gitelson, Spitz, Zetzel, Kanzer, Blum presented, and more. What Gitelson and others have presented is to me an affirmation that ego, autonomy, and the real self are primary, and that id and sick processes are a consequence of the blockage of the former.

The concept of the real self as primary and my formulations regarding communing and relating seem congruent with Balint's concept of "primary love."*(127, ch. 12)* Balint says that "The aim of all human striving is to establish — or, probably, re-establish — an all-embracing harmony with one's environment, to be able to love in peace."*(127, p. 65)* This is almost a restatement of Horney's urge toward self-realization and the goals of therapy. His concept of primary love follows, almost verbatim, Horney's concept of the real self. Balint feels that his theory of primary love can better explain many clinical conditions and "the feeling of ecstasy accompanying ... orgasm." Annie Reich compared "this *unio mystica* with what Freud called the oceanic feeling."

"This *unio mystica*, the re-establishment of the harmonious interpenetrating mix-up, between the individual and the most important parts of his environment, his love objects, is the desire of all humanity. To achieve it, an indifferent or possibly hostile object must be changed into a cooperative partnership by what I called the work of conquest (1948). This induces the object, now turned into a partner, to tolerate being taken for granted for a brief period, that is, to have only identical interests. Individuals vary greatly in the skills required for this 'conquest' and, in consequence, not everyone is capable of achieving periodically an orgasm, or, for that matter, a harmonious partnership. Still this is the most common way to re-establish the primary harmonious mix-up."*(127, p. 74)*

Balint continues: "In adult life there are a few more possibilities for achieving this ultimate aim, all of them requiring considerable skills and talents. These comprise religious ecstasy, sublime moments of artistic creation, and lastly, though perhaps more for patients, certain regressive periods during analytic treatment. Although in all these states the individual is on his own, creating the impression of narcissistic withdrawal, all of them have in common the fundamental characteristic that for these very brief moments the individual may truly and really experience that every disharmony has been dispelled. He and his whole world are now united in undisturbed understanding, in completely harmonious interpenetrating mix-up."*(127, p.75)* These "possibilities" are what I would call moments of communing. What Balint says about ecstasy in orgasm, religious ecstasy, and sublime moments of artistic creation are very close to the viewpoints I have presented. They are also congruent with what Masud Kahn presents in "Vicissitudes of Being, Knowing, and Experiencing in the Therapeutic Situation."*(254)*

In Grotjahn's technique of "responsive action," I find an integration and unification of the spectrum of viewpoints which have been presented here. It moves in directions discussed in this book and characterizes "the therapist's relation to the patient's unconscious needs." The term "responsive action" functions as "a unifying concept in contemporary attempts to understand the essentials of the therapeutic process. It relates to such concepts as corrective emotional experience, role-taking, therapeutic alliance, and other terms that indicate the analytic development from the study of transference neurosis to the role of countertransference, to the recognition of the interaction and human experience, and, finally, to the integration of all three."*(142, pp. 290, 295)*

Responsive action "should be genuine and spontaneous," a hoped-for consequence of personal analysis, and further disciplined thorough training. These should have made the analyst "more open-minded and tolerant of a manifold, multileveled, and multichanneled communication in human interaction."*(142, p. 291)* Such a hierarchical structure describes the symbolic spiral which, in turn, can serve as a model for the formulation of the structures subsumed under it.

Chapter 12

The Doctor-Patient Relationship II:
Communing and Relating

Goldstein says: "Communion is the basis of all communication; hence also of the communication that makes psychotherapy possible." *(178)* Communing is the basis of all communicating in a human sense. It occurs in infancy before awareness of otherness obtains, and exists thereafter, unconscious and conscious, at the prerationative, as well as at the rationative levels.

For basic trust to develop, it is essential that there be increasing openness to, experience with, and guidance by the prerationative levels of the symbolic spiral. This means that a deepening of basic and primordial trust must happen at, in, and through those levels of the spiral that are expressive of "communion of mother and child";*(178)* "of physiological continuity of child and mother, person and world"; *(179)* and of "the prototaxic mode" of unconscious processes. *(180)*

Even up to twenty months most communicating with the infant is via the prerationative, the demonstrable, the contactual, and the behavioral. In her communing, through the subliminal, the inchoate, the allusive, and the metaphorical, the mother is communicating, through her unique idioms, the idioms of the world, the extended family of persons, personing across time.

As there is sensitivity, respect, and love for what Scott calls that being's "Critical Periods of Behavior Development,"*(237)* what the communing ones communicate will be the most deeply and extensively embedded behavior patterns, the best "remembered" of those early learned idioms.

In the course of her analysis, Rose B. became aware of experiencing, almost literally for the first time, a mother's capacity of communing with her infant, only in this instance it was with her grandson. While a delightful experience, it also awakened painful recollections of her children's infancy twenty-five years earlier when she was unable to have such experiences with them.

What happened occurred after she had become acquainted with and had experienced feelings of rhythmicity in all aspects of her being. Being in tune with her natural rhythms, she could be aware of the disturbed natural rhythms in her grandson.

She had cared for her grandson frequently and with much pleasure from his birth. He was her first grandchild. His changing from day to day was an endless source of curiosity and joy to her. At the same time, she was poignantly aware of not having been part of this mutual process with her own children.

She communed with her grandson while both were silent, quiet, and still; and when he was awake and moving. She communed with him by holding his gaze when he first began to follow her with his eyes. She mimicked his facial movements, gestures, and sounds as he discovered and manifested them. There were also the many aspects of communing that went with being held, fondled, fed, diapered, and bathed. One outstanding form of communing was through cooing sounds and through singing to him in a soft, gentle voice. As he grew older, rhythmic sounds, such as gurgles and music, meant very much to him, and were the basis for endless little games.

One afternoon when he was four months old, she gave him his bottle. After finishing it, he fell asleep in his crib — only to awaken screaming a half hour later. She picked him up and patted his back to help him belch. He did burp some, and she put him back in his crib. When his screaming resumed, she looked to see if a pin was sticking him, or if he needed cleaning and diapering. These would be normal procedures of any mother, and Rose carried them out slowly and quietly. Because he enjoyed exercising his lungs from time to time, she allowed him to scream a bit longer before trying something else.

185

Rose now let him scream, but she held his gaze and made soft, cooing sounds. She then began slowly and gently to rub his belly, although she could not say why when I asked her later. As she did so, he became quieter, only to resume his screaming when she stopped. After several interruptions, she noted an increased intentness of his gaze which she returned. He then began to strain and flush which she also imitated. After a while, he passed some gas, and his face was immediately wreathed in smiles which his grandmother again mimicked.

As soon as she stopped rubbing his belly, he began to whimper. Rose resumed her belly rubbing. Again his gaze became intent, with straining, flushing and, this time, grunting sounds, all of which his grandmother repeated. After a few minutes, he passed a large hard stool, following which his face was again wreathed in smiles. These his grandmother mimicked while making pleasurable sounds of approval. She then cleaned and held him for a while. After putting him in his crib, he fell soundly to sleep until his evening bottle.

This happening was possible because in her analysis Rose had opened herself to, become acquainted with, and begun to enjoy the many dimensions of her biological rhythms. In this happening there was communicating by sight, sound, gesture, actions, and the many elements of her presence. Through all these means she restored the basic biological continuity of mothering one's and infant which is communing. Communing was obtaining.

Of crucial import in their communing were sounds and rhythms. The grandmother is talented musically and has musically talented children, one something of a prodigy. Her grandson, now fifteen years old, shows evidence of musical gifts. He has emotional problems for which he is getting help. His grandmother became aware that she had spoiled him. However, there is also a deep and special bond of love between them which is rare.

It is the analyst's task to learn the idioms of those seeking help so that he can hear, understand, and communicate ways of learning, so that his patients may unlearn their familiar idioms and their consequences and learn to learn new ways and new idioms appropriate to their uniqueness as changing, evolving human beings moving in the direction of straighter growing. This means the analyst must be alert to idioms pointing at his patient's assets, which he once knew and forgot, has known only distortedly, or has never known and experienced.

This openness to idioms, this comprehensive knowing essential to the development of healthy and harmonious human integrating, is evident in Horney's theory and technique. "The road of analytic therapy is an old one, advocated time and again throughout human history. In the terms of Socrates and Hindu philosophy, among others, it is the *road to reorientation and self-knowledge*. What is new and specific about it is the method of gaining self-knowledge, which we owe to the genius of Freud."*(49, p. 341)* Self-knowledge "is not an aim in itself, but a means of liberating the forces of spontaneous growth. In this sense, to work at ourselves becomes not only the prime moral obligation, but at the same time, in a very real sense, the prime moral *privilege."(49, p. 15)*

In reference to the working through of neurotic processes, Horney warns that *"becoming aware of all these factors does not mean having information about them, but having knowledge of them."* Furthermore, the neurotic's "knowledge of himself must not remain an intellectual knowledge, though it may start this way, but must become an *emotional experience."(49, pp. 341-42)*

Fromm-Reichmann also affirms this position: "Working through should be continued until the time is reached when the intellectual understanding of this problem, of its previously dissociated causes, and of its various interlocking mental and emotional ramifications is gradually transformed into real creative emotional insight."*(151, p. 95)* Alexander emphasized that remembering "an intimidating or demoralizing event" is not enough. There must be a "new experience," and it must be "corrective." It "must undo the effect of the old . . . the patient is suffering not so much from his memories as from his incapacity to deal with his actual problems of the moment."*(224)* This is reminiscent of Horney's emphasis on the actual situation and mine on here-now experiencing.

So that there will be more of comprehensive knowing, we must go the way of relating, exhausting its experiential possibilities.

Relating, a process, is an aspect of that moving matrix, the therapeutic process. While relating, patient and therapist are now subject and now object for each other. This is an expression of the human dilemma, says May. It arises out of man's capacity to experience himself both as subject and object at the same time. May uses the word dilemma in the sense of polarity or paradox. He makes it clear that he is not describing two alternate ways of behaving, nor does he feel it is quite accurate to speak of our being subject and object simultaneously. His focus is on consciousness where there is a process of oscillation between the two. From moment to moment, being subject or being object predominates in the foreground of our awareness. *(238)*

In their studies in "pure phenomenological psychiatry (ppp)," Brody and Oppenheim have attempted to confront the "Tension in Psychology Between the Methods of Behaviorism and Phenomenology." They recognize that "Whoever attempts to describe a non-conceptualized experience can do so only by a process of conceptualization which distorts and impoverishes the experience. Therefore, an experiencer who attempts to describe his conceptualized experience without loss of content must in fact be speechless." Nonetheless they feel there can be a "rapprochement . . . by assigning complementary roles for ppp and behaviorism."*(239)*

For explaining communing clearly, the tools are lacking, perhaps because at bottom it is unexplainable. I can attempt to communicate what it is by citing instances. In describing such experiences, I am immediately confronted with a paradox similar to those of May and Brody and Oppenheim. I must describe situations and events where and when there is no I standing outside and reflecting on the process.

With their limitations, examples can point a direction, illuminate the way to, and prompt recollections of similar experiences. The latter has happened following the reading or presentation of such instances. More often such awareness happens in a group situation. Most frequently it occurs in the one to one situation of therapy or in a crucial life situation involving an intense emotional upheaval.

In the following instance communing was most intense, mainly from my side.

The analytic work of Anthony V., a very intelligent, middle-aged married man, extended over seventeen years, with interruptions, in three continents with seven different analysts. A businessman, highly successful, his passion was painting. He would become intensely involved for varying periods and then not be able to touch a brush for years. People of discernment had said he could be a great painter if he devoted himself to it. One crucial interfering factor was a lifelong competition with a younger brother, his mother's favorite, over whom he must not triumph. Close to triumph, several times, he always destroyed the opportunity.

On a visit to New York, after a month of analysis, he interrupted because he felt his analyst had not been sufficiently attentive or interested when he showed him his paintings. He had brought them to New York at great expense. Because of his ambivalence, it required overcoming quite some internal blocks to dare to show them to someone. From what emerged, I felt he was not happy with his therapist even before showing him his paintings. That incident only hurried the break.

He suggested three sessions weekly, in the beginning, but soon asked for five because his time in New York was limited to a period of ten weeks. As the termination of his stay approached, I saw him on occasion six and seven times weekly.

Only after five weeks, when he had sufficient trust in me, did he bring in his paintings. On entering the office, he put them up one after another across the couch, on chairs, and on the floor. He then waited for my response. I was not interested in the chronological sequence, and he later told me they were not so arranged, although there were examples from the fifteen years that he had painted.

It was Saturday, when I rarely see patients. He was my only patient that day. I was aware; I was very open and receptive. I had no idea what would come out of me. Vaguely there were feelings of awe and unease as I communicated to him succinctly my feeling responses to what was in the bowels of each painting.

I could almost feel my whole being pointing at the depths of each painting. Sometimes it expressed itself as being focused on the bottom of a painting, and at others it felt like I was focusing through and beyond the painting. I was aware of not being interested in content and even being somewhat annoyed with it. I felt myself pushing content aside. It was as though I experienced it as an intruder on essence. This response was also slightly stimulated by Anthony V.'s focus on content and on interpretation.

I was definitely not interpreting but communing, responding and communicating my responding. My responding and the depths of what I felt in the paintings were one. I was communing with the paintings. No. Communing was obtaining. The paintings were the vehicles for contacting Anthony V. as he was at the time he painted them and now. Then and now were experienced as continuous and one.

The whole process of looking at, and commenting on, the fourteen paintings took about an hour and a half. As I went on, I was aware of Anthony only peripherally, while I centered on and in the paintings. As a response to being excluded, to the import of what I was saying, and to what was happening in him, from what he said and asked I knew he was becoming increasingly disturbed at the intensity of his being moved. From time to time he tried to get me to focus on content, but I kept pushing his suggestion aside and soon he gave up.

The next day he told me how stirred and disturbed he had been. He said that on occasion he had been moved in his previous analytic experiences by something that had been said; but thus far in his work with me, he had been moved more often and more deeply. This time, with the paintings, he had been moved more deeply and intensely than at any time in his life.

The day following he playfully and anxiously started to ask me for my responses to my own paintings. I was aware of becoming annoyed. I experienced what he was doing as cheapening what we had had together and that he was making a trick of something awesome. I didn't want to be sharp with him, but got across to him that my paintings had been acquired in quite different contexts and had quite different meanings for me. Our situation was unique. He had painted the pictures. I knew quite a bit about him. We were in an analytic situation.

At the close of the Saturday session he asked me to keep the paintings because he had to go downtown and didn't want to carry them with him. Actually, this was a deep declaration of trust. All this paved the way for the intensity of our work in the succeeding weeks, and particularly in the last week before he left for home.

Relying on the depth of his trust and the experiences we had had, particularly on that Saturday, I pushed him harder and harder into his past. I pressed him for recollections regarding three key female figures. They were caring, loving servants — simple people who had been with him from infancy into his teens. Many positive memories came through. There had been mounting annoyance at my pressure and as a repercussion to those positive recollections. Then came mounting irritation and anger against his father and his brother.

He next brought up his masochistic affairs with women. A breakthrough awareness followed concerning the intensity of his sadism and cruelty and his passion to dismember and to mutilate. These awarenesses frightened him because of their nature and intensity. He was also pleased because he somehow knew all his life that these feelings were there, like a deep festering abscess that had never been opened.

He now understood a crucial incident in his childhood when he had asked another boy to humiliate him, his terror of his passion in his first affair, his terror of triumphing over his brother, and the vicissitudes of his painting. There followed a flood of dreams replete with symbols related to his childhood, clearly dealing with and illuminating all the above. He commented that he felt lighter in his being than he ever had in his life.

As the time for his departure approached, he said each day that on the next he would take his paintings with him. On the last day, he almost left without them. Reluctantly, he put them in his new portfolio and departed. I never heard from him again.

I am highly interested in reading the changing patternings in paintings, in seeing the forms as arrangements, invested with color and content, as a process. I read them from my depths as a continuum;

hence, I prefer to look at, quickly in one session, a whole spectrum of paintings.

Over the years, as I have come to know myself as instrument better, I know when I am open and receptive and when not. In the latter case, I realize that it was not the time for me evaluate or purchase paintings, art objects, house furnishings, or clothes. When open, I can make decisions involving many purchases in a few minutes. In fact, when it is taking longer, and I begin to hesitate, I realize today is not the day and desist.

I spent a summer near an artist colony and came to know a number. One — Henry R. — I came to know particularly well. At one point he spread out before me paintings he selected from the previous sixteen years' work. There were over fifty. I looked them all over in less than an hour.

As I looked over Henry R.'s paintings I was very open and read my responses as they happened. I conjectured what he was feeling at various points and what might have been happening in human relations. At one point I experienced a passionate intensity of feelings. Later it was confirmed that he was having an intense love affair at the time. Not long after, my feeling responses were of disturbance, depression, and destructiveness, and I had it confirmed that he had ended the affair and broken off all relations with women.

Over the sixteen years represented, first the human figures disappeared, even in a diagrammatic form, then animals, and finally plant forms. The paintings became more abstract, broken up, and fragmented. I also followed the colors used and their intensity. He became more isolated and remote. A versatility, inventiveness, and virtuosity in the handling of materials and techniques which had been outstanding fell away. There was a dead remoteness about Henry when I knew him. His feelings would occasionally still burst through in the richness and violence of the colors red, green, and yellow, but the forms became more abstract and fragmented. I last heard about him ten years later, when I was told he had stopped painting.

During that same summer, another painter showed me a friend's paintings, charcoals, and pencils produced over fifteen years. I read them as I had those of Henry R. and Anthony V. His friend corroborated what I said about a man I had never seen.

Such experiences with artists and their productions are another evidence of the use of the person as instrument communing, responding, resonating, and communicating.

Since descriptions of actual instances help only to a point, the relating process must be relied upon. An experienced guide helps the novice relinquish his attachments to the dualisms and oppositional dichotomies of intellection. By rigorous disciplines, he drives the novice back more and more into the experiencing process which means total organismic participation. These practices have been used by sages in the various systems of yoga and Zen, by Sufi mentors, and by confessors in the Christian world. I feel they are an integral and essential aspect of the experiencing process in psychoanalysis. Pushed to the ultimate "there can be awareness without anything of which awareness is aware — hence, a state of pure lucidity."*(188, p. 187)* Then the dualisms and dichotomies in thinking, willing, feeling, and being will have ceased. Then there are only oneness feelings. More accurately this state of being might be described as secondlessness.

The poet, Burnshaw, for whom "words are also biology," presents a similar thesis. A poem is an involuntary expression of the poet's total organism. The poem is a physical assault on the reader's body. Poetry is opposed to the fetters of culture and science. The latter assume an "I," an abstraction made into a concretion, separate from the "continuity with the environment."

The poet in creating his poem is expressing his "drive to regain . . . his primary organic unity with the rest of creation: his 'dreamlessness.' " The creation of a poem is "an act of uniting." Burnshaw adds, "and to respond by experiencing its act of uniting is to relive for the duration and with the whole of one's being, an indefinable sense of organic creature unity such as pervaded our creature-existence when it 'knew' itself part of the seamless web of creation."*(240)*

Through the comprehensive knowing evident in Horney's theory via the relating process, one is more able to freely move up and down the metaphorical symbolic spiral and contact the ground of all knowing which is prior to all forms and intellection in the human sense. One becomes one with his own organicity, and with the wider organicity of others and of nature. He regains "continuity with" his environment, and attains biological "at-oneness" with the world, with "all that one senses and knows," in the words of Burnshaw.

I feel with him that the dreamer, in creating his dream, his poem, is assaulting his separateness. Further assaulting occurs via the relating process in which there is more of evenly hovering attending, of freer associating, and of contacting each other's unconscious processes. Communing becomes more possible through such eventing.

Just as analysts have been critical of my attempts to make possible communing because it might lead to psychosis, particularly with people with weak egos having ill defined boundaries, so have there been criticisms of Burnshaw. The issue of the *poète maudit* is a real one. There have been mad poets and poets who went mad through the exercise of the poetic vocation. What was developed in chapter 4 regarding the artist and the creative process may be a corrective to such fears. In my experience, madness and disorganization can but need not happen.

That large masses of people live constantly in the poetic mode without having a higher rate of insanity than other groups is evident in those who speak and paint Chinese, Japanese, and Korean. Their language is not written prose but painted poetry, a moving matrix of forms which describes a process. It is open-ended, allusive, poetic, and emphasizes the emotive and the intuitive. In the evolution of language, the immediate, the subjective, the concrete, the impressionistic and the pragmatic had primacy until the objectifying attitude gained ascendancy, an evolution necessary for the development of science.

In their current daily living, in their communications with one another, the Japanese rely very much on what Westerners name telepathy but what they call *i-shin denshin*. It means "heart-to-heart transmission." Another word for this everyday form of communication is *hara-gei*, or the "art of the belly." Rose B. used "the art of the belly" to communicate with her grandson. A young man said, "My golf is best when I hit the ball with my belly." This was no metaphor but a very real experience he had had on a number of occasions.

During his personal analysis and his work with patients, through comprehensive knowing and relating, during group, dyadic, and self-analysis, the analyst comes to know his person as instrument with wider and deeper intimacy. Through his evenly hovering attending and his contacting more dimensions of his depths, the gaps between the existing irrationalities and the ultimate of rationality narrow. He can avail himself of awarenesses formulated as techniques which will facilitate his contacting in and outside the analytic situation.

I have had such contacting experiences while running and swimming, and when experiencing the awesome grandeur of nature on lakes in high mountains. *(241)* In the analytic situation, some experiences which began almost thirty years ago have a significance of which I only gradually became aware. As I focused on them they became sharper. Gradually I could identify more pieces of the experiences. As I did so, I identified a whole process which I became more experienced in using in the analytic situation.

The examples to be mentioned are exceptional, used to highlight the points being made. Though out of the usual, they are prototypical of many less dramatic, quite subtle instances pointing at aspects of this total experience.

A patient comes in and lies down on the couch. I begin note taking and notice I am underlining certain words. This I often do quite spontaneously. The more unaware, the more valuable these underlined words tend to be as guides. When I look back over several pages, they often make a clarifying pattern.

Another sequence of note taking may also occur. I begin to notice the underlinings are coming too close together or are making quite irregular patterns. I get the feeling something is not making sense. I become restless, even anxious, and irritated. I may then stop the underlining and, in time, the note taking as well. I let go to be as open as possible to listening to myself and to the patient with the whole of myself.

Now listening, I become aware of something that had happened earlier in the session that had led to writing notes, at times excessively, and to underlining too much and rather haphazardly. Having become uncertain about what was going on and being anxious and irritable, I had resorted to these devices. When it was impressed on me that something was amiss, I *let go*. Let go is apt because I had been clutching and hanging on. That behavior had resulted in my becoming squeezed and constricted. As I let go, my awareness expanded, and what had been going on became clearer.

But at times this does not happen. I still cannot make sense out of what the patient was saying. I began to feel beaten upon by the barrage of sounds, words, and ideas and slowly become deaf to it.

What I now do is almost indescribable because to speak of *doing* sounds inaccurate. It is a different kind of doing by which I can let go still further. Sounds, words, and ideas become remote and vague as a consequence of letting go and through focusing more centrally. This process is aided by a concomitant blocking out of auditory impingements. There is a greater looseness and relaxation of my body. I melt into my chair. My eyes spontaneously close and block out visual distractions. I also become aware of withdrawing attention from my body sensations.

I am now more open and available for contact with what is deeper in myself and in my patient. As this is obtaining, there is more relating which in time passes over to communing. In an auditory sense, at times I am not hearing my patients. After this process has been going on for a time, what I begin to feel gets expressed as "So that's what he's talking about" or "So that's what he's trying to tell me." I then have feelings of relief, release, relaxation, and pleasure.

The possibilities of what I might say begin to suggest themselves. It might take the form of a question or comment. Not infrequently before the session is over, the patient will communicate, at times explicitly, that he now knows where he is going.

He may report feeling more relaxed and realize that he had been tense, anxious, and confused earlier in the session. He might add that as soon as I commented, or shortly thereafter, those earlier unpleasant feelings began to go. With more experience with these happenings, I can identify them earlier. My patients are thereby helped to experience their dilemmas sooner, and to more quickly and effectively resolve them.

In the next instance, I could in retrospect recall mild feelings of unease and awe associated with the pleasures of discovery. The unease was connected more with the awareness of my ability to let go of and block out upper noise levels and/or upper levels of my metaphorical symbolic spiral. The unease may also have been a response to letting go of the known and sinking into the unknown of my greater depths, leaving to chance what I might come upon.

When it will happen I can never predict nor can I make it happen. It is more likely to happen because of my readiness and openness for such experiences in the light of previous ones. Much of what is subsumed under communing is prepared for and present the more I can be the seven attributes and the nine modes of being. What I will describe is related to the whole realm of the paranormal and of psi-phenomenon — a field which becomes more respectable as more sophisticated research designs and refined apparatus to collect data and to test hypotheses are developed.

I begin to know the experience is happening when I become aware of an intense kind of total concentration and openness coming upon me. The experience can occur with the patient on the couch or facing me. I am more sharply aware of it in the *vis-à-vis* position. The feeling can be described as one in which the physical boundaries of the two of us are not relevant, nor is our concept of ourselves, nor our feeling of identity. This is negatively saying that to even feel or think in terms of separateness or togetherness is irrelevant. I am of course aware at all times that we have separate physical beings.

Attempting to describe this experience confronts me with the utter inadequacy of words. It is no evasion that so many speak of these states and other similar ones as ineffable and indescribable.

My patient is talking and I am listening and feeling my patient's being at the same time. I am aware of feeling this is happening to me. I am not simply listening to, but being at my patient's core of being and my core of being simultaneously. I am aware of the clarity and accuracy of what I feel and am going to say even before I say it. My patients confirm it almost every time, often quite explicitly.

This feeling of being at the core can last for a few moments to a whole session. As it is happening, I am aware of feelings of wariness, unease, awe, and maybe something close to dread. I feel that what is happening is not to my credit, but is rather a gift given into my keeping for the moment, and that it would be presumptuous to feel that it is mine. I am also aware of my aversion to talk about this experience. This is one of the very rare times I have written about it.

This feeling will continue in a session as long as I do not interfere with it by what might be called personal attitudes. When I say that what is happening has almost nothing to do with me and my patient, I mean by comparison with the vastness at which the happening points. Our share I feel is infinitesimal. All we can do is prepare ourselves for it to happen, be open to its happening, not interfere with it as it is happening, and be aware that the intrusion of the personal interferes with, detracts from, and may even prevent it from developing more fully or coming again.

This experience generally occurs only with patients who have been in analysis a number of years with me or with others. Our relationship is a deep and firm one in which there is basic trust and confidence. More important is the determination, tenacity, and incentive of such patients. The percentage of such happenings is higher with people having artistic sensitivity, but they may also occur with those having a deep creative wisdom. In my experience, it has occurred more frequently with women.

With these patients, I feel I can put considerable reliance on their being able to continue on their own as I leave them on one level to recontact them from a deeper one. This ability to stand on their own is rare. Most patients can sense this being left and become anxious, even panicked. Patients can sense my leaving even while on the couch. One patient could detect changes in my breathing patterns almost immediately and moments later pick up nuances of change in my ways of being. He could also pick up changes in the pattern of my note taking. Another who sat *vis-à-vis* went into a panic when I closed my eyes as part of the process of going into myself. I desisted thereafter because I saw his terror, his vulnerability, and because he pleaded with me not to close my eyes, unaware of what had really cued off his distress.

Since I first became aware of these happenings, major developments have gone on in the study of sleep, dreams and psi-phenomena. *(242)* Reports have gone from the anecdotal to the observation of spontaneous happenings and controlled experimentation. That such things happen is becoming acceptable. How they happen, and what brings them about is still conjectural. Formulations for conceiving these happenings are not yet available, but there are enough studies to show that people differ in their capacity for such happenings. In those with whom it can happen, the factors of rapport and emotional climate have been found crucial. Many other factors are being considered that might account for the higher rate of these happenings through enhanced mutual attunement.

These descriptions of processes going on in me in these happenings adds additional dimensions to the meaning of the person of the therapist as his most important instrument in therapy. As this instrument becomes more refined, more of these happenings do and can occur. The following example describes the effects of such processes on a patient who in the beginning of analysis and for some years was cold, callous, unfeeling, stony, and inaccessible. This example also describes aspects of the opening to process and of the "self-propelled feeling process" described in chapter 6.

In a session, Arthur G. said, "I wonder what it feels like to have my own feelings." At the same time he mentioned his tendency not to tell me facts about himself. He had been recognizing for some time his sullen, cold, and venomous ungivingness.

About a week later, Arthur opened the session with mention of a date with a passive girl the previous night. By her passivity she forced him to be active. "I know what you were talking about now when you say how active passivity is. That girl gave me a rough time the other night. She wouldn't let me be passive."

Later in the session he said, "I notice sometimes, like when you look at me and then you seem remote, but when you talk you are right there. It's like when you say something from your understanding to another me, a bigger me. I'm getting very anxious now. I'm feeling very scared. It feels like I want to run away. It was like when I was a kid and other kids were after me and wanted me to fight and I couldn't fight and I ran away."

Several weeks later in a session he said, "I feel a process in my chest. It's opposed to something and is pushing it back. I want free space in myself to move around. Now I feel feelings of feelings coming up in me." As he said this he had the fingertips of both hands pointing at his chest. "I feel that ague now." By ague, Arthur meant the shaking of his neck and head that soon involved his trunk and whole body. This had been occurring slightly for several years and with progressive intensity in the past year, up to two or three times each session. He continued, "I'm thinking now. I'm trying to figure things out and I hate it."

This sequence occurring over about a month was of course presaged by much experiencing of his passivity, the pull toward it and the beginning opposition to it. With this went his wondering what it would be like "to have my own feelings." These processes made it possible for him to experience my looking at him and then being remote as well as my talking to "another me, a bigger me." This was communing and contacting of each other's cores. What he said about "pushing" something back, wanting inner "free space . . . to move around in" made it possible for "feelings of feelings" to come up in him which were followed by intense, totally involving repercussions.

After years of a difficult analysis, a woman was in a group in which the discussion of the meaning of surrender in a mystic and spiritual sense come up, particularly as it might occur during a personal crisis. She was so moved that, even though it was quite late when she arrived home, she wrote out what it meant to her:

A feeling of surrender, in a mystic sense, as I have experienced it in analysis, is gaining a deep insight into oneself, as a result of great psychological stress. It is a feeling which is experienced from the inner depths, really from the bottom up, so to speak, real pangs of labor resulting in rebirth. [Later, on three separate occasions, she experienced on the couch the actual birth process, with sensations of a fetus moving down and out of the birth canal, followed by feelings of rebirth.] Genuinely felt as an act of creation, it bears with it a feeling of wonder and gratification — the wonder being of a mystical or spiritual nature which is inexplicable, derived from a feeling of humility from the rock bottom realization of the smallness of *I* midst the vastness of all. This is a feeling which reaches a peak of painful intensity, like an orgasm. It is yielding unconditionally and spontaneously to a feeling experience which, reaching its height, tapers off into an ensuing and all enveloping warmth of satisfaction and relief. The knowledge of a rare and fervent experience is left, to be treasured as precious unto oneself and forever contained thereafter. It is an incentive to living — life become invaluable and creation incalculable. Enjoyment and pain are intertwined and the discovery of how little the *I* is in the whole of life makes it more vital as a component of the whole, and as such it is to be respected, loved, cherished, and wondered about with faith in its integrity and hope in its identity with prospects for fulfillments.

In the next two years she had more such experiences. In time, they were less intense. In short, once having experienced the dramatic forms, she could experience the more subtle ones. One of them she described in a session right after having gone through it.

I see more and more that awareness is much bigger. Seeing something once is not enough. Something bigger is being born in me. Rhythms are becoming more important to me. As I'm talking I don't feel like I'm closing up. This week is associated with much suffering. I know now that it's attached to deeper awareness. I feel so much more relaxed than I used to feel. So much more a person than I used to feel. So much more with myself though I'm still running away. So much more part and parcel of everything now. Because I am a part of it, it is part of me. I feel so much more belonging to myself. So much more feeling I don't have to say something special which used to weave in and out. I still do evade things. I've got to keep tackling it. My sick part of me. There is still a lot more to that running away business.

She was more in and of what she described. It was less intense and dramatic. She knew where she was and where she had to go. A year later she said, "I am feeling a flowing apart and a coming together with you. But when I feel flowing apart and coming together in me, I feel it is all me. When I felt a flowing apart from you, I felt separate but not isolated, and when I felt a flowing together with you, I didn't feel submerged. I still felt me. Oh, it takes so many words to say it. And I felt it all in a moment and for several minutes."

Here is described separateness without isolation, coming together without loss of ego boundaries. Rather than schizophrenic panic or longer lasting episodes of psychic disorganization, there is evidence of increasing strength. Ultimately, this woman talked about these happenings less. During a session she would become silent for moments or longer. When she resumed talking, she told me more often by implication that there had been feelings of quietness, stillness, and serenity — feelings of secondlessness in which identity, continuity, and contiguity were not relevant. Communing was obtaining.

Communing is ultimately being — not the being of existential philosophies, although such being does participate in, and aid movement toward, that form of being to which I am referring. Communing might be pointed at by what is expressed in Hindu philosophy by "Atman is Brahman and Brahman is Atman." The sharpest and the clearest communications regarding the nature of communing are those available to a participant observer who can be open to the caring communion of mother and infant. This organic communion is widely evident at all age levels in the world of the so-called primitive.

In their world, all of nature, animate and inanimate is palpitatingly alive. It is a world of dynamic correspondences. The symbol and substance are identical. Knowing is nonconceptual awareness. It is having immediate knowledge. Knowing is influencing. The paranormal is normal. In this "society of life," our concept of self and identity cannot exist because, through initiation rites, one becomes identical with the collectivity without acquiring individuality in our sense. Through these rites, the myth of the "great beginning" is re-created. Time is cyclically reconstituted with recurrent sameness.

Anthropologists report that in pre-literate groups confirmed knowing of happenings at a distance and of happenings before they take place are not uncommon. In addition, they respond to what white men have dreamt without having been told. One bushman told van der Post "that there was a dream dreaming us." On this safari into the wild swamps of the Kalahari, a gigantic buffalo came straight at van der Post and still he withheld his fire. "Only one thing saved me. I was not afraid."*(243, pp. 261, 160)*

That night the scene of the buffalo was much with him. "I felt that the encounter had for a moment made me immediate, and had . . . closed a dark time-gap in myself. With our twentieth-century selves we have forgotten the importance of being truly and openly primitive . . . . We no longer know how to close the gap between the far past and the immediate present in ourselves. We need primitive nature, the first man in ourselves . . . . Of all the nostalgias that haunt the human heart the greatest of them all, for me, is an everlasting longing to bring what is youngest home to what is oldest in us all."*(243, p. 162)*

Man has created the magic world, the world of the East and the West, and the ways of communing and communicating in and with them. In the summer of 1967, on a visit through Indonesia, and again in 1969, I was informed by psychiatrists there that, because of Indonesian history, when sophisticated, westernized, Indonesians break down, it is essential to distinguish pathological thought content from what is naturally there of animistic thought, of thought of the East reflected through Hinduism or Buddhism, and of Western thought expressed mostly in Mohammedan, Christian, and atheistic forms. *(244)*

All these forms of thinking were created by man and are available to him. Piaget's genetic epistemology seems to support this contention. He does not suggest a naive ontological recapitulation of phylogeny nor that the possible resemblances between "the thought of the child and that of primitive man" with "some parallels with Greek physics are due to any kind of heredity. The permanence of the laws of mental development suffice to expose all these convergences and since all men, including 'primitive men' started by being children, childhood thinking preceded the thought of our most distant ancestors just as it does ours." The sensorimotor egocentricity of the infant and child results in animism, finalism, and artificialism.

"If the pre-Socratics created a philosophical system around ideas implicit in the thinking of modern-day children, then it is reasonable to suppose that, as children, the pre-Socratics had similar ideas which, as adults, they proceeded to elaborate into a comprehensive philosophy." The notion that "the movement of a body is explained by virtue of the combination of an external trigger and an internal force" present in a modern child's thought, was present in Aristotle's physics also. The child's conception of age is also "reminiscent of the ancient Greeks' idea of 'becoming,' and this similarity is yet another indication that childish thought resembles the static and relatively unoperational approach of the ancients."(244a, pp. vii, 27-28)

Arieti's views seem also to support my view that the sources for the creation of a fourth cosmic consciousness are inherent. Like Piaget, he does not believe in any literal recapitulation "but that there are certain similarities in the three fields of development [phylogeny, ontogeny, and microgeny], and that we are able to individualize schemes of highest forms of generality which involve all levels of the psyche in its three types of development." He indicates in a footnote that J. Huxley follows "a similar developmental approach in general biology."(153, p. 6)

My position is that a fourth cosmic consciousness, a new unitive world view, can and must be created. With the breakdown of the value systems of the West which have had obligating power for centuries and which were integral to the creation of science, there is now much greater availability for moments of communing and experiences of kairos (see chapter 26). Existentialism has returned us to the experience of dread. Awe and wonder has been maintained in the scientific spirit and attitude.

I believe that communing is a universal human possibility; that as a form of being, it is essential for being human, for self-realizing, for realizing others, and for openness to the cosmos and the spiritual dimension. Tillich uses "spirit" to mean that which characterizes "Man as man, and expresses itself as moral self-realization; as cultural production, and as religious self-transcendence. It is a power which gives liberation from the binding quality of law, culture, and religion." He urges the reestablishment of this doctrine of man as spirit, as the unity of all the dimensions of man. (245) Burtt affirms his philosophical position: "The whole structure of the science of man, theoretical as well as practical, must be reconstructed so that it will harmonize with our moral and spiritual vision, and will become an effective instrument for its progressive realization."(246)

I have presented my experiences with, and ideas on, communing and kairos in the United States, Europe, and Asia, before people guided by a spectrum of religions, ethical systems, and philosophies. In each audience, without fail, one or more reported such happenings in themselves and the existence of such concepts in their belief system. So often, at the moment of recounting their experiences, they were a manifestation of what they were telling me. The spirit and quality of their communication was not of an "I" who had had that experience communicating appreciation to a "me" for having recalled them to their experience. Their manner was a manifestation of those attributes and modes of being of the person of the analyst as instrument. This manner of being describes the being of the sage-guru-master-priest-teacher-therapist-helper-healer as he approximates the ultimate possible in communing while communicating his being *vis-à-vis* another.

Bally's views move in directions similar to mine. He evolved them against the background of his scholarship in philosophy and sociology, his ideas about Freudian psychoanalysis and the place of psychoanalysis in the context of our social structure. "Psychoanalysis today is confronted with a problem which at Freud's time was not yet as urgent as today," said Bally. "The fact that the manner of existing and the reality structure are now recognized to be complementary and that reality does not exist independently . . . pushes us to our interest in the existential problem and its interpretations. Our changing world teaches us to understand human existence as unity of being and world, as being-in-the world.

"The new challenge we have to meet thus confirms the original task of psychoanalysis: to reveal, develop and structure through analytic communication an appropriate character, able to live courageously in a changing world."(247)

In his "Sociological Aspects of Psychoanalysis," Bally amplifies his interpretation of human existence. It differs from that of Boss, with whom Bally was associated for many years. "The charisma of priestly authority," says Bally, "was . . . anchored in the common consent" of what was believed to be sinful and that is now gone. In a competitive, bourgeois society, "one's significance for others as well as for oneself must be achieved and sustained by performance. Health is the primary factor in the acquisition of status, that is, the maintenance and the improvement of the social position." Scientifically oriented medicine has made man's body healthy so it can serve the "tool function" of "performance." But because of psychic illness some do not "want" to recover and for this situation psychoanalysis becomes the medicine.*(248)*

But that can operate only so long as "the paternal authority" is instrumental in establishing "a success that gave inner and outer security." But even in Freud's time, sons were already freeing themselves from their father's authority. Today we not only have "fatherless" societies, but "motherless" and "parentless" ones as well. Bally continues: "The relationship to parents and siblings becomes meaningless. The relationship to peer groups . . . are decisive for the social role." Where the contact succeeds, whatever the basis, it provides "a feeling of absolute belonging . . . . The group is chosen in the passionate expectation that it will assign that status which gives basic security in the wider world, status through which we obtain 'primordial trust' (Erikson)."

When this does not happen, because of the failure of parents and of society, "Patient and doctor are . . . faced with the task of establishing self-assurance which is independent of achievement in order to provide the patient with the basic security in the society, the 'primordial trust,' which carries him through all the changing roles he will have to play." These parentless, homeless, societyless ones "must experience the analyst not as the authoritarian father-ideal, but as representative and spokesman for an ideal group which will finally receive him and give him meaning and purpose."*(248)*

Here Bally is describing what is reminiscent of Cassirer's *"society of life,"* with its deep conviction of a fundamental and indelible *"solidarity of life,"* so "characteristic of primitive mentality." *(249, pp. 109-10)* One is born into the collectivity of life. Each one's identity with it is recurrently revitalized with recurrent sameness through its myth which is thought to express the *"absolute truth"* because it narrates sacred history. "One magically re-enters the Great Time, the sacred time . . . the holy time of the beginning (*in illo tempore*) and unites with and becomes the mythic hero or God or exemplar."*(250, p. 23)*

Bally's ideal society is reminiscent of the so-called primitive society and the functioning of the analyst as "representative and spokesman" is very close to that of being exemplar, hero or God. As an introduction to this society, Bally suggested that in some instances a period of group therapy may be essential as preparation for individual therapy. The group situation is the ideal family situation that that person never had, and it is what youth across the world are creating for themselves. These groups, with their rites and myths, are attempting to create the vehicle and matrix of that communion of mother and infant which was all too little present, if not almost absent. For such communication, relating is essential until its possibilities are exhausted and there are more moments of communing.

Just as history had created that unique human experiment in Indonesia *(244)* it has done likewise in India. In India contact with the magic world was maintained through the guiding mind structure of Eastern thought. All otherness is held close and experienced as identical and juxtaposed, as in the extended family system in India. In the East, neither pleasure nor pain are exalted or degraded. Complementaries and contraries exist side by side. Time is as experienced in the lives of concrete individuals. Indian history is essentially a-historical, a composition of allegories about heroes who fight out the battles of good and evil. Indian cosmology is cyclical and recurrent. *(137, 251)* After eons of evolutions, through many worlds, all comes full circle to start anew. Western individuality is not possible

This became evident with the advent of psychoanalysis, introduced into India by the brilliant Doctor Bose of Calcutta. In an extended correspondence (1921-1938), he sharply differed with Freud regarding "the Oedipus situation" and "the wish to be female" in Hindu male patients. Bose's findings have been confirmed by others and myself, both in India and with Hindus in the United States.

Before the modern era, when an Indian sought help for his problems, he would go to an ashram, an ancient form of group therapy or community psychiatry. This move meant an attempt at contacting the Real. The methods and ideas used were referred to by Haas as *philousia. Ousia* in Greek means essence. Our Western notion of *philosophy* would not apply. In the West we seek knowledge through concepts; in the East the desire is for contact with "essence or Is-ness."*(188, p.134)* In the ashram, the seeker for the Real, the patient, lived with a sage or guru and his disciples.

Today Indians, who have become somewhat westernized, can no longer stand the rigors of an ashram. In some instances, they must first work for a time in analysis before they are capable of it. One Bombay analyst said he often refers his patients, after an analytic experience, to institutes of Yoga. *(253)* Because the westernized Indian has not developed enough ego strength in a Western sense, he can only tolerate short periods of analysis. By interrupting the analysis, he is given an opportunity to integrate what he has gotten and to develop greater ego strength through active living in the community.

This is something quite different from Freud's recommendation that people return for further periods of analysis every five years. This was suggested with the idea that still existing problems not currently available for analysis would become so through the process of living. They would have now evolved, become defined and be more accessible to be worked with.

The following reflects the reverse sequence. For two years, in her late twenties, Laurel Q. was treated by a Freudian analyst for intractable vomiting. In the process, she divorced her husband and the vomiting stopped. Seven years later she remarried; after a year the intractable vomiting recurred. Following two years of work with a second analyst, a neo-Freudian, the vomiting stopped, and after four more years, significant personality change had occurred. She became interested in Indian philosophy, and in the winter of 1967, Laurel spent six weeks with a guru in south India. On her return, the vomiting recurred. When associated with much anxiety, there was also severe diarrhea.

Her knowledge of my interest in the East, plus other factors, healthy and sick, led to her desire to work with me. Her stay in India, her prior and subsequent contact with Indian philosophy, and subsequent visits with her guru and his disciples in the United States have all been of help to her.

She, unlike Indians, had a Western ego, though underdeveloped, weak and malformed. She did not have enough strength to integrate what she had gotten from her first visit to India. Added to this was the debilitating effect of dysentery, which she had gotten in India. In Freudian terms, she was fixated at the oral and anal phases of development with much oral and anal sadistic behavior.

Within a month after her return, the vomiting and the diarrhea stopped. When she began to feel a degree of basic trust in me, there poured out, after several episodes of intense and devastating hatred and assaultiveness open demands to be taken care of like a baby by everyone. All her life she had been the strong giving one, on whom everyone leaned. She was revolted at the role and at herself for having been that way. Attempts to make the analytic relationship "more personal" brought out intense hurt pride and vindictive responses. She gradually became aware of her fear of doing anything for herself, for liking herself, and for being simply happy.

In the last six months of the second year of our work, she went through a long period of nausea, gagging, and anorexia before her evening meal. Gradually a chronic depression, present since infancy, became evident as did the sources of it. Following this came waves of hatred and rage toward her mother in particular, but also toward her father a sweet, weak, cruel man who always let her down when she needed him. Gradually, the terror at the intensity of these attacks and the fear of their disruptive power slowly abated.

She had been told about an extremely traumatic behavior

her mother had perpetrated on her when she was three weeks old. Although as such there had been no "re-experiencing" of those events, she was steadily feeling purged of wells of hate, self-hate, and anxiety never before contacted. There were concomitant radical changes in her feelings about herself. I believe I had been fulfilling the diatrophic functions of the analyst. Contrary to Anna Freud and in agreement with Gitelson and Zetzel, I feel I have been able to help her to the extent I have, although an underlying dependence had never been overcome—independence reached and then lost.

Psychoanalytic literature was first translated into Japanese in 1912, and Freud first appeared in 1930. Dr. Sakaki's *Study of Sexuality and Psychoanalysis* in 1919 was the first Japanese book on psychoanalysis. A few pioneers had very brief periods of analysis in Europe in the '30s. They and their students have analyzed all Japanese analysts. While interest is great, with twenty-five accredited members and eight associate members, there are no formal training analysts or formal training bodies. *(251)*

While Japanese have a deep belief that illness is a state of mind *(Yamai wa Ki kara)*, they reject psychotherapy and psychoanalysis in favor of somatic therapy. What they seek from the West is science, technology, rationalism, and materialism. Consequently, the rich get somatic therapy and the poor get psychotherapy. Besides, psychoanalysis *(sei-shin-bun-seki)* connotes something esoteric or religious, like "spiritual analysis." For such help, patients from lower socioeconomic groups seek the many varieties of indigenous individual and group psychotherapies rooted in traditional and religious practices. The wealthy receive psychoanalysis via the bridge of medication. *(25)*

Paradoxically, the approach to spiritual healing is via physical intervention. A somatic state of receptivity for *satori* is induced. Because of the commonly held belief that character *(seikaku)* is innate and immutable, the attitude toward basic personality change is one of hopelessness while the idea of finding symptom relief is acceptable.

Then there is the unique Japanese version of the Eastern mind structure and the unique structure of its language, ideographic in character, intuitive, aesthetic, emotive and allusive, hardly conducive for communicating concepts formulated in Western prose. Psychoanalytic technique could be applicable in Japan, but Freudian concepts of mind and motivation are still quite alien to the Japanese despite their westernization. *(251)*

And in the West, classical psychoanalysis is inadequate to the emotional and intellectual climate of our present context. The superego concept derivative of a Judeo-Christian ethic and of the primacy

206

of a male parental authority is outmoded. The notion of the id as rock bottom has been radically revised by classical theorists and superseded by ego psychology. The prerequisite of a transference neurosis and what it implies for basic personality change has been questioned by many. A new image of man, based on a new unitive world view derivative of the mind structures of the magic world, of the East and of the West, must emerge to again make possible those forms of communication leading to human communing.

Chapter 13

Blockages—
Resistance

From the moment the analysis begins there are impediments to moving toward its goals. The forces of spontaneous growth do not simply emerge and evolve as the analysis proceeds but are constantly blocked by patterns opposing change. It was Freud's great discovery that while the patient wants to get well he is unconsciously determined to remain ill. As the analyst attempts to help the patient move toward self-realization, he is confronted by the patient's determination to maintain his neurotic patterns. The "Consequences of Unresolved Conflicts" must be brought clearly and explicitly into his awareness. *(39)*

Among these consequences are "fears;" "hopelessness;" "sadistic trends;" and the "impoverishment of the personality" with the devastating *"waste of human"* energies brought about by *"indecisiveness," "ineffectualness,"* and *"inertia."* Moral integrity is impaired by the decrease in sincerity and the burgeoning egocentricity. What follows are innumerable *pretenses* of love, goodness, sympathy, interest, knowledge, honesty, fairness, and suffering. *(39)* An emerging awareness of how his neurosis impairs and impoverishes his life becomes a powerful incentive toward confronting those forces which obstruct his growth.

Blockages are defined as processes that maintain and increase sickness while obstructing growth and the urge toward self-realization. My viewpoint regarding goals in therapy is consonant with Horney's holistic theory of human nature. My goals are not symptom removal, syndrome alleviation, or amelioration of a disease entity, all of which do happen in the course of therapy, but which are incidental to the general goal of helping the individual outgrow his neurotic difficulties while concomitantly assisting his development in the direction of self-realization. The notion "cure" is appropriate to the goal of relief of symptoms. "We cannot 'cure' the wrong course which the development of a person has taken," but we can "assist him in gradually outgrowing it."*(49, p. 333)* There can be no tearing down first and then building up. The very resolution of the neurotic process, namely, the identifying, undermining, and resolving of these patterns is only possible as simultaneously there is an identifying, supporting, and extending of the growing possibilities of the real self system. *(75, 129)*

The real self is postulated as an integrating principle, an ongoing dynamism, not as an entity or a thing to be revealed. "The *real self*" is "that central inner force, common to all human beings and yet unique in each, which is the deep source of growth." By "growth is meant . . . free, healthy development in accordance with the potentials of one's generic and individual nature."*(49, p. 17)*

While at times the analyst may seemingly function like a mirror to reveal the patient's unconscious, much more is required of him. He and the patient are whole persons — not functions — integrating in moving fields and in oscillating equilibrium while mutually influencing each other. If a therapist hasn't grown during the analysis of his patient, I feel the therapy has fallen short of its possibilities.

With what is required of the holistic therapist, it is inevitable that his values will participate. The issue is not whether they should. The fact is they do, and he cannot operate without them. "Since neuroses involve questions of human behavior and human motivations, social and traditional evaluations inadvertently determine the problems tackled and the goal aimed at," Horney said. "My opinion is that an absence of value judgments belongs among those ideals we should try rather to overcome than to cultivate."*(35, pp. 296-97)*

Horney further elaborates her position on moral values: "Man, by his very nature and of his own accord, strives toward self-realization, and his set of values evolves from his striving. Apparently, he cannot, for example, develop his full human potentialities unless he is truthful to himself; unless he is active and productive; unless he relates himself to others in the spirit of mutuality. Apparently he cannot grow if he indulges in a 'dark idolatry of self' (Shelley) and consistently attributes all his shortcomings to the deficiencies of others. He can grow, in the true sense, only if he assumes responsibility for himself."*(49, p. 15)*

While a neurosis can be said to be an individually created value system, it lacks the freedom of creative self-realization. A compulsive pseudomorality, moralizing and moralistic, stems from the entire neurotic defensive system, and it must be distinguished from authentic, spontaneous morality which is the ultimate in being human, whole, and healthy.

The issues of authentic and pseudomorality sharply focus the need for rigorous determination of motivation, objective, means, and consequences. Good things can be done for bad reasons and bad ones for good reasons. The consequences may inadvertently be good or bad because of the operation of chance factors. We must also keep in awareness that motives and means, intents and consequences, whether conscious and unconscious, can be predominantly neurotic in one context, as determined by time, place, and circumstances and predominantly healthy in another. Content can only be understood in the context of the total process of the therapy embedded in, and expressive of, what has immediate, intermediate and ultimate relevance for those involved and participating.

> An example of pseudomorality was related to me by J. W. Vollmerhausen, M.D. The objective of the medical director of a private hospital had authentic values, but it later became apparent that his behavior was dictated by a pseudomorality and had the intent of enhancing the pride invested in it. The hospital was considering the admission of a group of insurance doctors to its staff. The medical director was very much in favor of it and tried to make the hospital board see his point of view which was rather constructive. They refused to go along with him and the admission of the group was blocked. Some time later the board reversed itself and now favored their admission.
>
> It now became a matter of "moral principle" for the director not to capitulate to his board and he now opposed what he had earlier wanted. His reaction was a mixture of vindictiveness for their earlier rejection of his idea, as well as an assertion of his own dominance and an affirmation of one of his very strong needs — "Nobody is going to tell me what to do" — he felt his responses to be morally correct and reacted with righteous indignation at the board's action. What was desired by him at one point became morally wrong for him when his pride in mastery and control were involved.

Horney's *morality of evolution* serves not only as a guide and a direction, but also provides the possibility for the formation of a new identity as the old (pride invested) identity is relinquished. The urge toward self-realization gives the motive power. "Outgrowing his neurotic egocentricity, he will become more aware of the broader issues involved in his particular life and in the world at large. From having been in his own mind the uniquely significant exception, he will gradually experience himself as part of a bigger whole. And he will be willing and able to assume his share of responsibility in it and contribute to it in whatever way he is best able."*(49, p. 365)* The medical director mentioned above was clearly not yet at this point in his development. He was still functioning as a moral automaton enslaved to his pride system, one aspect of what was his pseudomorality.

Horney's position regarding "abstinence," "privation," and "suffering" differs from Freud's because she assumes a momentum coming from the urge toward self-realization. I feel that the patient is *continually* re-creating his own privation, abstinence, and suffering.

With some patients the pressure for immediate relief from pain fills their consciousness and seems their only motivation for coming to therapy. Other patients, who may or may not have the experience of suffering because of their deadness, numbness, and inertia, need a higher level of pain and tension because for them it means aliveness, spurious though it is, until something more genuine replaces it. The analyst must also be alert to pain as an anesthetic and paralytic as well as an addictive narcotic as happens with so-called masochistic patients.

The aim is to maintain the pain, anxiety, and tension at a level most conducive to the work while avoiding unnecessary pain, economizing time, and helping the relationship to develop as rapidly as possible in the direction of basic trust, an issue dealt with extensively in chapter 12. Reviewing Erikson's contributions, Kanzer and Blum add, "Basic trust, not merely basic anxiety or basic sexual needs, should be included in the analysis of the transference neurosis."*(142, p. 122)* By ameliorating and mitigating pain that retards and obstructs, the analysis can be set moving. Diminishing unnecessary pain will be humanly appreciated. Such accruing experiences are essential for the time when the inevitable pain associated with experiencing basic and central conflict, as well as the accessions of anxiety and self-hate connected with the inevitable *"disillusioning process,"* become intense.

Such deepening of trust makes it possible for the patient to accept and seek the analyst's nonintervention in order to attempt being on his own for longer periods while struggling with his problems and knowing his depths.

Awareness that the analyst's values are involved and that counseling and "friendship in the best sense" participate is no false sentimentality or imposition of the analyst's values on his patient. Rather it requires the rigor and clarity of the scientific attitude and of the

211

phenomenologic approach essential to Freud's "evenly-hovering attention." It also asks for moral courage, a prerequisite to confronting human problems humanly and with humility. Then there can be that unity and harmony of dispassionate subjectivity and passionate objectivity in the analyst's use of his person as his most important instrument of therapy.

As he is that unity and harmony, he will be able to define the nature of his patient's pain, tensions, and anxieties. *(144)* He will be able to delineate the nuances of his patient's attitudes toward his pain and the proportions of his suffering which are sick and healthy in their functions, and sources. The issue then becomes how to deal with his patient's suffering so that its irrational proportions become less and the rational proportions increase in ways and intensities appropriate to the situation.

The aim in dealing with the patient's pain is to recognize when he is demanding relief and when he is working toward release from it. With the first goes a compulsion to solve, to deny, to disown his pain and experience it as alien and imposed which, when aided and abetted by his environment, leads to moral weakness, moral torpitude, and cowardice. A patient seeking release is working toward resolving, becoming more aware of, and owning, his pain. Then he will be experiencing it as "mine" and "coming from me." While working toward this end, he is seeking and accepting the help of his analyst in further identifying with and becoming his pain, with the result that he will become morally tougher, with increasing integrity and greater courage. "Self-realizing of human creative potentialities is only possible through daring to leap into the unknown, to threaten what has apparent subjective value, rational and irrational."*(144)*

In *New Ways,* Horney defined resistance as "the energy with which an individual protects repressed feelings or thoughts against their integration into conscious awareness."*(35, p. 34)* As Horney's theory evolved, while the notion of energy investment in hindrances to analytic progress remained, the mechanistic implications of the resistance concept were replaced by the holistic process concept of blockages. The holistic concept does not lend itself to finding the onus in the patient nor to abetting the analyst's acquisition of a halo of frustrated innocence. The comprehensive concept of blockages contains what is subsumed under repression. *(67)* It includes the various categories of resistance, and the processes referred to as defenses and defense mechanisms which are comparable to Horney's concept of the neurotic character structure.

Horney's concept of blockages would seem to deal with the phenomena defined as "defense and resistance." Kanzer and Blum state that "Although the terms 'defense,' 'defense mechanism,' and 'resistance' are sometimes used interchangeably," they make the "following distinctions: (1) a defense is a protective action or attitude directed against danger. (2) A defense mechanism is a specific technique used by the ego to ward off inner or external dangers (identification, projection, reaction formation, isolation, denial, repression, etc.). (3) A resistance is a departure from the fundamental rule or more broadly, the therapeutic alliance, through which the patient pledges his cooperation in the analytic procedure."*(142, pp. 109-10)*

Blockages may be experienced and seen as actively blocking and/or being blocked by patient and analyst. Blockages have both an inward and outward reference. The therapist must be attuned to the where, when, and why of blocking as well as to the what and how of it, not only after the fact but as it is beginning to happen. Horney's motto of "blockages first" becomes more understandable when connected with her focus on the rhythm, tempo, and direction of movement in the analytic process. The analyst must be constantly asking what's slowing, blocking, and stalling the process.

Horney saw blockages as very specifically related to the three major solutions for intrapsychic conflict — the expansive, the self-effacing, and the resigned. In these areas, blockages function to maintain the most deeply embedded solution and their main subjective values of mastery, love, and freedom. In a more general way the *auxiliary approaches to artificial harmony* and the *general measures to relieve tension* serve as blockages to the experiencing of unfulfilled shoulds, self-hate, anxiety, compulsiveness, and conflict. The greatest blockages are against the experiencing of constructive moves and assets, through the immediate glorification of what has just occurred in the analysis, its denigration, or its being politely ignored and denied. Blockages are most active in the doctor-patient relationship.

The forms in which blockages become manifest are myriad. The patient may be argumentative, sarcastic, and assaultive. He may take shelter behind a facade of polite compliance; or he may be evasive, forget the subject, or drop it. He may start talking in theoretical terms or treat the whole matter as if it were something that didn't concern him.

Special factors will operate in regard to the analyst, determining the climate of the relationship. If the patient's need is for love, mastery, or freedom he will become hypersensitive to what he regards as rejection, domination or coercion. In addition, "because his pride is bound to be hurt in the process, he tends easily to feel humiliated. Because of his expectations . . . he often feels frustrated . . . . His self-accusations and self-contempt" which have thus been mobilized make him "feel accused and despised." Finally, "patients regularly overrate the analyst's significance . . . . He is not simply a human being who may help him . . . . He is the magician who has the power to plunge them into hell or lift them into heaven."*(49, p. 339)*

While blockages are definite obstructions to progress and growth, they also point to what needs to be worked on in analysis. They aid in the process of working through, and act as a protection against the potential damage from premature interpretations.

In the earlier phases of the work, it may be in the interest of the analysis to go along with the blockages. It gives both patient and analyst the time and opportunity to get acquainted. The analyst can encourage this by responding to a demand and need for relief, and by going along with the patient's seeking help to "get rid of the bad parts of my neurosis while perfecting the good." Both of these are blockages which can be turned to constructive use in building the relationship and in helping the analysis gather momentum.

In the process of working through, patients will have a variety of reactions. The so-called negative therapeutic reaction may follow interpretations. *(220)* There may be what Horney called *repercussions* which can become serious blockages. *(49, p. 357)* The structure and function of blocking and blockages, their identification, their being worked at, with and through, are portrayed in detail in the following instance which was related to me by J. M. Davis, M.D.

One year before he began analysis, Samuel A., a young, married professional, had made a mild suicidal gesture. He suffered from moderately severe mood swings of short duration. His father also had mood swings, but they were less intense. Unresponsive to a year of supportive psychotherapy and medication, he was referred for analysis. Eight months after analysis had begun, it became obvious that blocking was becoming intense with a depressive phase setting in. Blocking had been previously identified and worked at.

On his way to a session, Samuel drove straight ahead instead of turning left to the analyst's office. "I found another way through the back streets but it took longer." He was blocked and conflicted about confronting the blocking. In that session he said he was "tired," "exhausted," "going to fall to sleep," "there's something weighing me down."

About the middle of it he associated. "I think the sessions are too much for me. I don't want to remember that I have to come here. My mind is blank. It's like something is trying to get out. There are people way down in a deep well. They are screaming for help and I can't help them. It must be me. I wonder if it's an ego knocking thing that wants to come out? It's me in the well. Possibly Rhoda and me. I pictured myself at the top looking down into the well, feeling helpless to help. I can't get any more. Maybe my motivation isn't strong enough."

Rhoda is a very sick young girl who has made suicidal attempts, and who he is trying to rehabilitate. He does so in the role of savior and martyr as well as in that of genuine interest. She is an externalization of his despised image of himself, but also of an aspect of himself struggling to get out of a deep well of self-hate and depression. He tries helplessly to pull himself out of it. Rhoda also stands for his intense dependency needs which he regards as unmanly, and which have a powerful pull on him. He has assumed the helper role with other young women but with none so intensely. With none is there sex. Some months later, Rhoda was able to accept an offer of marriage from which she had been fleeing.

The analyst, Davis, was aware that the patient was becoming anxious. Davis had an urge to speak after the above segment, but did not. The image and metaphor of the well with Samuel at the bottom, maybe with Rhoda, and with Samuel also at the top is a moving image of various levels of the metaphorical symbolic spiral, of aspects of the self-system, and of his experiencing of it at the moment and in process. The one screaming who is joined, maybe with his Rhoda aspect, and the one on top are all helpless. The patient continued:

"Rhoda was in the well, and others as well. They had their hands stretched up, their mouths open screaming, but they were so far away I couldn't even hear them. It was a round well with rock sides. There was no water in the bottom. It is too difficult to ask for help or get help. Help is so remote and far off. I looked. There was no derrick around. It almost doesn't seem worthwhile to try. Does this mean I don't believe in therapy, or that I'm playing down your part in the therapy. Recovery [one of the many mutual help groups spontaneously organized by laymen] calls these things sabotage."

The imagery becomes starker and more poignant: "others as well," namely more aspects of himself, which are "screaming" with "mouths open" and "hands stretched up." They are "so far away." The extensiveness of the involvement in helplessness, the intensity of the demands for help, and the inaccessibility to be heard and to get help are sharply portrayed. After a slight effort to get help, namely from something mechanical, something as powerful as a derrick, he sinks down into feelings of hopelessness and worthlessness. There is some self-questioning, however, as to whether he is sabotaging his efforts.

The patient continued. "I'm reversing the well. I can't reach the helping hands. I'm totally confused. I get up part way. I could reach the hands. It's like suspended animation. I don't know which hand to touch. I must stay there paralyzed. I'm trying to help Rhoda, but she has never asked for help. Once I got through to her that she needed help, and that night she wet her bed and became suicidal. She took an overdose of barbiturates. Another time I pushed her till she asked for help, but it came out weakly. Didn't even sound like her voice."

These segments are like a dream in which he is looking at himself as both subject and object from the subjective and objective poles of an oscillating equilibrium. Psychodynamically, his idealized and actual self are at the top of the well, and his despised self is at the bottom. In the reversal from the top to the bottom, his response is confusion which covers a dysequilibrium. Later in the analysis, with sharp confrontations and clarifications, he had short attacks of dizziness with nausea. The expression "totally confused" expresses how much of himself he feels is involved in this struggle. The confusion is contributed to by the conflictual situation. "I don't know which hand to touch." This leads to "paralysis" and "suspended animation" which are both consequence and defense. It is a further expression of his inability to deal with the conflictual situation.

Withal he becomes involved with the action. He defines what has to be done and he does "get up part way." That he becomes confused, paralyzed, and suspended at this point is understandable. He is sharply confronted with his Rhoda aspect who, when he got "through to her," responded with a *negative therapeutic reaction* — bed-wetting and a suicidal attempt. However, in this externalized form he recognizes that on other occasions he did get through to her. She did ask for help, although it came out weakly and the voice didn't sound like hers. It was too painful to Samuel to recognize that maybe the voice was his own.

Davis still curbed his urge to comment. "I'm scared of what I will be like if I'm cured. I'm afraid it may change all my relationships. Now I'm completely blank." That was the end of the session. On the way out he said, "Rhoda wants help so badly but something in her stops her from asking for it."

The fear of asking for and accepting help, hence, "cure," is intimately connected with the fear of changing. He equated changing with cure, an error often made by analysts themselves. Changing can be for the better or the worse. The very anticipation or threat of change can be most threatening to a rigid and precarious psychic structure. Changing must be clearly delineated in evaluating movement in the total analytic process.

With Samuel A., the very anticipation of changing triggered anxiety with his blocking out the anticipation and the anxiety as well. He clearly defined his struggle as he was leaving: "She wants help so badly, but something in her stops her from asking for help and accepting it." Opening and closing comments by patients are often most revealing. With sharp clarity, Samuel described and capsuled the total situation at the moment, the analytic process, the analytic relationship, and his dilemma.

The next session occurred three days later. He had begun analysis on a twice weekly schedule, giving a host of rationalizations for not coming three times. He had agreed, however, to do so about one month before the following session occurred.

He arrived unshaven, wearing a T-shirt and slacks. The first time he had come to a session dressed this way. Samuel usually dressed immaculately. It was also the first time in several weeks that he had been early for his session. His appearance might have suggested that he had gone into a deeper depression. The session revealed, however, that his appearance actually indicated a letting go of controls, of blocking, and of his opposition to deeper involvement. All these factors contributed to his being early for the first time in weeks. This "first" was combined with another first — the unshaven and relaxed appearance. There were at least two more in what followed.

He said nothing until he was lying comfortably on the couch. He was relaxed enough to take his time, a third first. It also felt as though he had snuggled into the welcoming soft arms of the couch, of the analyst, and of his dependencies needs which he had been fighting off, a fourth first.

"There is something new. I've blocked everything from my mind. I can't go to work and I don't even care. It's funny I'm so tired, but when I want to do something, I can do it. I've lost my desire to do anything, and I correlate this with something that's happening here. The closer I get to what's happening here, the more I run away outside. I have completely isolated myself against the outside world."

To the four firsts mentioned above he explicitly added a fifth, "something new." What was new was "I can't go to work and I don't even care." Before he was disturbed about it. Another first was the recognition that regardless how "tired" he felt, "when I want to do something I can do it." The seventh first was the closeness of the correlation with "what's happening here" to his loss of desire to do. This awareness he more sharply formulated in process terms, "the closer . . . here . . . the more I run away outside." How determinedly he defends where he ran away to, he makes explicit. It is to a position of isolation which is not isolation "from," but an isolation "against the outside world," namely, an embattled isolation.

A total of seven firsts were identified in this segment, an unusual number for just one hour, one being a lot for any one session. Firsts are of crucial import because they relate to the new, the different, the unfamiliar, to what was not known. Emerging from the forming aspect of the self-system and that area where associative connections are loosest, they may point at what is more plastic, dynamic, creative, and truthful. Pointing at firsts identifies change, helps to make comparisons with what was, underlines process, and supports the momentum and dynamic of the therapy. They help give the patient a feeling for the pattern of his process, embed the ongoing, and help him experience more of his totality. They enhance feelings of being supported, of confidence, and of trust and hope.

An analyst can bring firsts to a patient's attention in a variety of ways. When the patient has mentioned one, simple noting may be sufficient. Drawing attention to a first is another way. Asking for more about something new is also a technique for underlining a first. Saying, "Can you recall mentioning that before?" is still another. The latter is also a way of connecting what was with what is now. Identifying similarities and differences is a well tried method for gaining and embedding new knowledge. The more experience a patient has with firsts, the more attuned he becomes to them. He then begins to pick them up earlier, to search them out and do what he can to bring them about.

> "On Saturday night," Samuel said, "I had to go out or my wife would have been disappointed. I did go and had a good time. My wife is having a hard time with all this. I explained to her that I don't know how I will be from day to day."

This is a first. Before he could not have been open to a "had to." Before he was not cognizant of her disappointments, in fact, much earlier he was hardly aware of her existence except when he needed her. Not only did he note her disappointment, but also that she was having a hard time. And for the first time he was concerned enough to explain himself to her which he never had done before.

> Davis asked "What was your wife's response?" Samuel answered: "I don't remember how she responded. I know she wants to help,

but she doesn't know how." Davis said: "But you blocked out her response." Samuel was silent, then added: "I can't remember what you just said, I don't even know what we were talking about. I just blocked it all out." Davis added affirmatively: "And you are more able to experience your blocking."

The above mentioned firsts Davis underlined with "What was your wife's response?" The patient immediately blocked, so far as remembering specifically, but he did remember the spirit of her wanting to help while minimizing it with "but she doesn't know how." Davis did not let him remain blocked. By his question, "But you blocked out her response," he confronted Samuel with his "blocking." After a silence — an attempted evasion — Samuel tried even more intense blocking, this time by blocking out Davis's comment. Instead of saying, "You're blocking some more," which would have more deeply embedded the blocking, Davis turned Samuel's blocking to constructive advantage. He did so by underlining (1) that Samuel was generally "more able," (2) more able "to experience," and (3) "more able to experience your blocking." What could have been misused he turned to a triple advantage.

"Yes, I just did it again. Oh! Now I remember what you said. I do it in many areas, but I feel it as a passive process, something that happens to me. I'm fighting you. I just refuse to stay in the area you want me in." Davis interjected: "You refuse to stay in the area where *you* are!" Samuel paused, then said: "I blocked out your answer. What was it?"

Davis didn't answer, so he said: "Am I fighting you?" Davis countered with: "How does it feel to you?" Samuel answered: "My mind won't go into certain areas. It's a learned response."

The patient's response to "You are more able to experience your blocking" was to feel supported and affirmed and he responded with opening and recognition. "Yes, I did it again." The "I" also indicates more "I" feeling, and also an "I" who does and can accept responsibility for his doing. He not only remembered but widened out his awareness to "many areas." He then immediately began to block and deny responsibility by referring to it "as a passive process" and by calling it "something that happens to me." However, there is a basic honesty in Samuel and the relationship with Davis is one of trust. He can say, "I feel it," and admit "I am fighting you" and refusing to stay in the area where "you want me to."

Davis immediately placed the externalized responsibility right back in his lap. "You refuse to stay in the area where *you* are!" This stopped him in his tracks. He defended with blocking, tried to seduce Davis with "What was it?" and finally admitted by a question that he was fighting Davis. The analyst again put it right back in his lap with the open-ended question, "How does it feel to you?"

Samuel, while not conceding the fighting, unwittingly opened up some new areas by using another defensive maneuver. He did say his mind "won't go in certain areas," but he then tried to hide behind "It's a learned response."

After "learned response," a pause, and no comment from Davis, Samuel went on. "I could block out the whole world. I block out my wife a lot. This morning she asked my advice about the car. I blocked her out several times; I told her to do whatever she thought best. She said she didn't know what was best. I said to ask the man at the service station, but she said that the man had told her to ask me. I said just forget it. I was forced to make a decision, even if it was a decision by default. I just don't seem to care, but I know I really do."

Samuel had been pressed pretty hard, and was fighting back furiously: "I could block out the whole world." The whole world narrowed down to his wife who confronted his blocking at every step. Finally, he is forced to make a decision "even if it was a decision by default." This is quite an insight, particularly in the light of patients who scream "you can't hold me responsible. I didn't do anything," and remain obdurately closed to their responsibility for not doing. Samuel goes on to undermine his "I don't seem to care" with "I know I really do." Here are three "I's," with a "really" added, which makes for a lot of being responsible.

"Now I'm starting to think about going to work. I'm getting very anxious. I have blocked out all the bad things about not going. I'm concerned that I may be forced to go in. I've blocked out every responsibility and every worry. Then I start thinking about girls and the nice times I have had with them. I have to do this or other things will bother me."

Davis, while constantly confronting the patient's various forms of blocking, maintained a firm contact which created a tensional situation. It was supportive by intent and consequence. Too often firm and persistent confronting by the therapist to a patient's blocking is seen as negative by patients and some therapists. They fail to see the supportive and stimulating reciprocal values in a frictional tensional contact.

Out of such exchanges came the patient's "starting to think about going to work," which understandably triggered "I'm getting very anxious," the first block. Then he blocks out "all the bad things about not going." But all the blocks don't work. "I'm concerned I may be forced to go in." A further surge of blocking follows. "I've blocked out every responsibility and every worry." Now he is in full flight into the arms of "girls" and "nice times" which he justifies. There is also in his statements an inner wisdom about himself even though misused for defensive purposes.

Davis now pointed out that Samuel was experiencing some of the ways that he maintains his blocking things out. He answered: "Yes, that's right. I also use reading and sleeping this way. Sometimes sleeping feels like it's forced on me. It means that at those times I just have to cut out."

Note the analyst's emphasis on experiencing, on what Samuel is experiencing, on the ways he uses to support his blocking, and, finally, on the fact that he is the active agent in maintaining his blocking. Samuel's "Yes" is destructive in that it is followed by reminding Davis that he has a lot more ways of blocking, namely, by "reading and sleeping." To further defend the "sleeping," which at times he would do for most of the twenty-four hours of the day and for several consecutive days, Samuel tells Davis that "It feels like *it's forced on me.*" Nonetheless Samuel maintains a certain sense of responsibility by saying "it feels like," and by adding, with a certain wisdom, that he is aware that it gets to be too much for him and he has "to cut out."

Then Samuel started a tirade against himself. "Why did it take me so long to get to this point? I've cut out in many sessions. Why couldn't we deal with it before?" Davis pointed out the similarity of what was going on to a recurrent dream he had reported recently. This is both further working through of a recurrent dream, and using a recurrent dream as an interpretation of immediate associations and ongoing behaviors. Samuel answered: "What dream; I can't remember any recurrent dream?" Davis reminded him and he answered:

"Oh yes! But I had another recurrent dream. I was on the subway going backwards and forwards and I kept on sleeping past my stop. Now everything is blocking out again!" He sighed deeply, and after a pause continued: "I'm disgusted. I was hoping you would throw me out." Davis retorted, "Oh! I should feel as disgusted as you do?" Samuel went on: "I'm disgusted because I can't get any further into it." Davis pointed out: "You are getting further into your own need to block." Samuel snapped back: "So what! I am disgusted that I can't stand up to things."

The analyst's firm, persistent, confronting of Samuel's blocking maneuvers was becoming increasingly upsetting. Samuel resorted to the defense of self-hate. Often analysts do not recognize the integrating, unifying and defensive function of self-hate. It can also be a massive evasive maneuver. Davis was not seduced, and cut right through this maneuver by reminding him of the similarity of a recurrent dream to what he was doing. This ended the tirade. He genuinely asked for help. He recalled the dream and then tried to evade its impact by recalling another recurrent dream. Instead the latter illuminated what was going on, and he promptly blocked.

The subway dream is revelatory. Coming to a previous session he went past Davis's office, but did finally arrive by a circuitous route. In the dream, in the subway, in contact with his unconscious, he wants to use the defense of sleeping to keep passing his stop, his awareness of what he is doing. This would happen if he got off, came to the surface, into awareness, to the analyst's office where he would find clarification.

Samuel again tries blocking by self-disgust which Davis confronts with humor and irony. Samuel tries the defense of disgust a second time with real and apparent concern that "I can't get any further into it." Davis undercuts the attempted evasion and illuminates what he is doing: "getting further into your own need to block." This angered Samuel, and he fought back with self-disgust a third time. In saying, "I can't stand up to things," Samuel defines clearly what he knows is his next task.

In a friendly supportive tone Davis responded with: "You are standing up to your own need to block." Samuel responded much more quietly: "I feel like a flat battery in a car. I just have to wait for a recharge. I've got the world by the nuts, except my mind is all screwed up. I'm wondering when I will be able to go back to work." Samuel paused, and Davis made no comment. "It's rather early for me to be trying to make up my mind about that. I get so nervous. I feel it in my tummy and I have to rub it. Maybe I'll have to go to work tomorrow. I just blanked everything out." Davis then asked if Samuel could see the sequence of what was happening.

Again Davis illuminated and underscored what Samuel was doing and experiencing: "standing up to your own need to block." Exhausted and defeated in that exchange Samuel more quietly admits defeat, describing his feeling as being like a "flat battery" needing a "recharge." He even gets a bit expansive, as another defense, but quickly brings in some reality with "my mind is all screwed up," which is also used defensively. He more realistically wonders about work, but he is a bit premature. The proof of this immediately follows. He gets "nervous," feels it in "his tummy," a term a child would use, or one a mother would use to a child while she rubs it "to make the hurt go away." It is an expression of anxiety and of his tendency to somatize and externalize to his body. Even this was not enough to deal with his anxiety so he "just blanked out everything."

After Samuel blanked out, Davis asked if he could see the sequence of what was happening. He thought for a minute, then answered: "Yes, I come back to something, then I blank it out, then I come back to it, then I blank it out again." He paused, then: "I don't like this nervousness, these chills. It's like electricity running through my body. I hate having to make a decision even by default. I do all right just letting things ride. I don't really. Now I'm having difficulty concentrating again."

Having remained in tensional contact with Samuel and helped him experience aspects of his blocking and concomitantly more of his constructive forces, Davis now attempted to help him experience wider dimensions of his ongoing processes by asking him to look at the "sequences of what was happening." In asking this open-ended question Davis is saying it might be worth looking into. His question is a pointer and illuminator. It is indicating the value of exploring. Samuel looked, saw, described, experienced his sequences, and blanked out. But that was not a sufficient defense against his mounting anxiety expressed as "nervousness," "chill," and, ultimately, "electricity running through my body." He sharply states his hatred for making "a decision even by default" because of the anxiety it engenders. Again, he is for "default," "letting things slide." By adding, "I don't really," he gets back on the subway but now he is awake and aware. It's too much for him. He has "difficulty concentrating," which means he is riding by where he should get off.

In a questioning, humorous, and ironical tone Davis asked, "You're blocking again?" Samuel answered: "Yes! I can feel it, but it doesn't mean that much to me. I've known it all my life, but I never thought much of it. Is it that uncommon?" Davis countered again in a humorous, good natured tone: "You'll use that way to measure how important it is to you?" Samuel answered: "Yes! Now I've flipped again. I've got this feeling in my tummy again. I'll go to an internist for it."

The analyst's tone is face saving. Without clearly asserting "You are blocking," it leaves room for the patient to agree on his own initiative. He does, but immediately adds "What's more I've known it all my life," and, in addition, "I never thought much of it." This is another way of saying "And you haven't told me anything I didn't know already" and, besides, "What's so important about it?" This is a maneuver to deny, minimize, and undercut Davis and the importance of what he said.

After a whole series of "yes-buts," a blocking maneuver, which some patients use explicitly and repetitively, Samuel then moved to the wide-eyed innocent defense of "Is it that uncommon?" When Davis circumvented this, Samuel had to "flip," *somaticize*, and run to an "internist" from the analysis and the analyst. In this maneuver he is whining and threatening like a little boy: "If you won't love me, I'll go to someone who will rub my tummy and give me pills."

Davis again circumvented these ploys and brought Samuel right back to the analysis by saying, "And here?" Samuel finished the session saying, "When I face the blocking and stay with it, I become very uncomfortable and irritated." Then he walked out much more lightly than he had come in. Again Davis had confronted him in a humorous, kidding tone which stopped him in his tracks by sharply contrasting the analyst with the internist. This was confronting, supporting, and assuring. Samuel could save his face, and more matter-of-factly say, "When I face the blocking and stay with it, I become very uncomfortable and irritated," that is, "my anxiety rises, and I try to defend against it with irritation."

Through the analyst's effective conduct of the session, Samuel was helped to experience his blocking maneuvers more, worked them through in a measure, and became aware of the somatic consequences to mounting threats to them. Davis was very active this session, alertly following the patient's sequences so that his interventions could be appropriate, timely, and effective. The way Samuel came into the session, opened it, moved through it, and how he went out all reveal how much working through was going on and how effective it was.

The blocking continued to be worked at as he had elations and depressions with steadily narrowing swings. Four months after the above session, he said, "The fluctuations are getting closer and the bounces are getting smaller . . . ." Even at this stage, thirteen months after the analysis had begun, the blocking could still become intense when more embedded aspects of it were threatened. As the limits of the blocking as a defense were

224

reached, he would experience stomach pains, electricity running through his body, and, on occasion, pretty intense dizzy spells with nausea and vomiting on several occasions. The latter were also expressions of his anxiety which would break through with quite some intensity when his defenses were not sufficient to block it out.

Five months later, his mood cycles were almost normal. He could no longer avoid confronting his neurotic claims and the intense dependency needs on which they were based. His many maneuvers to avoid taking responsibility and to force others to make decisions for him were no longer effective. For two weeks he did not go to his business, stayed at home, slept most of the day, went out at night to entertain himself, and came to all analytic sessions on time. During this period, with even more intense determination he tried to force his business partners, his parents, and his wife to make all his decisions and to assume responsibility for him. This included his very young children.

By the end of the two weeks, his partners were opposing him with determination, as were his parents and his wife, who also interdicted his making servants of his children. He responded to his partners with some guilt, embarrassment and anger. His parents were the subject of mounting anger and resentment as he became aware of how they contributed to his problems. Toward his wife he felt increasing sympathy, understanding, and appreciation for what he had put her through and for how she had stood by him. In the next weeks, against great inner opposition, Samuel slowly took up his tasks at home and at work. He became more understanding and responsible.

In the next four months, before the summer holiday, on several occasions, Samuel followed the same pattern that he had for the two weeks he stayed at home, only this time the episodes lasted only one to two days. Concomitantly, more of his expansiveness, particularly his arrogant-vindictiveness, began to emerge as he became more constructive and responsible. A realistic situation precluded his continuing therapy in the fall, but analyst and patient felt he would continue to work on his own and would resume therapy at a future date.

This example illustrates the structure and function of blocking and blockages, how to work with and through them. It also is a demonstration teaching session, a microanalysis of a session which emphasizes process, experiencing, openings, closings, themes, and the crucial importance of the person of the analyst as instrument.

225

Chapter 14

Working Through

Horney made some formulations regarding personality change as answers to the difficult question, "What does what how?" They appear in her technique lectures, and in chapters devoted to therapy in her books. "What Does the Analyst Do?" and "The Road of Psychoanalytic Therapy" are examples of chapters devoted to the question. *(40, 49)* The latter describes "the disillusioning process" which is prerequisite to, and occurs concomitantly with, the strengthening of the urge toward self-realization and the turning toward health. Both chapters include some of what you do, how you do it, and what happens when you do do it. Her colleagues confronted these issues in a round table discussion of "What Is Effective in the Therapeutic Process?"*(255)*

Attempts to arrive at information, knowledge, and maybe even some wisdom in all human disciplines is via the six fundamental questions: why, who, what, how, where, when. They can all be used in psychoanalysis, explicitly and implicitly, formulated in words, expletives, tonal inflections, and gestures. The important issues of the form and structure of questions are elaborated in chapters 17, 18 and 22. As was demonstrated in the discussion of Samuel A. in chapter 13, questions are of crucial import for the working through process.

The psychoanalytic orientation and its concomitant theory regarding the nature of man determines what questions are crucial. If of a deterministic, closed system variety, the why question will be heard most frequently. How and what will seldom be heard. Freud's early work is prototypical of this orientation.

What and how have increasing import as theories become relatively deterministic, open-ended, and of the process variety. The why question comes up less frequently. Who, when, and where are asked in relation to the predominant import of what and how. Horney is a prime example of such theories.

The first group of theories tend to put greatest emphasis on cognition and least emphasis on emotion, with conation somewhere in between. Soma is seen in terms of a materialistic biology. In the second group, central importance is given to emotion intimately interconnected with conation and cognition on the one hand, and with soma on the other. This orientation is expressive of modern biology.

The developments of Horney presented in this book place herenow experiencing in the center, emphasize the what and how questions, use who, where, and when in intimate relation to them, and seldom ask why. These developments are related to the integration of post- and neo-Freudian theories with phenomenology, existentialism, and Eastern philosophies.

The concern with questions is intimately related to the notion of comprehensive knowing developed in chapter 12. Through the processes of relating and communing, while alone and with others, one comes to know the self immediately through numinous awareness and conceptually through phenomenal organization. For contacting and integrating these forms of awareness, questions are the stimuli, pointers, and illuminators.

What I mean by working through ultimately depends on what questions are asked, how they are asked, how the answers are expressed, and what changes occur as a result of the asking.

Working through, according to Kanzer and Blum, "is essentially the inner process by which the interpretations of the analyst achieve their effects leading to the abandonment of resistances and defenses, so that barriers within the personality can be reorganized in the direction of health rather than mental disorder." Kanzer and Blum add: "Insights are partly the result of interpretation and working through, and partly the instrument of interpretation in securing further working through . . . . The empirical limits of insight and working through in achieving effective change must be brought into relation to the theories of analytic goals and their attainment."*(142, p. 129)* These views are consonant with my own.

When the analysis is well under way and the patient has been "grappling with his conflicts," "constructive periods" begin which "are followed by *repercussions* in which the essential element is a renewed onrush of self-hate and self-contempt." Horney continues, "These self-destructive feelings may be experienced as such, or they may be externalized through becoming vindictive, feeling abused, or having sadistic or masochistic fantasies. Or the patient may but vaguely recognize his self-hate, but sharply feel the anxiety with which he responds to the self-destructive impulses. Or finally, not even the anxiety appears as such, but his customary defenses against it — such as drinking, sexual activities, a compulsive need for company, or being arrogant or grandiose — become active again."*(49, pp. 357-58)*

Aspects of working through have been discussed in the analyst's knowing himself as his best instrument of therapy; in the treatment of the doctor-patient relationship; in the elucidation of blockages; in the resolution of the autonomy of the self-system in its less plastic aspects; and in the delineation of the idealized image. More on working through will follow in the chapters on dreaming, the disillusioning process, interpretation, insight, change, and goals in therapy.

What we have mentioned compares with what Karush includes in his "Working Through." Using the language of the adaptional approach, he emphasizes the crucial import of the transference relationship and the therapeutic alliance. Processes in the patient aid the structural reorganization, thus freeing the adaptive functioning of the ego and superego. Then there are the technical exchanges between patient and therapist that help release and reshape dynamic processes. Karush refers to the arousal of the patient's reasoning and cognitive processes (the rationative levels of the symbolic spiral) and of the nonrational aspects (the prerationative levels) in which he includes the patient's trust, influenceability by suggestion, and ability to *realistically* idealize the *real* [emphasis added] aspects of the analyst. Most important are the new perceptions and the conflict-free affects appropriate to them. All successful working through involves the recognition and assimilation of newly learned truths, altered balance of defenses, neutralization of resistance, formation of new identifications and the reconstruction of the ego ideal. *(226)*

Brodsky's position is that the main goal of "working through" and all that subserves that purpose is the realistic mastery of suffering whether produced by anxiety, shame, guilt, or other painful feeling.

228

Brodsky mentions that, after a relative working through, residual conflicts when triggered by internal or external stimuli, become integrated in the ego's autonomous functioning rather than disrupting it. He also refers to the goal of analysis and the criteria for termination. *(257)*

Fleming and Benedict considered an analysis "well terminated" when there was a *"re-solution"* of the "transference neuroses," namely, when it had been worked through successfully. They used "the hyphen . . . and the long e" to "give a different twist to its meaning." By resolution they did not mean promises, as at New Year's, nor "dissolution," nor "dissolving." What they wished to stress was "that a problem is being solved in a new way." This did not mean that the problems were no longer present. They "still exist but are integrated into the total personality structure . . . under more effective ego control."*(258)*

I do not see resolution as "a new solution to an old problem," because of the importance of the real self in the theoretical framework. True, the problem is being solved in a new way, and there is a new integration of the organism's autonomy directed toward the goals of therapy. These can, however, be formulated differently; not only because of the concept of the real self, but also because of the different view of resolution. In fact, while Fleming and Benedict explicitly state that they do not mean by *"re-solution"* "dissolution" or "dissolving," it is exactly in these directions that Horney's ideas on resolution move. Horney was explicit about the differences between solving and resolving.

In *Our Inner Conflicts*, she said, "Throughout the text I shall use the term 'solve' in connection with the neurotic's attempts to do away with his conflicts. Since he unconsciously denies their existence he does not strictly speaking try to resolve them. His unconscious efforts are directed toward 'solving' his problems."*(39, p. 33)*

In "Resolution of Neurotic Conflicts," the last chapter, Horney states that "The task of therapy is to analyze the entire neurotic character structure."*(39, p. 220)*

By resolution Horney means first, the identification of those conditions that brought the neurotic character structure into being, that perpetuate, and maintain it, and which continue to contribute to its development. Prerequisite to that concept of resolution is Horney's formulation of the neurotic process as a special form of human development. With the identification, undermining, and resolving of the existing neurotic character structure must go the identification, supporting, extending, and expanding of constructive forces.

The various aspects of the neurotic structure do not suddenly disappear. What is resolved is their intensity, extensity, and embeddedness, with concomitant energy transformations taking place. Energy invested in neurotic patterns now becomes available for constructive living. As certain aspects of the comprehensive solution of self-idealization and of the major and partial solutions are resolved, other aspects can come to the fore to be identified, worked at, and worked through. *(49, ch. 7)* The analytic process is a dynamic process of emerging, unfolding, and resolving, which effects a shift of energy investment in neurotic processes to those favoring constructive growth.

Working through is more than seeing how a neurotic trend originated and how it functions in the patient. It means not only becoming intellectually aware, but also emotionally experiencing it as the patient's own, with its full intensity. A trend can only be understood by experiencing it in its many contexts.

An attitude of placating, for example, may originally be seen as part and parcel of the neurotic need for affection. When a patient's idealized image is under scrutiny, placating is then pointed at as an expression of his notion that he is a saint. When detachment comes to the fore, the placating quite obviously serves the need to avoid friction. The compulsive nature of the attitude is highlighted when the patient's fear of others and his leaning over backward from his own sadistic impulses come into view.

In addition to becoming emotionally aware of the attitude in its overt and covert forms, and of its compulsiveness, the patient needs to see and experience its subjective values as well as its adverse consequences. When a patient first becomes aware of a neurotic trend, he tends to look for a cause, usually in childhood. By turning to the cause, its historical origins, he hopes to remove it. He must be helped toward becoming more familiar with the trend — as an aspect of working through.

As an illustration, we will show how one aspect of the arrogant-vindictive character structure is worked through. "If, for instance, the patient's dread of being compliant has become clear, he must see the extent to which he resents, dreads, and despises in himself any form of self-effacement. He must recognize the checks he has unconsciously instituted to the end of eliminating from his life all possibilities of compliance and everything involved in compliant tendencies. We will understand, then, how attitudes apparently divergent all serve this one purpose; how he has numbed his sensitivity to others to the point of being unaware of their feelings, desires, or reactions; how this has made him highly inconsiderate; how he has choked off any feeling of fondness for others as well as any desire to be liked by them; how he disparages tender feelings and goodness in others; how he tends automatically to refuse requests; how in personal relationships he feels entitled to be moody, critical, and demanding but denies the partner any of these prerogatives."*(39, pp. 230-31)*

Working through the dread of compliance leads to seeing more of the patient's predominating expansive solution and his arrogant-vindictive solution. "Most expressions of vindictiveness have been described by others, and by myself, as sadistic trends," said Horney. "The term 'sadistic' focuses on the satisfaction to be gained from the power to subject others to pain or indignity. Satisfaction-excitement, thrill, glee — undoubtedly can be present in sexual and nonsexual situations, and for these the term 'sadistic' seems to be sufficiently meaningful. [*cf. 39, ch. 12*] My suggestion to replace the term 'sadistic' in its general use by 'vindictive' is based on the contention that for so-called sadistic trends vindictive needs are the crucial motivating force."*(49, p. 199)*

The attendant pride in the arrogant-vindictive solution with its great emphasis on strength, mastery, will-power, domination, and invulnerability as well as the passion for vindictive triumph, must be understood in connection with the dread of compliance. In addition, the patient's basic belief that it's a "dog eat dog world" must come to light. With the emergence of softer feelings — tendencies to be sympathetic, helpful, etc. — there will be accompanying feelings of chaos and profound anxiety. The emergence of anxiety frequently leads the patient to feel he is getting worse. It may be he has touched on attitudes and feelings which endanger his main defensive system. However, it may also indicate that the patient now feels strong enough to take the risk of facing his problems more squarely.

"Both the need to justify his claims and his responses to their frustration work like vicious circles, supplying constant fuel to his vindictiveness. So pervasive a vindictiveness naturally enters into the analytic relationship too, and shows itself in many ways. It is one part of the so-called negative therapeutic reaction, by which we mean an acute impairment of condition after a constructive move ahead." When the defense is "subjectively indispensable," failure to recognize its many forms "may not merely delay the analytic process but wreck it altogether."*(49, p. 201)* Such wrecking is an exaggeration of the so-called negative therapeutic reaction from masochistic patients. With them the implicit or explicit accusation is "you have ruined me" while the arrogant-vindictive patient's battle cry is "I will ruin you," which is his attempt at vengeance and vindication.

A paradoxical reaction to the decrease of anxiety seems to occur in the markedly self-effacing individual. While the arrogant-vindictive individual will tend to minimize anxiety, the self-effacing one will maximize it. "It is frequently observable that most of the activities of the self-effacing person will be carried out in a state of high tension.

Peaceful living seems almost unbearable and the creation of crises is a regular occurrence. This may not be seen in the early phases of the therapy of a self-effacing individual, but in time it will emerge. The sudden lowering of tension impairs his contact with reality and his sense of identity diminishes. He then experiences feelings of emptiness, loneliness, dissolution, wild disruptive anxiety, and suicidal self-hate."(259)

What needs to be worked through in the self-effacing person has been indicated in the description of the self-effacing solution, which is for Horney a more comprehensive term than masochism. The characteristics of this solution are most obvious in morbid dependency:

> Morbid dependency is one of the most complicated phenomena with which we have to deal. We cannot explain the total picture as manifold branches of sexual masochism . . . . Nor is it all the inverted sadism of a weak and hopeless person. Nor do we grasp its essentials when focusing on the parasitic or symbiotic aspects, or on the neurotic's drive to lose himself. Nor, finally, can we regard the whole condition as being merely an externalization of pride and self-hate . . . . All such explanations give too static a picture . . . . Morbid dependency is . . . a process in which all or most of these factors come into play [and] though relevant to the total picture, are, as it were, too negative to account for the passionate character of the involvement . . . . But there is no passion without the expectation of some vital fulfillment . . . this factor, which in its turn cannot be isolated but may be grasped only in the framework of the whole self-effacing structure, is the drive for total surrender and the longing to find unity through merging with the partner. (49, p. 258)

Characteristically such patients have extremes of irrational expansiveness to the point of not only encompassing but being the universe, with others being only aspects of themselves. The opposite extreme is irrational contracting to self-extinction and submerging in the all, which, at the same time, they feel they are. Such fluctuating processes evoke considerable anxiety and, to hold them in check, require an oppositional dualism with another person. This other may be factual or imaginary. The manipulation and control of this other becomes their consuming passion. Foreground anxiety may be used by the self-effacing person to control others and force his will upon them. More in the background is anxiety used as a motor force to catapult that individual against the significant other.

These are some of the difficulties that confront an analyst while working with so-called masochists: "Pain, past, present, and future, and relief and release from it almost totally fill these patients' mental and emotional horizons, and the analytic sessions. They are constantly demanding that the analyst do something about their suffering and berating him because he hasn't done enough to relieve their pain. Here we come upon several paradoxes. The very heightened state of tension becomes a numbing narcotic, which they need and unconsciously create. Quantity becomes quality. So more tension means more narcosis. This in turn means not only maintaining but exaggerating the masochistic processes. As the therapist helps in resolving these patterns, he is giving constructive help, but it leads to lessening of the tension and thereby increasing the pain. This is one of the crucial dilemmas in the therapy of such patients. They, who demand relief from pain, must be helped to tolerate transient, and even prolonged increases of pain for the ultimate resolution of their problems." *(259)*

> After eight years of a neo-Freudian analysis, Marion W., a young married woman is now beginning her fifth year of analysis with me. In the first year a pervasive and intensive masochistic defense became clearly delineated. At the slightest tension increase, she would, almost frantically, and in an increasingly rapid and louder speech, insist, in a variety of ways, that she was stupid, ugly, and, by implication, utterly amoral.
>
> My comments were rare and brief, usually a question or a statement suggesting that a slight change had occurred, something new had emerged, or that a movement in a positive direction could be seen. Not until the third year did she say, "I know what you're doing and don't give me any more of that constructive crap." She then continued her associations. After each summer interruption, she reported changes in the form of "I could do that better" and "I did some things I could not do before."
>
> In the second year, the intensity of the frantic flight to the masochistic defense slowly abated. Marion began to recognize it for what it was, and to talk about her fantasy life, another powerful defense. With increased distress, she would go off into fantasying which lasted for hours. In the second half of the third year, she let me in on its more secret details, aware that she used fantasying as she used tranquilizers and sedatives. The latter began to concern her in the second year, and by the end of the third, she got along without them for longer periods.
>
> The main fantasy involved a "brilliant, beautiful young boy who was crippled" in a variety of ways. Fantasies might also contain crippled older men. The crippling of women was in the form of fatness, skinniness, ugliness, stupidity, and looking like

hags or witches. She was fascinated by cripples on the street, and tried to work in a hospital for the crippled in her teens.

From earliest childhood she had been told she was difficult and different. Her father, who could be quite sadistic, treated her as a boy, but also as a mature, sexually experienced woman. Her mother was always depressed, very masochistic, and hypochondriacal. The patient's idealized image was of perfect brilliance, perfect beauty, and perfect grace. The needs to shine and be admired were passionate. She was slowly allowing herself glimpses of her hostility and rage, although she was terrified of both and immediately blocked them out.

Toward the end of the third year, Marion reported these two dreams. She had opened the session with a smile and a "hello" which were new, and informed me that she had stopped taking tranquilizers. "I realize now how much violence there is in me. I had a dream of a murderer. He was caught and put in jail. He was going to be put to death. I was a bystander, but I knew it was me. He had killed lots of people. He had escaped. Lots of people were waiting to see when he was killed. We all had something to keep him from killing us. I was on guard because he might kill me. In the process there was one person, his jailer. He was equally as hostile and ferocious as the murderer, and wanted to see him killed. He put handcuffs on him. The murderer was so violent he pulled the handcuffs off and was going to kill the jailer. The jailer violently threw the killer down the stairs. In the struggling I felt they were both right. The jailer won and put the handcuffs back on the killer. As I watched, it was two me's struggling with each other. I was terrified, as I watched, at the force in the two of then.. The jailer finally was able to get him back to his death cell."

"Then right after that I had another dream about women witches. This time it was a gang of women who were being tried for their life. In this dream, all the women were wearing clothes which were of the time of the witch hunts in Salem. They had hoods over their heads. Only the face showed. I was very tired. Our crime was we were martyrs. We were all being tried for our martyrdom. Here it was again, the feelings of violence and destructiveness. I saw their destructiveness and their appeal to martyrdom. I saw their evil, and their trying to look pathetic but it didn't come off. One of the women was called forth by the judge. She was going to be condemned to death. Her foot was bound up and it was swollen. [The crippled young boy of her fantasies often had a club foot.] Like it was a revolting, diseased, rotting part. She had to go by me and was awkward. I was covered and sitting on the floor. As she did her foot touched me. I felt horrid and afraid at the evil and the disease. I felt it was gruesome, that I was part of these martyred women. I felt a disgust at this whole bunch of sadistic martyred women. I was also waiting for death, and waiting to be condemned to die. When I woke up I felt very very frightened by the depth of feeling in both of the dreams. There was a part of the dream in which I was wanting the killer to be free to do as much violence as was possible. I do feel that my own crime feels like a disease of the will. If I could just will myself to do what I want to. In my most self-loathing moments I feel my lack of courage, as though I am a coward. In this dream my crime was being a martyr. This conflict is between wanting to be free and wanting to be in jail."

Marion later associated to "that martyred disease part. I'm glad she is going to be killed. I'm sick of her. I identify with that guy, rebellious, acting out, defiant. What's left I don't like. The guy of law and order is equally violent." She ended the session with "My crime is being afraid to make efforts in different directions." The experience of masochism and martyrdom were clear, her revulsion with both and her beginning open stand against them. With these awarenesses her violence and murderous rage were released. She identifies with them but fears them, and has to hold them in check. Controlling this conflict and the violence is what paralyzes her and causes her "laziness," inertia, and fear of doing. Her doing is frantic and compulsive, a flight from the pain of her paralysis of will.

One month later she woke from a dream in terror at the realization that if she didn't make efforts, she couldn't accomplish anything, but that making efforts means chancing failure — a terrifying possibility. But now she sees that by not chancing and by not making efforts, she will be sure to be a failure.

A month later, she talked about a dinner party. At it were men and women whom she previously classified as brilliant while she suffered horribly, in silence and felt "dumb." She talked with many of them. "I realized I had a body of knowledge underneath. I didn't buzz out, and I didn't get anxious. There was a woman at the table who was hostile, and I didn't hate myself in the light of her attack. It was a refreshing feeling to me."

Later in the session, Marion said, "I am beginning to sense what is called in dancing a turning. I feel I'm approaching a change in direction without it happening yet. It's ineffable. My feeling is it's pretentious to share this experience. Maybe I feel I'm pretending. When you said the contest between me and

Ruben [her husband] is sick, it lay very correctly. The image that came to mind is of laying on the water and letting it carry you; a feeling of letting go, and letting a deeper current carry you. I'm having a feeling for this but not in words. I'm beginning to realize that there are things that are not knowable; that can't be initiated; that are deeper and very pleasant. When I'm not talking I feel silence. I feel I can tell you I'm in the process of change . . . . For the first time I have a sense deep inside that if I stopped contesting with Ruben and wanting to be on top, it wouldn't be submission. What it would be I don't know . . . . Being without fighting is terribly sad to me. That gives me a real twinge of pathos."

She then related in detail an involved fantasy which contained an older man who was not crippled. The atmosphere was somber and ended in the man's loss of some illusions. She was also in it as herself, and there was another woman. She ended the discussion of the fantasy with "Lately I have been feeling the necessary separation of people."

After a year of analysis, there was the beginning experiencing of having boundaries, and a sense of identity started to take shape. After two years she had several dreams and one fantasy, in which it felt like I had reached down inside of her and felt the core of her. In the fourth year, there was further resolution of the masochistic defense and the negativistic position; greater experiencing of being separate and an identity; and increasing initiative and acceptance of responsibility, of taking chances, and of making mistakes. Feelings of liking herself increased and she felt herself becoming friendlier and even approached men and enjoyed their interest in her as a woman and a person.

Toward the end of the fourth year, over a period of several months, Marion made the following comments with a depth of feeling and connectedness with what she was saying. "I see how I have hung on to the negativistic position and wouldn't let go." "I love Ruben. I love you." "When I became anxious I felt plagued by those fantasies" which for years she had fled into as a narcotic. "I get frightened if I accept that I can do things, that I can enjoy myself. I want to take off all my clothes. I want you to see me. I want to see myself, all of myself. I get a message of a longing to get into life." For years she had had dreams of wandering through houses in which she unexpectedly discovered a room she didn't know existed, and always it had positive attributes. For the first time, she said, "If I dream those dreams, then that room must be in me and I want to be connected with it."

In the first session after the summer holidays, Marion said, "I had the best summer I ever had in my life. I enjoyed myself. It was a lot of fun. My relations with Ruben were much much better." Later in the session she added, "I see how interest, effort, and being connected make me anxious, but I know those are the directions I have to go." Following the first few sessions of moving into greater depth, she had a short-lived intense repercussion as a result of which she understood the narcotic and addictive pull of fantasying. These very recognitions led to its being further weakened as a defense.

By the end of the first month of our work after the summer holidays, she had more sharply experienced the extent of the alienation which terrified her. The summer progress further exposed and led to the resolution of more aspects of her sadomasochism. Frantic and desperate efforts to cling to it followed, throwing still more of it sharply into the foreground. As this happened, she became softer and relinquished more of her hostility. She noted that now people were more willing to do things for her.

More aspects of working through emerge as patients who fear unconscious processes can let go into them *(165)* and allow them to emerge: Compulsive intellectualizers and compulsive feelers can allow the emergence of the more spontaneous conceptual and perceptual; and patients who are compulsively wording, ideaing, and talking and who fear silence can let go into silence and experience its constructive values. This is more possible when a patient is effectively using the couch for working at his problems, for contemplating, meditating, opening himself to his depths, for letting be, so that he can be with himself, by himself, himself. Then the liberating and liberated unconscious processes can be predominantly manifestations of spontaneous creativity, of insight and outsight, of unified and unifying creative vision. *(168, 166)*

The many tries at formulating the masochistic defense could be a measure of the success of psychoanalysis, as theory and therapy. They could also be a crucial perspective from which to write its history. Most of this chapter has been devoted to this frustrating and often defeating neurotic problem. The above extended case citation was illustrative of sado-masochism. The microanalysis of the single session of Samuel A. concerned working through aspects of the masochistic position. Working through of masochism is also illustrated in many of the other cases cited, particularly in that of Rose B.

To further demonstrate the disillusioning process, the process of working through, the resolution of the neurotic character structure, and to further examine the concepts of the transference neurosis, regression, repetition compulsion, and stages of libido development, this capsuled analysis may be illustrative and illuminating.

Paul O. came from Europe to further his career. Descended from wealthy landed gentry, his father played the role of the lord of the manor, idealistically caring for his workers and the community at large. Often Paul complained about his father's largesse which prevented him from getting an even better education and doing more traveling. His father's favorite, and one of the younger members of a large family, Paul resented the ill treatment of his older, bigger brothers who were jealous of him, but he acted in kind toward his younger brothers and sisters not without pleasure and a certain arrogance.

In analysis, it became obvious that he had many of his father's attitudes. During World War II, driven by his idealism, Paul sacrificed his own food, and almost died of starvation coupled with a serious illness. His father, mother, and one brother died tragically during the war. He was deeply resentful of the traitorous behavior of many of those who his father had supported for so many years. In spite of adversities, he was very successful. Usually first in his class, sought after by men in friendship and women in love, and rapidly advancing in his career, his life appeared, on the surface, to be one of complete satisfaction and ultimate fulfillment. What made all this possible was an exceptional intelligence and unusual physical gifts.

Actually he was losing out in all kinds of ways because of an iron taboo on advantage, against getting anything for himself. It looked like a good natured, laissez faire attitude toward life. Many exploited him, and many more he encouraged to do so. He was living out the role of the self-sacrificing, self-martyring idealist as did his father. Of all this he was quite unaware.

What began to emerge early in analysis was the mounting resentment he felt at the jealousy of the many who had put obstructions in the way of his actualizing his idealism. His contempt for them, and for those for whom he had sacrificed himself became apparent to him as we proceeded. He was dimly aware of being involved in a losing battle in the role of the self-martyring idealist.

Once he decided to come to the United States, his problems became more manifest. He procrastinated, was slipshod about getting the necessary procedures completed, and did so only at the last minute at great cost to himself. On arrival in the United States, his procrastinating became more intense. Efforts in his own behalf were poorly thought through and effected. Money slipped through his fingers. He was an easy touch, and handled his banking, bills, insurance, and taxes in a vague, unrealistic, and disorganized way. Examinations which he could have passed with almost no studying he failed consistently. He sabotaged interviews to advance his career. He felt abused and unfairly treated by those who had interviewed him and by those who failed him in the tests.

In his analysis, begun over three years ago, his self-sacrificing idealism was soon identified and worked at. It was surprising and shocking to him to realize it. His procrastinating was next to emerge, which also distressed him because he had in fact headed large projects seemingly quite well, and saw himself as well organized, an efficient administrator. With the procrastinating, his not looking and not seeing, his not hearing and not listening, and his pushing aside became more obvious. Most reluctantly was he able to see how vague, disorganized, and unrealistic he in fact was. He found it harder and harder to deny the mess he was creating for himself. It was painful for him to realize how he had allowed himself to be used and taken advantage of, and how difficult it was for him to assert himself in his own behalf.

In time it was possible to bring to his attention, his narcissism and arrogance, his contempt for the ordinary, for the mundane, and for all the many details that make up daily living. The analysis had been a series of painful disillusionments. Following one session in which the realizations were pretty shattering, he rushed to the bathroom and vomited.

He is a person of great integrity. As a result, the analysis moved very rapidly. As we progressed, he became more and more depressed. His great charm and natural buoyancy were severely shaken.

After two and a half years, it was finally possible to put pressure on to investigate an insurance plan he had mentioned. He vaguely indicated that he would look into it. A month later, something he said stimulated me to ask whether he had done anything about it. Most reluctantly I got from him that he had found out he could not only save money, but even recoup some retroactively. He told me this with a lack of zest and even some irritation. With great difficulty could I bring to his attention the fact that he had not mentioned it; that he told it to me so reluctantly; and that he took so little pleasure in the success of his efforts leading to quite a monetary saving. I could see that he hated his involvement with reality. Being more realistic meant renouncing being taken care of by the world as if he were its favorite son. Understandably, he had been experiencing me as his father in the analytic situation.

He arrived several minutes late for the following session. On his way, he was aware of time passing, and of his reluctance, even resistance, to come to the session. He tried to think why but could not give himself an answer. "Then I began to think about a dream I had last night. I was sitting and defecating and not getting up to do anything, still being so passive, wondering should I do anything or not. Being so inactive. That is the real picture. Sitting in this dirt, not cleaning myself up, having difficulty getting up. I remember trying to find some other connection with the dream that would make it easier to accept."

Later in the session, he reported a second dream from the night before. It was set in his hometown. It took place during the war. There was a bombing raid, and by magic nobody was being hurt or killed although buildings were blowing up all around him. The dream brought up memories of the many tragic deaths in his family and the sufferings it had caused him. On the anniversary of his father's death during the first year of analysis he had burst into violent sobbing which startled and frightened him. Quiet crying and tears occurred on several subsequent occasions, particularly on this anniversary, but also as he related other events of those painful years. He needed to believe all that horror was gone and past, and here it had erupted from his depths.

Two months later, he dreamt that his mother had become ill and died. He was attending her funeral. He shed a few tears as he related the dream and added, "For years I dreamt about my father's death. It stopped about a year ago. Now my mother is dead. Finally, maybe I can leave all that and live my life now." He said this with a feeling of gratification, relief, and release. Although his mother loved him very much, and he her, she played a lesser role in his life compared to his father.

I asked him to repeat the dream of defecating. On occasion I have found it valuable to ask a patient to do so, saying, "it wasn't clear to me" or "I think I missed something as you told it to me," placing the focus of error on myself. I do this when I believe only part of the dream was told, and when I feel it is emotionally laden and of crucial import. The repetition is never identical with the first telling. Parts are dropped out, new ones added, and different emphases given. The second telling is like a series of associations to the dream as first told. Patients are usually unaware of these changes, but at times will spontaneously say, "Oh, as I'm telling it to you now I recall some more of it" or "It wasn't quite as I told you the first time."

He said, "It was very vague. I was sitting. I was defecating. I remember feeling something like sitting in shit. I remember a feeling of fury like I should get up and clean it and was sitting and not moving. I associate to my baby who defecates and sits in his feces. Maybe I identify with the baby, with being hopeless like a baby."

In a quiet, questioning tone I asked, "I wonder what you would say if I told you that three times you repeated 'hopeless.'?" His body jerked, and his voice revealed strong irritation. He said, "Maybe I feel hopeless. I'm annoyed how this slipped out three times. Calling him [the baby] hopeless when he is very hopeful. Maybe I'm talking about my helplessness. Maybe I'm feeling you didn't help me." This was almost the first overt criticism of me in analysis. Henceforth, it was easier for him to be critical and even hostile. He continued associating. "You should do my job." I asked, "What job?" "To clean up this mess. To take care of me as I am so helpless." To say he was helpless was humiliating enough, but hopelessness was intolerable because it went against generations of family tradition. Hopelessness did not exist in the dictionaries of their feelings and values.

He opened the following session saying he had been thinking about the dream and how powerful the blocking had been. "I felt it was a very good session on the one hand, and I feel very angry on the other because of the blocking. I should be able to see that first without any session. It suddenly came to my mind how it goes, opening, closing, opening, closing." He then related a dream which revealed his rage when his demands for instant gratification are not fulfilled. The night before, he wanted sex and his wife refused. He dreamt he was married, had no children (he has three), and was having affairs with several women, one of whom he brings into his home to live with him and his wife. In the dream he jokes about it with her.

He reported that that evening he had come home and gotten into comfortable clothes. About 8:00 his wife said, "Aren't you going to the meeting?" It was an important one, and he had scheduled it. He had completely blocked it out. I said, "Not only must big daddy take care of Paulie boy, but mamma must say, 'Paulie boy, wipe your ass, wash your face, put your clothes on, and go to school.'" His next associations indicated that the interpretation had been effective. To accept that this was what was going on was most humiliating and enraging. It had been taking quite a physical toll on him. He was looking pale and

241

drawn. As he got up from the couch, he was weaving as though quite faint and dizzy. He continued to do so as he walked out of the office into the foyer, supporting himself with his hand against the wall. He never mentioned it.

In a session one week later, he kept repeating how fatigued his wife was, and about how fatigued he was. From the beginning of analysis, he massively externalized to his wife. Gradually, he did it less intensively, and began more often to come directly to himself. He then related a dream in which he was talking to someone who could be of help to him. At no time did he ask for it directly but kept talking around it. The claim is "Others should know what I want and give it to me without my asking." To underline the point, I asked if he had asked Mr. P. for help. He mumbled something inaudibly, but it was enough for me to know he hadn't, and then went on to another dream. "I was going to Mr. M.'s house. I saw his baby. There was dirt all over the place. I thought, how much dirt this baby can make. The baby was five or six years old, but I thought it should be only one year old. I was impressed with the fact that he could talk and smile. I woke up and checked the baby and found that he was wet."

He associated to the baby being five or six years old and "all this dirty business." Only as the associations went on did it become quite obvious how much magical wishing and neurotic claims were present in the first dream of defecating, and how much "the dirty business" was pursuing him. He was trying to do away with it by making his baby, who was one year old five years old, but still he was making "dirt all over the place" — more than ever. He was still struggling against accepting the fact that he had to clean up this whole "dirty business," this "mess," he had created.

In the next session he kept talking about the necessity for "hard work" and "proper action." He kept fighting off both for another month. Then things started to move as he could let out how enraged he was that he had to become active and clean up this whole mess. Big daddy and big mamma were not going to take care of Paulie boy. As this was dawning, he looked worse, and on several occasions he went to the bathroom after the session. I can only conjecture that he was terrified, and that he wanted to hide his rage and shame and collect himself. This month was the low point. In the weeks thereafter, a slow development of being more active and organized began to manifest itself. He spontaneously said during several sessions, "I'm feeling more alive, I feel I have more energy." He was doing less selecting of associations, and more often was picking up what he was saying, particularly when his associations contained evidences of recurrences of his old patterns.

Two months after the dream of defecating and sitting in it, he spontaneously wondered how come the abrupt change, as he saw it, on coming to the United States. He did not pursue the subject, but something he said a week later gave me the opportunity to ask what had come out of his wonderings. He did not respond directly, but reported a conversation in which he mentioned an uneducated man who, due to war circumstances, had risen very high politically. This was a type for which he had contempt and hatred because they had blocked him so often in his idealistic efforts. They were also the kind of people who had exploited his father.

I asked if he hadn't dreamt about this man some months ago. He reported the dream, and I realized that he had previously related only a small part of it. Originally he told me that in the dream this man was extremely impolite and very abusive — so much so that Paul became furious and talked back, something most difficult for him to do because family tradition and his own structure demanded he always be the gentleman. This time he related that in the dream the man was screaming that Paul was a traitor and a betrayer. He had left his country after it had done so much for him. Paul went on to say that maybe he had done poorly in the United States because he felt himself a traitor and was punishing himself. He also was a betrayer of, and traitor to, his pride invested idealistic patterns. He was suffering the responses of self-hate as self-sabotaging.

With the dream of sitting in his own shit, after months of talking about the "mess" he had created, he was slowly opening himself to the sources of these problems. A week later, he soberly and with a feeling of owning what he said, reviewed his procrastinating patterns, his unrealistic attitudes, and his resistance to change. He said, "How sick this is. It's crazy." I had picked up a "had to come to the session" on several occasions in the week before. He commented, "What a difference it would make if I came here because I wanted to. What a different motivation. How sick my attitude has been." He was closer to reality — his reality — than he had ever been, and was planning more realistically the use of his time, money, and energies.

Shortly after the summer holidays, at the beginning of his fourth year, there was a breakthrough. There was a letting go of his defenses so that his alienating centripetal directedness was gone for about fifteen minutes. He became open to, directly in contact with, and a participant observer of his "self-propelled feeling processes."*(212)* He was surprised and pleased at his awareness, at this wholly new and different experiencing of what analysis could be. Thereafter it became an experiential reference point to which he could refer back — a point with which he could compare being far from and close to. He again contacted it in its many dimensions. As this was happening, he became more sharply aware of the violence of his opposition to assuming "responsibility" for himself and for taking over the "leadership" of his life.

From the evidence, the presence of a transference neurosis, of repetition compulsion, of regression, and of the anal stage of libido development would seem to be confirmed, as well as the working through of all of them to a degree. Samuel A.'s analysis had many similarities with Paul O.'s. In the case of Rose B., who had dreams of sexual orgasms, defecating in bed, and eating a meal with gusto, Freudian concepts would also seem to be validated.

In the discussion of the transference neurosis, however, I said one might more accurately speak of advancing toward childhood, childishness, and childlikeness. In the case of Paul O., what emerged had been evident and lived out all of his life. He simply had ways of hiding it from himself. Even before analysis, the forcible confrontation with the fact that his native country had rejected him as the favorite son intensified the demand that the new country should. In analysis, what had always been there was slowly brought into awareness. With support, he was integrating it and working it through while going through a painful disillusioning process.

How do I view what happened? Because of his intelligence, and other gifts, as well as circumstances, Paul could keep himself blind to his "Idealized Image" of himself as a saint, martyr, and an idealist who should be adored. In the foreground was much expansiveness mainly as narcissism. He was a charmer of the first order. Only later in analysis did the extensiveness of his arrogant-vindictiveness become obvious. Perfectionism was as yet minimally evident. But mixed with this foreground picture of expansiveness was much resignation. There was much of shallow living with an emphasis on fun, girls, and having a good time. Right below the surface was much rebellious resignation. Only after coming to analysis did his persistent resignation come to the fore. As this did so, the intensity of his self-effacement and dependency became evident.

Although all of this was present, plus alienation and a number of the other solutions, progress in therapy was quite rapid. This obtained because of his unusual assets. Exceptional intelligence and physical gifts were there in abundance. He had a flair for psychological thinking and dream interpretation. There was a basic integrity and a capacity for objectivity. He had a sense of humor and could laugh at himself. He had deep moral convictions. That he so easily could and did identify me with his father had its disadvantages but the advantages outweighed them. It brought him into a dependency relationship very rapidly. With it was a deep confidence and trust. In his life he in fact had been loved by his father and mother and all the members of the family even though his older brothers had been jealous. He was also loved by his many friends, male and female.

What was being frustrated were his neurotic claims based on his idealized conception of himself as so wonderful, so good, the favorite child. When they were not fulfilled at home he left, abused and in a rage, intending to extort it from his new father and mother. In the analysis, he resorted to the final defense of helplessness and self-hate, shitting all over himself and creating a mess all around him. When it still did not get him what he was demanding, he was able to begin to pick himself up, clean up the mess, bit by bit, and get on with being and becoming more responsible and more mature. Much work remains, and there will be difficult periods, particularly as he has to integrate deeper and wider dimensions of basic and central conflict. This I feel he will do because of the solid work already done, and the strength and depth of the analytic relationship.

Chapter 15

Dreams I: Formal, Phenomenological, and Psychodynamic

Horney gave many lectures and courses on dreams. She made many allusions to them in papers and in her books. In *"Neurosis and Human Growth,"* she capsuled some of her essential ideas on this subject:

> The greatest help at the beginning, as well as later on, comes from the patient's dreams. I cannot develop here our theory of dreams. It must suffice to mention briefly our basic tenets: that in dreams we are closer to the reality of ourselves; that they represent attempts to solve our conflicts, either in a neurotic or in a healthy way; that in them constructive forces can be at work, even at a time when they are hardly visible otherwise.
>
> From dreams with constructive elements the patient can catch a glimpse, even in the initial phase of analysis, of a world operating within him which is peculiarly his own and which is more true to his feelings than the world of his illusions. There are dreams in which the patient expresses in symbolic form the

sympathy he feels for himself because of what he is doing to himself. There are dreams which reveal a deep well of sadness, of nostalgia, of longing; dreams in which he is struggling to come alive; dreams in which he realizes that he is imprisoned and wants to get out; dreams in which he tenderly cultivates a growing plant, or in which he discovers a room in his house of which he did not know before. The analyst will of course help him understand the meaning of what is expressed in symbolic language. But in addition he may emphasize the significance of the patient's expressing in his dreams feelings or longings which he does not dare to feel in waking life. And he may raise the question of whether, for instance, the feeling of sadness is not more truly what the patient does feel about himself than the optimism he displays consciously. *(49, pp. 349-50)*

Some of what Horney is alluding to can be seen in the following instance given to me by J. W. Vollmerhausen, M.D. It also illustrates how dreams are worked with, and adds further understanding of the process of working through. It also shows some of the ways we use the *vis-à-vis* position and the couch.

The analysis of Sedra V., thirty-nine-year-old woman, had been proceeding in the *vis-à-vis* position for several years. Much of the content was related to her difficulties with her husband. She was spending considerable time trying to understand him, accuse him, excuse him, tear him down, and build him up. In the process she began to show increasing signs of moving closer to herself. With this she became more and more irritated with the various lights in the office, and over a series of sessions we dimmed most of the lighting so that a twilight atmosphere was created. Thereafter her eye movements became more wandering, and less focused on me. Sedra expressed greater feelings of relaxation, and mentioned in one hour that she thought she would use the couch next time. In this gradual movement toward relaxation of a strained and constricted consciousness, she expressed her needs to keep a watchful eye on people in order to see whether they meant what they said. She also brought up her fears of surrender, of letting go, of relying more on her own unconscious processes.

While at first quite anxious in using the couch, Sedra soon became comfortable in this position. There was a concomitant change in the feeling and tone of her hours. She developed a greater awareness of herself, as well as a sharply increased capacity to accept whatever was coming up in her without condemnation or criticism. This also reflected itself in a far less defensive attitude to interpretive comments.

About a week after she had begun using the couch, she opened her hour with a dream: "I had a strange dream. It made me think I was quite a prude. I was on a street with my son Tommy, and was about to get into a car with this woman who was attractive. She was rather vague and unfamiliar. You were on a porch of a house nearby. It belonged to an orthodontist. You were in a bathing suit, and scolding your small boy. Then there was another doctor, a very handsome man, a dermatologist who has all the women crazy about him, but he doesn't get close to anyone. I was stunned. His trunks were falling off. I got into the car to get away but the other woman was watching the scene with interest and unashamedly. She seemed intrigued by it. I was disgusted by her."

Sedra was silent for a minute. I [J.W.V.] asked her to look more at the woman and tell me more about her. I felt that if I were to see the other figures in the dream, we might first work through, as an opening, the symbol of the woman who can look, who does not turn away. In addition, she was an ambiguous figure who elicited feelings of attraction first and then disgust. The very ambiguity allowed for several directions of development. Since the patient is getting into the same car with her, we can continue with the movement already occurring in the dream toward this figure. At this point, she recalled several experiences with her mother.

Around the age of six, there had been some mutual genital exploration with a little boy who lived nearby. This had resulted in a severe scolding. She remembered her mother as always being very prudish, except when there was company in the house at night. Sedra recalled overhearing risque stories and jokes — especially an incident related in full by a visitor who had spied on her husband — my patient's father — disrobing.

As she related these memories, Sedra experienced herself as a mixture of being curious, fascinated, apprehensive, and disgusted. The conflictual attitudes which she had heretofore externalized to her husband, were now owned by her as she was experiencing here-now her own feelings toward the scene posed by her dream. She shifted away from the prude attitude to the underlying conflicts, and in subsequent hours continued in that direction. This way of working with a dream attempts to bring out conflict being experienced on all levels so that embedded positions (prude in this case) can be loosened and resolved; dilemma positions can be revealed, experienced, and reintegrated into new, more fluid positions.

This dream lends itself to a discussion of some crucial issues. It erroneously has been stated that Horney did not see childhood and the past as important. The cases presented, and the chapter on "The Actual Situation" should cast doubt on this assertion. Another criticism has been that Horney did not give sufficient weight to the importance of sex in her theories. The inclusive nature of the Freudian concept of sexuality with its special definition of biology in large measure accounts for this apparent lack on Horney's part. Again the clinical examples throughout this book — and particularly those in chapter 3 — would seem to question this conception. The discussion in chapter 3 of the philosophical and methodological issues pertinent to the concept of penis envy further clarify the significant place of human sexuality in Horney's theories.

Her position was that the total character structure, with its neurotic and healthy components, determines the nature of a person's sexual attitudes, the kinds of sexual behavior he will participate in, the function sex will serve, and the pains and pleasures he might derive from this whole area of humans being together.

Quite clearly in the instance of the nurse who suffered intense bladder pains on the couch and then enjoyed great relief at emptying it, there were extensive sexual implications *(p. 45)*. In Freudian terms, these behaviors and experiences would be regarded as reflecting "sadistic" and "masochistic" defenses. The so-called transference was highly eroticized and sexualized, not only in fantasy but almost in reality. She experienced sexual intercourse with the analyst in his bathroom with orgastic satisfaction, and shared with him this experience in fantasy, in feelings, and in words. In sexual terms, she was fighting her desires to be raped by him. From a wider perspective, she was experiencing conflict at many levels in terms of giving and receiving, in being closed to and open to, in opposing and surrendering, and in penetrating and being penetrated.

In the instance of Sedra V., who for some sessions struggled with, and in a measure worked through, her conflicting attitudes toward her husband and then mentioned that next time she would use the couch, there was also an intensely eroticized doctor-patient relationship (transference) being worked through. The romantic and seductive aspects were quite evident in the requests that the lights be dimmed, in her irritation that she had to ask, and that the analyst had not done so on his own, namely, succumbed to her blandishments. The twilight atmosphere and her wandering, unfocused eye movements, as well as the feelings of relaxation she felt, are a vivid description of a woman in love erotically aroused.

In the succeeding hours, she was more sharply aware of herself and more accepting of interpretative comments. In sexual terms, she was more womanly, more open to being penetrated. One could say her superego had become less stringent. But one has to stretch the sexual analogies and metaphors to discuss what was actually happening. She was allowing herself to be penetrated by herself, by her increasingly spontaneous feelings, in addition to her neurotic ones which had been kept out of awareness (repressed-blocked). In Horney's terms, she was becoming more compassionate and loving toward and of herself and concomitantly toward others. But in keeping with Freudian theory, this might suggest an increase in narcissism, the emergence of aspects of Hartmann's conflict-free sphere in his postulated autonomous ego, or the concept of her being raped by her unconscious.

Then a week after she lies down on the couch, she has a dream with frank and overt sexual content. Although she spoke about prudery, she also mentioned fascination, but with overtones of good nature and a bit of healthy bawdiness. There is quite some looking and seeing and being fascinated with an attractive woman who is openly and consciously interested in the frankly sexual. There are two little boys — her son and the analyst's — which connects with her looking and being looked at sexually by a little boy (the analyst in the doctor-patient relationship). Then there is the analyst scolding his little boy, a frankly symbolic representation of phallic stimulation, and a figurative offer of mutual touching and foreplay to an adult sexual act. The analyst is also her scolding mother who she is defying by bringing it all out in the open. There is the symbolism of straight teeth, and the dentist who looks into and explores, the dermatologist who is involved with skin and touching, and about whom women are crazy but "he doesn't get close to anyone." And who but the dreamer has his trunks fall off so that his genitals can be looked at?

Her associations clearly connect her with mother, with childhood, with the forbidden, with the organic, and with the child in her. They also connect her with her mother's hypocrisy regarding sex, namely, her mother's moral dividedness, as well as her own. She had externalized it to her husband, as accusing and excusing, tearing down and building up. In the process of moving to the couch, and in working with the dream, she had moved closer to herself and her moral dividedness and thereby deeper into the whole issue of being divided in so many other areas of her life. The sexual aspects were there as pointers to the past, the present and the future, in sex, in love, in the analytic relationship, in the whole of her human relations and the totality of her organicity as a sexual being, as a woman, as a person. Seen in this holistic light, sex takes its appropriate and proportionate place in the analytic process and in life.

Dreams are not the *via regia* to the unconscious, but they are one of the better ways of contacting it. Dreams (and fantasies) are extremely helpful for moving a patient toward freer associating, toward greater openness to the prelogical. The patient is helped to metaphorically move down the symbolic spiral to pure fact, to his ground of being. His acquired distortions can thereby be more quickly and effectively resolved and creative processes freed. Through focus on here-now experiencing, the patient's needs to see a dream as a thing, as unconnected with him, as something that happened in another place and time, can be more quickly resolved so that he begins to experience the dream's meaning in the ongoing context.

After years of analysis, this middle-aged married woman described this process most clearly and succinctly: "After all these years of analysis, only now do I feel I'm in analysis. I never felt connected to my dreams. I feel they're mine now. I wasn't interested in the processes going on in me. I never knew what working in analysis meant. I want to make efforts. I feel I can."

The "scientific, categorical, and phenomenal," as well as the "psychophysical" and the "descriptive" orientations which Weissman said the analyst could use to investigate his own and his patient's experience, can be effectively utilized in looking at, organizing, and understanding the human phenomena in dreaming. *(260, 128, pp. 7-8)* Rigorous phenomenological analysis of the evolving dreaming process leads to meaning which emerges through experiencing the interconnectedness of patternings. Further dimensions of meaning accrue through using the existential and psychodynamic approaches. Meaning has been measurably enhanced through these approaches after phenomenological analysis, and is greater than if either of the latter were used alone. This has been demonstrated in teaching situations in which a dream was presented without background material or associations. The therapist presenting the dream has often been amazed at what came out of the class's phenomenological analysis. Often they threw light on aspects of the dream of which he had been unaware.

The group first explores the manifold dimensions of space reflected in the dreaming process, then follows with a phenomenological analysis of time. Experience with space and time prepares beginners for more intricate phenomenological analyses. The emphasis throughout is on experiencing moving processes, namely, to become the dreamer dreaming his dream, reporting it to his therapist, and associating to it. Moving in the dimensions of sensing, perceiving, emoting, conating, and cognizing are next explored, each new dimension being imbedded in what has already been experienced. Such feelings as fear,

251

anger, joy, sadness, and anxiety, are descriptively explored as to their intensity, volume, and speed of appearance and disappearance. This is followed by explorations of conflict, dilemma, paradox, and polarities. Further dimensions, such as materiality, causality, atmosphere, climate, and modes of being, are gone into. Finally, the dreaming process is looked at from the viewpoint of integrating.

Integrating is the pattern of the process of living. " 'Life' may be regarded as the spreading of a pattern as it pulsates."*(176, p. 104)* All sequences involve disintegrating and reintegrating and are neutrally so described. The concept of integrating and all delineated aspects of it are psychophysically neutral. This means they are equally applicable to the physical and psychological aspects of systems in their internal and external reference, to individual and to environment. Systems are in equilibrium. They go through phases of disequilibrating and reequilibrating, disbalancing and rebalancing. All systems are in tension and torsion, going through phases of distensioning and retensioning, of distortioning and retortioning. This means the systems and the symbols representing them are periodically twisted and deviated from their rational and natural form. Analogous, but not identical, from a psychodynamic view, is the molding of the self by tyrannical shoulds, and of one's idealized image by the supremacy of the mind.

All symbols in a system hold particular positions. Their positions are altered through the process of dispositioning and repositioning. By a process of disproportioning and reproportioning the proportions of energy investment in symbols and the values reflected in them are changed. Symbols do not have inherent values in isolation and out of context. Because of their position in the system and the energy investment in them, the values they hold are changed by a process of disorienting and reorienting. The proportions of the values invested in symbols change as their positions change with each phase of disintegrating and reintegrating.

Our therapeutic effectiveness is enhanced by using the phenomenological approach to explore and experience the surface, the manifest, and the literal — the top, that is, of the metaphorical spiral. Boss devotes a quarter of his book, *The Analysis of Dreams,* to "the dream itself." After discussing a dream, he says, "Naturally our attempts to explain dreams phenomenologically in terms of their own nature and without any previous theoretical suppositions and reductions could equally well have been illustrated by means of another example."*(261, p. 80)*

Binswanger adds: "By steeping oneself in the manifest content of the dream — which, since Freud's epoch-making postulate concerning the reconstruction of latent dream thoughts, has receded all too far into the background — one learns the proper evaluation of the primal

252

and strict interdependence of feeling and image, of mood [*Gestimmt-sein*] and pictorial realization. And what is true of the brief cycles whose thematic reflection we can observe in the image and mood of the dreamer is, of course, also true of the larger and deeper rhythms of normal and pathologically exalted and depressive 'discords.' "*(191, p. 231)*

Hartmann had also been "seeking to bring depth psychology into a framework that reconciled it with a hitherto rather neglected general (or surface) psychology."*(142, p. 95)* With his concept of "reconstruction upwards," Lowenstein recognized "the need of the analyst to proceed not merely from the surface to the depths and from the present to the past, but also in reverse directions."*(142, p. 112)*

Through the phenomenological approach, there is experiencing of the forming process, the "formative tendency," thereby affecting a unity of the manifest and the latent, of the surface and the depth, of the literal and the figurative, of the metaphorical top and bottom of the spiral and the connecting levels. *(176)* The therapist attempts figuratively to work his way down the metaphorical spiral, to resolve incumbrances to contacting the depths. As a consequence, movement from surface to depth and depth to surface becomes easier and quicker.

With increasing frequency, the meaning of dreams is experienced as self-evident to the therapist and, in time, such happenings will occur in the dreamer. This also means that fewer associations and less theoretical reconstruction will be necessary for the dream meaning to emerge. The more the patient knows himself, the more he is his real self, the less his dreams will be attempting to solve, the more they will be concerned with resolving. Less of destructive patternings and more of constructive ones will become evident. In short, the gap between the manifest and the latent, between the top and bottom of the spiral, will have been narrowed and their mutual accessibility will have been increased.

In this context, in a formal sense, to say that one dream is more symbolic than another is illogical. All dreams are constituted of symbols as aspects of the symbolizing process. Experiencing the symbol sequences, as patternings, is determined by the nature and rigor of our method and our experience in using it. Viewed psychodynamically, one dream may require fewer associations and theoretical constructions to arrive at a relevant meaning. In this sense, one could say one dream is more symbolic than another, but I feel such a formulation is not productive and confuses.

In the phenomenological approach there is experiencing of emerging phenomena as patterned symbol sequences. The objective is to favor increasing proximity of the subjectifying and objectifying processes of phenomena. As this happens, there will be increasing experiencing of them in their continuity and unity. This procedure opposes the natural tendency in human intellection, made compulsive in sickness and exaggerated by the Western mind structure to artificially separate subjectifying and objectifying processes, to hypostatize them into static subjects and objects. In experiencing the connectedness of sequences, meaning emerges. This happens as there is more contacting of the deeper roots of the dreaming process in the organismic-environmental matrix.

Becoming grounded in the phenomenological approach helps undercut the tendency in beginners, as well as among experienced analysts, to ask automatically, when a patient relates a dream, "What does it mean?" If at all analytically sophisticated, patients do likewise. This fosters compulsive intellectualizing and interferes with freer associating. "What does it mean?" is asked before asking and knowing, "What is it?" The phenomenologic approach attempts to demonstrate and to help experience what the dream is, in its many dimensions, and to show that experiencing the what is to experience the dream's connectedness with wider and deeper aspects of that person's totality of processes. From such experiencing, meaning emerges.

In the described phenomenological approach, there is an experienced unity of the subjective and the objective pole of that organic, unitary process, human integrating. There are psychodynamically oriented dream theories (Silberer, Stekel, Maeder, Jung) which make interpretations from the "subjective" and the "objective" levels. On the objective level, the dream symbol stands for the actual object or person, and on the subjective level, the symbol stands for a concretization of the dreamer's subjectivity.

In dream courses, Horney included a lecture on self-presentation. My ideas evolved through a focus on self-dramatization, self-representation, self-presentation, and, finally, to subject and object presentation. What is presented are the products of the subjectifying and objectifying processes which are an expression of the inherent dualizing nature of intellection. In moments of communing, when there are only feelings of secondlessness, there are no products of subjectifying and objectifying processes, also no polarities or paradoxes. The mind is wiped clean of form, the objective of *The Zen Doctrine of No-Mind.* *(214)* In this sense there is formlessness but not chaos. The form is the absence of form, pure lucidity.

The subject of all my dreams is me in my world. My universe includes all that is subsumed in the creation of my symbolic self and is analogous to the existential domains of *Eigenwelt, Mitwelt,* and *Umwelt.* When Peter talks about Paul he is really talking about Peter. He will be seeing Paul through Peter's eyes, no matter how many people consensually validate the accuracy of his perception of Peter.

Every symbol has an I, or subject aspect, and an other, or object aspect. This means that the moment there is awareness, in sleeping, waking, or any form of consciousness, the moment there is an I who is aware, my awareness will have an internal and external reference. No symbol is pure I, pure subject, or pure other, pure object. The predominant aspect may be an I aspect or other aspect. All symbols should be looked at from both viewpoints.

The patient in the dream may stand for the analyst or anyone else, as the analyst in the dream may stand for the dreamer and anyone else. The meanings the symbol conveys are not determined by any immanent, inherent qualities in myself, but by the position I hold in the system of the whole as presented in the dream. One factor, determining the extent to which a symbol will be expressive of the subject aspect is the depth of sleep at which the dream was dreamed, namely, the degree to which the organism is being moved autonomously. As sleep becomes lighter, and as we are moved toward waking and being awake, the ratio changes in the direction of increasing heteronomous influences. Total separability of organism and environment is impossible, because the organism cannot exist in isolation.

Tortioning of objectified inner processes can lead to what is psychodynamically described as projection, externalization, and externalized living. *(148)* These are psychodynamic formulations, defenses, and blockages — all aspects of the neurotic character structure which are to be distinguished from the objectifying of inner processes which is a formalistic description. Horney did not develop concepts which would involve tortioning of subjectified processes leading to introjecting internalizing, and ending in internalized living. She did describe people who in their associations and dreams constantly talked about themselves and acted as if no one else existed. She referred to these people as being preoccupied with relations to self in contrast to those who are preoccupied with relations to others. The others may be limited to one person, wife, husband, or analyst who seems to fill their interpersonal universe.

In the dream of Sedra V. mentioned above, subject and object presentation are well exemplified. Clearly the woman is both herself and the attractive woman who got into the car with her. Her son Tommy also stands for various aspects of herself, as possibly does her husband and her father in her associations. The analyst is himself but also the dermatologist, the absent orthodontist, and the analyst's son. But the analyst could also be various aspects of herself as her husband, her father, and her son. All symbols had subject and object aspects of her, in her universe, of varying degrees of relevance and availability for experiencing in the ongoing contexts. This was an analytic relationship dream in which she was experiencing the analyst as he actually was and as various authority figures in her past, present, and possible future.

The mechanisms of projection, externalization, and — to a slight degree — externalized living are also portrayed in the dream. The subsequent associations revealed further working through manifested in her taking back some of her externalizations. The symbol of the other woman stands not only for her mother, but also for the woman herself. It stands not only for, and has reference to, the past, but also to the present. The analyst is not only the dermatologist, orthodontist, her son, her husband, and her father, but the analyst is also himself, a man, and she is she, a woman, enjoying a human situation with a certain good humor and ribaldry.

Boss, who incorporated phenomenological and existential orientations into his Daseinsanalysis, is critical of views by Freud, Jung, and others regarding symbols and subject and object presentation. *(262)* Boss said that both Freud and Jung are positivistic, hence rational, causal, reductionistic, and utilitarian in their approach to symbols. *(261, pp. 95-101)* They distinguish the "pure reality" of the symbol from its "psychological contents" or "representations." "Representations" refer to what transcends the symbol's "pure reality," and both must be understood from the viewpoint of the particular theory of human nature. Each theory has its own techniques for interpreting dream symbols. For Freud to have seen the transcending aspect of the symbol, Boss regards as quite an achievement, but it led to losing sight of the symbol as "the single and complete reality" that it is.

This splitting of the object opened the way to interpreting it from the objective and subjective levels of which Boss is understandably critical. "The more we divorce the phenomena of the dream" from such ideas, says Boss, the more we recognize their "quite original content and intrinsic essence" which corresponds "fully with the happy openness of the dreamer's existence."*(261, p. 111)* The phenomenological approach presented in this chapter has certain similarities to Boss's.

Forms expressive of the formal notions of subjectifying and objectifying are to be differentiated from forms carrying psychodynamic import. Failing to discriminate forms in their formal logical sense from forms as being the object, as vehicle for the object, as concept of the object, as experienceable phenomenal reality, and as concretization of the person's subjective experiencing of the object not only creates chaos, but also impedes the effective use of the various forms in diverse realms of discourse.

I agree with Boss regarding the possible dangers in interpreting from the objective and subjective levels, but I also believe that by clearer discriminations some problems can be avoided and advantages gained. I have included subject and object presentation in this chapter because of long usage. Familiarity with them can also serve as a bridge to the phenomenological approach which is much less known. From long experience in teaching this approach, I know that it evokes considerable anxiety and blocking when presented for the first time even after careful preparation.

Further, the notions of subject and object presentation can be valuable in therapy because patients are familiar with subject-object thinking. In fact they are often unaware that other intellectual and grammatical structures are characteristic of other societies. Western thinking is subject-predicate in form and noun oriented. That is the realm of discourse with which the analyst makes his first contact with patients.

From experience with patients and in teaching I know that the forms which they take as given and natural can function as bridges to a deeper experiencing and understanding of the phenomenological approach. When that happens, they can use — when appropriate — such approaches as the existential, the psychodynamic, and the Oriental, with greater facility.

Chapter 16

Dreams II:
The Total Solution of Magic

As a person abandons and turns his back on his real self in his search for glory and in his attempt to actualize his idealized image, he becomes alienated. His center of gravity shifts to the outside. Through the extremes of externalized living, he empties himself of his inner experiences and exists in terms of the outside. *(148)* Through the extremes of internalized living, he fills himself — more accurately, his imagination — with the outside. The ultimate consequence and manifestation of this sequence of processes is living by the total solution of magic. In this solution, the supremacy of the mind participates most actively and extensively. "The mind . . . is the magic ruler for which, as for God, everything is possible."*(49, p. 184)* These processes can be seen earlier and clearer in dreams than elsewhere. They are thus more quickly available for being worked with.

Angela P. was southern Italian and an opera singer of moderate ability. But this was hardly enough to account for her feeling every moment of her life that she was the *diva assoluta,* that her aria was being breathlessly awaited by the opening night audience of the

Metropolitan Opera. Comparable attitudes were manifested by Faye M., a delightful, childlike and childish, divorced Vermont woman who was a senior editor in a publishing house. For both, external realities as to time, space, causality, materiality, and money did not exist; nor did the reality of their own persons.

Angela not only felt she was a *diva*. According to M. Wainston, M.D., who related the case to me, she made a grand entrance at every session. The office, after she made the grand exit, and the office bathroom looked like a prima donna's dressing room, a shambles. Faye M. used my office as if it were her home, dropping in at odd hours and using it as a meeting place for friends. She exchanged and repotted the plants, and rearranged the paintings and furniture in my waiting room.

The analyst was not an extension of these two women, or an aspect of them, nor identical with them, he was them. These people are not overtly or predominantly psychotic. Their acting out is different than that of the so-called psychopath. Rather it is a way of life determined by their psychic structure. They have become so alienated, their reality has become so blurred out, that imagination dictates without restraint.

Such patients, extremely alienated and severely ill, within a few weeks or months of the beginning of the analysis have dreams involving me. We are in my office or waiting room, or in some other easily identifiable reality situation. Matter of fact conversations between us and other people of their daily life are going on. My general therapeutic experience has been that such dreams usually appear only after years of analysis and with patients who are not so sick. The contrast made me realize that here was something different. After ten years of such experiences, and by seeing these dreams as reflecting the total solution of magic, they become understandable. I *was* these patients, of their universe, undifferentiated from them.

To make the total solution of magic more understandable, the following dreams are presented in which the use of magic is flagrant, naive, and obvious.

"I had a box. If the wind was right, I could jump off the box and fly off into the air. If Bill [her husband] was watching me, I couldn't." This woman had no awareness of attributing magical powers to herself. She was quite righteously indignant with her husband who she felt was constantly thwarting her efforts to improve herself which meant taking flight into the stratosphere. Bill also stood for reality, whose very glance in fact did topple her from her airy heights.

Peter V. had a very high I.Q., and he was wealthy; but he held only a routine job and lived the life of a drifter. He married after three years of analysis. I experienced his dreams as an amalgam of science fiction novels and surrealistic paintings. The following dream is excessive, even for a proud father. Peter had it when his son, whom he adored, was eight months old. "I was discussing, in Greek, some abstruse philosophical problems with Bobby. My friend, Joe Reber, came in and was amazed. He asked, 'How does he do it?' I said, 'There is nothing to it. It was simple to teach him.' " He thought the dream was hilarious, and as he related it, I heard a half-believing tone of "You know it could be true."

"I just recall a dream with quite some feeling of reality," said Joel C. It was one of a long series involving the search for the magical answer. "Something about a key. Searching for a key. Being distressed that I can't find it. I woke, worn out and tired and feeling I wanted some rest." Joel's idealized image of himself was of saintly goodness and martyrdom, although he was aware of flagrant dishonesties and cruelties which were always justified. Because he had suffered so much, he felt entitled to a life of no pain, no friction, no conflict. Because he had struggled so hard, Joel felt entitled to results without effort. And because of all of these, he felt entitled to therapeutic help of magical proportions. There should be a magical key which would solve all problems.

When I indicated that he was still insisting there should be a magical key, that he was sure I had it, and that I was mean for withholding it, his response was an outburst of abused and bitter feelings. I also reminded him how upset and disgruntled he had been when I canceled a session because of illness. This enraged him because it meant I was human, no God, no magician, no king, and, hence, not omnipotent. He was surprised that he had blocked this out, then became irritated, promptly dropped the subject, and poured forth a shower of further abused feelings. Joel exemplifies an extreme of those who demand the answer "in a word" and insist that "there should be a law," "a formula." For them, the essentials of life, which are always complex, should be communicable in a few simple words.

After six years of analysis, he became less insistent on a magic key, and somewhat more comfortable with himself. Twenty-four years from the time of our first session, Joel is living a fairly full life, but he is still far below his potential. He remains filled with much bitterness and despair, although the latter has abated somewhat. After six years of analysis, the first man whose infant son spoke Greek went on to have two more children and increasing happiness from his family life. He changed jobs several times, each one more demanding of him, but they were still far below his potential. The woman who could fly if the wind was right was in analysis for seven years which were at times quite painful and turbulent. It is almost thirty years since I first saw her. She has gone on to raise a family of four children who are all doing well and to use her professional skills in a productive way in the field of education.

Angela, the opera singer, married, had two children, and continued her singing lessons. Through five years of analysis, she made steady progress, although there were many episodes of depression, severe anxiety, abused feelings, and violent outbursts of hostility toward the analyst. Ten years from the time her analysis began, she was a much more solid person, fighting against, but painfully accepting, her descent to being and becoming a better singer instead of a *diva*. After three years of analysis, the senior editor gradually went into a deep repression. Faye interrupted her analysis for three years during which she isolated herself, saying she wanted to struggle through it on her own. Seven more years of analysis followed, filled with much pain and struggle to find some ground in reality. It is twenty-nine years since I first saw her. Faye is senior editor in a much larger publishing house, more childlike than childish, more mature than unrealistic, still struggling against accepting the demands of reality.

This solution is referred to as total to distinguish it from what in psychoanalytic literature is referred to as magic in thought, the solution of magic, and magical solutions. Total is used because that is the aspiration of the person relying on this solution, and because he acts on the premise that not only is it possible, but he has actualized it. The illusion of omnipotence is evident because the slightest threat to it evokes terror, some of which comes from the immanent experiencing of feelings of abysmal impotence. The solution is referred to as total because it is so encompassing and comes close to taking over the total functioning of the person. What holds sway is the mind for which "everything is possible" including the impossible. *(8, p. 184)* A business tycoon who Horney saw in consultation had this motto on his door, "The difficult we do immediately, the impossible shortly thereafter."

The blurring out of reality is almost total. These patients approach being totally irrational, that is, totally out of ratio with reality. Because of this blurring out of reality, they are almost totally uninvolved with their daily experiences, and they therefore cannot learn from them. How early in life the total solution of magic began operating determines how many years of life experiences have actually been missed. This lack makes therapy all the more difficult because they have so little of learning from life experiences on which to fall back. As a result, one of the essential functions of analysis is to serve as a learning experience. They have to learn about so much of life, for the first time, long after the time it would have been optimal for them to have done so. Their psychic structure approaches being totally static, rigid, fragile, and vulnerable. Threats to it, and responses to such threats, are so terrifying and encompassing that they require very drastic organismal protective measures to maintain a state of wholeness, constancy, and integrity. For these additional reasons, learning is that much more difficult.

With people governed by the total solution of magic who have difficulty discriminating between reality, fantasy, and dream, affect-laden confrontations which are too quick or too strong can precipitate states of panic, of confusion, and of depersonalization. There may be suicidal episodes, psychotic breaks, and abrupt interruptions of therapy because of the therapist's unawareness of the structure of the problem with which he was dealing. Pacing of the therapy as to tempo, rhythm, and the timing of interventions is of crucial import. How one goes about helping them identify imagination, fantasy, dream, and reality requires the utmost sensitivity and caution.

The speed, mass, content, and emotional charge of the reality intrusion and the discriminations made determine the nature of their responses. They may respond with "I can't understand," "What do you mean?" "What's happened?" or "It's unbelievable!" The sequence of feelings may be fear, anxiety, panic, bewilderment, confusion, fuzziness in the head, vagueness, blankness. and falling asleep. As their distance making machinery starts operating they say "I feel funny;" "I feel dizzy;" "I feel unreal;" "I feel light;" "I feel I'm lifting;" "I feel I'm floating out of the room;" "Everything around me looks unreal;" or "You seem to be getting small and blurry." Hypnogogic reverie, depersonalization, and trance states reflect more intense responses. Ultimately there may be such extreme manifestations as amnesia, fugue states, furor states, dual personality, and neurotic and psychotic stupor states.

During the first visit of her family to her new home in suburbia. following a marriage they all opposed to a man they all detested, Linda C. became mountingly and unbearably tense and anxious.

After about a week Linda impulsively rushed out of the house and telephoned a neighbor who for some months had been trying to seduce her. Driving from the motel where they had had sexual relations, she exceeded the speed limit, went through red lights, and drove north on southbound streets in midtown Manhattan. At the periphery of her awareness Linda heard people on the sidewalk screaming at her, as did people in passing cars while wildly blowing their horns, "Lady, lady, you're driving in the wrong direction!" That she did not cause a serious accident is a miracle.

In her session the following day, Linda was very tense, and anxious. She rarely met my gaze as she sat on the edge of her chair opposite me. As the session proceeded, while glancing frequently at the door, she told me some of what happened with much anxiety and shame. More and more frantically she looked toward the door. She left ten minutes before the session ended, muttering something about not being able to stand it any more. In her year of analysis, this was the first time she had done this. It did not happen in the year and a half thereafter.

In the next session, two days later, Linda was quieter and, in the third, she had returned to her usual level of stability. In the first session, she blurted out, "Just because my whole family and my husband are sick doesn't mean I have to be so sick and have them as partners." Even before analysis, she had been aware that life without a partner was unbearable and unthinkable.

By the third session, Linda was recognizing that what had sent her into a panic was the sudden juxaposition of the reality of herself with how she had seen herself in her imagination and in her Idealized Image. Her image of herself was that she had complete control of herself and of the environment. She could always manipulate everybody. Right alongside this aspect of her image was another in which she saw herself as an innocent little girl. She recognized that she had been impulsively and compulsively driven to meet the neighbor at a motel. This contradicted her need for control and her ability to manipulate others to serve her needs. She now saw that she had been the helpless victim of her impulses. She also characterized her behavior as that of a slut and a whore, words she loathed and found most humiliating because they contradicted her image of herself as the innocent virginal maiden.

As we discussed what had happened she spontaneously said, "I hate analysis. I don't want to see you any more. Everytime I come here I see more about myself that I don't want to know about. I don't want to know any more about myself. Everytime I see the reality about myself it's something more that I don't like. But I know I will continue in analysis and continue to see reality."

The analytic work had been slowly confronting her with the reality of herself, but it was the sudden and massive reality intrusion of her family in conflict with her husband that had raised the level of her anxieties and her tension to unbearable proportions. Under those conditions, she fled from the external sources of tension increase, a solution she had used frequently. But flight did not suffice to allay her anxieties. She resorted to her most deeply imbedded solution, the need for a partner, a male partner, and a male partner in sex. When the reality of what she had done hit her, her tension and anxiety mounted precipitously, and she tried to flee from it. While her conflicts with her family and husband had increased the tension, she had herself brought about the sudden juxtaposition of reality, her reality, and how she saw herself in her idealized picture of herself. Linda also operated on the premises of the total solution of magic.

The confused state she was in after the meeting in the motel could be described as frenzied and clouded, a mixture bordering on a fugue and furor state. In this frantic flight from intrusive reality, there was also a violent attempt at denial. Prior to this episode, there had been several dreams in which she had portrayed and experienced herself as two different people. In the dream she became anxious and woke in terror. Later she wondered if she might not be a schizophrenic. She was not, although she was severely alienated, precariously held together, and at times somewhat paranoid. The presence of considerable assets kept her in balance and contributed to the unexpectedly rapid progress in the therapy.

Although I said that patients who live on the premises of the total solution of magic are not overtly or predominantly psychotic, the potential for transient and even extended psychotic-like and micropsychotic breaks is there. These possibilities are there because intensities and extensities of the psychotic process are present. The structure of the total solution of magic also helps make more understandable "The Intensity of Casual Relationships in Schizophrenia" and "The Communications of Psychotics."(263)

This solution is extensively discussed because increasing numbers of patients being treated analytically manifest it in their psychic structure. They have variously been diagnosed as severe character disorders, borderline syndrome, *(209)* and pseudo-neurotic schizophrenia, as well as occult *(264)* and compensated schizophrenia.

What I have described under the total solution of magic, Little has discussed as "Delusional Transference (Transference Psychosis)." *(265)* Her clinical observations and descriptions of what happens during therapy are very similar to mine. Although her orientation is Freudian, some of her theoretical formulations are very close to my own. She refers to one type of dream in which "the manifest and the latent content are one, and the manifest content is the dream thought." This I described in pointing out the difficulty such patients have in discriminating dream, fantasy, imagination, and reality. Little also refers to a "pan-autism," which would also fit with the extreme irrationality I have described. Little adds, "Acting out is violent, or the violence appears negatively as passivity. These patients call a good deal of attention to themselves, involve other people in their affairs, and interfere in the affairs of others." My case citations are illustrative of what Little describes, only I would speak of their acting out and acting in. I have spoken in several places of the amount of activity there is in so-called passive processes.

Little develops her ideas on the state of "total identity with the analyst, and of an undifferentiatedness from him" in "On Basic Unity."*(365)* I agree with her that symbiosis, a term some writers use, is misleading, and wish to add that parasitic is also an inaccurate description, as is the notion of fusion. All three imply prior separate identity and separation. Little uses the adjective total as I do. She makes identity with the analyst and undifferentiatedness from him the same. "The state of total undifferentiatedness I have called 'basic unity'; it is, actually a delusion, but a valuable one." To speak of identity, even when it seems total, is to assume a prior separation which beclouds the nature and structure of the undifferentiatedness. Empirically, of course, and to a real extent these patients can discriminate themselves from the analyst and others, but "this awareness of reality is used as a defense against the delusion."*(265)*

The subject/object dichotomy inherent in Freudian methodology and metapsychology accounts for so many speaking of fusion, symbiosis, and parasitism. It is also why Little makes identity and undifferentiatedness the same. However, in what follows in her paper, it seems that she has undercut that split.

Little presents a position which, if not the same, is very similar to my own regarding the essentialness of the mother-child unity as fact and as paradigm, and the undifferentiated continuum of the "all in the all," the ground of all being. From it the symbolic spiral emerges. From it emerge human autonomy, spontaneity, and creativity; the urge toward self-realization (Horney); and the autonomous conflict free spheres in the ego (Hartmann).

Little postulates "that a universal idea exists, as normal and essential as is the Oedipus complex, which cannot develop without it, an idea of the absolute identity with the mother upon which survival depends." She adds, "The presence of this idea is the foundation of mental health, development of a whole person, the capacity for holistic thinking. It is to be found not only in the delusions of the mentally sick, where it takes the form of transference psychosis, but also in the sane and the healthy.

"Within an individual both survival and the ability to find objects with which relationships can be formed depend upon the existence of a unity which comes from the entity mother-infant (or analyst-analysand). From it a rhythm of differentiation and reassimilation or integration comes. It provides the 'stillness at the centre' which allows of movement and perception; it is the *sine qua non* for living continuously in one's body, for having an identity, and for being identical with, and able to make assertion or statement of, oneself."*(265)*

In the history of psychoanalysis, it is noteworthy that therapists have agreed regarding clinical observations while, because of theoretical persuasions, their interpretations have been disparate. Also striking has been the recent transcending of existing theoretical positions and the increasing general congruence of viewpoints. Crucial factors have been a grounding and interest in other disciplines or a deep concern with a particular group of patients. Horney is an exemplar with her knowledge of philosophy, sociology, and anthropology. I feel Little's work with severely ill patients contributed to the widening of her theoretical viewpoints as it did for Fromm-Reichmann and Sullivan. Hartmann's background in the natural sciences and the humanities; Erikson's in anthropology, sociology, and history; and Anna Freud's work with children were significant factors moving them in the direction of holism.

What has been discussed regarding patients who live on the premises of the total solution of magic can be taught, as the following supervisory experience, related to me by J. R. Buchanan, M.D., illustrates.

The therapist presented his work with Millicent F., a young woman who was a practicing lesbian, living with her young lover. The patient had been in analysis three months on a three times a week schedule. In his first supervisory session, he told me something about his initial interview, continued discussing it in the second session, and also related a bit of her life history.

In that session I described to him something of the formal structure and the dynamics of this girl's problem and what he might expect in his work with her.

In the third session of his work with her, while relating life history Millicent reported this dream, her first during analysis: "I am mutilating my mother, and others are helping me to escape." This dream is illustrative of many of the points to be made regarding first analytic dreams. It gives a clear picture of how she sees herself, her mother, her world, and her mother in it. It describes how she sees analysis, the analyst, and what she wants from him. Among other things, she expected his help in mutilating her mother, which implied all mothers and motherliness, all females and femaleness. The theme of mutilating was explicitly defined: it would happen between mother and daughter, that is, between younger and older females. In this same session, Millicent mentioned that as a child she had frequent fantasies of mutilating her mother's genitals with a knife. This was a picture of herself with a penis. It was an indication of how she saw sexual intercourse specifically and human intercourse generally. It was also an expression of her hatred of female genitals, her own included.

Mutilating also implies being mutilated. Her mother and all females are externalizations of herself. The mutilating and being mutilated was very obvious in the sadomasochistic structure of Millicent's relationships, particularly with her lover. Her identity, sexual identity — and very specifically as gender identity — but also her core and real self identity are all experienced as mutilated and being mutilated. She experiences herself not only as mutilated, but also as basically defective. The theme of mutilation often goes with intensive masochism. Her sadism — also present — was concealed and subtle until it emerged with violence under special circumstances. This subtlety in sadism was present in the earlier phases of the analysis until she became surer of herself. Then it became more open.

Mutilation, with its implied hatred, cruelty, violence, and destructiveness, was directed toward herself predominantly in the early phases of her relationship with her lover. It appeared subtly against her partner at first and later became more overt.

Quite frequently in the dreams of homosexuals the theme of mutilation and its consequences appears. In extreme forms, their dreams may contain truncated bodies, only the torso present, dismembered parts, corpses, and dead babies. Such dreams may, of course, also occur with other severely ill patients and in those of psychotics.

267

As a child, Millicent did not simply want *to be* a boy, but *to turn* into a boy which meant a painful awareness of what she was and what she wanted to turn against and deny. She played boys' games with boys, often as the leader. Her behavior, thoughts, fantasies, and dreams revealed a preoccupation with sex, sexual behavior, genitals, and the body as a sexual vehicle, which is so frequently evident in homosexuals. In addition to the private language of the homosexual subculture, the language of homosexuals — male and female — is explicitly sexual and sexualized, with all manner of sexual innuendo and double entendre.

Almost exactly three months from the day he began work with her, my colleague opened our third supervisory session with surprise and delight. He informed me that on the day before "Millicent had a dream with me in it":

"I had a beautiful dream which took place in your office, but the office was different, like a motel. I was with a boy friend, maybe Bob. In haste, instead of knocking or waiting in the waiting room, we entered into the inner room. I was fifteen or twenty minutes early and burst in with him. A woman just finished having relations with you. She left hastily through the other exit with her bra and slip in her hand. I don't know if she was your wife or lover. I was embarrassed. We had the session. I referred to the woman as being annoyed, and you explicitly denied that you or she was annoyed. Somewhere along the way I caught you without your hairpiece I thought you wore. You were older and less attractive. [The therapist is young and good looking and with a full head of hair.] I was taken aback and surprised. In the dream it was obviously you; you were bald and less poised. For our next session the next day I had to wait all day long. You kept putting me off. I was finally put in with another patient who was in the next office, and you alternated between the two of us. I was annoyed. I also saw Raymond; he and Franklin were coming to see you. I told them they would have to wait all day too."

Bob is a young homosexual, younger than the patient, who is not a sexual threat. He liked Millicent's lover Lucy. Raymond works where the patient does in an advertising agency. She suspects he is homosexual, and that he is involved with Franklin, who works in another department of the same firm. The patient had dated Raymond several years before, and experienced him as trying unconvincingly to act flirtatious.

Right after the patient reported the dream, she continued with associations about the various figures in the dream starting with the therapist and the behaviors she manifested in the dream. On several occasions the doctor indicated support for her continuing to associate by saying, "Yes," "Um hum," and "Can you say some more about the dream?" Only once did he make a comment that could be regarded as explicitly interpretive. Millicent was talking about the way she burst into the office, and about other occasions of "catching somebody unawares." She had just talked of never having caught her parents unawares in sex, but how she had often seen her mother rushing to the bathroom looking as though she had just had sex. At this point, the therapist repeated the phrase "catching somebody unawares" with a questioning tone, indicating that she should explore this experience more. What I want to make clear is that it was the dynamism of the therapy, the emergence, and reporting of the dream which were almost solely responsible for what happened. The interpretive comment was minimal as a contributory factor.

In the session following the reporting and the discussion of the dream, Millicent experienced, described, and identified two short episodes of depersonalization. In the next session she reported a "vicious fight with Lucy" which the therapist accurately described as "an attempt at restitution." The following session, she was very depressed, felt fatigued, and requested tranquilizers. The next session, she wanted to give up her job, her apartment, her lover, the analysis, and go back home and live with her parents. In the following session, she was feeling much better. She and Lucy had had sex the previous night and both were satisfied. In the next months, she maintained a relative degree of stabilization, with a little more substantiality than previously, while living and working through this analytic sequence.

This progress was a response to the emergence, relating, and discussion of the dream and the many juxtapositions it created between dream, fantasy, reality, and living in imagination. This happened in the context of a beginning doctor-patient relationship (transference). As I have mentioned, the early appearance of a doctor-patient relationship dream frequently obtains with patients who are living through the total solution of magic.

Chapter 17

Dreams III: Self-idealization, the Disillusioning Process, and Working Through

Participating in and prerequisite to the evolution of the total solution of magic is all that Horney subsumes under the process of self-idealization. "Self-idealization, in its various aspects, is what I suggest calling a *comprehensive neurotic solution,* i.e., a solution not only for a particular conflict but one that implicitly promises to satisfy all inner needs . . . it promises [a person] an ultimately mysterious fulfillment of himself and his life." In this process, *"the energies driving toward self-realization are shifted to the aim of actualizing the idealized self."(49, pp. 23-24)* "We may consider the idealized image as a bit of psychosis woven into the texture of neurosis."*(39, p. 97)*

The following dream vividly portrays an undermined and collapsing idealized image. The disillusioning process is shown in operation, as well as the beginning shift of energies from the service of the idealized image to the aim of self-realization.

A middle-aged man, Martin C., opened the session with comments about an attack of anxiety, a response to his having been more open and involved in the previous session. He also reported an attack of fright after blowing up at his wife the night before. It made Martin sharply aware of his murderous rage. These opening comments reflected a positive dynamic in the therapy, an increased awareness of himself, and the repercussion to these healthy movements experienced as fright and anxiety.

"In a dream last night I was trying to inflate an image of myself. It was several stories high. Oh, yes, there was a recollection of when it had been inflated. It lay on the sidewalk in a heap. It had aspects of myself. It had served the purpose of a front at one time, and I felt frustrated and hopeless. I couldn't reinflate it. Maybe because there was a slit in it. It could be blown up by mouth. It didn't have the feeling of disintegration."

Martin went on to say that he had thought he had good relations with people. Here he found out that they are illusory and inflated because right after being close, open, and cooperative with me he became frightened and tense. His wife had also said that what he regarded as good relations with his son were in fact encouraging unhealthy compliance in the boy. Her evidence was that when the boy did not comply, the father went into a rage. For several weeks Martin had been talking about conflict between his compliant and aggressive trends. He was frightened at how he could lose himself in his violence. If he is compliant, which he calls his good relations with people, and they don't immediately respond, he blows up at them.

This dream portrays the illusory and insubstantial nature of an idealized image and the collapsed magical belief that it could be inflated by mouth. He knows he is a big talker, and that often what he says is a lot of hot air. Its size, two stories high, is also indicative of his grandiosity and of his investment in his image. He is aware that when it is threatened from without, when people do not immediately affirm that he is a nice guy, which is really a facade, he blows up in a gigantic rage which disrupts his whole precarious psychic structure.

Martin had hurt his neurotic pride by factually being more open and cooperative in the previous session. This means he had threatened his neurotic structure, his idealized image, and his neurotic pride in pseudo-goodness and in self-sufficiency. The result was an onslaught of self-hate, which he felt only indirectly as anxiety and as being in the power of that anxiety. The attempt to restore hurt pride by more hot air is frustrated. He feels hopeless about closing the slit, but Martin is the one who put the slit in his baloon in the first place. Tyrannical shoulds can be inferred. He should be a nice guy. He coerces himself to give a facsimile of being a nice guy and it boomerangs. Shoulds to be self-sufficient can also be conjectured. There is moreover not only the talk about struggle; it is also portrayed and experienced in the conflict between self-effacement and expansiveness. Beneath his pseudo-compliance are powerful dependency needs which terrify him. In becoming aware of them, he experiences their clashing with his needs for self-sufficiency. Finally Martin is terrified of the rages he has when his neutrotic claims based on dependency needs are not fulfilled.

Such naive reliance on magic to create and restore an idealized image when it is undermined is also evident in the next dream. Because of a host of factors, including seven years of analysis, and in spite of a poor initial prognosis, the man with the collapsed image did quite well in life, as I knew from a twenty-three year follow-up. He did better than the woman to be discussed.

The initial prognosis for Claudia S. was also poor, contributed to by extensive evidences of the psychopathic process. (153, 208) External factors, plus only two years of analysis, also accounted for the limited result which was affirmed in a twenty-six year follow-up. Four-year-old Dolly, her third and youngest child, was her adored — the child who was to be the actualization of her idealized image. Dolly, now a grown young woman, did much better in life than I would have anticipated. There is so much the analyst cannot identify that contributes to unexpected outcomes, positive and adverse. Maybe Dolly got something from her mother I didn't see, and much more from her father than I expected because, though a brilliant man in his field, he was dominated by his wife.

In the dream, Dolly is seen before three mirrors. In one she is seen looking at herself having a temper tantrum like she had had in the afternoon when she didn't want to come in and have supper and go to bed. In the second mirror, she is whining. "I [Claudia] said to her, 'Why don't you go into the third mirror where the more usual picture of yourself is, where you are constructive, pleasant, and lovable?' " This magic with mirrors is an attempt to restore her collapsing and collapsed idealized image, which are evident in mirrors one and two.

In the face of such powerful pulls toward the total solution of magic driven by the comprehensive neurotic solution of attempting to actualize the idealized image, what do the patient and the analyst have to rely on? Where can they look for help to begin the slow process of shifting the balance of energy investment back toward supporting the urge toward self-realization?

Horney said that "in dreams . . . constructive forces can be at work, even at a time when they are hardly visible otherwise . . . . From dreams with constructive elements the patient can catch a glimpse, even in the initial phase of analysis, of a world operating within him which is peculiarly his own, and which is more true to his feelings than the world of his illusions. These assets can be seen in constructive attempts at solutions in dreams. Horney said further that dreams "represent attempts to solve our conflicts either in a neurotic or in a healthy way."(49, p. 349)

Assets are reflected in dreams as specific symbols or symbol arrangements, as relationships of persons, places, times, and behaviors which have or have had constructive import. When one patient thought he might have to interrupt his analysis for lack of funds, he "recalled" through a dream, money he had secreted in a savings bank so successfully that he had "forgotten" about it. Another man "recalled" the promise of an uncle to help him if in great need. Through the symbolization of a visit to an art museum, and via associations to the watercolors he saw there, Chalmers A., a thirty-five-year-old man, "recalled" that between fifteen and nineteen he had done watercolors. In the following session, two days later, Chalmers reported this dream.

"I am in front of a canvas on which I was painting. There were various areas in color, including one of lavender in one corner. The painting was in the beginning stages. A voice close by said, 'You can paint.' Then, as if I said, 'How?' without verbalizing it the voice said, 'Keep on painting.' I thought, 'I'll put some green over that lavender.'" He recalled a friend saying, "To learn to paint, you have to mix your colors on the canvas." My patient, a writer, added, "I sit in front of a blank piece of paper on a typewriter until something comes."

In the following session, Chalmers informed me that he doesn't believe anything if I say it or he says it, but waits for it to be confirmed in a dream. He takes that as evidence and proof. Then he can go on. He resumed painting shortly after the dream. His professional writing also improved.

In dreams we are geniuses in memory. In books on dreams, many examples are reported of the vivid and detailed recall, verified as to their accuracy, of events that happened many decades earlier.

Dreams are an expression of the creative process. This one is pure poetry; it speaks universal truths with simplicity and wisdom:

"I am speaking with a girl. She seems attractive; is Jewish. Her fiance is somewhere about, but not visually present. I understand, know, that they are living together openly as man and wife, yet are not legally married. I seem to inquire somehow about the situation. She says: 'When his seed takes root and grows within me, then is the time we'll marry.' " The dream is saying that when the spirit is one with creation, then growth will take place which society will formalize.

This dream portrayed Rebecca Z.'s dawning wish to have another child with her husband in a spirit of union and communion. She is not Jewish. I am. She has many Jewish friends. She had been married ten years, and there were two children. Two years after this dream, she interrupted her analysis. Two years after that, she had a third child who has given her the greatest joy of her three children. By the time she left the city — the external reason for her interruption — she had begun, for the first time, in her fourteen years of married life, to feel "really married." It is twenty-one years since I last saw this woman, although I continue to hear from her from time to time. Her life, which had been destructive and filled with much pain before she began analysis, has steadily become richer with a deepening joy in her marriage and her children.

Bjerre was one of the first to write about the curative process in dreaming. *(266)* Horney also emphasized this process. The following example illustrates not only the curative process, but also the constructive momentum of analysis:

Aften ten days at her country home, Olive S. felt things were as bad between her husband and herself as before she had begun her analysis four years previously. Visiting them were old friends, the Grants. Olive had thought of marrying Sam Grant before she met her husband Jack. Sam's wife, Beatrice, was a brilliant, but very critical woman who had mellowed after about fifteen years of marriage. My patient was mentally comparing her husband with Sam Grant and feeling much abused by her husband's drivenness to have things go his way and his insensitivity to her and the children.

"I saw myself put upon, but did not see how I gave cause for his behavior. Finally, after a particularly nasty round of argument and bickering, I began to ask myself what was wrong with my position. Then I realized that I was constantly fantasying how things would be better if I was married to almost anyone else, including Sam Grant or Dr. Cranston. He had been our family doctor when we lived year round in the country and had become a family friend. I realized that my approach had been of trying to make Jack fit into my plans, rather than to get his cooperation in making them. I was just beginning to see things when I had the following dream:

"Dr. Cranston was asking me if he could marry Elizabeth within the next few months. I agreed, though I realized that she was only ten [in fact, her daughter was only five] and that there was a great age difference between them. I did not consult with anyone, nor did I tell Elizabeth until the day of the wedding. When I told Elizabeth, she complained, 'I don't want to stop playing yet.' I sympathized with her, but said there was nothing we could do about it since I had promised Dr. Cranston. Someone raised the question with me about whether I knew anything about Dr. Cranston. He might be syphilitic. Moreover, did he know that Elizabeth had not yet matured physically. I had a talk with Dr. Cranston in which he said that he had had syphilis, but was now cured; and that he was annoyed because he did not know that Elizabeth had not yet matured, but he supposed he would just have to wait for that. However, he wanted me to know that she would have to act as mature as a grown woman at all times."

"I awakened with a feeling of horror of nightmarish proportions. Here, because I was a manipulator, because I was compliant, I had involved Elizabeth in a situation which was horrible. In the dream, I saw no way out. Almost immediately, I connected the dream with the difficulties Jack and I had had. Without analyzing the dream very much, I felt somehow that my attitudes, which had compounded the situation, were somehow resolved — that my manipulation and compliance, my refusal to deal straight with Jack because of the presence of the Grants, had either caused or greatly exaggerated the way Jack felt toward me, toward the place, and toward his work there. From then on, I began to be able to relate directly to Jack, to love him for himself, and not for his appearance as a husband. Life became a much better kind of process. For some reason, the dream stayed with me as a perfectly remembered lump about which I did very little. I knew, however, that during it and through it certain kinds of conflicts had been resolved, that somehow the dream was a summation of negative attitudes which I had never seen clearly before as wholly destructive. Now that I had so seen them, they were to a large extent inoperative."

The above was reported in our first session in September. We continued to discuss the dream and her summer for the next few weeks. In a session in early October, Olive said, "In working through this dream with you, I saw that Elizabeth really stood for my newer self, the self emerging from analysis, and that there were apparently no lengths to which I would not go to prostitute that self in the service of older and neurotic trends. In the light of this, the dream took on much wider significance because I saw the trends already understood as destructive to be self-destructive. It seems that the unconscious reaction to the dream, inasmuch as my behavior became more positive immediately after dreaming it, was in line with this interpretation. For, what I seemed to be doing, and to connect with, was 'the cutting off my nose to spite my face' behavior.

"It occurs to me as I'm telling you this, that one reason it took me so long to get at this dream and what it meant to me is that the dream shocked me into forswearing some of the dishonesty in compliance and manipulation. While it is true that from then on I acted much more honestly in each specific situation, it was as if I did not wish to look upon that as a progress consciously achieved, but as a kind of coercion from within that I could not and did not want to understand. Hence my statements upon returning to analysis, 'I feel better but I don't know why,' 'I act better, but it's not because I have a clear goal in mind but because it is inevitable — I cannot do other — but I have no enthusiasm for it.' It seems to me that the positive advance which was presented in seeing the implications of the dream and the change in my behavior threatened the worthless feelings, so that I could not let myself enjoy the fruits of it completely even while I could not reject the immutable fact that the dream had had a powerful effect for the better."

Patients' dreams, and their comments about them, often speak with an aliveness of expression and poetry which is desiccated by theoretical constructions. This dream and what followed from it reveals that analysis has a momentum; that the momentum can be constructive; that dreams can be curative; that analysis goes on between sessions and during longer interruptions; and that self-analysis can go on against one's conscious will. Her words "a kind of coercion from within" are most apt and poetic. Often that is the way patients describe their response to the increasing dynamic and momentum of constructive forces in them. Another described it as "like being goosed from inside." What is feeling coerced are all those processes subsumed under blockages. She clearly identified a specific one, namely, "the worthless feelings."

It is very difficult to help patients see and experience that much as they bitterly complain about, and factually suffer from, feelings of worthlessness and expressions of self-hate, they can nevertheless have an integrating function for the patient, serve as most tenacious defenses, and have enormous subjective value, since they are heavily invested with neurotic pride. It is also most difficult to help both patients and beginning analysts experience that on the basis of these feelings, patients make inordinate or — to use Horney's term — neurotic claims. (49) Through such worthless feelings they act out considerable amounts of vindictiveness, hostility, and cruelty. They use such worthless feelings as a mechanism for guilt instilling purposes to which they remain adamantly blind. This is seen when the defensive or neurotic protective structure is shaken. There are not only "repercussions," but there may also be a "negative therapeutic reaction." This happened to the woman just discussed. Two years after interrupting analysis, as a response to interruption and to assuming fuller responsibility for herself and her self-analysis, she suffered from a gastric condition for about a year. It disappeared and never recurred. She and her husband went on to live increasingly productive and fuller lives, which I can confirm from a twenty-three year follow-up.

For movement to take place in the direction of self-realization, stands must be taken. It means there is a dilemma, at times with awareness of it. A stand is a confrontation, a saying yes to the more authentic, and no to the more inauthentic. It is often visible in dreams long before there is clear evidence of a stand in the patient's associations or in his daily living.

A middle-aged engineer, Luke C., had been in analysis for three years with quite some benefit. He was getting restless in the city, preferring to live in smaller communities which he had most of his life. He gave a number of other reasons, which were essentially rationalizations, for leaving New York and interrupting his analytic work. At the time of the dream, Luke had been designing a special piece of machinery for the plant at which he worked.

"As I began dreaming, the picture of the mechanism was blotted out by people moving in between it and me. I felt them as observing, but not as interferers. They were taking the place of something inanimate. I felt drawn to these people. I feel in the dream I'm in front of them when a cry comes from me. I don't know if I cried out in the dream. It's a cry of despair and defiance. I cry 'I must have another year in the city.' Then I am again a part of the moving mass of people, and again the idea of the mechanism is submerged in the people. There is no delight or fear in the dream only the feeling of something in process."

People take the place of an inanimate mechanism. The animate is poetically portrayed by a "moving mass of people." The cry of despair and defiance is clearly a stand for life against the lifeless, for the life in him and against flight. Luke not only took one more year, he took three. He remained in analysis a total of six years, with considerable benefit attested to by a twenty-one year follow-up.

Horney placed great emphasis on feelings, particularly in dreams. (74) The therapist asks, "What did you feel in the dream?" "on awakening?" "as you relate the dream now?" Then there are questions regarding feelings in connection with particular symbols or symbol arrangements in the dreams; comparison of feelings in dreams containing the same or similar symbols; changing feeling patterns in dreams, for example, the emergence of feelings where none had been present; the disappearance of certain feelings, and the appearance of quite new ones; and the changes in fear and anxiety dreams and the attitudes toward them.

"Jane [his wife] and I were out in the mid-West on a train. It was night and in the desert. We got out. There was a small mound of sand we had to climb. I said, 'Jane, the wind seems warm. The chill air is moist and chilly, but when the sun comes up it will be hot.' I seem to remember those feelings of warm and moist. Was a real barren place. That gave me the chills." "How were you feeling in the dream?" "I was chilly throughout. I am chilly as hell now. I kept thinking about those two feelings, warm and moist, and hot and dry. They seem to be due to the climate."

This was the first dream in Raymond B.'s barren inner and, in large measure, outer life in which some warm feelings began to emerge. But this could happen only under these stringently controlled circumstances; out in the midwest, while in transit, at night, in a desert, and in the midst of chilliness. The dream was so real and so alive that he kept having chilly feelings throughout the session. Raymond recognized the conditions required before he would let go of his control of his feelings. But the fact is he did. There is also the anticipation that when the sun rose it would be hot and dry. This is also a prophecy. At the end of the session, he said, "Strange. I woke Jane this morning [she usually remains asleep after he gets up] and stayed by the bed and kidded with her. I felt different toward her." In the morning the sun did rise, and Raymond was warmer toward his wife. More years of analysis and a twenty-year follow-up revealed the slow emergence of his feelings and an increasingly productive life. External, adverse circumstances slowed the pace of their emergence.

The following dream of John E. portrays the creative, the curative, taking a stand, the emergence of constructive forces, and "Finding the Real Self."(45)

"There is a long low island in the middle of the river which I identify as a river well known to me in my childhood. This island belongs to me, and I have known of it for a long time but never visited it. There is an inaccessible quality to the island. It is in the middle of the river and uninhabited. I approach the island, just how is not clear in the dream. I step ashore and start to explore. Much to my surprise, as I come to the side of this supposedly uninhabited island, I find a number of bicycle tire tracks running along the shore. I follow them and come to a doorway which is built into the side of a ledge of rock. I enter this doorway and come to a stairway which I start to ascend. At the head of each flight of stairs is a closed door. I know that behind each door there is a man lying in wait with a gun. He is waiting for someone, but it is not I that he waits for. I stop in front of each door and declare in a loud voice that it is I, and then enter and climb the next flight of stairs. I see no one, but I feel the presence of the waiting person behind every door and so I declare myself each time before I enter. In this manner, I mount through this darkly and apparently deserted building for some four or five flights."

This dream emerged in the fifth year of John's analysis which continued for two more. I have a twenty-two year follow-up. People whose opinion I respected said analysis was contra-indicated because of a possible psychotic break. This did not happen during or after analysis. His life became increasingly productive. Because of John's life history, temperament, abilities, and neurotic structure, what he gained in therapy and life is being tested as he passes seventy and cannot be as fully active as he used to be. John seems to be having mild, depressive episodes with some agitation. However, he continues an active life, possible through the continued support of his wife, children, and friends, both old and new, toward whom he has been able to reach out.

Just as the analyst can see in dreams earlier and clearer delineation of constructive attempts at the resolution of conflicts, so can he identify and encourage the undermining of neurotic attempts at solution. Their ebb and flow, portrayed in dreams, gives us clear guides as to what is happening in the analytic process and what is being worked through.

Aspects of the comprehensive neurotic solution of attempting to actualize the idealized image have been presented. Horney also identified major and partial neurotic solutions which became revised and amplified in their evolution from *Our Inner Conflicts* to *Neurosis and Human Growth.* She referred to the totality of neurotic solutions as the neurotic character structure. (She occasionally called it the neurotic protective structure.) Its function was to defend against the disruptive effects of basic and central inner conflict and to maintain a feeling of wholeness, constancy, and integrity, however precarious. In *Neurosis and Human Growth,* she delineated the major solutions of self-effacement, expansiveness, and resignation. Each solution has intrapsychic and interpersonal reference.

The partial solutions she referred to as "general measures to relieve tension." They are *alienation from self, externalisation of inner experiences, compartmentalization or psychic fragmentation, automatic control,* and *the supremacy of the mind. (49)* They represent a rearrangement and reformulation of what she had called in *Our Inner Conflicts* "the auxiliary approaches to artificial harmony." They are *blind spots, compartmentalization, rationalization, excessive self-control, arbitrary rightness, elusiveness, and cynicism. (39) Externalization* she dealt with separately, distinguishing it from projection. "Projection means the shifting of blame and responsibility to someone for subjectively rejected trends or qualities . . . . Externalization . . . is a more comprehensive phenomenon. The shifting of responsibility is only part of it. Not only one's faults are experienced in others, but to a greater or less degree all feelings."*(39, p. 116)*

All these solutions are supported by "the tyranny of the *shoulds.*" The solutions are invested with "neurotic pride." "Self-hate" is the response when the latter is hurt from within; when hurt from without, hatred is directed outward as vindictiveness. *(49)* The vicissitudes of these solutions, and responses to threats to them, are exquisite guides to the progress in the therapy. Some of these solutions have been portrayed in dreams presented thus far. Others will appear in dreams to follow.

Beginners in analysis unwittingly universalize the meaning of babies emerging in dreams and assign them constructive import. While the appearance of a baby in the following dream did reflect a movement in a constructive direction, what the baby stood for was something predominantly very sick, which emphasizes the need to view and understand dreams in the total context and the subsequent course of the therapy.

"Ruthie is a baby. She is beautiful and happy and I am enjoying her, not as my baby, but as my creation. Other parts to the dream I forgot. This was really the only part I was interested in."

My immediate feeling response to Myra J.'s dream was a hollow sick feeling in the pit of my stomach which for me was diagnostic. It was an instance of openness to the responses of the person of the analyst as instrument. Before this dream, there had been a long series of baby dreams in which they were dead, sick, black, or monsters. The babies gradually became healthier, but they always had some defect or other destructive element in them. Just before this dream, she had admitted to having some positive feelings toward me for the first time. The dream sequence and the analytic relationship would seem to indicate constructive changes in the therapy. They were there, but they had to be examined with caution.

Myra was extremely alienated, much dictated to by the total solution of magic. She had a most tenacious image of herself as being beautiful, romantic, and loving, with a feeling for the finer things. She was pervaded by pretenses in depth. She was egocentric, haughty, insensitive, and quite cruel. Myra talked endlessly about love. This image was a survival defense against experiencing feelings of self-loathing, cruelty, and moral torpitude which she could not allow herself to know about, much less feel. The evidences for this were in her life history, her current behavior, and in her dreams.

Myra's dream of her daughter and her admitting positive feelings toward me came at the point when there had been some slight constructive moves which might have opened her to what she was in terror of. She had taken about all she could of the destructiveness in herself which was reflected in her baby dreams. With the magic of her mind she recreated her creation, her daughter, age twelve, into a beautiful baby. There is no mention of her husband's part. With an icy, cold, queenly, haughtiness she said, "This was really the only part I was interested in." We were to be at such a point many times as the analysis proceeded by micromillimeters for the next four years.

I have fairly good evidence that this rate of growth continued for about the next ten years and then almost stopped. It is now twenty-six years since I first saw her, and I feel she has — at seventy — reverted to some of her old patterns as several illnesses and age began to take their toll. An able designer, she became more proficient and successful. The need for recognition and prestige became more urgent with years. She dissipated her energies in association with self-appointed poetry and art groups which gave her the quick empty adulation she so desperately needed.

The intensity of her neurotic pride and its vulnerability are evident as are tyrannical shoulds to buttress it. The dead, defective, and monstrous babies bespeak enormous self-hate from which she had to flee. Anxiety and despair were constantly imminent, if not present. Her foreground major solution was expansiveness. Also easily visible was self-effacement and very evident was severe resignation manifested mainly in a terror of friction. The partial solutions of the supremacy of the mind, externalization, psychic fragmentation, elusiveness (not only to others but also to herself), and alienation and cynicism were there. Obvious sadism was also present.

The evidence of self-hate as excruciating feelings of unlovability are present in the following dream, as was self-destructiveness in the life history. There had been a succession of suicidal depressions, each with diminishing intensity. There were several before I began seeing her, more during, and several after, while she was working with a third and fourth therapist.

"I had the most wonderful dream last night. I was a can of peaches. I was the one on top and I was going to be eaten." The dream was related with much hilarity, a tight smile, and horror in her eyes which was there most of the time. In the dream she is a thing, packed in a tin by assembly line techniques, and preserved in syrup, namely, concentrated sweetness. She is on top, where she is sure to be noticed and admired. Because of her deliciousness, she will be eaten with pleasure and gusto and end up inside of someone's stomach.

The degree of alienation from self is terrifying. She is a thing, an object. The best one can say about the objectification is that she is a fruit, eatable, enjoyable, and nutritious; but that is not what concerned her. Psychic fragmentation and externalization are also present to an extensive degree. The solution of self-effacement to the point of morbid dependency is obvious, that of expansiveness is also there but not so evident. While resignation was less evident, it was present in all three forms, with shallow living being the most obvious.

282

She must be overwhelmingly desirable so that people will want to take her in, that is, protect, love, and incorporate her. In fact, she would almost hug herself when she said, "I would like to be inside of him. Then I'd be warm and comfortable and safe." But this solution had its terrors. For, while she wanted to be safe inside, she recognized the pull toward self-extinction and oblivion. As a defense, with which she could only go so far before she became terrified, she needed to seduce, manipulate, paralyze with adorableness and love, and then swallow and devour. If she felt she had succeeded, and this of course particularly obtained with men, she would panic and make sure never to see the man again.

That this woman's life was saved through analysis cannot be gainsaid. It made possible marriage, children, and increasing success in her career, not without much pain and many hardships along the way. Withal, there has been a new ability to enjoy her marriage and her children, and to accept regard and recognition from her colleagues which had in earlier years been too frightening to believe or acknowledge.

In the second year of Eric I.'s analysis, which he terminated about six months later, he reported this dream: "I had a funny dream last night. A head on a stick. That's it." He had a very high I.Q., was gifted in mathematics and in many art forms. He suffered from a lack of self-discipline, a frequent characteristic of gifted people with facile minds. During the course of his analysis, he divorced his wife. Shortly after terminating our work, Eric married a wealthy girl he had known for some years. Eight years after I last saw him, Eric was doing the same kind of professional writing which he had bitterly complained about when seeing me. He had published a book which received fair reviews. I have not heard about Eric since.

The dream clearly indicates the solution of the supremacy of the mind and the need to deny not only all feelings, but also the total body. He felt it was fat and loathsome. It reminded him of sex, about which he had a great problem, and about his eating and drinking which were a source of anguish to him, because he gained weight. His body was the source of feelings which frightened him, especially his violent outbursts of rage and assaultiveness when drunk. Also evident in the dream are severe alienation and psychic fragmentation, as well as the resignation which was present with extensive and obvious shallow living.

283

He had been helped in analysis to be relieved of some of his worst tensions and anxieties, had gotten enough strength to divorce his wife, and gathered enough momentum to advance in his field of professional writing and to produce his book. The reviews corroborated what I felt. The book was intelligent, showed good reporting and attention to detail, but lacked aliveness and originality. Unless he returns to analysis, or life as therapist confronts and moves him, I feel this very gifted man will remain unproductive, driven primarily by the resigned solution of shallow living.

Horney said that dreams "represent attempts to solve our conflicts either in a neurotic or healthy way." A severely resigned and morbidly dependent woman had this dream one year after a serious attempt at suicide. She was just remotely beginning to find her feet under her.

"I was in an airplane between Bessie and Gertrude. I was frightened and woke up in a panic." Bessie is an older self-effacing sister who is ultra feminine and maternal. Gertrude is her oldest sister, expansive and very driving. This is a dramatization of basic conflict, of extreme alienation, of being out of contact with reality, and of extreme grandiosity, deeply buried. My patient had a terror of airplanes, of heights, of being heard, and of existing. In her dream she is trying to unify the two major solutions which are represented by her sisters. She is terrified that she will be pulled apart. In life, these two sisters were in fact constantly pulling at her from opposite directions with opposite attitudes. Her solution of resignation cannot work. Being up in the air, unconnected with the ground and away from her husband on whom she leaned is a picture of expansiveness and severe alienation. She also cannot call on that solution.

The following is another example of a dream which reveals the attempt to keep conflicting major solutions submerged.

Randolph F. had talked quite a bit about Henry and Gwen Saunders, old friends. She was "sweet, self-effacing and self-sacrificing." Henry was seemingly "friendly, but uses people right and left and gets what he wants." The patient had many dreams in which they were involved. Recently Randolph heard that they were having trouble in their marriage, and that there might be a divorce.

Randolph dreamed: "I rushed into their bedroom. Henry and Gwen were lying in bed next to each other. I placed myself across the top of both of them horizontally." My patient's outstanding solution was resignation. Through his friends, as externalizations, he was attempting to keep joined and submerged his self-effacing and expansive solutions. Before and after this dream, there have been many dreams of bridges. In one, the bridge ended half way across a stream. There were also many dreams of crossroads, of converging roads continuing on the same level, and of others where one road went down and one went up. He was deeply concerned about basic conflict breaking through. He kept holding it in check in all kinds of ways as we worked at the partial solutions of supremacy of the mind and automatic control. Earlier in analysis, arbitrary rightness was much in the fore with great intolerance to doubt and uncertainty. Randolph also constantly externalized many of his problems to his wife. This was also partially justified, which made the taking back of externalizations even more difficult. Through working on these partial solutions, his alienation became less. By the time he interrupted analytic work, there had been much resolution of basic conflict and of central inner conflict as well.

In the fourth year of another man's analysis, dreams involving friction, struggle, conflict, and violence began to appear. At first he was an onlooker, at a distance. Gradually he began moving closer, first to the bystander position, then so close he would wake up in panic as he was about to be drawn in the melee. He was finally confronted with staying with, experiencing, and working through the moral alternatives involved in a lifelong nightmare. As far back into childhood as he could recall, and he was thirty-five, he had had this dream:

In the dream there are two sets of parents. Both sets say they are his true parents. He does not know which is false and which is true. Both sets stand there waiting to be chosen by him. He feels that if he chooses the false set, he will lose his real parents whom he naturally wants, and if he chooses his real parents, his false parents will vindictively assault him. He wakes up in a terror, undecided, his dilemma unresolved.

He was seeing and experiencing his basic and central inner conflict, and his moral dividedness which had been the subject of many dreams and discussions. Over the years, he had worked through some of his immorality and cynicism, but when it came to taking a firmer and clearer stand for truth, he could not make it. About six months after his nightmare had come alive in him and in our sessions, he interrupted his analysis. That was nineteen years ago. I know that he has continued to grow within the limits possible, while still avoiding a confrontation with this dilemma in a fundamental way.

Chapter 18

Dreams IV:
Fear and Anxiety Dreams

Anxiety dreams presented a continuing problem to Freud's theory of wish fulfillment. "Lest it should seem that I try to evade this witness against the theory of wish-fulfillment whenever I encounter it, I will at least give some indications as to the explanation of the anxiety-dream."*(267)* Freud concluded that "a dream is an *attempt* at the fulfillment of a wish."*(268)* Horney spoke of attempts at solution in dreams.

Goldstein's ideas on fear and anxiety *(166)* influenced those which I presented in a "Unitary Theory of Anxiety."*(144)* They are basic to my understanding of fear and anxiety dreams generally. They are specifically applicable to "The Traumatic Syndrome."*(184)* Horney concluded that for an understanding of anxiety dreams one must ask and attempt to "answer three questions: What is endangered? What is the source of the change? What accounts for the helplessness toward the danger?"*(35, p. 195)*

"A Unitary Theory of Anxiety" postulates that all systems are in tension. Systems go through phases of distensioning and retensioning, with the tension level of the whole oscillating about a mean. Anxiety supervenes, becomes manifest, is prompted by but is not caused by the mean tension level being exceeded, whether below or above that mean. This is a reformulation of Goldstein's statement that anxiety becomes manifest when the organism and environment are no longer adequate to each other. "The basis of fear is the threat of the onset of anxiety."*(166, p. 291)* It is also a restatement of Horney's ideas. To understand anxiety and anxiety dreams, one must understand the sources of anxiety, the functions that anxiety serves, and the attitudes toward the anxiety. Anxiety is inherently neither healthy nor sick. Anxiety is rational and irrational according to the proportions of rationality and irrationality in its sources, its functions, and the attitudes toward it.

It is not necessarily the evidences of anxiety visible to the onlooker which wake a sleeping person, nor is it the restlessness, rage, laughing, crying, sleep walking, or violent activity. It is the exceeding of the mean level of tension for that depth of sleep, whatever it may be. Spouses have reported repetitive behavior during sleep which "should have awakened" the partner but did not. There may be no recollection of such behavior in the morning, no recalled dreams which could connect with it. Having anxiety dreams and waking from them, with or without experienced anxiety, does not mean something destructive is happening. I have worked with patients who have gone through phases of having nightmares which meant different things depending on the context.

> Nathaniel Y. had terrifying nightmares from infancy. As our work proceeded they abated. He became seriously involved with a girl, Anne. They planned to marry, but his nightmares returned in full force. He broke off the impending marriage at the last minute. For months thereafter he had nightly nightmares which could not be stilled even by drinking himself into a stupor. Nine years later, after about three years of fragmented analysis, he married Anne. The nightmares, almost absent for the previous five years, slowly returned, ebbing and flowing, but steadily building in intensity until the marriage broke up twelve years later. Nathaniel had to get out of the marriage, and Anne couldn't let go of him. Terror drove him to violent physical assaults upon Anne which resulted in a long prison sentence — an extreme solution to a desperate problem. Twenty years later his wife, whom I also treated briefly, informed me of her second marriage, a kind of numb existence. This was thirty-three years after I first saw her first husband. *(269)*

In another instance, a nightmare recurrent from childhood gradually disappeared. It was replaced by nightmares of ever changing content which dealt with ever new problems while the patient was making steady analytic progress. Anxiety dreams abated in frequency and intensity as fear dreams became more frequent.

A man woke at 2:00 A.M. in a panic, perspiring profusely. His wife corroborated his condition. He believed he was dreaming, but could not recall its feeling, tone, or its content. His mind was agitated with all the things he had to do in the next days to meet certain deadlines. After sweating for an hour — it was winter and the room very cold — he fell asleep and woke about 6:00 A.M. laughing uproariously with a very funny dream. He felt relaxed, and soon fell to sleep again. He awoke about 7:00 A.M. with the feeling of having had a good night's sleep. He felt that he had solved something during the night. He was not clear what it was that he had solved.

Another man woke in the middle of the night sobbing violently. The experience was confirmed by his wife. He woke with a dream which had given him "a feeling of having been purged." After half an hour, he fell asleep and woke in the morning tired but relieved. People have awakened in a panic and reported pleasant or innocuous dreams. Others have awakened quietly, calmly, and refreshed with dreams whose manifest content was panic. The central issue is not the dream content, the behavior during sleep, or the mood on awakening. What is essential is the adequacy of the organism and environment for each other.

When Burton D. began analysis he had severe insomnia and drank himself to sleep nightly. Sex, incessant talking, and a variety of physical activities were among the main ways he attempted to benumb himself, to avoid, and to flee from anxiety. Burton had many of the physical manifestations of anxiety, including urinary urgency and diarrhea. In time, with analysis, the amount of liquor required to knock himself out diminished. He was getting to sleep at one and two instead of five and six in the morning.

As our work progressed, he reported falling off to sleep and almost immediately awakening in a panic, falling off to sleep again after a while only to repeat the sequence many times during the night. Eventually, he became aware that he had dreamed. In time he could recall that the dreams contained a threatening figure. He first identified the figure as a man. In later dreams it might be a woman, an animal, an object, like an oncoming automobile, or various combinations of these. With the abating of his general level of tension, the dreams became more detailed and seemed to last longer. At first he fled in panic immediately and awoke. Later, Burton remained dreaming, and finally, he even moved toward the figure. Then he began to feel what he called fear, which changed to panic, followed by awakening with subjective experiencing and objective manifestations of intense anxiety. In one dream, he was arguing with the threatening figure while going through some rapid thought processes as to how to outwit him. Finally he said to himself, "I'll disturb myself too much if I keep up with this vociferating, and so I woke myself up."

In one phase Burton debated with himself whether he should stay in the dream or wake himself up. He had learned through many experiences that if he woke himself, turned on the light, smoked a cigarette, and perhaps read a little, he could then go back to sleep and sleep the night through. Sometimes he decided to stay in the dream. As time went on, he could more often ride through the panic and continue sleeping. The sequence might also go from panic to fear, with continued sleep, or back to panic with awakening. At times, the sequence panic, fear, panic might happen several times during one dream. Sometimes the panic in the dream reached frantic proportions. When he woke after such a dream, he knew that sleep was impossible for the rest of the night.

Other patients have described similar debates or actual physical struggles in dreams. They sometimes awakened themselves; at other times they decided to stay with it, successfully riding through the fear and anxiety; and at still other times, they awoke with varying intensities of anxiety. In some instances, having awakened, they would become infuriated and make themselves go back to sleep to finish or rework the dream so that it would come out a triumph. Others, while still awakening, would change the dream so that it came out with themselves the winner. Of this dream transforming process they became aware only later in the analytic work.

In the longer sequence of Burton D. who had to drink himself into a stupor and in the shorter instances I have described, the common denominators are a struggle between the dreamer and another figure, and a process ending in anxiety. The proportions of the anxiety described by patients in and after the dreams — and often while relating them in sessions — is predominantly irrational for long periods of the analysis. That was my evaluation. As far as they were concerned, there was only one kind of anxiety — the kind they were all too painfully aware of, which they attempted to avoid, and from which they attempted to flee. They had not yet experienced anxiety in which the proportions were predominantly rational, so they had nothing with which to compare the irrational kind.

After a number of years of analysis a man said in a session, "I feel anxious but it's different." There was a surprised, pleased tone in his voice. "It's different than the other kind of anxiety I used to feel. I feel warm, I want to stay with it. It feels like it's mine and belongs to me. That other anxiety was cold. It didn't seem to be mine. It was alien. It seemed to come from outside of me. I used to feel overwhelmed by it, helpless, paralyzed and wanted to run away. I'd get desperate."

A composite of patients' retrospective verbalizations regarding anxiety includes the following statements:

When the proportions are rational, they say, "It starts in me. It belongs to me. It is inside of me. I can stay with it. I want to stay with it. It's alive. I feel warm with it. I feel it gives me a push. It's uncomfortable, but I don't want to run away. My heart doesn't go fast like it used to. My guts don't knot up like they used to when I was anxious. My hands are warm and dry. I don't feel too restless with it."

When anxiety is present in irrational proportions, patients describe it as "That other anxiety I used to feel and still do. Sometimes it terrified me and I had to run. I'd get desperate and frantic. I'd get terribly restless. My hands would get cold and sweaty. My heart would race. My gut would go into knots. I'd suddenly have to make it to the bathroom. That anxiety was cold. It felt alien. It felt like it came from outside. I felt like it was pushed on me. It descended on me. I felt it as ominous, implacable. I felt helpless. I felt paralyzed. Sometimes I'd go rigid. In the nightmares it was the worst. I'd go rigid and paralyzed. I couldn't utter a sound. My muscles and my voice simply wouldn't function."

But these descriptions are reflections made after the fact. During the actual experiencing of irrational anxiety, they *were* what they described. I could observe it and infer it from their associations. The more intense the anxiety, that is, the more their totality was taken up in it, the less possibility there could be for that objectivity required for reflection and description. What they said expressed immediate direct experiencing of their feelings. At times, what came out would only be expletives or sounds. *They were anxiety.* Anxiety had them in its grip.

In anxiety dreams early in analysis, the dreamer appears as himself, is identied with himself, and experiences the vague other figure as threatening to him. The threat is actually to what is vital to him, to what has subjective value for him. But what he is not aware of is that what has subjective value for him are neurotic pride positions, a predominantly neurotic and idealized conception of himself in the maintenance of which most of his energies are invested. He as yet has little connection with what is healthier in himself, and there is all too little of it actually there and available. In the sequence of dreams just described, what threatened, in the symbol of the other figure, was simply other, or different, or slightly less neurotic patterns which at best contained some aspects of varying degrees of constructiveness. These patients were feeling threatened primarily by movement, change, and, in varying degrees, the dynamic of the analytic process.

In out-patient departments and in psychiatric hospitals I have seen massive anxiety expressed in homosexual and schizophrenic panics. On hospital night duty, I have observed patients, both military and civilian, suffering from a "Traumatic Syndrome."*(184)* Awakening from their recurrent nightmares, often with the wildest kind of mindless terror and disorganized panic, they attempted flight as well as assaultiveness. The latter occurred when they experienced impediments to escape from threats often visualized in the dreams as annihilating.

These patients reflect a picture of massive anxiety, the organism's response to threats to its continuity, consistency, cohesiveness, coherence, and identity, namely, to its familiar boundaries. Experiencing mounting anxiety geometrically intensifies it. This accounts in part for the wild disorganized attempts not only to flee, but also to find ways to grab hold of, splint, and hold together what is dissolving and disappearing. As the latter is happening the organism no longer *feels* anxiety, it is rapidly becoming mindless, I-less anxiety.

An instance of an ultimate expression of mindless violent anxiety, which I observed in 1941, is still vivid with me. A young seaman had been taken off a ship, in a state of disorganized panic. When I saw him on the open ward, his face was a picture of stark terror and wild horror. In a violent disorganized manner he kept reeling and thrashing around the ward clutching onto anything firm that came in his path, be it a bed post, the edge of a door, another patient, a nurse or myself. Never so dramatically have I seen the organism's attempt to splint and hold together an identity experiencing itself as fractured and fragmenting, facing impending dissolution and disappearance.

These disorganizing panic states can supervene as a person is gradually becoming sicker as well in response to an acute situation. They also occur in the phase of recovery. They reflect the organism's attempts to grasp for an identity momentarily glimpsed and then lost. This is observable when recovery occurs slowly. It is more obvious when it happens seemingly abruptly as a patient finally emerges into some semblance of health after long struggles to do so.

"In the state of fear, we have an object in front of us which we can 'meet,' which we can attempt to remove, or from which we can flee. We are conscious of ourselves as well as of the object, we can deliberate how we shall behave towards it, and we can look at the cause of the fear which actually lies spatially before us. On the other hand," Goldstein continues, *"anxiety attacks us from the rear,* so to speak. The only thing we can do is to attempt to flee from it without knowing where to go, because we experience it as coming from no particular place. This flight is sometimes successful, though merely by chance, and usually fails: anxiety remains with us."*(186, p. 293)*

As with anxiety, fear manifests proportions reflective of the proportions of rationality and irrationality in the sources of it, the functions it serves, and the attitudes toward it. The spectrum of fears ranges from the predominantly rational — such as an actual situation or object beyond the powers of a predominantly healthy person — to the increasingly irrational. At the irrational end of the spectrum of fears are what Horney described as fears that "the neurotic protective structure will be threatened; fears that its equilibrium will be disturbed." These fears are concretely expressed as the fear of insanity; the *"fear of exposure"* and the fear *"of changing anything in oneself."* *(39, pp. 144-52)* Going beyond these fears, being fearful is objectified into being fearful of someone or something. With increasing irrationality phobias and delusions occur.

Newer knowledge regarding sleep and dreams and electromyographic studies offer some support for the hypothesis regarding the mean tension level and the prompting of anxiety during sleeping and dreaming. *(242)* At the least, these hypotheses have proved useful as guides and as models. Whatever the evidence may be for or against such conjectures, there is increasing speculation regarding Meissner's "Dreaming as Process" — a formulation and position congenial to my orientation. Meissner offers some conceptualizations in terms of Freudian metapsychology. What I feel holds greater promise are his neurophysiological correlations with the dreaming process.

This comprehensive view of fear and anxiety dreams, in the context of the holistic approach, gives more guides for identifying the ebb and flow of the analytic process. Dream sequences that move from being predominantly filled with anxiety to demonstrating the experience of fear with an identifiable object, tell much about where the patient is in his development and the resources which are available to him. The phenomenological approach to dream interpretation helps make finer discriminations between fear and anxiety dreams. It helps to undercut the attitude that fear and anxiety in reality and in dreams mean only something negative, alien, and destructive. It opens the way to a wider understanding of their constructive significance in human integrating, and in human growth and development.

It is in the nature of the organism to be in tension. Conflicting and cooperating systems, healthy and sick, within the organism and between it and its environments are tension producing and tension reducing. The tension oscillations above and below the mean are also determined by the energy inflow and outgo. Contributory to the exceeding of the mean tension level are the rate, mass, volume and nature of the particular stimuli fed into or lost to the system of the whole and where in that hierarchy of systems, arranged in dominance order, the impact is felt.

As the tension mounts it may be experienced as being about to jump out of one's skin, as a fear of one's equilibrium being shaken, of being torn apart or of flying to pieces.

The dynamic of conflict is the one most frequently mentioned with reference to the disruption of the integrity of the organism and of its identity. As the patient is experiencing it, he attempts to ward off his feeling of being torn apart, split. You may recall from chapter 17 the dream of the man running in and lying horizontal across his two friends and holding them together. There was also the dream of the man caught in the agonizing dilemma which he could not solve or resolve. A final example is a man who woke in terror from a dream in which a tree split right down the middle with a resounding clap, like thunder.

That conflict will be tension producing and disruptive is obvious. This would also hold for a sudden accession of rage. Not as frequently observed, but also disruptive are sudden accessions of joy and of fright. Both can end in death by heart attack which ensues, possibly in some cases because of autonomic shock. A sudden access of self-hate leading to overwhelming anxiety can be disruptive. I have never seen sudden and/or massive sadness or depression lead to an obvious anxiety response.

In discussing the total solution of magic, mention was made of the variety of shattering impacts when there were sudden and powerful juxtapositions of dream, fantasy, imagination, and reality. There was the instance of Georgette T., the woman who went to bed with her neighbor. Her actual behavior was shattering to her identity as her Idealized Image. Less obvious are the cumulative effects which finally become excessive, and the sudden shattering effect of a number of simultaneous threats to what has subjective value.

The following instance illustrates the sources of tension producing and tension reducing, the cueing off of anxiety, and instances of wild disruptive anxiety when aspects of pseudo-identities were shattered as a new identity was being created. This happened through a series of crises and transitions, during which there was identity diffusion and confusion ending in new identity formations, each closer to the patient's actual self or real identity.

James O. was not James O., but one who lived under the shadow of his brother Steve, who died at age nine when James was three. Before the first half of the second year of analysis, James often remarked on how little he could recall about Steve.

Events about Steve's funeral began coming up as James wondered what Steve had been like and what their relationship had been. At first he talked of his brother's great love for him, mentioning an incident in which his action could have been life-saving to James. His mother told it to him, but he could never be sure if he also recalled it himself because it would have been before he was three. At the end of the first month in the second year, he wondered more to himself than to me, "Did Steve play with my little thing?" This was his mother's term.

Almost from the start of our work the metaphor "crossing over the line" was increasingly meaningful and affect-laden. By that we meant going beyond how he had perceived himself and behaved. This meant chancing and daring new things and, by implication, dropping previous ways of being. The dropping referred mainly to aspects of shallow living. The going beyond had also to do with confronting friction, conflict, and struggle and with becoming more expansive and assertive. On several occasions he said, "To hell with the goddam line," and promptly had a panic reaction. He had literally, momentarily, discarded all boundaries and was I-less.

After about six months of analysis James started using the couch, sitting up and lying down many times during a session while I continued to sit facing him. He sits in a modified lotus position which he had done as a child on his bed. He sat facing the bookshelves which are on the wall opposite the couch. I sat slightly to his left in a chair. He usually started the session recumbent, and as it proceeded spent more time in the modified lotus position.

In the second month of the second year, there were intense sessions. After an intense session, he was reluctant to come to the next one. He would arrive late with little inclination to talk. Concomitantly, the tempo of the sessions was steadily rising. One session began with an uneasy feeling about something "back there behind my head, and I can't see what it is." After a week it shifted to being behind the facing bookcases. Finally, "I can almost see him. He is going to come through there any minute. I don't know who he is." There were several particularly intense sessions during which he was restless and very anxious. At times, he looked the picture of stark terror, and he said he did not want to leave because he was afraid he'd "see him tonight at home." During this period he spent more time with his friend, Porter, and had urges to ask him to stay over in his apartment. Porter was going on vacation, and rather impulsively James decided to go also. It was partly through fear of letting go of him and the support he stood for, and partly flight from what was going on in the sessions.

Porter was with him one week. James was alone the second. As it emerged in sessions, he was scared and miserable most of the time. On the way down in the plane with Porter next to him he couldn't breathe. For two weeks before leaving, he had had difficulty in breathing while lying down. After he returned, for the first four weeks he clearly had the feeling of someone sitting on his chest.

In those four weeks, things moved very rapidly. More about Steve kept coming up. He had a torturing nightmare that seemed to go on a long time. He felt that someone was in his bedroom sitting at his desk. He woke up in terror but couldn't look. He felt it finally went away. Several nights later while awake in bed, he had the feeling, "He is there at my desk. He seemed to be sitting there writing something. I finally felt he is not going to harm me. Then I looked. He was a big man and then after a while he disappeared." It was shortly after this that things really exploded in a session.

In a wild-eyed panic, crying and almost sobbing he gasped, "I killed him. I killed him. I murdered him!" and with his fist he violently pounded the couch. Shortly after, he pounded his chest over his heart. In between blows, he sobbed in panic, "There is blood on my hands!" He could never definitely identify who was coming through my bookcases and who the man was sitting at his desk. At this point, he believed it was Steve whom he had murdered and whose blood was on his hands.

He asked for extra sessions which I was glad I had available. This was at the end of the third month, shortly before I was to leave for two weeks. In that last week, on several occasions, he had slept in Porter's apartment and spent more time with him. In the last session before I left, he closed down. Before he would refer to it as feeling "blah." Now he clearly knew he was putting the lid on everything and hoping it would stay put until I got back.

Shortly after my return, early in the fourth month of the second year, he began wondering what had moved him to pick up a man and put himself in the position of getting caught. He had known the consequences would be devastating, and they were. That it was an extremely self-destructive act and a cry for help became increasingly clear to him.

Two weeks later, he recalled that when he was about two and a half years old, traveling on a train with his mother, he was terrified and fascinated by a man having an epileptic seizure. Although his mother insisted he should look away, he would not. A few days later he recalled a dream he had had four years before, shortly after beginning his analysis. A homicidal maniac was loose in a house. James kept whispering to another person, male and ill-defined, asking the whereabouts of the maniac who was moving around in the house. James also kept moving about, and he finally left the house. He did not awaken with anxiety. Shortly after, he dreamt his father died. He woke feeling relieved and happy with the dream. It was so real he wanted to call home to confirm it.

In the seven weeks following my return, he literally discarded his father who had died in the dream and who, he added, "lost his balls in the depression and has been impotent since." His ties to his mother had been steadily weakening for over a year. Ridicule, disparagement, and hostility toward her emerged more frequently and freely. His hostility toward the values of the southern town in which he had been born became intense, markedly loosening his ties to it, to his past, his parents, and his origins. The time between calls home increased as his reluctance to visit home intensified.

In the beginning of the fifth month of the second year, he was feeling fragile and said just that. He burst out with annoyance at me when he experienced my voice as sounding like his father's. A few sessions later, he burst out sobbing as he mentioned how a number of underdogs in current competitive situations had come through unexpectedly at the last moment. He dreamt he found a dismembered female torso in his bathroom. A week later, he dreamt he went into the bathroom and found in an oversized tub a male corpse taller than himself, stretched out "under some kind of fluid." As he turned away, he threw in a gold coin.

When he turned back a few moments later, the corpse was sitting erect, and he could see it was alive by the color in its face though there was no visible breathing.

While he had earlier believed he had killed Steve, and that "the one" who was going to come through the bookcases and was sitting at his desk at night was his brother, now he felt it was another aspect of himself. This was after a number of questions and associations about schizophrenia. He believed it meant split personality. He then told me for the first time that he was convinced, from age three to nine, that all little boys whose last name was O. would die by age nine. Several years after he had passed the age, he was still incredulous that he was alive. At the same time, he mentioned a good friend who died five years previously of a brain tumor at age forty-nine. He was convinced he would die at the same age of the same condition. This time he allotted himself at least twelve years of future life.

In the last session of this five month segment before an extended interruption, he mentioned having gone to the Turkish bath three times in one week, and that each time after a few minutes there he got bored and left without any sexual experiences. The frequency of going there and to homosexual bars had significantly diminished, as had his sexual experiences. About nine months earlier, there had been a short affair with a man older than himself who looked like a little boy. He was very muscular, which James referred to as hunky — his condensation of chunky, and hunk of. In this session, he realized he had always been attracted to men with this physical attribute.

Shortly after he began working with me he had mentioned a picture of himself taken when he was about three. He always repeated, whenever mentioning the picture, "I loved that little boy. He was bursting with life. He was so full of life with his sparkling eyes, and his little white suit. What happened to him?" Often he would compare it with another picture taken at age five in which he looked sad, somber, and almost lifeless. About two months before the end of this segment, he mentioned that he had been a fat little boy filled with good humor and a joy to everyone. As he talked I asked, 'Could you be looking for that hunky, chunky, fat little boy?" With this he bounced up off the couch with a bursting "Yes," his face flushed, tears in his eyes, filled with a depth of appreciation.

Shortly after resuming in the sixth month of the second year, after the longer interruption, he reported, "I had a dream last night and when I woke I immediately realized. It's the story of my life. On turning out the lights just before climbing into bed, I had a strong premonition of something about to happen. I did not think specifically in terms of a dream, but I knew quite clearly that the night would bring something of importance.

"At about 1:20 in the morning, after having been asleep for nearly two hours, I awoke suddenly and completely with a vivid recollection of the dream itself and with the realization that the same thing I had expected had indeed taken place. I lay in bed several minutes, going over the dream in my mind, fitting the pieces together, reaching an understanding how this dream had been what I later called 'the story of my life.' I got out of bed, put on the lights, went to the bathroom, and returned to my desk to make some brief notes of the dream.

"The dream took place in a hospital. My notes in fact carried the scribbled heading 'Hospital Horrors.' In the opening sequence I am standing in a hospital room, empty except for a bed on which is lying a cadaver covered with a sheet. Only the face is exposed. I find the cadaver an object of indescribable horror, but I 'know' the horror without even feeling it. I am afraid to examine the cadaver closely, although I am aware that its face is somehow deformed or damaged in the area of the mouth. I want desperately to leave the room.

"Throughout this first sequence there is someone else in the room with me. We share our revulsion of the cadaver. In a sense, my companion seems to sense the horror of the situation more strongly. He starts to scream uncontrollably. I am aware of his screaming without even being able to hear it. I see his mouth open and his face contort in the scream, but I am deaf to it. Even during the dream I am aware that my companion is merely another aspect of myself. We are the same person.

"Almost instantly I find myself transported to a room directly across the corridor from the one containing the cadaver. It is a rather large room, perhaps a ward of some sort. There are several beds on one of which is lying a doctor. There is nothing to indicate that the man on the bed is a doctor, and there is more reason to assume him a patient, but I know that he is, in fact, a doctor.

"The screaming across the hall continues, although I am unable to hear it. I feel great pity for my former companion and want to help him, but I realize that there is little I can do by myself. I turn to the doctor on the bed. I cry out, 'Oh, doctor, please help him!' The doctor has heard him, but he chooses to ignore my plea. He shifts his position in the bed but makes no reply nor any move to help. I am unable to comprehend his inaction.

"At this moment a nurse saunters down the corridor and into the ward in which I am standing. I am unaccountably frightened of her. She is wearing a white nurse's uniform which has been lowered to midi length. Beneath it I see black knit stockings and black shoes. Her hair is hennaed a brilliant red orange. She wears black harlequin eyeglasses of the most extreme sort, and her face has been powdered to a pasty white that I associate with the rice-powdered mien of a geisha.

"I somehow make known to her the need to help the poor chap across the hall, although I do not seem to address her directly. She moves slowly — sashaying is the word that comes to mind — out of the ward and crosses into the room just opposite. The screaming stops. I have a sense of the nurse carrying and using a large syringe. She emerges shortly, and remarks to no one in particular, 'I just stick them and then they're O.K.' She wanders on down the corridor to my infinite relief.

"Soon afterwards I am besieged by several groups of grotesques. They remind me of the human monsters from Fellini movies, although mine have come from 42nd Street instead of from the streets of Rome. They are bands of Puerto Rican toughs, dwarfs, hustlers, derelicts, all sorts of human refuse. They threaten me, tease me, torment me. I feel like a complete outsider, totally alone, but somehow I am not truly afraid. At least I do not feel fear.

"Their tormenting turns abruptly serious, and I am being carried off by a group of dwarfs whose intent is to cut off my penis. I am now clad only in a T-shirt, and my penis seems to be shriveled so that it is incredibly tiny, as if I had just come out from a long swim in the cold Atlantic. They hoist me onto their shoulders and off we march. Through this final sequence, I am observing the action from outside myself. I do not feel myself being carried away. I see it as some third person would see it.

"When I awoke it was with no sense of fright. I did not think of the dream as a nightmare, but rather as a fascinating intellectual exercise. I was almost immediately aware that the cadaver must in some way represent my dead brother. The unresponsive and ineffectual doctor was my father and the nurse harridan my mother. The significance of the dream was immediately clear to me."

The following night he dreamed he was voyeuristically watching a couple having sex in all kinds of acrobatic positions in an apartment across the street. Suddenly the young man climbs into his window and lets him know in a friendly way that he realized my patient was watching and that he is a dirty old man. He then expresses admiration for the size of James O.'s genitals.

The dream of the first night — being "deaf to," not feeling "horror," and not being "afraid" clearly reveal the defensive function of the alienating process, the automatic checks on feelings, and the intellectualizing as he enters a horror-filled area of his life. The corpse of his brother is finally exhumed, and his parents seen in their true light. As mentioned earlier, gruesome and grotesque figures are often present in dreams of homosexuals. In the second dream, the forces are let loose by what he allowed himself to see in the first. The symbols of castration for having dared are obvious, but the following night he has "admirably large genitals." He also moves further in his interest in heterosexuality, albeit in exotic and grotesque positions.

That this was no "intellectual exercise" became almost frighteningly obvious a week later in the last session before the summer interruption. He began relating a call to his parents in which he literally experienced "the story of my life" as portrayed in the dream. In a few minutes he was in a murderous rage shouting, pounding the couch and tearful. He paced the floor, continuing with his outburst against them. Even a few months back, he would have been terrified to express rage of such violent proportions.

He kept repeating "What did they have against me?" "Why did they do such things to a poor little kid?" "They hung and quartered and cut me into little pieces." Grinding his teeth in a fury, he screamed, "Those S.O.B.'s!" He was not entirely quieted down when he left. Another evidence that the dream was no "intellectual exercise" was that after holding off a decision on a number of job offers, he decided on the one he felt most comfortable with. It also had the highest salary. He clearly thought of it as interim job until another one at a still higher salary opened up. This future offer was also to be a stepping stone to an even more important one at the head of a very large organization, all to happen within two to three years. These expectations and plans are quite realistic. James was really beginning to believe he had the exceptional abilities people had been telling him he had.

In the analysis thus far, in terms of identities James O. had moved away from being the one who lived under the shadow of dead Steve. Then he undermined that image and murdered it. Finally, he had the emerging awareness that all his life he had been searching for the little boy he had been before Steve died. His manner, voice, and behavior in the last five months had become more obviously those of a little boy. The self-destructive act was a cry for help. "Somebody please recognize what my dilemma is, and help me out of it!" It was part of his search to find that long lost little boy, so alive and so vital before his brother Steve died.

In the segment of analysis described, what was most clearly contributing to the anxiety curve were the successive threats to various identities, self-perceptions, and aspects of his self-system. During that period he was in almost constant terror, feeling as if he were without the boundaries of self-identity and his dreams clearly reflect his condition. First appeared an ominous male identity, next a homicidal maniac, and then a dismembered feminine identity. Next there was an outsize male corpse who came back to life. Finally, we found the long lost little boy. Then those aspects of his self-system represented by the "dear, sweet boy" and the dutiful son began to crumble.

Clearly, much had been accomplished in this six months, and James was on his way. There is a core of awareness and integrity in him which keeps telling him he is not what he could have become or still may be. Two months before this segment ended, there had been extensive discussions of such issues when he reviewed his educational and professional history. I feel the strength of the analytic relationship will carry him through the difficult periods ahead when he must experience the buried feelings of emptiness, meaninglessness, nothingness, and despair which had motored the unsatisfactory homosexual way of life.

What accounted for the mounting tension, the frequent outbursts of anxiety to the point of terror, the frequent nightmares, and the visual hallucinatory phenomena at night and in my office? What was being threatened and steadily eroded was the identity of the one who lived under Steve's shadow. Then there were all the recollections that threatened the one who could remember nothing about Steve. The one who could not cross the line, and the one who was his idealized image.

Specifically threatened in his idealized image were the various aspects of the solution of resignation. His shallow living began to fall away very rapidly and obviously. He noted he was not longer there with the "bon mot" and was getting bored with "superficial chitchat." Always gregarious and seldom at home, he found himself making more weekends and evenings "sacred" — to be kept for himself so he could stay at home, read, and "putter around." He also became much less polite. Crossing the line was going against his persistent resignation, and he was finding it a bore to do the things that had been motored by rebellious

302

resignation. He further found he was less interested in sex and was more easily and even brusquely saying no. After some weeks and no sex, he fixed me with a beady, threatening, and defiant look and said, "I don't want to be straight." This I have heard from many homosexuals as they feel their interest in homosexuality waning and externalize to the therapist by saying. "You are trying to make me heterosexual."

He showed an increasing interest in women and expressed his more obvious liking of certain of them: "She is one of my favorite girls." But I also picked up a poignant note as he talked about couples he knew and met. I was getting the feeling of his feeling that there were certain things you got in an association with a woman you couldn't get with a man. His wanting to spend more time at home had the feeling of wanting a home of his own and to feel more at home in his home and in himself. He was thinking of redecorating his apartment in more alive colors and giving it a feeling of being more lived in. Though remote, I had the feeling he would like to have a woman of his own in his home. It was companionship that he was wanting, to assuage his feelings of loneliness which were coming to the fore though still not sharply defined.

With these changes his pseudo self-effacement and deeply buried real self-effacement were being worked through. Not only was he less polite, he was also given to more frequent outbursts of irritability toward his staff. He began to drive them pretty hard. For him he was becoming quite tyrannical. He was able to say no in business situations also. He began to admire those who could do so "without any ifs, and, or buts." He also noted he was becoming capable of bursts of such productivity that he overwhelmed his staff with work.

As can be seen, the expansive side was coming to the fore, and he was now turning down jobs as head of projects which he felt were not big enough or challenging enough for him. For someone who earned only modest sums for his exceptional ability which he promptly spent, he now wanted to make a lot of money and "buy all the things I have always wanted." He did get a significant raise by going after it, something he had never done, and began to spend money he had not earned because he wanted some of those things to enjoy "now, not later." Before the past two years, he had had an abhorrence of possessions and of saving. When the fear of dying and the wish and possibility of living emerged, all this changed radically. As he put it, "I'm buying things like crazy."

All of the identities of his total self-system were constantly being threatened, and at an increasingly rapid rate. With all this, there was the emerging feeling that he had murdered Steve. Noteworthy was the speed with which he turned the knife on himself as an expression of self-hate for having imagined blood on his hands.

In his first session in mid-September, he angrily informed me he had been called back from his holiday abroad shortly after arriving. What enraged him was that it was taken for granted by his mother that he would immediately return. Besides, his return really was not necessary. His father had had a moderate heart attack. He wished he had died and felt, when he saw his father, that he also strongly wanted it over with. A week later his father had a serious heart infarct which almost resulted in immediate death.

Being at home became increasingly distressing. His death wishes toward his father and murderous rages toward his mother were getting him down. "I know how people become alcoholics. At first one Martini before dinner with mother was enough, and then it was two. If I had stayed there any longer, it would have been more, and even then I don't know if I could have controlled myself."

He had started his new job in the late summer and felt quite inept. Within two weeks after we resumed analytic work, he was feeling in good spirits, competent in his job, and the analysis was beginning to move forward. More aspects of the old themes began to emerge and also a new one, "flaunting authority."

In the analytic relationship, he acted out by needling me and in a staccato manner asked one question after another, many personal, immediately saying, "Why don't you answer me?" or "Say something!" But he also was experiencing what he was doing and was working it through. At a dinner party, seated opposite an imposing self-assured authority whom he had known for some years, to his surprise he was quite tense. A week later he walked out of a gathering where there were a number of people so sure of their authority they were unaware that they had it.

What James O. was confronting and working through was the authority of his pride system and the shoulds which supported and formed the many irrational identities of his self-system. Now beginning to oppose them, he was starting to experience their imperviousness, their intransigence, and his fear of them, rage at them, and his powerlessness to affect them. But the battle was now joined.

In the last weeks of his father's illness, he talked about the increased frequency and intensity of his mother's sweetly demanding long distance calls. He fought with himself and her not to "rush home and hold her hand." During this struggle he felt anxious, guilty, angry, and drained. This battle blocked out whatever feelings he was having about his father and his imminent death.

In the session before he heard about his death, while discussing the battle with his mother and how he would relate to her after "daddy's death," he suddenly said, "Has that book on 'Homosexuality' been there before?" Informed that he had been facing it from his very first session, he smiled knowingly and indicated in an ensuing exchange that he was aware how important his relationship to his mother was for his having become homosexual. Quite spontaneously he interjected, "It doesn't much matter which way it goes," meaning that if he became heterosexual, that would be all right too. Two weeks later he said, "Homosexuality is getting to be a bore." A week before saying that, he had referred one of his "favorite girls" to me for therapy.

At home for his father's funeral, James dreamt that his mother had died. Back in New York a week later, he dreamt she was about to die. He then dreamt he was in a church, about to marry his mother who appeared in a bridal gown escorted by his father who gave the "bride" to James. The dream clearly said what was making James increasingly furious — the burden of his mother. He also knew that the dream referred to his almost literal marriage to her — a seductive relationship forced upon James from infancy. He knew he would have to dissolve this "marriage" before he could become a mature male.

Although tight and feeling generally rotten in the first weeks of this phase, while acting out against me there was a gradual relaxation and, finally, a breakthrough as he experienced me as a rational authority who could support him in his battle against the system of irrational ones in himself. We were now approaching the close of the second year of analysis, during which there had been about 150 sessions.

In the case of James O., magical thinking had been intensively operating from early childhood. Because he wanted to murder Steve, he had blood on his hands, and he was going to die for it at age nine. It was a reality and hence had to be blocked out all these years. I have worked with four other people who had the absolute conviction that they had murdered. They lived in a state of frozen terror and/or numb deadness. They were severely crippled emotionally. All experienced occasional panic states. It took years of analysis before they could experience the depths of that conviction. During their analyses, anxiety and panic were constantly imminent and had to be warded off at times with severe paranoia. Based on magical thinking, this conviction had become for them a reaiity. Before it could be brought into awareness and resolved, the analysis had to go through some very tempestuous phases.

Magical thinking, the result of having lived practically all her life in a nightmare, was the fate of a fifty-five-year-old woman. The poignancy of the realization and the freeing from it, she worked through with me. After the death of her father she had become suicidally depressed. For the next twenty-five years, depressions occurred each year on the anniversary of her father's death. They gradually lessened via the help of three analysts and almost fifteen hundred hours of therapy spread over almost thirty years. Not long after her fifty-fifth birthday, the realization of her wish not only to murder her father but also to dismember him so that nothing would be left broke through. Although it had been a wish that had taken on concrete reality, she felt that now she was finally free.

All that happened with James O. could not have been possible without the fortunate coincidence of a right fit between therapist and patient. The fit was right with his first analyst, and would have been less right had it been me when he began therapy. When he began with me three years later I was righter for him than his first analyst. Certain analysts are righter than other analysts at different phases of therapy. A change of analysts can be helpful, but I do not recommend it lightly. What happened here was a chance happening coincident with an opportune time. Changing analysts because the patient feels the fit is not right or because the analyst believes the patient might do better with someone else more often happens at inauspicious moments.

Also accounting for the rapidity of change in James O. was his great trust and confidence in me. He obviously attributed magical powers to me. At one point I asked, "What makes you feel I know that?" His wide-eyed response implied that it was self-evident; "You know everything." This also indicated the intensity of his need. He was also saying, "only a magician or God could help me through what I have to go through."

The belief of having murdered, the fear of murdering again, the wish to murder, murderous rage and living in this nightmare of violence are relevant to my experience in the therapy of homosexuals. But first I should make clear that fears of being a homosexual, male or female, which at times can assume the proportions of a paralyzing

306

phobia, as well as transient and occasional homosexual behavior in childhood and/or in adolescence are to be distinguished from the pattern of living around which a homosexual person organizes his life, whether he acts it out continuously, occasionally, or tries to deny it altogether by marriage and children.

There is also a spectrum of motivations for help: The homosexual may want to get over his fears of exposure; he may seek relief from the depressions which often cover murderous rages when rejected; he may want help in the suicidal phases which follow rejections; or he may have a strong need for help which carries him beyond these immediate problems. And, finally, there are the differences in objectives, and the measure of success as defined by therapists. For me the criterion of having been helpful is not whether the patient becomes heterosexual. My objective is to help the patient become less crippled in his total functioning, to help him live with himself more happily when he interrupts the therapy.

The attitudes of society toward homosexuality, and the attitude of homosexuals toward society's attitude, as well as toward their own sexual attitudes and behaviors has gone through marked changes. In the forties, during the war, I saw about fifteen homosexuals in consultation. Half of them came with a mixture of concerns and guilt feelings because they had informed the examining officers of their homosexuality and were rejected. They felt guilty even though about five of them were doing useful work as medical orderlies or attendants in mental hospitals. Another small group had not admitted their homosexuality, but took the position that they were conscientious objectors. Another five had come at the suggestion of an older man with whom they all had been involved. I had seen him earlier. He had made several tries at analysis and marriage. All had failed. None of the latter group returned for a second consultation or entered therapy to my knowledge.

The first homosexual I worked with was twenty-five years ago. He had been married and had a family which he left. He had been actively homosexual before and after his marriage. He came in a moderately suicidal depression because he felt his partner was going to terminate the relationship which had lasted ten years. My patient was getting drunk more frequently on sherry. On one occasion because of an inability to urinate, and as a perverse form of sexual stimulation, he catheterized himself. He had to be hospitalized because of a severe bladder infection resulting from the unsterilized catheter. On recovery he called to terminate our work, which had been in progress some six months.

Another male homosexual in his late forties, suicidally depressed, also remained in therapy about six months. He had episodic affairs, but none continuously, as he began to feel a little bit better before he interrupted. I heard that he killed himself four years later.

Albert B. began his analysis at thirty-two. He had been homosexual since about age eight, and had the typical parental pattern of a dominating, seductive, mother and a remote father whom she disparaged. After four years of therapy, he married. When his first analyst died, he immediately continued with me for three more years, making a total of nine years. When he interrupted he had three children, was successful in his career, and it had been a year since any even remote impulse toward homosexual behavior had been present. However, I felt that the depth of his rage and self-loathing had not really been touched, and that the roots of his homosexual behavior had been inadequately worked through.

When it came time for Walter O. to experience his moral dividedness and his rages, he interrupted therapy. He continued a somewhat satisfying relationship with a slightly older man for ten years. From what I have heard indirectly, there has been a slight move toward admitting into private and public awareness his anger and furies. When he can admit into awareness, contain, and own his moral dividedness and his murderous rages, I feel he will be a happier and more productive person, utilizing his abilities in ways that have been blocked.

I have supervised the analyses of two lesbians over a period of a year and a half each. Although both improved, in that their anxieties are less, they have as yet gotten nowhere near experiencing and owning the intensity of their vindictiveness, hostility, and rage. Their lesbian patterns of relations had changed very little.

I worked with a third lesbian, Martha O., for eight years. Even before she interrupted her first analysis of five years her lesbian behavior had ceased. During her work with me, she married out of loneliness, morbid dependency, and masochism. She divorced as she grew stronger. It is five years since there has been even a remote impulse toward homosexual behavior. In the last three years, there have been no sexual impulses of any kind. She has been living out her maternal impulses by doing volunteer work at an orphanage for boys and girls.

Over the years, she has had to flee less impulsively after outbursts of rage toward me — rages which are mixed with quite some paranoid coloring. Now she can more directly be angry with me. She has been able to own the murderous rages she has had in the past. At one point she quietly said, "I know I could have killed him," and she meant just that. The changes in her I feel have been considerably determined by her ability to own these murderous rages. As a result she can be increasingly productive and creative in her career.

The responses to murdering impulses, past, present, and future, predominantly directed outward, are different than when the focus is inward. In each structure there is evidence of the other. Inwardly and outwardly directed murderous impulses are present in varying intensities and extensities in every neurosis. I am referring here to instances where it had a dominant influence on that person's life because it was the nuclear problem about which most of the neurotic protective structure was organized. In some instances it is obvious from the beginning of an analysis, and in others it only becomes visible years later. I am not referring to patients who are chronically suicidal, or who have made serious suicidal attempts and suicidal gestures, but to patients who have been and are out to destroy and/or keep secret what is authentic in themselves. This results in a condition equivalent to death, because it is an emotional, a spiritual death. These people are walking automatons, living zombies.

Very early in an extended analysis, one woman related a story about a man who perpetrated the perfect murder. It was discovered only years after his death. After some years of analysis, her murderous impulses toward her mother became clear, ultimately expressing themselves in murderous rages against her. More deeply buried were her murderous rages toward her father, which only years later emerged fitfully. Toward her mother the rages were pure and unadulterated. They were mitigated toward her father because he had at times shown her some understanding. But for his weakness and for his failure to protect her from her mother, she could never forgive him.

While these murderous rages toward her parents became obvious and in the foreground, what was equally obvious were the consequences of them for her life. Before they emerged, there was intense alienation and living on the premises of the total solution of magic. At times she seemed to be in a state of depersonalization and, of course, there was intense numbing, deadening, and checking of her feelings. An able career woman, she nevertheless lived far below her potential.

After about eight years of analysis there was a significant loosening of her defenses. She went into a disorganizing panic state which lasted almost nine months. During this period she was supported by extra sessions and medication. It was only after all these defenses lessened and the murderous rages had been long in the foreground that what was obvious all along became clear to me. All her life she had been out to keep hidden the perfect murder of her authentic self. As this became evident to me, the battle between us intensified and when it became clear to her, the measures she used to keep the nature of the murder from becoming clearer were desperate and diabolical. At all costs what had been buried and considered dead was not to be exhumed and brought into the light of day. Then she would have to face the extent of her crime, that she had been wrong in what she had done, and that it had been an even greater crime to have kept it hidden.

In all patients, in one form or another, and to different intensities, admitting to themselves that they had been wrong in their perception of others and of themselves must happen. The repercussions to such awareness can be very intense. I have had direct experience with some patients and know of many more where the pain of admitting that they have been wrong is more hurting than they can bear and they therefore break off their analyses. I know of a few who, after much anguish and suffering, returned to analysis because they couldn't live with themselves knowing they had run away from the truth.

While the masochistic component in the structure of the woman just mentioned was obvious though blurred by her alienation, her quite extensive sadism was harder to see. In a second woman's structure, the masochistic features were flagrant and in the foreground — most obvious in her marital relationship to an obviously sadistic man.

After four years of analysis, quite tempestuous at times, particularly during the third year when she was in an almost constant moderate panic state which was, at times, quite severe, and during which she persistently accused me of being a sadist while vehemently denying any hostility in herself except what was provoked by others, an old recurrent nightmare emerged. Now of middle age, she had had the dream off and on since she was a young girl. She mentioned it now for the first time as she began to admit that she also was hostile in her own right. It was at a point in her analysis where she knew she had to come to grips with a phase of almost total blocking. She also was aware she had stopped dreaming for months and knew it was related to this block. Intense blocking had waxed and waned throughout the analysis. During the sessions her mouth was so dry from anxiety she could hardly talk.

In the recurrent dream, a young girl has been murdered. She does not know who the girl is. She is accused of having murdered her. Although she knows she didn't commit the murder, she knows she is going to be punished for it.

To date she had only allowed glimpses of murderous rages toward an older brother, her mother's favorite, who took her father's place when he died. Deeply buried and still hidden were her murderous feelings toward her mother. They only came out indirectly toward her older sisters and, on two occasions early in life, murderously and directly against two girl friends whom she never spoke to again. Toward her husband they were still muted. Toward me the rages could only come out indirectly. When they upsurged violently, she dealt with them by silence in sessions or intense provocativeness to which she had to be blind. Even miniscule glimpses of what she had done against herself evoked panic and terror.

Whether she will be able to allow into awareness, work through, and integrate what she has done against herself is still in the balance. An extremely able career woman, she has lived far below her potential as a woman, wife, mother, and human being.

Chapter 19

Dreams V:
Technique, Attitudes to Dreaming,
First Dreams, and Dream Series

Begun as an experiment in 1941, I continued to omit giving, in the first session, the usual instructions regarding dreams and other practical matters. The emergence of a first dream, without prior instruction, makes for an undisturbed context and a climate conducive to raising questions regarding dreaming in general, the history of dreaming, repetitive dreams, and nightmares. Out of such discussion can come much information regarding the patient's attitudes to dreams, to working with them, and his possible flair for doing so. When dreams emerge naturally, they are least encumbered by extraneous influences from the analytic situation. They are more naive, more informative, and more easily understandable. Usually I do not make comments or ask questions directly relating to a first dream. More likely I will do so implicitly, and glean what I can from subsequent associations and the further evolution of the dreaming process in the analysis.

When months go by and no dreams (or a history of them) are forthcoming, I ask the patient simply whether he has dreamt recently.

I ask this question only if the analysis is not progressing. After such tentative tries I might ask first about dreams in general and then about anxiety dreams. I ask about dreams only if the analysis is becoming less productive or if I feel there is much blocking. I feel the rhythm and momentum of analysis should be respected. They are among our most valuable guides and constructive aids in the therapeutic process. This is not saying that the associations are sacrosanct, but that the task of analysis is to define and refine guides and aids to therapy. It is not productive to blur their outlines or interfere with their effectiveness.

It is a rarity when dreams are not reported spontaneously, and an even greater one when the subject has not been opened up by the first attempt to do so. Following such a successful initial effort, a host of attitudes may come to the fore. The patient has great fears of what is unconscious. There is a terror that dreams will expose him. He believes the analyst can read his mind through dreams and find out things known and unknown. He fears that the analyst will discover that he, the patient, is defective, a pervert, a criminal, or insane. Some patients, however, feel quite unconnected with their dreams, as though they come from and belong to another world. Another attitude is that they are either some kind of black magic or pure nonsense. If the analyst wants, he'll report them but don't bother the dreamer about them. Finally, some will bring dreams as a gift, as a bribe, or as a way to appease the analyst.

With some patients who report few or many dreams, early or late in analysis, I find myself paying little attention to them and have little desire to pursue them. I have learned that this is a telling response. Such patients may draw attention to my failure and ask for comments about their dreams. A patient's persistence may stimulate an attempt. I feel the strain of it, as I go on and as I attempt to enlist the patient's interest. What comes of this effort tends to be unproductive and soon the patient loses interest. There may be several more such trials at the patient's insistence, with similar sterile results. This may indicate great severity of blocking and a depth of illness. I further feel that some people, and this applies equally to analysts, simply communicate better in behaviors, in associations, and in fantasies than in dreams.

More troublesome are those patients who fill the sessions with reporting dreams, and who mail or deposit with you written ones they haven't had time to read in session. This can be a most tenacious blockage. The attempt is to fill the time, to shut you up, to literally swamp you. There are various things one can try. Requesting the patient not to write them up or mail them in is a beginning. Interruptions in the dream relating can be made with comments or questions as they proceed. Finally, one may be forced to exclude dream reporting. I have no direct experience with such patients, but I have supervised the analysis of others working with such patients. The usual outcome has been an interrupted therapy with little to no progress.

If I respond directly to a first dream, it may concern a symbol connected with a factual situation already discussed. "I recall your telling me about Mr. A." "That was the town you lived in from eight to twelve." I thereby indicate my awareness that the patient has dreamt; that I am interested in his dreams; and that they are connected with the reality of himself and his life. This technique is in keeping with the attitude of tentativeness, implicitness, and supportiveness. In teaching I use such metaphors as "getting the feel of the rhythm and flow as of a baby's first steps in learning to walk;" "having your hand close to his bottom, not touching it but being available in case there is faltering;" and "giving him support so that he is unaware of it and can feel that he did it all by himself."

The questions asked, when active work with dreams has begun, function to underline significant symbols and situations which already have appeared in associations and been discussed. (271) Underlining prompts associations connecting patients with the organic substrate of those symbols which leads to deeper and wider experiencing of them. My questions are to indicate to the patient "I am here;" "I am interested;" "I am listening;" "I have remembered;" and "I feel it might be worthwhile looking further into it." The questions are pointers and illuminators along the way of the ongoing direction of analysis. They are of the what variety, occasionally how, less frequently when, where, and who, and practically never why. The questions are implicit and open-ended. Statements as interpretations are rare and assertions even rarer. When I do make statements or assertions, their very rarity makes them all the more striking and effective so that patients may even spontaneously comment on their unusualness.

I almost never ask "why?" "What do you think about this or that?" or "What do you think it means?" Such questions aid, abet, and intensify the problem the therapist is attempting to resolve. The patient is automatically driven to intellectualize. Compulsive intellectualizing is one of the consequences of constricting spontaneous conceptual and perceptual awareness. Questions emphasizing feelings attempt to undercut that process.

Horney emphasized the importance of feelings in dreams. (74) Questions involving feelings can be varied: "What were you feeling in the dream? . . . when you woke? . . . as you are telling it to me now? . . . about this or that person or situation?" "How do your feelings now compare with those you had when you first dreamt about your mother (father, brother, sister, wife, partner, boss)?" Questions regarding feelings can be used to bring out nuances, differences, and discriminations in feelings. In this manner the richness of the life of feelings in dreaming, hence in all of life, can be explored. Going into feelings takes the patient deeper into his organicity, into the child within him, into the prelogical, into unconscious processes, and represents a movement down the metaphorical spiral. As this happens the contrast between psuedo- and authentic feelings begins to emerge. This is quite threatening to neurotic pride because it leads to experiencing self-hate, shoulds and should nots, as well as basic and central conflict.

Through what questions the therapist can explore the many dimensions of subject and object presentation and identify the many aspects of self-dramatization. "I was in the dream. There was a woman there and a man. I was both. And then I was there watching." Endlessly this young man was a bystander looking on. His dreams indicated severe alienation and resignation. His dreams also reflected a need to be both male and female, more accurately, to appear to be male and female; to be on the one hand all things to all people, and, on the other hand, to be sufficient unto himself.

These needs are often present in homosexuals. They think of it as a need *to be*, when in fact it is a need *to appear to be* all things to all people at all times regardless of age or sex. Although apparently oriented toward others, it represents a tremendous need for self-sufficiency, namely, to be all things to themselves and not need anyone because of the terror of discovering their emptiness and fragmentation.

This idealized image of being all things to all people is an attempt to unify a very fragile structure. It has been acted out by men, heterosexual and not psychotic, who attempted to perform self-fellatio; and by women also heterosexual, also not psychotic, who fantasied having a penis and using it for self-penetration. In these men and women, other feelings and attitudes reflected this need for omnipotence and self-sufficiency to stave off terrifying feelings of impotence and emptiness.

By asking, "What if we look at your father as standing for me?" or "What if I stand for your father (brother, mother, or myself)?" the symbol is thus looked at both subjectively and objectively. Creating such sharp juxtapositions by suggesting these opposite perspectives can have a startling impact and result in sudden illuminations.

Alertness for new symbol configurations leads to opening new avenues into problems previously untouched, history barely mentioned, and into childhood. The emergence in dreams of a new person, place, or number opens the way to asking, "What more about age

315

four?" "What about your teacher in the third grade?" "What did it feel like the first day you went to Newton High School?" Such questions can open the way to exploring the vast areas of sex, eating, defecating, sleeping, and human relationships.

In time, through what questions and questions regarding feelings, patients can be slowly introduced into the world of fear and anxiety dreams from which they may at first recoil. With care, caution, and support, desensitizing can proceed. These comments amplify the earlier discussion of fear and anxiety dreams and how I work with them. The results of such efforts were evident in a timid, terrified, fragile woman with almost no tolerance for pain, friction, or anxiety. She was helped to open herself to resting in panic. Because of her basic trust in me, herself and in the relationhip, she finally dared to chance it. With a feeling of revelation and release, she experienced the panic diminishing.

Phenomenologically, this happening is most difficult to describe. To formulate meaningful explanations is almost impossible because they are so distant from the immediacy being experienced. There is a letting go into a painful feeling which was feared. The fear had intensified the pain which in turn exaggerated the fear. The pain feared might be physical and/or psychological, fear itself, anxiety, even panic. With the letting go into the fear of the pain and then into the pain itself, following a transitional intensification of both, there is a slow diminution and ebbing away of both. The fear generally goes first. The painful feeling may remain for a shorter or longer time. When it is psychological and recurs, the patient now feels more able and potent to deal with it. As a result, the fear does not so quickly arise and the pain does not so acutely become intensified.

Where the pain is physical it may have to be lived with because the source of it is not reversible and may even become more intense. As the ability to bear with it and not fight it becomes greater, the pain moves away from the center of that person's existence. The pain does not dominate his life. This letting go into and bearing with the pain is no stoical enduring, no expression of pride in neurotic suffering, no indication of masochism, but an affirmation of human dignity and moral courage.

First dreams often reveal how a patient perceives analysis and the analyst. They also show how he sees himself; how he relates to people and to life; and what problems concern him immediately, whether current or of long standing. The latter problems are frequently reflected in a recurrent dream or a recurrent nightmare. When and how a patient brings up his first dream, and how he responds to it depends on factors such as whether or not he believes he has dreamt before, how far back he recalls dreaming, and the nature of his dreams.

Often a person who has had lifelong nightmares or a recurrent dream will mention them during the brief history given in the initial interview. Or he will bring in such dreams as soon as they appear, and expect the analyst or analysis to do something to make them stop because they are so painful. Some will soon bring in dreams because they think they should. They see it as part of the analytic ritual, and do so to please the analyst. Some patients will not bring in dreams because they cannot understand them, and because they fear anything unconscious.

One man, after three years of analysis, had two contradictory feelings quite clearly and simultaneously in the midst of a session. In the same moment he felt, with certainty, that he had never dreamt in his life and, if he had, he couldn't remember doing so, and the second feeling was, paradoxically, that all his life he had been a prolific dreamer. Up to that session he had reported no dreams. Thereafter, he reported many.

In our first session, after a few sentences about why he had come into analysis and a few details of his life history, Roland S. laughingly interjected, "I had a dream last night, with my sister of all people. We were walking down a long corridor. It was some kind of gathering. When I woke up I thought 'My God. It looks like it was a marriage!'" A few minutes earlier he had said that his sister had been a school teacher, had married late, and had adopted two children. "We got on wonderfully. She was much too devoted to her brothers and to my mother."

As our work proceeded, it became clear that Roland was trying to force me into the role of his sister, a role which he had attempted to impose on others, particularly on women, but also on men. I was to be selflessly devoted to Roland, in short, married to him. His sister had been more of a real mother to him than his own mother who he thought loved him but on whom he was deeply dependent. As it emerged that he had been in a lifelong love-hate bind with her, Roland felt relieved, released, startled, and disturbed. In the next seven years, he was in analysis about half the time. The interruptions had more neurotic than realistic components.

What also became evident as the analysis went on were fierce needs for self-sufficiency. While on the one hand he raged as not having his dependency needs fulfilled, on the other, as

317

they apparently were satisfied, his equally stringent needs for self-sufficiency were thereby threatened. When the tension became too great, he would find a good reason to interrupt, resolve the tension, save face, and return for another period of therapy. It is four years since the last interruption. On two occasions Roland dropped me cards saying he was making progress with ups and downs, a report which has been indirectly confirmed.

Albert W. had his first dream the night before his first analytic session. That analysis lasted four years, and was interrupted by his analyst's illness. The night before his first session with me, seven years after the interruption, he also dreamt. Both dreams Albert related in our first session. In the first dream before his first analysis, "I was boxing and had my opponent by the scruff of the neck and was beating the life out of him." Clearly, he was terrified of analysis and saw it as a violent struggle in which he would be hurt. He had never boxed in his life and was terrified of physical or emotional pain. Resorting to the solution of magic, Albert created a physical contest in which he apparently was winning. He was helped enough, in his first experience, so that he could avoid analysis for seven years until literally driven back by a recurrence of the old — and some new — disabling symptoms.

The night before our first session he dreamt: "I came in here [my office, where he had never been] and found Mr. B., senior vice-president of United Machinery, in your seat. He was the one I reported to when I used to work there. He said that you had told him that you could not analyze me and therefore had turned me over to him. I left to talk it over with Martha, my wife. She said, 'No, you can't do that. Don't work with him!'" He recognized that in the dream, before his first analysis, he was being his idealized image. About the senior vice-president in the second dream he said, "He was a tough no-nonsense guy." These were words he had heard others use in describing me. He also felt that he did not want to work with the vice-president because they had mutual acquaintances and he preferred to remain anonymous. Clearly, he experienced me quite differently from his first analyst.

There is a naivete about the way Albert tries to get out of analysis. He double-deals with himself behind his own back. By externalization, he puts himself in the hands of a man who is a replica of me. We know people mutually because he asked them, my patients, about working with me. His final evasive maneuver, and he was a practiced, tenacious, and ingenious

318

manipulator, was one he had used throughout his marriage. He constantly used his wife to carry out unpleasant tasks for him. She was also made to say what he wanted to hear. When she didn't, he became abused, hurt, and put upon, but still made it come out somehow the way he wanted to. Of course, when he wanted to do something of which he knew she would not or might not approve, he did not tell her.

Albert was clearly telling me of his need for anonymity. There was to be much of hiding, withholding, and secrecy, with considerable evasiveness and elusiveness to others which included himself. When he became aware of the latter it frightened him very much. With such a passion for anonymity, there were many pretenses and facades to be worked through with a great emphasis on performance and functioning. Only in the fifth year of his analysis did Albert glimpse the depths and intensity of his alienation and self-hate.

I had to proceed slowly, being supportive and cautiously analytical, because his motivation was limited and his tolerance to psychic pain minimal. At the same time I was not allowing him to become too comfortable. His disruptive manipulating and maneuvering became so intense on several occasions that I considered interrupting therapy. We worked through this block and a number more while making slow, steady progress. Five years after our first sessions, during a phase of very intensive blocking, he interrupted therapy. While much improved, there was much more to be worked through.

Violet H., a middle-aged married woman, had a first dream that sharply focused her presenting problem and revealed much of her current neurotic character structure as well as problems which had not been worked through in her first analytic experience which extended intermittently over eighteen years. The dream also showed what she hoped for in her work with me and what she was terrified of getting into.

Four years before our first session, Violet's urgent calls for appointments often came when she should have known that I was away for my summer holidays. When she did reach me I did not have open time. I sensed urgency, intense ambivalence, and fear of commitment. Violet said she didn't want any more of the "now there-there approach" — meaning she wanted someone who would be firmer, more authoritative in his conduct of the analysis, and also "someone whose intelligence I can respect." Both requests told me quite a bit about Violet and her expectations. Although I had no regular open time, after another call, I arranged an appointment. I felt she had become more receptive, and that irregular, widely-spaced sessions, available through cancellations, would suit her needs. She kept pressuring me, however, for more frequent sessions. When after six months it became possible, Violet eagerly accepted a regular once a week schedule. Some misgivings on her part soon became evident.

The conflict about coming and not coming to the regular session became intense. She kept "forgetting" the day and the time. There were intense fears of becoming involved and not becoming involved. There were blocking silences. She tried to force me to talk and answer questions, to stay superficial. Her moments of being open were immediately followed by closure and intense anxiety. Her body was in constant violent tension, and her eyes were always bleary and clouded.

In the first session of the regular schedule, her words of greeting were hardly out of her mouth before she told me she would like to take a holiday of unspecified length because it conveniently fitted her schedule. This sequence of a move toward, with an immediate violent pull away had occurred in every session to date. This time there was the additional factor of wanting to miss eagerly desired regular sessions. I pointed out her extreme oscillation. From additional associations, I mentioned her black and white thinking, Violet became quite upset and immediately said, "I know about my authoritarian rigidities," and followed with "I just recall a fragment of a dream" (the first in our work together). "What was in the dream was familiar, but everything was blurred and vague." As Violet said this, I noted increased bleariness, vagueness, cloudedness, and farawayness in her eyes.

Close to the end of the session, I called to her attention that she had not informed me of the length of her absence nor confirmed when her next session would be. Because of previous "confusions" and "forgetting," I had suggested it might be wiser to confirm the next session by writing it down immediately. When I said, "You have not confirmed your next session, as we have agreed, nor have you written it down," she responded with "Did I want it?" This came out in an anxious, bewildered tone of voice. I asked, "How come the need for blurriness and vagueness?" Violet immediately got the connection with the dream and smiled.

In the two and a half years since that first regular session, Violet has been more often and for longer periods "letting me in." Generally, there have been less powerful pullaways although there have been occasional violent upsets when she contacted the violence of her vindictiveness and rage of which she was terrified, and when she experienced greater intensities of conflict, anxiety, and self-hate. These feelings were usually intensified by external circumstances which she had shared in creating.

What was in the dream was indeed familiar, namely, the need to blur and make vague what would lead to involvement, friction, and conflict and to more actively blur them as they became imminent. Violet's desire for someone "whose intelligence I can respect," was intended to protect her from misusing, to her disadvantage, her own superior intelligence. Her need for someone firm whose conduct of the analysis she could rely on was to protect her from her needs to blur and vague out involvement, friction, and conflict, as well as to give her the support she needed during the repercussions to such involvement. The supremacy of the mind was also in the service of her resignation. With her self-effacement she was painfully familiar. She wanted someone to protect her from it while at the same time shielding her from her violent vindictiveness and rage. The latter Violet could only let out, as our work proceeded, in biting sarcasm and outbursts of vituperation. Her first dream indeed told much about her past, her present, and what was to be expected in the future.

This was the first dream of a young successful professional actor who came to therapy because of his homosexuality: "It's night and it's dark. Someone is roasting a horse over a spit." To my questions he answered, "The horse was wooden. There was no glow to the fire. I couldn't see who was doing the turning." The dream conveyed much regarding the diagnosis and prognosis of his illness and the future of his therapy. The eeriness, coldness, deadness, and remoteness in the dream apalled me. His second dream, not long after was a nightmare. "I was walking down some dark streets that had a surrealistic cast. Out of an open window came a horrifying nonhuman screech. I woke in terror." After six years of analysis he had advanced professionally, become much more comfortable with himself, ended his fleeting, fragmentary, homosexual relationships, and established a single, continuing, somewhat satisfactory one.

The following two dreams — the first of a series of five — took place about eight years apart in an analysis extending over twelve years but which involved only about eight years of actual work because of legitimate interruptions in the earlier phases. In the two dreams, which have almost identical settings and symbols, this man's attitudes toward analysis, the analyst, and himself in it are sharply portrayed, as are his changed self-perceptions. The differences between the two dreams informed us what had changed in him in the intervening eight years. The first dream took place about two years after I first saw William R.

The first dream: "I stood on the banks of a deep gorge. Looking down I saw a wide raging and torrential glacial river, dirty gray in colour. A wooden suspension bridge lay across the gorge at the top, about three to four feet in width, with a five to six feet high side railing. The whole structure was very rickety, shaking and swaying. My father was standing close to me, a little behind and to the right, urging me to cross over the bridge. I held back. A woman came walking briskly, passing us. She unhesitatingly continued walking lightly across the bridge. The bridge bore her weight well. I felt the railings were solely for the support of the bridge itself and would offer us no protection. I was very anxious."

The second dream, a little over eight years later: "I had come upon a stone bridge with a two feet high railing, on the left hand side, a kind of stone wall. It was about a foot in width, paved with flagstones. This was an arch bridge and in the dream it was covered also with flagstones. I had the feeling it spanned a fairly deep gorge with a glacial river at the bottom, but I never looked down into the gorge. Unhesitatingly I walked over on the railing, being careful to maintain my balance, placing my footsteps firmly on the flagstone ledge, and without a break in my measured pace, I crossed over to the other side and continued walking. The terrain on both sides was rocky and hilly, rather than mountainous, and the bridge was built of naturally available materials at hand. While crossing the bridge I felt purely but moderately anxious. This bridge can never be burnt behind oneself."

The bridges and terrain are like those in his native country. By "purely anxious," William meant the anxiety did not feel alien, but his own, created by him in his working at himself. It further did not have an admixture of hostility, a previously usual accompaniment. The constrictedness of the first dream contrasts with the expansiveness of the second, geographically and emotionally. The atmosphere of the first dream is brooding, filled with sick anxiety, with William "looking down" at the "wide raging and torrential glacial river, dirty gray in color." It contrasts with the more rational anxiety in the second where there is a gorge "I never looked down into." The bridge in the first is wooden and rickety contrasted with the stony, arched solidity of the second. The first dream portrays his life situation, constantly being or feeling pushed by his father, rebelling with anxiety and, as we came to know, with rage. Also, always there was his solution of a woman (mother, sister, girlfriend, wife) who should lead and take care of him, while he was constantly burning his bridges behind him in impulsive outbursts of self-destructiveness. In the first dream she crosses the bridge, and he can follow at the possible price of his life which he has almost literally done more than a few times. In the second dream there is no father or woman. He does cross the bridge on his own and continues beyond it. The bridge has been built of "naturally available materials at hand," that is, resources within himself.

But much work was still ahead of us. Rather than a bridge with two railings it has one, only on the left side. Rather than walking on an implied wider safer footpath, he chooses a more precarious ledge. He is not at the same spot where he was eight years before, but it is still quite similar. Bridges not only join but they separate. Although the split in himself was much less terrifying, it was still there although he "never looked down into" it. Conflicts of considerable depths and intensities remained to be experienced and worked through before he could go home and be at home in himself and with people on a quieter and more productive basis.

Five months after the second dream, William reported the third. "I was with some others in a car, a black limousine, driven by a man with a conductor's cap. We come to a long, low stone wall, one or two feet high, built from unhewn stone, similar to other rocks strewn around in the rough terrain we were traversing. We passed through an opening, rather than a gate, in the stone wall, and took a curving downhill course, ending up in a six foot gully. We got out of the car. I felt fairly comfortable, walking around in the gully, but the driver said: 'My heart won't hold out, staying here any longer.'

"He got back into the driver's seat, and I noted my son Henry [his second oldest child who is an excellent student] sitting in the front seat beside him. I got into the back seat, on the right hand side, next to my youngest son, William, Jr. A few feet further on to the right, the gulley was only four feet deep, so I thought the driver would go there to get out of the depression. Instead he drove straight up the almost perpendicular six foot high bank, with a mighty vehicular effort, apparently stepping on the gas to the bottom. The car ground up, out of the gully, and took a curve to the right, going uphill and on through the rough, pathless, and barren wilderness with its churchyard atmosphere."

The terrain is similar to that in the first two dreams as are the stones, this time used for a wall. There is no bridge now, but an opening in the wall (which he later mentioned was of a churchyard). The terrain has a "churchyard atmosphere" in addition to being a pathless and barren wilderness. His father suffered from religiosity and occasional deep and rather prolonged depressions. Several years back, the patient had become aware that in addition to conscious, occasional depressions he — the patient — had suffered from a chronic underlying depression all his life. In the dream he went down into and "walked around in the gully" which he later referred to as a "depression." Also the gully was the place where the "wide raging and torrential glacial river" had been which was "dirty gray in color."

William is now strong enough to explore these depths but under special conditions. He must be driven (carried), as a superior person, as one who has a private chauffeur but upon whom he is also dependent — an analyst, "a conductor." In the depression he "felt fairly comfortable," but only briefly because of the upsurging heart trouble. This he must externalize to his chauffeur, an aspect of himself as well as me. It is necessary for him to believe that it is I who can't stand it. When he gets back into the car his son (brilliant) already has the front seat, and he takes the "back seat," with his youngest son. He has moved back into the even more dependent "youngest" baby position. However, after the excursion through the gully, he was able to move into the depths through "the rough, pathless, and barren wilderness with its churchyard atmosphere" and continue on, swinging in a wide curve away from where he entered the gully. He came in one way and went out the other side having explored the sides and the depths of the gully, the "depression."

In the three weeks prior to the dream a vicious moral perfectionism was finally brought into awareness and worked at. Implied also were tyrannical moral shoulds. He said that in the past week he had been going through panic states. "There was a rapid spiraling down into them, but I didn't bounce right back out of them so rapidly." Earlier he would ward them off at all costs, one way being by evading issues which would provoke them. When they began, he would resort to automatic cutting off of feelings, massive denial, and — if necessary —

even go over into attacks of rage. He then spontaneously brought up the stone bridge in dream two and its arch with the two upward curves. He contrasted it with the curve down and the curve up in his third dream, and said that the four curves made the insignia of a fraternal organization guided by a strong ethical code with which he had been deeply involved.

Four months later, after the summer interruption, William reported, his fourth dream: "I am standing on the side of a dock near the ocean. In the harbor are two barges being pulled. One barge is covered with steaming cooked fish [at this point he mentioned that cooked fish and potatoes are his favorite dish]. There were also fish floating on the ocean which was calm. You were there to the left of me standing beside me. You were talking to me. You said, 'Let's go to X. There is good business there.'"

The dream came out in fragments. With each piece he went off on a current topic. He slurred and talked fast as he told me of the dream fragments. To get it clear, I had to keep asking him if there was more to the dream and to repeat what he had said. He mentioned the name of X in his native language (Breton dialect). I asked for a translation. He said, "It means horns of the dilemma."

We have finally arrived at the coast, past the barren, pathless wilderness with its churchyard atmosphere and are now looking out on the vast calm expanse of the ocean which provides his favorite food. Fish are floating on the calm ocean. There is a surfeit of good things, of love, floating on her calm bosom ready to be taken, even without asking. He says "You are to the left of me," which means he is on my right, the position of the favorite of the Lord, of kings, of parents. I am talking to him and I say, "Let's go to X. The business is good there." I take all the initiative. I still have my "conductor's cap" on. His reluctance to go there, in fact to get involved with the whole dream, namely, to even begin to consider going to X, let alone arriving at the horns of the dilemma, were evident in the way he related the dream and my difficulty in getting it clear.

Five months later William reported a dream, the fifth in this series: "I was on a battlefield. A train was going through it. There were all the survivors of the battle. They were silent. They were all standing up. The train was rounding them up and taking them off the battlefield. The war or battle was over. There was nothing in the dream about the fallen soldiers, if there were any. There were the survivors and all those that were

325

standing up. This dream was different than all my other dreams. It was purely visualized. It was not thought but visualized. I didn't seem to visualize myself." He did not associate directly to the dream, but to a project he had been working on for some years. He made reference to his many struggles to develop it and thought of the survivors as being what was left from each of his efforts.

After these associations, which were not proving to be very productive, I asked William if he could recall the dream about "the barges and the steaming fish and potatoes." I wondered if he felt there was any connection. I purposefully avoided any mention of "the horns of the dilemma." This is how he repeated it:

"We were on the north shore of Long Island. There was a wharf. The ocean was calm and unruffled. There were mildly undulating waves. There was a barge being towed by a boat. It was moving toward the side of the dock or the wharf. It was filled to the brim with stacks of fish like halibut. They are steaming hot and ready to eat. They had come from a place on the south coast of where I used to live in my early thirties. It was called X. That means the horns of the dilemma. The boat was at an angle to the wharf. You said something to the effect that maybe we should go there where the fishing was good or where business was good."

From "the horns of the dilemma," he has arrived five months later on a battlefield. He is still warding off being in the battle because he arrives after it is over. He does not visualize himself in the dream. There are survivors who are all standing up and there is "nothing in the dream about the fallen soldiers, if there were any." He is using alienation and externalization to ward off still more intense involvement in conflict and struggle but the fact is that between the fourth and fifth dreams there had been increasing depths of experiencing dilemma, conflict, and struggle which he could own consciously bit by bit.

The dream being "purely visualized . . . not thought" represented a significant advance. In childhood, frequently required to remain in bed for long periods alone in his room, William used his very good mind as a survival necessity to entertain himself with thoughts, ideas, and words. As an adult, when anxious, his intellectualizations flowed long and sententiously to the annoyance of his listeners. To let go of this defense and "purely visualize" — not think — represented real progress.

There are some crucial differences in the relating of the fourth dream a second time. He tells the whole dream without hesitation, and included reference to the horns of the dilemma spontaneously. There is one barge, not two, and it is "filled to the brim with stacks of fish," as if to make up for the absent one. He said "dock *or* wharf" because of his lack of familiarity with these words in English. To "where business is good" he added "where the fishing was good," which adds many more dimensions of meaning to the dream.

The most crucial addition to the dream is "We were on the north shore of Long Island." When first related we were on the coast at the dock. Though not stated, it was clearly implied that it was in his native country. I feel this was a clear dramatization of how much William had experienced of our movement in the intervening five months. We are now in the United States where we both live. His home is in fact close to the north shore of Long Island. He is finding his home in the United States, is feeling more at home with me in my home, and he has moved from the past into the present, into here-now experiencing.

From what has been presented, there is sufficient evidence to explain why there had to be such a long and careful preparation for movement from what was portrayed in the first dream to what we see in the second dream. From then on the movement and change is steadily more rapid. In the third dream, the bridges are gone and he can go into the gully, "the depression," where the "dirty gray, wide, raging, torrential river" was. In the fourth dream, he finally does confront himself with being on "the horns of a dilemma" with which he must become involved. He can do so now because he feels himself my favorite and receives the fulsome love of the bosom of the sea. There is reluctance evident in the relating of the dream and in having me assume the main initiative, but the direction he must go is clear. Conflict and struggle in depth must be experienced, owned, and resolved.

Up to the second dream his life and the analysis had been pretty tempestuous with much acting out. From then on there was gradually less of acting out and more of acting in. The shift from feeling out to feeling in was slower and the movement from thinking out to thinking in was slowest of all. His high development of thinking and thought as a survival necessity makes this understandable.

In the months before and after the third dream, much came up about his depressions and those of his father. In between the second and third dreams his mother died. After a period of mourning and separation grief, there gradually emerged increasing bitterness and hostility toward her because of the crippling effect on him of her excessive, overprotective "love" which had made him so narcissistic and so dependent on her and on women in general. In the next two years there was more of working through of his intense dependency needs.

In the months after the fourth dream, much more about William's perfectionism emerged. In the earliest phases of our work, narcissism had been in the fore. Still more about his dependency needs appeared, and more intensive work on his arrogant-vindictiveness was done. Following the fifth dream, his externalizing began to fall away, and what remained of resignation was more in view. Present in all forms from the beginning, particularly the rebellious form, resignation had been worked at all along. Once William had arrived on the horns of the dilemma, the evidence was there that resignation — the defense against conflict — had considerably lessened, but that much more had to be resolved for him to arrive on the battlefield. In the months since the fifth dream, more of the perfectionism, particularly its moral aspects, buttressed by powerful moral shoulds were worked through. Identifying the problem as moral masochism had an illuminating impact on him. William was sophisticated about psychoanalytic literature. Our work on this problem involved further exploration of his dependency needs and arrogant vindictiveness.

Six months after the fifth dream and after the summer break, as a result of his own considerable efforts at self-analysis, William brought up and pieced together many events of a sexual nature from infancy and childhood. There had been much seductiveness on his mother's part and strong incest wishes on his own. Much about his so-called homosexual submissiveness to his father and his repressed rage toward him emerged. Much of the material could be organized and understood in terms of Melanie Klein's notions of the depressive and paranoid positions of infancy. With these realizations and experiences the analysis was moving toward a resolution of deep-seated, lifelong problems which had caused William much anguish and suffering.

These five dreams have been discussed from the phenomenological, existential, and psychodynamic approaches simultaneously. Taken without any background knowledge or associations (individually or in series), they serve as an exercise in the phenomenological approach. Immediately obvious in the five is all that can be seen and experienced from the viewpoint of space and human relationships.

In space there are the aspects of motion called forward, backward, sidewards, upwards and downwards. There is the speed, rhythm,

328

momentum, mass, volume, and direction of movement in space as an experiencing process. The analysis of space is intimately related to the analysis of time as a space-time unitary process. There are all the dimensions of past, present, and future as movement in space with all of its attributes. There are all the dimensions of time genetically, developmentally, historically, ontogenetically, and anterospectively as anticipations.

The relationships involve age, and age difference; kinship, friendship, and acquaintance; the personal, the functional and the authoritative. To concretize some, they are father, grandfather, sons; mother, grandmother, daughters, girlfriends, and wife. Some of the authoritative aspects are submission, domination, cooperation, and opposition. Personal aspects include dependence, independence, and interdependence.

From experience of the evident phenomena, the therapist can move on to a more difficult phenomenological analysis involving viewpoints of conation, emotion, sensation, perception, materiality, and causality. In the series of the two first dreams eleven years apart, and in the first two dreams of the five above, which were eight years apart, a picture of the big sweeps, a macroanalysis, of the analytic process is portrayed phenomenologically and psychodynamically. The little sweeps, a microanalysis of the analytic process, can give the most minute guides, particularly in analyses moving at a snail's pace.

In an extended analysis, a young homosexual had well over five hundred dreams involving obvious psychopathic figures or persons having evident psychopathic traits. These are some of the sequences observed, indicating steady, though minute, progress in our work: older men were slowly superseded by younger ones, eventually teenage boys; single persons were replaced by groups; from manifestations of intense violence, gradual changes to borderline mischievousness occurred; his dream's position evolved from being absent and waking in a panic, to being first a terrified onlooker paralyzed or in flight, and then to remaining, participating, and finally attacking these figures. As these patterns disappeared, they were replaced by dreams reflecting increasing dimensions of conflict, ways of avoiding it, dealing with it, and, ultimately, attempting to contain and experience it.

In a dream series of over a thousand during the extended analysis of a young man, what was revealed, in addition to the minutest evidences of progress, were endless variations on one theme, on one solution. He was the spoiled first son of a *nouveau riche* family, undisciplined by his remote and generally absent father, adored and seduced by his hysterical, possessive mother. In one night, there would be two to three dreams involving one or several women of varying ages, often his mother. They were always making the moves toward him, doing for him, making themselves available sexually or in other ways. He was always the passive recipient. The imbeddedness of his demands to be taken care of by the whole world were fantastic and tenacious. The sadism, masochism, and paranoia let loose when these needs were frustrated was considerable, as was the panic when these latter defenses began to be undermined.

With some patients, almost continuous active interpreting of dreams is about the only way the therapy can be kept moving:

Ruth T., a very sick, extremely sadomasochistic woman, came to me after two long tries at therapy and many individual consultations with therapists whom she had rejected. Many times I felt like interrupting our work. She was extremely provocative in ways that were both subtle and flagrant. She did, however, bring in dreams, although most of the time she barely associated to them.

The first three years of our work centered almost totally around how Ruth's father had mistreated her. In the next two it shifted to her stepmother. In the next three, more about both of them came up, but, in addition, there was much about her mother, whom her father had divorced, and many other figures in her life. Almost all were brought up through dreams. In the last two years, what had begun to be evident, even in the previous three, was now clearly and frequently present. Ruth's father, most obviously, but also her stepmother were becoming increasingly supportive and helpful, as were a number of other figures in her dreams. She was also showing increasing initiative and assertiveness. Her attitude had considerably softened. Her humor, previously sharp and hurting, now became good-natured. There was still a wide gap between what her dreams revealed and what she could do in daily life.

Ruth began this session in the sixth year of our work with "I don't know why I can't remember my dreams. I remember parts of one." After she had related it, she added, "This is part of another dream." This contradictory, jerky, choppy way of talking was characteristic, and intensified if her usual high level of anxiety rose even higher. Part of the first dream related to having received a miniature set of library books. In associating to library books, she mentioned her own library and said, "I have them on my shelves here." As she said this, I saw her looking at my bookshelves. I asked, "What do you feel about saying 'here'?" A tirade of anxious, irritable comments followed. "You know by 'here' I mean at home." "What about feeling at

330

home here?" I replied. Another rapid, anxious, irritable outburst came at me during which she slowly loosened up. Her smile became softer and she said, "That just came out. I hadn't realized I have been feeling more at home here until I said it, but I feel that's been gradually happening."

I then picked up other aspects of the dream relating to the fact that Ruth had received a very large box with many supplies, in addition to the set of library books. From her associations, I could introduce her words, "whole lot," "very much," "abundance," pointing out the contrast to the usual scarcity reflected in the words used, the mood of her associations, and in so many aspects of her life. She more relaxedly smiled, said, "Yes," and quickly went on to talk about how she was going to arrange her own summer holiday so that she would be back before I returned.

It had been an absolute certainty for her that, when I went away on vacation, I would be killed in an accident. Her husband had been killed in an air accident eighteen years before she began seeing me. She had been convinced all her life that nothing positive could continue to happen to her. She also experienced my leaving as a rejection, and she would become intensely provocative in the weeks before my departure, particularly in the first four years. For the first time she had hope that I would return. More accurately, she had the courage to dare to hope. She dared to feel in terms of the possibility of more, of abundance, of continuation and development.

Right after telling me about her summer plans, Ruth said, "Oh, by the way, I just recall I had another dream. There was a ledge. On it was a box in which things had been stored. I discovered cupcakes there. There were too many to eat and I was going to take them with me. I sort of hoarded them I guess." I very actively asked for associations to various items in the dream but particularly the cupcakes, and then continued with active interpretation about how hoarding leads to things sweet turning sour. "Oh, yes, I recall some of the cupcakes were stale. Yes, my stepmother tried to turn me sour and bitter against my husband before I married and after he was killed." I emphasized that she had an abundance of sweetness in her which she had hoarded. Now maybe she was ready to come out in the open with it and share it. Instead of her usual almost automatic, bitter, tight smile and pullaway, Ruth remained soft and friendly.

This example illustrates the most active kind of interpreting, of weaving associations into the fabric of the therapy and connecting them with and through the dreams. It also shows how a dream comes as an association which is immediately pertinent and continues to move the therapy still further in a constructive direction. A dream is an association like any other association, except that it requires more associations for its meaning to be experienced.

Chapter 20

Dreams VI: Technique, Crucial Dreams, and Termination Dreams

Some dreams are termed "crucial" because they tell so much about how a patient perceives himself in his world, the analysis, the analyst, and the patient's expectations of both. They reveal much for the diagnosis and prognosis of his illness. In this sense, they may be referred to as "crucial." They are also "crucial" because of the clarity with which issues are delineated for the therapist and the patient, and because their meaningfulness is experienced by the patient with sharpness and immediacy. This can come out in a single symbol, or symbol arrangement, a whole dream, or constellation of them. Certain dreams may demarcate phases and identify significant points in the therapy and in life. They may function as reference points throughout the therapy.

Crucial may mean that the dream is of vital import for moving the therapy in a constructive direction, as in the dream of Olive S. who was going to marry her five-year-old daughter to elderly Dr. Cranston *(275)*. Crucial is not limited to mean conflict, but also refers to imminent or present dilemmas, struggle with alternatives, and a stand taken from among several choices. Dreams may be crucial because of their informativeness, dimensionality, and dynamic import as with first dreams, dream series, and sequences of fear and anxiety dreams. Dreams can crucially inform us of how a patient is experiencing unilateral termination and/or therapy interruption by mutual agreement. And to begin before the beginning, dreams can be crucial in their impact on a person, moving him to seek help.

Sixteen years before I first saw Serge J., he awakened with the terrifying nightmare that his oldest and favorite son had fallen or jumped in front of a subway and had been killed. So powerful was this confrontation and the awareness that something was radically wrong with the way he was living, that within minutes after he had awakened he was on his way to getting the help he knew he needed.

Shortly thereafter, he began an intensive analysis which lasted five years, followed by ten more years of less frequent sessions. I saw him one year after he had last seen his first analyst. He was in despair and was seeking help for unresolved problems. He soon mentioned the nightmare, but only after eighteen months of analysis, spread over three and one-half years, did he understand some of the deeper dimension of that dream.

It was now twenty years since he had a major kairos. (272) Serge had confronted himself in his nightmare with the question: "What are you doing to your life?" Now he was asking, "What do I want to do with my life?" For the first time he was experiencing the meaning of wanting and of feelings of being able to act on his wanting. He was also feeling able to assume responsibility for his actions. How he lived out the answer to his second question he told me in the equivalent of a year of intensive analysis spread out over the next four and one-half years, a total of eight years from the time I first saw him.

In the sixth year of her analysis a woman reported a long harrowing dream in which a shark kept coming at her. This crucial symbol she immediately identified with her mother's life-long carping, "sharklike" criticism of her. She soon experienced, with greater terror, that the shark also stood for vicious onslaughts of self-hate when she failed to fulfill her own neurotic pride-invested character attitudes. Self-hate was intensified, leading to even greater terror, when she failed to hold in check murderous rages which would throw her into conflict and disrupt her whole psychic equilibrium. The many dimensions of meaning

334

in this dream, and what followed from it could only slowly come out as this symbol kept appearing in more years of analysis.

The many changing dimensions of meaning in the same symbol, same dream or same constellation of them, as they appear in associations extending over a number of years is further demonstrated in the next example. This is to say that there is no single, right, or final interpretation to a dream. The meaning of each dream is unique to its context. The same symbol or dream may mean similar or different things in similar or different contexts. Different symbols in the same or different contexts may point at the same, similar, or equivalent meanings. Dream symbols may portray universal happenings such as birth, courtship, marriage, aging, and death. They may portray basic biological facts such as eating, defecating, urinating, sex, and sleeping. Despite these commonalities, there are no universal symbols — symbols, that is, which mean the same thing to all people, in all cultures, across time.

Rose B.'s sexual orgasm dream opened her to an interest in sex after fifteen years of frigidity. In addition, there were the many meanings the dream had for her when she spontaneously recalled it a year and a half later. The orgasm aspect of the dream opened the way to a discussion of orgasms during other physiological functions such as defecating, urinating, and eating. Then there were the dreams reflecting these functions and developments in them. Finally, discussions of these functions led to explorations of further aspects of the total organismic response in orgasms, namely, in the whole realm of feelings.

The shift from orgasms in dreams and during sessions to orgasms of rage was presaged by a dream in which she had a virtual orgasm of vindictiveness and assaultiveness toward her mother and hated daughter-in-law. This dream occurred six years after the original sexual orgasm dream. It was eight years after the original sexual orgasm dream before she was able to have an orgasm of fury at me in a session. This breakthrough was followed by quite significant changes in her whole psychic structure.

This example might look like a validation of Freudian theory regarding stages of libido development, fixation, and regression. It may well have been from such material that Freud arrived at his theoretical formulations. But there is a vast difference between working with what turns up in the foreground as phenomena, and giving those phenomena causal and explanatory significance in a theoretical structure. I believe the model I am using has wider and deeper dimensions which can include, where appropriate, the values from a variety of theoretical orientations — Freudian, post and neo, phenomenological, existential, and oriental. The sexual orgasm dream, about eight years before the orgasm of rage, was crucial in what it opened up. It was a turning point, a touchstone to refer to in the rest of Rose's analysis.

A dream may be crucial to illuminate sharply what had been unclear regarding our position, the direction, the goal, and the possibilities of reaching it. What might eventually be the outcome of work now in its fifth year was indefinite to me, although I had some indications that progress was being made. I lacked something concrete and precise as a guide until my patient reported this dream:

> "The dream took place somewhere in the center of Europe. How, I do not know, I came upon an isolated monastery somewhere in the middle of a forest. After entering, I came upon a monk who asked me to follow him. After passing through many doors and many rooms, somewhere near what must have been the center of the monastery, we began to descend stairs. After having descended seven levels of stairs, we came into a large room with a dirt floor in which the monk dug a hole. About seven feet down he found a box. When he opened it, it contained seeds which had been there for thousands of years. They were still vital and well preserved and he was going to plant them. They were wheat seedlings."

> The dream told me quite clearly what was ahead of us, what had to be worked through, how extensive were the doors and floors between us, what was vital and well preserved, what had been dug for and was to be planted by someone else which would then produce wheat — bread, the staff of life. I now knew our direction and our goal. Because of the depths of what had to be worked through, and because of external circumstances which contributed to our work being interrupted, we were still far short of the Promised Land, though we knew what we would find when and if we or she ever got there. She unilaterally interrupted the analysis two years later, at the end of the seventh year. This may be an example of dreaming as prophecy and of a self-fulfilling nature. Her progress slowly continued, coming almost to a halt, with some old patterns again becoming manifest.

A dream may illuminate the inner structure of the crucial decision to unilaterally interrupt therapy. *(271)* For some months, sitting up on the couch, after six years in the reclining position, a female patient had been talking about wanting to terminate analysis.

At the beginning of this session she went directly to a chair and sat down, facing me at a distance. She was obviously quite disturbed and immediately began talking about terminating. In the midst of her talk she said, "I had a dream of an old house on a lake, way up high on stilts. It was very precarious. It began to crumble and I climbed down very carefully. I had known that there were jewels there. I looked for them and found them, and they were no more and no less than what they were." She made no explicit associations to the dreams. Toward the end of the session I asked, "How have you been having me in the last few days?" Belligerently, she responded with, "I wasn't having you anything." Her voice was high pitched. With great effort, she was trying to control herself. Reluctantly, she agreed that her decision to terminate was unilateral.

She admitted to the significance of the word "precarious." Jewelry for her was a many-determined symbol. The expression, "the jewel in the crown of her idealized image," had often come up. She had quite some understanding of what the dream meant. Though well aware of the precariousness of her neurotic structure and what her decision would do to it, she was insistent she could still get out of the analysis with the crown jewels intact. But a deeper wisdom had broken through when she said, "They were no more and no less than what they were." This meant "reality is reality." During analysis, her war with the reality of the facts of herself, of life, and of the world had been a long and painful one, and she was still fighting it desperately.

I saw her again four, and then seven days later. In her last session, to which she came seven minutes late, I experienced her as less defensive and less belligerent. Shortly, she said, "I had a dream of being in bed with the idiotic son of my next door neighbor." She made no reference to the dream, but its meaning was quite clear to her. She continued talking about terminating, and said that this would be her last session.

During analysis, we had dealt extensively with her emphasis on intelligence (hers being of a high order), and on her need to control through intellect. When pregnant with her first child, she had a continuing terror of its being born an idiot. The emphasis on intelligence, brightness, and cleverness in her child was enormous. For her, anything less than perfection equalled idiocy. Her dream about her neighbor's son said it and she knew it — someday she would have to go to bed with her idiocies, understood in the broadest sense. Terminating analysis was not going to fore-stall this eventuality.

It is ten years since I last saw her. Through friends, whom she referred to me for analysis, I knew of her progress. In the first year, she had some severe repercussions. Thereafter it was far from smooth. In the past three years, she had begun to consider resuming analysis. Each time, there was a violent repercussion to contemplating the possibility. It would have been easier, quicker, and less painful if she had continued in analysis. She was still trying to hang on to some of the jewels in the crown of her idealized image, but she was losing her grip on them in spite of her best or worst efforts. The eventuality of her resuming analysis is there.

In the following example, the termination of analysis was sharply defined in fact and in a dream, both of which concerned her first analysis. It had to be interrupted for legitimate reasons after five years. "I felt he was a nice man with certain positive human qualities . . . . I don't regret the time spent there. I have the feeling I couldn't have gone any further. I feel pretty definite about that."

Her analyst, Dr. Arnold, had recommended his own analyst, Dr. Dorimer, with whom he had terminated. My patient found out about Dr. Arnold's termination later. For the break with Dr. Arnold, which had not been a happy one, my patient blamed Dr. Dorimer. In addition to the recommendation, Dr. Arnold had given her some advice about her future. She did not go to Dr. Dorimer, and also rejected Dr. Arnold's advice regarding her career.

In the first five years of our work there were some quite distressing phases because of the impact of some painful life circumstances and confrontations of deep-seated problems. In the last four years, progress has been slow and steady with clearer feelings of emerging into the light after lifelong depression, suffering, and emotional and relational constrictedness. Early in the tenth year of her analysis she had this dream.

"I was someplace away from New York City. I went to this house which was quite an elegant home, Bronx renaissance, and I came in with a sense that I was going there purposefully, and I met Dr. Arnold. It was his home. To myself I thought, 'So this is where you are!' He was quite smooth looking. Mrs. Arnold was there, smooth looking and prosperous looking. We were talking polite chitchat. All the time I was thinking and looking and thinking, 'These are your values!' I said, 'Oh, Dr.

Dorimer is seriously ill with cancer.' Dr. Arnold didn't seem particularly disturbed. I thought, 'Oh you quit going to him.' She then recalled the conversation of ten years previously when she had listened to his recommendation of Dr. Dorimer and to his career advice to which she had not verbally responded. I said to Dr. Arnold in the dream, 'I didn't agree with you about your values and about Dr. Dorimer.' In the dream I had feelings of distaste. I had feelings of inadequacy and superficiality, and I wanted no part of it. I was very pleased with my values and my feelings about those middle-class values which I grew up with."

I asked her to repeat the part of the dream relative to her conversation with Dr. Arnold. She added that she was struck by the pomposity of the home and of Dr. Arnold and his wife. "In the course of the conversation it turned to the time I interrupted my work with him. We talked about his recommendation of Dr. Dorimer and his advice regarding my career, and it was then I said that Dr. Dorimer was seriously ill. Dr. Arnold went on to indicate that he had recommended Dr. Dorimer and to repeat his recommendation to me about my career. I said, 'I disagree with you.' There was more about the disagreement. I don't know whether the dream went on and the subject of how come he interrupted his work with Dr. Dorimer came up."

In this dream there is a definite confrontation about a factual interruption. She sought out Dr. Arnold and defined his values. Having done so, she reminded him of the advice that he had given and openly asserted her disagreement. In addition, she felt and thought of saying, although it was not clear if she did say, "I blame Dr. Dorimer for your interrupting your work with him. How come you recommended him and gave me the advice you did?" She described the values he stood for. She defined them as smooth, superficial, and middle-class. With such values she had been brought up, and against them she had all her life ineffectually rebelled, at great cost to herself. In the month before the dream, the confronting and open opposing of those values was going on at an increasing pace. Concomitantly she was affirming her own values more clearly as a person, as an identity, and as a woman.

This dream was reported a month after the summer vacation, during which she completed a paper. A physician, she had a number of publications to her credit, many of high caliber. Some of her work was quite original. When she completed the paper, she wrote:

"As I work on my paper I have become for the first time

339

truly aware of the meanings of working through, experiencing, and being aware. I am watching each phase of the writing. But, I am not writing a paper, despite the fact that it is a good, and maybe even excellent paper. I am creating me: me as a human being, a part of the human race, and an individual; me as a physician, and I can assume this title for the first time; me as a theoretician, utilizing other theories, other formulations, but making my own therefrom. I do not belong to any set of ideas, any formulation, any theory; I do not belong to anyone; I am grateful and not obligated for others and for their ideas, their similarities, and their differences. These are mine; integrated. I feel somewhat guilty about all this; I feel somewhat perpetrating of myself onto others. Yet, what else is the creative process if it is not presenting oneself? Finding oneself? Expressing oneself? I am also writing a paper to present these experiences and these formulations to others."

In this instance, the writing of the paper, her experience of it and the termination dream of her first analysis presaged the interruption of regular work with me. Termination of her work with me will be next. Tapering off of sessions by mutual agreement has already begun.

The dream reported below crucially informed me of an interruption of analysis five months before it happened. It occurred in a ten year analysis which had extended over fifteen due to unilateral interruptions. This young man was a spoiled darling, intimidated by an uncommunicative, remote, critical father and almost devoured by an omnivorous, possessive, hysterical mother. Self-effacement, with intense masochism, filled the picture.

In September, after the summer break, he was in despair about his own violence, on which he still kept a tight rein. He had worked through his fear of friction and conflict to a considerable extent. He was also in despair because he felt he was a born loser. He had a dream of winning in tennis over a very poor player and then losing. In the dream, the losing feeling became transformed into a sexual feeling. This change illuminated much about his fear of "killing" the other guy "six love," of assertion which had become transformed into passivity, and of dominating males which switched over to being passively seduced by females. In the next few months, his tennis improved to new peaks.

By now, considerably disentangled from his mother, having worked out many of his problems with women via many affairs (including three lengthy ones), he had been standing up to his father. That fall he acted out against his father in a publicly defiant way, and told off his older brother and sister in ways he never could before. He was now struggling with breaking off his third relationship, with Beth, who had many similarities to his mother.

Five months before our mutually agreed upon interruption, he reported, "I don't dream very often, but I had a terrifying dream the other night, one of the most terrifying I ever had. It was mother or Beth. I couldn't be sure which one. I kept screaming at them, 'Don't go making something subjective objective!' I kept screaming louder and louder and finally people from the ground floor apartment came up the stairs to find out what was the matter. I felt people were hearing me out on the street and that any moment they were going to call the hospital and take me away."

He realized that in the dream he could not discriminate Beth from his mother. For the previous four months, we had been discussing making discriminations, and for four years the subject of making subjective objective had been in the fore. In our very first session, he told me of his need to watch himself fall asleep. His compulsive need to objectify his thoughts, his feelings, and everything inside of himself was powerful, consuming, and desperate. He simply could not contain anything and loathed himself for being unable to keep his private affairs to himself or to keep the confidences of others. He constantly had to "shoot his mouth off." To be alone meant being lonely, being confronted with his feelings, having to contain them and not have someone to unload them onto, in short to remain subjective to and with himself.

A crucial source of this problem was his mother. She adored him and made him into a thing. Every word and behavior of his she immediately took away from him by naming it, describing it, wonderfulizing it, and reporting on it to the world at large. He had almost no experience with anything subjective remaining subjective, private, nor of developing feelings of anything uniquely his, as belonging to him. He was now finally and forcibly opposing his own driven tendency to objectify his subjectivity.

In doing so he was contacting the suppressed screaming he had held back all his life. He never had had a court of appeal from his mother. He couldn't scream at her. His father rarely listened, was not available, and, when around, was critical. In his dream he screamed louder and louder. His concern was

"What would people say?" Clearly he also wished they would think he was crazy which is what both parents, always in essence, did say when he tried to assert his feelings. He was saying he was crazy to take a chance on letting go and letting come out his screaming opposition to objectifying his subjectivity. He also was stating it was crazy and terrifying to let go of his compulsive intellectualizing, his automatic control of feelings, his alienation, the residuals of his idealized image, namely, of being such a good listener and so likeable. But at the same time he was coming out with the well of lifelong screaming, held back, which he wanted the whole world to hear. He was announcing his opposition to, and his impending separation from, Beth-mother.

Over the years he complained, in an abused way, that I was always against his interrupting analysis which he had unilaterally acted out on three occasions. In the three months previous to the dream, he had said, as though he meant it, that he was going to interrupt his analysis at the end of June. Not long after this dream, his haunting obsessive fear, which began about age fourteen, that he might be homosexual began to disappear.

Shortly after his public defiance of his father, because I had not been sufficiently alert, the session degenerated into an argument. I then told him where I felt I had been wrong. Maybe I had more brains in my bowels than in my head, for out of this argument and my admission of error came something quite positive. He then talked about power struggles with his father, and was surprised when I said that such power struggles could happen with me and that they would have to be worked through. He heard this with a response of revelation, and then realized, "of course." He had not been aware that I had not been opposing his comments about his interruption. I had even implicitly been supporting them since his screaming dream. When I explicitly said it was up to him, he was taken aback. He had had his power struggle with me-father, who had admitted his fallibility, and who was now saying his future was in his hands.

Also in previous months, he was feeling more strongly that he was coming to the end of his relationship with Beth, that he was ready for a different kind of woman than he had ever been involved with before, a more mature, more rounded person with whom he could feel communion, comradeship, and continuity. He now experienced sex as but one aspect of a relationship. His desperate need for a pretty woman to bolster up his low self-esteem had almost disappeared. The so-called masochist component in his character had been considerably resolved.

The night before his last session he dreamt that Peter, a young close relative, died. In the dream, he had a feeling of indifference and added he never really had liked him. This was a quieter defiance and rebellion against family and self-imposed shoulds going back to childhood. Almost his first comments in the session, which he kept repeating, were that this was the last session, that he should feel sad and that he didn't, the reasons for which became clearer toward the end of the session.

Shortly after he mentioned the above dream he reported a second of the same night. He had been indicted for some crime, and wasn't allowed to leave his home city which was in the midwest. He was at the airport and thinking of escaping. He immediately added an association: "But if I did, I could never come back home again." The symbolic significance of his association he immediately saw. He continued, "Maybe it was a marijuana charge." He smokes it once in a while, partly because he likes the effect, but mainly as rebellion and defiance against authority in general, and against the authority of his family mores, which had become imposed shoulds. He added, "The death of Peter means the end of an era." He went on with "I feel I want to face my crimes and not leave," — one crime being killing off this relative, and the second being the rebellion against his family and self-imposed shoulds. He felt a new phase in his life was beginning because of a new way of working which he had never dared, namely, extended isolation and immersion in his work. This new phase was also indicated by increased activity and violence in his dreams.

Throughout the session he kept commenting, in a wondering way, about not being sad at this being the last session. As the session was closing, he said so again, and added that he knew there was something to his inability to say goodbye, awake or in his dreams. He can say it in at least five foreign languages, as came out in our exchange. But the languages are foreign, alien, and hence don't touch him so closely. The parting expression in all these languages is, in addition, not goodbye, but peace, peace be with you, I'll be seeing you, and until we meet again.

The connection between not being sad and not being able to say goodbye revealed his still existing problems with decision and finality. He has not really accepted this as the termination of analysis but as an interruption. He is not yet able to stand the pain of a definitive separation. While he was not sad at the death of Peter and the many crimes against old patterns, that is, rebelling against and murdering them, the actual experience of leaving me was too new an idea after so many years of an intensive relationship. Also leaving me was on his motivation and choice and therefore not a crime. This he was as yet unable to integrate.

I certainly had served the diatrophic functions of a mother and father to this man. Without having done so this result would not have come about. When he left I conjectured that he would return to see me from time to time for an occasional visit or a short period of analysis, but that it would have new attitudes of seriousness and self-respect. Just this happened a year and a half later when he returned for eight weeks of analysis. The break with Beth was moving to a close, and he had begun a relationship with the most substantial girl thus far in his life.

In this period of eight weeks of analysis the attitude was clearly one of being intensely motivated and of serious work. The working through of the ending of his relationship with Beth meant painful exploration and resolution of the deepest roots of his "masochistic" ties to his mother. Also during these weeks, particularly the last four, he experienced mounting generalized rage which he welcomed, from time to time letting it loose against me freely, and with less and less concern. As a consequence, it became easier for him to be assertive and simply angry with someone if he did not like what they said. In the last year he has finally received the satisfaction of public recognition, but more important is the feeling of self-respect for himself as a person and as a professional in his field. In the spirit of wanting to see an old friend and a wiser older counselor, when he left he said he wanted to keep in touch from time to time.

A dream can be crucial in poignantly and clearly telling of the ending of a long painful fantasy in addition to prophesying the interruption of analysis. Sara C.'s first analysis, of ten years, had been most supportive and helpful. She was unsatisfied, however, when it ended. After four years of struggling with and by herself, she continued analysis with me. She talked about the pain of her struggle. She felt disloyal to Dr. Demstedt, her first therapist, and had great difficulty speaking openly, not only about her positive feelings toward him, but also — even more difficult — her critical ones. She had to be able to be quite critical of me before she could speak negatively of him. This she was able to do in the course of four years of analysis. In the process, her terror of friction and conflict began to be resolved. This morbidly dependent, resigned woman discovered a well of hate and vindictiveness in herself. Finally she was able to become more freely assertive. Blocked for almost thirty years in the expression of several art forms in which she was gifted, they again became available to her with a new kind of pleasure.

In the fourth year of our work, Sara related this dream which she immediately understood. The dream setting was pleasant and enjoyable. Dr. Demstedt and Dr. Whitestone are standing there. She is going to leave them and they both know it. "Dr. Demstedt says, 'Will you kiss me goodbye?' At first I was going to shake his hand but then I decided to give him a goodbye kiss and noticed that he was not shaven. He walked away, and then I left." About a week later she mentioned Dr. Demstedt in her associations and I asked her to repeat the dream to see what changes would appear in the second telling, and to explore it further. "I was in front of the house of a man to whom I was going to say goodbye. I was going to just shake hands with him but then I decided to kiss him on the cheek. As I did so, laughing, I said, 'You are not shaved.' As I woke up I knew that Dr. Demstedt also stood for Dr. Whitestone."

Dr. Demstedt had been Sara's first analyst. She had been in love with Dr. Whitestone in her youth. He was to have been her Sir Galahad and to have taken her out of the prison of her family, which she realized in analysis was also the prison of herself. He was to take Sara into what she felt would be heaven. He told her there was no chance of their ever marrying, although yearly they continued to exchange greetings on holiday occasions. Ten years ago he finally married and is now a well known biochemist. She next cast Dr. Demstedt in the Sir Galahad role. While seeing me, the rage at him for failing to fulfill this role came out. But it happened only after she had raged at me because I wouldn't fulfill it either. Then her productivity returned, and her relationship to her husband radically changed. Where she had always been the weaker member of the partnership, Sara now was emerging as the dominant and stronger one.

This was one of the clearest instances of a significant resolution of an ancient problem as I have ever seen portrayed in a dream. She had resolved her false loyalty to some false loyalties. Now she could be more truly loyal to what was worth being truly loyal to in herself and in others. She could do it pleasantly and with good nature. Although there was a bit of disparagement in making her old analyst need a shave and look a bit down at the heels, it was a pleasant ending to a long and painful life saga. One year later, Sara interrupted her work with me. She had quietly announced her decision several sessions before the last one. I agreed with her decision because I felt she could effectively continue on her own. The first two years were very painful, physically and psychically. Four years after our last session, I met her at a meeting. She looked better than I had ever seen her in the fifteen years I had known her. She spontaneously expressed her appreciation for the help she had received.

Chapter 21

The Initial Interview I:
Opening Contact, Aims,
and Practical Arrangements

The initial interview is pregnant with therapeutic possibilities. *(70, 203)* The first session is a critical moment in a patient's life. How the session is conducted greatly determines the future course of therapy. While the ultimate of openness and sensitivity to the patient's needs may start the therapy off most auspiciously, their lack may cause it to founder or to fail. In the first session a patient can be most open and revealing of himself, whether he is aware of it or not. Usually he communicates more about his sickness and less about his assets. Often in a first meeting, the therapist is most open in his perceptions of his patient. Too frequently these initial perceptions are not heeded. The first session is a unique opportunity for starting the relationship off in a constructive direction and creating an attitude of trust.

Clues which determine how the therapist responds in that split second when the patient sits down in front of him, may have come from a letter, a telephone call, or from his first view of the patient in the waiting room. Is he preoccupied, maybe overconcentrated on a magazine, or looking out the window, so that he does not see the therapist come in? Is this unawareness more apparent than real? If a patient faces the therapist, a smile and "Will you come in please," can be enough to make the contact.

I generally say, "Are you Mr. Smith? I'm Dr. Kelman," in a voice audible enough to be heard but not to startle. Adding the mutual identification enhances my move toward a patient; it helps him relax and respond.

I usually extend my hand, but on occasion I do not if I feel it will be too intrusive and frightening. The responding handshake can be most informative. Is it natural or forced? Is the hand warm or cold, dry or moist? Is it firm or like a fish? I usually shake hands before and after the long summer holidays. On a rare occasion I may do so after a particular session. As a result, because of its infrequency, it has quite an impact. I may do so to concretely underline my awareness that it was a very difficult and/or productive session or to indicate support when a patient is having a very difficult time of it in analysis or in his life circumstances. An appropriate accompanying facial expression is all that is necessary. Added words are usually superfluous and may make the whole gesture awkward, even trite.

A turn of my head or the extension of my hand in the direction of the office door indicates the next step. Some immediately rush ahead, and others remain unmoved. Both responses are informative. In the office, after taking a chair behind my desk, I wait a few seconds to give the patient an opportunity to reveal himself through the choices he makes. He may remain standing, take a chair opposite me, move it to various distances to and from my desk, or sit in a chair at the opposite end of the room. At times a patient will sit on the couch — at either end or in the middle. On other occasions the patient will rush into the office and lie down on the couch because he thinks that's what he is supposed to do.

A patient may also walk into the office, before or after you, and remain standing frozen in the middle of it, his face suffused with a spectrum of emotions. Sometimes a smile, nod, or gesture are enough to set him moving. At other times, such accompanying words as "Would you like to sit down?" are necessary. They help guide and support him into moving toward and sitting.

The analyst must determine at the time whether to wait only a few seconds to give the patient the opening to begin talking or to wait longer to allow a moderate tension to build up which will propel him into speech. He also must be sensitive to the patient's tension rising to the point of blocking, paralysis, and terror. There is not only what the therapist does and doesn't do, says or doesn't say, but also how he is and is not as a presence. In those first seconds it is urgently necessary that the therapist's attitude approximate that composite of attributes and modes of being described as the analyst as instrument (p. 147).

That this composite was required, and in a measure fulfilled, when I saw this twenty-five-year-old girl appears confirmed by what followed. Almost the moment Sonia V. sat down she said, "Of course you know Dr. Kelman, that I attend all your lectures and that you're always talking directly to me." She went on to tell me that for some years she had attended lectures and courses I had given in the adult education division of the New School for Social Research in New York. Attuned to when she was slowing down, I said, "Um huh" or "Yes," prompting her to go on and indicating that I recalled the lecture or course she mentioned. My intent was to help her keep talking through affirming my totally being there for her, through my attention, my interest, and my wish for further information.

At no time did I allow any intimation of doubt about what Sonia said, or any suggestion that I thought that what she was telling me was strange or odd. I most definitely did not indicate that there was anything sick about what I felt was a loosely organized paranoid system involving me. The climate and mood of the session was of a pleasant chat about events in which we had mutually participated. As the interview was drawing to a close I said, "I'm sorry. We will have to stop now." She thanked me, asked me my fee, and paid me by check. No mention was made of helping her, or of her needing help, or her wanting to see me again. She shook my hand and departed with a smile which could have meant many things.

During the next seven years, I saw Sonia approximately once a year. The pattern of the sessions gradually changed. With each one, more about her current and past life emerged. She had a high school education and some credits toward a college degree. Holding a secretarial job but actually doing executive work, she occasionally was asked to do modeling because her job was with a clothing manufacturer. She hated the approaches of the married men.

In her early twenties, she was married for one year to an immature man whom she had divorced. Sex with her husband had been satisfactory at first but it soon became distasteful. In her mid-twenties, in a panic, she married a second time. It lasted only a few months. Sex was bad from the start. Although Sonia was intelligent, well groomed, very attractive, and had a perfect body, she felt herself a failure and ugly. She constantly feared rejection by men. She lived with her family in a hostile dependent relationship, having moved out twice during her marriages. She deeply resented having to return after what she experienced as her failures. She had a few girl friends. She visited with them and with some of her relatives. During the time she saw me she rarely dated, because she was terrified of men and of repeating the same mistakes.

In the course of these seven visits Sonia became more relaxed. She almost stopped attending my lectures and courses. After about four visits, she no longer maintained that I talked only to her. That she knew she was sick was clear from the way she spoke. Toward the end of the seventh session, I asked her quite casually how she would feel about seeing someone regularly. And, as if it was the most natural thing in the world to do, she said yes. I referred Sonia to a younger female colleague, B. J. Harte, M.D., who had had experience in working with problems such as this girl presented. As an older male authority figure, she could cast me in the supportive role of father. I definitely did not suggest a younger male colleague — the possible hazards for this patient were too great.

Dr. Harte and the girl worked together for about seven years on a three and two times a week schedule. She moved up to an executive position in the company she worked for. At the same time, by going to evening classes, she completed her college work. She then became a high school teacher, work she thoroughly enjoys. She dated men occasionally and broke off a satisfactory sexual affair with a married man because of guilt. She developed a number of very close relationships with women. After literally setting up her own apartment within her parents' home, she finally got the courage to move out into one of her own. My colleague continued to hear from her for the next five years. She wrote — seventeen years from the time I first saw her — that she was happy, was teaching, and had a number of friends and some relatives whom she saw quite frequently.

Such opening comments as "What are your complaints?" and "What'se troubling you?" are not recommended. I avoid saying, "Tell me about yourself," and "Start anywhere." I don't remain silent for an undue period. Such openings structure the situation into a complaining, troubling, and telling, or a painfully lost and silent one. I do not wait very long for the patient to begin talking. What I often start with is, "Can I help you?" or "What can I do for you?" Sometimes these offers are not necessary because the patient starts talking the moment he sees you in the waiting room.

Peter V. was a young man of thirty when he briskly marched into my office ahead of me on his own initiative, sat down, and began a barrage of words in a wise-guy, bantering, cynical, and disparaging tone with a partial facade of good-natured kidding. He was quite sophisticated about analysis, although he had had no previous analytic experience. He said he had read a lot about analysis, knew many people who had been in analysis, had heard about me through friends who had worked or were working with me.

He said he thought he would like to come over and see who "this guy" was who his friends talked about so much. He'd like to find out about analysis. He was curious. He'd like to talk to me about it. Of course Peter wasn't interested in analysis for himself, but he might try it for a short period to see what it was like. He also named a fee which he thought he might be willing to pay for such visits.

After Peter began to slow down a bit, his fright, anxiousness, and brittle defensiveness emerged more clearly. I then began asking him some questions about himself which he answered with the same cynical attitude and bantering tone. Clearly I was not going to ask him, "Can I help you?" As we approached the end of the session, I said to him that I wasn't sure I wanted to work with him, and if I did, the fee would be double what he quoted. With a visible, though only momentary, show of relief, he said, "When can we start?"

Maybe not consciously, but pretty close to awareness, I felt Peter experienced support and reassurance by my having called his bluff. This was also a small kairos experience. My confrontation opened to him a new vision of possibilities for himself. The fee I quoted was well within Peter's means. He could have afforded more financially, but definitely not emotionally.

We worked together for over six years. At the start, he was drifting in life, wasting his time in a low-paying minor executive job. It interested him little, and required almost none of his considerable ability. He was a college graduate with an extremely high I.Q. He filled his nights with card playing in which he gained a certain prominence. From infancy he had had asthma and hay fever. He was obese and talked with a lisp. Tied to his possessive mother, he perpetually rebelled and defied her in endless, ineffectual, petulant, and annoying ways.

During analysis the above described manner slowly changed, but it never disappeared. Firmly yet flexibly, with moral compassion and moral toughness, I had to communicate continually to Peter that I was conducting the analysis, and that I knew what I was doing. Behind his brittle defenses was a terrified little boy, despairing, hopeless, and cynical about himself and about life. The record of what he had done with his unusual gifts was there for him to see. For the whole six years we sat *vis-à-vis*. He of course knew about the couch. Even the remotest intimation that he might use it terrified him. I never suggested it.

After about three years of analysis, he married and a year and a half later, his wife had a little boy whom he adored. When he was eight months old, my patient had the dream *(p. 260)* in which he was discussing with him, in Greek, abstruse philosophical subjects. His despair about himself had lessened. He had affirmed himself as a man. He had moved to a higher paying job in a private industry where he could better use his talents. The motivation to continue therapy began to wane. I knew his wife was pressing him to discontinue. She was also responsible for his curtailing his card playing for the past year. After he terminated his analysis, his wife had another child. It is now twenty-five years since that first visit. He was getting much more out of his life when I recently heard about him.

To have asked this man Peter V. "Can I help you?" or "What can I do for you?" would have both frightened and angered him because he felt both beyond help and above it. It would have invited a response of ridicule. But that does not mean I did not continue with the helping orientation. I did so in the spirit and form that the situation required. My confronting statements at the end of the first session are examples of what I mean.

Many examples could be cited to contradict the belief that a helping attitude supports the patient's neurotic dependency and interferes with his analysis. When a helping orientation interferes, it is because the analyst's own neurotic dependency needs have not been sufficiently worked through in order that he may spontaneously and appropriately respond with human help and assurance. *(40, p. 202, 221, 222)*

In the beginning of the analysis it may be necessary to go along with neurotic dependency needs as well as with other kinds of sick patterns until the patient has become strong enough to begin to relinquish and resolve them. This does not mean that the analyst is entering into an unconscious collusion with his patient.

During the first session, a patient who has been talking may suddenly stop. A nod, a smile, "Um huh," or a "Yes" often are enough to help him begin. "Can you say a little more about this or that?" or "I wasn't quite clear about what you said about your wife (boss or partner)?" may be necessary to maintain the flow of associations. When a patient is blocked, he may say, "Will you ask me some questions?" Something concrete like, "What kind of work do you do?" or "Where were you born?" may start him going. Further questions may elicit a life history, but the primary purpose is helping the patient start and continue talking. When a first session ends with a patient saying, "I didn't know I could talk so much," I feel that the analysis has had an auspicious beginning. In the first session, I may also make a diagnostic and prognostic evaluation, not only in terms of psychiatric nosology, but also from the viewpoint of assets and liabilities for self-realization. I try to evaluate the patient's incentive for analysis, healthy and neurotic. What, for example, brought him to analysis at this time, and what went into his choice of analyst? *(273)*

The conduct of the initial interview and particularly the first few minutes of it reflects the clinical attitude. *(274)* The importance of this orientation has been impressed upon me by many years of practice in the fields of clinical medicine, clinical neurology, clinical psychiatry, and clinical psychoanalysis. The focus is on the whole patient. The clinical attitude involves the use of the person of the analyst as his most important instrument in therapy, trained, disciplined, and matured.

From the viewpoint of the clinical attitude and the *Clinical Judgment, (219)* which Feinstein has refined, the meaning of the term palpate takes on many dimensions. It involves not only the touching of an abdomen, the percussing of a heart or a chest, but also the use of one's whole person confronting a whole patient. One can palpate his mood, his atmosphere, his climate, and his level of tension; the tempo and rhythm not only of his gait, speech, and gestures but of his life processes as well. Reusch has expressed mounting concern about the "Declining Clinical Tradition."*(275)* Clinical medicine and clinical psychoanalysis in particular are in need of much more clinical research. *(276)*

First visits often evolve in quite unexpected ways, and with unpredictable outcomes. Because of a letter, a telephone call, or information from another patient, a certain kind of meeting may be anticipated and certain objectives projected. One measure of an analyst is his ability to deal flexibly with a quite unexpected turn of events in a first interview.

On the basis of prior contact, by telephone or through letters, the stated purpose of the session may have been to discuss an acute situation, a specific problem, or to be a consultant concerning the possibility of therapy. More frequently, in recent years, people come because they feel unfulfilled, experience their lives as meaningless, aimless, empty, and boring. They want to talk with someone who might give them some perspective on themselves. In the following instance I literally had nothing to go on. This woman called and said she wanted to see me that day or the next because she would be in New York only briefly. She did not tell me why she wanted to see me or how she knew of me.

In my waiting room I saw a woman who looked to me to be in her late fifties, but was forty-eight. Though well put together, Gertrude B. had the atmosphere about her of the malignantly ill, deteriorating psychotic patients I had seen in earlier years on the chronic wards of a mental hospital. She was in deep despair and kept repeating in an unbelieving tone of voice, "I couldn't be that kind of person, could I?" meaning so loathsome, so degraded. This was Gertrude's response to the sexual interpretation of a dream her therapist had made some months before. A severe puritanical upbringing, the nursing of a sister, obviously schizophrenic, on and off for the previous ten years, and severe financial reverses had all had their impact.

My help consisted in listening, showing an interest in her detailed history, and assuring her that she had gone through some very trying times. I also assured her that her dream, which she did not relate could be looked at from different perspectives.

Gertrude lived in the midwest and had come to see me on her way to visit her daughter, a student in a New England college. When I saw her a year later, I could hardly recognize her. The atmosphere of malignant illness was gone. There was an aliveness and openness about her — an expression of happiness on her face. Her appreciation for the help she felt I had given her was great, although she did not specify the nature of my help. External circumstances had obviously contributed to the change. Her sister was in a recovery phase. The family financial situation had improved. Her daughter was graduating from college and was soon to be married. She had also gotten the courage to break off her unproductive relationship with her therapist.

What happened with this woman is to be distinguished from those instances, familiar to experienced therapists, of patients having an "acute attack of health" following a single interview. This is clearly an acute blockage or defense in the service of flight from analysis. Such patients are frantically and overwhelmingly appreciative of all the help you have given them. They can't get out of your office fast enough after the first session or terminate the telephone conversation soon enough when they call to cancel the scheduled second visit.

There are, in contrast, patients who have struggled and suffered on their own. They have made great efforts at self-analysis without having talked themselves out to anyone before. This they do in an initial interview, and much that they have struggled with and worked through is verbalized. The human help from an interested listener, an expert in eliciting life history who perhaps makes a few interpretive comments, may be of considerable value. The effects of such an interview may keep reverberating for months thereafter. The appreciation these patients feel is solid and real as is the help they received. Further help may not be necessary or sought.

What happened with the woman above is of still another order. She had an authentic *kairos* experience. *(272)* She came under the conditions favourable for such a happening. She was in deep despair, to the point of exhaustion, having struggled with moral self-loathing for months. Because of her puritanical background, she literally had to hit bottom before she could be disloyal to her therapist and ask for another opinion. She was trapped in and drained by a whole series of adverse circumstances. Under these conditions, I presented her with a new and different therapeutic perspective. Crucial was my comment about her dream. I did not excuse or accuse her or her therapist but suggested alternative perspectives. I opened other doors and threw light on other possible ways of seeing her dream, and hence herself in her world. I had seized the auspicious moment. *(272)* My intervention was effective as the evidence showed a year later. I have not seen or heard from her in the twenty years since that visit.

How a patient sees the first interview must be taken into account. I may be the first or fifth analyst he has consulted with the hope of finding someone who had the time to see him, who wanted to work with him, or whose fee he could afford. He may also not have found the therapist with whom he felt congenial. It is of crucial importance that there be a mutual willingness to work together and some measure of liking for each other. A patient legitimately may have difficulty finding the therapist with whom he wants to work. The nature and difficulty of the problem he presents may, however, have caused analysts to decide not to work with him.

There was no question about the severity of the problems that Nina R., a thirty-four-year-old single woman presented, nor was there any doubt that the right fit of therapist and patient had occurred in her previous analytic attempts. Her history attested to the strength of Nina's urge toward self-realization, and the tenacity of the human spirit to find surcease from human suffering. What happened also exemplifies the value of a test interpretation for validating a patient's complaints.

Nina R. contacted me after having worked with nine different therapists over a period of fifteen years. *(277)* Her complaint against all of them was that they had not allowed her to express herself. By this she meant they had not made it possible for her to come out with the full intensity of her feelings of hostility. Although she felt she had not been helped, she clung to the hope of getting help and was willing to try again at quite a financial sacrifice. This I saw as an asset, as well as an indication that her previous therapy had not been as unsuccessful as she claimed:

After she had assured me several times that I had not in any way blocked her from expressing her feelings, I made this interpretation: "Could it be that you might have a fear of letting your feelings go and expressing them?" Nina flushed, became tense, and anxious. I saw forceful pulsations in her neck which became very red. After a few moments she said that she was afraid of the violence of her feelings. For her to accept such an interpretation and to respond as she did indicated to me that she had quite some assets, namely, the willingness to switch from the attitude "What they didn't do, it was their fault," to the recognition that "This is a problem, and it's my own."

Nina accepted my recommendation of one of my colleagues, and made slow, steady progress with him for about six months. Due to an error in technique, and his compulsive need to be helpful, this therapeutic venture ended. She promptly called and asked me to make another referral, explicitly stating she wanted someone very experienced regardless of the financial burden. She worked with this therapist, her eleventh, about five years, the longest she had ever worked with anyone. Her progress was substantial.

The severity and/or the special nature of a patient's problems make the necessity for the most congenial fit between patient and therapist all the greater and so much more difficult to arrange. Very often the most suitable therapist does not have open hours because of his very competence or special ability with certain patients.

For a number of years, steadily more of my analytic hours have been spent with patients who have had one to five previous analytic experiences. *(278)* When meeting such a patient, I nevertheless assume nothing regarding their knowledge of or experience with analysis and analysts. These patients represent a highly selective group, and my comments about them should not be generalized. They represent a group of people with a high degree of constructive motivation and/or with an intensively neurotic involvement with analysis. From my side they represent a challenge.

As a group, all had benefited in some measure from their previous work. Although some started out bitterly complaining about their previous therapists, it was not long before this issue was dropped and they devoted themselves to the tasks at hand. Just as therapists differ in competence and experience, so do patients vary in their availability for receiving the help of a particular therapist, at a particular time, in the natural history of their illness. I feel that without their previous help the patients in this group could not have contacted me, could not have worked with me the way they did, and could not have benefited from our work as they have.

In many instances, a first interview is for purposes of a referral. Generally, this interview will be with a person of greater experience than the therapist with whom the patient will work, and the contrast with the therapist to whom he is referred may be quite sharp and disturbing to the patient. He may erroneously exaggerate the superiority of the referring analyst to his own therapist, creating problems for both.

Being in the position of frequently being contacted for referrals, when I am quite certain I will not be able to work with that patient, I avoid arranging a session. With experience, a referral to fit the patient's needs can be made without detriment to him. When I receive the call, I ask him to call back. When he does, I carry on a brief initial interview over the phone. It takes but a few minutes of my time. The patient is saved the fee and has had a brief telephone consultation. He has had a hearing, but he has not had an opportunity to develop an exaggerated feeling about me. Also a call to the analyst to whom I make the referral makes the situation helpful to him and his patient. The patient becomes aware that I spoke to his potential therapist. Where I feel it necessary and of help, during his first telephone conversation with me, I may tell him I will make such a call.

Because of my experience I have had consultations with patients unhappy about their analysts. It is important to give them a hearing, but they must clearly realise that I am only hearing their side of the story. There are several alternatives open to them. They can interrupt their work and seek a therapist on their own, ask me for a referral to someone else, or make a further attempt with their present therapist. These alternatives are opened up at opportune moments during the consultation. In almost all instances, after such a consultation, patients return to their own therapists for another try. When warranted, I add that after a further try, if they still wish to interrupt, they can call me for a referral, and for a second consultation if we feel it necessary. On a rare occasion, when it is obvious that their decision to terminate has been made, I mention that it might be wise to wait a while before resuming therapy, if they are considering interrupting their work. Only in rare cases have I suggested an interruption and made a referral in the same session.

Practically all such patients try to pressure me into making a decision for them. Effective conduct of the interview results in this pressure gradually waning during the consultation.

Regarding the usual instructions given in a first interview, there is general agreement among holistically oriented analysts as to what may be mentioned and when. Most would not mention the couch or the fundamental rule in the first session, while many would mention the importance of dreams, the twenty-four hour rule, arrangements regarding hours, fees, and payment. These instructions are used toward the same end, helping the analysis start in a constructive direction.

I am more flexible in these matters. My aim is to use instructions — or the lack of them — to facilitate the emergence of "Freer Associating" of fantasies and of dreams (76, 182) and to more effectively use lateness, missed sessions, and delays in payment. My feeling is that much can be done toward helping patients become freer in their associating, without explicit mention of it.

This flexibility has come out of the experiment begun in 1941. I do not give the usual list of instructions during or at the close of an initial interview. A patient is distressed as it is — a list of complex instructions might only further disturb him. He will forget some and be confused about others. The main reason for the omission of formal instructions is, as previously mentioned, to avoid interfering with what will naturally emerge in most instances. When it does, it will be a concrete unique instance of mutual concern, to be discussed and worked with in its immediate context. The freeness, freshness, and firstness of these instances adds much to their worth for effectively moving the therapy.

I do not mention absences until the first absence has occurred. The specific instance is discussed, sometimes analyzed, and used as an opportunity to explain the rule regarding absences. I may then ask the patient for twenty-four or forty-eight hours' notice for session cancellations. If the patient misuses this rule, I may ask for earlier notice of cancellations.

The issues of timing and frequency of visits, as well as the size of the fee are used to effectively further the analysis. There are instances where I raised or lowered fees because a patient misrepresented his finances. On occasion, I have lowered them because of the patient's financial reverses or other medical expenses. Partial payment of fees and postponement have been agreed upon with analytic benefit. At times, when the initial fee arrangements are made I inform a patient that the fee can be rediscussed from time to time. I may explicitly state that it will be done at the end of six months or a year. Whatever arrangement is suggested, the patient is informed that rediscussion can be initiated by either one at that time. Insurance coverage by industry or through individual or group arrangements for limited, partial, or total payment of fees raises special problems. These problems can be present in patient or therapist or both. The contrast in attitudes of analysts working with patients in their private offices, in low-cost psychoanalytic clinics, *(278a)* like the Karen Horney Clinic, and in public agencies with fewer sessions and short term therapy are often quite evident. I only refer here to the attitudes toward fees and money. Where the analyst has the total responsibility, in his private office, fees and money are very much in the picture and much more discussed practically and symbolically. In the psychoanalytic clinic setting where the administration investigates the patient's finances, sets the fee, and establishes the rules regarding missed sessions, number of sessions, and duration of treatment, fees as an issue practically disappear from the associations and dreams and money is perhaps all too little discussed. In the public agencies the fee question does not appear. Money is discussed much more, but primarily from the viewpoint of practicalities. Supportive psychotherapy is the rule, with emphasis on problems in everyday living which naturally includes handling money

The central point is that all these arrangements regarding the number and time of sessions, the size of the fee, and the schedule for payment should be discussed in the analysis and be considered as analytic material. From the training analyses of over thirty psychiatrists, and my experience with over three hundred training supervisions over the past almost thirty years, I am acquainted with the many problems beginners — and even experienced therapists — have with setting fees, particularly in analyzing the meaning of the fee to each individual patient.

In many instances, because of being informed about analysis, having been in analysis, or being clear about what they want, arrangements are made with patients for intensive analysis in the first session. In those instances, I inform my patients of my vacation schedule which now includes a winter, spring, and extended summer holiday and suggest they arrange their holidays to coincide with my absences. When they do not, there is almost always a problem of blocking or acting out.

If I am contacted shortly before one of my holidays, I will not begin to work with, and at times not even see in consultation, someone who is acutely disturbed. When it is someone who will require intensive help for some months, I will not begin to see them during the two to three months before by summer holiday. It definitely is not fair to them. With such patients, asking a colleague to take over in my absence would be putting an excessive burden and responsibility on him. When patients are anxious about my absence, or when I feel it is wise for them to see someone while I am away, I introduce the subject at an opportune occasion if they do not ask. They experience my concern as supportive. Having the name of a colleague whom they may call is usually sufficient assurance. It is rare that they avail themselves of such help.

I usually see patients three times weekly for about thirty-six weeks — an average of about 110 hours yearly. Although most analytic patients will sooner or later have this arrangement, there are a number of them, as well as others preparing for such a program, who will not. I may not have that number of hours immediately available or if I do, they may not fit the patient's schedule. Analysis is difficult enough without unnecessary burdens. I try to arrange a schedule which interferes least with the patient's daily program. In this way, analysis more naturally becomes part of the patient's life.

At times, it is wiser, and a crucial part of the therapy, to begin with an occasional session at irregular intervals. I do this because regularity and commitment terrify some patients. Others feel not only coerced, but literally strangled by a regular schedule. In time, as the work requires and the practicalities allow, the sessions are increased to three times weekly. There have been a number of patients I have seen four and five times weekly, on a rare occasion, six and seven. In two instances, for extended periods, I have seen patients for double sessions five times weekly. It took one patient the entire first part of a double session to get started because she was so literal and circumstantial. The other's anxieties were so great it took a double session for her to quiet down enough for some kind of analytic work to be done. Very often I have seen patients once or twice a week for double sessions because I felt analytically it was the better arrangement. At times this schedule coincided better with the patient's life circumstances.

Although a patient may begin his or her work on an infrequent and irregular schedule, as soon as possible a regular one is arranged, even if it starts on a once a week basis. Regularity, continuity, and

360

consistency are the basis for forming and developing deep human relationships. It is what has been lacking in practically every patient's life.

Regularity, continuity, and consistency underline that therapy is a mutual contract, compact or agreement, with mutual responsibilities. The therapist by being there and available solely for this patient at these times communicates itself to the patient which in time he expresses: "It's good to feel that you will be here every Monday, Wednesday and Friday at 3:00. Just knowing it means so much to me." For these reasons, I keep the same hours for as long as possible; do not change them easily at my patients' request or my needs; and if I have to, I inform the patient as long in advance as possible. My dependability and responsibility with regard to hours sets an example. It also acts as a brake on the patient's tendency to request appointment changes and cancellations.

This regularity and consistency also carries over to the payment of fees. After discussion with my patients regarding what is convenient for them, we agree on what is mutually satisfactory. A pattern is set, which when deviated from, is immediately evident to both. When the patient requests a change in the basis of payment or a delay, he is aware he is asking for something out of the ordinary.

Continuity, consistency, and regularity on both sides impress and imbed the feelings of the mutual seriousness of the work to be done. These attitudes are there to reflect contrasts with the qualities of their relationships in the past and in the present. It also helps to identify changes. It often contrasts with the sick, compulsive dependability a patient has known.

The requirements of continuity, consistency, and regularity in the analytic work can, however, be experienced as coercive and suffocating. Also, because it is experienced as alien, it can be quite frightening. This is particularly so when psychopathic processes predominate. Continuity, consistency, and regularity are a threat to their learned patterns of irregularity, inconsistency, and fragmentariness. At times, the analysis can allow for and contain such patterns. However, in working with such patients, it is both wise and productive to allow for interruptions. The anxieties generated by these new strange patterns become unbearable. They may have to have a period away from analysis to integrate the regularity, continuity, and consistency they have experienced thus far. When the psychopathic process is not too intense, by thoughtful pacing and timing on the analyst's part, patients can emotionally act out interruptions while factually continuing in the therapy. Worked through in the therapy, an actual interruption might not be necessary.

Chapter 22

The Initial Interview II:
The *Vis-à-Vis* Position and the Couch

With few exceptions the *vis-à-vis* position is better for the early periods of therapy. It gives patient and therapist an opportunity to get a clearer picture and feel of each other. Contact at more levels is possible. The therapist has more obvious clues to guide him, and his total person is visible to his patient. A patient may be kept in the *vis-à-vis* position when it becomes evident how elusive and evasive he is and/or how compulsive is his intellectualizing.

For similar reasons, when a patient is feeling isolated, when he is floundering and going into a panic, when he is escaping into fantasy, or when I realize that he simply needs to see me *vis-à-vis* I may ask him to leave the couch. Because of such defensives, I may use a patient's body gestures, and autonomic responses to connect him with his own organicity by firmly drawing his attention to them. In these ways I hope to undercut the many defenses he uses to keep away from his body and his feelings.

The *vis-à-vis* position gives a basis for confronting the multidimensional blockage of "How can I talk so personally about myself when I don't know anything about you?" Clearly the patient knows a lot about the analyst, and he learns more with each session. He can form opinions about him from his waiting room and office, the periodicals and other literature present. Clothes and grooming through the four seasons is revealing. Then there are the analyst's facial expressions, gestures, his voice, word selection, and grammar. In short, all that an analyst can observe about a patient, the patient can observe about him. While the analyst does not see the patient's home or office, the patient generally has at hand this knowledge. In the *vis-à-vis* position, the patient can see all the nonverbal metacommunications which the analyst is both aware and unaware of.

There are many misconceptions about the analyst's neutrality and the reflecting mirror technique. The latter was an expression of nineteenth-century science which assumed that the influence and error introduced by the experimenter could and should be eliminated. Scientists now recognize an irreducible margin of error, even in physics. The analyst should, however, try to keep his influence, which causes error, to a minimum, with the constant awareness that the attempt is an aspiration with perfection an impossibility.

McAlpine's statement that "The analyst . . . is never a co-actor" is a definition of an ideal transference. She clearly recognizes "that an analysis is a 'team-work.' "*(235)* Tarachow emphasizes "the inherent difficulty of doing analysis at all, and the pecular antithesis in the psychoanalytic situation which makes ideal psychoanalysis impossible and which introduces a degree of psychotherapy into every analytic situation." He amplifies why the analyst cannot avoid being a "co-actor," contrary to McAlpine, and why ideal psychoanalysis is impossible: "The analyst is confronted by a paradox. Analysis can take place only in abstinence, that is, if both renounce the other as object. Yet at the same time there is an important archaic object relationship between them without which analysis cannot take place. This sets the limits to analytic technique. It is the very object relationship which interferes with abstinence and at the same time supplies the motivation for analysis. The imperfections of the analyst make analysis possible, strange but true."*(222, p. 208)*

Through his contact with the analyst, the patient builds up an image of him which is constituted of the images operative in the doctor-patient relationship and based on rational and irrational perceptions. While the *vis-à-vis* position favors imagery formation based upon immediately available reality perceptions, it does interfere with free play of fantasy and the emergence of the so-called transference neurosis. However, as the analysis proceeds and the patient is helped to avail himself of the couch in optimal ways, he takes with him perceptions of the analyst more solidly based in reality. These perceptions can thereby more effectively be in the service of the "therapeutic alliance" and the "real" relationship. They can also act as a bulwark against the more malignant forms of "regression."*(127, p. 146)* They make the patient's "Responsive Action" that much more realistic and productive. *(142)*

That the patient is building an image of the analyst, whether he is aware of it or not, reveals itself in his associations and dreams, implicitly and explicitly, as well as in his behavior. He may start assuming a cringing posture and tone of voice as he did toward his father. If female, the patient may refer to him in ways identical to the ways she did with her mother whom she adored but of whom she was also in awe.

While still in the *vis-à-vis* position, and also after the patient has begun to use the couch, there are various ways to confront the blockage of "I don't know anything about you" and turn it into an asset for moving the therapy forward. The use of the following questions accompanied by a variety of intonations has proven helpful. Implicit, open-ended, feeling questions are most productive. They are intended to show and to expose the limitations of telling and being told.

Some of the questions that can be asked are "What is knowing?" "What comes to you about information?" "What are your feelings about knowledge?" Then there is another category of questions which opens up wider possibilities for fantasying. "Do you have me being single, married, divorced, or separated?" is a question more pertinent to a blocked single female, while a man might be responsive to "How tall do you have me being?" "What do you imagine my weight is?" Only with experience and talent can one use humor, irony, and bantering in one's questions to expose the limitations of what patients refer to as "I don't know anything about you." "What does it tell you about me that I was born in Smithville, New York on July 8, 1910 at 2:05 A.M.?" "Will it help you if I tell you my passport number is 247934 and my New York State Physician's License is 76382?" These questions expose the absurdity of knowing through what patients refer to as facts about you. All of these ways of questioning create a tensional situation requiring patients to confront what it is that they feel they are seeking by "wanting to know you more personally so that I'll feel freer to talk about myself."

As these moves toward the analyst are exposed and resolved, opportunities for helping patients experience the crucial differences between information about, knowledge of, and wisdom emerge. They become more acquainted with the knowing process experienced as a spectrum of processes from the ultimate of subjectivity in increasingly authentic dimensions to the ultimate of objectivity in becoming increasingly rational. Then there is a widening of perceptual and conceptual horizons, a harmony and connectedness between the two, and an increasing spontaneity of both. As this happens, patients speak less about wanting to know the analyst because they are knowing him more in a root sense, as they are knowing themselves more. They become more focused on the task at hand and learn the crucial difference between authentic self-interest and sick self-centeredness.

The couch is a multidimensional fact for the patient when he comes into the office. He has heard much about it in the mass media, in cartoons, and in speaking with others. It is there to be seen, moved toward, avoided, ignored, talked, or joked about. The first glance toward it, accidentally bumping up against it, commenting on it, or even trying it out by sitting on the edge of it doesn't mean the patient is ready to use it or explore his feelings about it. Such moves, carefully palpated, can be guides as to how and when to approach the subject. It is essential to keep in awareness the context of the whole analysis to date; the particular session in the context of a sequence of sessions; and the context within the hour in which the issue of the couch becomes manifest. A spirit of tentativeness, openness, and flexibility in the analyst's approach to the *vis-à-vis* position and the couch is of paramount importance. The move to, and the use of, the couch is multifaceted and emotionally laden.

Patients in the *vis-à-vis* position sit opposite me across the desk. When they move to the couch, they may sit or lie down. In all positions, they continue to face me as I continue to sit in my chair behind the desk. When they discover that I remain in my chair, which I do in most instances as a transitional phase, they are surprised and then assured. Then follows a period of fear about my imminent move to a chair behind them. This I do after their fears regarding the supine recumbent position are, to a degree, worked through.

When I feel they can integrate the shift, most often at the beginning of a session, I will take my chair behind them, the possibility having been discussed off and on. Rarely do I say, in the session before, that next time I will sit in the chair behind them. The patient, already on the couch, hears me come in and waits for me to take the chair facing him. After some sentences, he suddenly turns around with a startled look and a forced smile as if to say, "Aren't you going to sit in that other chair?" I smile noncommittally, and he turns back. There may be several more such turnings and quite some restlessness and difficulty in proceeding for varying periods of time in that and succeeding sessions. Eventually he settles into the couch position, using it more and more effectively.

The couch is not a fixed coordinate in a closed system which we attempt to arrange so that the patient is the only variable. Such thinking is another expression of nineteenth-century notions of science, of the attempted mirror technique, and of the need to see the analyst as "not a co-actor" in the development of the transference neurosis.

Since I see analysis as a bipolar unitary process, moving in phases of oscillating equilibrium, with patient and therapist mutual influencing each other, with each being now subject and now object for the other, my view is different. I not only use the chair in front and behind the patient, but I also move between both as well as in and out of the office. The meanings of the *vis-à-vis* position, the couch, and the many other positions a patient might take in reference to the analyst are seen in process terms and as aspects of moving fields. The question is not which position is better, the *vis-à-vis* or the couch, but which position and which movements between them, is most effective for productively moving the therapy in a constructive direction. The analyst must ask which is most effective at a particular time, in a particular analysis, for that unique combination of patient and therapist.

The physical positions taken and the movements between them are a fact, a manifestation, and a symbol of mobility in all dimensions of being in the moving process called analysis. Such physical moving can define and facilitate moving in the dimensions of thought, feeling, conation, and action within the boundaries of effective therapy. Such flexibility can allow for much acting out within the session where it can be identified, analyzed, and contained. This picture of what might obtain in an analytic session may be experienced as quite threatening to some. The widest variety of possibility has been presented, and it suggests more of the extreme and the dramatic than most analyses have. Being more open and receptive, however, to such moves results in their happening less frequently and with less intensity. What may prompt feelings of unease in some analysts are comparisons with what should be according to an illusory picture of analysis. Culturally required attitudes and personal blockages with regard to expressing oneself in the motor spheres may also contribute to such discomfort.

Freer expression of motor behavior gives the therapist that much more with which to identify what processes are obtaining. As these restricted and constricted motor patterns are expressed and resolved, the patient is better prepared for freer associating, for self-contemplation, and self-investigation in the recumbent position.

Human beings have always sought ways to improve self-contemplation and meditation. The use of different positions has been resorted to — kneeling, the lotus position, and lying prostrate or supine. Isolation and silence are also characteristic — Jesus in the mountains, Mohammed in the desert, and Buddha sitting under the bo tree. The use of the supine position on an analytic couch is a rediscovery of this ancient wisdom. It affords the opportunity for greater relaxation and a greater possibility for physiological rest with minimal distraction from outside stimuli. Some patients close their eyes until the intensity of their inwardness no longer makes it necessary.

Attitudes toward the use of unconventional positions and the movements between them vary. Although the classical model of analysis makes the couch more acceptable, it is alien to what was once natural such as sitting on the ground among primitives. In the whole eastern world, the complete or partial lotus position or sitting on one's heels is still the natural position in daily living for most.

There are also individual attitudes which influence a patient's or an analyst's aversion to movement toward the couch and to mobility in the physical dimensions mentioned. In some instances, both patient and therapist cannot remain long enough in the *vis-à-vis* position. In others, the patient can't get to the couch fast enough and the analyst can't have him there soon enough. I am referring to neurotic attitudes in both which determine these preferences. They should have been worked through in the analyst in his personal analysis, and they have to be in a measure resolved in the patient before he will be able to become more effectively moved to the couch.

Naturally, those analysts trained according to the classical model have had much more experience of being on the couch. Increasing numbers of analysts and psychotherapists are having less and less of this experience, which I feel is a loss.

The values of the couch and other positions for meditation have been arrived at and affirmed across time. A patient can learn about his tensions and experience the processes of letting go, relaxing, surrendering, giving in, and total giving which is receiving. The possibility of using the analyst for working out fantasies is enhanced. Dreams more easily emerge to be recounted. Freer associating is supported and extended. The range of forms of consciousness can more easily emerge: hypnogogic reverie, mild trance states, states of depersonalization, drowsiness, and sleep, for example.

On the couch the patient has a better opportunity to learn to discriminate sick feelings of aloneness, loneliness, and isolation from healthier being by oneself, with oneself, oneself. Concomitantly, he experiences how he has used compulsive being with others. As a patient on the couch comes to learn and experience what he is and that he is, the analyst's silence becomes less of a disturbance and a distraction. The patient begins to know the constructive values of silence and how to use it constructively. His silences are no longer evidence of resistance.

Not fearing silence, in fact welcoming and accepting it, he learns to listen in silence and to listen to his silence. In constructive silence, he begins to experience being quiet not only in his mind but in his body and in his feelings. He becomes acquainted with Lao Tzu's

"Creative Quietism." Through being silent, quiet, and still, that rare experience serenity more often happens. The more all these are possible to him, the more that vast "beyond which is within" (J. Huxley) opens to him. As one patient began to glimpse such feelings, he experienced them "like the beginning of a voyage into the unknown of myself. It may be like what a musician or an artist feels when he begins to write music or paint a picture."

He has an opportunity to become better acquainted with his boundaries, as they become defined, change, extend, and expand. He will come to know his boundaries in thought, feeling, willing, and action in reference to himself as a social being and as an aspect of the cosmos. He will experience his contiguity, continuity, and connectedness with others. He comes thereby to know himself more clearly as an autonomous being, as a self, as an entity, as an identity, as a self-responsible agent in his life. In approximating these feelings he will go through those experiences described as losing oneself to find oneself. As he does, he will use whatever words are available and appropriate to him, religious, ethical, or philsophical, to describe his experiences. As he does so, whatever remains of feelings of unconventionality and artificiality about the couch will fade away.

The process and the experiencing of the ultimates possible on the couch are best expressed by a patient who said, "I am feeling a flowing apart and a coming together with you. But when I feel flowing apart and coming together in me, I feel it is all me. When I felt a flowing apart from you, I felt separate but not isolated, and when I felt a flowing together with you, I didn't feel submerged. I still feel me. Oh, it takes so many words to say it. And I felt it all in a moment and for several minutes."

Not everyone can or will use the couch in the course of his therapy. For some it would be unwise; for others, more limited objectives would preclude its being used. Some having arrived there, have to leave it or be asked to do so. Others cannot make constructive enough use of it. It is my conviction that for those who can, what is possible through the productive use of couch, is not possible in the *vis-à-vis* position.

With optimal use of the couch, I look for freer associating, more effective utilization of dreams, fantasies, and slips of the tongue. I also find that greater regularity occurs in the frequency and attendance at sessions and in the payment of fees. In such an atmosphere the patient is feeling more trusting and secure. He knows where he stands with himself and his analyst regarding time, place, person, and function. The patient can now more and more wholeheartedly continue to focus on the task at hand. As this state of affairs is reached, he is preparing for interruption of the regular schedule of sessions.

As a patient approaches the ultimate possible in therapy through the use of the couch, he will have reached a measure of rational faith in unconscious processes, in his innate constructiveness, and in the autonomy and spontaneity of his nature which is beyond good and evil.

No one, however, ever fulfills the mythical end point of a completed analysis. When viewed from the holistic orientation there is no termination to analysis because "man can change and go on changing as long as he lives."*(39, p. 19)* The issue becomes how best to gradually taper off the regular work with mutual agreement. The practical application of the theoretical premises for interrupting therapeutic work will be discussed in chapter 25. The notions of a "completed analysis," "undergoing analysis," and of "making a patient see" are in concept, language, and spirit mechanistic, derivative, and expressive of methodologies in science applicable to inanimate matter. Regrettably these expressions are frequently found in publications on technique and are often used by experienced analysts. Consonant with such attitudes, animate and inanimate nature is made into objects. Things are done by material forces to which patients are supposed to react as if they were material things. These operations are hardly consonant, congruent, and congenial with the mutual human endeavor which is analysis.

The further a person goes along the path of the ultimates possible through analysis, the more effective he will be in his self-analysis after analysis. Should he return for a single session, a few, or another period of analysis, the gains from such experiences will be far greater. What will come out of such meetings will accrue mainly from what he has done on his own in between and during such contacts. Talking it out and formulating it in the trusting atmosphere of the analytic situation will require much less from the analyst.

Just as I feel it essential that every analyst of whatever persuasion have the experience of treating patients intensively over a long time, so do I feel he should have had the experience of having personally experienced analysis conducted according to the classical model. By the classical model, I refer to those arrangements and techniques which characterize it, but used according to the theory of the nature of man and the theory of technique presented here.

I also feel that a therapist should have had the experience of treating at least one and preferably several patients according to the classical model. This work should be supervised by an analyst experienced in the use of that model. Without having had such experiences, the therapist cannot have that gut guide of total organismic participation which such a process makes possible.

This experience personally and with patients is essential to the use of psychonanalysis as an investigative tool. Its research possibilities are at their very beginning in clinical research, in experimental research, and in research relating to theory formation regarding the structure of psychic life. *(276)* While comparatively fewer patients are being treated according to the classical model, the number of people treated psychotherapeutically mounts significantly. Then there are the many other forms of therapy — group therapy, conjoint family therapy, the therapeutic community, and the many aspects of community psychiatry — in which psychoanalytic principles are crucial guides.

The analysis of Waldo K., a thirty-five-year-old married man, illustrates many aspects of the issues of frequency of visits, fees, the *vis-à-vis* position and the couch. He called for an appointment, after I had been working with his wife for four years. Of inherited means, which he invested wisely, he devoted himself mainly to philanthropic work, using his specialized training in long term projects which he could in large measure control himself. When his wife entered therapy, at his insistence, he assured himself that she was the source of their marriage problems. With her developing strength and independence, and her determination to continue in analysis, he became increasingly disturbed. When he finally called for an appointment, he thought it was to come and vent his feelings about what I was doing to his marriage.

My seeing him and his wife was not conjoint therapy of marital partners. It was working with two people in individual analysis, who happened to be married. In my thirty years of psychonanalytic practice, I have done so on twenty-two occasions. Twenty of these couples have remained married.

I only accept a spouse in therapy after the other member has been in analysis with me for several years. More important than the duration of therapy is the strength and depth of our relationship and of the patient's motivation for therapy. This means that accepting the partner has to be in a measure genuinely acceptable to my patient. I also have to feel convinced that it will not be too disruptive to the work, and that the advantages of working with the partner significantly outweigh the disadvantages.

In such marriages, the pattern that usually evolves is for the actually or supposedly sicker partner to enter therapy first. This often happens partly due to the pressure of the other. At times one partner, supposedly the healthier, begins analysis first because they feel they might be contributing to the marital problems. They enter therapy to find out about themselves in order to help the other with the hope that maybe later the other partner might be willing to accept therapy. What usually happens is that the process of change, not necessarily

370

of improvement, of the one in therapy, upsets the equilibrium of this sick relationship and the other partner becomes increasingly distressed. Attacks on analysis, on me, and on the one in therapy begin. Attempts to break up analysis might go to the point of threats of divorce and suicide. Psychotic breaks occasionally occur which are necessary before the sicker one finally accepts the need for therapy. I want to emphasize that it is not only because one partner becomes healthier, but also because the dynamic of change, the rate of change, and the feelings of being excluded and isolated all combined in a geometrical progression to present a mounting threat to the other partner in the relationship.

Once the other partner enters therapy, the following pattern emerges, mainly from the side of the one who has just begun analytic work. There is a defensiveness and fear that I am biased in favor of the partner. At times the concern is that I favor the one who told the story first. Naturally they believe I have been given an inaccurate picture. The question of talking and opening up comes and goes in many forms. There are periods of intense needs for secrecy, withholding information, and resentment. This occurs because of the feeling that their privacy is being invaded. I have two sources of information. They have a feeling of being at my mercy. Endless maneuvers are used to try to get me to tell them what the other says or to trap me into affirming or denying what they are attributing to the partner or to me. To all these blandishments and attacks I remain firmly friendly. In time these fears and maneuvers fall away, and both proceed with their analyses as individual patients who happen also to be spouses.

At home the following patterns emerge. The partner just starting has the fear that any new patient has entering upon this frightening and strange experience. There are pressures to want to talk to the partner and to withhold, to confess and to attack, to try to get him or her to talk about what they say and what I say. Naturally the one longer in therapy is at an advantage. Usually he or she takes the position that the other should talk it over with me, except when his or her own neurotic needs are threatened. Then the situation can be difficult, but no different than other patients just starting analysis who begin acting out with a spouse not in analysis, with a family member, a friend, an employee, or an employer. Naturally the more recent one in therapy has the more difficult time. He or she is less experienced, and more often the more troubled one who has fought off going into analysis. Again, in time, this need to find out, to talk it over at home begins to wane. What happens eventually is that months go by and the subject of analysis rarely comes up in their conversations. They arrive at the feeling that analysis is serious business, that it is their business and not a conversation piece. To work simultaneously with husband and wife rigorously tests how closely the therapist has approximated the ultimates described in the chapter on "The Analyst as Instrument."

In his first session Waldo K. was violently controlled and hardly as attacking as he had threatened to be in his discussion with his wife. In fact, terror was the feeling that I experienced dominating his being. I let him choose his topics and set the pace, occasionally asking him to elaborate. He said most positive things about what had happened with his wife through analysis. At the end of the session, he asked when he might see me again. I said maybe in two or three weeks, whenever he felt moved to do so. He called in two weeks and I gave him an appointment for the week following.

I had known from his wife that some had advised that Waldo should not be analyzed. These were people whose opinion I respected. Their concern was that his equilibrium was too precarious, his structure too fragile. A serious break might occur. I knew that his whole protective system had to hold in check and in balance not only violent rages which terrified him, but also violent conflictual feelings, feelings of self-hate, and violent anxieties. I felt that there were sufficient assets in him, in his wife who was becoming stronger, in his family, in his environment, and in his life circumstances, to make a cautious tentative approach. Supportive therapy was always available and interruption could be resorted to if necessary.

It was eighteen months before we had a regular three times a week schedule. In the early phases of our work, each time I saw Waldo he asked for an appointment and each time I asked him to call several weeks hence, giving him an appointment a week to several days thereafter, each time shortening the time slightly. And each time when I gave him an appointment, to which he felt committed, I would experience the terror that pervaded his being. It was six months before I gave him a definite once a week appointment. Although he had been pressing for each appointment and for a regular one, each time there was panic when he got it. There was terror of commitment and involvement and panic about what he was finding out about himself. There was a terror that his controls would not hold him and that the violence of his feelings would shatter his shaky equilibrium.

The question of the fee was a far more complex one. The issue of money suffused Waldo's whole existence. There was inherited wealth, the accumulation of more, the giving it away, and the careful accounting for it. Money was his language for communicating, for relating, for controlling the world, for holding himself together, and for affirming his idealized image. In fact, almost from the beginning of our work, discussions about money took up a good part of each session. A good part of the discussion of money was taken up with the fee. When he began seeing me, he asked me my fee. I said it would be the same as his wife's which had been raised once. I purposely set the fee the same as his wife's to avoid making them different in this crucial way.

Not long after arranging for a definite weekly appointment, Waldo began pressuring me to raise his fee. To see this behavior, as happened with the appointments, solely as a power struggle would be too limited a viewpoint. He also wanted to feel my strength to determine if he could rely on it. Also in pushing against me, he was defining his own boundaries and gaining support and contact. It was also a form of relating, of touching, contacting, of being in tension and in friction with me. Money was also a medium of asserting his worth about which he had grave doubts. He was driven to pay me off, pay me back, buy me off and buy me out, out of power motives, fear, self-loathing and appreciation. At the same time he was terrified I might exploit, cheat, and take advantage of him. But then, in refusing to accept his money, he was experiencing me as powerful, as having contempt for him and for his money. His most potent weapon and support was ineffectual, and it left him in impotent terror.

From our first regular session until the last time I saw him this struggle went on. In the last five and a half years of our work, I agreed to raise his fee on three occasions. It was still a moderate fee for a man of his means. Each time the sequence was the same, increasing pressure to raise the fee, my finally agreeing, the terror and all the other feelings for some months thereafter, and again a gradual building up of pressure for a further fee increase.

Just as there had been frictions, confrontations, and resolutions over the frequency of sessions and fees so there were about other issues. In the beginning it went on quite covertly, as to whether he would allow himself to become involved in the therapy. Later it concerned the use of the couch which began about four years after his first visit. Certainly there was the need to compete with his wife and to prove he was like any other analytic patient, but there was also a need to test himself to the breaking point out of a courage of despair. He also genuinely wanted to explore and experiment and get the most out of his experience while in terror of it, he constantly pressured me to let him use the couch. The struggle regarding using the couch went on for over a year before I finally felt it was safe to say it was up to him. I made it clear that he was free to sit up any time he wanted to.

As could be expected, Waldo responded to using the couch in his usual violent way, with violent anxiety, violent restlessness, alternating with violent frozen rigidity and violent laughing, joking, and booming, staccato speech. Even up to the time he interrupted our work, his fears of the couch and of attack from behind, while in this recumbent defenseless position, were still present, though considerably less intense. However, when subjects which were threatening came up, the tensions described above would again become manifest.

Seven years after our first visit he interrupted his analytic work. His wife had done so three years before. Fear of deeper involvement was not the only reason for his decision. It was time for him to try himself out on his own. This could be done better outside of New York. It is almost thirty years since I came to know him through his wife, and twenty-three since I last saw him. He continued to grow and get increasing satisfactions from his life, his married life, his children, and his interests. He never did have a serious break, though in recent years with age curtailing his activities he has periods of anxiety and mild depression.

Many analysts might say that somehow I should have prevented him ever getting onto the couch. As I saw it, his using the couch and working it through was part of the therapeutic process as it had been with the questions of sessions and fees.

Those who would be absolutely against the use of the couch in this case overlook the possible and probable serious consequences of not allowing him to use it and of his interrupting therapy if I had not permitted it. There is the possibility that the dangers of following such a course could outweigh those of going along with the analytic process as it was unfolding. Analysts often overlook the great wisdom that patients may have about their tolerances and possibilities and about what is wise for them. They will often communicate this inner wisdom, gained from their pains and sufferings, if we can but listen and hear what they are saying in their unique idioms and languages.

Chapter 23

Aids—Parameters

Sometimes I prefer that a patient remain in the *vis-à-vis* position or return to it from the couch so that I may observe what his body and confronted presence communicate. I may for the same reasons extend investigation of the life history for weeks, and at times months, as a way of widening and deepening communication, gaining information, and enhancing the relating process. Just as the person whose bodily expressions may constitute the main avenue of productive communication will slowly increase his verbalizing, so will the continuing elaboration of life history be a vehicle and a guide into the patient's past, present, and future. It will widen and deepen the patient's contact with himself and make increasingly productive his involvement in the analytic process.

I have asked patients to write their life history when an opening has presented itself, and when I feel it will help resolve blocks to communicating. No time limit is mentioned. When requested by a patient, a general outline is given. The request to write a history is made as a suggestion to avoid making it a *cause célèbre*. This might happen with patients whose need for control, whose hypersensitivity to coercion, and whose authority problems cause them to feel threatened. With perfectionists and obsessive patients, a history can result in self-torture or a never-ending task blocking the therapy. If disadvantages become apparent, the patient is encouraged to drop the project.

Many character problems emerge from life histories, and many aspects of the analytic relationship are brought into sharper focus. Whole areas of life history previously blocked out open up, often with intense emotional repercussions. Some discover, with shock, that whole life areas remain unavailable to recall, whole time periods, personal relationships, and crucial events. Others are confronted with the realization that progress slows and productivity slackens as the present is approached. It persistently remains in the distance. Others become aware that they seem unable to move out of the present.

Some will bring in their life history the next session, usually it will be brief, and then drop the whole subject. The heart-rending tragedy and meaninglessness of one man's life was portrayed by the single, small sheet of slightly torn stationery on which he had written his life history. It consisted of about ten lines — his age and one or two words about a few listed events — a whole life in less than one hundred words bleakly annotated.

At times patients will spontaneously bring in aids to help them talk. One analysis proceeded for months via notes on bits of paper brought to sessions. Then followed several years of discussion of original poems being written as the analysis proceeded. In this process, a childhood passion was rediscovered — she could create jingles in her head for her private pleasure.

Patients may start writing their dreams or use the device of a night table pad and pencil to catch the dreams before they are forgotten. If productive, these aids should be continued. They should be dropped when patient and/or analyst realize that the dreams written down and reported still elude productive exploration. Such a confrontation can have value as part of the working through process. The issue with all aids is whether they are used to help confront blocks or to exaggerate or to circumvent them. This should become clear and worked through so that the blocks are resolved. Then the need for the aids will fall away.

Helen Z., a nineteen-year-old college drop-out with considerable artistic and linguistic ability, spontaneously and on request made use of a number of such aids in her analysis with J. W. Vollmer-hausen, M.D. She had extreme difficulty in talking and moved from moments of deep silence to sudden explosions of speech which would then subside into a blocked silence. On one occasion she brought, at Dr. Vollmerhausen's request, some compositions she had written in college. After reading them, he commented on them. His interest in her compositions led her to write down whatever she experienced in one session and bring it to the next one. She always wanted the analyst to read what she had written while she quietly sat there. The meaning of this behavior became clearer when she revealed that she could experience the essence of her father and mother as they were quietly sitting, doing whatever they were doing and not talking. Language was generally confusing for her. Helen expressed this by saying, "Words are liars." It was quite true that words had been used deceptively in her experience with authority figures.

In addition to her writings, she soon brought in or talked about pieces of sculpture that she had modeled out of clay. In each instance she would readily describe the sculpture and her thoughts about it. Then she would wait for Dr. Vollmerhausen's response. One was a rather stiff rigid figure. She said, "You know when I can put stiffness into the figure, I can begin to feel my own stiffness inside."

Helen had other ways of communicating. She represented the therapeutic relationship in a series of sketches. She would freely talk about whatever she had sketched and was always delighted when the analyst had something to add that she hadn't seen. Body gestures and movements were other forms of communicating that she used. On one occasion, the analyst had cajoled her about something which was quite serious to her, of which he was not aware. He had a dim feeling at the end of that hour that she was angry and that he had done something wrong.

The next hour Helen came in carrying a cracked pod containing two chestnuts and asked Dr. Vollmerhausen to feel them and look at them. He held them, felt them, and gave them back to her. Material connected with the last hour began to come up, and he suddenly realized the mistake he had made. Dr. Vollmerhausen told her he had been wrong and in addition insensitive to what she was feeling. As he said this, she began to rub the rough surface of the chestnut pod against the side of her face that was nearest the analyst. Her face was shining with pleasure. He looked at her quizzically at this point, and she said, "Whiskers." Immediately, the analyst had a vague feeling and image of a loving rubbing of whiskers against her face which she liked. Quite quickly and directly he said, "It seems to me you liked what I said about making a mistake." She responded very brightly, "Yes I do. My father would always say, 'Yes, I'm wrong, I'm wrong but so what.' I knew that he never really accepted the fact that he was wrong."

It is striking how deeply patients wish to be understood. They constantly hope the analyst will be available to the various ways they are trying to communicate. Most painful are the fears that they will be ridiculed and laughed at, that their efforts and the forms of them might be regarded as silly and childish.

On a later occasion, Helen mentioned that she was afraid that Dr. Vollmerhausen would consider her writing, her sculpture, her sketches, as well as her chestnuts, as only aspects of her symptoms and sickness, to be patiently tolerated. The analyst made it quite clear that his feeling was one of wonderment at the many ways she could find to communicate with him. He did not consider these as symptoms, but as expressions of her deep desire for understanding. This was very relieving and helpful to her.

I feel that being open, alert, and available for utilizing such aids is not giving patients crutches. Nor is it tolerating and enduring these modes of communication while patiently waiting for the "real" free associations to emerge.

The question form of communication, whether as verbalization, intonation, facial expression or gesture, can be one of the most effective aids for helping patients become more productively involved in the therapeutic process. Patients respond to questions literally and conclusively, even though they are asked figuratively and open-endedly. They often experience a question as being questioned, doubted, criticized, examined, and put on the spot. What I am out for with my questioning is to help them open themselves to questing. Patients are driven toward telling and being told, and I am out for showing, so that the patient becomes open to being shown. I want him to look at what and thereby experience what and how. Such experiencing will undercut the compulsion to ask, "Why?" "What does it mean?" "Who did what to who?" in order to place blame there and then.

An interpretation, in the question form, may also be communicated in other ways than a verbalized question. Questioning is confronting. It helps to create a juxtaposition, as a polarity, a paradox, a dilemma, a conflict. It causes a momentary arrest and leads to tension producing. It creates doubt, uncertainty, reflection, and questing.

Why and who questions are almost never asked. The what question is asked because it is an invitation to look and see, listen and hear, the actual, the real nature of ongoing processes. It asks for

378

detailed observation and description with all the senses and functions. There is thereby an experiencing of the multidimensionality of the what as a moving process. It teaches the patient more ways of self-observation. It also directs attention away from who, which usually means compulsive personalizing and blaming. Finally the where and when questions also become less urgent. As there is increasing experiencing of what, there is greater experiencing of what and how in the here and now.

There is a particular preference for questions asking for greater experiencing of feelings. Feelings connect us immediately with the worlds of the emotive, the intuitive, and the conative — the sensory in all its modalities, special, general, and autonomic. Feelings spread out in many directions, to thought as feeling-thinking, to conation as feeling-willing, to organicity, as feeling-sensing-perceiving, to the intimate relationship of soma with psyche, to values, values as fact, aesthetics, morality, and spirituality. Feelings are at our core and emanate from it, connecting us with what is imminent and emergent in ourselves and in the whole of creation, numinous and phenomenal. With the focus on feelings the possibilities of resolving blocks to what has been dissociated becomes greater. Feelings of wholeness, unity, oneness, and identity are fostered. This comes about because in touching feelings and their connections, contact is made with the ebb and flow, with the tempo and rhythm of organic processes as they are emerging into appropriate symbol forms.

What questions pointing at feelings also influence attention which can focus now inwardly and now outwardly. While "Attention is only a transitory focusing of the extended system of processes which guide behavior,"(176) effective use of it can develop the therapist's "focal attention"(218) and "evenly hovering attention." Through attending, looking and seeing, defining, clarifying, illuminating and investigating, a wider and more rational creative vision is opened.

The emergence of such insight and outsight is facilitated not only because the communication has a question form directing attention to what and to feelings, but also because its structure is implicit and open-ended.

Questions are not only actions to cause reactions but also stimuli to prompt responses. Questions may be asked to obtain information, but the intent of what questions is to function as pointers. What I want is for the patient to let go of the pointer, to open himself to contacting and allowing his "self-propelled feeling process" to move him in the direction of what is being pointed at. (212)

The more implicit and open-ended the pointer, the more loosely organized the field remains, with a wider spectrum of creative possi-

379

bilities, and with that many more open spaces to be filled. It is attempting to work at life's growing edge, in the realm of prelogical experience where "paradox forming and paradox-resolving is greatest," where tension-producing and tension-reducing is constantly happening, where logical associative connections are loosest and prelogical forms maximal.

All my questions ask about processes and are aimed to prompt processes. "What is going on?" "What is coming up?" and "What more about . . . ?" are designed to urge the patient toward deepening and widening his experiencing of his processes. The questions are prompted by the analyst's responding at all levels of his symbolic spiral. Resonating to his responses and reactions, his person becomes an ever more effective instrument of therapy. These processes enhance the possibilities for patient and analyst being attuned to and more extensively in contact with the unconscious and prerationative processes of each other.

What do the analyst's questions mean to a patient? That the analyst is present — a presence that carries weight; that he is attentive, interested, and wants to know more; that he is moving with the patient, willing to help, and illuminate the way; and that what he is asking has value and is worth looking at, going into, and exploring. All of these are stimuli to greater trust and productivity and help the analysis become that much more a cooperative venture.

But these attitudes do not emerge without prior mistrust, irritation, struggle, and blocking. A professional writer expressed his feelings about my what questions, their intent, and how his attitude shifted. "Your questions annoyed the hell out of me for a long time. Now I know what you are doing with your questions. It's like the difference between good and bad writing. Good writing is showing while bad writing is telling. Good writing says to the reader 'Look at it for yourself and come to your own conclusions.' "

The question form of interpretation does not preclude "I wonder what you feel about this?" referring to a possible meaning of a dream or sequence of associations. The analyst might say, "This is a possibility," "I am not sure what it might mean," or "Maybe if we look at the dreams you brought up today (last week, last month) and compare them, we might get a feel for what is going on." On occasion the analyst might conjecture that a problem is being evaded, defined, or being struggled with; or that this is the first time this situation, solution, or person has appeared; or conversely that there is an absence of anxiety where it would have been present in a similar situation; or that there is less of destructiveness and more of constructiveness. These interpretive questions are used to make comparisons, to indicate movement and the direction of it. They are aimed toward identifying and fostering process. But as will be noted in all the forms just mentioned, there is always a spirit of tentativeness.

Menninger asserts "Everything is to be considered 'tentative' — an opinion as of the moment only."*(200)* Middleman suggests that societies characterized by "heterogeneity" (Mead) and "discontinuity," where tentativeness is a way of life and where an individual may develop a "tentative ego-identity" (Erikson) the concept of tentativeness is likely to be relevant to many aspects of the psychotherapeutic process. Feeling out and trying out serve to resolve many of the oppositional dichotomies which characterize neurosis. *(279)*

Lifton describes a "new psychological style . . . emerging everywhere" which he calls "Protean man."*(280)* Protean man experiences "an extraordinary number of beliefs and emotional involvements," each of which he "could readily abandon in favor of another." He can move from being a revolutionary youth through a sequence of roles to being a substantial married careerist without finding his rapidly changing behaviors incongruous. He is an expression of the rapid changes in our present day which requires "heterogeneity," "discontinuities," and a "tentative ego-identity." Lifton's views are consonant with those developed by Bally and those evolved in this book *(p. 202)*.

Questions, as interpretations, arise out of the emergent immediacies. They come out of the context of the mutual confrontation in the ongoing therapeutic process, and are an expression of the totality of the analyst's orientation and experience up to that point. This means he is guided by an image of man, of what is a therapist, what is a patient, what is therapy and what are its objectives. It assumes an image of technique and a theory of it. It might be more accurate to speak of images because I have been attempting to convey the need to rely on the kind of images that come out of the so-called primitive mind, the mind of the East, and the mind of the West. Expressive of the latter are Freudian, post-Freudian, neo-Freudian, phenomenological, and existential images regarding the nature of man.

In the usual sense of interpretation, my activity is limited, but from the viewpoint of interpreting by open-ended questions I am very active. I have tried to indicate how intensely the analyst attends to himself as instrument in response to himself and to his patient. "Evenly-hovering attention" is a most active process. There is the therapist's interpreting to himself, what he interprets to the patient, and the patient's interpretations of what he — the analyst — intended to be interpreted. The preference for activity by the methods of open-endedness and indirection does not preclude interpretation as statement, nor forceful intervention which some patients require.

I have stressed the productive possibilities of the question form of communication because its misuse is all too common. The analyst who asks his patient, "What is on your mind?" or "Tell me what you are thinking?" is directing his patient to focus on the top of the metaphorical symbolic spiral, on higher order abstractions of the rationative aspects of the spiral. He is reinforcing the almost universal tendency to compulsively intellectualize — a neurotic problem the analyst hopes to help his patient identify, undermine, and resolve.

Martin elaborates this point. "In the present-day glorification of the mind and intellect, modern man grossly deceives himself and confuses compulsive and healthy intellectualism. . . . In the healthy individual the Socratic dialectic, logical process complements the mystical, the intuitive, non-teleological process. They are not in conflict."*(166)* But as Martin pointed out, and I agree, such integration can only be realized through and in the whole person becoming and being involved in inner friction, struggle, and conflict.

That the misuse of questions is no caricature or rarity is demonstrated by Glover's "Questionnaire Research" and "Common Technical Practices": "The form of the association rule most frequently communicated to patients seems to be: 'Say what is in your mind.' And this is taken by the patient to mean: 'Say what you are thinking.' Whereas if the instruction were: 'Tell me also all about your *feelings* as you observe them rising in your conscious mind,' in a great number of cases the ideational content would follow of necessity."*(281)*

Glover's instructions are in the right direction, but they still seem to overstress intellectualization. Prefaced by the word, "also," Glover's request for "your feelings" implies prior statements regarding thinking. The concluding words "your conscious mind" again draws attention to thinking.

Of note also are the assertive forms of the comments used as examples. Two of them open with "say" and the third with "tell." Patients react to assertions and statements as assertions as if they were commands and feel coerced by them. They respond with fear, resentment, and closure. The contrast with the holistic emphasis on questions rather than statements, on being implicit rather than explicit, on remaining open-ended rather than specific, and on being tentative rather than assertive are evident.

An overemphasis on language goes with an overfocus on thought. There is then an insufficient utilization of all the other possible ways of communicating that have been mentioned — the nonverbal forms, the metacommunications, and the many other aids which can help prepare a patient for greater availability for therapeutic procedures approximating the classical model. Many patients who would have dropped out or been terminated have continued in therapy through the use of such aids. Prerequisite to the productive and meaningful use of such aids is the broadened concept of awareness that I have presented. Associated with and integral to it are the attitudes of being respectfully vigilant and wondering while being threshold conscious. Depending on the degree of the illness, circumstances, and the objectives in therapy, some patients can be helped to the point where they become available for treatment according to the classical model. In short, the dictum unanalyzable, which at one time meant unhelpable, must be applied with much more tentativeness than heretofore.

The following instance illustrates how tenacious the problem of compulsive intellectualizing can be, particularly when there is the self-deception of being "a feeling person," "a good person."

Seymour W. was extremely alienated and resigned, with a deeply embedded façade of pseudo- and also real self-effacement. He had an iron conviction that he was a very sensitive and feeling person. His sensitivity was mainly a neurotic hypersensitivity. He in fact was driven by his neurotic pride to believe he was a very feeling person. Actually he was a compulsive feeler as well as a compulsive intellectualizer. An aspect of his idealized image was that he was brilliant. By order of his brilliant mind he was to produce immediately the feelings appropriate to the situation. In short, he had intellectually seduced himself into the conviction that he was a friendly, feeling person.

After several years of analysis, when I felt our relationship was strong enough to withstand and be strengthened by the repercussions Seymour might have, I asked him little else but variations on one question, "What do you feel?" I thought this technique would only be necessary for a short time but as it turned out I remained with it for over a year. All of the questions contained the words "what" and "feel." Some of the variations were, "What are you feeling?" "What were you feeling?" "What feelings are stirring in you?" "What feelings are coming up?" "What feelings are coming up now?" "What were you feeling earlier in the session?" "What were you feeling yesterday?" "What are you feeling about your mother (your father, me, the analysis)?" "What do you feel about what we have been talking about?" "About what you said?" and "About what I said?" In response to every question, he immediately came back with an "I think."

When I gathered from his associations that he was somewhere becoming aware, though still only remotely, that I had been asking "What are you feeling?" and I felt he could take the confrontation, I told him what I had been doing for more than a year. He was startled and frightened which showed in his voice and his face. Subsequently, to my continued variations on the question "What are you feeling?" He attempted to respond with "I feel." He became aware, over the succeeding weeks, that he simply could not. This panicked him because here was the concrete evidence that there were aspects of his being, unconscious processes, that were beyond the control of his mind and beyond the power of what he referred to as his will power.

In the next phase of our work he became aware that he had contempt for feelings and that the glorification of his intellect far exceeded what he had imagined it to be. Next began to emerge his terror of feelings and also an awareness of the patterns used to cut off his feelings. At first he argued that the feelings that would emerge if he let go of his controls could only be destructive. Hence, if he worked toward loosening and letting go of checks on feelings, the consequence would be "Who knows what kind of harm I might do to myself and others?"

Historically there was a very real basis for this statement. At age eight, when he had been tormented beyond endurance by a playmate, he went berserk and almost killed his tormentor. Several playmates could barely drag him off of the boy whose head he was mercilessly banging on the pavement. Since then he has had a terror of struggle, fighting, friction, conflict, and violence.

In time, in response to my feeling questions, he became aware that his deepest terror was of spontaneous feelings. He ultimately saw that most of the terror was the consequence of experiencing spontaneous feelings as a threat to his neurotic character structure. What he felt as most precious and, hence, most in danger from spontaneous feelings were his needs to be brilliant and absolutely original, immediately and effortlessly, and to be able by order of this supreme mind to issue directives as to what and how he should and should not feel, think, do, and be. This emphasis is understandable in view of all that he experienced as conflict and violence. Intrapsychically by order of his mind, all intense feelings were controlled and appropriate facsimiles were produced in their stead. Interpersonally, he was able to argue himself out of every fight and make everyone be reasonable.

This man's problems exemplify Martin's position regarding "The Fear of Relaxation and Leisure." Interventions help the patient's fears to diminish and his relaxation to increase. "By relaxation, I have in mind mainly mental, or emotional, relaxation rather than muscular relaxation, although from a holistic viewpoint, I do not lose sight of total relaxation as the desired and natural phenomenon . . . . True relaxation in the sense of surrender to one's own basic, intrinsic, unique rhythm is not an escape, but brings us in touch with the darker reaches of ourselves and gives us a greater sense of our totality. Here surrender does not mean submissiveness."(165)

An ultimate expression of relaxation is experiencing that "giving is receiving as receiving is giving," a single unitary process formulated as an apparent paradox. In holistically giving to others one is concomitantly giving to oneself. In being able to receive fully, a rare human attribute, one gives to oneself and to the giver. Predominantly healthy, whole persons operate on the premise of abundance. People who are sick, hence, constricted and restricted, are driven by an economy of scarcity. The genuine giver lives in feelings of abundance; hence, he more likely will feel his giving as enhancing, not depleting. The receiver more often is in the human condition and experience of scarcity. He tends to take rather than to receive, and feels small by comparison — feels indebted, obligated, burdened, and humiliated. Also from experiencing himself as wanting, lacking, and meager, such giving, abundance, and opulence is threatening and frightening. He often misuses the abundance of others against himself in vicious comparisons.

These views become sharply apparent when the analyst attempts to help patients driven by an economy of scarcity to relax, to let go, to yield, to surrender, and to give in, not only to the totality of their thoughts but also to their bodily sensations, feelings, and conative processes. They find this most difficult and experience it as almost impossible. These problems become sharply focused as I ask, "What more about giving out (giving way, giving in, giving into)?" In my questioning, I use a variety of expressions involving letting go, yielding, submitting, and surrendering.

As patients experience this spectrum of feeling processes more widely and deeply, I may gradually introduce them to the feeling process of being open and opening, being closed and closing. These processes happen more and more spontaneously. Then patients become more available for the feelings of resting in panic. What before was frightening and rejected now becomes welcomed and accepted. They will then experience and understand how Alexander arrived at his notion of the "corrective emotional experience" and Fromm-Reichmann said, "A patient wants an experience, not an explanation."(224, 151, 198)

Chapter 24

Interpretation and Insight

"In its classical sense, interpretation refers to a verbal intervention by the analyst into the process of free association in order to demonstrate and remove a resistance."*(142, p. 113)* Assuming the orientation of the most evolved Freudian ego psychologists, our viewpoints on interpretation include what is subsumed under this rigorous definition. I want, however, to underline several key terms in this definition which are opposed to the holistic orientation. They are "verbal" with no mention of the nonverbal; "intervention," which unwittingly conveys a quality of relatively intense willed action; and "demonstrate," which implies showing with which I agree, but as I shall indicate in an example below there is much more of telling with which I differ.

The analyst gets his understanding from his observations of his patient and his responses to what is being communicated verbally and nonverbally. From these he draws his inferences. From this totality of processes which involves all levels of the symbolic spiral he makes his interpretations. This viewpoint is evident in Horney's statement,

"When he [the analyst] tries to convey his understanding, or some part of it, to the patient, he is making an interpretation."*(68)*

With her emphasis on feelings and understanding Horney points up the need to be aware that knowledge is only tentative. Interpretations are stimulating and revealing, merging into one another, all aimed at activating a forward move. In interpreting, Horney indicates the importance of "striving toward a democratic spirit," toward "clarity and precision," toward becoming "more and more sensitive to what the patient feels at the time being."

With her motto of "blockages first," the immediacy and need for their interpretation has primacy. Timing of an interpretation is determined by the possibility for resolving existing and impending blocking and for moving forward whatever, of a constructive nature, is already in process. This is done within the patient's tolerance and possibilities, with an economy of time, with the avoidance of unnecessary pain, with the knowledge of the patient's character structure in awareness, and with a depth and clarity of feeling for the strength of the analytic relationship. In short they are directed toward "The Aims of Psychoanalytic Therapy."*(65)*

Premature interpretations may cause unnecessary pain, upset the patient beyond his tolerance for effective working, slow up the process, waste time, disturb the relationship, or even lead to an interruption of the analysis. It is fortunate that most patients have built-in self-protective devices and ways of disregarding premature interpretations. Delayed interpretations, because they come out of context, after the clarity and intensity of the optimal context is gone, usually have little effect. At times they may, to a degree, be effective but after quite some time has been lost.

"The ideal response to an interpretation would consist of the following. The patient would take the interpretation seriously, think and feel about it, have a conviction it was right, and test it. This would lead to change." The responses might be "anxiety, hostility, and an attack against the analyst," as well as "pseudo-acceptance," "temporary aroused interest," and a "reaction of relief."*(68)* Although the immediate form of these responses ranges from the apparently positive to the apparently negative, only further follow-up can determine whether the interpretation was productive of change and movement. After the responses of anxiety and hostility, there may either be acceptance and often aroused interest with change, or a pseudo-acceptance and a relief without change.

What I am describing here are the overt and obvious responses to interpretations. They are the exception. Most interpretations are implicit and the responses to them are subtle. Analysts attempt to rigorously identify and define as many responses as possible. But patients often respond as if practically everything the analyst says and does is an intended interpretation. Then there are the analyst's many metacommunications that he does not observe and identify. Patients often attribute communications as if the analyst did make them and had said them with intent when to his awareness neither was the case. At times such communications are so remote from the analyst's awareness that he can with justification ask what in the patient could have moved him to see the analyst in this light.

In short, most of the analysis and change goes on out of awareness. It is a consequence of communications identified by neither patient nor therapist and is not produced by conscious intent. It is the analyst's task to define as rigorously as possible what he does while hoping to effect and to refine methods for delineating responses to what he intended.

To illustrate the meaning of interpretation, Kanzer and Blum give the example of a patient who described "a stern man who is devoid of human feelings." The patient then became silent. Shortly he said, "Nothing comes to my mind." The interpretation is made. "This man reminds you of myself." The patient's response is considered "confirmatory." This is called "a 'confrontation' because it only deals with the surface (conscious and preconscious)." Kanzer and Blum continue, "Other aspects of the resistance may now be examined in a stratified and systematic 'approach from the surface'" to reach unconscious material and the genetic antecedents of what had been happening in the transference. *(142, p. 113)*

These are some holistic approaches to a similar instance. Assuming the silence as resistance (blockage), I start with implicit open-ended questions focused on feelings. If no or limited associations were forthcoming, and if I sensed present or increasing tension or tightness from the cues given by the patient's voice and body posture, I might continue with "Can you describe the sensations you are having in your shoulders, chest, arms, stomach, back, legs?" Such questions draw the patient's attention away from his mind, from the constrictedness of his consciousness, to his bodily sets maintaining such attitudes. If such approaches did not lead to a relaxing and a flow of associations about the "stern man," I would pick up associations remotely connected with the feeling image of the "stern man." There might have been some associations to the time, place, or circumstances under which the patient had that particular contact with him. Exploring these associations might open the way to his associating further and more freely to this "stern man" on his own.

The contrast between these implicit open-ended approaches and the assertive statement as interpretation, "This man reminds you of myself," are clear. I rarely make an interpretation in this form. I feel it too forcibly confronts. It is felt as a coercion and a criticism and triggers closure and defensiveness.

"The interventions of the analyst are not limited to the interpretations." Among these, Kanzer and Blum include interventions to deal with acting out. When these are not sufficient, "the preliminary rules of the treatment may be invoked, such as the admonition to avoid important decisions while motivations and values are undergoing change." The therapist may state that "a divorce is incompatible with the continuance of treatment. Here he invoked the 'principle of abstinence,' which, like the fundamental rule, is an indispensable instrument of analytic therapy."*(142, p. 115)*

Here the term "intervention"*(283)* means explicit, concrete, and specific conscious behaviors with the intent to create a confrontation which is immediately apparent to the patient or which would become so in time. The intended result is the discontinuation of the patient's threat to divorce when confronted with the possibility of therapy being discontinued.

These interventions described by Kanzer and Blum offer an opportunity for comparison between classical and holistic techniques. Differences are immediately apparent. A highly selected group of patients are being discussed, namely, those considered analyzable according to the classical model. While some of my patients might fulfill those criteria, I would not begin the analysis by informing them of the usual rules and what would follow from their being broken. I would wait for the emergence of a situation which according to the classical model would require a confrontation or invoking a prohibition. This means that while the classical model required a certain ego strength in the patient before therapy began, in the holistic approach the focus is on the therapist of whom much more ego strength is required. I refer here to the attributes of the therapist I have so frequently mentioned.

In the case of acting out, verbally, in gestures, and in movement about the office in relation to the analyst, I have indicated in the discussion of the *vis-à-vis* position and the couch how these and other dimensions of being are supported and analyzed. This approach makes for greater demands on the analyst's ego strength, versatility, and inventiveness. With his more fluid field of operation, it is he who must give increased guidance, necessary cohesiveness, and meaningful coherence. Much greater alertness is required of the holistic analyst. He must sense the emergence of disruptive possibilities and conduct the analysis so that the development of insupportable tension is forestalled. The possibilities of acting out are diminished, and the analysis is conducted in such a way that areas of personality problems feeding into such possible destructive behavior are brought into focus and worked with.

This gives some context and flavor to what I mean when I refer to conducting the analysis. The major responsibility for its productive continuation, progress, and outcome is the analyst's.

According to the classical model, when a hasty marriage or divorce is entered into during the course of analysis, the analysis is terminated. Only a careful follow-up, with research tools not yet available, could tell which, continuation or termination, is better for the patient. In such a hypothetical follow-up, one group would consist of those whose analysis was terminated. In the other would be those who have gone on to carry out what was regarded as an ill-considered major life decision and who continue to get help from someone with whom they have had a meaningful and trusting relationship.

Important decisions involve not only marriage and divorce but also breakups of other crucial relationships, such as a business partnership, an important job, a profession, or analysis itself. One important form of help is to keep raising alternative possibilities; another is to keep open as many options as possible. In short, the situation should be kept fluid to foster the tentative and the provisional. In every instance, it is crucial to forestall the formation of an "either/or," an "or else," an impasse situation — namely, an oppositional dichotomy in which the patient feels forced to act, and to act generally in opposition. This precludes the possibility of continued effective working together. When the patient begins to have second thoughts about his decision, which apparently or in fact was contrary to yours, his guilt, shame, and hostility must not be of such proportions that he cannot continue to talk to you. Succinctly put, the analyst does everything possible to avoid the confrontation in which someone must obviously back down or be defeated.

"The variations of character structure and the changes in external circumstances, with respect to each patient, bring unique factors and experimental conditions into every analysis and usually require, at one time or another the use of different agents of psychotherapy." I agree here with Kanzer and Blum, and underline the words "unique" and "experimental," which emphasize the tentative and the provisional. Kanzer and Blum add, "The analytic setting and its rules . . . can only set up a harbor for temporary protection and repair work." In analysis which assumes operations in moving fields this apt analogy must be stretched: the analyst must be more than a stationary repair harbor — he must be a floating drydock.

"External and internal storms must be met with understanding and helpfulness, which require the analyst to utilize the routines as an aid, not as an artificial restriction, in achieving ultimate goals." With all this I concur. Artificiality comes from limited experience and the misuse of the findings and conceptualizations of experienced therapists. What are offered as aids and guides are often turned by others into constricting restrictions. "There must be a balance, which each analyst in each case finds for himself, between flexibility and firmness, between inventiveness and tradition, in coping with the demands made on his therapeutic equipment."*(142, p. 115)* With all of this I agree, particularly with the emphasis on the uniqueness of the therapist, of the patient, and of each therapeutic venture.

The classical definition of "interpretation" states that it is "a verbal intervention." Horney's more comprehensive notion is that interpretation is a conveying of understanding to the patient.

The analyst communicates in and out of awareness with and without intent. The patient is constantly interpreting all of these communications and metacommunications. Among the forms of intended communications by the analyst are silence, "Um huh," "Yes," "I see," a question, an expletive with a variety of intonations, a comment, and what is usually referred to as an interpretation. The latter generally means a statement, often as an assertion, about the meaning of a sequence of associations, a fantasy, dream, or behavior. As has been indicated, I rarely make what is classically defined as an interpretation. I am most inactive with regard to making statements as assertions as interpretations. As I have indicated I feel implicit, indirect, open-ended questioning is more effective and productive. Because it is verbal, because it demonstrates, and because it has the aim of resolving (not "removing") a blockage, I feel it is an interpretation still within the classical meaning. But I feel for conveying understanding, many more forms of communication can be regarded as interpretations, among them silence.

Silence may be intended or unintended — as a communication and/or interpretation with and without awareness.

I may be silent because nothing comes to me, or because what does I do not feel will be helpful to say. I may be silent as a response to a patient asking questions in an attempt to manipulate me, because I recognize that he needs me to remain silent to keep me at a distance, or because I know he has felt my silence as supportive of his working on his own.

The patient on his side may be silent as a form of evading and blocking and to be provocative. He may also be silent because, as he later states, his mind was blank. The analyst can generally infer that it wasn't, although it may actually have become blank — a condition which terrified him. At times anxiety, panic, or a variety of intense emotions and sensations may make a patient speechless. Among them might be choking with tears or rage. At times patients do not know that they are silent. This may obtain when they suddenly go into fantasy, hypnogogic reverie, or trance states. When asked what is going on, they come to so fast they cut out recollection of the state they were just in. A patient also may be silent while feeling something through. Finally, he may be silent to experience listening to his silence, to experience going into himself, maybe even to experience being serene.

To my intended silence and nonverbal communications, Rachael F. had an intense emotional response. This silent communication was my interpretation of a dream she had just reported. Before working with me, and extending over the previous twenty-five years, this middle-aged woman had had about ten years of analysis with three different analysts.

Rachael dreamt that a young girl was telling her about her feelings of hatred toward her father. "She was telling me, and I answered her and said, 'You know it intellectually, but you have never felt it,' and I got mad and screamed at her, 'You don't know the least thing about what real analysis is! You know a lot, but you have never felt anything in your analysis!' I was quite furious and banged my hand on the table."

When Rachael finished relating the dream, she looked at me with a look of "It makes no sense to me," but also with another facial expression, the meaning of which became clearer to her in the ensuing year. This meaning was "Give me, do for me." We came to call it "the greedy wide open mouth look." After a series of associations or after relating a dream, she would look at me for some minutes saying nothing. When I did not comment, she would look away, continue being silent, and then begin to talk about a topic distant in time and relevance to what we had been discussing.

After about a minute of looking at me after she related the above dream, I imperceptibly smiled and slightly raised one eyebrow. In about five seconds Rachael burst into violent laughter which continued for almost five minutes. She laughed so hard her cheeks were covered with tears. She told me that her sides hurt, and that she had almost wet herself.

It had struck her forcibly that of course the girl was she; that what the girl had said to her in the dream, and what she had said to the girl was almost verbatim what I had said to her many times in response to her intense compulsive intellectualizing. This problem as well as the intellectualizing of her feelings we had discussed for months.

Why was her response so violent? It had much to do with her shallow living in which "fun" and "laughing" were extensive and embedded neurotic solutions. Also determining was the intensity of her alienation. Because of the extent of her living on the premise of the total solution of magic, the sudden juxtaposition of the dream and her intellectual realization of its meaning contributed most to this violent response.

What contributed least to the violence of her response was insight. Rachael had had endless seemingly deep insights with very little change. To the extent that insight had moved her, it evoked anxiety. The anxiety was prompted by threats to her precarious structure from the sudden juxtaposition and from feelings breaking through which threatened the neurotic solutions of the supremacy of the mind, externalization, resignation, and alienation.

There was ample evidence for her depth of insight being limited. It was two more years before she could really begin to contact her feelings. They were years of much pain and struggling, particularly in the area of the analytic relationship. Rachael had to give me up as a magic savior figure and see me, bit by bit, realistically. Then she could experience the real help she was receiving and see me as being simply human.

Was my imperceptible smile and raised eyebrow an interpretation? This is what I felt I was attempting to communicate, "Come now. Don't you realize that that is what we have been talking about for months?" If verbalized, my tone would have sounded like good-natured kidding with an edge of sharpness. That she got nonverbal messages close to this verbal description was indicated by her response and by what she said after she stopped laughing. I feel that what I did and what happened fulfills the criteria of an interpretation.

Balint cites an instance which contributes to the discussion of silence as interpretation:

The patient, who at that time had been under analysis for about two years, remained silent, right from the start of the session for more than thirty minutes; the analyst accepted it and, realizing what was possibly happening, waited without any attempt whatever at interfering, in fact, he did not even feel uncomfortable or under pressure to do something. I should add that in this treatment silences had occurred previously on several occasions, and patient and analyst had thus had some training in tolerating them. The silence was eventually broken by the patient starting to sob, relieved, and soon after he was able to speak. He told his analyst that at long last he was able to reach himself; ever since childhood he had never been left alone, there had always been someone telling him what to do. Some sessions later he reported that during the silence he had all sorts of associations but rejected each of them as irrelevant, as nothing but an annoying superficial nuisance. *(127, p. 142)*

In the patient's statement "that at long last he was able to reach himself," and in his relaxing sufficiently to sob and be relieved, the objectives and the results of analytic therapy are identical with what I would seek. There are, however, a number of terms which bear examination. Balint speaks of being "under analysis." I have already spoken of the medical model and the mechanistic orientation that prompts language such as "making the patient see," being "under analysis," or of "undergoing analysis." It sounds as if surgery were being performed on an unconscious patient or as if an inert object were being manipulated. I also would have "accepted" the silence "without . . . interfering," but would have described my inner state as being moved to remain silent and hence not feel in terms of "not even feeling uncomfortable or under pressure to do something." I feel somewhat uncomfortable with the expression "some training in tolerating." I find this phrase dubious and dangerous. Too often tolerance is concealed contempt. I prefer describing this process as becoming familiar, experienced, and relaxed with silence, with naturally and spontaneously resting in it.

Was Balint's being silent an interpretation? From experience he realized what was "possibly happening," that is, he understood and communicated his response through being silent. The effectiveness of his intervention is evident. This does not fulfill the classical criteria of an interpretation. It does Horney's and it does my own.

Balint's example appears in his book *Therapeutic Aspects of Regression*. He arrives at two "clusters," or forms of aggression, "benign and malignant." He says that "regression is not only an intrapsychic phenomenon, but also an interpersonal one; for its therapeutic usefulness, its interpersonal aspects are decisive." Regression "depends only partly on the patient, his personality, and his illness, but partly also on the object; in consequence it must be considered as *one* symptom of the interaction between the patient and his analyst. This interaction has at least three aspects: the way (a) in which regression is recognized by the object, (b) in which it is accepted by the object, (c) in which it is responded to by the object."*(127, pp. 146-48)*

394

Although the terms used are different, what is being described is a holistic process having an intrapsychic and an interpersonal reference. Clearly Balint feels that the analyst is "a co-actor" in the transference and transference neurosis. Contrary to MacAlpine, he feels it essential that he be a "co-actor."*(235)* In fact, he says that he sees the "interpersonal aspects" of regression "as decisive" for "therapeutic usefulness."

In discussing the instance of silence quoted above, Balint said that it "belongs to what we call transference, and constitutes a piece of acting out." It is an "emergence of a primitive form of behavior after more mature forms had established themselves." This means the so-called more primitive can emerge only after there is a strong enough relationship established on the ground of basic trust. In this instance, I feel that the operation of the "therapeutic alliance" and the "diatrophic functions" were essential, considering the intensity of feelings (the sobbing). Balint adds that he felt his "technique" of continued silence "helped the patient toward a better integration, by removing some of his inhibitions or even repressions."

What follows indicates how much Balint has moved in the directions I have concerning the concept of regression. Referring to the instance of silence he says, "But, can this episode be called a regression or a repetition? My answer is . . . that logically it cannot. One can repeat something only if the something existed at least once before; and on the whole, the same holds true for regression. Instead of these two misleading terms, I suggest calling this episode a 'new beginning' or a new discovery, leading to a different, more satisfactory, relationship to an important object."*(127, pp. 142-43)* His book is an attempt to clarify the "misleading term" regression. In doing so, he felicitously names episodes "new beginnings" or "new discoveries" which were formerly referred to as regression.

I have frequently remained silent for an entire session and for several in a row, for the variety of reasons I have mentioned above. I was told of a post-Freudian who worked with a patient for four years without saying anything other than the initial greeting and a parting comment. At the termination of the analysis, the patient shook the analyst's hand and thanked him saying, "You are the first person who has ever listened to me." Assuming the accuracy of this story I would regard the result as successful.

The longest time I have been continuously silent in therapy has been three months, a total of fifty-five sessions. This man had one year of classical analysis fifteen years earlier and three years of neo-Freudian analysis prior to his work with me.

Up to the beginning of my silence, which occurred in the beginning of the fourth year, I had often been silent for one or several sessions. Soon after I began to work with Matthew V., I became aware that he had been upset by what he experienced as the excessive talking of his previous analyst. I knew from his history that throughout his childhood it had become a survival necessity for him to remain silent, unobtrusive, unseen, and practically nonexistent. He had a fear of people at times amounting to a terror. As Matthew became aware that my comments were limited, and that sessions passed without a word, his fears lessened and his appreciation for my conduct of the analysis increased. A clinical psychologist, he was quite well informed on the structure of his problems.

At a crucial point in the analysis and in his life, I remained silent for several sessions. As the silence continued, I felt "I should say something," but nothing came. This impulse to speak receded within a week. From then on I remained comfortably silent and listening. Every few sessions I wondered with diminishing intensity when something would come to me to say that I felt would be helpful.

After about five sessions, Matthew began to comment on my silence. At first he was appreciative. Then he anxiously said he hoped I would not say anything. After the third week, he rarely mentioned it. During these three months of silence he worked through, in associations, fantasies, and dreams, deeply embedded and disturbing problems which went back to his earliest years. He had not been able to allow himself to experience these problems before. Cyclically he would let himself into his depths, become anxious, defensive, and defiant, then gradually relax and slowly begin to move in greater depths than had been attained in the previous cycle. It was the most productive period of Matthew's analysis to date, and much more productive than any equivalent period of our work.

Was my prolonged silence an interpretation? It was based on our mutual understanding of the old survival necessity to be silent and practically nonexistent and of his terror of people. I could not find a louder, clearer, and more definitive way of saying to him session after session that he did not need to remain silent, nonexistent, and fearful of people than to give him all the time to say or not say whatever he wanted to while being the center of my complete attention and support. Material which could be defined as transference and the transference neurosis emerged with great clarity. He was manifesting basic trust in me, and I was serving the diatrophic function in ways his mother and his father never had.

Since I believe my silence was an interpretation, how do I define interpretation? I feel that the term as generally understood and in classical theory reflects an emphasis on reason, intellect, and conceptualization. In this sense its function is to tell according to concepts. It focuses on thinking, on why, on motivation according to a theory, and on who, where, and when. Interpretation tends to focus attention away from feelings, conation, bodily processes, and the total sets maintaining character attitudes. In place of interpretation, I suggest the holistic term *illuminator*. What I call illuminators function to sharply light up nuances of the what and how of compulsive and spontaneous processes.

By demonstrating, by showing, and by focusing attention, experiencing is fostered and enhanced. The "self-propelled feeling process" is stimulated, freed, and supported. Experiences of letting go, giving up, surrendering, and accepting are set in motion and expanded. Compulsiveness in conceptual and perceptual processes is lessened. Spontaneous processes are identified, extended, and expanded. Change takes place in and out of awareness in varying degrees.

These ideas on interpretation are intimately related to my ideas on insight. The example of Seymour W. *(p. 557)*, who was a compulsive feeler by order of his mind, illustrates many issues relevant to the notion of insight, a hoped for outcome of interpretation and the effective use of illuminators. One of the crucial objectives of insight is relaxation. Increasing relaxation makes possible freer associating. Both open the way to more insights.

Relaxing and "freer associating"*(76, 182)* are intimately related. As Martin points out in discussing the "inability of many patients to relax during the psychoanalytic hour," it is important to "see our whole problem primarily as one involving consciousness during which thinking tends toward the perceptual, mystical, alogical, and non-teleological . . . . A patient can be helped to relax consciousness by the non-teleological approach which means less, and less questioning in terms of 'why' and 'how,' and more direction of the patient toward 'what' is going on . . . to bring about what Goethe called 'living in the all.' "*(165)*

Martin develops the relation of holistic relaxation to the "Dynamics of Insight." " 'Insight' should be reserved for the phenomenon that accompanies some greater and richer awareness, some revelation of the self, some growth in consciousness." In discussing the "aha" phenomenon in psychoanalysis, creative insight in creative people, Freudian "abreaction," the insight therapy of French and Alexander, *(284)* and "excitation abreaction" as produced by either, Martin says that: "The emotional picture that accompanies this wide range of integrative reactions . . . depicts conflict involving the whole individual . . . . The whole being's involvement in inner friction, struggle, or conflict reaches consciousness at the time integration and insight occur."(166)

Martin's description of the processes through which insight is prepared for, moved toward, and experienced presents certain similarities to my notions regarding experiencing as expressive of movement up and down the metaphorical symbolic spiral when there is simultaneous participation at all levels of the spiral by patient and therapist. My ideas are also in the direction of Gendlin's notion of experiencing as the creation of meaning. (212)

In discussing the process of working through, Fromm-Reichmann has this to say regarding insight: "The actual character of the experience of creative 'insight' into, versus the rational understanding of, an interpretation is as difficult, if not as impossible to define as is the nature of creative processes at large at the present state of psychological knowledge. That was why Freud despaired of coming nearer to it than describing it as 'Aha-Erlebnis' an experience of 'Oh, that is it!'"

The concept of insight has created problems because of the tendency to connect unwittingly insight and intellect. Attempts to meet this problem may be seen in the emphasis on the awkward notion of emotional insight and the admonition that both intellectual and emotional insight are essential. This split is artificially created by the dichotomy of feeling and thinking. As I have attempted to indicate with the concept of the symbolic spiral, feeling-thinking and thinking-feeling are continuous and connected unitary processes.

I feel that the notion of experiencing many levels of the metaphorical symbolic spiral is a more helpful one than that of insight. In the spectrum of dimensions of paradox-forming and paradox-resolving, tension-producing and tension-reducing, conflict and cooperation forming and resolving, the person creates himself and the world of which he is an aspect. He experiences the unity of insight and outsight, of feeling-thinking and thinking-feeling, and of holistic seeing. The notion of experiencing the continuity and connectedness of emerging forms from all levels of the symbolic spiral as the creation of meaning appears to be a more productive way of looking at the phenomena referred to as insight.

Is there a term that can make a bridge from the concept of insight to experiencing the symbolic spiral? Creative vision may meet these needs. It unifies intellect and feeling. Vision can refer to and contain insight and outsight and oscillation between the two. It undercuts the dichotomizing of thinking and feeling. Unitary processes which have inward and outward reference are not split.

The adjective creative is comprehensive. It does not separate self-creation from creation of others and the world. Authentic creation is not possible without all aspects of the unitary process involving organism and environments being influenced. Creating involves the resolution of compulsive processes and the enhancement of constructive ones. It involves cooperating and conflicting patternings and all those steps delineated in the creative process. Such creative vision evolves and emerges in and out of awareness. It does so through obvious experiences like the "aha experience," which is a burst of vision, and through decreasingly subtle ones to those that go on out of awareness. The latter contributes the most to the many aspects and moments of creative vision. This awareness, identified immediately or over time, is the criterion of an interpretation having been productive, of illuminators having been effective in contributing to the disillusioning and self-realizing processes.

The ideas of the post-Freudians who give primacy to ego over id, and to primary love over secondary hate [Balint], imply many of the functions of interpretation and the objectives of insight as I have defined them. This position seems supported by Kanzer and Blum's statement that for insight to occur, contact had to be made with "particular memories in their causal contexts" and the "entire psychological climate of the family would have to be reconstructed as the background for an understanding of the maturational tendencies that were revived and guided in new directions through the analysis . . . . It may not be a particular event that is forgotten, but rather the effective and behavioral associations, which have to be restored by insight."(142, p. 123)

These comments suggest that the post-Freudian intent of interpretation and insight seems to be in the direction of holistic experiencing. Hartmann's thinking tends in a similar direction. Because of his "emphasis on evolutionary changes of function and shifting relationships between defense and adaptation," he does not feel that "preoedipal, and especially, preverbal, experiences" can be modified by "isolated reconstruction and recapitulation of early infantile memories."(142, p. 124)

What has been developed regarding creative vision takes into account what is subsumed under the therapeutic alliance, the *real* relationship and the diatrophic functions. The analyst's functions expand not only "beyond that of the object and interpreter of the transference neurosis," of being "a participant in reliving experiences that revise the personality," but also in experiences that help his patient to belatedly live for the first time. Through functioning like a "successful parent," and what follows from moments of creative vision, the analyst helps to bring about movement in the patient from the so-called pre-verbal and pre-oedipal phases where he was fixated into "mature genitality."*(142, p. 125)*

In the light of the above, I would characterize Dr. E. M. Loutsch's comment — and what followed from it — as fulfilling the criteria of an interpretation-illuminator, of an intellectual-emotional-insight-outsight, of an *aha* phenomenon, and of an *Erlebnis* experience as an instance of creative vision:

> Nancy W., a young married woman, divorced and with one child, came into therapy because of homicidal rages and a terror that she might impulsively act them out, particularly against her infant child. Initially the therapist was frequently frightened of these outbursts and her frequent micropsychotic episodes which occurred during and between sessions. He also became anxious and defensive when she resorted to a spectrum of sadistic maneuvers with reference to him, which she used with diabolical ingenuity.
>
> In the four years of their work, they came to know each other in depth and to establish a very productive working relationship. The rages and the homicidal impulses and micropsychotic episodes gradually diminished. As the therapist came to know the rages and episodes in increasing detail, he could more easily sense when they were coming and at times head them off. His feelings toward Nancy became less fearful and defensive and increasingly friendly, and compassionate with quite some sensitivity and understanding. Good-natured kidding, chiding, banter, and irony which the therapist could communicate with subtle nuances of tones and facial expression became an increasingly effective therapeutic technique.
>
> In a session toward the end of the fourth year, Nancy was extremely restless and unable to decide whether she was going to let herself go into teasing, being sarcastic, sadistic, and frustrating or if she was going to allow herself to free associate and enjoy her session without wasting time. Then, as Dr. Loutsch describes it, "She demanded that I make a choice for her. I remained silent [which he was able to more comfortably and relaxedly do as he experienced more and more how supportive it could be to her and how effective it was as an interpretation]. Nancy called me 'superhumanly superhuman,' 'the perfect Dr. Loutsch,' 'Buddha.' I replied matter of factly, 'You are being a pain in the neck, Nancy.' She couldn't believe that I had said what I had said. 'I'll store that up against you . . . . That really throws me, really overwhelms me.' Suddenly Nancy started sobbing violently,

then laughing, then both at the same time. 'It's ridiculous but I feel it's the nicest thing you have ever said to me.' "

Chapter 25

Objectives and Termination

Aids as parameters and interpretations as illuminators have the ongoing objective of helping to make possible more episodes of creative vision of varying dimensions. Toward this end all techniques participate. The one ongoing comprehensive objective of all therapeutic efforts is to support the urge toward self-realization while undermining the drive toward actualizing the idealized image.

In "All Dis-Ease Is Not Disease," Pleune states that the clinician has "three increasingly difficult and sometimes incompatible functions: (1) to *study* (scientifically) . . . man in his environment. (2) To *treat* (scientifically) . . . to remove, relieve, or prevent disease. (3) To *help* (as a human being) in the sense of caring for and about people while . . . healing through loving."

Pleune contrasts psychoanalytic therapy "with physical, chemical, and other forms of *behavioral engineering* . . . . The doctor is more candid and more accurate if he takes the position 'I will try to be helpful to you as a person,' rather than 'You are sick and I will cure you of your illness.' Moral regard and integrity are not merely desirable additions or guides to scientific knowledge, they are rather the substance, the essence of the work of the psychological therapist, who ideally possesses the maximum of both.

"A suitable prayer for the scientific psychotherapist would be: May I achieve the skill to discover and aid those who can benefit from increased self-knowledge, the skill to relieve those who cannot, and the wisdom to know the difference."(285)

The concept of objectives is used rather than that of goals because it helps to maintain the therapeutic focus where it should be, namely, on the immediate ongoing task of moving the therapy forward in a constructive direction. I feel the notion of objectives is more precise, rigorous, and productive than that of goals. The concept of goals often carries with it the idea of something out there at a remote distance, in a faraway future, away from what is given in the immediate here and now. Goals also imply ideals which, though desirable and necessary, unwittingly stimulate feeling and thinking in absolutes, such as shoulds and should nots. (49) Such activity creates additional problems.

But changing words will not change a person's needs to create shoulds, but I feel the notion of objectives does not lend itself as easily to that tendency on the part of a patient. Being moved by the concept of objectives, the analyst's ways of operating in therapy also may be significantly affected. Objectives bring in the feeling of steps along the way, connected with the immediacies in and of the therapeutic process. These moment-to-moment efforts are in the service of the ongoing comprehensive objective which implies and requires immediate, intermediate, and ultimate objectives.

To help make conscious what is unconscious, to help make known what is unknown, and to help a patient become aware of what he is unaware of are aspects of this continuing comprehensive objective. Other aspects are the continuing identifying, undermining, and resolving of obstructive or destructive patterns, while concomitantly identifying, supporting, extending, and expanding constructive patterns, namely, all that supports growing possibilities. In being focused on and working at the comprehensive objective of helping move the therapy in a constructive direction, analyst and patient actualize a whole range of objectives they have tentatively set for themselves in the early phases of their mutual work.

The objective of helping a patient experience what he is unaware of, while helping growing possibilities emerge, requires planning. Too often planning has meant some rigid, preconceived outline in the therapist's head to which the patient must conform. Patients never fit textbook descriptions. Patients also reveal their sensitivity to such preconceptions by rebelling against them. A rigid notion of planning assumes that predictions can be certainties, whereas a realistic spirit of planning is characterized by tentativeness, a feeling for plastic possibilities, and probabilities. The spirit of planning I am suggesting is not that of following certain rules, so that something *should* happen, but of doing what can be done now, so that the likelihood of certain probabilities happening increases.

In planning therapy, objectives range from the immediate to the intermediate to the long-range to the ultimate, which may be formulated and aspired toward, but which are unattainable. In the context of helping a patient become aware of what he is unaware of, the analyst is helping him experience his assets and liabilities. This is in keeping with the ongoing objective and process of diagnosing and prognosing the patient. The analyst concomitantly focuses his efforts on giving human help, building a relationship, allaying overwhelming anxiety, or trying to help a patient who is falling to pieces to become a bit more unified. This may not only be humanly required, but also an essential precondition of analysis.

More specific objectives might involve helping a patient with a particular problem, such as to whether, when, and with whom he might start analytic work; with a practical problem, like a decision to marry or a change in profession; or a psychological problem, such as an inhibition in work or a recently manifested phobia. Objectives may have to do with known past occurrences or imminent possibilities. The analyst's objectives might be: to prevent a hospitalization; to keep a patient out of a hospital after he has been in one, once or several times; to mitigate the severity of depressions or elations; or to prevent a precipitous divorce, marriage, or breakup of an important business relationship until analyst and patient have a more solid and extensive basis for diagnosing and productively dealing with the situation.

Objectives can be formulated in theoretical terms: to undermine neurotic pride and self-hate and to strengthen real selfness; to help work through major neurotic orientations toward life; to alleviate excessive anxiety; or to build the analytic relationship so that it will be strong enough for the patient to rely on in the more difficult periods which occur in almost every analysis. Other objectives are: to help a patient become more connected with the whole range of his feelings, to help him become connected with his body, his organicity; and to help him improve his relations with others in their personal and functional aspects. All along, one holistic objective is to educate our patients in self-analysis as a preparation for another objective — the interrupting of regular work.

I feel that the concept of objectives focuses the analyst's and the patient's attention on the immediate, continuing present and on the tasks at hand. It does so in a sequence of their probable realizability. It also helps both to obtain a deeper feeling for beginnings, for what is immediately available, for what might be possible, and focuses away from endings and results. It also helps both develop a feeling of and for process, of progressing from one objective to another, of knowing and experiencing where they are in this process. Such a focus on work being done gives to each satisfactions from the smaller and occasionally larger successes along the way.

This means working with a spirit of humility, an essential ingredient to effective therapy, particularly for the analyst. An analyst in training complained of his patient's lack of progress; in fact, the analyst was convinced that the analysis was at a standstill. After I had identified a number of nuances of change in the sessions, he burst out in surprise and disbelief not without an edge of contempt, "Are you satisfied with such crumbs?" "Of course," I replied. It was some years before he could experience the full impact of this humble truth.

Among the successes along the way are firsts *(p. 217)*. They become small milestones and points of reference to locate beginnings and endings of smaller and larger phases of the mutual therapeutic work. The success may be the first time a shy young girl accepts a date with a young man; the first time a man does not panic before a conference with the boss; the first time a woman has a fairly good night's sleep without pills; or the first time a male patient does not experience the analyst as a malignant authority. Guided by such objectives and ways of working together, the focus becomes less and less on working and suffering toward some ideal goal out there, and more and more toward realistic objectives in the here and now, in the realm of the probable and the possible.

From time to time patients will report firsts such as I mentioned above. The feeling that goes with such incidents is that of discovery and of a gift from emerging growing possibilities. These happenings can and do occur because both patient and therapist are no longer focused on proving and on improving. They are attending to the tasks at hand. Spontaneous emerging real selfness is the consequence.

Working in this spirit, the analyst continues his diagnosing of past, present, and future growing possibilities in himself, as well as in his patient. He finds or does not find verification of his previously made diagnosings and corrects them with regard to future growing possibilities. The accuracy of diagnosing future growing possibilities in general depends on the competence of the analyst and the patient's ability to make increasingly available to the analyst a picture of his assets and liabilities.

Accuracy in diagnosing and prognosing naturally decreases with an increase in unknown events. The probability of inadequate information and openness to it increases, the further the analyst gets away from the individual concerned, into his familial and working relationships, and into the effects of societal, political, economic, and cultural changes. Analyst and patient become aware of what was unknown in both only as they proceed from surface to depth in each other. This pertains not only to psychological, but also to organic, factors as they influence the patient's and the therapist's total physical state. In other words, the weight of chance influences affecting a particular analysis steadily increases the less those factors are known, explored, or influenced.

The notion of chance and its implications can be misused for neurotic purposes. Some misuse it by making it a justification for jumping into the lap of the gods or for tenaciously clinging to a neurotic pessimism or optimism. Others respond with abhorrence to the idea of chance because of their need to hang onto a notion of self-sufficiency or an arrogant certainty that they are the masters of their destiny. All therapists have had experiences with patients who insist that certain occurrences were matters of chance when it is apparent how much the patients had to do with their coming about. There are also many patients who insist this or that was of their own making when, in fact, the event was most likely chance.

"What we call chance," says Angyal, "are not random happenings. They are only beyond the control and foresight of the individual. Chance occurrences, in spite of the fact that they are strictly lawful processes, are practically incalculable factors in the life history, because it is impossible to know all those external factors which may become relevant for a person's life."(162)

Chance factors and fortuitous events are more frequent in the patient's environment than within himself. An unexpected opening of a better job opportunity, the changing of a law increasing benefits or diminishing burdens, or the termination of a war, all could give an individual an added lift. Being struck down by a reckless driver, the sudden illness of a wife with an unknown or untreatable malady, or an economic depression could have most disruptive effects. The death of a parent or a child could have both negative and positive consequences, immediately and ultimately.

The impact of chance factors in the individual's environment often depends on how far along in analysis the patient is. Early occurrences can be devastating. If the patient has grown in analysis before the painful event, he will be better able to integrate it.

Chance factors also occur more often in the analyst's environment than within himself. Those in himself are mostly related to unexpected, adverse, internal physical occurrences. There are also those in himself which he couldn't have known because of his neurotic involvement. Neurotic optimism early in analysis can be helpful but it carries with it the danger of pushing a patient too hard. When periods of difficulty do occur, such an analyst may be in for a very disturbing time of it, as may his patient. Neurotic pessimism in an analyst can be quite a drain on a patient. *(286)*

There are other problems in the therapist which may interfere with the fulfillment of the patient's growing possibilities. He may not be able to stick with an analysis which turns out to be too difficult or painful for him. He may not be able to admit he can't take it and was in error in his original evaluation. Sometimes, in the latter instance, he works through his personal problems, although at a cost to his patient. In other instances, the patient breaks off the therapy. A bad start can be saved if the analyst can ask for help; but if he cannot, both he and his patient suffer. Because of inexperience and other pressures, the analyst may have taken on too many patients, too many very sick patients, or too many from whom he derives too little satisfaction. Some therapists grow in working their way out of such situations, while with others it has quite a retarding effect.

As analysts develop, they become clearer in their interests, and have greater opportunities for selecting their patients. Previous misjudgments have varying adverse effects on them. The knowledge that unfortunate selections do occur generally helps therapists to choose more carefully and wisely.

A candidate-in-training kept repeating. "I always do my best for my patients." From time to time over a period of months, with a quizzical tone in my voice, I echoed, "Your best?" Finally one day it got through to him. He paused and then asked with an anxious, doubting, assertive, and accusatory tone, "Don't you?" In a matter-of-fact way I responded, "No." He almost levitated off the couch, looked at me with anxiety and bewilderment, and asked, "You don't?" Again, I said, "No, I do as well as I can," in the same quiet tone. After some minutes, he lay down on the couch to struggle with his anxieties and disbeliefs.

This exchange immediately opened up the issues of neurotic standards, perfectionism, neurotic ambition for his patients, and tyrannical shoulds. It was quite some time before he could let in, experience, and appreciate the radical difference between having always to do "Your best" and "Doing as well as you can." The first is static, absolute, indiscriminate, compulsive, and closed, the latter is dynamic, relative, discriminate, spontaneous, and open-ended. Driven to do the best, we block ourselves from the possibilities of doing better and better and better.

Operating with the objectives previously outlined, what criteria are available to ascertain whether change is taking place and in what direction? One guide is the patient's immediate and continuing responses to interpretations. The evolving patterns of "Freer Associating" afford another guide. *(76, 182)* The patterns of change in a patient's associations as the analysis progresses are participant in working through and expressive of it. They reveal, confirm, or disconfirm the validity and effectiveness of interpretations.

"The Evaluation of Change" requires the most careful scrutiny, according to Slater. "The patient's own statements concerning the ways he has or has not changed are often unreliable . . . . The analyst's neurotic tendencies, to the degree that they persist will warp his judgment and make it difficult or even impossible for him to estimate the extent and nature of the patient's change . . . . External changes may affect the patient, making it difficult for the analyst to determine whether the person's improvement (or his worsening) is due to them, or to the analytic process, or to both in varying degree." Put in Horney's terms, the analyst seeks evidence of "less of the neurotic" and "more evidence of healthy thinking, feeling, and acting in the patient," and is alert for changes, in "the evolving doctor-patient relationship." *(73)* To effectively evaluate change, it must be done with regularity, every three or six months, so that there are clearly defined bases for measuring increments and directions of change.

Against the background of the foregoing, Horney's valuable discussion of "the road of psychoanalytic therapy" is more easily understandable. Since neurosis "is a *process* that grows by its own momentum . . . with a ruthless logic of its own" and "envelops more and more areas of personality . . . we must be clear about the seriousness of the involvement" and "guard against false optimism envisioning quick and easy cures. In fact the word 'cure' is appropriate only as long as we think of a relief of symptoms, like a phobia or an insomnia, and this as we know can be effected in many ways. But we cannot 'cure' the wrong course which the development of a person has taken. We can only assist him in gradually outgrowing his difficulties so that his development may assume a more constructive course."*(49, p. 333)*

To help the patient to outgrow the wrong direction his life course has taken, the analyst must first estimate the difficulties involved and the patient's available assets in the service of our mutual efforts. He must learn how he denies his anxieties and conflicts and avoids experiencing his self-hate which is the product of his unfulfilled shoulds. The analyst helps the patient become aware of how he attempts to maintain what has subjective value for him, how he attempts to maintain the *status quo*. The analyst must differentiate what the patient is driven to say and to have from his real incentives, the objectives in therapy, and what the analyst sees is in the patient's interest.

The analyst must get a picture of all that obstructs the forward movement of the analysis, all that the patient invests with neurotic pride. The patient must not only gain information about all these factors, but also have a knowledge of them — knowledge derived from emotionally experiencing them. He must feel their impact and their consequences. Then he will be able to take a stand against them in an understanding way. This is a *"disillusioning process"* because it involves an undermining of false values in order that real values may take their place. *"The therapeutic value of the disillusioning process lies in the possibility that, with the weakening of the obstructive forces, the constructive forces of the real self have a chance to grow."* (49, p. 348)

While the forces of the real self are operating from the beginning, they are weak, and the patient is unconsciously opposing their operation since he is bent on actualizing his idealized image. But bits of constructiveness appear in his associations, in dreams, in breakthroughs of feelings, and in the doctor-patient relationship. A patient's interest in working at a neurotic problem which impedes his actualizing his Idealized Image may be an opportunity for setting a constructive process going. As there is some strengthening of his constructive forces, he will find himself involved and *"grappling with his conflicts."*

At first, the patient will be caught up with *"basic conflict."* Ultimately, he will be concerned with *"central inner conflict."* The patient, of course, attempts to keep the conflicts blurred and in separate compartments because of a deeper awareness of their disruptive and anxiety-provoking possibilities. There are moments of increased tension and great struggle, which may become moments of *kairos.* (272) These can become turning points of minor or major proportions. They may happen before, during, or after analysis. When they occur, all dimensions of human being participate, including the spiritual. Following such *kairoi,* patients have a new view of themselves, of their world, of the world.

As a patient approaches and enters the phase of analysis in which the struggling with conflicts becomes intense, there are many ups and downs. It is a phase during which many patients interrupt their analytic work. How far and how deep a patient can go depends on him, the analyst's training and experience, the work that has been done, the strength of the relationship, and environmental factors.

Constructive periods are followed by *"repercussions"* which may have the extreme form referred to as the negative therapeutic reaction or there may be a flight into health. (49) Participating in such repercussions are intensities of anxiety and self-hate which the patient finds unbearable and attempts to avoid. Depending on the above-mentioned factors, he might and often does work them through. These are what Horney called the *"growing pains."(49, p. 357)*

As a patient experiences the phase of "I never felt so good and I never felt so awful," he is on his way to accepting pain more and fighting it less. As he can more often with foreknowledge and choice enter anxiety-provoking situations, which is courage, he will be able to accept with humility and humor the analyst's response that he "never felt so good and so awful" because he was "never able to feel so much."

When the work has progressed to this point, patient and analyst will discuss possibilities regarding interruption of regular work. They will consider arrangements for tapering off the sessions, the possibilities of further work, if and when the patient desires it. I do not speak of termination or completion of analysis because the first does not happen, and the second is not possible. Analysis with a therapist is followed by self-analysis and analysis through the therapy of life. Completion is therefore impossible because it would imply finality, perfection, or a static state, the latter hardly desirable. Horney says, "I believe that man can change and go on changing as long as he lives and this belief has grown with deeper understanding."*(39)*

By the time the agreed-upon interruption takes place, the patient will have defined his objectives in life which will be toward affirming and fulfilling the urge toward self-realization. He will have moved in that direction and have glimpsed what Horney formulated as the aims of therapy in *Our Inner Conflicts:*

> The patient must acquire the capacity to assume *responsibility* for himself, in the sense of feeling himself the active, responsible force in his life, capable of making decisions and of taking consequences. With this goes an acceptance of responsibility for others . . . . Closely allied is the aim of achieving an *inner independence* . . . . This would mean primarily enabling the patient to establish his own hierarchy of values and to apply it to actual living. [These objectives could be defined] in terms of *spontaneity of feeling,* an awareness and aliveness of feeling, whether in respect to love or hate, happiness or sadness, fear or desire . . . . The most comprehensive formulation of therapeutic goals is the striving for *wholeheartedness.*
>
> These goals are not arbitrary, nor are they valid goals of therapy simply because they coincide with the ideals that wise persons of all times have followed . . . . We are justified in postulating such goals because they follow logically from a knowledge of the pathogenic factors in neurosis . . . . Such high goals rest upon the belief that human personality can change. [While]

neither the analyst nor the patient is likely wholly to attain these goals, they are ideals to strive for."*(39, pp. 241-43)*

In *Neurosis and Human Growth*, Horney further elaborated her ideas on objectives in therapy. "Outgrowing his neurotic egocentricity, he will become more aware of the broader issues involved in his particular life and the world at large . . . he will gradually experience himself as part of a larger whole . . . . This step is important not only because it widens his personal horizon, but also because the finding or accepting of his place in the world gives him the inner certainty which comes from the feeling of belonging through active participation." *(49, p. 365)*

In 1913 Freud said, "He who hopes to learn the fine art of the game of chess from books will soon discover that only the opening and closing moves of the game admit of exhaustive systematic description, and that the endless variety of the moves which develop from the opening defies description; the gap left in the instructions can only be filled in by the zealous study of games fought out by master-hands." *(131, p. 342)*

"We want to emphasize that separation into phases does not imply clearcut or rigid boundaries between them," caution Fleming and Benedek. *(258, p. 81)* The analogy with chess fits, says Hollender, "only if the patient immediately sets to work on a pressing problem, but it does not fit if he first seeks to find out more about the therapist and about the various ways in which this new 'game' of psychotherapy can be played."*(287, p. 56)*

Regarding the opening phase, from the side of the therapist, there are well known, less known, and exceptional moves he can make. Then there are frequent, less frequent, and entirely unexpected things patients might do. For precision and rigor in the planning and conduct of the therapy, a knowledge of and experience with these moves is essential. But each patient is unique, as is each therapist. The inventiveness and ingenuity on the part of the latter to deal with the permutations and combinations of moves and responses becomes increasingly possible for the therapist as he learns and has confidence in his person as instrument.

"It is in the middle phase of an analysis where, as in a chess game, the variety of therapeutic problems multiplies. The opening moves may be fairly constant. The end-game may be predicted with some confidence if all goes well in the middle phase," say Fleming and Benedek. Their "if" about the middle phase is a very large one leading to wide spectrum of influences on the end phase. And about the latter, their viewpoints differ from my own.

"The flow toward the end-game may be described in general

terms, but the variations caused by resistances, regressions, and the impact of current life situations on both patient and analyst cannot be foreseen. Only 'living it through' in a situation where experience can be simultaneously objectified will enable a student-analyst to understand the psychoanalytic treatment process and develop his equipment for its myriad challenges."*(258, p. 120)*

"Every psychotherapist would agree that the variety of moves for the middle game is practically endless," said Hollender. "For this reason it is difficult to know where to open or to close a discussion of this aspect of psychotherapy."*(287, p. 70)* Still there are the knowns and knowables to be learned from the experiences of "master-hands" to be tried and tested in the crucible of experience under supervision and later on one's own. But precision and rigor should concern not only the knowns, but also the unknowns and the possibly unknowables.

"In the initial and middle phases of an analysis," Fleming and Benedek continue, "the short term transactions claim the bulk of the analyst's effort as he follows the patient's responses to his interpretative work. Yet this concentration on the day-to-day cycles of changing resistances and the regressive behavior of the transference neurosis may cause him to lose sight of the subtle signs of progressive movement toward the end-point of therapy. It is this long-range movement which serves as a kind of obligato to the dynamic themes as they vary from moment to moment, and it is in the end phase that the underlying curve of progression becomes traceable through the whole analysis."*(258, p. 172)*

The focus on the step-by-step work in the here and now and the identifications of the ebb and flow of the progression in analysis I have mentioned, emphasizing the need for evaluating the immediate, intermediate, and long term objectives from time to time. The purpose of this way of proceeding is to insure that the analyst does not lose sight of the ongoing progression. It also derives from a different perspective on resistance, regression, the transference neurosis, and the "end phase" of therapy.

"The most common formulation of the criterion for considering an analysis as well terminated" is "the 'resolution of the transference neurosis.'" I have discussed *(p.229)* Fleming and Benedek's meaning of "re-solution." But "not all analyses terminate in this way." Some are "only partially terminated" by external necessities because of finances, illness, and enforced geographical separation. There are also many internal psychological reasons for interruption.

It may be abruptly ended by the patient in a state of intense "resistance" which drives him "into a 'flight into health.'" It may be prolonged forever by the patient who sinks into the couch and enjoys the game of emoting, or sparring with the analyst. It may be abruptly ended by the analyst in a moment of intense irritation and frustration . . . . It may be prolonged by the analyst whose therapeutic ambition expects more from his patient than is reasonable — or who gets gratification from him and cannot let go of him."*(258, p. 174)* Abrupt termination or endless prolongation by the patient are, according to Fleming and Benedek, due to "transference" resistances and "countertransference" problems.

I want to reformulate these various categories of termination (which I refer to as interruption). My different views on resistance, regression, and transference neurosis are crucially contributory. Interruption occurs when it is known that the contact will be limited to one or a few sessions or when the help sought is for a crisis situation or a specific problem. These contacts make up a significant percentage of the analyst's practice and usually end mutually and fairly agreeably.

Therapeutic ventures which become long term after the acute situation or acute problem has been dealt with, as well as those entered with the intent of a long term analysis, can be interrupted by patient or therapist or both before the analysis has been "completed." The patient interrupts because blockages are not being effectively dealt with and resolved. He solves them centripetally by interruption or centrifugally by prolongation. To both solutions, the analyst contributes his share.

The patient's motivation may not be as great as he thinks. He comes in a crisis situation, and once it is over, his motivation ebbs. External factors which have maintained and increased his anxieties abate and give him an out, or they become so intense that they are a block to productive analytic work. The very dynamic of therapy stirs up so much anxiety, conflict, and self-hate that he has to flee. A physical condition begins to develop and cause anxiety which confuses the whole picture before it can be clarified in the analysis. The patient's total person as vessel and vehicle of the process reveals that its simply cannot take what is required to continue therapy. Finally, because of some or all of these, in spite of the best will and competence of the therapist, he can't help the patient work these problems out in the therapy. As a result, the patient had to leave either in an acute attack of health or in one of resentment.

From the side of the therapist, he and his patient are not a good fit. He does not pay attention to his first adverse impression, or he does not have experience with such problems as the patient manifestly presents. He does not recognize his limitations and cannot ask for help. External factors in his life, as well as internal, psychological, and/or physical factors, begin to impinge on him and affect his abilities. Things begin to get out of hand and he cannot rectify the situation. Finally he allows the patient's anxiety to abate too rapidly, or he anxiously participates in bringing it about. He thus dilutes a productive level of anxiety and tension which is a crucial stimulus, a source of energy and motivation.

When a patient "resists" by prolonging the therapy, which is not uncommon with morbidly dependent women and passive, aggressive males, the therapist may blow up and terminate — another not uncommon occurrence.

While the predominance of the problems might be either on the side of patient or that of the therapist, it is only in a holistic evaluation of their interactions that one can understand what has happened. An interruption might then be seen as a salutary happening for both. The patient may have benefited more than he thought, the therapist did better than he believed, and both got more out of the experience than seemed to be the case when viewed from either side alone.

The student-analyst in training wants to finish his required "completed case," and the therapist wants to see his cases "well terminated." The student is certainly influenced by the social context of an institute and his desire to graduate. (258) The therapist is moved, guided, or constricted by his theory which requires that he "resolve the transference neurosis" and "complete" the analysis.

The notion of "completed" or "terminated" analysis does not take into account the natural history of illness; the cyclic nature of many psychiatric and physical disorders; the fact of spontaneous recoveries; the philosophy of biology that nature tends to mend rather than to end; the ancient notion of the urge toward self-realization; and that complex of helping and healing agencies, the therapy of life. This means to me that most analyses are "partially terminated." The happening of a "well terminated," or "a completed analysis" must happen, even within the context of its definition, in only a very small number of the cases that fulfill the criteria of being analyzable according to the classical model.

Some of Hollender's comments on resistance, regression, and transference neurosis are pertinent to the "end phase of analysis" and a case being "well terminated" or "completed." He finds "the road block picture of resistance" with the necessity for "circumvention," "breaking down," "pushing through," and "battering away" hardly congenial. This leads to an "angry analyst" in an "interpersonal battle" with his patient. "Unfortunately the term 'resistance' is a one-sided term, focusing on the patient's reluctance to look and to learn and away from his desire to do so . . . . In ascribing problems to resistance, the role of the therapist in impeding progress in psychotherapy is sometimes overlooked."(287) Much of Hollender's position I find congenial with my own.

Hollender says regression should not be "induced." He does not

414

believe it occurs "spontaneously" in every therapy nor is it "essential for therapeutic purposes." Since the shift from "id to ego psychology" and the "focus . . . on the here-now instead of on the past and on resistances," certain conflicts and patterns are discovered and worked through "without having the patient regress and relive his childhood conflicts." Hollender questions whether everyone has "the desire to regress." He feels the generalization inaccurate and misleading, and thinks that if there is that tendency, it is an "idiosyncratic" problem which has to be "dealt with only in some analyses."*(287)* Hollender's views regarding regression are close to my own.

With his questions regarding resistance and his doubts about regression, Hollender's ideas about the transference neurosis can be anticipated. He does "not agree with" the "contention . . . that regression is a prerequisite for the development and resolution of the transference." Patterns of relationship which evolve in the analysis with reference to the therapist and others, "taken as a whole . . . can be viewed as an unfolding of the prototypical relationship of early childhood or of the transference neurosis." In the light of his views on resistance, regression, and transference neurosis, what are the possibilities of the end phase?

Since Hollender does speak of an "end phase," when does he decide to "terminate?" After reviewing the literature on the subject, he concludes that it is a decision based on "clinical impressions, not precise measurements." Essentially it is when the therapist feels the patient "is feeling and functioning well (or at least better than formerly) as a result of certain fundamental changes in his personality." He makes this evaluation on the basis of what "the patient reports," what the therapist "observes, and what he can infer or read between the lines." Hollender adds that, while supposedly making an objective evaluation, the therapist cannot help but be subjective.

He concludes that while "descriptions of change expressed in terms of id, ego, and superego or in terms of the resolution of the transference neurosis sound more scientific than those worded in everyday language, the result is somewhat akin, however, to precise measurements of inexact data. In the final analysis, the therapist has offered nothing more nor less than a clinical impression or an educated guess."*(287)* While I also would not define change in terms of the tripartite classical structure, I do not go as far as Hollender does. I do feel that in the light of the detail and rigor of Horney's description of the neurotic process, and in the light of my delineation of assets and liabilities as well as the detailed guides regarding process and change, clinical conclusions are more than educated guesses.

What does Hollender do in the end phase? He makes a crucial point when he stresses the patient's participation in the matter. The patient knows what he came in with, what he went through, and where he is now. He can also initiate the decision to terminate on the background of quite some experience and evidence. The patient may bring up the subject just to try it out for size as it were. On one of these occasions, the therapist will pick it up. The patient will back away, say he didn't mean it, or begin to engage himself with the possibility. In the course of these discussions there is often a reconsidering of old problems. The need to defer becomes intense, and the reluctance to relinquish the relationship can become quite stubborn.

Once the agreement to terminate is reached, a date is set of one to several months and it is rarely changed. Feelings of grief and anger at the separation have to be worked through. In the process the patient asks if he can return, and that possibility is left open for a single appointment or two, or an extended period when necessary. This helps the patient accept the parting. *(287)*

All that Hollender has mentioned I have observed and done. Because of my ideas about interruption and the open-ended nature of the relationship, my end phases are not so sharply delineated, as interruption of analysis is to me only one more interruption in a long series of them. As the work proceeds, for example, and the relationship deepens, a patient's responses to my vacations begins to be sharper, particularly before my long summer vacation. Feelings of anger and rejection can become quite intense. These may be veiled and not so veiled suicidal threats and exacerbations of physical symptomology.

By the time a patient has worked through his problems to a significant degree, he has experienced a number of these separations and becomes aware that he no longer responds as he did. He begins to regard the summer and other interruptions as a challenge and an opportunity to see what he can do on his own. How patients respond and work on their own during these interruptions forms a crucial basis for our mutual decision to interrupt.

Another reason why my interruptions are neither sharp nor dramatic is because the issue has been discussed. I often explicitly ask, "What do you want?" In discussing "the patient's desire to regress," Hollender has made this point in another way. He said that therapists "have not focused sharply enough on the patient's wishes for learning and mastery."*(287, p. 112)*

In June, shortly before my summer vacation, a patient implicitly asked and responded to the question with regard to his fall program. "On one level I want to cut down and in another I want to come more often. I want to get the feel of my own healing processes. I want to get the ultimate of help possible with you, to get the maximum strength. For strength there is no substitute." He had started analysis on a three times a week schedule increased it to four, then cut it to three and after the above comment decided to leave cutting to two weekly for further discussion in the fall. All decisions were arrived at with mutual agreement.

The question, "What do you want?" confronts patients with the fact that they come on their own initiative and remain on their responsibility. Raising the question of interruption is their decision. The issue is, do they feel they have gotten what they wanted at the time they raised the question? "What do you want?" is an existential question. Being confronted with it helps to sharpen live and living issues with which they must deal. Having confronted and responded to the question during phases of blocking of varying intensities, and responded to it they are not unfamiliar with it or its implications.

The question brings vague and unconscious issues out in the open. It forestalls and makes it more difficult for the patient to create the *cause célèbre* that the analyst wants to hold onto or to get rid of him. There have been a number of analyses where this question opened up severe blocks. After I had asked the question two or three times over several years one patient said, "Yes, I know you're going to ask me, 'What do I want?' so I'll ask myself first, what *do* I want?"

The need for and value in stating my position explicitly comes when I see the patient is being moved to interrupt. I will try to avoid his becoming locked in so that he feels he has to interrupt in opposition to me. My hope is that he will leave in an amicable mood so that he can return to me or someone else when he feels he needs help. I will try to get the discussion to the point of his amicably accepting that he is going to interrupt, and then say, "It is your decision to interrupt at this time." I may add, "I feel that what is moving you to do so at this time is so and so," but more likely I will leave such comments for later. I will continue with, "I want you to know that I feel your decision is unwise, and that I do not agree with it because I feel we can work it out."

Making quite clear that their decision is in opposition to mine gives most patients considerable pause. To leave on their own is easier when I am not clearly opposed and I leave it up to them. I may take this position because the disadvantages of explicitly stating my opposition are greater than the possible gains. When, however, I say I am opposed the full responsibility is on them. They then often go through all kinds of maneuvers to blur that fact or push it back onto me. They will insist that I created the situation which is making them leave, and no matter what I say, they are certain that I want them to leave and that is what they are going to do.

A further reason why most of my interruptions are neither sharp nor dramatic is because of the focus on here-now experiencing and the process orientation. Patients are helped to feel more deeply and widely the ebb and flow of the processes in themselves. This is imbedded through the experience of their having been identified by the analyst which is communicated more often implicitly than explicitly.

What has been enumerated thus far implies another reason why interruptions are not so sharply experienced. As early as possible patients are educated in working on their own. When they do so in the course of sessions, their efforts are supported and recognized. Self-analysis becomes an ongoing experience at which they become more adept. By the time there is an extended interruption, they have a strong feeling that they have themselves to rely on.

Finally because of the open-ended, matter-of-fact attitude toward interruption, the idea of being able to return if and when they might want to is clearly experienced. I say: "Call me if and when you might want to see me." "We can talk it over." "If I have the time and circumstances permit, we will try and see how it goes." "You may decide to stay and I feel it's a good idea." "You might continue on your own a bit longer." "After reviewing what you have done on your own for a few sessions, you might realize that's what you wanted and that is all you need."

To some my attitude toward the end phase may seem rather lax and unstructured. Others have not only differed with me on this matter, but also accused me of prolonging my analyses, holding onto my patients, and making them dependent on me. I have been diagnosed as suffering from a bad case of the Pygmalion complex. Audiences hearing of my experiences with long term analysis often imply or state that both my patients and I are masochistic, sadistic, addicted to analysis, or all three. Also frequently mentioned were megalomania, on occasion courage, and, rarely, humility. There may be a certain truth in all these criticisms.

My response to these objections is in "The Chronic Analyst" to which I will allude only as it pertains to the "end phase" and the "completed" analysis. This article does contain many examples of extended analysis and of long term follow-ups. (278) The latter indicates that I continue to hear from and about some of my patients for long periods after they have interrupted. But I regret that they are all too few. With more such follow-ups, to which there is an awakening interest, analysts might gain a better perspective on what they do.

When I have presented my findings on long term therapies, a number in the audience have confided in me that they also had such patients but never had had the courage to publicly say so.

The span of these long term analyses, that is from the time they began to the present, ranges from fifteen to thirty-three years, with most between fifteen and twenty-two years. The actual time in analysis, regardless of the number of hours per week, is from ten to thirty-three with most between ten and fifteen. This I call duration. The actual number of years of analysis on a three times a week basis is from two to twenty-five with most between seven and twelve. This I call calculated years in analysis.

One man had been in analysis off and on from age sixteen to age fifty-four. He had had over twenty-five analysts. The estimated duration is about twenty-five years. The calculated time in analysis is about fifteen years. I have been seeing him almost three years, the longest he has been with any analyst.

Another man has had twenty calculated years of analysis with three different analysts over a period of thirty-three years. The first ten years were with me. I still hear from him and it has been thirty-three years since I first saw him.

My longest continuous therapy has been for twenty-four years. The calculated time is about twelve years.

Most of these patients had seen two to four therapists before me. For the past fifteen years more than half of my practice has been made up of such patients and their number is increasing. Attitudes toward their previous analysts include vicious hostility with feelings that they have gotten nothing from their work, feelings that they have been harmed, and feelings of anger and sadness at the time they feel they have lost. Not expressed but close to awareness are feelings that maybe they were not ready for analysis, or that the previous therapist was not the right person for them. In some I sense the feeling of "That's past, let's get on with the job."

I should emphasize that these patients were highly motivated or compulsively driven to have what they felt analysis could give them. Their symptomatology and suffering were of such a nature that it moved them to continue to seek therapy.

I found as a group all have benefited in some measure from their previous analytic work. Without that help they would not have contacted me, would not have worked with me as they did and would not have benefited from the work as they had. I felt their previous analytic experiences, their self-analysis, and their continuing life struggles with life as therapist, had led to further growth, greater maturity, and increasing availability for therapy.

As I presented my work with these patients, over the years and to a variety of groups, certain impressions became stronger. I feel that comments and criticisms to the effect that the therapies were too long, that more patients could have been helped, and that I was encouraging a dependence on me or satisfying an addiction of the patient, often concealed some very intense fears. They were fears of involvement, of friction, of struggle, of frustration, of depth, and of long term commitment. A few analysts have said privately, "When I get to a certain point I quit. Beyond a certain point I can't or don't want to take it." A spectrum of motivations, healthy and neurotic, can determine such attitudes.

I have been confronted with these fears again and again in analysis, in supervisions, and in teaching courses. Candidates, as they went on in their training, often became increasingly critical of me. They felt I overfocused on sickness in people. They believed that they were both more optimistic and realistic than I, and wanted to give the patient the benefit of the doubt. "Who can know," they would query, "what patients can do on their own after having been given the tools to work with by themselves?" With effort, pain, and years of experience some come to learn that only by a rigorous, precise, and thorough delineation of sickness and its resolution is it possible to concomitantly identify what is present of emerging health which can be supported and affirmed.

In this special group of people were a few who had been informed that they had "completed" their analysis. A few more were told, "This is as far as you can go." A few others heard it put as, "This is as far as we can go, maybe you better try it on your own." Only one patient reported an analyst saying, "This is as far as I can go," or "I suggest you try working with someone else." A very few were abruptly terminated when the analyst lost his patience, his interest, or his vigor. But more than three-fourths terminated unilaterally. They did so when they felt the analysis wasn't going anywhere. Others felt mounting frustration with their analyst and some became quite hostile. What these observations indicate is that the burden of "terminating" had been thrust on the patient in most instances because of a host of contradictory factors operating in the therapist.

From all that I have said about this group of patients, from what they told me, from what I could conjecture with varying degrees of probability, and from what happened as I worked with them, a deep and abiding caution has become ingrained in me about "terminated" or "completed" analyses, and about the "final" or "end phase" of a therapy.

Chapter 26

Phenomenology and Existentialism I:
History, Description, and Theory

Throughout her work Horney makes use of concepts from phenomenology and existentialism. There is her detailed phenomenologic analysis of the neurotic process in *Neurosis and Human Growth* and the existential orientation in her concept of basic anxiety in *The Neurotic Personality of Our Time*. She makes frequent reference to the influence of existential writers throughout her publications.

The differences in *being, having,* and *doing* are crucial in existentialism. In "The Dread of Women," Horney discussed their implications for men and women in the sexual act. *(63, p. 133)* The woman "performs her part by merely *being,* without any *doing* — a fact that has always filled men with admiration and resentment. The man, on the other hand, has to *do* something in order to fulfill himself." It is not enough for him to *have* a penis in the sexual encounter, his *being* and that of his partner must be affirmed in his *doing.*

Survival on this planet depends on the emergence of a fourth cosmic consciousness. Phenomenology and existentialism are a partial response to the urgent need for a new global mind structure. The fourth form of awareness will evolve from the three main mind structures man has created but which have lost their vitality and obligating power: the magic world of tribal life, that of the East, and that of the West.

Erikson states that mankind's current task is to form increasingly "inclusive identities."*(288)* He echoes Gandhi who emphasized that all the participants in "The Event" — the 1918 strike in Ahmedabad — all had membership in a common human species.

The symbols of transition and crisis in life's great events — birth, adulthood, marriage, and death — have become shallow and meaningless to "Protean Man."*(280)* Man is confronted with the necessity of creating *rites de passage* into a new cosmic order. To experience a "sense of immortality . . . a fundamental component of ordinary psychic life," which is now being threatened by nuclear annihilation, solutions are being sought for in nature (hence the concern with ecology) and in "experiential transcendence" with its imagery of rebirth, the sources for which may be "from ideas, techniques, religious and political systems, mass movements, and drugs" or from individuals who they believe have "the gift of prophecy."*(280)*

In *The Ritual Process,* Turner develops his concepts of *liminality* and *communitas. Liminality* occurs in the middle phases of the rites of passage which mark changes in social status. Such rites characteristically began with the individual or group being symbolically killed or separated from ordinary secular relationships and conclude with a symbolic rebirth and reincorporation into society. The intervening liminal phase is thus betwixt and between the categories of ordinary social life.

Turner extends the concept of *liminality* to refer to any condition outside of everyday life. It is a sacred condition, and one in which *communitas* is most evident. The bonds of *communitas* are anti-structural in the sense that they are undifferentiated, equalitarian, direct, and nonrational I-thou relationships.

Ordinary, everyday social life is rapidly disappearing. Man can either descend further into the profane, or rise to the sacred toward which many are aspiring. With the remnants of the ritual process of ordinary social life, no longer viable, man is literally being thrust into a continuing condition of being betwixt and between.

Pappenheim asserts that "the alienation of modern man" moved apace when life as *Gemeinschaft* moved to association as *Gesellschaft,* a process accelerated by the Industrial Revolution. "The purest form of *Gemeinschaft* is within the family, particularly between mother and child where unity is the first stage in development and separateness is a later phase . . . . *Gesellschaft* is a relationship contractural in its nature, deliberately established by individuals who realize that they cannot pursue their proper interests effectively in isolation and therefore band together . . . . Individuals who enter a *Gesellschaft* do so with only a fraction of their being, that is, with that part of their existence which corresponds to the specific purpose of the organization . . . . In the *Gemeinschaft,* unity prevails, in spite of occasional separation; in the *Gesellschaft* separation prevails, in spite of occasional unity."*(290)*

The *Wissenschaften* appeared in the later phases of the transition from the predominance of *Gemeinschaft* to that of *Gesellschaft.* The *Wissenschaften* include the *Naturwissenschaften* and the *Geisteswissenschaften.* The former may be translated as natural sciences, and the later as the humanities or, more recently, the behavioral sciences. *Geisteswissenschaften* are concerned with the spirit and mind of man in the broadest senses. In the late nineteenth century, interest in natural and moral philosophy lessened as the sciences, particularly the physical sciences, became dominant. Concern with technological applications crowded out humanistic considerations.

Kierkegaard, the forerunner of modern existentialism, opposed these materialistic tendencies. In 1900, Edmund Husserl put phenomenology on a solid foundation with his *Logische Untersuchungen* which appeared the same year as *The Interpretation of Dreams.* Heidegger gave phenomenology and existentialism a tremendous impetus in 1926 with his *Zein und Zeit (Being and Time).*

Phenomenologists asserted that they could restore to "the term 'scientific' its traditional broader meaning," provide a methodological basis which would satisfy the criteria of precision and verifiability, define the limits of the *Naturwissenschaften,* reinstate the scientific status of the *Geisteswissenschaften,* offer "a new dimension of human life, *Existence,* and a new non-physicalistic conception of the world."*(291)*

Existential analysis relies on the various forms of phenomenology — descriptive, structural, and categorical — to study in detail man's inner states and forms of consciousness. Existential analysis directs itself to man's being-in-the-world, his *Existence,* in contrast with the natural science approach of classic psychoanalysis which concerns itself with essences. Existential analysis affects the therapist's attitudes, interests, and ways of using familiar techniques. The patient's experiences and worlds are entered into with other forms of participation and objectives. Between existential analysis and the classical psychoanalytical model, there are considerable differences.

In the natural science approach the hallmark of investigation and experimentation is objectivity; in existentialism it is subjectivity. In science each instance is to reflect or help create a generalization, an

423

essence, while in existentialism, existence precedes essence, and each event is experienced as unique and original. In the one, the predictable, repeatable, controllable, and quantifiable is sought, in the other, the unpredictable, uncontrollable, qualitative, and spontaneous is openly sought and confronted. Natural science is concerned with factually valued phenomena. Existentialism, with equal rigor and vigor, describes and utilizes all phenomena in terms of their factual, moral, aesthetic, and spiritual valuations. Public verifiability of aspects of external reality through concepts characterizes the one, validation through consensual experiential referents happens in the other. The literature of one is written in a literal prose style, the other in a poetic one replete with the figurative, the metaphorical, and the paradoxical.

In existentialism a new concept of disease emerges "as a restricted way of life . . . a greater rigidity" in a human being's "potential designs of existence." Etiology is not an isolable cause or causes but the result of "all factors shaping human existence."*(292)* Diagnosis holds a less significant place. Prognosis depends on the patient's capacity for containing suffering, his ability to assume the fullest possible responsibility for his life, to make free decisions, and to experience all of these in his encounter with his physician, healer, priest, friend, or nature.

Kairos means crisis in the sense of auspicious moment. *(272, 293)* There may be many, small and large, before, during, and after therapy. The latter involves the patient's changed attitudes toward suffering, guilt, and responsibility in encounter *(Begegnung)* with his helper. "The patient remains the sole and competent witness," Riese says. The patient must give "an unprejudiced and faithful picture of his inwardness," and "make the greatest contributions . . . his own free decisions."*(292)*

The extensive theory revisions in psychoanalysis and the many modifications in technique make the diversity in practice between the classical model and holistic analysis significantly less.

The therapeutic application of phenomenology and existentialism has many exponents. While some would have the philosophical aspects mark an entirely separate field from that of their application, others believe that it is a unique form of therapy requiring special training programs. Although some assert that it is utterly techniqueless, Boss says that "It is by no means unusual to find Daseinanalysts who adhere more strictly to most of Freud's practical suggestions than do those psychoanalysts whose theoretical orientation remains orthodox." *(142, p. 446)*

Existence contains an excellent review of existential approaches. *(293)* Most familiar are those of Binswanger (Existential Analysis) and Boss (Daseinsanalysis). *(191, 262)* Discussion here will be limited to three existential concepts which can be effectively integrated into the philosophy, methodology, and technique presented in his book. They are existential neurosis, encounter *(Begegnung)*, and *kairos*.

"*Existential neurosis*" arises "not so much from repressed traumata, a weak ego, or life stress, but rather from the individual's inability to see meaning in life, so that he lives in an inauthentic modality. The problem for him is to find meaning in life and to pass to an authentic modality."*(293, p. 119)*

Meaninglessness, aimlessness, boredom, and emptiness are the complaints analysts hear from increasing numbers. To speak of alienation is a commonplace. The hysterias and the classic obsessionals have practically disappeared. Character disorders and *The Borderline Syndrome* are increasing. *(209)* Many of these complaints can better be described as existential neurosis.

The second pertinent existential concept is the encounter, often referred to as "*der Begegnung*." Encounter is not so much a meeting of two individuals, but the "decisive inner experience resulting from it for one," sometimes both. "Something totally new is revealed, new horizons open, one's *weltanschauung* is revised, and sometimes the whole personality is restructured . . . . An encounter can bring a sudden liberation from ignorance or illusion, enlarge the spiritual horizon, and give new meaning to life."*(293, p. 119)*

Encounter is an interpersonal experience which has little to do with transference in the strict sense because it works through its very "novelty." Through and in the encounter, the therapist acts as a catalyst. He helps the patient "to realize his latent and best abilities and to shape his own self."

Kairos is the third pertinent existential concept. Taken from Hippocratic medicine, it refers to "the typical moment when an acute disease was expected to change its course for better or worse; 'critical' symptoms would appear at this point for a short time, indicating a new direction; and the proficient physician would prove his capacity by his way of handling the situation."*(293, p. 120)* Without an existential neurosis there would not be an encounter. Without an encounter there would not be the possibility of a "proficient physician," analyst, or friend to contact and intervene on the side of the new direction. The concept of *Kairos* includes the other two existential concepts; I will therefore devote more detail to it.

The Greek god of opportunity, Kairos, is often represented with a long forelock and with the back of the head bald, from which comes the expression "to take time by the forelock." If the psychologically opportune, auspicious moment is missed in the face to face encounter, there is no place to grab in making a second attempt.

"Kairos points to unique moments in the temporal process, moments in which something unique can happen or be accomplished. In the English word 'timing' something of the experience which underlies the term kairos is preserved. Timing means doing something at the right time . . . Kairos emphasizes the qualitative experiential unique element . . . in the temporal process."*(294)*

Hippocrates immortalized the *kairos* experience in physical · medicine in his famous Aphorism I. "Life is short, the art long, the opportunity elusive, experience fallacious, judgment difficult." Translations in England and the United States from 1708 on, have rendered *kairos* as opportunity fleeting and elusive, the psychological, the favorable moment, the right time, the *kairos* instantaneous, the season sharp, or the season soon past. A footnote to one translation suggests that *kairos* may mean the danger attending a crisis in a general sense.

Kairos is a universal human possibility, expressed throughout time, East and West, in a spectrum of religious faiths and ethical systems. In presenting this material throughout the United States, Europe, and the Far East, I have everywhere found echoing responses of recognition. On one occasion in Lucknow, India, Hindus, Muslims, Jains, Protestants, Methodists, and a Nestorian from Kerala participated in a seminar and all responded with feelings of recognition and personal examples.

In ancient Hindu scriptures the idea of *kairos* is designated in Sanskrit by the word *desakalajnana* which means "the man who knows the right place and the right time for taking action and for deciding on a course fitting to the occasion."*(297)* Related to *kairos* is *Ausar* in Sikh scriptures. *(298) An* appears in Sufi writings with meanings similar to *kairos. (299)* The state of readiness in Morita therapy with its crucial concept of *satori* based on Zen Buddhism is equivalent to *kairos.*

The term *kairos* appears often in the Old Testament, and even more frequently in the New Testament. New Testament scholarship revived the concept and defined its place in our time. "Kairos, for biblical writers," said Tillich, "is fulfilled time — the time in which the appearance of the Christ was possible because, in spite of actual rejection, all conditions of his reception were prepared . . . . The great kairos presupposes many smaller *kairoi* within the historical development by which it was prepared . . . . Christianity needs not only the consciousness of the central kairos, but also of smaller kairoi and their prophetic interpretation. Otherwise, the central kairos loses its concreteness and applicability to future history."*(294)*

Kielholz of Basle introduced the concept of *kairos* into psychotherapy. In discussing a suicidal schizophrenic, who had been hospitalized several times, he mentions what others had advised. He made

426

exactly the same recommendations at a later date and immediate improvement followed. He states that the effectiveness of his advice could only be partly explained by the fact that he had helped the patient's stepmother. "This only partly explains, moreover, the success of my advice. It must be answered that the *kairos* came to my aid and this caused me to give my attention to this remarkable phenomenon."*(301)*

Kairos implies a right time in the course of events to do certain things that will favor a crucial happening; the necessity to be aware that there is such a right time so that it might be prepared for; and that it is an opportunity which must be immediately recognized and seized upon. The context of *kairos* must be experienced to be acted upon. Such opportunities are not things that can be possessed, saved up, and used on the occasion of one's choice. A person may be prepared in the sense of being aware of, open to, and trained to seize the opportunity, and environmental aspects may favor the factor of chance. The individual concerned, however, may seem to have earned the right to at least some favorable opportunities and yet they appear never to come his way, while opportunities seem to drop into the laps of others after little preparation and with chance seemingly against them. I here touch upon the concept of grace so perceptively discussed by Aldous Huxley in his *Perennial Philosophy. (302)*

Kairos involves total participation of being in a succession of shifts, minor and major, in the meaning of existence and of illuminations of wider and wider aspects of a unitive world-view. Those aspects of environmental intervention which are under some measure of control, such as those coming from the therapist, require optimal timing to be effective. Interventions may be made at a wrong as well as a right time. Interventions may be premature, too late, or disastrous. With some, who have determinedly turned their back on life, it may not only be fruitless but also dangerous to attempt to awaken them. Some who, because of genetic and constitutional makeup, because of what life has done to them and what they have done with their lives, find themselves in circumstances which, were the awakening to succeed, might cost too high a price.

Kairos is a living palpitating process having direction leading to a peak of heightened tension following the relaxation of which new patternings obtain which have the characteristics of being more open, more flexible, more dynamic, and more spontaneous. There are certain similarities to Maslow's concept of "peak experiences."*(303)* In this living process, organism and environment participate.

The therapists's effectiveness with regard to *kairos* requires that he have learned and experienced personally and with patients the value and limitations of theories regarding the nature of man which are dualistic and teleological. He should be open to what Existentialism and Eastern wisdom can offer, learning and experiencing the possibilities and limitations of these non-dualistic and non-teleological theories. In the process he should have experienced in himself and his patients integrations in the physical, psychological, moral, and spiritual dimensions. To still further help himself to become open to *kairoi,* he might work with someone experienced in this human phenomenon in a supervisory or personal analytic relationship.

With such experience and training, a therapist would earlier and more often sense the possibilities for a *kairos.* He would see when it is necessary to press forward with quite some firmness even to the point of evoking considerable anxiety and despair in his patients. Such a therapist would be able to take chances and calculated risks. He would not only have a knowledge of how that person's heredity, endowment, and life history might participate, but could also intuitively gauge his patient's ultimate responses of both a retarding and a forward-moving nature.

Such prior training and experience should be so much a part of the therapist that he can rely on its being spontaneously available. He will thereby be all the more self-reliant, flexible, versatile, and inventive. These attributes are of the authentic modality, essential because of the suddenness with which opportunity for a kairos may confront him and because of the immediacy with which his intervention must happen. The requisite authentic modality is the ultimate of the personal because it is the ultimate of the impersonal. It is beyond why and who as well as beyond what and how. It is the "one in all things," the always here and now — the phenomenological, the existential, and the oriental attitude.

Erikson's studies of development rely mainly on the phenomenological approach, illuminated and enhanced by the artist's eye. In his use of the term crisis, there is a meeting of phenomenology, existentialism, psychodynamics, and anthropology.

With his psychobiographies of Maxim Gorky, George Bernard Shaw, and Freud, Erikson prepared the way for his book-length psychobiography of *Young Man Luther. (306)* A European, steeped in European history, politics, and culture, with a longstanding personal interest in Luther, Erikson as person, as his investigative instrument, had been long and rigorously prepared. Empathy does not adequately convey Erikson's being moved as he heard, as a young man, Luther's Lord's Prayer in Luther's German. Similarly, identification does not explain Erikson's *feeling with* Luther in the latter's dissatisfaction with the Lord's intermediaries as Erikson was with the intermediaries, and the interpreters of Freud. The spirit of the East in the experience of identity and juxtaposition in the connection of the subject and all otherness are more adequate and comprehensive explanations. Erikson arrives at such a concept in *Gandhi's Truth* when he speaks of humanity's necessity to form more "inclusive identities."*(288)*

In *Gandhi's Truth*, a unique conjoining of happenings demonstrates the *kairos* experience in Gandhi and in Erikson. Erikson had long been interested in Gandhi. He was invited to Ahmedabad to give a seminar on the human life cycle by Ambalal Sarabhai, the benevolent industrialist who had been Gandhi's protagonist and host in the 1918 wage dispute. Erikson went to the scene, interviewed the main protagonists, and talked to many of Gandhi's disciples. He steeped himself in Gandhi's writings, the history, and the traditions of India. He then created his confrontation with Gandhi in a letter to him which is immediate, critical, and respectful.

But to understand "Gandhi's Truth" one must be aware of Erikson's "intellectual discipline" which is reflected in his "hidden method." Lifton writes: "Central to that discipline is his continuous concern with the self of the investigator. For that self, as many of us working in psychohistory have come to realize, is the investigator's research instrument, and it must be scrutinized as it records and recasts that which it encounters." Many of the early chapters of this book are devoted to the person of the analyst as his most important instrument of investigation.

There are many congruences in Erikson and Gandhi's life according to Elkind. Gandhi was forty-eight in 1918 when he reluctantly became involved in politics and Erikson at forty-eight reluctantly published his first book, *Childhood and Society. (306)* "While Erikson's affinity with Luther seemed to derive from comparable professional identity crises, his affinity for Gandhi appears to derive from a parallel crisis in generativity."*(308)*

Gandhi's Truth is about an event which was a crisis and a transition. In a truly holistic manner. Erikson's starts from the here-now experience, moves forward, backward, sidewards and in depth, in space, time, and persons. Erikson uses the genetic orientation as developmental genetics, as historical genetics, and as ontogenetics. Put otherwise, he uses the psychosexual, the psychosocial, and the psychohistorical approaches.

Lifton continues, "Ultimately he [Erikson] seeks an integration of Gandhian *Satyagraha* with Freudian psychoanalysis in a *'universal therapeutics' which would be committed to the Hippocratic principle that one can test truth . . . only by action which avoids harm — or better, by action which maximizes mutuality and minimizes the violence caused by unilateral coercion or threat."(307)* This is existential neurosis, *Begegnung*, and the possibility of the *kairos* experience raised to the level of politics and history.

Central to the method of *Satyagraha* (truth force, militant non-violence) is "Gandhi's sure sense that he could and would take care of the consequences of his actions." Gandhi also said that in order not to kill, but be killed if necessary, one must "cease to fear," while simultaneously insisting that "the ability to strike must be present when the power of the soul is demonstrated."*(307)* While the therapist may not put his life at stake in the usual therapeutic confrontation, there are occasions when it is put at stake by the patient. However, the demands on the therapist in helping to make a *kairos* experience possible are much beyond those expected of a participating observer.

While a person of Erikson's stature can use classical psycho-analysis for his "psychohistorical confrontations," Lifton adds that "to avoid merely shifting from one system of self-analysis to another," others "may find it necessary to anticipate the new combinations they grope toward by moving further away from that classical psycho-analytic idiom."*(307)*

For some years Grinker felt its inadequacies, and, as a consequence, he developed his "Transactional Model for Psychotherapy." *(310)* Trained by him and later a co-author with him, Spiegel, a student and colleague of Grinker's, moved into the areas of culture and sociology and now devotes himself to the study of violence guided by the transactional perspective. He sees the limitations of a simple cause-effect stimulus-response paradigm to understand the phenomenon of violence.

Spiegel postulates systems having six foci: "The universe (physicochemical and cosmic systems), the soma (biological systems), the psyche (cognitive and emotional systems), the group (small face-to-face organizations), the society (government, economic, educational religious, recreational, intellectual-esthetic and family systems) and the culture (language, technological, value and belief systems)."*(311)*

He describes four stages of interaction for a solution to be arrived at in a confrontation between groups. In doing so, the culture explicitly states its preference for collaterality in the decision making process, but lineality or dominance is what in fact obtains.

The bringing together of existential neurosis, *Begegnung,* and *kairos* with "Truth Force," "militant non-violence," and violence I feel can be productive. The evidence, as earlier stated, is that many theoreticians are moving in this direction because the problems of violence are so obviously pressing.

In "Student Unrest," Eisenberg has indicated that while it would seem that the biological stages of development are givens, over the past three centuries biological and sociological changes have occurred. Nutritional changes have led to earlier physical maturation as well as size and weight increases. *(312)* At the same time, Western societies have revised their concepts of the various stages of psychic maturation. The concepts of adolescence, postadolescence, and *youth* reflect this trend.

Educational, religious, and familial institutions which previously were the conveyors of societal value systems have lost their obligating power. While children growing up today go through developmental phases with identity crises or transactions, there are no socially acceptable or even formulated *rites de passage*. Lifton has spoken of modern "Protean Man;" Erikson of the increase of "tentative identities." I have underlined the ease and frequency of anxiety being cued off. The boundaries of identity are disrupted, diffused, and dissolved because they are so insubstantial. The frequency of anxiety appearance leads to its eruption in violent proportions.

The authority of the older generations and their value systems are suspect to the young. An effective therapy must therefore rely more and more on wider and more "inclusive human identities." The therapist must be exemplar and representative of a non-existing ideal society to obtain the basic trust of his younger patients. *(328)* Psychodynamic theories having only intrapsychic reference are inadequate. They must include also an interpersonal reference which extends from the family to society to the cosmos. In such models, values of fact, aesthetics, morality, and spirituality must all be integrated. Phenomenology, existentialism, and the three concepts developed in this chapter are crucially important for a comprehensive understanding of human being and being human.

Chapter 27

Phenomenology and Existentialism II:
Human Instances

A *kairos* can occur through an encounter *(Begegnung)* with life: "I was desperate. I was becoming nothing. I was wiping myself out. Then I began having nightmares. They became more frequent and vivid. Then in the middle of the night I had this nightmare of my oldest son [the favorite] jumping or falling in front of a train." Within hours he was on his way to getting help.

This patient described an existential neurosis in which alive despair was a crucial ingredient. A cold deeply embedded lifeless despair blocks the possibility of a *kairos* occurring. Vital despair opens the way to help of a genuine nature whether it be in seeing the sun burst through the clouds, the smile of a child, or the help of a person.

The patient's existential neurosis and the life circumstances in which he found himself created the encounter and the *kairos* experience which moved him to get the help he needed. Twenty years later, in a session, when he was feeling hope and was being able, he could recall the dream which he had had in the depths of his despair. Having confronted and worked through the question, "What am I doing to my life?" he could ask, "What do I want to do with my life?" and answer it effectively.

In a session with me, after eight years of analysis and five with a prior analyst, Daphne B., a woman in her fifties, recalled this dream. "I don't think I ever told you this dream. I had it before I began my analysis. I was touring Vienna. I wanted to visit Freud's house with more than a tourist's interest. I found it and it didn't have any windows. My feeling was disappointment. It's what in this country would be an old house sitting back on a lawn and off the street and no windows. That's how I was feeling then. That I wasn't finding any windows. That dream reminds me how I was feeling last week talking with them [members of an organization]. We go so far and then we are talking another language." This is how she always felt with her parents.

Daphne had had the dream twenty-five years earlier when she felt dead inside. After struggling with herself for five years, in deep despair and hopelessness, more dead than alive, she approached an analyst. The experience was very traumatic, and it took her three more years before she would again call another analyst. The structure of her world was of houses with no windows which faced her after she went out of her way to face them.

Duerckheim's ideas on form and counterform throw additional light on the existential neurosis, *der Begegnung,* and the *kairos* phenomenon. He speaks of the "Great Experience" in which our "spatiotemporal person encounters our metaphysical self; about the enlightenment which results from this encounter; and of the greater and deeper reality to which this experience awakens us."*(313)* Hoch's understanding of Duerckheim from personal contacts with him, and her knowledge of existentialism and of the East further clarifies Duerckheim's views. In discussing Duerckheim with me, she said, "In whatever form life offers itself to you, you have to try to find the appropriate, right, counterform *(Gegenform),* which together with the 'forms' makes a harmonious whole likely to reveal the *'Sein'* [being] in more and more transparence."

Put otherwise, one first has to be aware of and define one's life form. This is often portrayed for the first time in dreams. This definition of form is one aspect of dreams that makes them so valuable for helping direct constructive energies. The response to the form, the problem, and the structure of it may be alive despair, as with the man above, or as with the woman who was up against a house without windows in which the as yet unavailable Freud lived.

Sometimes life's form is presented with intrusive violence. This seemed necessary for the following man who was blocked in defining, in creating, and in asking for help to create his counterform.

Twice divorced at thirty-eight, and severely alcoholic for fifteen years, Burton D. was ending up nightly (6:00 a.m.) on the bar table or floor. His father, a paranoid schizophrenic, had committed suicide, and his mother, a hebephrenic praecox, died in a mental hospital when he was twenty-five. He was in deep despair which he could admit only indirectly in the form of seeking help. He was in an almost constant state of agitated hypomania.

I saw Burton three times weekly for three years, once weekly for four more, and occasionally for the next nine. His drinking diminished considerably. He used a lifelong obsession with health, food, and diets to defend himself and keep in check his compulsive alcoholism. At age fifty-two he married for the third time. Certain aspects of his wife he could transform into the image of a homeloving, protective mother figure. Other sides of her he only gradually saw: that she was a very destructive and self-destructive woman, extremely possessive, and demanding. The disillusionment was painful and after about three years, they did not simply separate, he fled from her.

After a three year interruption, knowing that I would soon leave for the summer, he came to see me for six sessions. Burton informed me that when drunk the previous summer, which was several years after having left his wife, he was robbed and severely beaten up by two sailors and left in a ditch. Most upsetting about this happening was that after years of planning, effort, and expense he had finally completed extensive and expensive dental work of which he was very proud and it had been smashed. This event led to a major *kairos*. He never drank again, further fortifying himself by becoming a compulsive nondrinker and by intensifying his fanaticism about diets.

He appeared for short periods of therapy before my vacation for the next two years. For the next three years, he would occasionally telephone me. At about age sixty-two he took an early retirement, hoping to complete several projects he had been working on for over twenty-five years. From his calls thereafter, widely spaced and bunched, I felt he was getting worse and becoming more intensely agitated and hypomanic. He also sent me very long letters which we discussed over the phone. At age sixty-five, during my summer absence Burton came back to New York in connection, I believe, with arranging a legal separation from his wife. He jumped or fell in front of a subway train.

Burton knew he had an existential neurosis. The pattern and tragedy of his life and his drinking confronted him with the fact that all was not harmonious in the form of his life. In coming for help he was trying to at least diminish the disharmony and in a measure he was succeeding. Always gregarious and needing "the love of a good woman," he married. His drinking increased and then came his major *kairos*. But it was a year before he could return to see me and then only for three years for five or six times each and then no more. Owing to his heredity and the accumulation of tragedies in his life, the vessel was too weak to produce, to support, and to contain the monumental efforts necessary. He was also past sixty and felt time was running out on him. Despite his great *kairos,* he did not have it in him to carry through to a more harmonious existence.

A *kairos* can occur in the presence of another person, and both will be unaware that it took place. Later, the experiencer identifies the *kairos* by its effects.

After his wife had been in therapy for six months, Eric I. asked for a consultation "to see if what I was doing was making it more difficult for my wife and if there was anything I could do to help." Four months later his wife was away visiting her parents for two weeks. Eric thought he might take his wife's hours "to see what analysis was like." Eight months later he thought he "might try it for himself." After six months his therapy was proceeding at a rate much beyond my expectations. A crucial factor for this perplexing progress emerged a year later.

Two years before his wife began therapy everything looked pretty black. Eric was in deep despair and didn't know it. He felt he was stagnating in a job doing hack work. Instead of helping, a move to a new apartment was followed by a worsening of his wife's condition.

Since childhood it had been drilled into him. "Keep your feelings to yourself!" — never communicate what is deeply meaningful to you and always be there selflessly for the other. To go against these dicta and visit an old friend, a woman recently divorced, to discuss his problems was only possible through despair. The moment he arrived, she started telling him the hell she had gone through before, during, and after her divorce. Now, six months later, she was seeing things quite differently and finding a new life for herself. Six hours later, he left without mentioning his problems although he felt as though he had. He had gone in deep despair and left feeling renewed and fortified, that he could divorce also if necessary, come through it, and have a different life. As later became apparent, these realizations meant something more comprehensive and fundamental; a divorce from old ways of orienting himself toward life and people which had been ingrained since childhood.

This was a major *kairos,* its effectiveness enhanced by a very vital, though deeply buried, determination to break out of his family imposed patterns. The despair that he might not, the *kairos* experience, and the re-emergence of the old determination, plus his wife's improvement and the help he got from analysis, all come together to account for the rapid and unexpected progress in his therapy.

While Eric was unaware of the extent of what had gone on in him, the next instance — described to me by E. Enczi, M.D. — is of a man who literally had a *kairos* while in a state of physical unconsciousness.

A Hungarian refugee, he had found a fairly comfortable life form in his new country; but seven years after his arrival, he still was not studying to pass the examination necessary to obtain a license to practice his profession. He was struck down by a drunken driver and lay unconscious for four weeks, hovering between life and death. After four months, he left the hospital and a year from the date of his accident he knew that the decision had been somehow made. He went on to its actualization shortly thereafter and found a more harmonious life practicing the profession he had before his enforced emigration.

A person can have a deep dissatisfaction with the form of her life acutely and intensely brought into awareness by a dream.

Olive S. was feeling that things were as bad between her husband and herself as they had been before she had begun analysis four years earlier. In this context she had a *kairos* experience through the tension created between the forms and counterforms of her life and through the impact of the curative effect of a dream. In the dream *(p. 275),* she had promised her little daughter in marriage to their elderly family physician. Olive was aware of a change in her attitude toward her husband, herself, her family and friends after the dream. Its fuller implications and effects came much more to the fore on resumption of her sessions in the fall.

436

A person can be conscious of dissatisfaction with the form of his life, be vaguely aware that he is doing something to bring about circumstances that will break up that form, and ultimately find his way to a more harmonious one.

Two years after interrupting nine years of therapy, Alexander H., a young married man, was in a deep depression. Another mild depression occurred a year after he began work with me. Progress was very slow. An executive in an old conservative organization, advancement into higher echelons had been expected of him but was not happening. He had the potential and an uncanny ability for seeing the essentials of complicated transactions, but didn't communicate these assets or, when he did, he spoke in such a sullen, irritable, and abrupt way that people were put off. He had been given one advancement partly to serve as a stimulus, but he didn't move. More accurately, he wouldn't budge.

Alexander's father, a brilliant man, had not fulfilled his potentialities because of his sadistic behavior toward subordinates. He treated my patient similarly, favoring his sisters. His mother was never there for him. I had to prove to him I could be the good father he never had, but that was not enough. He had to have it from the fathers of the organization even though he had proved a recalcitrant, bad, sullen, nasty little boy. In a succession of departments in his organization he had made life for his superiors very difficult, the more so the more they resembled his father. He was aware he was doing it, but he had no impulse to stop this behavior. He also realized they might finally get fed up. In the last few years on several occasions he was convinced they had reached that point and were about to fire him. On other occasions he was close to resigning because he felt he was an absolute failure. If he resigned, he saw himself as drifting through the rest of his life on inherited income while filling some minor executive position somewhere.

In the ninth year of our work, there were two breakthroughs of panic and despair seemingly unconnected. Alexander couldn't break his old form of little boy recalcitrance. He demanded and forced the fathers of his firm to give him the support and the love he so desperately needed after almost literally kicking them in the teeth. He was finally asked to see the head of personnel who suggested he see a psychiatrist in consultation. He was relieved and surprised at their supportiveness when he told his story to his superiors. As we discussed the situation, he experienced an awareness of what he had been doing, namely, pushing them so they would be forced to do something to break him out of the deadlock in which he felt trapped.

In the following year he became increasingly active. The frequency of the panic and despair episodes increased, became more alive but less intense. He reached the point of welcoming them, realizing their positive significance. Gradually they abated. In the second year after the psychiatric consultation, his functioning improved and he became increasingly competitive, taking over senior responsibilities. By mutual agreement, we interrupted our work with the long overdue possibility of an advancement in his job in the offing. Alexander was pleased at what was happening, as were his superiors, who were recognizing his exceptional abilities as he was allowing himself to use them openly.

A *kairos* can happen at any age from eight or nine, into advanced years and just before death. After seeing Violet E., a nineteen-year-old girl who was living the life of a Greenwich Village hippie, about fifty times over a period of six months, Dr. N. J. Levy had agreed to interruption because of mutual feelings of hopelessness. A college dropout, she was doing the whole scene, including promiscuity and mainlining. Dr. Levy describes her *kairos* experience and the events leading to it:

During the course of our work, she became increasingly aware of the fact that the sessions made her think and that the act of taking drugs was a form of "no thinking." She became increasingly disgusted with herself. With this disgust came increasing depression, apathy, and a frenetic period of drug taking.

About a month before she developed hepatitis, Violet felt that she had "hit bottom." As she put it, she became aware one night while in the depths of despair that drugs don't create life, "that I was depending too much on something so artificial. The people I had been seeing were all on the way out to nothing. I knew I really didn't enjoy drugs, but there didn't seem to be any alternative to the situation. For about a month I wrestled with these thoughts and feelings. I moved uptown, began to see new people, but continued shooting up amphetamine. When I got hepatitis I was, in a way, glad. Not being near those others helped, but I really thought I would probably be too weak to resist when I got out of bed.

After interrupting with Dr. Levy, Violet had the following dream: "Suddenly, one evening I thought I'd rather be unhappy without drugs than happy with them. I felt all choked up and then calm. I felt like something was opening up, like becoming unconstricted. I stopped feeling hopeless and I thought, 'I'm just

438

going to have to suffer with my boredom until I can get myself to move.' In other words, before, when I was in therapy, I had wanted the doctor to be the force to direct me and get me out of my feeling of indifference. Now I wanted to help myself. From that time on I began to look forward instead of just living each day as it came. I planned for and got a job where I am fast, efficient, and bored stiff, but at least I am supporting myself instead of sponging off my parents. I have my own apartment and my own special boy friend instead of just indiscriminately sleeping around.

"As the weeks went by, I could look back on that period with a kind of detachment. It seemed like a new me looking at the old one. I knew I had felt and done all those things, but I couldn't exactly remember how I had felt or why I had to do them. I felt different inside, more whole, like the decay had stopped and healing was taking place."

This girl, a confirmed drug user, had a *kairos* experience during an interruption in her therapy. Her phrase, "hit bottom," is an expression workers with alcoholics are familiar with. After such happenings, alcoholics are generally available for help. The authenticity of the experience is supported by what happened to Violet after interruption and by the fact that she resumed therapy on a regular basis.

This next instance of *kairos* was described to me by Y. Moadel, M.D. It occurred at age forty-nine in a severely masochistic woman. One could hardly have expected such a happening, particularly after so brief a period of therapy. It would seem that much of the work of preparation for this event had gone on far out of awareness.

Anne J., a forty-nine-year-old woman, married eight years, began therapy because of a moderately severe depression and somatic complaints. Her husband had indicated that he no longer loved her and was taking steps to arrange a separation. She was nevertheless satisfied that he remain. Anne felt he needed her, and that she could still be of service to him. She wondered what more she could do to "make him" love her. She also said that she loved him "too much." She tried very hard to explain that she did not resent him in any way, and that her only wish and goal in life was to see him happy.

Her husband was a heavy drinker and spoke only when absolutely necessary. Every weekend and on holidays he absented himself without explanation. Her response was, "I understand that he needs this rest and I don't question him. My problem is that my headache and dizziness get worse when he returns. Even if he wants to see his ex-wife, it is his business and I can understand it."

This was her first marriage and his second. She had worked in one place most of her life, a typical loyal employee. Her husband was a gifted engineer. She tried to be extremely pleasant and ingratiating. Anne said she never thought of herself as an individual but only in connection with her husband. "When he is happy, this is all I want. I never think of myself. I don't know how to think of myself." She refused to think about what she would do if her husband left her. As she described her husband it was apparent that he was resigned, perfectionistic, and extremely sadistic. She suffered from the ultimate of masochism and morbid dependency.

This neurotic pattern was present from her earliest years. Anne identified with her weak father. Father and daughter were dominated by her mother and intimidated by a younger sister who was a bully and a nasty child. She never recalled being angry. Although her family and friends and employers had given her a hard time, she was sure they were all concerned for her welfare and "never meant any harm."

In the first months of therapy Anne talked mainly of her symptoms. In the third month she began questioning her husband's weekend absences, and began to feel entitled to an explanation. By the fourth month, her somatic symptoms became secondary. That month she was delegated workers' representative to negotiate salaries, although she couldn't understand why they had selected her. When pressed, she related times in her life when she had been able to stand up for her rights "with her father, mother, and sister."

In the next session she looked rather pale. She showed Doctor Moadel the new scarf and hat she had bought for herself, then talked about her husband and a trip they had made. At one point, with hesitation she said, "I wanted to tell you something, Doctor. When I was getting off the bus coming here it just hit me. I felt for the first time that I am a human being too. For some reason, I never looked at myself that way. I began to feel nauseous and cold all over my body. It is coming now. It was a feeling that all the people I knew never looked at me that way. I never thought of myself as equal to other people and it just never occurred to me. It frightens me. I feel like vomiting now." Here she suddenly began vomiting and continued to do so for the remainder of the hour. Dr. Moadel finally helped her to a taxi where she said that she thought she would "eventually be all right."

440

In the following session, Dr. Moadel noticed a special glow and a happy smile on Anne's face. She first apologized for the last session and stated, "You can be sure that it won't happen again." In that session and in the following ones, the nature of her attitudes was clearly more assertive and less self-minimizing. She stated that her husband had gone away again, but that she spent the time with girlfriends and had a "wonderful time." She had started to make a few new friends. She had decided to have a haircut for the first time in years. Anne said that she was frightened because she felt that she was not "equipped and was too uncertain" about her feelings. She reminded Dr. Moadel that she was forty-nine years old, and asked whether she was not too old to change. It occurred to her that never in her life did she question things and always accepted them as they came. She continued, "I feel I have a right to question things and to be curious; why not?" At one point she stated, "This has to change, and I must have a chance for a half-way decent life."

In the following session she reported dreams for the first time, two of them. First she related a dream she had a month after she began therapy. "A cat was run over by a car and was crushed." She awakened in a panic. She identified with the "helpless cat" and felt her husband might throw her out of the house any day. That would have been the end of her life, and she would have felt really "crushed" with nowhere to turn.

Then Anne said she also had a "good dream" to report from the night before. "There I saw a large egg. The egg suddenly hatched and a kind of gentle pheasant came out. It felt good. Something was being born out of this hard shell." In her associations, she indicated that she felt that she had been coming out of her shell, that she has been trying to express herself more and that she had felt positively about it. She felt that a pheasant is a beautiful bird which is kind, gentle, and never harms anyone.

The picture of this woman's psychodynamics and her relation to her husband is given in detail to indicate the deep severity of her problems as does the pattern of her life history. What happened is unexpected and startling. That she had a deeply moving, organically involving *kairos* experience is unquestionable. To feel for "the first time that I am a human being too" after existing only in terms of her husband and others is a striking change. She was helped to dare to have a new and different perception of herself and of her place in the world.

The two dreams are reminiscent of what I have observed in many *kairos* experiences. The despair is alive and extensive. In her case, it was there but not in the foreground. After such patients have had a new and hopeful perception of themselves, they are able to recall their despair. This happened in the instance of the man who had the nightmare of his favorite son falling or jumping in front of a subway. Another example is the woman who dreamt of Freud's house without windows twenty-five years before she felt enough hope to experience the painful and anguishing hopelessness she felt then.

A forceful confrontation of the patient's self-destructive and suicidal tendencies may be the encounter necessary for turning him toward life and living and for a *kairos* happening. The therapy of Rose B. is an example of this process.

> Beginning therapy, after fighting it for ten years, meant a stand against powerful pulls toward death and dying. Continuing in therapy and communicating "family secrets" created an exacerbation of Rose's symptoms requiring hospitalization after six months of therapy. A year later, during a cholecystectomy, for the first time, she did not want "to drown" in her own blood or "die under the anaesthesia." These had been powerful wishes during three previous operations.
>
> Six months later, again due to the dynamic of therapy, her steady improvement and my absence, which she experienced as a rejection, she became suicidal. Her intent was manifested in diminished food and water intake and an increase of barbiturate and codein consumption to almost lethal doses. She also fell and banged herself so that she was covered with black and blue marks. In one frenzy she beat her legs with a wooden stool "because they wouldn't carry me," and in another, she beat her head against the wall "because it wouldn't think straight."
>
> On my return, my interventions were immediate and forceful. I visited her at home and put her under twenty-four hour surveillance. This enraged her. Later she expressed her appreciation for my having done so rather than sending her to a hospital which she hated. Among the many things I said, two statements definitely got through her confusional state created by anemia, dehydration, starvation, and drug intoxication: "Do you realize you are trying to commit suicide?" and "I will not allow you or anyone else to destroy what we have worked so hard to build!"
>
> These confrontations had a deep and lasting impact. Later she told me that the word suicide concretized to her what she was doing, and it horrified her. Although she often expressed a desire for a "good rest," or "a long sleep," she had never said, "I wish I were dead" or "I want to kill myself." My determina-

tion not to let anyone destroy what I had built, the fact that I valued what I had worked for, and the realization that I had said "we," which meant that she had worked and that I valued her efforts, were most meaningful to her. She had always had the absolute conviction that she could do nothing, that if she did do anything, it wasn't worthwhile and certainly that no one would ever value her efforts. The fact that anyone would fight for what they had helped to build was a new and utterly alien idea.

From that date, progress was slow but steady with fewer, more widely spaced, and less severe repercussions. Rose mentioned my two statements for years thereafter and had a deep feeling for them and their meaning to her. Also striking was the fact that though in a clouded state at the time of her suicidal attempt, over the years Rose recalled in minute detail and with accuracy most of what went on during that episode.

This is the most dramatic instance of a *kairos* in all my years of practice. It is a clear instance of the impact of firm and pertinent interventions helping to create a turning point in a person's life. In her case it was crucial in determining the creation of a life. Up to then, Rose had not lived, as she often said spontaneously in the succeeding years.

Without so designating it, Bleuler described the *kairos* experience in somatic illnesses associated with acute psychic symptomatology. "The experiencing of these (acute exogenous) psychoses can be understood as a dreamlike working through of a threatening life situation, namely, a working through which often leads to the patient's ultimate acceptance of the threat or of the definite impairment of health and his making peace with it. In this the physician who is on his side can be of help to him."*(314)*

In the same book, Bleuler describes his experience "with fifteen moribund patients for whom a close contact, lasting for weeks, was not harassing or burdensome but meant comfort and help to them." Through that help each patient gained "tranquility, peace and confidence by fighting." He felt assisted "in all this even during his death struggle."

Willi wrote that "During the agony (of death struggle) the exogenous psychosis follows a certain closed pattern, corresponding to the acceptance and mastering of an initially unacceptable fate or life situation. The temporal sequence runs as follows: rebellion against fate — great anxiety — appearance of the exogenous psychosis — despair and restlessness — acceptance of his fate — quieting down — fading of the exogenous psychosis. We have found such sequences in our patients during the agony when during the struggle outspoken deleria arose which subsided after the patient accepted his death so that he could die with a peaceful smile."*(314)*

The classic example from literature of this process is Tolstoy's "The Death of Ivan Ilyich." After a life that "had been most simple and most ordinary and therefore most horrible," he became afflicted with cancer. Ivan's slow deterioration and struggle against accepting it and his death are brilliantly described. At the end of the death agony, "There was no fear because there was no death . . . . In place of death there was light . . . . To him it happened in a single instant and the meaning of that instant did not change . . . 'It is finished,' said someone near him. 'Death is finished' he said to himself. 'It is no more.' He drew in a breath, stopped in the midst of a sigh, stretched out, and died."*(315)*

In recent years our dehumanized attitude toward terminal patients, particularly those with cancer has evoked a response. It is beautifully contained in "On Death and Dying" by Kübler-Ross. *(316)* The terminal patient has been studied, understood, and the possibility of dying with dignity returned to him. Such dying is preceded by a *kairos* experience — an event which used to be much more common when people died naturally in their homes surrounded by their friends.

Kübler-Ross's stages have a similarity to those of Jurg Willi mentioned above. The person is shocked by the realization that he is going to die. There is denial, anger, feelings of injustice, depression, bargaining with fate, acceptance, decathexis, and death. After the denial ends, to the last moment, patients have hope some cure will be found. It is the caring concern of a good friend, a wise spiritual counselor, or a Hippocratic physician who humanly and realistically supports that hope.

A patient, Sally F., lucidly and sympathetically described her father's last days. In his seventy-fourth year, he was an able, perfectionistic, silent man whose feelings were held in and buried. Dominated by his anxious, obsessive, and restrictive wife, contact between him and my patient had been limited, although she lived at home until her marriage and close by thereafter.

Her father became seriously ill on a holiday trip. His lungs were affected and he had a shortness of breath that limited his locomotion. In the months before his death, he had respiratory infections and high temperatures. He spent his last ten days in a hospital. My patient was with him the last eight days. He was mentally clouded part of the time, and tried to get out of bed and dress himself, not realizing how serious his condition was. In the last days he remarked several times that he felt he was not going to recover.

Two nights before his death, "He suddenly in a very clear voice asked if I was sleeping. He then said, 'It is written that God created out of nothingness. How can anything be created out of nothing?' I answered that I thought it must happen in a long development process. He went on saying, 'It is difficult to imagine nothingness, that one shall go on falling forever and forever.' He had never spoken to me about religious or existential questions.

"On the fourteenth he woke from his sleep with an expression on his face that I had never seen before. His eyes were light and clear. He looked like he had been just born, reborn in a new and fresh way. He looked as if something had clarified. I shall have this picture of him in my mind forever. He then went to sleep again and slept most of the time until he died.

"On the morning of his death he was very weak and couldn't speak. Just before twelve o'clock he turned his face toward my mother and me. We were sitting in the next room. The door was open. We were talking. I rose and went to his side and took his hand. He impatiently shook his arms. I asked, 'Do you want us to be quiet?' I got the feeling that through his shaking he was wanting to get rid of his body. He then turned his eyes to the window and went into a coma which lasted for a few hours. His last respirations were very deep and intense. He didn't suffer from breathing difficulties those last days. He got oxygen most of the time."

What my patient described was a commonplace before the advent of our modern mechanized medicine which tries to save by molesting patients up to their last breath. This man had accepted his death and had arrived at an inner peace. His arm shaking I felt was a response both to the sounds of his wife and daughter's speech and expressed his wish to get on with his death. This has been described in detail by Kübler-Ross as decathexis. Once a patient has accepted death, the work of withdrawing into themselves and dying proceeds. Interference with it is resented. That is why simply quietly sitting beside a dying person's bed, and holding his or her hand is appreciated.

It is perhaps prophetic that Kierkegaard had a *kairos* before he died. It is also in keeping that he was finishing the last pages of *Ojeblikket* (Danish), *Der Augenblick* (German), *The Instant* when he fell unconscious and was taken to the hospital.

It seems more than coincidence that the last entry in his *Diary*,

September 25, 1855, reads "The purpose of life here below is to carry us to the highest degree of *taedium vitae.*" Kierkegaard distinguished "three categories of human beings: 1) those bereft of spirituality, whose lives are so empty that punishment will not apply to them, wherefore they are lost; 2) those who eventually may receive mercy and be brought to *taedium vitae* (become utterly fed up with life), but who are scandalized and rebel against God; 3) those brought to *taedium vitae* who maintain that God acts as He does from love. Only the last are ripe for eternal life."*(307)* And for this Kierkegaard was "ripe," as his life history cried out, and his dying days in the hospital affirmed.

In those last weeks of his life, "his friends and relatives saw him free from anxiety, though he was fully aware of his closeness to death." He said, in fact, on entering the hospital, "I have come here to die."*(318)* "Unanimously his physician, nurse, and visitors experienced a radiant serenity in the dying man."*(319)*

Chapter 28

What is Technique?

The term technique has been used as if everyone understood what they meant by it. For most, an intuitive formulation may have functioned as a more or less effective guide. Some papers, as well as books on psychotherapy and psychoanalysis, only implicitly indicate what they mean by technique. Others make attempts at a loose formulation. Rarely is there a rigorous effort at definition.

With our modern emphasis on technology it seems surprising that so little attention has been given to definitions of technique and to theories of technique.

Freud wrote six brief papers on technique between 1911 and 1915 and little on the subject thereafter. On several occasions, he toyed with the idea of writing an *Allgemeine Technik der Psychoanalyse*, but he did not realize this hope. Strachey noted "some feeling of reluctance" on Freud's part to write of the subject systematically. *(320)* He gave a variety of reasons for not doing so, but his underlying premise was that psychoanalysis could only be learned from experience and mostly from one's personal analysis. The recommendation in 1937 that every analyst have further analysis every five years reflects Freud's emphasis on personal experience.

In 1941 Fenichel felt psychoanalysis was too young a science for a book on technique. *(132)* In the fifties, Hartmann and Rapaport noted the lag in regard to expositions on technique by comparison with those on theory. *(321, 322)* Horney never wrote the book on technique she had long promised herself.

In his review of Menninger's *Theory of Psychoanalytic Technique,* Alexander said that "the author stresses that this is a book on the theory of psychoanalytical treatment but the assets of the book lie more in its practical recommendations and vivid descriptions of the fundamental psychodynamic phenomena of treatment . . . . The crucial issue of psychoanalytic treatment remains essentially unanswered — namely why, after a certain period of regression, when a point is reached, the patient turns around to more adequate forms of organization of his impulses, feelings, and object relations. The author is frank in admitting that his theoretical framework cannot provide a cogent answer to this question."*(323)*

A recently compiled list of Freudian techniques and their definitions offers an opening into this complex subject.

"Techniques involve," Bibring suggests, "any purposive, more or less typified, verbal or nonverbal behavior on the part of the therapist which intends to affect the patient in the direction of the (intermediary or final) goals of the treatment . . . . [There are] five basic therapeutic techniques, each with its curative agency: (1) suggestion, acting through resultant beliefs, impulses or action; (2) abreaction, producing relief from acute tension; (3) manipulation, favoring the progress of treatment or producing changes in adjustment; (4) clarification (Carl Rogers), providing insight into phenomena that operate on the conscious and preconscious level; and (5) insight through interpretation of unconscious material, producing deep-seated changes within the personality. (George Devereux's concept of 'confrontation' has much in common with 'clarification'.)"*(142, p. 102)*

In the light of the evolution of post-Freudian theory, with the concomitant innovations in technique, the operations involved in the above-described techniques and their objectives approximates, in some instances, holistic technical maneuvers. Elsewhere the gap is wide. This position is taken with awareness of Eckstein's caution "that technical issues cannot be discussed fruitfully if . . . derived from significantly different theoretical frames of reference."*(324)*

The gap between post-Freudian and holistic positions is least regarding "clarification" and "confrontation." The difference concerns the frequency with which they are used, the importance put on them, and the range of the effectiveness assumed for them. I feel they not only affect "phenomena on the conscious and preconscious level," but also on the unconscious. Also they help to bring about creative vision which comes out of that unity and harmony of insight and outsight.

While there are many similarities regarding the use and meaning of "abreaction," there are differences. That there are urgent occasions and emergency situations when the prompting, even the provoking of an abreaction is essential, is unquestionable. The term abreaction, however, is an unfortunate one. It focuses on reaction rather than on response and resonation, on relief rather than release. Reaction is an expression of the oppositional dichotomy, of the automatism, action-reaction. Relief expresses the urgent need of a person compulsively driven and demanding surcease from pain. The overfocus is on that immediate objective, obliterating the long-range ones and the consequences of action and reaction. The holistic objective is to help patients accept and contain pain and tension toward the fulfilment of immediate, intermediate, and long-range objectives. There is a diminishing focus on relief, and an increased one on release, a diminishing need for abreaction, and an increased wanting to contain tension toward the end of transforming it into less destructive and more creative forms.

The concept "abreaction," with the overfocus on relief, is a reflection of a hedonistic philosophy and, in psychoanalysis, an expression of Freud's "pleasure principle."*(325)* As formulated in 1922, it is a restatement of Bentham's principles of economic democracy and hedonistic utilitarianism.

"Nature," says Bentham, "has placed mankind under the governance of two sovereign masters — *pain* and *pleasure*. It is from them alone to point out what we ought to do, as well as to determine what we shall do. On the one hand the standard of right and wrong, on the other the chain of causes and effects, are fastened to their throne . . . . A man may pretend to abjure their empire; but, in reality, he will remain subject to it . . . . *The principle of utility* recognizes this subjection, and assumes it for the foundation of that system, the object of which is to rear the fabric of felicity by the hands of reason and law. Systems which attempt to question it deal in sounds instead of sense, in caprice instead of reason, in darkness instead of light."*(326)*

The concept of "suggestion" as used in classical theory departs further from the holistic view because it is based on "resultant beliefs" regarding images of man, of therapy, and of technique.

In the light of the rather different holistic concepts of "insight," "interpretation," and the "unconscious" which have been previously developed, the divergences begin to become quite significant. With Horney's emphasis on feelings, aids to widen and deepen the ongoing multidimensional experiencing process received greater attention. Her comprehensive notion of "Understanding the Patient as the Basis of All Technique" was one response. *(66)* Insight is now seen as a process with an internal and external reference (insight and outsight) with intellectual and emotional components. Because the aim of understanding is seeing, out of which comes comprehensive experiencing, the notion of creative vision more adequately conveys this process than insight.

"Interpretation, in its classical sense, refers to a verbal intervention by the analyst into the process of free association in order to demonstrate and remove a resistance."*(142, p. 113)* Horney's definition of interpretation presents a contrast. "When he [the analyst] tries to convey his understanding, or some part of it to the patient, he is making an interpretation."*(68)* Developing her ideas of understanding and interpretation, I arrived at the comprehensive concept of illuminators of processes which maintain and extend spontaneity and undermine and resolve compulsiveness.

The greatest gap between holistic and post-Freudian views has to do with "manipulation" and "adjustment." Manipulation is contrary to the spirit and practice of holistic psychoanalysis which is also antipathetic to the notion of adjustment, a hard, coercive concept. Adapting and coping are less distressing terms and concepts than adjusting. However, I feel the holistic term, integrating, is a more comprehensive and humane one.

In the statements "make the patient see" and "undergoing analysis," frequently found in literature on therapy and technique and used by experienced therapists, the issue of manipulation is sharply focused. The analyst cannot make the patient see. His task is to help him see through illuminators and creative vision. Analysis is not a process a patient undergoes as if an anesthetized object. He should become an aware and active participant in a cooperative venture which is also a learning experience toward becoming more effective in his self-analysis. Likewise the analyst does not "cure" his patient nor is an analysis ever "completed."

The phrase "curative agency" implies that sickness is some circumscribed entity that can be completely eradicated without consequences when the acute manifestations are past. The patient is not as "good as new" after a cold. His organism is now different by virtue of having gone through the illness and healing processes. Likewise a person is not cured after an acute psychotic break, neurotic depression, or anxiety attack. He is a different person, maybe sicker and maybe healthier, by virtue of the relative weights of the rational and irrational processes in him and in his environments and the nature of their participation in those happenings.

What I hope for from my technique is that, in participating in the unitary process of therapy, it will aid the identifying, undermining, and resolving of irrational, sick, destructive, compulsive processes while simultaneously aiding the identification, supporting, extending, and expanding of rational, healthy, constructive, and spontaneous processes.

From some perspectives, Eckstein's caution "regarding making comparisons of techniques based on significantly different theoretical frames of reference" seems excessive in spite of the differences just described. This gap is not so wide as it might be because psychoanalytic technique is dependent "on three variables" which reconnect us with human essentials. These variables are "1) the patient's disorder and personality; 2) the present circumstances; and 3) the personality of the analyst."*(142, p. 100)*

Techniques are not something fixed, specified, and circumscribed. They keep being modified. Their specificity resides more in the loosely defined conditions they are intended to affect rather than in the all too unclearly delineated operations and inner processes that go on between their application and the outcome. How much the "patient's disorder" influenced psychoanalytic technique is underlined by Wolman. "A close study of Freud's clinical work discloses a definite and quite consistent pattern. It was not the analyst who changed his attitude. Distinct categories of patients developed certain attitudes toward the analyst, and the analyst, in turn, had to modify his therapeutic technique. The reactions of the analyst were determined by the patient's disorder."*(142, p. 241)*

Technique is dependent on "the present circumstances." The evolution of theory and technique determine how one defines and what one considers as "present circumstances." Horney's definition of "the actual situation"*(33)* gives quite a different picture of the area of operations in the analytic process than what would be subsumed under the classical model. (See ch. 7).

Then there is "the personality of the analyst." Historically, the changing categories of patients not only caused the analyst to modify his techniques; they effected changes in his personality as well. The changes in theory and technique, reciprocally influencing each other, further determined how this changing "personality" was defined, which effected still further changes, in a geometric progression of influences. All this has led to an increasing focus and emphasis on the person of the analyst as his most important instrument of therapy. *(142, p. 414)*

Most analysts concur on the importance of the analyst's personality in therapy and emphasize specific aspects of its impact. Hollender says, "The therapist's personality, and specifically his mode of expressing himself, will determine the style suitable for him."

451

(287, p. viii) Freud says, "I must, however, expressly state that this technique has proved to be the only method suitable to my individuality."*(130)*

It bears repeating at this point that phenomenology and existentialism are not a reaction to being scientific, to precision, rigor, and verifiability. They are an objection to reductionism, to the turning of human into objects, and to the overemphasis on technique. Phenomenology and existentialism assert that they can restore to "the term scientific its traditional broader meaning."*(291)* Quantification is, for example, a special case of qualification and according to the Eddington Principle, "all the quantitative propositions of physics, that is, the exact values of the pure numbers that are constants of science, may be deduced by logical reasoning from qualitative assertions, without making any use of quantitative data derived from observations."*(327)*

Teachers and students are constantly confronted by the difficulties in organizing available knowledge and communicating it in an open-ended spirit of tentativeness. *(279)* They are caught in the unhealthy attitudes towards discipline. They have difficulty discriminating between control and coercion. Other difficulties beset them in separating license from freedom. Discipline is essential to teaching and learning. It helps bring about that harmonious balance between spontaneity and rigor, intuition and precision, to the productive benefit of all concerned.

The terms "automatic," "instinctive," "innate," and "given" also create problems in teaching and learning. In both, practice and drill are essential. The term "automatic" is an unhappy one. It gives the impression of the analyst reacting like an automaton rather than through disciplined spontaneity based on training and experience. Through practice, drill, and experience, wisdom is hopefully attained. This means the analyst no longer has a certain constrictedness which is the result of having to hold theory and technique in the foreground of awareness. Then, filtered through the prism of the analyst's unique personality, theory and technique are immediately available with inventiveness and ingenuity, evolved, as they are, at the moment, for the needs of unique patients in unique situations.

Mitigating the mechanistic attitude reflected in the terms "standardize," "calibrate," and "automatic," is Weissman's statement that "The ideas and practices of psychoanalysis emerge from an existential attitude within the psychoanalyst . . . . The existential attitude . . . recognizes that each person's version of reality is determined by his unique way of polarizing existence." From that position the analyst can investigate his own experience and that of his patient from a number of vantage points and with a variety of methodologies. The existential attitude is at the core. Increasing significance is given to the uniqueness of each one's experiencing of himself, of the process and of the other. *(128, p. viii)*

Integral to the existential attitude is the experiencing process. In *Psychoanalytic Supervision,* Fleming and Benedek emphasize the importance of "the experiential nature of psychoanalytic learning." They "attempt to distinguish the elements of learning-by-experiencing from learning-by-cognizing, and the part played by each in the education of the analyst . . . . Cognitive processes are essential but play a role secondary to learning by experience during the greater part of the development of a psychoanalyst." Their "thesis" is that "to make self-analytic functions readily available equipment for working as an analyst is the basic and continued goal of psychoanalytic training." *(258, pp. 20, 34)*

Experiencing reflects human uniqueness more closely than do cognitive processes which are more readily influenced by others and environments. Because of the prevalence of alienating processes and dissociation from organicity, thought processes become increasingly remote from a person's core. In the experiencing process that person is closer to his uniqueness experienced in the form and content of his feelings as well as through the conative dimensions of his being. For these reasons, experiencing, as trying and testing, not only includes the processes of arriving at, and the use of known techniques according to that therapist's individuality, but also the processes of being open to using variations of them, to improvizations on those techniques, as well as to doing what might be regarded as unorthodox. But even beyond all these there are all those effects of the therapist's being as influences, metacommunications, communications, and interventions which are techniques unique to that therapist, at that time with that patient.

In the light of what has been said about the "experiential nature of psychoanalytic learning," the historical distinction between psychoanalysis as research tool and as therapeutic instrument may be reconsidered. Freud said: "It is indeed one of the distinctions of psychoanalysis that research and treatment proceed hand in hand, but still the technique required for the one begins at a certain point to diverge from that of the other . . . . The most successful cases are those in which one proceeds, as it were, aimlessly, and allows oneself to be overtaken by any surprises, always presenting to them an open mind, free from any expectations."*(130, p. 326)*

I have attempted a reformulation of Freud's statement: "Being guided in the psychoanalytic setting by the pure research viewpoint and the unbiased approach — that is, observing by introspection and inspection the forms as they arise in awareness, and experiencing them

— is therapeutic. Formulating these emerging forms into patternings of different orders of abstraction is theorizing. What we name 'therapy' (healing, helping, technique) and 'theory' (systematizing and interpreting in their broadest senses) are both rooted in and derive from the experiencing and conceptualizing aspects of what I have defined as the universal forming process."*(229)*

Concerning "the certain point" at which research and treatment begin to diverge, I feel that as the analyst is guided by the seven attributes and the nine modes of being described in chapter 9, the point of divergence is put off, the gap between the two becomes narrower, the mutual enrichment persists, and the possibilities for productive clinical research remain great.

The differences between Freud's model of research and treatment and the one I have suggested need clarification. The ultimate of the classical model, as suggested by McAlpine, is that "the analyst . . . is never a co-actor" and that "the psychoanalytic technique may be defined as the only psychotherapeutic method in which a one-sided, infantile regression-analytic transference is induced in a patient (analyzed), worked through, and finally resolved." Her position is that "the analytic transference relationship ought, strictly speaking, not be referred to as a relationship between analysand and analyst, but more precisely the analysand's relating to the analyst."*(235)*

Her definition represents the ultimate desired in the mirror technique. In it the patient is clearly viewed as an object, a thing, as the only variable being examined in a closed system: Many Freudian analysts would disagree with this, and it is radically at variance with Horney's position and my own.

I concur with Freud's statement that "the most successful cases are those in which one proceeds, as it were, aimlessly." Creativity in psychoanalytic investigation, as research and therapy, is possible only as there is openness of mind which allows for being "overtaken by any surprises."

Some Freudian analysts see differences between psychoanalysis and psychoanalytic psychotherapy. About the differences Hollender says, "I am not sure if they are sufficiently distinctive or significant to justify the choice of a separate name." *(287, p. 9)* For Hollender there is only psychoanalytic psychotherapy.

Tarachow insists that the terms have different meanings. *(142, p. 474)* In "The Limitations of Technique" he does, however, warn that "ideal psychoanalysis is impossible." "A degree of psychotherapy" is introduced "into the analytic situation" because while the latter moves toward "psychic fusion (symbiosis)," the psychoanalytic work of interpretation antithetically "drives toward separation."*(222)*

Rapaport reminds us that psychoanalysis is not orthodox science.

This fact, he adds, says nothing about its value and effectiveness. It could be called a "protoscience" on the basis of its present values and could become scientific, he says. For this to happen therapy and research must not be separated. Otherwise objective psychologists will concern themselves more and more with trivia and the subjective psychologists move in the direction of untested dogma. The model of science to which Rapaport is referring is that of the modern experimental physical sciences. *(330)*

Among modern scientific models, that of biology is most akin to holistic psychoanalysis. *"Biological knowledge is continued creative activity, by which the idea of the organism comes increasingly within reach of our experience,"* says Goldstein. *"The symbols which biology requires for the coherent representation of the empirical facts are of a kind other than those in physics . . . . The symbols,* the theoretical representations in biology, *must in principle, include quality and individuality in all its determination . . . .* The symbol must have the character of a *Gestalt . . . .* In practice, we usually proceed in such a way that, from the facts gained by analysis, we sketch a picture of the whole organism, which in turn instigates further questions and investigations, so long as we encounter discrepancies between this picture and factual experience . . . . The material is essentially supposed to demonstrate over and over again *that method as well as theory must originate from nothing but the most concrete evidence."* *(186, pp. 403-13, 507)*

Goldstein's picture of biological knowledge and its acquisition could well apply to psychoanalysis as research, as therapy, as creating process. Its rigor, method, and theory formulation could well be a guide.

"Biological knowledge is continued creative activity." It is self-knowledge, self-creating, and creating the world of which one is an aspect. The structure and meaning of knowledge have changed across time shifting from a focus on knowledge as wisdom to knowledge as knowledge to knowledge as information. This shift reflects the movement from a focus on subjectifying to one on objectifying, from seeing the world through the immediacies of the so-called primitive and the contemplative vision of the East to the conceptualizing mind of the West.

These lines of movement reflect the movement from depth to surface and surface to depth ontologically in the holistic metaphorical symbolic spiral. They reflect what happens in the therapist as he becomes more capable of using the whole of himself as instrument, as creator and effector of technique. This holistic approach includes techniques exemplifying subjectivity, as in moments of communing and in the *kairos* experience, and techniques approximating objectivity. With increasing dimensions of objectivity, the therapist is increasingly able to formulate his experiences and to validate them with the methods of sciences.

In addition to viewing psychoanalytic investigation, research, and therapy as a biological science concerned with "the phenomena of life"*(331)* with appropriate symbols which give a "coherent representation of the facts," there are other concepts of modern biology relevant to a holistic theory of technique.

Mayr emphasizes the rich possibilities of taxonomy in teleonomic, not teleologic (or directed), processes. He adds that evolutionary biology could be scientific without recourse to explanation, prediction (other than statistical), or causality. *(213)*

Regarding causality, Bunge states, "Nothing is inherently causal or noncausal"; and "strictly causal laws are never exactly operating . . . but rather *causal ranges* of scientific laws . . . . A more fertile approach should be to group scientific laws into those which contain determination categories, for example, causation, interaction, triggering, blocking, global dynamics, statistical dynamics, dialectics, and teleology and those free from determination categories, for example, laws of irrelevance, statistical correlations, functional relations, structural statements, and transformation formulas."*(332)*

Phenomenology and existentialism are congenial to this new picture of a science. Boss explored *"The fundamental difference which separates the natural sciences from the Daseinsanalytic or existential science of man."* He emphasized that "Daseinsanalytic statements . . . are at all times 'nothing but' references to phenomena which can be immediately perceived, but which as such, can neither be derived from something else, nor, 'proved' in some way."*(262, pp. 30-31)*

May's comment is worth repeating here: "Our Western tendency has been to believe that *understanding follows technique; . . .* The existential approach holds the exact opposite; namely, that *technique follows understanding." (293, p. 77)* In Horney's "Understanding the Patient as the Basis of All Technique," this existential position is clearly delineated.

The West with its emphasis on why, on theory, on the notion that science means the exact sciences, tends to see technique as preceding. Existentialism, focusing on the phenomena of life and rigorously adhering to perceiving them in a holistic way, gives primacy to understanding.

Ehrenwald asserts that magic, myth and faith, participate in all psychotherapies, scientific and prescientific. The guiding principles in all are: (1) myth present in the therapist's motivation and the patient's expectations; (2) re-education, "working through" and learning theory; (3) psychodynamics. He suggests four models of psychotherapy indicating the proportions of the three operative guiding principles. *(336)*

He concludes that "the therapist capable of manipulating both his myths and scientific concepts, of effecting what [he] described as the existential shift from magic to science — and if need be, back from science to magic and myth — may find that his patients will do more than merely comply with his doctrine. They may indeed be helped by his motivation to help, and unless he is deceived by his own myth, he may even come closer to knowing how and why myths (or theories) happen to be therapeutically effective."*(336)*

Keeping the existential viewpoint in mind, what is technique? In *Systems of Psychotherapy,* Ford and Urban give a definition of technique that is the most rigorous and comprehensive one I have found. It goes beyond those given by the academic psychologists and logical positivists who will consider only observables verifiable by an external observer.

Ford and Urban "espouse a monistic view of human behavior." By "behavior" they mean not only a person's "overt actions . . . but also what he thinks, how he sees, and what his emotional reactions are like. . . . The term includes the more complex patterns of response, such as the attitude of one person to another." Behavior also "encompasses the antecedents to overt behavior, that is, 'personality organization,' as well as motor and glandular events."

They utilize three classes of behavior: (1) objectively observable; (2) subjectively observable; and (3) unobservable, e.g., presumed chemical changes. The content of these responses "is the 'what' of a response" emphasized in "personality theory."*(337)* They add that the "what" of behavior is of equal critical importance in the individual psychotherapy interview.

Ford and Urban see the practice of psychotherapy as based on theories of therapy which are themselves the outcome of theories of behavioral change imbedded in general theories of behavior. Ford and Urban see psychotherapy as a special case of planned behavior change. They define psychotherapy, which for them includes all forms of psychoanalysis and psychotherapy, as *"a set of procedures for changing behavior."* They add that *"the techniques of therapy, or perhaps more accurately the behaviors of the therapist, constitute a set of conditions that can be varied by the therapist."(335, pp. 71, 85)* Referring to technique as *"behaviors of the therapist"* which are procedures, operations, a set of conditions which the therapist can vary, as constitutive of him and constituted by him, helps to undercut the mechanistic notions of technique and represents a move closer to the holistic position that the therapist is technique. His person is his instrumentalities and their effectuation. He is a techniquing process.

Ford and Urban ask why techniques are de-emphasized? They allude to the viewpoints of existentialists and also to Rank and Rogers who, they note, abandoned "specifying techniques." They feel "that more specification rather than less is required." This specification is made possible for them by the following stated position: "It is what the therapist does, not what he thinks and feels, that directly affects the patient. It is true that patients make inferences and guesses about the therapist's subjective responses, but one must assume that these are based on the therapist's objectively observable behavior."*(337, p. 667)*

Although their "monistic view of behavior" includes subjective and objective observables and unobservables regarding patients, Ford and Urban omit subjective observables and unobservables in considering the behaviors of the therapist. They also assert that his behaviors are limited to his observable doings, and that these are the only ones that influence his patient. Left out of account are the happenings in moments of communing, during a *kairos* experience, and when both are silent and experiencing each other's presence, *vis-à-vis* or on the couch.

The holistic definition of technique then as applied to therapy, is a continuum from moments of techniqueless therapy, as in moments of communing when there is pure lucidity, formlessness, and secondlessness, to the impossible of therapy which is pure technique. That would imply form without content, the mind facing itself in pure abstraction. Put otherwise there are hierarchies of interconnected kinds of technique between these two extremes of absolute subjectifying to ultimate objectifying.

This is a restatement of Northrop's position that there is no single scientific method but many methods appropriate to different stages of inquiry in different disciplines from biochemistry to poetry, from astrophysics to theology. *(339)* The described structure of this spectrum specifies a movement from the most qualitative to the most quantitative, from the acausal to the absolutely deterministic, from what cannot be validated except through faith and through having had a similar experience to what can be confirmed mathematically.

This technique can be taught and learned through utilizing the many dimensions of the comprehensive knowing process, through practice and drill, and through experiencing what has been taught in the context of a preceptorship. The more teacher and student move toward the subjectifying pole of the spectrum, the more is required of the person of the teacher as an instrument of instruction and the person of the therapist as practitioner. The more precision, rigor, and clarity there is in defining teaching methods and utilizing techniques appropriate to different levels of therapeutic dialogue and discourse,

458

the more accurate and adequate will be the application of the techniques to what each moment is requiring.

Such a definition of technique fits into Ehrenwald's expanded version of psychoanalysis which accepts and accounts for myth which is man's creative vision produced by the universal forming process. *(336)* It formulates and expresses how man sees himself as an individual *vis-à-vis* another individual, groups, society, culture, and cosmos. Myths are the expression, the repository, the communicators of the deepest wells of human being.

This definition is congruent with Heuscher's three categories of psychotherapy: (1) those based on a deterministic world like psychoanalysis and so-called organic therapies for the emotionally disturbed; (2) those based on communication or transactional analysis which focus on the interactions in groups larger than pairs; (3) "existential psychotherapy" which aims at explaining "the human being out of himself."*(340)* In the third category there are practitioners who insist therapy must be absolutely spontaneous and utterly techniqueless; those who assert that it has not yet evolved its technique; and still others, like Boss, who assert that they use orthodox techniques more effectively than classical analysts do themselves.

Heuscher says existential psychotherapy means "to prove oneself helpful *(therapeuo)* to a soul *(psyche)*" in furthering "its authentic experience and expressive of its existence." Pure, continuing, techniqueless spontaneity with one patient after another would not only be exhausting but impossible. Among analysts there are no saints or gurus. It can obtain in techniqueless moments of communing and in the *kairos* experience which, however, are helped to be brought about by techniques based more on disciplined spontaneity than learned rational manipulations.

The process of arriving at techniqueless technique which continues beyond the moment is beautifully described in *Zen and the Art of Archery. (341)* Although the context is not that of therapy, it is one of comprehensive knowing carried out in an atmosphere of devotion to the task and to the master. Being an Occidental, Herrigel brought to the task his experience and understanding of technique into which he transformed the master's instructions. Driven by his failures he became frantic and began to cheat. The master immediately sensed this and turned his back on him. In despair, the humbled Herrigel begged for another chance. At the ultimate of exhaustion and despair all that he had learned as technique dissolved into genuineness. He *became* technique and the bow and arrow and the target. He did not bend the bow and shoot the arrow. All in a spirit of communion joined, and the arrow found the target. This happening continued with effortless effort with continued devotion thereafter.

The need for explicit, rational, describable interventions is greater in the teaching and learning phase of psychoanalysis and psychotherapy. As there is increasing experience and expanding knowledge, the disciplined spontaneity in the use of the formulated techniques increases. They are also more quickly available with inventiveness and ingenuity. Then there is an accrual of wisdom which allows for increased reliance on a more widely and deeply imbedded disciplined spontaneity. As this happens, the ultimates possible, as attributes and modes of being, will manifest themselves through the person of the therapist's unique personality, uniquely applicable to the unique needs of that patient at that unique moment. Then that therapist will experience, will know, will be the embodiment and the answer to the question, "What Is Technique?"

Chapter 29

Teaching Technique I:
History and Training Analysis

Freud first used the term "psychoanalysis" in 1895. In July of that year he began occasional casual analysis of his dreams. He became the first analytic candidate-in-training in July 1897 when he continued this practice as "a regular procedure with a definite purpose . . . . He never ceased to analyze himself devoting the last half hour of his day to that purpose."*(343, pp. 323, 327)*

The beginning of psychoanalytic training of others can be dated at 1902 when Freud came out of his "splendid isolation," when his lonely but glorious "heroic age" was interrupted. "From the year 1902 onwards, a number of young doctors gathered round me with the express intention of learning and practicing and spreading the knowledge of psychoanalysis . . . . On the whole I could tell myself that (the group) was hardly inferior, in wealth and variety of talent to the staff of any clinical teacher one can think of."*(344)*

What came from that original group and those Wednesday evening meetings (1906–1915) substantiates Freud's assessment of their quality. Many were mature and experienced psychiatrists and people who had evolved their own ideas on therapy. They were moved by a pioneering spirit. "It took courage to become associated with someone who had been excluded and whose ideas were anathema if not considered scandalous."*(344)*

The first training analysis occurred "During a fortnight in January, 1907," when Eitingon "passed three or four evenings with Freud . . . on personal analytic work during long walks in the city."*(343)* In 1912 Freud recommended that "anyone who wishes to practice an analysis of others should first submit to be analyzed himself by a competent person."*(130)* Nunberg "declared that no one could any longer learn to practice psychoanalysis without having analyzed himself." *(345)* Nunberg's position was formalized at the Berlin Congress in 1922.

However, when Bernfeld suggested in 1922 that he should have a personal analysis before practicing Freud answered, "Nonsense. You go right ahead. You'll get in trouble. Then we will figure out what to do about it." When Freud sent Bernfeld his first case he went to Freud alarmed by the task. Freud responded "Don't you know more than he does? Show him as much as you can."*(324a)* This was no expression of casualness on Freud's part but a recognition of the caliber of the man.

In 1907 Brill came to Freud after a stay with Bleuler. In 1919 Dr. Adolph Stern was the first American to go to Vienna for a didactic analysis. The first analysis in New York was begun three years later. In the 20's many Americans went to Berlin and some to Vienna.

I began my analytic training at the New York Psychoanalytic Institute in 1936 with Dr. Abram Kardiner as my personal analyst. Most of us had training not only in psychiatry and neurology but also in neurophysiology and neuropathology because tradition still saw them as two aspects of one speciality. Others had had years in the general practice of medicine and in specialties. It was still a pioneering venture and there was a spirit of enthusiasm.

After the war, the number of training analysts and teachers was inadequate. Most applicants were older men with years of practice in medicine. They had matured through their war experiences. The demands for psychiatrists had forced some of them to practice it on military order with no training. World War II had brought psychiatry into an equal place with medicine and surgery. In 1945 almost every psychiatric resident wanted psychoanalytic training. By 1960 the ratio had dropped to 1 in 7, and by 1970 to about 1 in 20, while the number of psychiatric residencies mounted precipitously.

By 1950 the quality of the people seeking analytic training had changed. Referring to the golden era of the 20's and early 30's, Knight said that they were of a "somewhat different breed from the current crop of candidates . . . . Many gifted individuals with definite neuroses or character disorders were trained . . . . Many of these became our best teachers, theoreticians, and clinicians." Some, however, turned out to be "problem children" for their institutes and the association (A.P.A.) and "caused raised eyebrows in the general public."*(346, p. 218)*

About this different breed, Eisendorfer said in 1957, after ten years on the admissions committtee of the New York Psychoanalytic Institute, "I do know it required a different type of character to be attracted to analysis when the pressure of society was opposed to it than the type of personalities who are now attracted when psychoanalysis has seemingly become the holy grail of psychiatry and the intelligentsia. That something extra, the sublime courage which seeks truth in the face of whatever counterpressure, is indeed rare among the candidates in this age of psychoanalytic affluence."*(345, pp. 245-46)*

Eisendorfer found an increase in applicants with a "façade of normality (about 10%)" and a picture of what "I call 'the all-American normal' " who come to be known as the "normopath."*(345, p. 229)* They caused quite some difficulties once admitted. They began to reveal "severe latent depression," "schizophrenic processes," and "a propensity to acting out" behind this façade of normality. They were motivated by an "intense ambition" which coincided "with a narcissistic omnipotence and delusional grandeur."*(345, p. 146)*

By 1968 the situation had gotten worse. Bird commented on "the large number of unsuitable 'normal' applicants being allowed to slip through not . . . by accident but . . . on purpose." These normal graduates with "normal character disorders" with their façade of normality were "relatively unanalyzable," said Bird, and "seldom skilled at conducting an analysis."*(347, p. 515)*

The reasons given in 1968 for this situation were that psychoanalysis had become a profession; that there were demands for services; and that such "normal, stable, attractive, and essentially nonscientific people" can produce such services. *(347, p. 515)* Formal evaluation procedures fostered their acceptance. The institutionalization of psychoanalytic education favors their graduation. Soon they are on the admissions committees themselves, and do not find creative mavericks congenial applicants. Nonetheless a few of the latter are accepted. Maybe they and those residents who self-select personal analysis and supervision are of the breed who sought analytic training in the golden era.

Other factors contribute to this situation. Psychoanalysis is no longer the holy grail of the young psychiatric resident. Only 1 in 20 seek training. Now psychiatry can compete with its many effective drugs. Anna Freud added that the acceptance of psychoanalysis by academic psychology and the pressure to be more scientific "was caus-ing problems. Also psychoanalysis has lost the allegiance of the young, no longer concerned with man's struggle with himself, but with man against society."*(348)* The senior members of the American Psycho-analytic Association are concerned that it is becoming a profession of older people. Graduates become older and older. After a specialty training they have to take, in addition, a long, extremely expensive postgraduate training.

It took a special breed of candidate-in-training to leave the pres-tige and security of New York Psychoanalytic Institute and join the Association for the Advancement of Psychoanalysis in 1941. It took courage and rebelliousness. From two splits in that group (A.A.P.) came the William Alanson White Institute and the Comprehensive Course in Psychoanalysis at the New York Medical College. Those qualities were also present in those that formed the Columbia Group which trained the people who began the Psychoanalytic Program at Tulane. Among these pioneering groups were many people of com-petence and originality. Such groups would understandably attract a different kind of candidate than those who joined institutes associated with the American (A.P.A.).

My knowledge of the evolution in the kinds of applicants is greatest about those who came to the American Institute for Psycho-analysis (A.I.P.). Because of my activities in the American Academy of Psychoanalysis, I was informed about other institutes whose gradu-ates were not eligible to join the American (A.P.A.).

Because of courage, rebelliousness, and independence, some psy-chiatrists interested in training would not consider institutes affiliated with the American. Some found orientations other than the classical more congenial. Others did not apply for monetary reasons, because of long waiting lists for training analysts, or because they regarded the classical training too demanding. A small number came to the A.I.P. after being rejected by American institutes. These were often the kind of people we preferred.

This preference in applicants followed from the philosophy of the American Institute of Psychoanalysis — a philosophy which con-tinues in the Specialty Training Program in Psychoanalytic Medicine at the Postgraduate Center for Mental Health with which I am now identified. It is important that the applicant realize that he has per-sonal problems; that he show a genuine interest in them, and an active incentive to resolve them; that an awareness of his own suffering has made him more sensitive to it in others; that he has a serious motivation for self-investigation and for training in order to become more effec-tive in the alleviation of human suffering; that such training would lead to an enhancement of his capacities for compassion, concern, and

464

firmness in therapy; that such therapy is possible after he has made significant progress toward becoming a whole person; that for such an outcome a deep and extensive therapeutic analysis is essential; and that such qualifications, motivation, therapy, and training make more possible the fulfillment of the applicant's original interests and his potential contribution to the advancement of psychoanalysis.

In the early years of analysis it was sufficient if one senior person with *Menschen-Kenntnis* made the decision. As time went on, the decision was made by a committee and criteria began to be evolved as to who was a suitable candidate. With the development of tests much greater use of them, individually and as a battery, followed. After a few years tests were dropped because it was felt that they contributed little. A committee of experienced senior analysts ultimately made the decision. Seminars were held on what determined these selections and often the answer predictably turned out to be "someone like me."

According to the requirements of the classical model, the "analyzable patient" must have sufficient of the following: "a reasonable tolerance for frustration," "ability to accept a passive role and passive position," "ability to tolerate a reasonable amount of anxiety," ability to free associate, introspect, self-observe, self-appraise, a "potential range of adaptability," satisfactory capacity for reality testing, ability to establish "a transference relationship . . . a *sine qua non* of analyzability," satisfactory motivation, "the psychosexual development not too disturbed, the id not too strong, the superego too harsh, and the ego too weak or defective . . . and finally the external factors of time, money, family, and work situations which would make the analysis possible and not obstruct it."*(349)*

The contrast between what Freudian institutes consider to be an analyzable candidate and our own is immediately evident. They understandably formulate requirements in terms of their theory which includes the concept of id, while we focus on the viability of the real self-dynamism, on the strength of the urge toward self-realization, and on the availability of constructive forces. We look for people with problems who are aware of their suffering and want to do something about it and to help others similarly afflicted. While the issue of not too harsh a superego is important in Freudian criteria, the concern with authentic moral issues and the possibility of moral compassion is of interest to us.

At the A.I.P. each member of the admissions committee, of three, which rotated between the six members of the faculty council, evolved his own style of interviewing reflective of his personality, interests, and experience. Because the faculty personnel changed slowly over the years, we got to know our individual styles quite well. They tended to complement each other. Some did open-ended interviews, others conducted more systematic ones. Some might ask for more life history, others focus on a recent or recurrent dream, some were more motivated to investigate psychosexual development while others focused on how the applicant was dealing with his current life situation.

What often proved very valuable was to ask an applicant to describe a patient with whom he was working or to talk about the kind of patients he enjoyed working with, the kind he found most difficult, and the kind he positively disliked or was afraid of. Asking the prospective candidate how he responded to the previous members of the committee was usually very helpful. How he saw and responded to each of us was like an ongoing human Rorschach test. What was told to each one of us and the sequence in which it came out was most informative. Responses to how he felt about his interviews was particularly revealing. Did he feel he would be accepted? How would he respond if rejected? A picture of the kind of training analyst he would like to work with told us very much as did his preference in sex and age.

At times, as subsequent events showed, there was much that we hadn't picked up. On a few occasions we were seriously handicapped in our evaluation by withheld information and in others the seriousness of the pathology was so covered that none of us sensed it. In those cases a battery of tests might have been helpful. Once accepted, there was still a trial period of analysis to be evaluated and, if necessary, a further trial in therapy and in the training program.

In about half the instances mentioned above, training proceeded moderately well; in the other half the situation was most difficult. We all found it more or less painful to drop a candidate. The net result was that we lived with our mistakes throughout that candidate's course in training.

Such crieria as expressed in the Institute's and Program's philosophy of "living, while learning, while growing" imply a definition of education. Participating in being analyzed and trained, as aspects of daily living, involves sequences of bringing up, bringing out, and bringing into manifestation what is potential, probable, and possible. Included are the acquisition of information about, knowledge of, and possibly the beginnings of wisdom. *Information about* not acquired in the context of *knowledge of* is empty intellectualization. Learning, happening as a sequence of growth experiences, becomes integrated and embedded in that person's total personality. This means that "a successful analysis" is proceeding as sequences of growth experiences in candidates and training analyst are happening and as both are acquiring increasing wisdom in living and proficiency in their profession.

466

On one issue all institutes agree, that an analyst cannot help his patient beyond where he has progressed in his own development. The necessity for a deep and thorough personal analysis is essential. Criteria for how successful it has been are the capacity for and interest in continuing self-analysis and a recognition that he is learning and growing as his patients confront him with their problems. I have repeatedly stated that an analysis in which the analyst has not in some measure grown with his patient is an analysis that has fallen short of what it should have been.

The insistence on a training analysis began with the founding of the institutes in Berlin (1920) and in Vienna (1921). Personal analysis — *Lehranalyse* — was a vital part of the training program. Before 1923, the society approved the training analyst selected by the candidate. In 1923, in Berlin, Hanns Sachs became the first training analyst. Thereafter each society had a roster of approved training analysts from whom the candidate selected one. At times and in some places he was assigned a training analyst.

In 1929, "didactic analysis, over a regulated period by an officially recognized senior" became a prerequisite for admission to the New York Psychoanalytic Society. *(350)* In 1938 the American Psychoanalytic Association formulated "minimal standards for the Training of Physicians in Psychoanalysis," a second and third edition of which appeared in 1950 and 1956. In its 1956 ruling, "at least 300 hours of analysis, and usually more are required" for the training analysis. *(345, p. 456)*

In *Psychoanalytic Education in the United States,* Lewin and Ross discuss the difficulties in arriving at a figure for hours of training analysis because of "(1) hours of therapeutic analysis before admission; (2) hours of training analysis while a student; and (3) hours in analysis and after the official training analysis." They concluded they "could use 700 hours as the probable average . . . . The intuitive impression that training analyses were becoming longer appeared to be justified."*(345, pp. 172-77)*

They add that "The stated minimum plays little role at present among institutes' educational problems . . . . Other factors have seen to it that short analyses have not driven out long ones . . . . In some groups . . . well over half of the local society members have been thus 're-analyzed.' The periodic postgraduate analysis of the analyst which Jones refers to as a common practice, was recommended by Freud in 1937 . . . . The institute atmosphere rather than any formal rules, plays a part in establishing the desirability of longer analyses and second analyses."*(345, pp. 227-28)*

Other factors since 1960 have begun to shorten the length of

467

personal analyses. In the early years, a training analysis was referred to as a didactic analysis, *Lehranalyse,* although it was clearly felt that it had a therapeutic function. "Of the student's preparation for the acquisition of technical skill we believe today it should be based on a thorough personal analysis; and although we retain the name of training analysis, we are agreed that his experience must be a therapeutic one."*(324a)*

From 1941, when the American Institute for Psychoanalysis was formed, through 1958, there was no numerical requirement as to the number of hours of personal analysis or time limit for completing training. Up to that date all graduates had significantly exceeded that number.

In 1958 a six-year program was instituted with a minimum requirement of 750 hours of personal analysis. This was stimulated by the indefinite prolongation of training occasioned mainly by the requirement of a final thesis. That requirement was dropped and a time-limited, more structured program was instituted. This was a response to the increased institutionalization of psychoanalysis and the demands on the part of applicants to know beforehand what would be required of them.

In 1964 a five-year program was begun with the requirement of 600 hours of personal analysis, and in 1967 a four-year program started with the requirement of 500 hours of personal analysis. This is also the requirement in the Specialty Training Program in Psychoanalytic Medicine. Although the American stated a minimum of 300 hours of personal analysis was required, as have a number of institutes outside the American, in practice what has happened is that analyses finally exceed 700 hours and the years of training often extend to five, six, and more.

While in the beginning training analysis supervision and courses ran pretty much concurrently, with the institutionalizing of analytic training the tendency in Freudian institutes has been to require the completion of personal analysis before courses and supervision begin. I can see the wisdom of such an ideal structure. The candidate is more mature and free in himself, and can get much more from courses and supervision. It does, however, lengthen the time of his postgraduate training, and it has meant that he is often middle-aged when he completes his training. I have mentioned the recent mounting concern by analytic bodies over the predominance of older people.

I have stated our philosophy of living while learning while growing. In the earlier years our graduates also were in their mid-forties and older, but this was primarily owing to their beginning their training in later years. Here also our philosophy differed from American institutes. We accepted for training people close to fifty and, on a rare occasion, beyond. These were people who had done a lot of living and growing through their experiences and their suffering. We felt they had much to contribute, and this occurred in most instances. Gradually the age of graduation dropped to the middle thirties and at times even in the early thirties when training started as early as age twenty-seven or twenty-eight.

That the families suffered while the father, and on occasion the mother, were in training is well known, particularly in the years from 1945 to 1960. There was the draining expense, the time required for personal analysis, evening courses, and supervision. Besides these very real problems of young families with absent fathers, there was an atmosphere of living in limbo and postponement. There was something quite unnatural about the whole situation. In recent years, there is more of a tendency to begin courses and supervision earlier and to lessen the burden in other ways.

In the years before the founding of the Karen Horney Clinic in 1955, it was usually only after two or three years of analysis that the first supervision began. Three supervisions of fifty hours each was required. Since most candidates had full-time jobs, they did their analysis, courses, and supervision in the evening.

Soon after 1945, clinics were founded by most American institutes. Working with clinic patients became an integral part of the training of candidates, a practice begun in Berlin in 1920. In the years immediately after the war, when there was a shortage of therapists, many began their private practices as soon as they finished their psychiatric residencies, and some even started part-time practice before the end of their three-year appointments. In later years, as there was increasing difficulty in finding private patients who could come to three or more sessions weekly, more of the required supervisions were done with clinic patients. At the A.I.P. by 1965 candidates were treating patients soon after beginning their personal analysis. This meant they might ultimately have two hundred or more hours of supervision.

In the Specialty Program all candidates, referred to as Fellows, are required to work with clinic patients a minimum of ten sessions weekly. For these services they receive courses and supervision without fee, although they are personally responsible for their fees for personal analysis. The patients are supplied by the Center. The Fellow is required to give ten (patient) hours (forty-five-minute sessions) of services to receive one intensive supervision of a three-times-a-week patient, and one supervision on the remainder of his patients (seven sessions). A few Fellows elect to work twenty hours (fifteen clock hours) a week with clinic patients. In addition to courses and supervision, these candidates receive a stipend. They are required to have supervision of two three-times-a-week patients. This means that Fellows working in the clinic ten hours weekly receive 360 hours of supervision in four years, while those working twenty hours receive 540 hours. Supervisions run for forty-five sessions. The place of the therapy of patients and their supervision reaches almost as significant a position in a Fellow's training as that of the Fellow's personal analysis. This strong emphasis on supervision is somewhat unique in analytic training programs.

The philosophy of living while learning while growing gives to the whole training program an atmosphere of growth and process. Practically it lessens the financial burden because soon candidates are able to earn from their private practices. The time when they can expect to graduate is foreseeable. More time is made available to be with their families, although the pressures are still great. But it is the experience of a training program which is growth- and process-oriented that has the greatest impact. Rather than a feeling of suspension and postponement, an experience of ongoingness is felt in all aspects of the training.

As my yearly schedule began to be established at thirty-six to thirty-eight weeks yearly, in order not to unduly prolong their analyses, I offered candidates the opportunity of four sessions weekly. In time I saw almost all candidates working with me four times weekly.

One extremely circumstantial and elusive candidate I started with at three times weekly and went to five. This was not sufficient to work through his problems, and for over two years I saw him for double sessions five times weekly. Another became so anxious after analysis began that I went first to five times weekly and then to double sessions five times a week. Several, because of severe repercussions to the analysis, I saw four and five times a week for periods of weeks to months until the acute phase passed. Another wondered what it would be like to come daily. She was also motivated by the dynamic of the analysis, increasing anxiety, and a feeling of loneliness. I saw her five times weekly for five months. She, as did the others who came more than three times weekly, spontaneously commented on the difference between four and three, five and four sessions. There is no question that the experience of daily sessions is different from three times weekly. When at all possible, I prefer this arrangement.

At the beginning of training, most candidates in their private practice see the sickest patients once a week. As they gain experience and make progress in their analysis, they begin to have a wider range of patients and see more of them for two and three sessions weekly. However, a number complained that it was difficult to get "good" analytic patients to come privately at three times a week. This led to greater reliance on the Karen Horney Clinic for patients for required supervision.

470

Although there were differences among the candidates, those who had had the experience of four or more sessions weekly also began to have patients whom they saw four sessions weekly. They were reluctant to see patients once and twice a week, and spontaneously commented on how different it was to work with patients at least three and particularly four times a week. They often used the expression "This is real analysis."

Clearly the factors of imitation or identification with their analyst was there, but more fundamental was their own experience of the difference between three and more than three sessions weekly, both for the patient and the therapist. The tempo, rhythm, mood, and atmosphere are different. There is not the pressure of time. Things can evolve more naturally. Time is saved because pressure and constrictedness are absent leading to deeper and broader experiencing and observing. As a result, more is seen accurately and in detail. The feeling of "I'll see my analyst tomorrow, after today's session" is a very powerful support. Having had such experiences as a patient, the analyst can improvise from a broader base and take more chances than he can if he only sees patients infrequently over an extended period.

Just as the personal analysis is a crucial learning experience with regard to number of hours, so it is with regard to how the training analyst conveys his attitudes toward money and fees, practically and symbolically. These are ongoing problems for many candidates and also graduates. Also during his own analysis, the candidate learns how his analyst deals with missed sessions, lateness, and vacation schedules.

It is common for candidates to try to take mental notes for longer and shorter periods on how their analyst works with them and to apply it directly to their patients, often without discrimination. This kind of mental note taking in time drops away. The analysis they tried to make didactic gradually becomes more therapeutic. They unwittingly began to remember from experience how their analyst dealt with silences, compulsive talking, blockages, relationship material, and dreams.

In all analyses of candidates I have used the couch for an extended period. With a few I have done so from the very beginning. I feel this experience is essential for every candidate-in-training. He should have had some experience with the use of the classical model with himself as patient. He will then be experienced in its limited and more extended uses.

Because most candidates had the experience of the *vis-à-vis* position and the experience of moving in whatever variety of ways unique to them before they arrived on the couch in the recumbent position with me behind them, they had gone through the experience at their tempo and pace. They experienced what they concomitantly heard of in courses and supervision. Because they had an extended period of working on the couch, the movements to, on, and from the couch became familiar.

In the actual therapy of candidates I use all that I have described in this book; the technique of free association, analyzing dreams, the working through of blockages, and the analysis of the doctor-patient relationship. I work toward and hope for a more thorough analysis than I would expect with most patients. A crucial outcome is the experience of self-analysis and a capacity for growth through therapeutic experiences. Another outcome I hope for is a desire for further periods of personal analysis, further supervision, participation in teaching and training, attendance at scientific meetings, and a concern for the future of psychoanalysis in general. I believe this objective has been realized at least to a minimum with most all of the candidates I have analyzed. Some have made real contributions to their profession.

It is very difficult to keep training and organizational aspects separate. This problem has been recognized since the beginning of analysis and has created no end of problems, never satisfactorily resolved. There are the problems created by the training analyst being also a teacher of his candidate, a member of committees, and an officer of his organization. The personality of each training analyst has much to do with how he handles these problems within the context of his institute.

Just as there are problems during the training, so will there be with regard to interruption. How is one to conduct oneself with a candidate who will be a colleague, a co-worker, a co-contributor, and, from time to time, a student and a patient?

Hanns Sachs, the first training analyst in Berlin (1923), withdrew from all activities except training to separate himself from all other aspects of the institute, but he later involved himself again. Many others have had similar impulses. Two institutes outside the American rigorously held to the policy of excluding the training analyst from any aspect of his candidate evaluation during training and at graduation. He still was involved in general instruction and administration. He also had to say if his candidate had advanced sufficiently in his training analysis to be considered for graduation. Willy-nilly he had to consider his patient's future from an institutional and administrative viewpoint.

What was surprising was that although the candidates knew of this policy, they still didn't believe it. It is quite understandable that they did not. My experience, first as training analyst, then as Dean, evoked these responses. "I'm afraid to tell you because you are my training analyst and you'll tell the Faculty Council (the Educational

472

Committee) and I won't graduate." Substitute Dean for training analyst, add greater certainty to the candidate's voice, and the problem becomes greater. The fact is that the training analyst is a member of a training body selected and elected by an institute. This obtains everywhere. The candidate simply will not believe the training analyst will not communicate confidences until he no longer needs an authority on whom he must externalize his irrational attitudes toward authority. When and as these attitudes are worked through, the concern with analytic confidences preventing his graduation lessens.

That does not mean that the confidences of candidates-in-training do not play a part in the training analyst's evaluation. The policy of the A.I.P. has been for the faculty council to discuss the candidate's progress with the training analyst. The training analyst has the advantage of the help of a body of experienced training analysts. Such discussions occasionally led to the transfer of a candidate to another training analyst because the first was not happy with himself, his patient, and their work. Sometimes the faculty council decided a change should be made. The candidate had the opportunity of a second try. In more recent years, particularly regarding evaluations at graduation, the training analyst has become even more rigorous in giving only essentials.

This experience of pooling experiences by training analysts is done all too infrequently. When I have conducted such meetings they have proven most valuable. I refer to discussion of general problems in training not about specific candidates. Psychoanalysis is a lonely profession and all analysts unwittingly form all kinds of habits of which they are unaware. These meetings evoked responses of surprise that others had had similar problems. From such discussions came new methods of approach.

Chapter 30

Teaching Technique II:
Supervision and Teaching

A fter training analyses began, the analyst — who for a long time was Freud — also did the supervisions. When institutes began in Berlin and in Vienna and there were enough senior personnel, training and supervision were done by different analysts. There was the *Lehranalyse* or *Kontroll-Analyse* (Didactic Analysis) and the *Analysen-Kontrolle,* which was called control analysis for a long time. The term and the attitude it conveys often brought out sharp reactions and deep problems regarding supervision in some candidates. Later control analysis was called supervisory analysis or supervision. Obviously changing the term did not make the problem disappear. What did help was the accompanying shift toward an attitude of cooperative participation. In my supervisions I attempt to convey that the candidate is not being supervised but participating in a mutual discussion of therapeutic work.

Once established the separation of training and supervisory analysis was taken for granted as preferable. In 1953 Blitzten and Fleming said that problems of countertransference made it desirable that the supervisor and training analyst get together and discuss the candidate's difficulties. *(352)* They felt the candidate should be mature enough at that point to allow for such contact. Grotjahn went further and suggested the candidate join the conference. *(353)* The Los Angeles Institute reported that most colleagues found such arrangements helpful. Eckstein wondered whether these issues represent the replacement of individualized by institutionalized teaching which requires the collaboration of different teachers. *(324a)* Although analysts are not known to function well together in groups, younger teachers and candidates are finding such arrangements more congenial.

The early papers on supervision focused on the candidate's countertransference problems. There was much discussion of note-taking in sessions. In recent years, a similar issue — that of tape recordings — has come up.

I am not happy with the use of tape recorders. This attitude is doubtlessly influenced by an aversion to gadgets in general. On the part of the candidate, I feel, all too often tape recording is used as a substitute for hard work. They also put something between himself, his patient, and his supervisor. There is a consequent disruption of the natural flow of the supervisory sessions. The therapist asks a patient, who has difficulty refusing, how he feels about it. A third person who he never sees is introduced. The patient can then ask "And what did the supervisor say?" The patient begins to consider the supervisor his therapist and his actual one only an intermediary. This process is an all too frequent occurrence. The artificiality, distortions, and complications of tape recording outweigh the gains as I see it.

Problems in supervision are generally seen as an expression of countertransference and the candidate's need for more analysis; as a lack of didactic information which should have been imparted by the supervisor; or as a specific problem between the supervisor and the candidate. These problems do come up in supervision and the supervisor should know how to deal with them.

There is much that I find congenial in *Psychoanalytic Supervision* by Fleming and Benedek, particularly their emphasis on the "experiential nature of learning."*(258)* Although there are a number of places where I differ from their position, it is striking how comfortable I feel with their protocols of supervision despite our differences in theoretical orientation.

In addition to their emphasis on the experiential aspect of training, Fleming and Benedek see the supervisory situation as a process. They quote from Whyte's *The Unconscious Before Freud,* a book by one who has made valuable attempts to evolve a language of process. *(354)* They also refer to and make use of literature on system thinking. The model of supervision they suggest could very well be illuminated by Koestler's open-system hierarchical model of the *holon. (304)*

Their "attention became concentrated on the processes of inter-action between communicating systems in the teaching-learning relationship." They were "struck with the parallels between the analytic and supervisory situations . . . . What stood out in great clarity were the phenomena of process — that is, the sequential series of actions linked in a continuing pattern of shifting balance of tension moving toward goal directed change." They observed what facilitated and what disturbed "the balance of tensions" and that the factors producing both "made up the content of the communication between student and supervisor. The student's learning difficulties and mistakes with his patient were targets for corrective supervisory activity." I would add *corrective emotional experience.*

They stated they found useful the "concepts of structure, system interaction, and process" to convey the idea of movement and change toward long-term goals and to describe the "interactions betwen systems in communication with each other and of processes which alter dynamic equilibria."*(258, pp. 50-56)*

Fleming and Benedek see the psychoanalytic situation as an ex-periment in which "its conditions and procedures are relatively constant." Within this structure there is a triadic system composed of subsystems operating between analyst (A) and patient (P); between supervisor (S) and analyst (A). I would add a third subsystem, between supervisor (S) and patient (P); and a fourth subsystem between super-visor (S) and the candidate's training analyst (T).

They add the intrapsychic systems of the triad which for me would be a quartad. Also to be considered are the systems of the environments — immediate, intermediate, and remote — which im-pinge on each of the four participants mentioned. There are the per-sonal environments of each (A), (P), (S), and (T), and the functional ones, namely, the relations of (A), (S), and (T) to the respective insti-tutes, to the supraordinate organizations, to the psychoanalytic move-ment, and to the position of psychoanalysis in the current social context.

Paralleling the therapeutic alliance, Fleming and Benedek refer to a *"learning alliance,"* "Motivation for health or learning, trust in the mutuality of goals and confidence in the ability of the helper to help are the factors which patient and student bring to these respective relationships. When coupled with the motivations to help on the part of the analyst and supervisor, an alliance is established and a state of rapport is manifest in each situation." Intentionally and with ap-propriate timing the supervisor upsets the equilibrium of the dyadic system (S⇄A) which opens learning possibilities and encourages the candidate "to regard psychoanalysis as a process . . . the most important and probably the most difficult of the supervisory tasks" — a statement with which I agree. *(258, p. 53)*

Procedures and techniques are not process but "are integral to the movement of the process." Fleming and Benedek make use of two excellent terms, "system sensitivity" and "system responsiveness," which they have adopted from Lennard. *(355)* The former relates to the "quality of the analyst as 'instrument' which intuitively registers the quality of rapport in the therapeutic alliance and the intensity of resistance, source of anxiety, frustration tolerance, and level of regression in the intrapsychic system." "System responsiveness" concerns the analyst's task "to remain oriented to the therapeutic goal while he simultaneously takes into account the stresses in the system and responds appropriately." The analyst's "system responsiveness will enable him to regulate the timing and dosing of interpretations to facilitate the analytic process rather than to impede it."*(258, pp. 54-55)*

The supervisor "becomes a 'participant observer' in the treatment process as he influences the student's understanding, his attitude toward his patient and his technique of interpreting . . . . As his own scanning, hovering attention covers the interaction in the triadic S⇄A⇄P system, the supervisor becomes a resonating instrument on two levels."

Fleming and Benedict sharply confront the controversy concerning the "double role of the supervisor [therapist or teacher] as if the two roles were mutually exclusive . . . . The difficulty seems to us to be not so much in defining a difference in role as in being able to reconcile the factors that are common to the goals of therapy and education." The goals of both have much in common, since both experiences may deal with irrational neurotic obstructions to progress. "Close examination discloses that the same philosophy underlies both education and therapy — that is, the values of integrating impulse, affect, and intellect for the mature individual."*(258, pp. 56-57)*

Shifting from the role of therapist to that of teacher does require some reintegrations. The educative function is, however, a fundamental part of therapy, both on the simple informational level as well as in helping a patient to develop his capacity for reality testing, to learn to reason effectively, and to become involved with problem solving.

In these quotes and comments on *Psychoanalytic Supervision,* a valuable and provocative book, I have indicated how some Freudians have moved in holistic directions.

When the American Institute of Psychoanalysis was founded

(1941), the requirement was for three supervisions of fifty hours each to be done sequentially with three different supervisors none to be the candidate's training analyst. The first supervision was usually started after completion of the junior courses which were mostly theoretical and reading courses and after two to four years of personal analysis.

While Horney was alive practically everyone wanted to do their third supervision with her. If this could not be arranged, they often had Horney do a supervision after graduation. It was a unique experience, because she had a special talent for supervision and teaching.

Implicitly throughout all her works Horney was process and system oriented, with an emphasis on structure and function. This became most explicit in her phenomenology of the neurotic process and in the pride system. In the light of her emphasis on constructive forces, the real self, the real self dynamism comes close to being explicated as the real self process and system.

Communication of a feeling for process thus occurred at all levels of training. Since we were all influenced by her thinking each in his way communicated it, in training, supervising, teaching, at scientific meetings, and in publications — mostly in the *American Journal of Psychoanalysis*.

When the Karen Horney Clinic was founded candidates received supervision on their clinic patients. They usually started seeing clinic patients after a year or two of analysis. As the Clinic became more integrated with the Institute training program, treating of patients started earlier. In time, it began within three to six months of beginning training. Candidates would concomitantly start supervision. This meant they were having 200 hours or more of supervision. In 1960 Lewis and Ross reported that the national average for individual supervision of American institutes was 247. The proportion of hours in supervision to those in personal analysis was one to three.

The structure and function of the first supervision is quite different from the second and the second is quite different from the third. The years in personal analysis, the influence of courses, the concomitant effect of psychotherapeutic efforts in residency training, and the therapy of life all have their impact on the candidate-in-training and determine his attitude toward supervision. The earlier supervisions he will see as more didactic, and his attitude toward his supervisor will be more one of awe, anxiety, and distance.

My experience as a supervisor began in 1943 and concerns over 150 supervisions. As I did more final supervisions and supervisions of new training analysts with their first candidate, I began to have a feeling of restrictedness and discomfort when doing a first or second supervision.

Part of this feeling was owing to the didactic process itself. It was, however, increased by my administrative position as Dean of the A.I.P. Candidates had a picture of me which was often quite exaggerated and distorted and which at times they gave up most reluctantly. A sense of humor on their part generally led to considerable relaxation of the supervisory atmosphere with much learning and enjoyment for both. In short, I feel supervision can and should be fun.

For me, the supervisory experience reflects my attitude toward analysis in general. Our relationship and the relating process are crucial. My intent is to deepen and foster them as the first priority, to make them explicit to the candidate, to constantly palpate and test them toward deepening trust and confidence. Also crucial to this context is the nature, mood, and place of the institute in the total context of the psychoanalytic movement.

In 1943 I wrote a syllabus for a course on the psychoanalytic process which I expanded into a manual, *The Process in Psychoanalysis. (203)*

The supervision begins and continues with the development of the relating process in the context of process and system. The candidate follows the format of the process manual; the initial interview, the life history, the process of the analysis to date, the individual sessions, and, finally, the session which contains a dream. These are five vantage points for viewing, teaching, and experiencing process.

The number of sessions devoted to each of the above varies according to its value for deepening and widening the relating process. By the use of questions, the candidate is involved in giving information about his patient; the dynamics of his patient's problem; the plan of his therapy; the objectives he seeks; the blocks to their being realized; what he considers as interpretation (illuminator); insight (creative vision); and the doctor-patient relationship (the relating process). Many questions are directed toward his experiencing of himself as instrument in the therapeutic and the supervisory situation.

From my side, in addition to questions, I may indicate pertinent reading material, make brief comments on a variety of current topics, and encourage the candidate to ask questions. I continuously palpate the candidate's level of tension, his tolerance for anxiety and criticism, and his need for support and encouragement. What is named countertransference will be pointed out to him. Suggestions will be made as to what he might bring up in his analysis. Interpretations are made as they pertain to blocks between candidate and me, between him and his patient, and those of an intrapsychic nature which I feel he has not been bringing into his personal analysis. When timely, how he feels about supervision, what being supervised means to him, and what he feels he is getting from supervision are discussed.

What should obtain as we proceed in the supervision is that the candidate, as he reads his notes, returns unselfconsciously to his session with his patient. For this to happen there must be trust and confidence in the relationship with his supervisor so that he literally forgets he is being supervised. As he does so, and more of what he naturally is with his patient begins to emerge, with nuances of expression and feeling responses, many dimensions of communication are thereby added.

My evaluation of what the candidate gets out of the supervision is much determined by his ability to be with his patient right there before me so that I feel I am also there with his patient in the candidate's office. When this does not eventually happen, there are usually blocks in the supervisory process from one or both sides. The failure of the candidate's patient to come alive in the supervision is not always owing to an inadequate presentation, or an absence of feeling toward his patient. There is the real possibility that the presentation accurately portrays a patient who has much deadness, a frantic elusiveness, and a passion for anonymity.

Notetaking does create problems for the candidate, the patient, and the supervisor. If for example the candidate does not take notes from the outset and then begins to do so for supervisory purposes, his patient will notice it, begin to wonder, and, if he can, ask why. In such cases I generally suggest that we drop that patient for supervision and for the candidate to use another patient on whom he took notes from the start.

Out of such happenings a discussion of notetaking and the uses and abuses of notetaking can be timely and productive. Many candidates hide behind their notes. Some take few and others are compulsively perfectionistic. When I feel they are used as a barricade to keep me out, I have asked the candidate to put his notes aside and describe what went on as well as he can. Where I feel it is blocking the patient's therapy, I suggest that the candidate devote himself totally to the patient, and make a few notes after the session is over. Such suggestions often evoke considerable resistance and anxiety. The candidate feels naked and exposed. Out of such efforts have come much better therapy and learning.

As the circumstances arise, I discuss my own attitudes toward notetaking. With some patients I do so regularly, with others once in a while, and with some I have never written a note. This obtains whether patients are *vis-à-vis* or on the couch. The conduct and progress of the therapy hold priority. If notetaking interferes, it is dropped. This may happen because I see or sense the patient is experiencing me as giving him less of my attention. But notetaking also has its values. It helps to keep me in contact with a patient who is frantically elusive, or who needs to push me away or bore me to sleep. Referring to notes during a session may help me see patterns I did not previously identify. Reading notes immediately after a session can be most helpful. And finally there are the scientific purposes that notes serve.

Earlier I mentioned my lack of congeniality with tape recorders. I feel they interfere with the development of a productive and conductive flow in me, in the candidate, in the supervisory process, in the fullest use of both of us as instruments tuned in to the alive patient right there in the office in front of both of us. This does not deny the great value they and a one-way mirror can have for teaching purposes.

Generally at the midpoint of the supervision, the candidate and I have a mutual evaluation. All aspects of what goes into a supervision are reviewed — the candidate's feelings about his patient, his progress as a therapist, and his work with me as a supervisor. The candidate is also asked what he feels the supervision lacks, what he feels is being overemphasized, and what he would like to discuss further. Upon completion of the supervision, I write a graded report. Reports are discussed with the candidate although he does not get a copy.

It has been the practice of the Faculty Council of the A.I.P. to send a letter to the candidate after he has been officially informed of his graduation by the Board of Trustees. It contained a description of his course in training. The focus was on progress, process, and change as gleaned from his work in courses and supervisions. It also indicated where further change was needed and desirable. Suggestions for further personal analysis, supervision, and courses, were made. Attendance at scientific meetings, and involvement in the teaching, administrative, and organizational aspects of psychoanalysis was recommended. The letter also offered the graduate an opportunity to discuss the letter with his faculty advisor who was also a member of the Faculty Council.

The immediate response to these letters was often negative. At such times, when they contacted their faculty advisor, candidates often complained. Over the years graduates often informed us that their perspective on the letters had changed. The letters were reread over the years and many of the suggestions were implemented.

In retrospect candidates came to understand what went into their immediate negative response. No matter how far they had gone in the resolution of their problems, which were often intensified by the notions of a "completed analysis," "a successful analysis," and "a graduate analyst," the irrational image of what an analyst should be still remained. Their training was "over," yet they were being asked to work at themselves for the rest of their life. There were also residual authority problems. They experienced such letters as being pushed back into the role of schoolboys. Then there were the unworked through relationship problems and what remained of neurotic dependence/independence difficulties. In addition, there were of course the uniquely individual problems which were touched on by such letters.

The pain and difficulty experienced by candidates and supervisors alike were both individual and general. This is due to the dualistic structure of intellection, the fact that our language is noun-oriented, hypostatizes processes into a subject-predicate structure, and creates oppositional dualisms within this structure where process in fact obtains. We also tend to think in categories of isolates, of things, of point-for-point correlations, and of simple cause-and-effect relationships. All these are antithetical to process both in the abstract and in the concrete experience.

Teaching and experiencing the phenomenological approach has been of crucial importance for resolving some of these blocks. It has aided candidates to get a feeling for the interconnected patterns and their flow as process leading to emerging meaning. The focus on here-now experiencing has additionally contributed. These approaches, the use of questions, and looking at the analytic process from the five vantage points developed in *The Process in Psychoanalysis* have all been useful in experiencing system sensitivity and system responsiveness. Candidates also become sensitive to the ebb and flow of tension levels, of systems in equilibrium constituted of hierarchies of dominant and subordinate, autonomous, and integrated systems.

Freud's writings were the original curriculum. Programs of theoretical and clinical courses were developed with the advent of institutes. Freud and the pioneers were the first teachers. Criteria for the selection of teachers and programs for their training emerged very slowly.

I have found no better way of teaching teachers than by practice, drill, and experience with experienced teachers in a sequence of different courses. Depending on their experiences, sooner or later assistants are asked to take over one or more sessions and conduct them with the senior instructor as participant observer. What makes these experiences valuable is that at the end of the course there is a required evaluation of the course by the students and by the instructors, individually and together. In addition to the group evaluation, at the Postgraduate Center candidates also individually evaluate the course on a questionnaire as a part of a research project. During the course I also ask the students to spontaneously evaluate each other.

The following description of how I conduct an advance seminar is typical of instruction at the Postgraduate Center.

The seminar on analytic process may have from six to a maximum of twelve participants. Three of the members make presentations. The others submit a written case. They include their impressions, the dynamics, and interpretations, as well as the comments they made in the individual sessions with and without a dream. They also include the patient's dreaming history.

The course meets fifteen times. I select from the most experienced students the ones I feel will make the best presentations. I select the cases to be presented on the basis of their diversity and value for teaching purposes. Five sessions are given to each presentation. I only hear a little about each case, sufficient to get a general picture. To the class I ask the presentor to read a presentation of about 1500 words for four of the sessions, and one of about 2000 words to cover the analytic process to date. The presentor is urged to include only data and impressions, but no interpretations. The class has no prior knowledge of the patient. This gives the presentation the freshness of being there with the patient as the material is being communicated.

Before each class, for the first five sessions, I give a thirty minute lecture on relevant topics. Each session lasts about one hundred minutes. The last seventy minutes of the first five are devoted to presentation and discussion. For the last ten meetings, the whole time is available for presentation and discussion. The lectures contain much that candidates have heard in other courses, but they receive it and respond to it because of its immediate relevance to the evening to follow.

Many aspects regarding process are included in the first lecture, but I particularly emphasize the analyst's tendency not to listen to their first impressions and feeling responses which so often turn out to be so accurate.

The second lecture is on the dialectic of the genetics of the life history. In it I indicate how the character structure develops and give instances of shifting neurotic solutions during various age periods. I also include discussions of the variety of cultures there are in the United States, so many of which are present in New York. I show the changes in cultural patterns and value systems in first, second, and third generation immigrants and point out that these considerations also hold for people who move within different parts of the United States. I indicate the uniqueness of idioms and other forms of communication in different parts of the United States.

This is also an opportunity to review medical history. It is striking how often candidates forget that they are doctors and miss some very obvious medical conditions. They describe them but do not take the next step and diagnose them. During this lecture I also often say, "You are clinical dynamic psychiatrists. How would you diagnose what the patient is showing?" It is as if suddenly they forgot all their psychiatric background and, as with the medical conditions, they are startled at what has happened to them. They are suffering from the common affliction of analytic candidates, "mania psychoanalytica," from which hopefully they will recover in the main, though regrettably a number do not. Then sometimes I say, "You are an untrained person, a simple human being. How would you respond to what is happening with this patient?" This reminds them of their simple humanity.

The third lecture on the analytic process is an opportunity to introduce candidates to the functions and uses of theories and to review in outline Horney's work. The methodological implications of theory and its organizing function is usually quite new to most. I indicate to them the many levels on which several years of analytic work can be organized and communicated so that the listener familiar with the theory can have a feeling picture of how the analysis began and proceeded.

The fourth lecture conveys some essentials about individual sessions. There are the openings and closings as well as the themes of content, relationship, and feeling. The microanalysis of an individual session is compared with the macroanalysis of the analytic process to date. The little sweeps or nuances are compared with the big sweeps of the total analytic process. All that was presented in the third lecture is applied in finer detail to the individual session.

The lecture on dreams — the fifth and last — is mostly devoted to the phenomenological approach. It evokes the most intense response of being illuminated. No matter how I impress students with the fact that they have used the same approach as physicians and were taught it in medical school as the natural history approach, it comes to them as something startlingly new. Every candidate I have known has gone through the phase of *mania psychoanalytica,* an aspect of which is *mania psychodynamica.* They become obsessed with the question, "What does it mean?" and have lost sight of the question, "What is it?"

In addition to the three presentations and the papers from the other participants during the fifteen session course, the students may be asked to write six to eight one-page, 350 word answers to a specific question. The shortness of the assigned papers undercuts the candidates' tendency to build it up into a big project and so block themselves. Because it must be handed in the next week they can't get involved in procrastinating or become obsessive about it. It must be done on the weekend between classes. There are always a few who do it the last minute, the night before the class. Sometimes I make general comments about all of the papers after the first assignment. More often I wait until two or three have been handed in. Then I can talk about the spectrum of responses and the evolving patterns I have observed. This is to help undermine egocentric responsiveness and to teach objective evaluating.

The questions are open-ended which evokes considerable anxiety and, at times, violent attempts at closure. The question is almost always one sentence, given orally. There are always one or two who change the question into a static closed question as they are writing it down. Reading these variations — without identifying the authors — can be a valuable learning experience for all.

Some typical questions are: "What were your responses to the last session?" "What were you experiencing in the last session?" "What is your feel of the patient being presented?" "How did you experience Doctor A. in the last session?" "How do you feel Doctor A. experienced his patient?" "What have you learned in this course thus far?" "What has been your experiencing of the instructors?" "Devote one paragraph to your experiencing of each of the participants."

Following each lecture, questions pertinent to that lecture are asked. The questions include: "What have you learned from my comments?" "What's familiar in what I said?" "What's new in my lecture?" "What value do these lectures have for you?" "Have they stimulated you to read on the subjects discussed?" As the course proceeds, there is an anticipation and acceptance of these questions and students write their answers more spontaneously each time.

Understandably, why questions are rarely asked. The focus on feelings indicated throughout this book is stressed during the seminar. The attempt is to help candidates become aware of their blockages to being open to their feelings in immediacy. In a variety of ways I attempt to help them experience immediacy of feeling. By asking, "What are you feeling in response to X?" I can demonstrate that their responses tell me not what they *immediately* felt but what they are feeling *for*, feeling *with*, feeling *against*, and feeling *about* which are all different categories of feeling responses each successively further away from the candidate's center and his immediacy.

The three presentors read prepared material. The assistant lecturer and I are given copies. The reading is frequently interrupted by questions relevant to the material. What immediately becomes obvious are the silences and pauses before anyone says anything. After it has happened a number of times, I ask if it has been noticed. What do they feel accounts for it? What do they feel goes on in those that don't speak and those who are the first ones to speak?

Later in the course, by implicit questions I bring out who holds back most and longest, who is first and overtalkative, who speaks briefly and to the point, and who speaks all around it. In time it begins to break through into awareness how much blocking is going on, how difficult it is to initiate, and how threatening the open-ended position is, how much anxiety it evokes, and how plentiful are the many forms of defending against it. By questions the participants are helped to become aware of their somatic expressions of anxiety. It is one more method of helping them to know themselves as instruments.

Naturally the conduct of the sessions reflects a system or process sensitivity and responsiveness to the tolerance of the group and the individuals in it. Tension and anxiety steadily builds as the class proceeds. As the material lends itself, to lessen excessive tension, to inform, and to bring out responses, I make comments on a variety of topics. Included is an attempt to show how no theory has all the answers, that a theory is a tool, and that one tool cannot serve all purposes. Horney's theory is emphasized, but other theories — Freudian, Jungian, Adlerian, Existential, and Oriental — are shown to bring light and sometimes more of it on certain issues. Such discussions are sometimes formulated as disloyalty to Horney, but the deeper issue is that students feel threatened by being asked to be open to a spectrum of views.

Blocks to openness are constantly being confronted. This continuing activity is prerequisite to feeling and experiencing which is basic to learning. In this way, the participants learn about rationalizing, denying, evading, intellectualizing, externalizing, alienating, and all the mechanisms for blocking out feelings and denying to themselves the fuller use of their persons as instruments. I occasionally begin a class with a simple "yes," said in a questioning tone, with my palms out, eyes closed, and an expression of questioning on my face. The variety of ways of asking a question in open-ended ways is thus demonstrated. It also asks for increasing responding and greater intensities of initiative.

All that I have described aims at helping each participant gain information about process, acquire knowledge of it, and have immediate experience of it in the presence of others who are having similar experiences while struggling against it. This is a continuing human experiment in group teaching and learning. This form of teaching is premised on the following assumptions about groups.

I see groups as constituted of individuals continuous and contiguous with each other. Participant in group teaching and learning are confronting, experiencing, and practicing toward the acquiring of information about and involvement with knowledge. I see meaning as emerging in the group from the individuals in it, each according to his nature and according to his pace. I see this meaning emerging out of their experiencing of the interconnectedness of ongoing patternings which are forming, disforming, and reforming. In these patterns, physical and psychological, individual and group hierarchies of systems participate. Out of this experience, system sensitivity, system responsiveness, process awareness, and a truly holistic orientation evolves.

There is a pattern in the evolving group dynamics. It is dependent on the size, the experience and the competence of the group. The evolving pattern is also dependent on the instructor, on the assistant, and on the era in which the course is given, namely, as the social context influences the institute and its functions.

In general what happens is that tension begins to mount, with anxiety manifestations. They are defended against by blocking, withdrawal, denial, and externalizing. All these do not suffice, and irritability begins to come to the fore. The various mechanisms for avoidance are confronted by the instructor which leads to higher levels of tension and anxiety. The first outbursts of irritability are usually against the patient being presented, then at one another, next at the presenter, and finally at me. As this is evolving, coalitions and alliances occur, break up, and re-form. Finally the group unifies around a mounting irritability which breaks through as intense outbursts of hostility toward me. Each time the outburst or irritability has been intense there have been fright responses at this open demonstration of hostility which all were attempting to hold in check, some more successfully than others.

After an intense outburst at me there is a feeling of surprise, relaxation, and well-being in the group, as well as an increased openness toward each other and toward me. They all comment on it with pleasure and often say, "This is the best learning experience that I have ever participated in."

The violent outbreak may occur as early as the seventh or eighth session or as late as the thirteenth or fourteenth. Sometimes there may be several minor outbreaks which may go in any direction and never become fully mobilized around me. This happens because the group never develops cohesiveness and solidarity.

In one instance the presenter of the first case blocked out what was required of him and came to the first session completely unprepared. He defended himself with the most naive rationalizations. I became openly quite angry. The group as a body immediately attacked me, saying, "You had no right to be angry." They could not and would not look at what one of their colleagues had done. It was a tempestuous first session which released and resolved many tensions.

One crucial reason for the high tension level of the process seminar is that the participants are close to the end of their training. Each candidate has an image of what a certified analyst who has "completed" his training should be. This image contains, however, many residual irrational elements. In the course this image is called into question from many sides and with great rapidity. Integrating the many threats and bruises to their pride can be quite difficult even with the concomitant help of their personal analysis, supervision, and participation in other courses. Fifteen weeks does not give them enough time to do so. The result is that the tensions build faster than they can be resolved.

There are other reasons for the rapid tension building and the intensity of outbursts in the process course. A high level of participation inwardly and outwardly directed is required of the participants cognitively, conatively, experientially, and somatically. A very high energy output at a very high speed is expected. What also contributes to the high tension level is the use of implicit open-ended questions and constant confronting, implicitly and explicitly, which leads to conflict and paradox formation. While this is going on, the participants are being asked to respond directly and immediately. They are asked not only to contact and describe their experiencing, but also to formulate their feelings descriptively, to conceptualize them, and to describe what is going on from a theoretical and technical viewpoint.

This form of teaching can be used only because the group is a highly selected one. The participants are men and women of mature years, who have had years of experience in medicine and in psychiatry. They can be assumed to have a high level of ego strength or real selfness, and enough self-confidence and flexibility to integrate the experience and resolve the anxieties and tensions which are, in part, purposely engendered.

The course is conducted as it is because I am aware that in their analysis certain problems have been touched on only in a limited way. Because the participants in the process will soon be completing their formal training, there is a responsibility to sensitize them to new problems and old ones. The group situation has potentialities for doing this in ways which the one-to-one personal analysis cannot.

Finally, having had a long experience in doing supervision and in treating people who have had a number of prior therapists, I have observed that supervisors and analysts often have a limited tolerance for anxiety and hostility. Not a few patients have told me that their former therapists could not take their hostility and discharged them. They gave the patients messages informing them that they could not take their hostility. Because the patients had to restrain it, the situation became intolerable.

Many borderline, compensated, and openly psychotic patients can be treated in the office situation. All have high levels of anxiety and hostility, particularly the psychotic ones, and of their hostilities they are particularly terrified. If a therapist can be open to and live with such intensities, he can be effective with such patients and they know it. Such patients also know when the therapist cannot live with their hostilities. There was the woman who said, "I couldn't work with the man you sent me to. He was too anxious. I have enough trouble dealing with my own without having to worry about his." Her therapist later told me that he was indeed frightened of her.

In the process course the participants have an opportunity to feel intense anxieties and hostilities, to see them expressed and acted out directly toward a therapist. They have it concretely demonstrated to them that he did not go to pieces, but became stronger, that the therapist could accept it, deal with it, and continue to be supportive of them.

The final objective of the course is hopefully to stimulate greater enthusiasm for reading, particularly about the issues dramatized and discussed in the course.

Despite the demanding nature of the course, the fact that some elect to repeat it suggests that they feel they have benefited from the course and from this way of teaching. In my estimate, those who have repeated the course have often become excellent teachers. That they use so many of the techniques learned there is perhaps an indication of the value of such a teaching and learning experience.

The continuous case seminar on the relating process is conducted in a similar way to the process course except that only one person presents for the entire fifteen sessions. He is carefully selected, as is the case. He must be able to take the criticism of his colleagues for the whole course. He must also be able to communicate both what he did and felt with relation to himself and his patient and what he is feeling toward the group and instructors as the course proceeds.

The case is presented with the focus constantly on the relating process. Thirty-minute lectures are given before the first five sessions with the emphasis on relating. Step by step, dimensions of relating patternings and systems of relating are identified and introduced. Out of such emphases, the connectedness of systems is brought into awareness This awareness leads to experiencing movement and change in all systems, in process, in the dimensions of time and space, in the structure of the analytic situation, and in the patient's life as a whole.

The one-page answers to the one-sentence questions to be handed in the following session move in a sequence similar to that in the process course. At first the questions are general such as, "What are you feeling?" "What are you experiencing?" and "What are your responses to this?" Gradually the questions become more focused on relating and on relating to a specific person or aspect.

"What is your experiencing of the patient's relating to his father (mother, sister, brother, wife, children, boss, neighbor)?" "What is your experiencing of the patient's relating to Dr. A.?" "What is your experiencing of your relating to the patient (to Dr. A., to one another, to me, to the co-instructor)?" "What is your experiencing of the relating process in this session?" "What is your experiencing of the patient's relating to his dreams (to the people in his dreams, to Dr. A. as he related the dream)?"

The group dynamics and tension building evolve in a way similar to what obtains in the process course, however, with some crucial differences. Because the focus on the relating process is constantly in the foreground, and on the participants' feelings pertaining to relating, the tensions build up more slowly and less intensely because they are constantly being drained off. As a result the criticisms and attacks on me are less frequent, less intense, and only rarely occur in the form of a violent outburst.

Another reason that the levels of tension, anxiety, and irritability never get high is that the course is focused on one topic, one patient, and one person who is presenting. On the one hand, having to remain open to their relating feelings and bringing them out is demanding. On the other hand, the opportunities offered for resolution of tension, and the number of times they are confronted with having to do so drains off the tensions before they become intense. Also the ways they use to defend themselves against their awareness of these tensions and their expressions of them are more rapidly exposed. The greater demands of the process course are not there, namely, to respond quickly and well to three different patients, to three different presentors, to the five shifts of focus for the three cases, and to the many different topics brought up for discussion.

In the light of what has been described about teaching and learning in training, supervisory analysis, and courses, I feel that psychoanalytic education needs to be and can be integrative. This means that the here-now experiencing process can be taught and learned via a spectrum of different structures and methods.

In the chapter "Psychoanalytic Education: Syncretism," Lewin and Ross define the current scientific meaning of syncretism as "the *use* of conflicting and irreconcilable assumptions."

Lewin and Ross assert that "psychoanalytic education, as a concept is a syncretism . . . . The two models 'psychoanalytic patient' and 'student' complement, alternate with, and oppose each other." The training analyst's dilemma most sharply focuses the issue because he must be "analyst and judge"*(345, p. 48)* unless he gives up being a supervisor, a teacher, and administrator and gives no information of any kind by request or requirement of the institute or at the suggestion of the student. *(356)*

Lewin and Ross report "several very experienced training analysts" stating that "under institute auspices," training analysis "is generally limited and that many persons cannot be 'really' analyzed until they have graduated." This may be a response to the increasing institutionalization of training, the focus on the number of hours in training and supervision, and the emphasis on rules, regulations, and procedures. Other training analysts report "great resistance all along the way" in the undergraduate situation but "believe they have been successful in individual cases."*(345, p. 231)*

Add to these problems the appearance of increasing numbers of graduates who are unanalyzable, and of analyzed normal characters who are incapable of being scientific but can be therapists. The result is a picture of sterilization and mechanization which either reflects the unrealizability of a brilliant idea, psychoanalysis, or indicates that radical changes are necessary. *(358, 359, 347)* The fact is that some are finding ways of solving the problem. A careful study of Fleming and Benedict shows that they are adopting a process and experientially oriented form of teaching and training and that it is working. *(258)*

Chapter 31

The General Practice
of Psychoanalysis I:
The Chronic Analyst

Working for extended periods with a variety of patients — particularly with those of advancing years — requires of the analyst special attitudes toward past, present, and future time. Will the finiteness of linear abstract time narrow his view? Will the possibilities opened up in experiencing multidimensional concrete time light his way? Will he arrive at that integrated perspective of both which is an aspect of creative vision? His own years will also influence his responses to age, aging, growing, maturing, dying, and death. His experience of time, his years in practice, his own age, and other factors determine his qualifications for becoming a "Chronic Analyst" who is concerned with continuously confronting challenges presented by the manifold aspects of psychoanalysis. *(278)*

Many long term therapy patients manifest what Little defined as a "transference psychosis." They "develop a sort of addiction to analysis" which "leads to a ruthless repetitive searching for something, at any cost to either patient or analyst." Little adds, "But this very quality sometimes makes an unpromising looking analysis successful

492

in the long run, if only that 'something' can be recognized and got, at least in token measure. The gap between the need and what is got has to be fully acknowledged by the analyst."*(360)* It is my conviction that the "chronic analyst" has what is required for helping the patient to recognize and get that something.

That Solomon W. was ruthlessly searching there was no question. He saw his first analyst at sixteen and at least twenty-five more since. He saw twelve analysts for more than three months, one for nine months during a voluntary hospitalization when he was forty-three, and five for at least two years. He is now fifty-four. The analytic span is thirty-eight years, the duration about fifteen, and the calculated years in analysis about ten. *(p. 419)* He has been with me almost three years, the longest he has worked with any analyst.

One could say that Solomon has "a sort of addiction to analysis" and to analysts, that as yet the outlook does not look "promising" although there are glimmerings that the gap between what he needs and what he should get is beginning to be narrowed.

Solomon was absolutely convinced no one had helped him, that no one had understood him or "they wouldn't have said such stupid things," that he had no other choice but to continue because "What else was there but to commit suicide?" He felt that time was running out because of his number of analysts, his years in analysis, and his advancing years. His desperation was increased by the image he had of me. Solomon had been told, in essence, "If he can't help you, nobody can." As the therapeutic test will show, he experienced me as his last chance. This attitude contributed to the depth and courage of his despair and to the tenacity with which he clung to analysis. Despite negative aspects, this attitude made for a measure of positive motivation which I counted on. It also heightened the challenge and at the same time, in an odd way, gave me the feeling that time was on my side if I had the patience, tenacity, and acumen to effectively use it.

I saw Solomon twice a week for the first fifteen months. Then he began to express doubts about the value of continuing to see me, and decided to come only once a week. He then began provocatively to prod me about possibilities other than psychoanalysis, saying it had certainly not helped him thus far. I suggested hypnosis. He said he had tried it and could not be hypnotized. He added that when he was hospitalized in 1948 narcosynthesis had been tried on a number of occasions and had also failed. He didn't talk. I then raised the possibility of group therapy. "Are you crazy? I can't even talk to one person. I'd be terrified. I've gone to those advertised parties and I stay in the corner and don't talk to anybody." These discussions extended over several months.

To confront him with his motivation in seeking other possibilities, I raised the question of L.S.D. He became cautious and wary and asked many questions indicating he knew a lot about it. I gave him the details. What upset him most was that there might be a psychotic episode and "I might have to go to a hospital. What about my mother? What about my job?" After talking about it for several more weeks he dropped the subject. That summer, the second, he asked for the name of someone he could see in my absence and did so on three occasions.

When he began seeing me his foreground problem was his inability to talk openly. He had been discharged by a number of analysts because of it and was bitter about it. "That's my problem. I'm sick. If I could talk I wouldn't be going to see them." Another problem that led to his dismissal by other analysts was his hostility. Even silent, Solomon bristled with hostility. He was constantly disparaging analysts in general. "But what can I do? I'm sick. I need help." When he began to talk, he reported several other analysts discharging him because "they said I was an empty can and they couldn't do anything with me."

What was immediately evident the first time I saw Solomon was that he was massively and brutally anxious, a fact I determinedly kept in the foreground of my awareness. As a result of his anxiety the odor of his perspiration, which varies between neurotics and psychotics, was an important guide to me. When the odor was very strong and had a stale metallic smell to it, I could be certain he was practically rigid with anxiety.

Solomon used four to six packs of cigarettes a day, smoking hardly a third of each cigarette. His throat was sore, his cough was intense. He also ate compulsively. He regularly consumed a quart of ice cream and a whole cake after dinner. He made rare attempts to join classes but he soon dropped them.

I sat with him through long silences, asking a question or making a comment perhaps two or three times in a session. They were often about his eighty-five-year-old mother, her health, or his job. An only child, his father had died twenty years earlier. Very cautiously and rarely I asked what he did with his evenings and weekends.

My intent was to continue to be there for him and with

him and to help him say something once in a while. He at least had someone to come to regularly and to talk to if he could.

After a year and a half, he became more and more openly hostile and talked much more, repeating frequently that some of the analysts had said they couldn't take his hostility. I felt he had made quite some progress when he began to question me about other forms of therapy. It was important for him to feel he could reject me and that he was doing so, not I. His hostile commenting went on up to the second summer interruption. After the last session, it dawned on him that I would be gone. He called me for someone to see after a year and a half of disparaging everyone associated with me. He saw my colleague three times and never made a negative comment about him. In fact he spontaneously mentioned, without being critical, several things he had said.

That fall he began to talk more and longer. Also he began to write me letters. Letter writing was an old pattern which I later learned about. In several letters he complained about seeing me only once weekly, implying that I had taken away his second session, although he never asked for it back. I never raised the question because I felt he was not ready for it. He would only vindictively reject it and then be terrified. By the end of the second year he occasionally talked steadily for a whole session and finally brought up the subject of sex about which he was terrified. Off and on in the prior six months he had mentioned his masturbation and the one occasion on which he had a call girl come to his home. His main source of information was gained from underground newspapers. He kept talking about David Reuben's *Everything You Always Wanted to Know About Sex,* but it was four months before he dared to go into a store and buy it. *(361)* Then he could only read a few pages at a time, it was so upsetting to him. He kept talking about how ignorant he was, and how the matter-of-fact style of the book seemed to assume that everyone was familiar with all aspects of sex. This tone further impressed him with his own naiveté and ignorance.

By the third summer interruption, he had talked for the whole session many times. I inferred from what he said that he realized and appreciated that I had not been disturbed by his silences or his hostilities. At one point he openly asked, which took great courage for him, "Why do you allow me to come?" Not long after he pointed to a new green shirt he was wearing and indicated it was the color of my carpet, of my walls, and of the plants I have in my living room. This for him was the ultimate of trust and confidence as was his telling me about his rages at his mother, that at times culminated in his striking her for which he felt horribly guilty. At one point he bitterly said, "It's the old story of an old mother and an only son." Just before we interrupted for the summer, he wrote a letter in which he got very close to asking for two or three sessions because one wasn't enough. "1x week — insufficient? 2-3x week?" Shortly after his anxiety and hostility fell away. He showed and expressed feelings of depression and sadness at his life situation and hopelessness about his future. This was the most trust and the deepest feeling he had shown and voiced. His sadness also covered feelings of being deserted, abandoned, and rejected. From what he has told me he has remained with me longer than with any therapist and shown me greatest confidence and trust. He did not ask for someone to see while I was away because I believed he would return to see my colleague, something he had never done before.

By occasional side remarks Solomon showed himself to be very perceptive about himself. He is a college graduate, but his knowledge consists of bits and pieces. He can't stay with a task, a course, a book, or a relationship.

When I saw Solomon in the waiting room after the summer holidays, I sense a significant relaxation in him. He looked up at me from the waiting room divan with a look of affection. He is about five feet three inches tall, small-boned, and looks like a little boy. I moved toward him and offered my hand, something I had not done before because I felt it would be too shattering. He looked surprised and pleased, and sort of tentatively offered his hand without a responsive grip.

He immediately started talking and did so steadily for that session. He soon commented that I had never offered my hand before and perceptively conjectured about it, giving a number of possibilities, one of them being, "I suppose you did it because you felt I was ready for it." Solomon conveyed a vague implication that he appreciated it, particularly because it meant he was better. Although still quite anxious, he was much less so. Hostility, biting bitterness, and criticism were almost absent.

Solomon launched into a report of the summer. In early August at a vacation spot, he had met a divorced woman who had been helped out of a depression through analysis. She made the moves toward him, very cautiously and supportively, with the result that within a month they had gone to bed several times. He was able to tell me that she inserted his penis in her vagina and that he was not too upset that he could not get a full erection. She talked much more and helped him to open up a bit.

496

"But you know how wary and suspicious I am." He is also extremely stingy and always fears he is being taken. He cheats constantly, and withholds payment of debts if at all possible. This has gotten him into a number of lawsuits. Knowing of this propensity which had destroyed his relationship with several therapists I firmly laid down the basis of his payment. He tried to deviate a number of times. At first he was very hostile about it. Subsequently I sensed his relief at not being able to push me around.

In the next month he continued to talk about his relation with the woman he had met on vacation. He asked me if it was safe to take marijuana because he read in David Reuben's book that it was an aphrodisiac. "I know L.S.D. is not for me." I told him that if he wanted to try marijuana which his girl friend had, to do so on a weekend and have someone with him when he did. He was appreciative of my having hedged it with so many safeguards.

In this month he steadily relaxed, was increasingly open and told me things about his daily and past life he never had before. With quite some poignancy he also talked about his failures and his yearnings and how he wished he had been able to marry, have children, and a home of his own. He also talked with more sadness and shame about how he had mistreated his aged mother.

Because of his stinginess, his failure to initiate evening and weekend entertainment, his suspiciousness, and his noncommunicativeness, his girl friend began to pull away, ending the relationship about ten weeks after it began. I sensed he couldn't be sure if he was glad or sorry it ended because of "her empty frigidaire" and "aging, fat body." The fantasy of finding a young beautiful girl who will love him and ask him to marry her still has a powerful hold on him even though he repeats, "I know it will never happen."

Solomon has become less resentful about caring for his aging mother, now even feebler and almost blind. He arranged for a companion to be with her during her annual southern stay. The previous summer he arranged for the first time a stay in a country place and on her return in a rest home when recovering from an illness.

Following these months of steady progress, for a month, Solomon reverted to sessions of silence, hostility, and bitterness about the "failure of analysis as a method. Maybe it's not for me." This was followed by increasing volubility mixed with threats to quit analysis.

I knew that most who had seen Solomon W. felt he was a compensated schizophrenic. Only in schizophrenia have I experienced such brutal and massive anxiety which literally fills the room with the stale metallic odor of intense sweating. Only at times and then not too definitely did I have the "schizophrenia" experience, the *"praecox-gefühl"* which Rümke regarded as "the most pathognomonic sign." *(362)*

In the light of what has happened in the course of therapy, is Solomon still a compensated schizophrenic? Wasn't he one to start with, or did therapy and the natural history of his disease effect a change? Is a schizophrenic helped by therapy no longer a schizophrenic, or is he only hopefully a "cured" schizophrenic?

I feel such questions arise because analysts cannot accept the fact that before the test of therapy and/or the natural history of an illness has gone its course there can be no certain diagnosis. Rümke perceptively touches on these issues in his "Contradictions in the Concepts of Schizophrenia."*(362)* In it he discusses twelve pairs of contradictory theories and concludes that the contradictions are more apparent than real and that many of the concepts are accurate but apply only to an aspect of a highly complex problem.

My feeling is that without therapy Solomon W. could have become a deteriorating or a functioning burnt-out schizophrenic. I feel therapy has positively influenced some aspects of his illness process and at least slowed his movement toward greater illness. It may even have promoted some healing and restitution. If he stays in therapy I feel his anxieties and hostilities will considerably abate and he will be able to integrate the imminent death of his mother without a serious break. Without continued therapy this event will more likely accelerate Solomon's illness process.

The time in which he lives, his era's attitude toward time, toward age and youth, toward getting older and being younger all influence how a patient sees his past, present, and future.

I have worked with many males who were sure they would be dead by age thirty-three. In their neurotic structure there was much of Christly saintliness and martyrdom. Still alive after thirty-three, they often went through depressions of varying intensities. The false meaning they had given to their lives was gone. "Now what?" they had to ask themselves.

"I'm getting older" or "I'm not getting any younger" expresses the impact of time on people in their forties. I have yet to work with a patient who did not have a very strong and special feeling about his fiftieth birthday. "Half my life is over" is one expression of it and "From here on out it's downhill" is another. The reality of "I'm fifty" and "I don't have all the time in the world" can have powerful repercussions and provide strong motivation, as can the despair it may engender.

Patients reaching sixty in the course of analysis have the support of a relationship and of a dynamic process to rely on. Some past sixty coming for therapy after earlier analytic experiences, even when they felt they hadn't been helped, find they have a familiarity with the process which is supportive. Older patients coming to analysis for the first time occasionally do so with the feeling of "There is time." When they come in a crisis situation, another kind of approach is required.

I saw a married man of sixty-three twelve times over seven months. It was his first analytic experience. His guilt feelings covered intense death fears and a deep depression. These symptoms erupted as he contemplated ending a twenty-three year affair with a single girl twenty years his junior. By the last visit he was able to tell the girl he never had intended to leave his wife on whom he was helplessly dependent and, I gathered, the girl could admit she never really expected him to marry her.

He had come in guilt and panic, and as he began to feel more comfortable his urge to continue began to diminish. Following a southern vacation, he called to say he was not returning to therapy.

I saw Sophia Z., age sixty-four, on four separate occasions over a four-year period: four times during a six-week period; six times in six weeks ten months later; nine times in ten weeks twenty-two months later; and once seven months later. She had an acute agitated depression with moderate paranoid ideation, both mildly present for years. She had never seen anyone for therapy before. Needing to be used and abused by her husband, son, and daughter, she was almost suddenly confronted with the fact that they didn't need her in these ways anymore. Feeling cast aside, useless, and bereft, she realized that her artistic abilities and interests, and her joys in travelling were not enough to fill her life.

At the end of the first six-week period she was somewhat less anxious and less paranoid. When Sophia returned ten months later, she dropped in as though she hadn't left and did not explain her interruption or her return. This time she was not as anxious or as paranoid as she had been initially, and she was quieter and less suspicious after these four visits.

When Sophia returned twenty-two months later, she was even less anxious and suspicious. In between she had nursed a favorite brother when he was sick, and buried him when he died — a problem that has to be dealt with as people get older. She had dropped by in the same casual way, but by now there was a relationship of quite some depth and trust. She had now accepted getting older and being old which she realized she had been fighting. In a more active way she was trying to make meaning out of her life outside of her family and within it with different attitudes.

After a few sessions, quite unexpectedly I found we were doing some solid analytic work. It was giving her quite a lift. She understood herself better in her relation to her husband and as a result was less dependent on him. She had even moved over to being the dominant one in the partnership after almost forty submissive years of marriage.

Seven months later Sophia called. "Doctor Kelman, I want to talk to you. I have some decisions to make." Her dominant position in the marriage had become more evident. Faced with retirement and having to relinquish a position in which he had functioned as an adored potentate, her husband was beginning to more openly lean on her.

She wanted to discuss a boat trip and holiday in Europe. On previous occasions she had always insisted on having a female friend with her. This time Sophia emphasized her wish to go alone so she could do as she pleased. She also had wanted to discuss with me decisions about her future in the light of her husband's impending retirement. She left with the possibility of calling me once more before her trip. She didn't. I believe she will call again sometime in the next six months or two years, for one or several visits.

This capacity for change in a person of sixty-four who had always been considered "a little bit odd," was quite unexpected and heartwarming. Sophia had come in a crisis situation with feelings of uselessness. She returned to reveal changes that only the therapeutic test can verify.

Hyman D. was married and had two grown children. I first saw him at age sixty-two after fifteen years of therapy on and off. He spoke fondly of his first psychiatrist whom he saw when about forty-seven for five to seven years. He was hit very hard by his doctor's sudden death. After a hiatus of several years he saw another therapist for two to three years, but he was unhappy with him, and left although he returned for occasional periods of several months with him and other analysts. He came to me because of his high regard for another man I was treating.

His previous therapy had been mainly supportive. His coming to me after many tries demonstrates the tenacity with which human

500

beings persist in their search for help to alleviate their suffering. My effort at depth therapy was his first. It reveals, as with the woman of sixty-four whom I saw on four different occasions, that productive work and fundamental personality change can be an unexpected outcome of such attempts.

As his opening comments indicated, Hyman was in chronic panic. It was also a crisis situation, but to what extent became evident only as we proceeded.

"Dr. Kelman, I'm scared, scared, scared, scared. I've been scared all my life" were almost the first words out of his mouth. They were repeated frequently in every session during the first six months. I saw Hyman once weekly which was about the frequency he had seen the other therapists. In nineteen months of therapy I saw him thirty-one times because of my schedule and because he interrupted for three months in flight from what was coming up in our work. After six months he didn't appear for several sessions. This was a pattern he had acted out all his life with others.

Hyman's story is a classic instance of the saga of a first generation New York lower East Side Jew in the early 1900's. His father was a bitter, angry man and his mother sick from his earliest years, in and out of hospitals because of tuberculosis. Shunted off on relations who didn't want him, he was generally ill-treated. In addition, Hyman was forced to become father and mother to his brother, two years younger. After several months a memory emerged from age five of his mother almost choking to death on blood from a lung hemorrhage. At the same time, he recalled the slow death from a brain tumor of a distant male relative who lived with them. These recollections came up as more of the determinants of his throat tic were explored. It would manifest itself as repetitive clicking sounds when he became tense. As our work proceeded, it became a crucial indicator that we had touched on emotionally-laden areas. As this happened, more of the mechanisms perpetuating it were clarified.

After two years in high school, because of poverty he left school. Even before age ten he had begun crawling, scratching, and scrounging his way to a fortune in the New York garment industry with its fierce competition, jungle philosophy, and violent swings of fortune. Salesmanship meant lying, cheating, promising and not fulfilling — all and anything, in short, that the industry allowed and accepted as sharp business practices. These patterns of relating he acted out with me. Forcible and regular confrontations were necessary to convince him that I would not go along with such practices which I firmly implied were also expressions of his personal problem.

As his scared feelings abated and some solid analytic work began to be done, what emerged was a stark terror of making any decision because of a literally murderous perfectionism. Because of this and a terror of involvement and trust, Hyman could not commit himself to anything. The moment he did, he had to undo it. If something I said touched him, he would blank it out and then plead, beg, and "cry," as they say in the garment trade, for me to repeat it. He was extremely bright, quick in his thinking and movements, and capable of a high order of psychological perceptiveness. It is tragic that a man of such abilities was able to do so little with them and derive so few satisfactions from them. Once he got an idea, it stayed and he was deeply appreciative.

After about six months, Hyman began to experience the remote edge of conflict. He didn't turn up for two sessions. He was almost impervious to examining what he had done and what it meant. The pressure was relieved by my absence for three weeks shortly thereafter. A month after I returned, he suddenly announced that he was leaving for an extended winter vacation and implied that he was interrupting therapy.

During this three month absence his anxieties mounted and he urgently wished to return. He sent a letter indicating when he would be back and enclosed payment for all the missed sessions. When he called and was told he had forfeited his time and had not been definite about his continuation in therapy, he was jolted. Again he pleaded, begged, and "cried" to be taken back. I told him I could only see him on an irregular basis. This was a practical necessity from my side, but I felt in addition that more effective work could be done this way. Now he was willing to come at any time. Originally after saying the same thing, he had insistently demanded sessions to fit his convenience. These demands also expressed his need to drive as hard a bargain as possible — an essential part of his way of life.

What had an even more powerful impact on him was my returning his check. This went absolutely contrary to the mores which made the accumulation of his fortune possible. It also meant I could not be bought or bribed, and that I would not enter into any collusive arrangements with him. The already great trust and confidence in me was considerably enhanced as a consequence.

In the next ten weeks before I interrupted for the summer, unexpected analysis in depth began to occur. In that period I saw Hyman eleven times, six of them in the last two weeks. In the third week he suddenly discovered that he was talking freely in a way he never had in his whole life. "Doc, I'm talking. I'm not thinking. I'm saying whatever is coming." He was giggling like a child. A few sessions later he became aware of "a lock in my mind." He also realized there had always been a dim awareness of it. In the next weeks he began to experience the opening and closing of that lock.

About the fifth week, Hyman reported that he had gotten sick after two drinks of Scotch. For years he had consumed up to a quart a day. By my questions I embedded his experience of feeling sick and his aversion to drinking anymore. From then on his limit was one, at most two drinks a day. He also told me that because of increasing business tensions in recent years, his blood pressure had gone up to 190/110. His cardiologist had warned him that if he didn't relax, he might have a heart attack. A year later he sold his business but his tensions remained. Since therapy began, his feelings of tension have much diminished. His headaches have disappeared, and symptoms associated with his hypertension are no longer present. Eighteen months after I began seeing him, in a panic state Hyman saw his local physician who found his blood pressure to be 155/90.

As we continued, more about his early life and the determinants of the throat tic emerged. One was of his mother screaming that she would commit suicide by jumping out of the window and of his crying, pleading, and screaming for her not to do so. Another memory was of having been locked in a dark closet by relatives when he was four years old. He also recalled screaming in terror for hours before they let him out.

The unlocking of his mind led to the association of having been in jail all his life. As a result of having been dominated and imprisoned by his fears, he always felt "like a scared kid."

He then recalled that at age seven, a kid had challenged him to a fight. Hyman gave him quite a beating. He also recalled his father's store being held up by three gunmen. He was calm and collected, while his father shook like a leaf. Hyman realized that when challenged and he can't avoid it, he can fight like hell. But he cannot challenge, initiate, or assert on his own. He is afraid to challenge the day. To get out of bed in the morning has been a lifelong torture.

Immediately on my return in the fall, he called to resume our work. After a month, Hyman became aware of a terror of enjoying anything. Two weeks later a major breakthrough occurred. He realized that all his life he had experienced himself

503

as a terrified little kid pleading with his mother not to jump out of the window. It suddenly hit him that she had used it as a threat and never really intended to do so. The anguish of uncertainty and doubt that had pervaded his feeling and thinking all his life suddenly fell away.

A month later he discussed in detail a nephew who used to live with them and then moved to a cheap hotel. He lay in bed all day until hospitalized. As he related this, he became enraged at his father who used to take him, a child, to visit this nephew in this sleazy and dark hotel. It suddenly hit him that all his life he had been in terror of going crazy. With this awareness he burst into a fit of convulsive sobbing. Soon after he became more sharply aware of his fear of life and his fear of the future. With this insight his maddening ruminating and obsessing regarding having enough money to live on the rest of his life fell away.

Hyman exemplifies how powerful the urge toward self-realization is, and how great the possibility of change is in a person in his sixties. My prediction is that Hyman will continue therapy and continue to improve although there will be tempestuous periods in our relationship for some years to come.

I saw one man once a week for three years. He was thirty when he began therapy. Obstipation was the presenting complaint which cleared up after two years of therapy. Before coming to see me he had applied for a private flying license and was rejected for a supposedly unusual congenital form of yellow color blindness. In the third year of our work he reapplied and passed. The color blindness was gone. This created consternation in the federal examining board. Such a happening had never been seen before. It did not show up in the next twenty-five years in the regular re-examinations.

Thirty years after I last saw him he returned because of intense guilt feelings caused by an affair with a young married relative. He returned a year later, at age sixty-four, again for a single visit. Six months after I had last seen him he suffered a severe coronary occlusion. He was experiencing this happening as a punishment for his misdeed and was more frightened than depressed. His focus now was on survival and on trying to make some kind of a more amicable life with his wife.

Three years later I heard from him that he had almost died of complications following a prostectomy. He had retired a year after I last saw him. His interruption of thirty years has been the longest in my experience.

Horney firmly believed "that man can change and go on changing as long as he lives."*(39)* This growth oriented, life affirming philosophy, which regards constitution as a spectrum of dynamic possibilities, was made explicit in 1917 and reached its most detailed development in 1950 with the concepts of the real self and the urge toward self-realization. *(2,49)*

In the history of psychoanalysis as well as for medicine generally, patients do not respect textbooks, theories, or techniques. All require continual revision. Erikson felt that his epigenetic psychosocial model of the "Eight Stages of Man" was a necessary addition to Freud's psychosexual one. First formulated in 1950 and revised in 1963, he assumed for each stage an appropriate form of growth and maturing as the crucial issues of that phase were met and solutions were found. "Generativity" or "Stagnation" are solutions for the middle-aged. For the oldest age groups there are "Ego Integrity" or "Despair." *(306, pp. 266-68)*

Always contributory to theory and technique reformulation are social, cultural, economic, political, historical, and cosmic forces. The latter forcibly obtrude themselves on "Earth Man" with his narrow vision. Since 1850 the percentage of population over sixty-five has gone from $2\frac{1}{2}$ to 10 percent. There are the beginnings of a geriatric psychiatry, but it is crucially necessary to evolve a growth oriented, life affirming psychotherapy for older age groups. Programs appropriate to the continuing vitality of citizens advancing into their sixth, seventh and eighth decades must be established. If these steps are not taken, the confrontation of *youth-ism* and *age-ism* already apparent may become one of the most painful and serious crisis of the near future. *(363)*

The issues of age, aging, growing, and maturing at whatever age raise the question of duration. The longest continuous personal analysis I have conducted was twenty-four years. I have described my experience with Solomon W., fifty-four, who was in therapy almost continuously from age sixteen. A vital and productive woman began her first analytic experience at age seventy-two. Another person whose therapeutic span is thirty-eight years is a woman of seventy-three whom I saw for six months during a difficult phase following which she returned to her therapist.

Long term therapies and extended follow-ups offer unique opportunities to check on early diagnoses and prognoses and to observe the results of the therapeutic test: (1) in effecting improvement and fundamental personality reorientation; (2) in maintaining the status quo; (3) in arresting an illness progression; and (4) in slowing its progress.

The history and thirty-four year analysis of one man who I considered a compensated schizophrenic has been presented. *(p. 97)*

Without therapy, it would not have been possible to slow the process, to maintain him, to increase his feeling for life, and to change the diagnosis from compensated schizophrenic to borderline syndrome of the mildest variety. *(209, p. 89)* The same diagnosis would hold for the woman I saw seven times over seven years and who was eventually treated by a colleague. *(p. 349)* I believe Sonia V. could well have deteriorated and became a paranoid schizophrenic.

In 1931, at nineteen, Grace H. attempted suicide by gas. In the hospital we could not agree whether she had a psychotic depression or was a simple schizophrenic. An enthusiastic psychiatric intern, I saw her daily. Hospitalized for fourteen months, she left three months after my appointment ended. In 1935 she was again in a hospital following her mother's almost total disability. She was morbidly dependent upon her mother. For one and a half years in 1938 and 1939 I saw her privately once weekly. Grace improved steadily.

In 1939 I saw her older sister, Gwendolyn I., after a suicidal attempt. In 1945 her sister was again hospitalized with a psychotic depression or early schizophrenia. By 1954 Gwendolyn's husband had to hospitalize her permanently as a deteriorating hebephrenic praecox. Grace's older brother died in 1940 at thirty-three of a coronary thrombosis from which her father also died at thirty-eight. Her youngest brother, hospitalized at nineteen, was diagnosed a psychopathic personality.

Self-supporting by 1938, in 1945 Grace was an office manager of a large industrial firm. I last saw her because of an involvement with a married man. She recognized the neurotic nature of this affair, such relationships having happened several times before. Three months later she wrote that she had broken off the relationship. I heard she was in a hospital from June 1956 to February 1957. I was not told the diagnosis but learned that she had moved south on being discharged.

When I first saw Grace I could not have made the prognosis that her life course demonstrated. The first one to break, and at the youngest age in a family with poor physical and emotional endowment, Grace did better than all of the rest with the minimal help she obtained.

At twenty, Bernard F. had his first panic in a theater. By twenty-five he had been diagnosed schizophrenic during two hospitalizations. After three years of analytic therapy, I began seeing him when he was twenty-nine. The picture was one of chronic schizophrenic panic. For nine years I saw him three times weekly and thereafter for six years once a week. Married at thirty-three, his wife died three years later. He remarried at thirty-eight and separated at sixty-one.

From age thirty-four to thirty-seven he held the first job in his life. Because of a mild agitated state he did not work for the next two years. Thereafter he made steady advancement until age forty-four when he again broke down and felt he was as sick as he had ever been in his life. From age forty-five to forty-nine, Bernard worked with another therapist, a woman whom he experienced as most helpful. She noted changes in him at age forty-eight which he began to experience a year later.

At forty-nine Bernard completed his college work and courses for a master's degree. At fifty-nine he again broke down and had to be temporarily hospitalized. He went on to get a Ph.D. and to become a specialist in his field. Now at sixty-three, he is having the best years of his life. I have continued to hear from him and have seen him three times in the last fifteen years.

Bernard's life pattern of growth and illness could hardly have been predicted forty-two years ago when he first became ill or thirty-four years ago when I first saw him. The diagnoses of remitting or non-process schizophrenia though descriptively accurate leave many unanswered questions. What part did the psychotherapy and the hospitalizations play? Marriage and a son and a daughter from whom he derived much satisfaction I feel were of vital importance. Crucial was his potential for struggle which could only show in the testing. Several years ago he said, "There is one thing I've learned in life. What it is to suffer. Most people don't understand it and can't take it." I feel that at present the most appropriate diagnosis is "Borderline Syndrome: Group IV."*(209, p. 89)*

Seven patients — three men and four women — who could be diagnosed occult *(264)* or latent schizophrenia showed manifest illness from twenty-nine to fifty-six years with an average of forty. Three of them had one to sixteen years of therapy with an average of 5.6 years and one to four hospitalizations due to panic states. Six are now living fairly productive lives. I am convinced that deterioration has been forestalled.

Four women whose total spans were thirty-four, twenty, eleven, and eight years respectively; and who had fourteen, nine, five, and two calculated years of analysis revealed schizophrenic thought processes. The prior analysts of two thought that they were definitely schizophrenic. These processes slowly disappeared in two or three years as their anxiety level gradually diminished. The fourth whose thinking was the most scattered and fragmented also had the least therapy. I occasionally see her in public. She has become very obese and gross with a flatness of expression. While the first three might have been diagnosed schizophrenics, their present diagnoses would be "Borderline Syndrome, Group II: The Core Borderline Syndrome" for one, and "Group IV" for two. The fourth one (with the minimal therapy) might now be considered a "Group I: The Psychotic Border" whose deterioration had been slowed by therapy. *(209)*

Sabrina Q., now fifty-two, who had a brutal childhood and a tragic marriage began therapy twenty-eight years ago. She has been in therapy fifteen years with me, and had eight years of analysis with two previous psychoanalysts. Often during the first four years, because of her intensely provocative and frustrating behavior, I wanted to interrupt our work. Slight changes, however, began to be evident. From the seventh through the ninth year she suffered from severe back muscle spasms and excruciating pain. For six months of this period she could hardly get out of bed. She walked bent over almost double. Thereafter her rate of change steadily increased. Two years ago the pace of change further quickened. Originally considered a compensated schizophrenic, I could now see her as a "Borderline Syndrome: Group II."

In her early thirties, after three and one-half years of analysis, Bertha D. suffered a schizophrenic break requiring twenty months of hospitalization and a year and a half more of a slow return to health. Now in her mid-fifties, a married woman with two children, Bertha has arrived at a significant awareness of her emotional problems and an ability to live with them. She now has a feeling of identity, of belonging, and a level of maturity she never had. A creative urge and talent evident since childhood are still there and unrealized. Her diagnosis would now be "Borderline Syndrome: Group IV."

I realize that these reports are impressionistic and without controls. But how are the factors of the urge toward self-realization and the tendency for nature to mend rather than to end evaluated? They involve the issues of the natural history of limiting and limited illness, of spontaneous recovery, of hereditary endowment, and of the many helping agencies which make life itself a therapist. The specific therapy used — human help, individual, group, and community, with and without drug therapy — is also of paramount importance. The following instance confronts but does not answer these many questions.

I last saw Louis B. when he was forty-one. The only child of a disturbed marriage, his father remote, his mother clutching and hysterical, he was disturbed from childhood. By sixteen his schoolwork was becoming erratic. There were frequent interruptions for one to several years with periods of working in between.

As a result he completed college in his early thirties, got his master's in the late thirties, and is still struggling toward his Ph.D. at forty-one. He has attended about ten different colleges, three of them on three different occasions.

After seeing four analysts for shorter and longer periods from sixteen to twenty-one, Louis was hopitalized for about a year. He always had difficulty making friends. He was aloof, stiff, and uncommunicative, especially with girls. His intellectual ability was superior, but he panicked before examinations in a rather bizarre and histrionic way.

At twenty-four, after his hospitalization, Louis resumed analysis. The above problems slowly abated although his therapy was punctuated by intense outbursts from time to time which almost necessitated hospitalization. After eleven years with the same analyst, Louis began to have doubts about him and thought he should make a change. He asked his therapist whether he thought he should make a change. After some time, he asked to be referred to someone for a consultation. I saw him in the spirit I have described regarding such consultations. (p. 357) He continued with his therapist for three more years up to age thirty-eight.

At twenty-six he married a quite schizoid "helpless" girl who found the demands of marriage too great a burden and asked for a divorce. His first sexual experience was with her. After the divorce there were prostitutes now and then. At thirty-nine Louis met another girl, separated from a "hippie who had disappeared" and by whom she had had a child. Louis had a number of urges to marry her, but as he got close to a decision he panicked. He finally married her several months before I last saw him. He called me because he felt this marriage was breaking up. The girl was also quite schizoid and finding the closeness of a marriage too binding. But Louis was also talking about it himself.

A year before his last visit with me, I saw him three times over a period of two months. Striking was how little feeling he had for the therapist with whom he had worked for fourteen years. He told me that he had been impressed during his consultation with me six years earlier, but he saw a number of other analysts before he returned to see me. Disturbed about whether or not to marry, he called me. When he decided to marry, he canceled his appointment. Again he called me when he felt the marriage was going on the rocks. In the interim he had seen someone once who suggested he contact me because of the way he felt toward me.

509

The last time I saw him, a year after the previous three visits, I was struck by the change in Louis. There was a greater openness, responsiveness, and availability of feeling which he could touch and describe. I felt a much closer contact with him and he with me. He asked whether I thought he should return for intensive therapy. I told him I felt it was better if he called me whenever he felt moved to do so. This touched him, and he smiled quite openly which was rare for him. He agreed it was a good idea and felt quite appreciative.

Three months later I heard that six weeks after seeing me, at the suggestion of a senior analyst he had consulted once before, Louis began working with a younger colleague. He was in need of support in the crisis of deciding to divorce his second wife which both wanted and which happened six weeks later. Having reintegrated himself as a single man, Louis was loathe to continue with self-investigation in depth. He gave finances as the reason for wishing to interrupt.

Louis B.'s diagnosis I feel is "Borderline Syndrome: Group III: The Adaptive, Affectless Defended 'As if' Persons."*(209, p. 89)* From their protocols and a follow-up study after six months and after five years, Werble concluded that "There has been little individual change in their social functioning" and in their life styles. Also they "gave no evidence . . . of movement toward schizophrenia" which was one of the chief concerns. *(364)* Grinker found no change in any of this group while others have, including myself. There is always the question, "Are we dealing with Borderlines who in fact improved with therapy or with a different group of patients?"

In their sample, thirty-nine patients when hospitalized were less than thirty, twelve were older. Louis B. was in a hospital from age twenty-one to twenty-two. Their follow-ups are only after five years and the findings are as indicated above. Would longer term follow-ups show some of what Louis B. is showing? Or is what I observed a momentary breakthrough of "as if," rather than something more substantial? Perhaps all his years of therapy have finally borne fruit, aided by the therapy of life, and the remitting nature of his illness. I incline to the opinion that the years of therapy were a crucial factor in what I observed on his last visit and that what I saw has something substantially healthy in it.

This same series of questions comes up in regard to certain psychopaths whose illness seems to wane with age as they become quite rigid and conservative.

510

Frankie T. was a musical prodigy, evident by age six, a pathological liar by age eight, and a severe psychopath by age seventeen. At age twelve his dog, a fearless mongrel, toward whom he had a deeper attachment than to any human being, was killed. He cried bitterly for several days and from then on became numb and remote and seemed to have locked up his feelings, according to his mother.

A year of psychoanalysis at age seventeen was unproductive. I saw him from age twenty-one to twenty-five. In a session when the subject of his dog came up, he became tearful, but soon choked down his feelings. A year later he interrupted therapy. Married at twenty-one, his wife abruptly left him four years later. Frankie went into a deep depression. He became involved with a very psychopathic girl with two children who was separated from her husband. She was killed in an automobile accident for which he somehow blamed himself. When he returned to therapy after an interruption of two and a half years, I learned he had been suicidal for almost a year after this happening.

After four months of therapy, Frankie burst into tears as he mentioned his father's impending operation. Three days later he came down with virus hepatitis. Two years later, he interrupted his work with me and began seeing another analyst. This change was made at the suggestion of an older man with whom Frankie worked and to whom he had become quite attached. He saw this analyst for about six years fairly regularly.

Three years after I last saw him, Frankie became involved with the law and was hospitalized. He had played around with drugs since he was nineteen. In his early thirties he was severely addicted to amphetamines. This hospitalization in a large public hospital had a deep impact on him. By age thirty-seven the intensity of his psychopathic behavior began to wane.

At forty-two he is a very conservative and staid professional in the musical world. Frankie is now contemplating marriage to a previously married woman with three children from a very conservative background. At times he is given to long righteous diatribes of a virulent reactionary nature. He has many features of a reformed drunk. Similar to the reformed compulsive non-drinker, he seems to be a reformed compulsive non-psychopath.

Frankie has had *kairoi* of major and minor dimensions. *(272)* The first was when his dog was killed; the second was when his feelings burst through in a session with me in his recollection of his dog; the third was when his wife left him; the fourth was when his girlfriend was killed; and the fifth was when he was hospitalized. After his serious and dangerous brush with the law and with human misery in a large mental hospital, he was finally touched in a fundamental way.

I have presented my work with Frankie to colleagues in Switzerland, Germany, and Sweden. Some felt that analytic therapy was a factor in the changes, some were sure it was crucial, and others felt it was incidental — they had seen similar patients go through this cycle having received little or no therapy.

I feel equally important with the individual therapy were the *kairoi*. Of almost equal import, from age twenty-five on, was his relationship with his mother. She had been in therapy with me for years and had become painfully aware of her part in her son having become a psychopath. She spontaneouly realized that she had not only aided and abetted his psychopathic behavior, but she had also stimulated its happening and gained vicarious satisfaction from his rebelliousness against authorities. During his most difficult period of drug taking she confronted him with what he was doing, stood firm when he was hospitalized, and continued with these attitudes and her supportiveness thereafter. In the years since his hospitalization, Frankie and his mother have developed a deep and affectionate relationship. He has great trust in her as well as great respect. His relationship with his father which had been bad since infancy has steadily improved in the last five years.

The enigma remains. How *much* of *what* contributed to the evolution of this picture? Is what I have described a picture of the natural history of a certain type of illness, and are his individual therapy, his *kairoi,* and his mother's support only incidental or slightly important? Someday long term follow-up studies will give analysts a more substantial basis for confronting and answering such questions.

The question of diagnosis remains. Is Frankie a pseudo- or symptomatic psychopath? *(153, p. 243)* Is he a true or idiopathic psychopath? There is much to suggest that he suffered from a psychoneurosis or character disorder with psychopathic features. He was capable of intense object relationships, his dog, his wife, and his girlfriend. He also remained in analysis for long periods with me and his second analyst. Is he a pseudo-psychopath because psychopaths rarely respond to analytic therapy? But then, did he really respond to therapy? If he didn't, is he a psychopath?

Some practical considerations bear mentioning in connection with the therapy of borderlines, compensated psychotics, psychotics in a recovery phase, and those whose progressive deterioration I hope to slow or forestall. Much more flexibility is essential with regard to hours

— the number, double sessions, evening and weekend sessions, lateness, and absences. The use of the telephone, letters, notes, and dreams and the use of drugs, shock therapy, and hospitalization must also be made more flexible.

Some times it is better to keep a patient out of the hospital with drugs, shock therapy, and more sessions while he's going through a panic state or a micropsychotic episode. One patient who had been hospitalized several times turned her home into a private sanitorium. Friends in the building and close by acted as her nurses and brought her food. She spoke to me by phone three times daily. After about six months she resumed her sessions.

In other instances hospitalization is the better choice because the physical and emotional burden of remaining out is too great and is impeding effective therapy. One woman who had been in hospitals several times and didn't like them said, "Doctor Kelman, I want to go to a hospital for awhile. It's too much for me. I can't take care of myself. I don't know if I can keep control on myself. I want to let go and be taken care of for awhile," and she was right.

Another instance involved a boy in late adolescence. His schooling was becoming erratic. Two attempts at therapy had been unproductive. I told him and his parents that I would try therapy but if it didn't work I would suggest hospitalization. After five months I made that suggestion. Both his parents and I were surprised at his response. He was relieved and pleased. "Nobody has had the courage to tell me that before." He willingly entered a psychotherapeutically oriented private hospital where he remained for twenty months during which time he occasionally called me when rashly about to sign himself out. When discharged he resumed work with me for nine months until he went to college outside of the city. In our last session there was quite a breakthrough of feeling at leaving me. The depth of feeling surprised him. I made a recommendation for a continuation of therapy which did not work out. On two occasions in my absence he called. It is six years since I last saw him and two years since I last heard from him. The hospital made the diagnosis of schizophrenia, simple type. I believe he is a "Borderline Syndrome: Group IV" with much immaturity which he will outgrow.

Chapter 32

The General Practice
of Psychoanalysis II:
Being and Appearing Healthy and Sick,
Thin and Fat

Of keeping healthy Henry Z., a capable deck officer on passenger ships, had made a life career. At least yearly he checked into the hospital for a thorough examination to insure that he was maintaining his perfect health. He neither smoked nor drank and took sparingly of tea and coffee. Henry did calisthenics daily. At sixty-five, he looked fifty and had the body of an even younger man. His hair was still jet black, and he had all his teeth and no cavities. He had never had a serious illness. Five feet ten inches tall, he weighed about 165 pounds.

Henry had been referred to me because he was regarded as a "health nut." Although married with children, I experienced him as unconnected with human beings and humanity. He obviously was intensely narcissistic about his health and his body. He smiled and laughed, but right below the surface I sensed intense anxiety. I experienced him as a hollow man.

In contrast to Henry, the focus in some people is not on keeping healthy but on the terror of becoming and being sick. Their feelings, thoughts, and behaviors may be directed toward maintaining health, but only in a minimal way. Becoming ill means having to admit the existence of their body. They have lived almost entirely in their minds in an alienated way. In therapy, the pride in having a body which functions like a machine which never needs oil comes to the fore. They should be effortlessly self-sufficient. Soon the Peter Pan fantasy emerges, and the demand for perennial youth becomes apparent. Becoming ill means having a body, and with that there is the horrible specter of aging which means life and living, death and dying, the existence of which they must deny.

Their terror when they have to admit illness has many sources. They failed to control their body through their intellect. They failed to protect themselves against the intrusion of the reality of their body, of reality in general as of time and space and other people. Now they have to depend on another, a physician, for help. About medication such patients regularly ask, "I won't become addicted, will I?" Some viciously disregard their bodies and have claims for immunity from the consequences of such attitudes.

There are some striking attitudes toward the body, the organic, and the earthy in people who live predominantly in their minds. One woman was in constant fury that she could not get along on five hours sleep a night. She hated the fact that she had to eat and that if she didn't, she would get colds which meant her body had struck back at her for maltreating it.

Another woman arrogantly proclaimed that she really didn't need any sleep and was proud that she got along fine on five hours sleep a night. She was in a constant, mild hypomanic state. As her hypomia began to abate, she was first angered, then enraged, and finally panicked to find that she needed more sleep. Where previously she had been extremely gregarious, she found herself going out less and seeing fewer people. Over a period of nine months she became isolated and withdrawn, sleeping eight and twelve hours daily. She saw this as evidence that she was deteriorating. In the following year she slowly became more active, but in a more balanced manner. She continued to need seven to eight hours sleep nightly, but she was no longer raging about this fact.

Both of the above women were exceptionally bright. One arrogantly flaunted her intelligence. The other's intelligence was hidden by a compelling need for love. They regarded their bodies as despised objects because they reminded them of their femaleness and because various attributes of their bodies failed to measure up to their imaginary requirements.

One man talked endlessly about keeping fit but actually didn't do too much about it while shamelessly abusing his body. He also had the Peter Pan fantasy with a vengeance. Needing to prove his virility constantly, he slept with a succession of women, and swam in dangerous places. His son's surpassing him in tennis was a painful experience. He became quite vicious toward his son and the rest of his family. Only with a feeling of bitter resignation did he accept the fact that his son could "beat him every time." In addition, for years his pattern had been to take a psychic energizer in the morning to wake him up and several during the day to keep him going "at top speed." He took a sedative at night "to hit myself on the head and put myself to sleep." It took many years of analysis before he could relax some of these patterns, accept his passing years, and begin to respect his body's needs, at least in small measure.

People who never have been seriously ill become quite disturbed with the first evidence of body involvement as an aspect of progress in therapy. This pattern is obvious in certain types of men. They are usually quite alienated, resigned, and cerebral. The body that had functioned like a machine with a minimum amount of care is suddenly reminding them of its existence. What is worse, it is breaking down as they see it, both of which experiences are frightening to them. They have no experiential referents to deal with these strange happenings. They are being called to areas of their being they had locked out: their organicity as soma and — in the offing — feelings fostered by the dynamic of the therapy.

"I have never been sick in my life before I came into analysis. Now I'm having one illness after another and this is supposed to mean I'm benefiting from analysis," and equivalent statements are not uncommon. When there is insomnia in a person who "slept like a log," fatigue when "I never felt tired," and inability to concentrate when "my mind was always as sharp as a razor," that's bad enough; but when there are a variety of ailments such as frequent colds and recurrent dental trouble, the situation can become terrifying. Worse still is when they are brought low by a required hospitalization for a complete study because nothing specific has been identified. The direst threat of all is a required surgical intervention.

Pride in never having been sick when there never has been illness is one thing, but trying to be healthy where there is continuing physical illness is quite another matter. At forty Bessie R. discovered she had malignant hypertension. From then on her life was consumed with keeping herself from getting sick and preserving her health. Her thoughts, feelings, and behaviors were filled with devotion to taking care of herself, getting enough rest, not overtaxing herself, not being out late more than one evening a week, limiting her activities, insuring she had enough restful holidays, frequently visiting her internist for checkups, and, of course, religiously following the prescribed diet and medications.

At seventy-five, still devoted to her career of preserving her health, she carries on her profession in a similarly measured way with her blood pressure well-controlled. She has never married and never becomes deeply involved with anyone. She looks to be about sixty and has a childlike mien about her. Although she would say her life has been happy and meaningful, it has been in fact a very restricted and constricted one. Her analysis, while it did not effect fundamental character changes, helped considerably in mitigating her intensive fears and anxieties and aided her in becoming less cramped. Combined with considerable hygienic efforts, therapy also may have contributed to keeping her blood pressure within limits. The fact is, except for the hypertension, Bessie R. has never been seriously ill in all these years.

During an initial interview, when a patient brings up previous illness, or at the time of an illness, I may ask for a medical history. *(365)* On such occasions the possibility of hereditary illnesses is gone into, as well as familial tendencies to certain diseases, to obesity or thinness, to longevity, or to early loss of hair on the part of the males.

Discussion of physical illness offers an opportunity for asking about the last physical examination, whether the patient has a regular physician, whether he is connected with an organization from which he can get needed medical services, and whether he carries health as well as life insurance. In a city like New York, the number of people without a personal physician is very high, and many do not have membership in insurance plans for health care. In general, all too few people on their own initiative insure their health needs.

When the subject arises, I suggest that the patient arrange for medical care and consultation. Much about the patient's problems may immediately come to the fore: an awareness of health needs, an inability to feel concern for his body, blocks to initiating on his own behalf, taboos on self-concern to the point of interdiction, or, various intensities of self-destructiveness where health is concerned.

Brought into awareness, these issues can act as a significant dynamic for the analytic process. At first indirectly and then occasionally explicitly, I raise the issue. At times I have had to use methods of direct confrontation. It is rare that a patient will not ultimately make the necessary contact. In three different instances I informed the patient that if he did not seek medical aid, I would interrupt therapy because I would not be a partner to his irresponsibility. All three finally did so.

When I feel the patient really does not have the resources for finding his own physician, which is rare, I may suggest one. I will only do so when I feel it will take the patient a long time before being able to act on his own, when I feel there might be a current medical condition, when it has been a long time since he has seen a physician, or when I feel it will further the therapeutic work.

The number of patients who do not have their own dentist is much larger than those without a private physician. Everyone has mixed feelings, rational and irrational, about going to the dentist.

The commonest problems are fear and intolerance to pain. With a few, the sound of the drill is unbearable. While others demand "plenty of novocaine", some, much as they want it, simply can't take the pain and penetration of the needle.

The loss of teeth implies oral and facial disfigurement and, worst of all, irreparable and irreversible aging. Then there are attitudes connected with being out of control and helpless. One woman found the experience of "me there with my mouth open and him looking down my throat simply revolting." Another experienced it as helplessly being intruded upon, invaded, and of being utterly exposed and naked. I prefer, if at all possible, not to make dental referrals.

Patients with hypochondriacal symptoms are most difficult for both physician and analyst. In my experience, analysis rarely improves hypochondriacs. There is a vicious tenacity about their focus on physical symptoms which is, in some instances, a survival defense against a psychotic break. Where possible, referral to an internist who has experience with such patients can at least protect them from unnecessary medicating and operative procedures.

Other occasions when I make the referrals are when I am dealing with so-called psychosomatic disorders which need continuing surveillance such as malignant hypertension, ulcerative colitis or anorexia nervosa; when the matter is urgent and will take months before the patient will be able to do so on his own; when I feel the patient's physician is not giving adequate care; and when he is involving himself with the patient's emotional problems and acting as a surrogate or competing therapist.

Because of the foregoing, I feel it imperative that an analyst have a continuing relationship with an internist of competence who is respectful of the analytic relationship. Once he has seen the internist, the patient can be referred back as occasion warrants, or seek help on his own. Once he has established a relationship with him, the patient does not have to go through me. This pertains to all medical conditions including the prescribing of sedatives.

The internist feels free to call and inform me of findings I should know but which the patient has not or could not acquaint me. I feel free to call the internist for findings and guidance if I feel something might be physically amiss. What may be involved are the treatment of acute illness, the alleviation of chronic illness or the slowing of its progression, the prescribing of medication or health regimens necessary for short and long term health needs, and the ongoing treatment of so-called psychosomatic disorders until such therapies are no longer necessary.

Rose B. had been physically ill almost from birth. A close relative was her physician. The relationship was sadistic and highly eroticized sexually. She was emotionally bound to him and terrified of him. Only his death freed her from this malignant relationship. Through a fortunate set of circumstances she reached her present internist who referred her to me when she was more dead than alive. Only our close cooperation, particularly in the first two years of our work, made her survival possible. Thereafter, with the urgent need past, his continued physical ministrations and emotional support made analytic therapy possible through a sequence of repercussions, often manifested physically. With the passing years one medication after another was dropped and her visits to him diminished to once or twice a year.

In women the patterns and the emphasis regarding keeping and being healthy focus on looking well. This is partly due to an awareness and denial of being indisposed due to menses, often referred to as being sick, having a sick headache or being unwell.

There is a shift from being to appearing and to the preservation of appearances. "You have a perfect figure" is the ultimate accolade from one woman to another, not "You look in the pink of condition," or "How do you keep yourself so fit?" which are male comments. The number of women I have worked with who were deeply disturbed by becoming misshapen by pregnancy are not few.

The commonest forms of female preoccupation relate to flabby breasts, misshapen figures, varicose veins, abdominal striae, getting fat, and getting and looking old. This emphasis on appearance and bodily perfection can extend to their offspring. Several women insisted on Caesarian sections to insure having the perfect baby, particularly if they wanted a girl. A strikingly beautiful Amazon of a woman demanded she have spinal anesthesia for the birth of her child. She simply found being unconscious and out of control unbearable. She not only wanted to observe the birth, but also to supervise it and insure that no harm came to the perfect product she would produce.

After her daughter was born, her mother showed limited interest in her and regarded her as an interference to her social activities. She had come to me after a serious suicidal gesture which terrified her because it meant her impulses had gotten out of control. She was afraid she might damage her perfect mind and her perfect body. This was almost thirty years ago, and I was too inexperienced to deal effectively with such a formidable patient. After she interrupted, I realized that one crucial source of the difficulties in our tempestuous relationship of two years duration was that she saw me as imperfect. She continued therapy with a famous analyst for about four more years. In him she sought the perfect analyst to whom the perfect patient felt entitled.

Stephanie W. boasted that she had the "most beautiful breasts in Cleveland." She paid for her vanity with her life. For three years surgeons had been urging mammary biopsy because of bleeding from both nipples. When I saw her, my task was to help her accept surgery as soon as possible. Four months later a bilateral mastectomy was performed. Disseminated carcinoma of the lymph glands was found. I continued to treat her as a physically-well patient. She soon married and had the five happiest years of her life before she died at age thirty-four.

A very sick young married woman who was practically flat chested insistently demanded that her therapist agree and help her make arrangements for silicone injections. Through my supervisory help, this demand was postponed and ultimately dropped. Since adolescence she had avoided public bathing. Salesgirls in the women's section of department stores were a torture to her. In bed with her husband she wore falsies and insisted on having the lights out during intercourse.

When treatment began, she was on the verge of suicide or a schizophrenic break. After several years of therapy she could do without falsies in bed with her husband and could go bathing with her children who for years had been begging her to do so. Her life which had centered around her absent breasts was now concerned with herself as a whole person in relation to the many aspects of her living.

One of the most difficult consultations I ever had was with a practicing lawyer in his thirties who was a compensated schizophrenic. He had seen two other psychiatrists before me, one for a period of treatment. He was quite personable and fairly good looking but not outstanding. Quite blandly and smilingly he told me he was convinced that if he had plastic surgery on his nose and on one of his ears, both of which showed nothing beyond the average norm, he would be as handsome as any male Hollywood actor and that he would then become a star. He wanted my acquiescence to this idea following which he would proceed with the operations. How to insure that he would not take my comments as confirmation on the one hand and how to encourage him to give the matter more careful consideration before proceeding on the other without having him discard what I said or become paranoid was what I attempted while walking this razor's edge.

I did have a ten year follow-up on a front row Ziegfeld Follies chorus girl who became obsessed with an imaginary mole on her chin. She came from a family in which a number were physically and mentally ill. I saw her several times and again five years later for several sessions. Five years after that, her husband informed me that she had to be hospitalized because of a rapid deterioration. She was diagnosed hebephrenic at age thirty-five and her husband was told that her condition was hopeless.

Those aspects of the self-system which are formed through interactions in the life course and lead to the development of identity, as body image or sex, gender, core, and real self identity, are crucial and determining for life patterns. *(366)* They frequently become woven into pathological patterns which tenaciously persist even after fundamental personality change has taken place.

At age twelve Monica S. was five feet eight inches tall. In addition she had protuding teeth, wore braces, was extremely thin. Her mental gifts created problems for her with girls and caused boys to avoid her. Essentially she was an only child, her next sibling being a brother nine years older. An older sister was thirteen years her senior and completely uninterested in her. In addition, although there were plenty of women around — her mother, grandmother, and aunts — no one seemed to be there for her. Her adored father was seldom available. She remembers a succession of big houses and no children to play with. Monica clearly recalled that at seven, "I decided I had to grow myself up because there was no one to help me do it." She had felt ugly, awkward, skinny, and lonely as long as she could remember.

From ten to twelve, when she shot up ten inches, life was a torture for her. In private schools from eleven to eighteen, she had practically no dates with boys. In her late teens her roommates were the "oddballs," and the "lame ducks." The school was run by rigid spinsters against whom she was in constant rebellion. In the last two years of college, Monica fastened onto a boy whom she saw constantly but who broke off the relationship after graduation.

Sex with her boyfriend was the acting out of a fantasy supposed to signify love. Back home her problems with men became excruciating. Six feet tall since age eighteen, still rather thin, but with her teeth somewhat improved, she became involved with a succession of brilliant, sadistic young men who used and abused her. Following an episode with one she developed hemorrhagic colitis. That fall she had a cholecystectomy at age twenty-three.

Feelings about her height and her unattractiveness and

problems caused by her intelligence came painfully to the fore. In three years, she interrupted therapy twice. She also announced long weekends or vacations at the last moment. This was both an acting-out against me as her father and an expression of her terror of closeness from which she had only known pain.

After a year of therapy she interrupted right after my winter holiday. She had experienced my leaving as a rejection. Five months later she resumed therapy, and again interrupted right after my winter holiday. This time it was because of a fear of deeper involvement which would entail painful feelings with reference to herself.

Eight months later Monica wrote, "I see now that I left out of anger 1) that you were leaving; 2) that I was at the point in analysis where I had to make the leap of faith, to trust you or else go no further; and 3) fear that you were going to die. The last being the most potent fear." She realized the profound effect on her of so many in her family dying of cancer. All leavings were painful, and all were associated with cancer and death.

She also realized the necessity for paying for her analysis from her own earnings. "Please try and take me back . . . . It's you, and my relationship with you that's at stake, not just any doctor or the rightness of analysis which I've never questioned." We resumed, and she became more solid in herself, more open with me, and worked with greater understanding and fewer repercussions. For the first time she continued therapy after my winter holidays.

Clearly many factors other than her height determined her feelings toward herself, but it did limit the number of available men. *(366)* Her height and the changes it had effected in her life were indelibly impressed upon her. Other physical features contributed to the most excruciatingly painful feelings of female unattractiveness.

A young man in his early thirties, after an extended analysis with interruptions, is now quite happy with himself and his career. In moments of tension and turmoil, however, he can still vividly experience himself as small and fat. Up to age twelve he was the smallest in his group. He followed "big guys," especially athletes, around like a puppy. In his teens he reached his present height of five feet ten inches, became deep chested, and quite an athlete in his own right. Nude in bed with a girl he has a mixture of feelings when the girl says matter-of-factly and also admiringly, "Gee, you are a big guy." His reaction is a combination of "Who me?" disbelief, unease, and "They must be talking about some other guy." These feelings persist in the face of having accepted, liked, and felt comfortable with many aspects of his being.

He has never been fat, yet throughout our work whenever he disliked himself he would feel fat. This was a condensation of feelings of passivity, inertia, block, and what he called his "slovenliness." He also experienced being fat when he would feel he would never get over deeply embedded and extensive manifestations of self-effacement, masochism, and immaturity. In my foyer is a floor-to-ceiling mirror. When he felt this way, the reflected image of his being fat was very real. "With my head I know it isn't so, but I still have the feeling that maybe it is."

During his teens another man, about five feet eleven inches tall weighed 260 pounds. After an extended analysis, now in his late forties, he weighs around 160. When he had feelings of self-disgust, he would have feelings of being "fat and a slob." In my hall mirror the image of himself at sixteen was very real and it was hard for him to shake the feeling that visually that was what he was seeing.

Another man, now past fifty, also had an extended analysis with several interruptions. He had been thin, small, and sickly most of his early years. When I first met him, he was almost six feet tall and weighed about 165 pounds. He was quite athletic, well-proportioned, and quite strong. When assailed by feelings of low self-esteem, even after considerable personality change, he experiences himself as "skinny," weak, small, and sickly. His difficulties with my foyer mirror are not as intense as with the other men but they are there.

To understand the problems of people who are thin by intent, the psychodynamic, the phenomenological, and the existential approaches are essential. Knowledge regarding identity in all its aspects particularly as it pertains to body, sex, gender, core, and real self identity must also be utilized. Palazzoli emphasizes these issues in her study of "Anorexia Nervosa." She questions "interpreting anorexia nervosa as a defense against the oral sadistic impulse. I consider this interpretation arbitrary because it does not take into account clinical and phenomenological observations, the only reliable foundations on which to base a psychodynamic explanation."(367)

Palazzoli distinguishes true anorexia nervosa from various manifestations of pseudo-anorexia. In true anorexia, there is generally neuromuscular hyperactivity and food is of central importance. Palazzoli agrees with Bruch that the main issue is "a struggle for control, for a sense of identity and effectiveness." Keeping food out serves "the singular goal of achieving autonomy through this bizarre form of control over the body and its functions."(381)

In pseudo-anorexia, neuromuscular hyperactivity is usually absent and food is of only secondary or symbolic concern: in depressives, lack of appetite is but one aspect of a general disinterest in vital needs; in certain schizophrenics, food and bizzare eating habits become symbolically associated with such delusional ideas, for example, as poison and decay; and in neurotic reactions, mainly of the hysterical type, where food reduction is aimed "at controlling the environment — to attract attention, to blackmail, to obtain the desired responses. . . . After a brief period of reduced food intake, these patients cannot endure this renunciation."

Simmonds' disease and chronic anorexia must also be distinguished from true anorexia. With the latter, patients "show an early onset in childhood on the basis of the typical conflicts of the oral and anal periods, improve temporarily at puberty, and later give rise to chronic conditions of an asthenic hypochondriacal type."

Palazzoli delineates two types of true anorexia: "1) a stable type, characterized by constant limitation of food intake, and 2) a type that presents dramatic alternations between fasting and overeating. The latter group also includes patients who show overt terror of overeating attacks."*(367)*

Palazzoli mentions many other facets of true anorexia which I can confirm.

Thin, nervous and a difficult child, Marion W.'s relations with her parents and the world were much determined by her physical attributes. In analysis, the picture presented and conveyed was how much she had suffered from being "skinny." Only after many years of therapy, when she began to relinquish a deeply embedded and extensive masochistic pattern mixed with much sadism, did it become obvious that she had powerful vested interests in remaining thin. In fact, she despised fat women and enjoyed their discomfiture about their weight.

Not to be thin was quite frightening to her. It meant that the many ways she used being thin to justify her biting bitterness and to make people uncomfortable would now have no basis in fact. How she wove her skinniness into many aspects of her fantasies associated with her body would also have to be relinquished. Being skinny was intimately intermingled with feelings of being crippled. To be of average weight, to have good relations with her husband and children and get satisfaction out of life meant to give up many feelings of uniqueness and to become average, ordinary, "a slob like everyone else."

In the fourth month of the fifth year of our work, when Marion began to let in that liking people was fun although she was still frightened of doing so, much more material about her thiness came out. Its relation to her identity problems also became clearer.

As a female physical model, her mother was of average proportions, but everything about her "sagged — her breasts, her stomach and her behind. She was always tired." In retrospect Marion recognized that her mother was hypochondriacal and constantly depressed. Her mother had plainly indicated she had never wanted children, informed Marion that she was a difficult child, and that she "didn't know what to do with her."

Her father, though he had "scrawny thin arms," was athletic. He was extremely insecure, constantly inflating himself by talking about imaginary "big deals and important people he knew." He demanded that Marion be a boy and participate in athletics with him. At the same time, he treated her like a grown woman — a big blowsy "dame" with whom he cracked risque jokes which were beyond her.

Although there was a maternal grandmother in the household and other women around, they were not available. Her parents were rarely at home in the evening. When she came home from school her mother would be resting or out shopping. Her parents didn't actively treat her badly. They simply weren't there, and when they were, their identities were confusing. At times to get a response, she would provoke her father into beating her. She felt this was worth the price because during these physical confrontations he was palpably there for her. How much she longed for warmth, contact, and a feeling of identity was evident in how she held and cuddled her sister five years younger. They slept together and she spent much time playing with her.

Her mother did not like to cook and her food was tasteless. Marion was a poor eater and her mother constantly picked at her about it. Over the years, her mother became increasingly obsessed with the possibility of a sudden food shortage and stored food. The house became stocked like a warehouse.

Marion has a sense of rhythm, a love of dancing and music. She practiced the piano for hours so that she would become famous. She is a very good tennis player and ice skater. She had a passion for the theater. Concern with what shows, what it looks like, appearances, and recognition filled her earlier actual existence as well as her fantasy existence which was extensive and involved. But there was another aspect to her rhythm and love of motion. She had the characteristic neuro-muscular hyperactivity of true anorexia. Her mother constantly scolded her for her restlessness. She could never sit still for more than a few minutes.

After her marriage she learned to be a good cook, but was indifferent to food. She always complained about her husband's demand for eating meals at home together and for having a variety of foods always available. Though she had told me about her concern regarding her skinniness, only now did she tell me that she had had episodes of gorging in frantic, desperate attempts to gain weight. She even drank pure cream. Some of her conflicts about gaining weight now became clearer.

She believed she had a large behind which was not so. What disturbed Marion was the obvious evidence that she was a woman. For a long period she had a powerful desire to be a "dyke," and acted as if she were one "coming on strong." There were of course intense sexual problems which she blamed on her husband. She considered herself so loathsome "who would want me."

Through extensive discussions, it became clear that Marion wanted to gain weight, but not in her behind. It did not concern her that her breasts were small. If they did not become larger with weight gain that was all right. Large breasts could be seen, revealing her as a woman. About being seen as a woman she was divided. The weight gain should show in her face because "it is what shows, people see it, and you can't hide your face."

In Marion many aspects of the picture of true anorexia can be identified. There is the secrecy about many aspects of her attitudes toward food — eating and not eating and attitudes toward food in references to others. Lifelong poor appetite is there. There were taste-less meals at home and constant criticism about her being a poor eater and always being skinny. Her becoming a good cook and pre-occupied with menus as well as the constant talking about her husband's wanting all kinds of foods also fits the picture. The evidence for inadequate and confused real self and core identity, sexual and gender identity is all there.

The true anorexic feels bound to her mother and enters adolescence lacking deep peer relationships. As Marion's body assumed curves, it became alien — one she could not accept as her own. She experienced it as a concretization of her mother which she had introjected. She fought against her internalized mother, and maintained her identity, autonomy, and effectiveness by starving that internalized object. In consequence she starved herself. *(367)*

Rose B. was always a poor eater and easily lost weight. Five feet

526

five inches tall, Rose weighed eighty-eight pounds when she began analysis.

In her sixty-eighth and sixty-ninth years, her husband was in and out of hospitals eight times in one and a half years. After two years of her husband's illness, she began to have violent hunger pains. As she attempted to satisfy them, she had excruciating stomach and bowel cramps followed by diarrhea or constipation. As this went on she became frightened. "These hunger pains and my bowels are becoming an obsession with me. That's all I talk about." All forms of medication and palliation were of no aid. Barium studies revealed that her hyperirritable bowel emptied four times faster than normal. After this had gone on for four weeks, I again reviewed in detail her life history of gastrointestinal disturbances. This brought forth much new material and some alleviation of the intensity of the hunger cramps and the alternating diarrhea and constipation. She indicated that our discussion had been helpful through clarifying the meaning of her gastrointestinal problems.

A poor eater since infancy, she was aware of having used eating as a way of controlling her mother. At table when the patient was forced to eat, she covertly spat it out. Her mother constantly gave her enemas and laxatives. She also slept with her to keep her husband out of her bed. Rose had a constant fear her mother would roll over on her and crush or smother her. Clinging to her mother, she also hated her. Out of fear, she hid these feelings and silently adored her father.

Her mother was of her height, but food conscious and very fat. She had diabetes in later life and always cheated on her diet. Rose recalled that after her mother had a stroke in her late sixties, "she became like an animal the way she ate. She was revolting."

Rose B. suffers from chronic anorexia from childhood and shows the stable type of true anorexia nervosa. There are also aspects of the alternating fasting and overeating of true anorexia. The latter was evident in adolescence when she ate before supper, refused to eat at the table, and secretly gorged from the ice box. But the sharpest evidence of the latter is in her present state of intense hunger where she has urges to gorge herself. As soon as she begins, violent spasms of pain force her to stop.

For understanding Rose B.'s anorexia, a holistic approach including the phenomenological and existential orientations is necessary as well as newer knowledge regarding identity in its many aspects. Many aspects of true anorexia defined by Palazzoli are evident. Muted is

527

the neuromuscular hyperactivity which only occasionally broke through. Her hatred of her femininity, her curves, and her body like her mother's is evident.

Palazolli states that the incorporated bad object is experienced as "powerful, indestructible, self-sufficient, growing, and threatening" and that the pathetic weak ego of the anorexic "feels helpless in every sense, biological and psychological, before the imperious object."*(367)*

Horney's concepts of the pride system, the tyranny of the should, *(40)* and the dictatorship within illuminate these aspects of true anorexia and are most helpful in the therapy of such patients.

Laurel Q. had a perfect figure of which she was very proud. I was the third analyst for the treatment of her pernicious vomiting. Her thinness was partly a consequence of the vomiting and occasional nausea which interfered with eating. The nausea followed a period of feeling depressed toward evening. This brought up recollections of the tortures suffered at her mother's hands when, as a child, she wanted to stay up and be alone in her room, the only time she was free of her mother's vicious diatribes. The nausea appeared also with recollections of the fights at the table at the evening meal. What emerged was that nausea, vomiting, and an inability to eat were Laurel's ways of rebelling against her mother. Underneath her depression were intense feelings of hostility and rage.

With her increasing ability to experience and own her feelings of murderous fury, there was an increasing ability to let herself enjoy and like herself. Laurel began to feel hungry in a new way and to enjoy eating with a new spirit. As she began to gain back the weight she lost, she began to become concerned about becoming fat. She began to restrict her food intake. At this point, much about her perfect figure came out, about people's comments on it, particularly when she was younger, and about her daughter who also had a perfect figure with whom elements of competitiveness began to come to the fore.

In the last three months of the third year of our work, the effects of my having fulfilled the diatrophic functions of a successful parent became evident. This came through more sharply after a tempestuous period during which she let go of a deep and tenacious need and demand to be taken care of like a baby. Her inability to eat returned and her weight dropped to 105, low for her five feet three inches.

She had been told that when her mother brought her home from the hospital, she locked herself in the bedroom with Laurel for three days so that no one could interfere while Laurel cried herself out. At six months they called a pediatrician who said Laurel was hungry and underfed. Laurel was breastfed but, as she expressed it, "I feel my mother's milk poisoned me. With her hatred for me her milk must have been bitter."

Her mother was always fat with big breasts. "She eats constantly, anything and everything, and between meals lollipops." She belched and passed wind loudly, laughing uproariously about it. Her father also belched loudly, but went to the bathroom to pass wind. Her mother was a poor cook, and her meals were tasteless. She insisted that mustard, ketchup, and any other condiments "were bad for you." There were never any "goodies around, like cookies or cakes. All that was available were apples." Laurel's school lunches were either dry or soggy "while the other kids had good lunches." Her mother kept the ice box locked because she was sure the maids stole the food. She threw out edible leftovers because she was certain stale food would poison you.

Her mother was constantly talking about food poisoning. She recited a long list of foods which weren't good for you because they would "poison you or you could get botulism and die from it." She fired Laurel's beloved maid because her mother insisted she fed her brother poisoned food and "made him almost die." People "disgusted" her, or made her "sick to my stomach." She uttered these statement loudly with vicious, revolting sounds.

She would wake Laurel up on weekends with a tray to have in bed so the maid could clean up the kitchen and leave. Laurel hated this. Laurel was always a poor eater and thin. As she sat at the table, her mother screamed at her constantly. The only times she enjoyed eating were when she went to her colored maid's home and when the family summered in the mountains at a small hotel or at the beach which she loved.

After her marriage, Laurel became an excellent cook but didn't eat what she cooked. "Whenever I talk about cooking and anyone says 'You're a good cook' I always say, 'I hate cooking so much I can't understand how it can taste good when all the poison of my nature goes into it.' " All her life Laurel has been hypersensitive to smells.

During her first — eighteen months — and second — six years — analytic experiences, the vomiting stopped after several months and she had no further problems with eating. Since working with me, it has never been entirely absent for an extended period. In the last three months of the third year, it was often quite intense although there were times when she could eat with pleasure. During these months, more of the roots of her anorexia became clear and were worked through. Between sessions she immediately wrote down what would suddenly break through and then read it to me later. This was a great help to her. In this way she experienced me as always available and there for her. Over a period of a month she wrote:

"I have to go to school. I have to behave. I have to. I have to. I have to." This describes an external imposed and learned dictatorship of oughts and musts which she internalized and against which there was no rebelling. Horney's "Tyranny of the Should" makes this dictatorship within more understandable. This coercing of self also illuminates the neuromuscular hyperactivity of the anorexic. They are driven by internal obligations. It is psychodynamically determined, and can be resolved. Then they can feel they have the "right to sit and do nothing," which still made Laurel unbearably anxious.

"She makes me — no use to fight — no use to rebel. I'll still have to do whatever she wants, be like she wants." This is the imperviousness anorexics experience and rebel against in their mothers which Palazzoli describes. Horney's concepts of the "Tyranny of the Should" and "The Pride System" illuminate it further.

"She can make me do anything no matter how much I hate it EXCEPT she can't MAKE ME EAT." By opposing her introjected mother, Laurel starves. "I have such an overdeveloped sense of responsibility to everyone. Even to strangers. I have to eat or I'll die. I can't, I can't, I can't anymore. I can't fulfill my obligations and responsibility and I don't want to. I never did want to." The struggle between introjected shoulds and dimly felt, genuine *not wanting to* is clear. Genuine *wanting to* is still too weak.

"I feel like those skinny starving mongrel dogs you see foraging around garbage cans and running off with any scrap of food they can find to hide and eat it alone. I always said I'm greedy for life. I want to know and be and smell and taste and have everything. Am I afraid to eat because I'm so hungry I'll gulp and guzzle like an animal? Forget my good manners?" The hunger and greed for life and the fear of it are exquisitely described. The confusion of being like her mother, gorging food, and the genuine desire to eat leave Laurel in a dilemma.

The connection of food and sexuality is evident in her mother's statements. "Don't take food from strangers. It may be dope and they will kidnap you and sell you into white slavery. . . . My mother was always very disgusted by people who showed any sexuality publicly. She said they were like animals, like dogs, I want to be like an animal. To snarl and bite, to eat like an animal, greedily, hastily, to steal food and gulp it down, (I used to steal money from her purse) to howl and bite anyone who tries to take food away from me — to fornicate publicly and freely 'like a dog' — to be like an animal not a human being — like an animal is free — free to defend myself — free to demand — free to protect myself — free to have no manners — free to tend for yourself at all costs and to hell with anyone else — free to be *aggressive — free to frighten people, free to abandon everyone and run away.* Without a role to fulfill I don't have the strength *or is it the inner resources — for life to be worthwhile.*

"Is the only way I can assert myself, feel myself, *feel me —* be me — is the only way I can feel my center of being by not eating? She used to talk a lot about people being 'eaten up' by envy — 'eating themselves all up' with jealousy, etc. When I can't eat food my stomach feels like it's eating itself up. I sometimes feel, when I'm starving myself, that I'm 'eating myself up.' If I had ever been fat, there'd be something to 'eat up' you might say I could live off my body fat — but I've always been thin — so I'm really eating myself up — instead of eating food — but this destroying myself and yet I must be getting something out of it? Am I doing it to *survive* rather than to die? I don't know. It's irrational and dangerous.

"I am willing to face the pain and suffering because I believe a new, free woman can come out of it — and the sick childish slave will disappear.

"Have irrational feeling I'm afraid to eat . . . . Don't let me starve to death. That was another one I frequently heard about. 'The poor children all over the world who are starving to death. You ought to be ashamed that you didn't eat the good food I gave you.' But this was contradicted by being punished by sending me to bed without supper and being told she would punish me by giving me only bread and salt water like the prisoners got if I didn't behave myself. Also somewhere in here comes a memory of washing my mouth out with brown Octagon kitchen soap for talking back to her, for being impudent, for talking ugly.

"I want to stay in bed all day today. I feel guilty for having nothing to get up for except the housework and cooking and walking the dog. But all the things I can think of to *do* are not for the *sake of doing* but to have something to do. Realize how I must be doing something or I become miserable, can't just sit quiet doing nothing — get very depressed and nervous. Don't understand this at all.

"I want to have a sense of existence. When Bob [her husband] was home *I didn't exist*. This not eating is really crazy. It's now an obsession. I never realized not eating is a real OBSESSION. It is a fixed idea — a persistent and inescapable preoccupation. She has an obsession about eating too. But it's the other side of the coin. Do I use it not only to fill my existence but also as a weapon against the people whom I feel deny my existence by their behavior? I seem to be able to be myself, to feel, to exist only in misery and unhappiness — panic, anxiety, and depression. I'm very worried about myself — I want to eat intellectually — but emotionally I can't.

"When I was a child and didn't want to eat, but knew I'd have to sit till I did, or be yelled at till I did, or force it, and I couldn't slip it into my pants to throw it away later. I pretended the fork was a woman and the food on the tip was different kinds and styles of hats. By thinking of the game I forgot the food and then I would eat.

"I hate feeling I'm being watched when I eat. I think that's why it's easier to get a little something *into* myself when I'm alone. I ate three meals today — small ones but nevertheless 3 — lunch and dinner at table with Bob.

"Now if I could only work through my *own* unreal fantasies which I am trying so hard to do. At least I do feel that I am opening up to myself and looking at all the mess inside. I can hardly believe the mess I am but I can't deny it. I see it clearly and it's horrifying to know I'm obsessed, crazy in certain areas, and doing these terrible and unreal things to myself for so many years and never aware they existed till now.

"I am very constipated. Haven't been able to go for three days. This seems to happen when I begin to eat a little." Laurel wanted to take in and hold onto what she had taken in by and for herself. When she couldn't take in food, she was against being penetrated sexually. Both Laurel and Rose recalled their mothers forcing enemas on them and literally forcing them to give up their stools. Laurel more clearly felt the helplessness and the humiliation.

"I just started to remember that she used to hold my nose so that I couldn't breathe, and would choke or suffocate unless I opened my mouth. I would hold out as long as possible. But in the end I would have to open it. Then she would stick the food in my mouth. She always did this to give me medicine. I remember spitting out the medicine. Then she hit me across the face and I had a terrible nosebleed. *BUT I DIDN'T SWALLOW IT OR TAKE IT IN THAT NIGHT AT LEAST.* What were my feelings about all this kind of forced feeding? Utter defeat, hatred of her, fear of her, humiliation and determination that I should be the victor, not her.

"So how have I perverted this wish to assert myself and ruined my life by trying to be alive — for if she is the victor I am KILLED — MYSELF IS NOT *ME* BUT HER? But my way of trying to live is DEATH — NOT LIFE — SELF destructive. Not self ALIVE — must go into this at length with Dr. K."

In the two months that this battle raged, images of a mad dog running amok as a symbol of freedom emerged. But she recognized he was sick and would be killed. Then followed images of wild horses and wild birds who were free and in contact with their natures, hence healthy. Then came an image of a baby wetting, soiling, and spitting out its food; enjoying the warmth of its urine and feces, and smearing it and food all over itself, everyone, and everything.

All the while "A great battle is going on within me. To *GIVE UP* the 'obsession' and *TO CLING* to it." She became aware of how she had been used as a football in constant battles between her parents and felt it was all her fault. It began to dawn on her that it wasn't her fault at all, and that she had erroneously blamed herself. I have worked with many patients who felt they were the bad ones. It was their fault because to find the problems in their parents would leave them without parents, abandoned, bereft.

During this raging battle Laurel was learning to become the mother to the child in her that her mother never had been. She always tried to get some nourishment into her to conserve her strength, even if only liquids. She appreciated the days she could eat three meals at the table with her husband. She learned how to conserve her strength and rest by staying in bed most of the day. Likewise she became more experienced in using medication to hold her anxieties in check. She had previously been most reluctant to use any. She indicated an awareness of her learning through suffering and through accepting her suffering. All this she realized was preparation and training for a battle that may go on for some time. Now it was a battle to become more continuously what she had begun to feel for moments and hours.

"I am relaxed and happy — a few hours ago I was feeling a failure. When will I level off and quit swinging to extremes? I feel calm and rested. Tomorrow I plan to stay in bed all day and sleep and continue to rest myself until I go to Dr. Kelman. I need the rest badly. Today was a horror till the evening." when

533

she was with her husband, son, daughter, and her daughter's boy friend. "It was our little family. Happy together and relaxed."

A woman and a man both protested that they suffered much pain and anguish not simply because they were thin, but because they always looked frail and in ill-health. Their frailty and ill-health were more apparent than real. The woman's face was thin and gaunt, giving the picture of emaciation and possible fatal illness. She had, however, a sturdy body, enormous stamina, and could, in her youth, successfully compete with her brothers in wrestling and in mountain climbing. The man was a lawyer who had been a long-distance runner in college. He could run for hours in the hot sun. Onlookers became anguished because they expected him to drop at any moment from exhaustion or ill-health. Both, particularly the man, could eat for three and never show it.

In analysis what emerged was that both used their looking frail and sick for intimidating people and extorting advantages. The man had a martyred, sweet, all-suffering look when his intense bitterness did not show through. The woman had the expression of an all-suffering, "sweet dear" who would say, "Oh, it's all right, don't bother about me" while making you feel guilty and intimidating you into going along with her coercive demands for attention and understanding. Both had extended analyses. The woman I knew for seventeen years and the man for twenty-one. Although both had gained from their analyses, their body habits did not change in the least. The way they used their apparent frailty and looking ill was moderately leavened.

Another woman enjoyed ill-health, but not too much of it. All that was necessary was for her to have a slight cold and she would take to her bed. From there she queened it over her friends from whom she now felt free to extort all manner of attention. She quite openly told me how she would call them far and wide, using her illness to justify demands that they come visit her, send her flowers, and chocolates.

While she and the people who looked frail and sick could be said to have gotten secondary gains from illness, this dynamic is usually more complex and interwoven with the whole neurotic structure of so-called psychosomatic disorders. Of a different order is falling ill when psychically threatened, and using such illness as a defense and a threat. These issues are related to the "giving up-given up"complex studied by Engel and his associates. (368)

In the above examples of looking frail and sick and of looking and being skinny, I of course do not overlook hereditary factors and the influences of life's vicissitudes. The work of Draper *(369)* and others on body habitus has indicated that some people are thin but should be fat, and some are fat but should be thin.

One woman who should have had average proportions had been thin all her life, always in good health, very athletic, and, according to her own statements, was "strong as a horse and could eat for two." As a woman she liked being thin because it made it possible for her to be something of a clotheshorse. She had good taste in clothes and wore them well. Always intense, restless, and hyperactive, she had become much less so during analysis. It represented a great change in her when she could lie on the couch for some minutes quietly relaxed without moving and not talking. I would doubt whether after years of analysis and follow-up that there would be any change in her body habitus, eating, or activity habits. Her brothers and sisters as well as her parents tended toward being somewhat heavier than she.

Though the fear of getting fat is a concern of nightmare proportions with most women, I have never analyzed one whose obesity was a central problem. I have known, however, many women who gained and lost from five to fifteen pounds during the menstrual cycle.

Many of them reported a diminution in urinary output before and during menstruation, as they were feeling heavier, more bloated, and their breasts were getting sore and painful. One woman said, "After my period I seem to pee and pee and pee." While these changes are clearly connected with the hormonal cycle, they are also intimately related to how these women feel about being women. Weight changes due to water retention, however, are not limited to women.

A chemist, athletic and well-proportioned, brought this fact to my attention. In the next twenty-six years I observed it in a number of other men. In every one the water retention was concomitant with holding in, holding back, and not giving out. The chemist became aware that this happened when he was enraged with his wife and didn't want to have anything to do with her. Also it was connected with his fear of his rages, his need to control them and hold them in check. Finally, it was related to his pride in intellect and self-sufficiency. To be out of control and show an impulsive outburst of feelings was humiliating to him. When his rage at his wife subsided, he passed quantities of urine and his weight dropped five to seven pounds.

When I first saw Abraham B., in his early thirties, he was six feet tall, and had weighed 260 pounds since his early teens. Samuel G. was almost five feet eight inches tall and weighed 220 pounds, also since his early teens. They were both the most

535

obese in their respective families. Both were painfully shy and anxious. Abraham B. dealt with his suspiciousness, secretiveness, and withdrawal; Samuel G. by expansiveness and boisterousness. He had suffered much more from being a fat boy and had had difficulties in athletics because of awkwardness. Both perspired in winter and seldom wore overcoats. With Samuel G., the element of rebellious defiance to his mother played a crucial role. Both had extended analyses without any effect on their weight.

In the case of Benjamin L., fluctuations in weight occurred in his thirties and forties. As his personal life became more difficult, he gained until he weighed 235 pounds. He was five feet eight inches tall. Even with the greatest effort, he could not get below 210 for almost fifteen years. When anxious and feeling abused, he would insist to himself that he had the right to indulge himself with sweets or extra helpings of rich food.

It was only after years of working through his neurotic claims that his weight dropped below 210. On several occasions he even went below 200.

With Simon D. a very special factor obtained. Before the age of four months, he had almost died of what was called summer diarrhea. It was actually a case of marasmus due to hostile rejection by his mother. Added factors were a familial tendency to easy weight gain, low blood pressure, and low basal metabolic rate. His own was so low that he had to take thyroid supplement. Five feet ten inches tall, in his teens he weighed up to 220. Then gradually in five years his weight dropped to 170 where it remained until his late thirties when it again went as high as 220. Dieting was a torture for him. He would become exhausted, develop colds, and stop the diet.

He has had many years of analysis. In the last five, as his life became easier, fuller, and happier, he had the feeling that he was approaching a resolution of the psychic sources of his weight problem. In the last year, dieting became easier, and he noted the absence of the previous anxiety and restlessness as he did so. He observed that getting through the first difficult two-week period was less difficult. He was about 200, and had the conviction that in the next several years he would drop to 170 which he felt as his natural weight. He experienced himself as of average proportions; and so visualized himself, even when his weight was fluctuating wildly.

Although familial and constitutional factors were present, the special factors of a very traumatic infancy, an unhappy childhood, and a difficult adolescence were the crucial ones. As Simon's dependency needs were resolved, so was the weight problem.

Irving W.'s weight gains were mainly associated with binges of chocolate eating and hors d'oeuvres at cocktail parties. He recognized the self-destructive nature of these binges. Since his earliest years he had been fond of chocolate and chocolate cake. There was very little of human sweetness in Irving's life. His mother was consistently critical. His father was remote and dominated by his mother after he had failed in business when Irving was ten. The family atmosphere was barren.

Strict adherence to diets would bring Irving's weight down to 210. These were followed by a chocolate or food orgy which would bring him back to 260. As his massive depression began to lighten, the intensity of the binges became less, but predictably, after a lift in his mood, a repercussion and a binge of chocolate eating would follow.

As we explored the inner feeling structure of what went on in these binges, Irving first became aware of a gloating vindictiveness against himself as if there were two sides of him. He could almost hear a voice saying with gleeful derision, "Go ahead and gorge yourself!" Next he became aware of an intense anxiety followed by an uncontrollable compulsiveness to head for a candy stand. These binges often happened just before seeing me. He would sit and literally smack his lips, derisively smiling and challenging me to do something about it. When he became aware of the uncontrollable and violent nature of these binges and their connections with episodes of opening up and feeling better, he began to get frightened and concerned. Their intensity began to fall away with this awareness. His mood became more elevated. He also became more active, with much more open hostility and vindictiveness. The binges became less frequent and less intense.

These case citations can be subsumed under an expanded notion of so-called psychosomatic disorders, under what Engel designated as *somato psychic-psychosomatic,* and certainly under what is now referred to as comprehensive medicine. Understanding of such patients can further be enhanced by the holistic approach, medical and psychoanalytic.

Chapter 33

The General Practice of
Psychoanalysis III:
The Holistic Approach

According to Engel, there are three historical phases of "the psycho-analytic approach to psychosomatic relationships." Engel further states that this approach rejects the notion that certain diseases are psychosomatic while others are not. "It attempts to identify what bodily systems may become activated through psychologic mechanisms and then to assay what part the consequent physical changes may play in the series of processes which may ultimately culminate in an organic disease state."*(368, p. 252)*

The first phase of psychosomatic investigations began with Freud's study of conversion. The second started with World War I when it was thought "that certain somatic conditions might be conceptualized within the psychoanalytic framework and perhaps also might be amenable to cure by these means." The third and present phase began in the late forties when psychoanalysts began to "apply psychoanalytic know-how to the bedside and the laboratory."

Although through great ingenuity psychoanalysts have been able to devise experimental models to use psychoanalytic know-how and have gained solid information, this direction of research is open to further possibilities. Engel feels that "Patients in psychoanalysis offer the best source of material for gaining insight into the unconscious determinants and metapsychology of the critical psychic states involved in the genesis of somatic disorder." He adds that "Rich lodes have been uncovered during this third period, begging for mining in depth by practicing analysts."*(368, p. 268)*

Psychosomatic Specificity by Alexander, French, and Pollock, is the result of fourteen years of work (1951-1965) by twenty medically trained psychoanalysts, thirteen internists, and one statistician on 149 patients. In his review of their book Engel stated that while the work is not conclusive, it is important because it shows "that specificity is by no means a dead issue in the psychosomatic field."*(370)*

In "Education in Psychosomatic Concepts," Wittkower and Aufreiter mention that "Freud's model of conversion hysteria is usually listed as the first model of Psychosomatic Medicine." They note, however, that he restricted his theory to the body changes having a symbolic meaning in conversion hysteria. Freud never used the term "psychosomatic medicine" and "never concerned himself with the psychoanalytic study of somatic diseases." This lack may have been occasioned by his bitterness at being rejected by academic medicine and by "his preoccupation with the elaboration of psychoanalytic principles."*(371)*

It was thirty years from the beginning of the psychoanalytic movement to the start of the psychosomatic one. Flanders Dunbar, one of the pioneers, did not mention the contributions of psychoanalysts to the field in the first edition of *Emotions and Bodily Changes* (1935). *(372)* She did include them in the second edition, three years later. With the appearance of the journal *Psychosomatic Medicine* in 1939, created mainly by psychoanalysts, the second phase of the psychosomatic movement was in full swing. But by the late forties "the honeymoon" between psychoanalysis and psychosomatic medicine was over.

This sequence of development was to "some extent . . . reflected . . . in the teaching of psychosomatic concepts at psychoanalytic institutes." To get exact information, Wittkower and Aufreiter sent questionnaires to eighteen institutes in the American and got seventeen replies. Ten said they had never given courses on psychosomatic medicine, and two no longer did. The views of the seventeen respondents went from (1) opposition to teaching psychosomatic medicine as a separate subject to (2) initial hopes about psychosomatic medicine being disappointed to (3) those who felt "The traditional psychosomatic approach was too narrow" to (4) a preference for the integration of psychoanalysis within medicine via the psychoanalytic approach. *(371)*

Grinker, Founding Director of the Institute for Psychosomatic and Psychiatric Research (1946); Daniels, Millett, and Rado, Founders of the Psychoanalytic and Psychosomatic Clinic for Training and Research (1944); Alexander, Engel, and Wittkower are all pioneers congenial to the above fourth viewpoint. Wittkower formulates it as the need for the "development of comprehensive research as a counter move aimed at encompassing, without bias, a broadening spectrum of biological, psychological, social, and cultural aspects of disease and the transactions between them."*(371)* This volume is congenial to the holistic approach. *(371)* Studies in depth of diverse populations with organic disease have led Engel to the inescapable impression "that psychological characteristics and disease processes are by no means randomly distributed" even though the meaning of such associations cannot yet be clarified. *(370)*

Against this background and in the light of Engel's above statements regarding psychosomatic specificity I want to include some of my experiences with patients who suffered from so-called psychosomatic disorders. These findings, though uncontrolled, may serve to stimulate not only an interest in psychosomatic specificity but also an enthusiasm for the natural science and history approach to health and disease.

The psychosomatic disorders most usually mentioned are "peptic ulcer, colitis, dermatitis, rheumatoid arthritis, asthma, hypertension, and hyperthyroidism."*(371, p. 253)* I have had experience with all these physical problems as well as some not usually included.

Jake B., age twenty-nine, was diagnosed generalized eczema, type Prurigo Besnier, on eight hospitalizations over three and a half year for this condition. During his eighth hospitalization I saw him thirty times. *(373)*

Jake was married with one son. His father, sixty-seven, a man of few words and broad interests, was respected but not loved by his children. His mother, also sixty-seven, was an intelligent, generous, kindly woman full of fun. However, Jake could say nothing about his feelings toward her or her feelings toward him. An older brother and sister were fairly well educated and were happily married. Another brother, thirty-two, unmarried, was poorly educated and always sickly. To him the patient was indifferent, but he had a fair relationship with the older two. Another sister, age thirty, a grammar school graduate, and unhappily married, was his father's favorite and Jake resented her. The youngest — a brother, age twenty-five — had done fairly well in grammar school and toward him the patient felt kindly.

Born on the Lower East side of Manhattan in 1905, Jake began school at seven and failed four times in his earlier grades. At fifteen he left school and continued to work full time in a shoe store where he had been an errand boy. His I.Q. was 94 but the examiner felt it was much higher.

Jake gave his mother his complete salary for several years. When he took part of it, he spent or gambled it all. He never saved and was never satisfied with the size of his earnings. After five years in the shoe store he and his brother borrowed money and bought a truck. After initial failure, they did exceptionally well. They broke up the partnership, and Jake continued to do well until the pre-Christmas lull when he became ill.

From age ten homosexuals had approached him. "I had a rosy complexion and they seemed to like me. They would flirt with me like a woman before as well as after I was married." Masturbating started at fifteen with much anxiety because he had heard "it goes to your head and you become a nitwit." His wife was his only sweetheart from fourteen until they secretly married at twenty-one. While masturbating he had fantasied coitus, but never with his sweetheart. At sixteen, following his first heterosexual experience with a prostitute, he stopped masturbating. He had gone with a group of fellows but could not recall who went first. "If there had been a fight for first, I would have remembered it. I went up to her like experienced man with my clothes on. It was over in a half minute. I was satisfied." He continued to go to prostitutes twice monthly with some other fellows, never using condoms by preference and always having premature ejaculations. At nineteen, first through curiosity and the second time at the request of the prostitute, he experienced fellatio.

When he married, there was no sex the first two weeks and there had been none premaritally. On the first attempt, he had sex seven times with seven premature ejaculations. It was two months before there was penetration. His wife never requested relations. He believes she never had an orgasm. Relations were once nightly and always ended in premature emission.

After the ordeal of his wife's first pregnancy, Jake went to sleep in his mother's apartment rather than his own. "I slept well. They consoled me. I didn't have the itch. I was healthy." In addition to a flight from the new responsibility and the competition from his newborn son, the move was an infantile rush into mother's arms. Obtaining the history of his relations with his wife was most difficult. He constantly asked if I wasn't tired of trying to find something wrong with his mind, and he admitted several weeks later that he was "nervous, jittery, and high-strung."

For six months before the Christmas lull, he had been nervous and worried, sobbing hysterically "for no good reason." He later asked if nagging could have "an effect on the human body. As soon as there is no income, even if there is money in the bank, my wife starts worrying and that makes me worry. When I missed a job I did not worry. I would say I might have gotten killed or wrecked on it. When will I see you again?" He was disconcerted when I told him three times weekly.

The above and other material indicated powerful masochistic and self-destructive pulls toward total incapacitation and death. "I am a glutton for punishment. When I was four I almost had my leg twisted off but that didn't frighten me from hitching the same wagon. Between five and seven many times I had head cuts, bruises, and my arms twisted in gang fights. I have taken lots of abuse and after it I felt like a whipped dog. Nobody ever gave me anything because no matter how bad I needed it, I would refuse it even if it were offered." Between fifteen and twenty as a shoe salesman his boss abused him shamelessly. Jake excused it all for the little kindnesses he was occasionally shown. This employment situation also tells much about his relationship to older men. "My wife abused me a little but it is necessary because I give her all the money and with it the worry of paying the bills." This was a replica of what he did with his mother when he started to work at fifteen and gave her all his salary.

Toward the end of his hospital stay with his skin clear and feeling much betetr, he was asked if he felt our discussions had anything to do with his improved physical state. "Does it mean I'm licked? Why is it I can't refuse to do things people ask me to, even though I hated to and was burning up inside while I was doing it?" Each time he had been told he didn't have to come to see me and could terminate the interview at any time, neither of which could he do. He also had to deny what his relationship to me meant to him.

He showed a most naïve, immature expansiveness, narcissism, and exhibitionism, the roots of which he was painfully aware of. "I would like to have a nice income, be a big shot." In the fifth session he reluctantly admitted dreaming and then mentioned one in which he was the hero of a boxing match. He also admitted that all his fights when young were because he was extremely sensitive and had a strong feeling of inadequacy. If anyone, no matter how fond he was of them, used the word stupid even in jest, Jake would brood about it for hours and hate them without giving vent to his feelings. He said he had never talked intimately with anyone, and was averse to continuing to do so with me because I might think some of the things he said were foolish, which meant mental derangement to him.

Three months after his first hospitalization, suddenly overnight "pimples appeared" on Jake's chest. Within a week the rash covered his whole body and itching developed. Seven hospitalizations followed including a trip to a professor in Chicago and a move of the family to the West Coast for some months. The pattern was repetitive. Skin tests were always negative and the treatment non-specific. Soon after coming into the hospital his skin cleared up and promptly on leaving and on several occasions at the imminence of leaving, he broke out again. On one occasion when he was about to be discharged, he rubbed perfectly clear skin on his arms for two minutes and said, "You could see the pimples coming on." The doctors discharged him anyway, and on the way home his skin broke out.

Jake observed that "The parts that are most active seem to break down first," and that if he lay perfectly still he was not bothered by the itch, but if he moved where the skin got warm it itched. Absolute stillness, lifelessness, helplessness, passivity, and even oblivion and death were the necessary defenses against the itching and the rash. While the rash would go away in a hospital, after the first hospitalization the itch never left except under the very special conditions mentioned above. "The itch feels like something crawling under the skin that wants to come out and I am not comfortable until it has broken through so that sometimes I tear the skin off and then I feel all right until it heals up. In fact, I feel better when my skin is broken out."

Before the itch Jake felt mountingly helpless and enraged, conflicted and hating himself, which promoted more anxiety and increasing tension as he attempted to contain, control, and deny them. As a consequence and as part of the active alienating process he became increasingly remote from himself almost to the point of depersonalization. In the process he concretized, objectified, projected, and ultimately externalized the itches which he had vitalized into a living something. The struggle now was outside of himself. The pleasure in gouging at the almost personified itch came from having alienated himself from it and having externalized it. From being powerless he now became powerful. The very tension which tortured him now became energy transformed into action and thus diminished. From being the passive victim, he became the active victimizer. In tearing at his skin, the itch and pain increased. What was painful to Jake became pleasurable, at times eroticized to the point of orgastic sexuality. The net result was that Jake was now obviously sick, crippled, and had to be taken care of. People now had to pay close attention to him (even with magnifying glasses) and treat him gently with the most soothing lotions. He began to "sob hysterically" through his weeping skin wounds and was "consoled." The burden of life was no longer his.

In the instance above I referred to mounting tension as a consequence of increasing feelings of helplessness, anxiety, rage, self-hate, and conflict and the patient's efforts to control, contain, and deny them. This is the organism's attempt to maintain itself as an autonomous identity in a state of relative constancy. I prefer the term tension to stress because it has subjective and objective reference. I feel the term tension is more comprehensive than stress. The findings regarding stress in the work of Selye and H. G. Wolff can be incorporated into the concept of tension. *(374)*

It is not tension *per se* which is sick or healthy, but the proportions of rational and irrational aspects of the tension as determined by the rationality and irrationality of its sources, functions, and the attitudes toward it. *(144)*

Toward the end of his eighth hospitalization, Jake asked to see me on several occasions. A month later, Jake was hospitalized for three months. Discharged, it was again only a month before he was hospitalized for the tenth time, a period of seven months. In the tenth he said, "I don't miss my wife and child so much," and "I am really afraid to leave here." His wife had gone back to work without asking him and the child was boarded out. Shortly after leaving the hospital after the ninth hospitalization, he arranged to spend the night with his wife in a hotel rather than going to either parents' home, Their last sex relations had been a year previous. He fortified himself with beer, a friend having told him it prevented premature ejaculation. On his three attempts that night his control was better but still premature. "The very next day I got much worse" and soon he was back in the hospital for the tenth time.

"By this time my wife was fed up. Somehow I lost faith in her," an obvious and immediate defense which evolved into suspicions of infidelity of which he accused her. He asked me what I felt about a separation or divorce because he was convinced she was the source of "all my problems." Then he told me that two days before she had asked for money for a divorce. His skin promptly got worse, but it soon improved.

During his tenth hospitalization, Jake had a very severe recurrence right in the hospital. He had discovered that, two days before, his brother had sold his truck and given the money to his father. It was two weeks before he had a full night's sleep. His weak, sickly older brother was now his father's favorite, and Jake had been made completely helpless without even a chance to fight back against the brother toward whom he had felt indifferent, that is, he hadn't considered him a competitor for his father's affection. The loss of his truck, a most precious love object, and rejection by his father, were shattering blows. "I feel I'm doomed. I am getting used to this disease, I'm getting used to being an institutional bum. I feel in years to come I'll be all right, but it will be too late when I am forty-five. I used to worry about my wife and child but I don't anymore."

Engel and his associates delineate the "giving up-given up" complex which develops in a setting of mental and physical illness. *(368)* "This is an ego state during which for shorter or longer periods of time, often in a waxing and waning manner, previously effectively used defenses and adaptations are perceived as ineffectual and current sources of gratification as unavailable. In phenomenologic terms it has the following features": (1) A feeling of "It's no use," made up of helplessness felt as due to the failures on the part of the environment and hopelessness as due to failures in oneself; (2) feeling less intact and less able to function relatively autonomously; (3) relationships with objects are felt as less secure; (4) the environment is no longer what it was so far as expectations were by oneself or for guidance; (5) there is a loss of feeling of continuity between past and future and an inability to project into the future; and (6) there is an inclination to revive feelings, thoughts, and behaviors connected with past events which had a similar quality. *(371, p. 266)*

The "giving up" phase is ushered in by a failure of defenses and the "given up" one "marks the apparent finality of the loss of gratification as a psychic reality." Engel and his associates report the manifestation of this complex in 80 percent of patients and their relatives before the obvious onset of disease. They "differentiate women with cervical cancer from those without on the basis of the presence of the complex," although they caution that their evidence is presumptive. "Nor can it be regarded as either necessary or sufficient for the emergence of somatic disease, but only as a contributing factor and then only when other predisposing factors are also present and operating."*(371, pp. 266-67)*

Four months after his tenth hospitalization, Jake came for an interview at my request. One week after his discharge against his wishes he had dreamt, "I was in a tight place, a cave or woods, and was being chased by an animal and couldn't run. I had that horrible feeling like being paralyzed." He recalled having similar dreams many times during his illness. Trapped, powerless, and alone, the overwhelming animal forces constituted of a host of feelings and symbolizing many things were on the loose. His only protection was to "sob hysterically" in the "consoling" arms of his mother and/or father and neither was there or could be there because of his intense fears, hostilities, and conflicts.

On leaving after his tenth hospitalization Jake had returned to work in the shoe business for his old boss who was disappointed in him. "I don't want to go back to trucking. I hate dirt. I want to be a gentleman."

Ten months later, Jake returned for a second interview at my request. Things had gotten worse. His wife had started divorce proceedings, but gave it up and accepted separation by common consent. He saw his child once a week and filled the time by going to the movies at the child's instigation. He had insomnia and nightmares. His skin had broken out occasionally. Sensitivity tests remained negative. A month before our interview, Jake had gotten a new job with brighter prospects, but he was afraid of failure. Now he was convinced his skin condition was definitely related to his mental attitude. However, he still vacillated about the necessity for psychotherapy.

Three months later Jake voluntarily returned for psychotherapy. His mental and physical condition improved. He broke off therapy after six months. Six months later, his wife divorced him, and he left for a southern climate where he remained symptom-free for six months.

None of his family had skin conditions, hay fever, or asthma. As noted, sensitivity tests proved negative. Besnier conjectured that the condition was a "prurigo diathesique." Jake did have a "rosy complexion" which suggests a possible constitutional factor in his skin. The etiological factor verified again and again was psychogenic. Engel said regarding psychosomatic disorders, "a basic premise is that the degree and extent to which somatic systems are mobilized in response to psychological stress is inversely related to the success with which stress can be dealt with by purely psychic processes."*(371, p. 252)*

This certainly holds for Jake B. He showed the characteristic intense craving for closeness combined with conflicts about exhibitionistic tendencies.

All sons with silent, withdrawn, hostile, or absent fathers and domineering and seductive mothers obviously do not become homosexuals. This configuration is, however, a valuable clinical guide when the patient withholds information or unconsciously holds such propensities in check.

Jake B.'s history illustrates this configuration, although he never acted out homosexually, at least to my knowledge. There was the noncommunicative father whom the children respected and the mother who obviously was the dominant one. In addition, Jake had to compete with the favored sister, a little over one year older. The rejected male baby, Jake in turn rejected his masculinity and tried to be a little girl so his father would love him. This conflicted with his need for his mother's love. He clearly stated he never saw them show affection which also tells how much touching, holding, fondling, and caressing he himself missed. With no male love and support, an older brother who was sickly and to whom he was indifferent, he had to find his male images in the brutal life of the streets.

Jake B. was hysterically sobbing and nervous six months before his skin broke out. There was no special or crisis situation, but I feel there was an accumulating tension from many sources with which he finally could not deal. Once he was psychically and dermatologically conditioned, his skin easily responded to sudden or even mild accessions of tension. Once the tensions concretized in marriage and a family were removed, they no longer triggered his conditioned skin. What psychotherapy he received involuntarily and voluntarily aided in diminishing the sources of tension. But when he approached deeper problems he fled cold New York and the scene of his failures for the consoling arms of the sunny south and what he imagined would be easy living.

While psychosomatic specificity is neither proven nor disproven, I feel at the least it can serve as a valuable clinical guide. The concept makes use of the guiding notions of configurations of personality structure, of conflict patterns and of specific forms of response to tension. Alexander attempted to widen the concept to include physiological variables. *(370)* I feel that a comprehensive concept of tension combined with greater experience in using system thinking will help to explain the "by no means random" distribution "of psychological characteristics and disease processes."*(370)*

For the whole sixth year of her analysis Rose B. had a maddening scalp eczema. Since infancy she had one illness after another, beginning with "weak kidneys" at age two, wheezing and asthmatic attacks at age four, and migraine at nine. Later, there were menstrual problems and sexual frigidity. Psychic means for dealing with her problems were definitely not available to her.

As a child, a blonde, blue-eyed, doll-like creature, she was oohed and aahed over, the center of attention. She hated to be touched, and raged inside when anyone did so. She choked her rage back and clearly recalls the first attack of wheezing on such an occasion. The youngest, she was her father's favorite and treated like a fairy princess. Her pride in her blonde hair and how youthful she looked were extreme.

In the fifth year of her analysis, her princess attitudes came more clearly to the fore and were analyzed. They included no awareness of the meaning of money and how to use it realistically. At the same time her husband's and son's financial irresponsibility had come more sharply into focus which forced her to deal with money matters. This meant renouncing her fairy princess role.

During this year much about her morbid dependency had been discussed, her emphasis and pride in her intellect and her need to control her feelings and her body through intellect. While she had renounced much of her crowning glory as the fairy princess with the beautiful blonde hair, her head was now being further assaulted. During her suicidal phase she had taken her head in her hands and banged it against the wall because "that darn head wouldn't think clearly." At the same time she was renouncing her beloved mother and her image of herself as so sweet and gentle. The rages in her toward three father figures and two mother figures who had failed her were considerable. In addition she was having to renounce her pride in intellect and in controlling her feelings.

At this point the intolerable eczema disappeared. Local applications had been ineffective except as palliatives. Twelve years later, there was a mild recurrence for about three months. It occurred just before and during a period when much material which could be seen as body as phallus emerged. Her father wanted a boy and in many ways he treated her as if she were one. She wanted to become an athletic instructor until she broke her ankle in the gymnasium. She married a very athletic man. Her father had bought him as a son for himself, a playmate in athletics, a husband for his princess daughter, and an heir to manage his estate. Also at this time much material emerged concerning her clitoris as a weapon of assault, and her conviction that at one point, when taking stilbesterol, it had become very long. Shortly after, in the most intensely experienced rage Rose ever had toward me, she said she wanted to kick me, a pattern present since childhood when enraged. She also had a violent clitoral spasm.

In November of the eighth year, Rose had a dream she could not tell me for three weeks. Vaguely I was there in bed with her. She had an orgasm with which feeling she awoke. It was a half hour before she could turn the light off and dare to go back to sleep. Right after the relation of the dream came discussions of her lifelong urinary problems of her adolescent, feeling that she had to hide her breasts with tight bras and walk round-shouldered, and of her need to choke down all feelings regarded being a woman, being attractive and being noticed by men.

By the end of the sixth year of her analysis the scalp eczema had disappeared. She had an even better summer than she had had the year before. That fall there were intense repercussions, to her "well adjusted daughter's" marriage. She developed acute intestinal intussusception confirmed by X-ray while hospitalized. A spastic obstruction of the bowel occurred two years later, again under distressing situations. With the first illness, her history of lifelong constipation, bowel problems, use of cathartics, and enemas came out. As they were discussed, the conditions improved and shortly thereafter they practically disappeared.

The geographic localization of the eczema is specific from the viewpoint of her areas of pride investment, explicitly and symbolically. There was neurotic pride in her hair and in her head, and pride in control by her head over her body and over her feelings.

As Rose's tension generally lessened, so did her constrictedness, crampedness, rigidity, and the physical symptoms of her frigidity. By the fifth year she was noting changes in her feeling cold in summer and frozen in winter. By the seventh year, her allergies and migraine headaches were almost gone and her interest in sex was beginning to emerge after fifteen years of frigidity. By the ninth year Rose had only occasional mild wheezing and only an occasional mild tension headache.

549

Her hands in the beginning of analysis were clammy, white and cadaveric looking. She told me they were almost always ice cold as were her feet. In the third and fourth years, they began to look a bit mottled — white, pink, and purple. She noted how she was generally warming up over the years. About the ninth year, she drew my attention to how her hands would be cold at the beginning of a session and by the end they would begin to be warm. In the next two years, this warming happened faster — ten to fifteen minutes after the session began her hands were pink, warm, and dry. Rose told me this happened also with her feet. By the fifteenth year, her hands and feet were warm, dry, and pink most of the time. She could now wear light dresses in summer and proudly announced that she was not going to get a fur coat because a cloth coat was sufficient for the coldest winter days even though she was now in her early sixties.

I feel that the comprehensive concept of tension helps to explain the phenomena described as a response to therapy. Rose's general level of tension steadily lowered, and with it there was a general warming up as her symptoms steadily dropped away. Increasing knowledge of the psychophysiology of the arterioles in the extremities, and their relation to skin temperature will illuminate this process. Rose B. illustrates the fact that therapy can have an effect on seemingly intransigent and even apparently lethal physical processes in people who do not have psychic processes to deal with their conflicts.

Skin conditions, cold hands and feet, tension, and migraine are often associated. I have treated seven women and one man who suffered from migraine. Laura T. and Rose B. both literally froze during the hottest days in summer. Both had severe migraine, Rose B.'s being almost lethal. Although Laura T. looked of normal weight, she was on the thin side. Rose B. was thin and underweight all her life. Laura T. revealed and lived out many psychopathic features. For Laura T., the fantasy of having been a changeling of royal birth had a reality that almost amounted to conviction.

Both women were strikingly attractive. Rose B. unconsciously seduced attention which got her into difficulties. Laura T. had the charm of a psychopath and treated people shamelessly. Both women were exceptionally intelligent — Rose B.'s covered over and Laura T.'s quite obviously shown. The need for control through intellect of others, of their bodies, and of their feelings was powerful in both. Rose B.'s rages were violently controlled and only emerged with violence after years of analysis. Laura T.'s temper was constantly at the erupting point. Both were sexually frigid while looking so sexually desirable. Messages demanding attention were misinterpreted as interest in sex which when so responded to were met with rage in Laura T. and abused feelings and withdrawal in Rose B. With the violent demands for attention, to be taken care of and served, were the needs for self-sufficiency, control and distance.

Laura T.'s therapy lasted only three years, one or two sessions weekly. Mild depression, restlessness and in time anxiety and rage about to erupt were her presenting complaints. When our work was interrupted by her there was slight improvement in all her symptoms; the migraine, the freezing in summer and the painful sensitivity to it in winter, the depression, and the anxiety. Another patient, Pauline A., came into therapy at fifty and remained for less than a year. She was slightly more comfortable when she interrupted. She did so, she said, because of the demands of her sadistic husband. Her migraine was only slightly mitigated.

If anything, Monica S.'s migraine became slightly worse during therapy with nausea, vomiting, hemianopsia, and scintillating scotoma. Less intense attacks would come and go during a single session while more severe occurrences would prostrate her for twenty-four to forty-eight hours. I felt her migraine got worse because of mounting rage against me for unfilled neurotic claims, rage with which she could not deal. She had interrupted therapy for a few months on a previous occasion but before her rage had emerged so clearly. The second time it had begun to move into awareness. She could not let it loose against me and departed instead. I clearly stood for her father and his world which had fooled her. During our work, her problems in areas which had concerned her most when she began had been somewhat worked through. Nine months after her second interruption she returned with a deeper awareness of her rages, her self-destructiveness, and her lack of commitment to therapy which she realized was due to her fear I might die. Many meaningful people in her life had died, and she was terrified of committing herself or having faith and trust that they would continue to be there for her. Her migraine had become less intense in the nine-month interim. I feel, however, it will become and remain much worse until the sources of her murderous rages are worked through.

Rhoda R., now fifty, has had infrequent migraine with prostration, hemianopsia, and scotoma since she was a little girl. In four years of therapy the migraine remained unchanged while radical personality changes occurred. Highly accident prone, this and many other evidences of self-destructiveness considerably diminished. I feel she is close to the resolution of a major perpetuating factor, a murderous rage which she must deny as her own. She can now admit she has such feelings, but still insists that others provoke them in her.

Myra C.'s migraine began in her teens with nausea, vomiting, prostration, hemianopsia, and scotoma. Her main physical symptoms were, however, asthma, hay fever, and sensitivity to a host of substances. As with Rose B., the foreground picture was massive self-effacement and masochism. Other usual aspects of the personality picture associated with migraine were very much buried. She had had asthma and hay fever since infancy and came into analysis in her early thirties several months after ten days in an oxygen tent because of status asthmatics.

It was six years before her constant and powerful suicidal urges disappeared. By this time, the asthma was also almost gone. When she interrupted therapy three years later, she had only occasional mild attacks of wheezing. Her hay fever had become much less intense. Even the scratch tests evoked less of a response. Her migraine was much less frequent and much less intense. For about six months at one phase of the therapy, she was diagnosed as having renal hypertension which never recurred. It developed at a point of mounting unconscious rage at unfulfilled claims and unfilled shoulds. She could not become aware of her rage and had to somatize in this way. Although her self-effacement and masochism had been considerably worked through, her expansiveness did not come to the fore. She never was able to fully utilize her exceptional intelligence and other gifts.

Similar to Myra C., transient tension rise was reflected in a glaucoma of six months' duration in a woman of forty. Pain in one eye, eye strain, blurring and fading vision, and one-sided headaches brought her to an ophthalmologist. He asked if she had been emotionally disturbed recently. Although she had been in analysis for some years, she was unaware that in the past six months there had been an accession of rage at her husband. More because the acute external reasons for her rage were gone than because of any real personality change, the glaucoma disappeared. It has not recurred in the fifteen years since it happened. She is now in her mid-fifties.

Although widely spaced, Vivian O. had vicious and prostrating attacks of migraine with hemianopsia and scintillating scotoma to the point of blindness. The migraine pattern was obvious and clear. Of superior intelligence and authentic sensitivities, Vivian could not effectively use them because of her persistent and rebellious resignation which was in the foreground. In the background there was self-effacement to the point of morbid dependency.

In eight years of analysis, the psychological problems were much mitigated as were her headaches. Recurrent chest colds, not asthma, persisted, occurring when she was particularly upset. They expressed held back murderous rage. Vivian was intellectually aware of her rages and their intensity. Until she can dare to emotionally integrate them, however, there will not be a resolution of the dynamic factors manifested by her colds and her migraine.

Irving W. had migraine headaches since the age of ten. At times there was slight hemianopsia and scintillation. By his late teens he had learned that if he took an Anacin at the first sign of the headache, he could abort it. He insisted that "Nothing else would do the trick." He had seen many therapists for shorter and longer periods before he came to me because of depression, irritability, and difficulty in "getting on with people." In two years his depression lifted and he began to be more active and more hopeful about himself. He knew he was nasty, hostile, sarcastic, and even vicious, but he was not emotionally connected with these feelings. In the last few months as he was coming to life these feelings became more alive in him as his. Now when he said, "I know I'm a S.O.B.," Irving felt it and meant it.

He had the usual personality picture of the migraine patient. Of superior intelligence, he knew he stood in his own way and loathed himself for it. The intensity and frequency of his migraine attacks have become slightly less frequent and less intense. Again I feel that only as Irving can let in and own his murderous rages, vicious vindictiveness, and the sources of them will his migraine be significantly affected.

The above patients were not angry — they were simply in murderous rages. Awareness of these rages varied. Vivian clearly recognized them and made monumental efforts to contain them which exhausted her and kept her silent. Rose B. was utterly unaware of hers. To maintain her unawareness, she had practically killed herself with lethal migraine and other somatic disorders combined with intense deadening mechanisms. The foreground pattern of Vivian O. was of haughtiness, colossal arrogance, manipulativeness, and violent claims. Rose B.'s self-effacement had gone to the point almost of self-extinction. Myra C. was on the verge of wiping herself out by suicide. All were using enormous energies and a host of different mechanisms to control, contain, and deny these rages. The consequence was alienation and irritability with extreme constrictedness of feelings. They lived far below their resources, abilities, and gifts. All had high intelligence. All were violently ambitious and all were in violent conflict because of the contradictory nature of their needs and the power of them.

It is usually stated that migraine patients have guilt feelings because of their murderous rages. I feel Horney's concept of the pride system of which self-hate is one aspect is a more productive concept for understanding these rages and the consequences of them. The first source of rage is unfulfilled claims on the basis of their idealized image of themselves. Then comes vindictiveness from that pride being hurt by others. Intrapsychically, there is rage at the self for failing to fulfill shoulds and should nots as standards demanded of them by their perfectionism. There is also self-hate for failing to fulfill simultaneously their contradictory expansive, self-effacing, and resigned solutions. Then there are the general measures to relieve tension which they make use of and which also prove inadequate and engender even more self-hate. Sometimes this self-hate is of such proportions that it is expressed in suicidal impulses, accident proneness, and other self-destructive acts. Another way to deal with this enormous self-hate is to externalize it and add it to the already formidable rage at others. Various mechanisms are used to release it, and it is acted out through irritability, nastiness, and downright viciousness.

Although the group is selective, the picture is specific enough to be a helpful guide in working with patients with milder forms of migraine or with less severe headaches where the diagnosis is not clear. This does not exclude the possibility of hereditary and constitutional factors. In the families of two of the women mentioned above, female members on the maternal side had migraine. As a somatic solution to psychic involvement, migraine may be used moderately or extensively. These and other factors may account for the speed of influence of analytic therapy.

Myra C. had asthma and hay fever, Rose B. wheezing attacks, and Vivian O. had chest colds. Ernest O. had hay fever since childhood and asthma since his teens. In seven years of analysis, he became more aware of the dynamics of the attacks of both. They became less frequent and less intense, but they were still present when he interrupted therapy. His dependency needs were still intense and had been insufficiently worked through. Peter V. had been fat from infancy, and, in a lifelong, little boy rebellion against his overprotective mother, he showed little change in his mild asthma and hay fever during his six years of analysis. During therapy he married, improved his employment status, and lived a much fuller life. Fundamental character changes did not occur, although he was happy with the results of our mutual efforts.

One woman's hay fever, though mild, revealed a unique pattern. Because of her work and public activities, she was often at committee meetings. When things were not going as she would have wished and her mounting resentment reached a peak, she would have explosive sneezing attacks, blow the papers off the table, and generally disrupt if not terminate the meeting. By the fourth year of her analysis, the violence of these attacks considerably abated as she could open herself to the violence within her. After eight years of analysis her hay fever was much mitigated and has remained so in the twenty years since she interrupted.

By the seventh year of analysis, Samuel J.'s hay fever had entirely disappeared, as had his back spasms and episodes of intense gastric discomfort associated with aerophagia and pylorospasm. In the five years with me after an earlier therapeutic experience of two years, Marvin O.'s hay fever had considerably abated although there was only moderate fundamental personality change. The same obtained with Rubin Z. who, after therapy, could do without his shots which had been necessary for the previous ten years to get him through the hay fever season.

Sydney F. had had hay fever since age eight but had never been skin-tested or treated for it. Although there was a fundamental personality change in an extended analysis, the sneezing fits did not change until he was finally able to own his hostility and be able to become openly angry and assertive.

Arthur G. had had very mild hay fever for which he was never treated or skin-tested. Under tension his nose clogged up. At times he felt his chest closing down and at others he felt a violent urge to sneeze. He had had these symptoms off and on since childhood. After years of analysis, he admitted to a cold cruelty of which he had been long aware. Then came a phase of experiencing murderous rage toward his father. Much more difficult to contact and open himself to was one toward his mother who had cruelly tied him to her in bondage. It was most

555

difficult for him to open himself to his murderous rage at his brother to whom he felt helplessly and hopelessly bound in a vow of everlasting loyalty and love. Only as this was worked through did the symptoms of blocked nose, chest closing down, and impulse to sneeze begin to abate.

This is again a highly selected group. All were from upper middle or upper socioeconomic groups. All were well-educated, and all were of superior intelligence. All had some problem with their respiratory passages, nose, throat, or lungs. Every one was tied to his or her mother in the most primitive kind of symbiosis, induced by overprotectiveness, seductiveness, manipulativeness, rejection, or terrorizing. They were all in a constant rage because they had been so tied and could not get free and because their intense dependency needs had not been and were not being fulfilled.

The intensity of the bondage and the struggle against it were closely correlated with their rages. How successful they were in working through and resolving this bondage depended upon a variety of factors. To the extent they were able to do so, their symptoms abated, their dependency needs lessened, their feelings of independence increased, and their rages reached awareness and were worked through.

These men and women tied to their mothers were literally and figuratively in a survival struggle. Alexander and his co-workers have pointed at the fear of biological survival as a typical psychic stress precipitating thyrotoxicosis. (370) One of my experiences was in supervising the therapy of a girl in her early twenties a year after she had had an emergency operation for an acute fulminating thyrotoxicosis. She clearly recalled that at age twelve she had promised herself that she would always be first in her class. Regardless of ability, one would have to be driven by the furies to decide on and attempt such a solution. Only a threat to biological survival or its equivalent would drive a person to such lengths. She came into therapy because after her surgery she noted increasing apathy, withdrawal, fear, and a reluctance to take up that driveness to be first. A good deal of her motivation for therapy was her fear of her mother who constantly tried to interfere with her therapy. Ultimately, her mother insisted on going into therapy with her daughter's therapist — an invasion which he did not have the strength and experience to prevent. The mother succeeded in disrupting her daughter's therapy and then left herself.

In the middle of the sixth year of his wife's therapy, right after she had the dream of sex with me, I saw Rose B.'s husband Chester for the first time. His depression was just beginning. Two years after his first visit and deeply depressed he had a

556

right herniorrhaphy at fifty-eight. Six months later, he had a partial thyroidectomy because of tachycardia and heart pains. At sixty-three there was a question of carcinoma of the kidney or adjacent areas. A watery cyst was found and removed. A prostectotomy was performed at the same time. At sixty-four carcinoma of the lung was suspected but not confirmed. At sixty-nine mild hypertension and a high blood cholesterol were discovered. The hypertension was controlled by diet and drugs. Six months later he had a serious coronary thrombosis, having had a mild attack the year before. At seventy he admitted that he had to retire from his business, and his depression increased. At seventy-one he began a series of hospitalizations, a total of eight in eighteen months because of nephritis. With each hospitalization, the depression became deeper and the "giving-up" became "given-up." Only the constant support of his wife and his internist brought Chester out of a determined pull toward death which he repetitively and tenaciously expressed.

The "giving up — given up" complex is very obvious in this instance. As Rose became dominant and her desire for sex returned, his depression increased. In two years he was completely without desire even with his wife's support and help. At that time he had the right herniorrhaphy. The symbolism is fairly obvious. Six months later came the partial thyroidectomy. He clearly felt his biological survival was threatened as he gave up piece after piece of his body and his manliness. The development of hypertension at sixty-nine fits the rest of the picture. The quite definite renal damage and renal hypertension aspect as well as the high cholesterol must also be included.

At sixty-four John R., hypertensive for twenty years and alcoholic, was referred to me because of his terror of having a sympathectomy, a last resort measure to relieve his hypertension. What became obvious was he had a terror of dying focused around a specific terror of dying from the operative procedure. But the real terror was that he would die and go to hell because of enormous guilt feelings about his marital transgressions and his failure as a husband and a father.

He had the personality picture and psychic structure associated with hypertension. Unique was the point at which he came for therapy. It was late in life with feelings of failure and guilt, with physical death facing him, and hoping against hope that he could make amends. I saw him about ten times over three months.

Before ten Merwin D. was told his blood pressure was labile.

By twenty-five he was definitely hypertensive (180/100). When I first saw him at thirty-four, it had reached 260/120, with the diastolic steadily creeping up. He was obese, given to secret drinking. In the fourth year of analysis, after telling me he had given up excessive ingestion of barbiturates, he informed me that he was even increasing his intake. Chronically anxious, painfully shy, with intense feelings of weakness and helplessness, his dependency needs were enormous. His controlled rages even greater. He lived an isolated existence made worse by a barely compensated, paranoid schizophrenic wife and no children.

Analysis had helped to decrease his anxieties moderately, his shyness, his mistrust, and his suspiciousness somewhat more. At times his blood pressure dropped as low as 220/100 but did not remain there. His wife's mental illness which necessitated several hospitalizations kept him in a constant state of anxiety and controlled rage for which he had no outlet. In the sixth year of analysis, he had a hemoptysis from esophageal varices. In the next two years these episodes became more frequent and severe. He had serum hepatitis following a blood transfusion, became jaundiced, developed a toxic confusional psychosis, and died at age forty-two.

Elmer M. was given to violent homicidal rages and equally violent suicidal impulses. Since childhood he had had a labile blood pressure which was 260/110 by age thirty-five. He was over six feet tall and thin. Different from other hypertensives, he was quite overtly megalomanic, suspicious, and quite paranoid.

He had been helped over the most violent aspects of his emotional illness in his first analysis of almost ten years. I saw him for three years more, and another analyst saw him for an additional two. In these years his violence subsided, although he never mellowed. He remained seclusive and isolated. His blood pressure was generally below two hundred.

Meyer D. came to me at age fifty-one following a hospitalization due to two severe clonic seizures with a high level of protein in his spinal fluid, nicking of his retinal arteries, and sclerosis of the arteries of his lower extremities. (376) Six feet four inches tall, Meyer had had a lifelong battle with obesity. He knew there had been essential hypertension in his family for at least three generations. This was noted at age eight. In the hospital his blood pressure had been 240/120 and he had known it to be

260/130. The only medication prescribed was moderate doses of Luminal.

He revealed the characteristic psychodynamic picture of patients with essential hypertension. *(375)* The prognosis was poor because of his heredity, constitution, and the advanced sclerosis of his cerebral and peripheral blood vessels. Acute brain damage may also have occurred during the seizures which lasted some minutes. The prospect of improvement was also poor because of the severity of his psychopathology and a terror of illness and of physicians, with whom he had had many painful experiences.

When he interrupted analysis five years later his anxiety had considerably diminished. He could now be assertive and even aggressive with pleasure. His inability to communicate with his wife had changed to a touching mutual friendship. His blood pressure for over two years had ranged around 160/90 and he no longer used any medication. His phobias about physical illness had disappeared. I last heard about him seven years later when he was sixty-three, still well and active in his business.

Rose B. had hypotension all her life and only in her mid-sixties developed episodic hypertension up to 180/100 controlled by moderate doses of depressive drugs. She spontaneously correlated the rise of blood pressure with difficult life circumstances.

In her sixties her life was happier than it had ever been. Her lifelong migraine was now entirely gone and the many illnesses she had had — scalp eczema, anorexia, and insomnia — were long past. Her increased blood pressure became manifest as she mobilized greater amounts of rage and resentment at what she didn't like but still could not let herself feel and express it fully. On several occasions, she became aware when it had risen spontaneously, made the connections as to when and why, worked it through in her sessions with me, and experienced a resultant drop in blood pressure without medication.

Hypertension is a physical expression of tension manifested through the cardiovascular system. In all cited cases, the contribution of psychic factors to increase and maintain the blood pressure increase was evident. Where successful, therapy has been able to resolve the processes elevating it. Hypertension presents an excellent opportunity to identify and maybe in time measure the sources, the functions, and the attitudes toward tension in its physical and psychological aspects in the individual and in his environment. *(374)*

In the cases of Chester, Rose, and Meyer, an acute crisis situation was connected with the blood pressure rise. In all the others there was a chronic crisis situation with acute ones interspersed.

What is present in all hypertensives is rage which cannot be dealt with in psychic ways. To keep it at levels below the explosive level, John R. tried alcohol and women. He ended with monumental feelings of guilt. Merwin D. used alcohol and barbiturates in increasing amounts until they killed him. He couldn't let out his rages on his schizophrenic wife. Therapy helped him allay some of his anxieties and tensions but not fast enough. Analysis helped Elmer M. so that his homicidal and suicidal rages slowly abated. Constrictedness characterized all of these hypertensives socially and sexually.

Their rage was fed from many sources, and they had to hold it in check for fear of its consequences. These consequences were rejection by those whom they imagined they needed to fulfill their dependency needs. As a result, submissiveness was very evident, but it was with the stubbornness of submissives who use it as a way of releasing some of their aggressions. Their submissiveness made them feel weak and defenseless and, in fact, they were. All were easily given to acute anxieties and different intensities of depression. As a result of all these, their relations to people and their environment were disturbed. They couldn't and didn't dare to communicate their wishes and needs and they could easily be taken advantage of.

There was a lifelong struggle with their aggressive drives. They were in a constant struggle with adults whose love they needed, the loss of which they feared if they dared to assert their wishes, criticism, or rebellion. As a result they constricted themselves, backed down, and felt more and more defeated. There was a "giving up" — Merwin D. had "given up" and was literally in a suicidal rage until he died.

Such a suicidal rage can be in awareness, with the intent clear and explicit, or it can be an instance of unconscious, somatic hara-kiri. In this case to be described it was to retain possession and to maintain as close to a biological symbiosis as I have seen between a mother and son.

My patient's mother felt violently threatened when her only child, a son, contemplated marriage. His father had deserted her before her son was born. Twice before the son had broken off with a girl when his mother became ill at the possibility of his marriage. On this occasion he held fast. His mother became steadily worse and had to be hospitalized. Her physician could find nothing physically wrong. He recognized that she was dying and that she was determined to do so. My patient visited her at the hospital and told her unequivocally he was going to marry the girl. His mother got the message that he meant business this time. She promptly began to recover.

I have mentioned secondary gain from illness where minimal physical indisposition is used for maximal gain. There is also somatizing because of the failure of previously adequate psychic mechanisms with secondary gains of other dimensions and character. Then there is the extreme situation of the death threat where the gain sought is clear and the price to be paid quite evident.

In the "giving up — given up" complex studied by Engel and his associates (368) there is secondary gain of a different order intent, and consequence. With Chester B. there was a sequence of episodes when he recognized the structure of his relationship to his wife had become reversed, that she was now dominant and he dependent. There was a piece by piece giving up of parts of his body as a suicidal act, as an expiatory offering, as a gesture of despair, and as an expression of rage against the world. He almost killed himself in "giving up" with such lethal determination.

The relationship of psychic factors to malignancy has often been conjectured. Over the years, the possible correlations become increasingly detailed and verified. Engel mentions a case of virilizing due to an inborn defect in the production of adrenal steroids resulting in a disproportionate output as a "nonspecific pituitary-adrenal response triggered during a period of psychologic decompensation." (368, p. 265) He also reported on the use of the "giving up — given up" complex to differentiate women with and without cervical cancer. Engel mentioned that this complex appears when previous "defenses and adaptations" are experienced as no longer effective, and "current sources of gratification are no longer available." In this complex he describes six phenomenological features.

After years of analysis from which she derived much benefit, Helen R., married with three children, was finding her therapy increasingly less rewarding. She was finding that certain problems were not being dealt with and was experiencing her analyst as being incapable of doing so. Concomitant were mounting feelings of frustration, anxiety, hopelessness, and despair leading to an outburst of explosive rage which frightened and bewildered her. She was surprised that she did not feel guilty. After this explosion, she felt even more frustrated, desperate, and hopeless. For almost a year, she struggled with the decision to interrupt her analysis.

At the same time, she completed a project on which she had been working for years. Completing this project meant she could be free from a longstanding burden. It also meant that she symbolically was no longer a child and could function as an adult. This meant rejecting her internalized mother. Her mother had in reality tied her daughter to her in an intensely symbiotic relationship.

At the peak of this struggle, she discovered a lump in her breast and immediately acted to have it examined and treated. Surgery and radiation therapy insured an excellent prognosis. I feel she acted so fast and effectively because of a courage of despair, because the problem was physical, not psychic, because it was concretized and externalized, because she experienced it as self-destructiveness in herself, and because she could get immediate help to extirpate it. Also through her explosion of rage without guilt, she had already relinquished her analyst; hence she was no longer afraid of rejection which would previously have been experienced in life-threatening dimensions.

On recovery from surgery and radiation therapy eight months from the discovery of the lump and about a year and a half from the peak of her struggle and the depths of her despair, she interrupted her analysis and came to see me. In our work the themes of survival identity, of despair and the courage of despair, hopelessness and hope, disappointment in her therapist, and frustrated expectations were much in the picture. In her struggle she had worked through much of her grief and mourning at the loss of her love object who she experienced as rejecting her because of unfulfilled expectations and, in turn, whom she herself had to reject. In rejecting her therapist she was now left with the full burden of her introjected mother to whom she had been helplessly and hopelessly tied. Now she was left with experiencing that all adults, male and female, had failed and rejected her. She now felt she had to reject them also, but this left her an isolated, lonely child, unprepared for the demands of adulthood. I, in functioning not only as the bad mother and bad father but also as the good ones, helped her to slowly begin to work through and resolve her destructive relationship to male and female adult authorities.

The conjecture is that in this despairing and grieving process, the malignancy began to form as the lump in her breast. One can wonder about the organ specificity, the possibility of hatred toward the internalized maternal object which had failed to be nurturing. I was struck by the lack of feelings of regret at the loss of her breast. In fact, she was pleased to be rid of it because it concretely stood for and contained destructiveness. There was almost the feeling of an expiatory offering gladly made to be rid of an evil that had invaded her.

Her malignancy developed in the process of "giving up." In the process of our work, she was able to contact areas of herself that she had kept inviolate from her mother and almost secret from herself. It was these wellsprings of the will to live and a hunger and feeling for the spiritual that kept her from "giving up."

This instance and others strongly suggest a connection between psychic factors, malignancy, and the crucial role of grieving and mourning, though as yet, they have not been scientifically substantiated.

Gifford and Gunderson offered the "clinical hypothesis" that "Cushing's disease represents a psychosomatic disorder, defined as a patholophysiological reaction to bereavement that occurs in predisposed individuals with lifelong disturbances in personality structure, homeostatic self-regulation, and neuro-endocrine responsiveness."(377, p. 169) They based their hypothesis on the ten most completely documented out of sixty very well decumented cases of Cushing's disease and reviewed a number of other large, carefully investigated series. The study is an exercise in caution and rigor. They worked out many of the biochemical and endocrine correlations, namely, some of that "vast area of the in-between" which legitimately concerned Grinker. They found that nine of the ten patients showed diffuse bilateral adrenocortical hyperplasia at adrenolectomy or subsequent autopsy. "The tenth patient had a large unilateral adenoma of the adrenal cortex."(377, p. 215)

Excess of response to the point of exhausting that particular function, inhibition of productivity, and chain responses affecting interrelationships between functions as a concomitant of psychic disturbances have been identified and worked out in many conditions. In the above group, this was done with reference to many biochemical, metabolic, and endocrine factors as well as to the histological pathophysiology in the form of adrenocortical hyperplasia in nine and a large unilateral adenoma of the adrenal cortex in the tenth.

In all ten a significant correlation was made between the precipitating event with the responses of grief, bereavement, and depression and the improvement of the acute symptoms with little to no changes due to the premorbid personality following adrenolectomy. The closeness of the responses of "giving up" and "given up," and of helplessness and hopelessness are evident. The fact that one case was an adenoma makes one wonder. Could there be a correlation between the grief, bereavement, and self-destructive psychic factors and a stimulation and fostering of malignancy?

Because of urgent personal circumstances, some years ago I had to interrupt my work with a number of patients. I explained the reason to them and arranged for their referral to someone with whom I felt they could work.

I had worked with one of these patients, a young married woman, for about four years, and she was beginning to hope. When we started her picture was one of hopelessness and depression mixed with borderline schizoid features. During our work she made a suicide attempt which by accident was not successful.

Two years after her transfer, after an illness of less than six months, she was dead of a fulminating malignancy diagnosed only at autopsy. I have the strong feeling that her transfer just at the point when she was beginning to hope was experienced as a rejection. Also it had always been difficult for her to form relationships with people and to trust which she had begun to do with me, particularly after the suicidal attempt. To make a new try was perhaps just too much for her. There was no question of the competence of the therapist to whom I had referred her. He also was convinced that the interruption of her work with me was more than she could take, and that his efforts were not sufficient to help her over this overwhelming feeling of black despair and hopelessness, grief and mourning at her feeling of having lost me and been rejected by me.

An overwhelming, fulminating, black despair, combined with determinedly turning her back on life can be conjectured. Of a different order are the deaths from black magic where the picture is more of futility and powerlessness. Then there are the marasmic children who die from the lack of nurturant loving which is as essential as food if not more so. In these instances, death occurs because human dignity was violated.

But what about Mrs. Frazer? There are many such instances, but none quite so dramatic. The wife of Sir James Frazer, author of *The Golden Bough,* was, although a virago, nevertheless devoted to his welfare and reputation. When Frazer died, she gave her last orders to her servants, took to her bed, turned her face to the wall and died the same night. *(378)* The frequency with which the fact and the metaphor of turning his or her face to the wall is striking and meaningful. I would say Mrs. Frazer died with dignity. Somewhere she knew herself well. Is her death so different from those who choose voluntary euthanasia, *(379)* who choose to die in battle for a meaningful cause, or who choose suicide with dignity in concentration camps.

All this is pertinent to dying with dignity, an issue I discussed in chapters 27 where I spoke of those with an incurable illness who are allowed and helped to go through the process of decathexis according to Kübler-Ross. *(316)* They had done the work of dying, of withdrawing from a life no longer meaningful, and wanted to be left alone to die with dignity. *(380)* Maybe as we confront our increasingly aging population and we rediscover human dignity at all age levels, such dying will happen more often, adding to the dignity of their families, their physicians, and themselves.

References

Karen Horney

1. *Ein kasuistischer Beitrag zur Frage der traumatischen Psychosen* [A Casuistic Contribution to the Question of Traumatic Psychoses]. Berlin: H. Bode, 1915, 1-34.
2. "Die Technik der psychoanalytischen Therapie" [The Technique of Psychoanalytic Therapy]. *Zeitschrift für Sexualwissenschaft* 4 (1917): 185-91; in *Bericht über die Fortschritte der Psychoanalyse 1914-1919*. Vienna: Internationaler Psychoanalytischer Verlag, 1921; *American Journal of Psychoanalysis* 28 (1968): 3-12.
3. "Zur Genese des weiblichen Kastrationskomplexes" [On the Genesis of the Castration Complex in Women]. *Internationale Zeitschrift für Psychoanalyse* 9 (1923): 12-26; *International Journal of Psycho-Analysis* 5 (1924): 50-65.
4. "Gehemmte Weiblichkeit. Psychoanalytischer Beitrag zum Problem der Frigidität" [Inhibited Femininity: A Psychoanalytic Contribution to the Problem of Frigidity]. *Zeitschrift für Sexualwissenschaft* 13 (1926): 67-77.
5. "Flucht aus der Weiblichkeit" [The Flight from Womanhood]. *Internationale Zeitschrift für Psychoanalyse* 12 (1926): 360-74; *International Journal of Psycho-Analysis* 7 (1926): 324-39.
6. "Diskussion der Laienanalyse" [Discussion: Symposium on Lay Analysis]. *Internationale Zeitschrift für Psychoanalyse* 13 (1927): 101-7; *International Journal of Psycho-Analysis* 8 (1927): 255-9.
7. "Der Männlichkeitskomplex der Frau" [The Masculinity Com-

567

plex of Women]. *Archiv für Frauenkunde* 13 (1927): 141-54.

8. "Die monogame Forderung" [The Demand for Monogamy]. *Internationale Zeitschrift für Psychoanalyse* 13 (1927): 397-409; *Psychoanalytische Almanach* 3 (1928): 38-54.

9. "Psychische Eignung und Nichteignung zur Ehe" [Psychological Suitability and Unsuitability for Marriage]. In *Ein biologisches Ehebuch*, edited by Max Marcuse. Berlin und Köln: A. Marcus und E. Weber Verlag, 1927, 192-203.

10. "Uber die psychischen Bestimmungen der Gattenwahl" [On the Psychological Conditions of the Choice of a Marriage Partner]. In *Ein biologisches Ehebuch*, edited by Max Marcuse. Berlin und Köln: A. Marcus und E. Weber Verlag, 1927, 470-80.

11. "Uber die psychischen Wurzeln einiger typischen Ehekonflikte" [On the Psychological Roots of Some Typical Marriage Conflicts]. In *Ein biologisches Ehebuch*, edited by Max Marcuse. Berlin und Köln: A. Marcus und E. Weber Verlag, 1927, 481-91.

12. "The problem of the Monogamous Ideal." *International Journal of Psycho-Analysis* 9 (1928): 318-31; "The Problem of the Monogamic Statute." *Psychoanalytic Review* 15 (1928): 92-3.

13. "Die spezifische Problematik der Zwangsneurose im Lichte der Psychoanalyse" [The Specific Problems of Compulsion Neurosis in the Light of Psychoanalysis]. *Archiv für Psychiatrie* 91 (1930): 597-601.

14. "Das Misstrauen zwischen den Geschlechtern" [The Distrust between the Sexes]. *Psychoanalytische Bewegung* 2 (1930): 521-537.

15. "Der Kampf in der Kultur, Einige Gedanken und Bedenken zu Freud's Todestrieb und Destruktionstrieb" [The Role of Aggression in Civilization. Some Thoughts and Objections Regarding Freud's Death Instinct and Drive for Destruction]. In *Das Problem der Kultur und die ärztliche Psychologie* [The Problem of Civilization and Medical Psychology]. Vorträge der Institut für Geschichte der Medizin, University of Leipzig 4 (1931): 105-18; *American Journal of Psychoanalysis* 20 (1960): 130-8.

16. "Die prämenstruellen Verstimmungen" [The Premenstrual Emotional Disturbances]. *Zeitschrift für psychoanalytische Pädagogik* 5 (1931): 1-7.

17. "Das Misstrauen zwischen den Geschlechtern" [The Distrust Between the Sexes]. *Die Arztin* 7 (1931): 5-12.

18. "Zur Problematik der Ehe" [Problems of Marriage]. *Psychoanalytische Bewegung* 4 (1932): 212-23.

19. "Die Angst vor der Frau. Uber einen spezifischen Unterschied

in der männlichen und weiblichen Angst vor dem anderen Geschlecht" [The Dread of Woman. Observations on a Specific Difference in the Dread Felt by Men and by Women Respectively for the Opposite Sex]. *Internationale Zeitschrift für Psychoanalyse* 18 (1932): 5-18; *International Journal of Psycho-Analysis* 13 (1932): 348-60.

20. "Erhöhung und Erniedergung der Frau" [Adoration and Degradation of Women]. Unpublished lecture before Berlin General Medical Society for Psychotherapy, 1932.

21. "Can You Take a Stand?" *Journal of Adult Education* 11 (1932): 129-32.

22. "Die Verleugnung der Vagina. Ein Beitrag zur Frage der spezifisch weiblichen Genitalängst" [The Denial of the Vagina. Contribution to Problem of Genital Anxieties Specific to Women]. *Internationale Zeitschrift für Psychoanalyse* 19 (1933): 372-84; *International Journal of Psycho-Analysis* 14 (1933): 57-70.

23. "Psychogenic Factors in Functional Female Disorders." *American Journal of Obstetrics and Gynecology* 25 (1933): 694-703; *Medical and Professional Woman's Journal* 40 (1933): 319-24.

24. "Maternal Conflicts." *American Journal of Orthopsychiatry* 3 (1933): 455-63.

25. "The Overevaluation of Love. A Study of a Common Present-Day Feminine Type." *Psychoanalytic Quarterly* 3 (1934): 605-38.

26. "Concepts and Misconcepts of the Analytic Method." *Archives of Neurology and Psychiatry* 32 (1934): 880-83.

27. "Restricted Applications of Psychoanalysis to Social Work." *The Family* 15 (1934): 169-72.

28. "Personality Changes in Female Adolescents." *American Journal of Orthopsychiatry* 5 (1935): 19-26.

29. "Conceptions and Misconceptions of the Analytical Method." *Journal of Nervous and Mental Disease* 81 (1935): 399-410.

30. "On Difficulties in Dealing with the Transference." *News-Letter of American Association of Psychiatric Social Workers* 5 (1935): 1-12.

31. "The Problem of the Negative Therapeutic Reaction." *Psychoanalytic Quarterly* 5 (1936): 29-44.

32. "Culture and Neurosis." *American Sociological Review* 1 (1936): 221-35.

33. *The Neurotic Personality of Our Time.* New York: W. W. Norton & Co., 1937.

34. "Das Neurotische Liebesbedürfnis" [The Neurotic Need for Love]. *Zentralblatt für Psychotherapie* 10 (1937): 69-82.

35. *New Ways in Psychoanalysis.* New York: W. W. Norton & Co., 1939.
36. Letter to the Members of the American Psychoanalytic Association by Five Resigning Members of the New York Psychoanalytic Society, Signed by Harmon S. Ephron, Karen Horney, Sarah R. Kelman, Bernard S. Robbins, Clara Thompson. Reprinted in *American Journal of Psychoanalysis* 1 (1941): 9-10.
37. "Psychiatrist-Social Worker Interrelationship." *American Journal of Psychiatry* 98 (1942): 504-8.
38. *Self-Analysis.* New York: W. W. Norton & Co., 1942.
39. *Our Inner Conflicts.* New York: W. W. Norton & Co., 1945.
40. *Are You Considering Psychoanalysis?* Edited by K. Horney. New York: W. W. Norton & Co., 1946.
41. "The Future of Psychoanalysis." Contribution to a Symposium. *American Journal of Psychoanalysis* 6 (1946): 66-7.
42. "Inhibitions in Work." *American Journal of Psychoanalysis* 7 (1947): 18-25; *Psyché* 3 (1947): 481-92; *Psyché* 4 (1949): 581-95.
43. "Maturity and the Individual." Contribution to a Symposium. *American Journal of Psychoanalysis* 7 (1947): 85-7.
44. "The Value of Vindictiveness." *American Journal of Psychoanalysis* 8 (1948): 3-12; *Psyché* 6 (1951): 159, 230-50.
45. "Finding the Real Self." Foreword to a Letter: *American Journal of Psychoanalysis* 10 (1950): 64-5.
46. "The Search for Glory." *Pastoral Psychology* 1 (1950): 13-20.
47. "Psychoanalysis and Moral Values." Contribution to a Symposium. *American Journal of Psychoanalysis* 10 (1950): 64-5.
48. "Was tut eigentlich der Psychoanalytiker?" [What Does the Analyst Do?]. *Psyché* 4 (1950): 1-10.
49. *Neurosis and Human Growth.* New York: W. W. Norton & Co., 1950.
50. Tenth Anniversary Address. The Association for the Advancement of Psychoanalysis. *American Journal of Psychoanalysis* 11 (1951): 3-4.
51. "On Feeling Abused." *American Journal of Psychoanalysis* 11 (1951): 5-12.
52. "The Individual and Therapy." Contribution to a Symposium. *American Journal of Psychoanalysis* 11 (1951): 54-5.
53. "Ziele der Analytischen Therapie" [Goals of Analytic Therapy]. *Psyché* 6 (1957): 463-72.
54. "The Paucity of Inner Experiences." *American Journal of Psychoanalysis* 12 (1952): 3-9.
55. "Values and Problems of Group Analysis." Contribution to a

Symposium. *American Journal of Psychoanalysis* 12 (1952): 80-1.
56. "Human Nature Can Change." Contribution to a Symposium. *American Journal of Psychoanalysis* 12 (1952): 67-8.

Karen Horney—by Others

57. Karen Horney Memorial Issue. *American Journal of Psychoanalysis* 14, 1 (1954).
58. Weiss, F. A. "Karen Horney — a Bibliography." *American Journal of Psychoanalysis* 14 (1954): 15-18.
59. Weiss, F. A. "Karen Horney — Her Early Papers." *American Journal of Psychoanalysis* 14 (1954): 55-64.
59a. Kelman, H. "The Holistic Approach (Horney)." In *American Handbook of Psychiatry,* Volume 2, edited by S. Arieti. New York: Basic Books, 1959.
60. Karen Horney. Seventy-fifth Anniversary Issue. "Alienation and the Search for Identity." *American Journal of Psychoanalysis* 21, 2 (1961).
61. *Advances in Psychoanalysis. Contributions to Karen Horney's Holistic Approach.* Edited by H. Kelman. New York: W. W. Norton & Co., 1964.
62. *New Perspectives in Psychoanalysis. Contributions to Karen Horney's Holistic Approach.* Edited by H. Kelman. New York: W. W. Norton & Co., 1965.
63. *Feminine Psychology.* Edited by H. Kelman. New York: W. W. Norton & Co., 1966.
64. "Karen Horney — The Cultural Emphasis by J. M. Natterson." In *Psychoanalytic Pioneers,* edited by F. Alexander, S. Eisenstein and M. Grotjahn. New York: Basic Books, 1966, 450-6.
64a. Kelman, H. and Vollmerhausen, J. W. "On Horney's Psychoanalytic Techniques: Developments and Perspectives." In *Psychoanalytic Techniques,* edited by B. B. Wolman. New York: Basic Books, 1967.
64b. Rubins, J. L. "A Holistic (Horney) Approach to the Psychoses: The Schizophrenias." *American Journal of Psychoanalysis* 29 (1969): 131-46; 30 (1970): 30-50; 31 (1971): 136-51.
64c. Brés, Y. *Freud et la psychoanalyse américaine Karen Horney.* Paris: Librairie Philosophique J. Vrin., 1970.
64d. Kelman, H. "Karen Horney." In *Major Contributors to Modern Psychotherapy.* Nutley, N. J.: Roche Laboratories, 1971.

Karen Horney On
Psychoanalytic Technique

Compiled and edited from "The Lectures on Psychoanalytic Technique" given by Karen Horney at the American Institute for Psychoanalysis during the years 1946, 1950, 1951, and 1952.

65. Slater, R. "Aims of Psychoanalytic Therapy." *American Journal of Psychoanalysis* 16 (1956): 24-5.

66. Metzgar, E. A. "Understanding the Patient As the Basis of All Technique." *American Journal of Psychoanalysis* 16 (1956): 26-31.

67. Zimmerman, J. "Blockages in Therapy." *American Journal of Psychoanalysis* 16 (1956): 112-7.

68. Slater, R. "Interpretation." *American Journal of Psychoanalysis* 16 (1956): 118-24.

69. Azorin, L. A. "The Analyst's Personal Equation." *American Journal of Psychoanalysis* 27 (1957): 34-38.

70. Cantor, M. B. "The Initial Interview." *American Journal of Psychoanalysis* 27 (1957): 39-44; 121-6.

71. Willig, W. "Dreams." *American Journal of Psychoanalysis* 28 (1958): 127-37.

72. Cantor, M. B. "The Quality of the Analyst's Attention." *American Journal of Psychoanalysis* 19 (1959): 28-32.

73. Slater, R. "Evaluation of Change." *American Journal of Psychoanalysis* 20 (1960): 3-7.

74. Sheiner, S. "The Importance of Emotional Experiences in the Analytic Process." *American Journal of Psychoanalysis* 26 (1966): 88-90.

75. Cantor, M. B. "Mobilizing Constructive Forces." *American Journal of Psychoanalysis* 27 (1967): 188-99.

76. Sheiner, S. "Free Association." *American Journal of Psychoanalysis* 27 (1967): 200-8.

Annual Karen Horney Lectures

77. Cameron, E. D. "Karen Horney: A Pioneer in the Science of Human Relations." *American Journal of Psychoanalysis* 14 (1954): 19-29.

78. Whitehorn, J. C. "The Scope of Motivation in Psychopathology and Psychotherapy." *American Journal of Psychoanalysis* 14 (1954): 30-9.

79. Appel, K. E. "Principles and Practice of Psychotherapy." *American Journal of Psychoanalysis* 15 (1955): 99-106.

80. Allen, F. H. "Horney's Conception of the Basic Conflict Applied to Child Psychiatry." *American Journal of Psychoanalysis* 16 (1956): 99-111.

81. Hill, L. B. "Psychotherapy of a Schizophrenic." *American Journal of Psychoanalysis* 27 (1957): 99-109.

82. Kardiner, A. "New Horizons and Responsibilities of Psychoanalysis." *American Journal of Psychoanalysis* 18 (1958): 115-6.

83. Kanner, L. "Centripetal Forces in Personality Development." *American Journal of Psychoanalysis* 19 (1959): 123-32.

84. Rioch, D. McK. "Recent Contributions of Neuropsychiatric Research to the Theory and Practice of Psychotherapy." *American Journal of Psychoanalysis* 20 (1960): 115-29.

85. Weigert, E. "The Function of Sympathy in the Psychotherapeutic Process." *American Journal of Psychoanalysis* 22 (1962): 3-14.

86. Tillich, P. "What Is Basic in Human Nature?" *American Journal of Psychoanalysis* 22 (1962): 115-21.

87. Maslow, A. H. "Fusions of Facts and Values." *American Journal of Psychoanalysis* 23 (1963): 117-31.

88. Alexander, F. "Neurosis and Creativity." *American Journal of Psychoanalysis* 24 (1964): 116-30.

89. Masserman, J. H. "Anxiety Revisited." *American Journal of Psychoanalysis* 25 (1965): 115-28.

90. Grinker, R. S., Sr. " 'Open-System' Psychiatry." *American Journal of Psychoanalysis* 26 (1966): 115-28.

91. Lidz, T. "Psychoanalytic Theories of Development and Maldevelopment: Some Reconceptualizations." *American Journal of Psychoanalysis* 17 (1967): 115-26.

92. Bettelheim, B. "Personality Formation in the Kibbutz." *American Journal of Psychoanalysis* 29 (1969): 3-9.

93. Arieti, S. "The Meeting of the Inner and the External World: In Schizophrenia, Everyday Life and Creativity." *American Journal of Psychoanalysis* 29 (1969): 115-30.

94. Wynne, L. C. "Variations Within and Between Families of Schizophrenics: Implications for Etiology and Treatment." *American Journal of Psychoanalysis* 30 (1970): 100-14.

94a. Keniston, K. "Youth as a 'New' Stage of Life." *American Journal of Psychoanalysis* 31 (1971): 115-31.

Karen Horney Biography

95. Horney, K. Autobiographical Material. Found in her files; possibly prepared for organizations and press releases, 1932.
95a. Zuckmayer, C. *A Part of Myself.* New York: Harcourt Brace Jovanovich, 1970.
96. Karen Horney's Biography. In *Current Biography*, Volume 2. New York: H. W. Wilson Co., 1941, 27-9.
97. Freud, S. *The Ego and the Id.* London: Hogarth Press, 1923.
98. Kretschmer, E. *Physique and Character.* London: Kegan Paul, Trench, Trubner, 1925.
99. Bally, G. "Psychoanalysis and Social Change." *American Journal of Psychoanalysis* 24 (1964): 145-52; "Sociological Aspects of Psychoanalysis." *American Journal of Psychoanalysis* 26 (1966): 5-19.
100. Freud, S. "Some Psychological Consequences of the Anatomical Distinction Between the Sexes (1925)." *Collected Papers,* Volume 5. London: Hogarth Press, 1956, 197.
101. Freud, S. "Female Sexuality (1931)." *Collected Papers,* Volume 5. London: Hogarth Press, 1956, 254, 258, 271-2.
102. Jones, E. "The Early Development of Female Sexuality." *International Journal of Psycho-Analysis* 8 (1927): 459.
103. Freud S. *An Outline of Psychoanalysis.* New York: W. W. Norton & Co., 1949, 29, 107.
104. Sherfey, M. J. "The Evolution and Nature of Female Sexuality in Relation to Psychoanalytic Theory." *Journal of the American Psychoanalytic Association* 14 (1966): 28-128.
105. Freud, S. "Analysis Terminable and Interminable." *Collected Papers,* Volume 5. London: Hogarth Press, 1956, 356, 357.
106. Zilboorg, G. "Male and Female." *Psychiatry* 7 (1944): 275-96.
107. Van Leewen, K. "Pregnancy-Envy in the Male: Case History." *International Journal of Psycho-Analysis* 47 (1966): 319-24.
108. Applegarth, A. Review of *Feminine Psychology* by K. Horney. *Archives of General Psychiatry* 18 (1968): 124-5.
109. Jones, E. Review of *Neurotic Personality of Our Time. International Journal of Psycho-Analysis* 20 (1940): 240-1.
110. Alexander, F. Review of *Neurotic Personality of Our Time. Psychoanalytic Quarterly* 7 (1937): 536-50.

574

111. Stern, A. Review of *New Ways in Psychoanalysis*. *International Journal of Psycho-Analysis* 21 (1940): 360-3.
112. Fenichel, O. Review of *New Ways in Psychoanalysis*. *Psychoanalytic Quarterly* 9 (1940): 114-21.
113. Green, M. R. *Interpersonal Psychoanalysis. The Selected Papers of Clara M. Thompson*. New York: Basic Books, 1964.
114. Thompson, C. "History of the William Alanson White Institute of Psychiatry, Psychoanalysis and Psychology." *W.A.W.* [William Alanson White] *Newsletter* 3 (1968): 406.
115. Marmor, J. "The Pre-History and the Founding of the Comprehensive Course in Psychoanalysis." *Newsletter, Society of Medical Psychoanalysts* 5 (1964): 1-3; September 1964; "Origins of the Institute." *W.A.W.* [William Alanson White] *Newsletter* 3 (1968): 6-7.
116. *Newsletter*. Society of Medical Psychoanalysts, Volume 9, Number 3 (September 1969).
117. Rioch, J. "Origins of the Institute." *W.A.W.* [William Alanson White] *Newsletter* 3 (1969): 3.
118. Roazen, P. *Brother Animal. The Story of Freud and Tausk*. New York: A. A. Knopf, 1969.
119. Oberndorf, C. P. Obituary on Karen Horney. *International Journal of Psycho-Analysis* 34 (1953): 154-5.
120. Tillich, P. Funeral Services for Karen Horney. December 7, 1952. Unpublished.

Additional References

121. Freud, A. *The Ego and the Mechanisms of Defense*. New York: International Universities Press, 1946.
122. Hartmann, H. *Ego Psychology and the Problem of Adaptation*. New York: International Universities Press, 1958.
123. Munroe, R. L. *Schools of Psychoanalytic Thought*. New York: Dryden Press, 1955, 488.
124. Tarachow, S. In *Current Approaches to Psychoanalysis,* edited by P. H. Hoch and J. Zubin. New York: Grune & Stratton, 1960, 45.
125. Lomas, P. "Passivity and Failure of Identity Development." *International Journal of Psycho-Analysis* 46 (1965): 438-54.
126. Apfelbaum, B. "Ego Psychology: Critique of the Structural Approach to Psychoanalytic Theory." *International Journal of Psycho-Analysis* 47 (1966): 451-75.
127. Balint, M. *The Basic Fault: Therapeutic Aspects of Regression*. London: Tavistock Publications, 1967.

128. Weisman, A. D. *The Existential Core of Psychoanalysis: Reality, Sense and Responsibility.* Boston: Little, Brown & Co., 1965; "The Right Way to Die." *Psychiatry & Social Science Review* 2 (1968): 2-7.
129. Kelman, H. "The Holistic Approach (Horney)." In *American Handbook of Psychiatry,* Volume 2, edited by S. Arieti. New York: Basic Books, 1959.
130. Freud, S. "Recommendations for Physicians on the Psycho-Analytic Method of Treatment (1912)." *Collected Papers,* Volume 2. London: Hogarth Press, 1933, 323.
131. Freud, S. "Further Recommendations in the Technique of Psycho-Analysis (1913)." *Collected Papers,* Volume 2. London: Hogarth Press, 1933, 342.
132. Fenichel, O. *Problems of Psychoanalytic Technique.* New York: The Psychoanalytic Quarterly Inc., 1941, 1.
133. Freud, S. *The Complete Introductory Lectures on Psychoanalysis.* New York: W. W. Norton, 1966, 645.
134. Boss, M. and Condrau, G. "Existential Psychoanalysis." In *Psychoanalytic Technique,* edited by B. B. Wolman. New York: Basic Books, 1967.
135. Kelman, H. "Psychoanalytic Thought and Eastern Wisdom." In *Science and Psychoanalysis,* Volume 3, edited by J. H. Masserman. New York: Grune & Stratton, 1960, 124-32.
136. Kelman, H. "The Changing Image of Psychoanalysis." *American Journal of Psychoanalysis* 26 (1966): 169-77.
137. Kelman, H. "Toward a Definition of Mind." In *Theories of the Mind,* edited by J. M. Scher. New York: The Free Press of Glencoe, 1962, 243-70.
138. Ciardi, J. "Internal Man and External World." *Saturday Review* (June 11, 1960): 15.
139. Salzman, L. "Socio-Psychological Theories in Psychoanalysis." In *Science and Psychoanalysis,* Volume 7, edited by J. H. Masserman. New York: Grune & Stratton, 1964, 82.
140. Fenichel, O. *The Psychoanalytic Theory of Neurosis.* New York: W. W. Norton, 1945, 573.
141. Jones, E. "A Valedictory Address." *International Journal of Psycho-Analysis* 27 (1946): 7-11.
142. Kanzer, M. and Blum, H. P. "Classical Psychoanalysis since 1939." In *Psychoanalytic Techniques,* edited by B. B. Wolman. New York: Basic Books, 1967.
143. Martin, A. R. "The Body's Participation in Anxiety and Dilemma Phenomena." *American Journal of Psychoanalysis* 15 (1945): 28-48.
144. Kelman, H. "A Unitary Theory of Anxiety." *American Journal*

of Psychoanalysis 16 (1956): 127-52.

145. Portnoy, I. "Anxiety States." In *American Handbook of Psychiatry,* Volume 1, edited by S. Arieti. New York: Basic Books, 1959.

146. Willner, G. "The Role of Anxiety of Schizophrenia." *American Journal of Psychoanalysis* 25 (1965): 171-80; "The Role of Anxiety in Obsessive-Compulsive Disorders." *American Journal of Psychoanalysis* 27 (1968): 201-11.

147. Bychowski, G. "The Archaic Object and Alienation." *International Journal of Psycho-Analysis* 48 (1967): 384-93.

148. Kelman, N. "Clinical Aspects of Externalized Living." *American Journal of Psychoanalysis* 12 (1952): 15-23.

149. Martin, A. R. "The Whole Patient in Therapy." In *Progress in Psychotherapy,* edited by F. Fromm-Reichmann and J. L. Moreno. New York: Grune & Stratton, 1956.

150. Sullivan, H. S. *The Interpersonal Theory of Psychiatry.* New York: W. W. Norton, 1953.

151. Fromm-Reichmann, F. *Principles of Intensive Psychotherapy.* Chicago: The University of Chicago Press, 1950.

152. Fromm, E. *Man for Himself.* New York: Rinehart & Co., 1947.

153. Arieti, S. *The Intrapsychic Self.* New York: Basic Books, 1967.

154. Gershman, H. "Reflections on the Nature of Homosexuality." *American Journal of Psychoanalysis* 26 (1966): 46-49; "The Role of Core Gender Identity in the Genesis of Perversions." *American Journal of Psychoanalysis* 30 (1970): 58-67.

155. Weiss, F. A. "Some Aspects of Sex in Neuroses." *American Journal of Psychoanalysis* 10 (1950): 27-37.

156. Rubins, J. L. "Sexual Perversions: Some Psychodynamic Considerations." *American Journal of Psychoanalysis* 29 (1969): 94-105.

157. Erikson, E. *Identity: Youth and Crisis.* New York: W. W. Norton, 1968.

158. Gergen, K. J. "Self-Theory and the Process of Self-Observation." *Journal of Nervous and Mental Disease* 148 (1969): 437-48.

159. Stoller, R. J. *Sex and Gender.* New York: Science House, 1968.

160. Schilder, P. F. *The Image and Appearance of the Human Body.* New York: International Universities Press, 1950.

161. Knapp, P. H. "Image, Symbol and Person." *Archives of General Psychiatry* 21 (1969): 392-406.

162. Angyal, A. *Foundations for a Science of Personality.* New York: Commonwealth Fund, 1941.

163. Fairburn, W. R. D. *An Object-Relations Theory of the Personality.* New York: Basic Books, 1954.

164. Martin, A. R. "Psychoanalytic Contribution to the Study of

Effort." *American Journal of Psychoanalysis* 10 (1944): 108-21.
165. Martin, A. R. "The Fear of Relaxation and Leisure." *American Journal of Psychoanalysis* 11 (1951): 42-50.
166. Martin, A. R. "The Dynamics of Insight." *American Journal of Psychoanalysis* 12 (1952): 24-38.
167. Martin, A. R. "Self-Alienation and the Loss of Leisure." *American Journal of Psychoanalysis* 21 (1961): 156-65; "Idle Hands and Giddy Minds." *American Journal of Psychoanalysis* 29 (1969): 147-56.
168. Kelman, H. "Creative Talent and Creative Passion as Therapy." *American Journal of Psychoanalysis* 22 (1963): 133-41; "Oriental Psychological Processes and Creativity." *American Journal of Psychoanalysis* 23 (1963): 67-84.
169. Huxley, A. *The Perennial Philosophy.* New York: Harper & Bros., 1945, 166.
170. Sorokin, P. "The Factor of Creativity in Human History." *Main Currents in Modern Thought* 18 (1962): 99-104.
171. Weiss, F. A. "Dreaming: A Creative Process." *American Journal of Psychoanalysis* 24 (1964): 17-27.
172. Hulbeck, C. R. "Three Creative Phases in Psychoanalysis: The Encounter, the Dialogue and the Process of Articulation." *American Journal of Psychoanalysis* 23 (1963): 157-62.
173. Wenkart, A. "Creativity and Freedom." *American Journal of Psychoanalysis* 23 (1963): 195-201.
174. Gershman, H. "Homosexuality and Some Aspects of Creativity." *American Journal of Psychoanalysis* 24 (1964): 29-35.
175. Kelman, H. "Life History as Therapy." *American Journal of Psychoanalysis* 16 (1956): 145-69. Compare with reference 137.
176. Whyte, L. L. *The Next Development in Man.* New York: New American Library, 1950.
176a. Whyte, L. L. *Accent on Form.* New York: Harper & Bros., 1954, 105.
176b. Whyte, L. L. *Aspects of Form.* Bloomington: Indiana University Press, 1961.
177. Northrop, F. S. C. *The Logic of the Sciences and the Humanities.* New York: The Macmillan Co., 1947; *The Meeting of East and West.* The Macmillan Co., 1949.
178. Goldstein, K. "The Concept of Transference in Treatment of Organic and Functional Nervous Disease." *Acta Psychotherapeutica Psychosomatica et Orthopaedagogica* 2 (1954): 334-53.
179. Burrow, T. *Preconscious Foundations of Human Experience.* Edited by W. E. Galt. New York: Basic Books, 1964.
180. Mullahy, P. *Oedipus, Myth and Complex.* New York: Hermitage Press, 1948, 286-91.

181. Tauber, E. S. and Green, M. R. *Prelogical Experience. An Inquiry into Dreams and Other Creative Processes.* New York: Basic Books, 1959.
182. Kelman, H. "Freer Associating: Its Phenomenology and Inherent Paradoxes." *American Journal of Psychoanalysis* 22 (1962): 176-200.
183. Ehrenwald, J. *Psychotherapy: Myth and Method.* New York: Grune & Stratton, 1966.
184. Kelman, H. "The Traumatic Syndrome." *American Journal of Psychoanalysis* 6 (1946): 12-19; "Character and the Traumatic Syndrome." *Journal of Nervous and Mental Disease* 102 (1945): 121-52.
185. Ferreira, A. J. *Prenatal Environment.* Springfield, Illinois: Charles C Thomas, 1969.
186. Goldstein, K. *The Organism.* New York: American Book Co., 1939, 118; "The Smiling of the Infant and the Problem of Understanding the Other." *Journal of Psychology* 44 (1957): 175-91.
187. Krishnamurti, J. *The First and Last Freedom.* New York: Harper & Row, 1954, 96.
188. Haas, W. S. *The Destiny of the Mind, East and West.* New York: Macmillan Co., 1956, 187.
189. Sullivan, H. S. "Conceptions of Modern Psychiatry." *Psychiatry* 111 (1940): 1-117.
190. Vico, Giambattista. *Autobiography of Giambattista Vico.* Translated by M. H. Fisch and T. G. Bergen. Ithaca: Cornell University Press, 1963.
191. Needleman, J., trans. *Being-in-the-World. Selected Papers of Ludwig Binswanger.* New York: Basic Books, 1963, 23.
192. Kuhn, T. S. *The Structure of Scientific Revolutions.* Chicago: The University of Chicago Press, 1964.
193. Caws, P. "The Structure of Discovery." *Science* 166 (1969): 1375-80.
194. King, L. S. "Cecil-Loeb Textbook of Medicine." *Journal of the American Medical Association* 202 (1967): 151-2.
195. Ramo, S. *Cure for Chaos.* New York: David McKay, 1969; *Medical Opinion and Review* 5 (1969): 96-133 (September), 100-61 (October), 98-145 (November).
196. Bruns, B. D. *The Uncertain Nervous System.* Baltimore: Williams & Wilkins, 1969. Reviewed in *Medical Opinion and Review* 5 (1969): 92-6.
197. Miller, N. E. "Learning of Visceral and Glandular Responses." *Science* 163 (1969): 434-45.
198. Fromm-Reichmann, F. *Psychoanalysis and Psychotherapy:*

Selected Papers. Edited by D. M. Bullard. Chicago: The University of Chicago Press, 1959, 311.

199. Angyal, A. *Neurosis and Treatment: A Holistic Theory*. New York: John Wiley & Sons, 1965, 286.

200. Menninger, K. *Theory of Psychoanalytic Technique*. New York: Basic Books, 1958, 11.

201. Manuel, F. E. *Shapes of Philosophical History*. Palo Alto, California: Stanford University Press, 1964.

202. Zelmanovits, J. Review of *The Collected Papers of David Rapaport*. *Psychiatry* 31 (1968): 292-99.

203. Kelman, H. *The Process in Psychoanalysis*. New York: Postgraduate Center for Mental Health, 1969.

204. Kelman, H. "Diagnosing and Prognosing in Psychoanalysis." *American Journal of Psychoanalysis* 15 (1955): 49-70.

205. Kelman, H. "The Doctor-Patient Relationship." A Round Table Discussion. *American Journal of Psychoanalysis* 15 (1955): 16-19.

206. Rapaport, A. *Operational Philosophy*. New York: Harper & Bros., 1954, 230.

207. von Bertalanffy, L. *Problems of Life*. New York: John Wiley and Sons, 1952, 181.

208. Kelman, H. "The Uses of the Analytic Couch." *American Journal of Psychoanalysis* 14 (1954): 65-82; "The Psychopathic Process." Unpublished manuscript.

209. Grinker, R. R., Sr., Werble, B., and Drye, R. C. *The Borderline Syndrome*. New York: Basic Books, 1968.

210. Wenkart, A. "Self-Acceptance." *American Journal of Psychoanalysis* 25 (1955): 135-43.

211. Rubins, J. L. "On the Early Development of the Self: Its Role in Neuroses." *American Journal of Psychoanalysis* 22 (1962): 122-37.

212. Gendlin, E. "A Theory of Personality Change." In *Personality Change,* edited by P. Worchel and D. Byrne. New York: John Wiley, 1964.

212a. Gendlin, E. *Experiencing and the Creation of Meaning*. New York: The Free Press of Glencoe, 1962.

212b. Gendlin, E. "Values and the Process of Experiencing." In *The Goals of Psychotherapy,* edited by A. H. Mahrer. New York: Appleton-Century-Crofts, 1967.

213. Mayr, E. "Cause and Effect in Biology." *Science* 134 (1961): 1501-6.

214. Suzuki, D. T. *The Zen Doctrine of No-Mind*. London: Rider & Co., 1949.

215. Kelman, H. "Training Analysis: Past, Present and Future."

American Journal of Psychoanalysis 22 (1963): 205-17.
216. Watts, A. *The Wisdom of Insecurity*. New York: Pantheon Books, 1951.
217. Waldhorn, H. F. "The Silent Patient." Panel Report. *Journal of the American Psychoanalytic Association* 7 (1959): 548-60.
218. Schachtel, E. G. *Metamorphosis*. New York: Basic Books, 1959, 251-78.
219. Feinstein, A. R. *Clinical Judgment*. Baltimore: Williams & Wilkins, 1967. Reviewed in *Journal of the American Medical Association* 201 (1967): 985.
220. Ivimey, M. "Negative Therapeutic Reaction." *American Journal of Psychoanalysis* 9 (1948): 24-33.
221. Martin, A. R. "Reassurance in Therapy." *American Journal of Psychoanalysis* 9 (1949): 17-29.
222. Tarachow, S. "The Limitations of Technique." *Israel Annals of Psychiatry and Related Disciplines* 3 (1965): 197-212.
222a. Tarachow, S. and Stein, A. "Psychoanalytic Psychotherapy." In *Psychoanalytic Techniques,* edited by B. B. Wolman. New York: Basic Books, 1967.
223. Ruesch, J. *Therapeutic Communication*. New York: W. W. Norton, 1961, 31.
224. Alexander, F. and French, T. R. *Psychoanalytic Therapy*. New York: The Ronald Press, 1946, 22.
225. Freud, A. "Problems of Technique in Adult Analysis." *Bulletin of the Philadelphia Association of Psychoanalysis* 2 (1954): 607-20.
226. Karush, A. "Working Through." *Psychoanalytic Quarterly* 36 (1967): 497-531.
227. Greenson, R. R. and Wexler, M. "The Non-Transference Relationship in the Psychoanalytic Situation." *International Journal of Psycho-Analysis* 50 (1969): 27-39.
228. Goldstein, K. *Human Nature in the Light of Psychopathology*. Cambridge: Harvard University Press, 1946, 153, 154.
229. Kelman, H. "Psychoanalysis and the Study of Etiology: A Definition of Terms." In *The Etiology of Neuroses,* edited by J. H. Merin. Palo Alto, California: Science and Behavior Books, 1966.
230. Freud, A. "The Theory of the Parent-Child Relationship." *International Journal of Psycho-Analysis* 42 (1962): 240-2.
231. Gitelson, M. "Curative Factors in Psychoanalysis." *International Journal of Psycho-Analysis* 43 (1962): 194-205.
232. Spitz, R. "Hospitalism." In *Psychoanalytic Study of the Child I*. New York: International Universities Press, 1945, 53-74.
233. Zetzel, E. R. "The Theory of Therapy." *International Journal*

of Psycho-Analysis 46 (1965): 39-45.

234. Bibring, E. "Symposium on the Theory of Therapeutic Results of Psychoanalysis." *International Journal of Psycho-Analysis* 18 (1937): 170-189.

235. McAlpine, I. "The Development of Transference." *Psycho-analytic Quarterly* 19 (1950): 501-53.

236. Strupp, H. "Psychoanalytic Therapy of the Individual." In *Modern Psychoanalysis,* edited by J. Marmor. New York: Basic Books, 1968.

237. Scott, J. P. "Critical Periods in Behavioral Development." *Science* 138 (1962): 949-58.

237a. Scott, J. P. and Fuller, J. L. *Genetics and the Social Behavior of the Dog.* Chicago: The University of Chicago Press, 1965.

238. May, R. *Psychology and the Human Dilemma.* Princeton, New Jersey: D. Van Nostrand, 1967.

239. Brody, N. and Oppenheim, A. "Tensions in Psychology Between Methods of Behaviorism and Phenomenology." *Psychological Review* 3 (1966): 295-305; "Methodologic Differences Between Behaviorism and Phenomenology in Psychology." *Psychological Review* 74 (1967): 330-4.

240. Burnshaw, S. *The Seamless Web.* New York: George Braziller, 1970.

241. Kelman, H. "Communing and Relating." *American Journal of Psychoanalysis* 18 (1958): 77-98, 158-70; 19 (1959): 73-105, 188-215; "Communing and Relating." *American Journal of Psychotherapy* 16 (1960): 70-96; "Communing as Witness Consciousness" (Communion et la conscience Témoin). In *Roger Godel — De L'Humanisme à L'Humaine,* edited by S. Nacht. Paris: Les Belles-Lettres (Association Guillaume Budé), 1963; "Communing and Relating." Unpublished manuscript.

242. Ullman, M. and Krippner, S. "An Experimental Approach to Dreams and Telepathy: II." *American Journal of Psychiatry* 126 (1970): 1282-9.

242a. Piaget, J. *Six Psychological Studies.* New York: Random House, 1968.

243. van der Post, L. *The Lost World of the Kalahari.* New York: Pyramid Books, 1966.

244. Kelman, H. "Indonesian Psychiatric Services." *Transcultural Psychiatric Report and Newsletter* 5 (1968): 206-7; "Indonesia: Some Psychiatric Impressions." *Indonesian Quarterly of Psychiatry* 1 (1969): 65-79.

245. Tillich, P. "Toward a New Image of Man." *Main Currents in Modern Thought* 16 (1960): 114-6.

246. Burtt, E. A. "The Value Presuppositions of Science." *Bulletin*

of the *Atomic Scientists* 13 (1957): 99-106.
247. Bally, G. "Psychoanalysis and Social Change." *American Journal of Psychoanalysis* 24 (1964): 145-52.
248. Bally, G. "Sociological Aspects of Psychoanalysis." *American Journal of Psychoanalysis* 26 (1966): 5-17.
249. Cassirer, E. *Essay on Man.* New York: Doubleday & Co., 1953.
250. Eliade, M. *Myths, Dreams, Mysteries.* New York: Harper & Bros., 1960.
251. Kelman, H. "Psychoanalysis in Cosmology." *Comprehensive Psychiatry* 9 (1968): 581-607.
252. Bose, G. Bose-Freud Correspondence. *Samiksa* 10 (1956): 155-66. Bose's letter of April 11, 1939.
253. Kelman, H. "Psychotherapy in the Far East." In *Progress in Psychotherapy,* Volume 4, edited by J. Masserman and J. C. Moreno. New York: Grune & Stratton, 1959, 296-305.
254. Khan, M. M. R. "Vicissitudes of Being, Knowing, and Experiencing in the Therapeutic Situation." *British Journal of Medical Psychology* 42 (1969): 383-93.
255. Van Bark, B. "What is Effective in the Therapeutic Process?" A Round Table Discussion. *American Journal of Psychoanalysis* 17 (1957): 3-33.
256. Weiss, P. "Beauty and the Beast. Life and the Rule of Order." *Scientific Monthly* 81 (1955): 286-99.
257. Brodsky, B. "Working Through. Its Widening Scope and Some Aspects of Its Metapsychology." *Psychoanalytic Quarterly* 36 (1967): 485-96.
258. Fleming, J. and Benedek, T. *Psychoanalytic Supervision.* New York: Grune & Stratton, 1966, 173, 174.
259. Kelman, H. "Masochism and Self-Realization." In *Science and Psychoanalysis,* Volume 2, edited by J. Masserman. New York: Grune & Stratton, 1959.
260. Kelman, H. "A Phenomenologic Approach to Dream Interpretation." *American Journal of Psychoanalysis* 25 (1965): 188-202, 27 (1967): 75-94.
261. Boss, M. *The Analysis of Dreams.* London: Rider, 1957.
262. Boss, M. *Psychoanalysis and Daseinsanalysis.* New York: Basic Books, 1963.
263. Sheiner, S. "The Intensity of Casual Relationships in Schizophrenia." *American Journal of Psychoanalysis* 28 (1968): 156-61; "The Communications of Psychotics." *American Journal of Psychoanalysis* 29 (1969): 11-16; "Investigation of a Learning Block in a Schizophrenic." *American Journal of Psychoanalysis* 30 (1969): 205-11; "The Psychoanalytic Approach to the Psychoses." *American Journal of Psychoanalysis* 26 (1956): 76-80;

"Schizophrenia." *American Journal of Psychoanalysis* 22 (1957): 110-4; "On the Therapy of Schizophrenia." *American Journal of Psychoanalysis* 24 (1964): 167-83.

264. Cantor, M. B. "Problems in Diagnosing and Prognosing Occult Schizophrenic Patients." *American Journal of Psychoanalysis* 29 (1969): 36-46.

265. Little, M. "On Delusional Transference (Transference Psychosis)." *International Journal of Psycho-Analysis* 39 (1958): 105-9; "On Basic Unity." *International Journal of Psycho-Analysis* 41 (1960): 377-84.

266. Bjerre, P. *Das Träumen als Heilungsweg der Seele.* Zurich: Rascher, 1936.

266a. Weiss, F. A. "Constructive Forces in Dreams." *American Journal of Psychoanalysis* 9 (1949): 30-7.

267. Freud, S. *The Interpretation of Dreams,* third edition. New York: The Macmillan Co., 1945, 534.

268. Freud, S. *The Complete Introductory Lectures on Psychoanalysis.* New York: W. W. Norton & Co., 1966, 493.

269. Kelman, H. "A New Approach to Dream Interpretation." *American Journal of Psychoanalysis* 4 (1944): 89-107.

270. Meissner, W. W. "Dreaming as Process." *International Journal of Psycho-Analysis* 49 (1968): 63-79.

271. Kelman, H. "Techniques of Dream Interpretation." *American Journal of Psychoanalysis* 25 (1965): 3-20.

272. Kelman, H. " 'Kairos' and the Therapeutic Process." *Journal of Existential Psychiatry* 1 (1960): 233-69; "Kairos: The Auspicious Moment." *American Journal of Psychoanalysis* 29 (1969): 59-83; " 'Kairos': The Auspicious Moment." Unpublished manuscript.

273. Kelman, H. "What Are Your Doubts About Analysis?" and "Who Should Your Analyst Be?" In *Are You Considering Psychoanalysis?* edited by K. Horney. New York: W. W. Norton, 1946.

274. Sandifer, M. G., Hordern, A. and Green, M. "The Psychiatric Interview: The Impact of the First Three Minutes." *American Journal of Psychiatry* 126 (1970): 968-73; Pittinger, R. E., Hockett, C. F. and Danehy, J. J. *The First Five Minutes.* Ithaca, New York: Paul Martineau, 1960.

275. Ruesch, J. "Declining Clinical Tradition." *Journal of the American Medical Association* 182 (1962): 110-5.

276. Kelman, H. "The Role of Psychoanalysis in Psychiatry: Present and Future." *Bulletin of the New York State District Branches.* American Psychiatric Association 11 (1968): 1-3; "The Clinical Tradition and Clinical Research." *Newsletter, American Aca-*

demy of Psychoanalysis 13 (1969): 1-3; "How Does Psychoanalysis Fit into the Total Concept of Care?" Read before New York District Branch, Biannual Meeting, November 15, 1969.

277. Kelman, H. "Prognosis in Psychotherapy." *Samiksa* 12 (1958): 29-48; *Psychiatria, Neurologia, Neurochirurgia* 63 (1960): 81-92.

278. Kelman, H. "The Chronic Analyst." In *Science and Psychoanalysis*, Volume 16. Edited by J. H. Masserman. New York: Grune & Stratton, 1970.

278a. Lorand, S. and Console, W. A. "Therapeutic Results in Psychoanalytic Treatment Without Fee." *International Journal of Psycho-Analysis* 39 (1958): 59-64.

279. Middelman, F. "Linguistic Relativity in Psychotherapy." *Comprehensive Psychiatry* 10 (1969): 31-43.

280. Lifton, R. J. "Protean Man." *Yale Alumni Magazine* 22 (1969): 14-21.

281. Glover, E. *The Technique of Psychoanalysis*. New York: International Universities Press, 1953, 300.

282. Heinemann, F. H. *Existentialism and the Modern Predicament*. New York: Harper & Bros., 1958, 1.

283. Kelman, H. Moderator. "Intervention in Psychotherapy." *A Round Table Discussion. American Journal of Psychoanalysis* 22 (1962): 43-83.

284. Alexander, F. and French T. *Fundamentals of Psychoanalysis*. New York: W. W. Norton & Co., 1948.

285. Pleune, F. G. "All Dis-Ease is Not Disease: A Consideration of Psycho-Analysis, Psychotherapy and Psycho-Social Engineering." *International Journal of Psycho-Analysis* 46 (1965): 358.

286. Kelman, H. "Neurotic Pessimism." *Psychoanalytic Review* 32 (1945): 419-48.

287. Hollender, M. H. *The Practice of Psychoanalytic Psychotherapy*. New York: Grune & Stratton, 1965.

288. Erikson, E. H. *Gandhi's Truth: On the Origins of Militant Nonviolence*. New York: W. W. Norton & Co., 1969, 433.

289. Turner, V. W. *The Ritual Process. Structure and Anti-Structure*. Chicago: Aldine Publishing Co., 1969.

290. Pappenheim, F. *The Alienation of Modern Man*. New York: Monthly Review Press, 1959.

291. Tymieniecka, A. T. *Phenomenology and Science in Contemporary European Thought*. New York: Noonday Press, 1962.

292. Riese, W. "Phenomenology and Existentialism in Psychiatry: An Historical Analysis." *Journal of Nervous and Mental Disease* 132 (1961): 469-84.

293. May, R., Angel, E. and Ellenberger, H. F. *Existence.* New York: Basic Books, 1958.

294. Tillich P. "Kairos." In *A Handbook of Christian Theology.* New York: Meridian Books, 1958.

295. Hippocrates. *De Affectionibus.* In *Oeuvres Complètes d'Hippocrate,* Volume 6, edited by E. Littré. Paris: J. B. Baillière, 1849, 270-1.

296. Delling, G. *Theological Dictionary of the New Testament.* Edited by G. Kittel and G. W. Bramley. Translated by G. W. Bramley. Grand Rapids, Michigan: W. B. Erdman, 1964-1967, 455-64.

297. Hoch, E. "Desakalajnana: An Indian Contribution to the Discussion on Kairos." In "'Kairos': The Auspicious Moment." Edited by H. Kelman. Unpublished manuscript.

298. Neki, J. S. *"Ausar* (Kairos: and Its Place in Creative Psychotherapy)." In "'Kairos': The Auspicious Moment," edited by H. Kelman. Unpublished manuscript.

299. Arasteh, R. A. "Greek *Kairos* and Persian *An* (The Climax of Being)." In "'Kairos': The Auspicious Moment," edited by H. Kelman. Unpublished manuscript.

300. Kondo, A. "Kairos Experience in Japanese Culture." In "'Kairos': The Auspicious Moment," edited by H. Kelman. Unpublished manuscript.

301. Kielholz, A. *"Von Kairos — Zum Problem der Kurpfuscherei"* (Concerning *Kairos* and the Problem of Quackery). *Schweizerische Medizinische Wochenschrift* 86 (1956): 982-94.

302. Huxley, A. *Perennial Philosophy.* New York: Harper & Bros., 1945.

303. Maslow, A. *Toward a Psychology of Being.* New York: D. Van Nostrand, 1962.

304. Koestler, A. "Beyond Atomism and Holism — the Concept of the Holon." *Perspectives in Biology and Medicine* 13 (1970): 131-54.

305. Whyte, L. L., Wilson, A. G. and Wilson, D. *Hierarchical Structures.* New York: American Elsevier Publishing Co., 1969, 4.

306. Erikson, E. H. *Childhood and Society.* New York: W. W. Norton & Co., 1963; *Young Man Luther, a Study of Psychoanalysis and History,* New York; W. W. Norton & Co., 1958.

307. Lifton, R. J. "On Spiritual Innovators: Erikson and Gandhi." *Psychiatry and Social Science Review* 4 (1970): 3-8.

308. Elkind, D. "Erik Erikson's Eight Ages of Man." *New York Times Magazine* (April 12, 1970): 25-119.

309. Whorf, B. L. *Language, Thought and Reality.* New York: Wiley & Sons, 1958.

310. Grinker, R. R. "Transactional Model for Psychotherapy." *Archives of General Psychiatry* 1 (1959): 132-48.
311. Spiegel, J. P. "Anatomy of Student Revolt." *Roche Report: Frontiers of Clinical Psychiatry* 7 (1970): 5-11.
312. Eisenberg, L. "Student Unrest: Sources and Consequences." *Science* 167 (1970): 1688-92.
313. Willner, G. "Duerckheim's Existential Philosophy." *American Journal of Psychoanalysis* 18 (1958): 38-51.
314. Bleuler, E. *Acute Psychische Begleiterscheinungen Koerperlicher Krankheiten.* [Acute Psychic Symptomatology Associated with Somatic Illness]. Stuttgart, Germany: Georg Thieme Verlag, 1966.
315. Tolstoy, L. *The Death of Ivan Illych and Other Stories.* New York: The New American Library, 1959, 95-151.
316. Kübler-Ross, E. *On Death and Dying.* New York: The Macmillan Co., 1969; Weisman, A. D. "Misgivings and Misconceptions in the Psychiatric Care of Terminal Patients." *Psychiatry* 33 (1970): 67-81.
317. Kierkegaard, S. *The Diary of Soren Kierkegaard.* New York: Philosophical Library, The Wisdom Library, 1960. 201, 242.
318. Hohlenberg, J. *Soren Kierkegaard.* Translated by T. H. Croxall. New York: Pantheon, 1954, 394.
319. Weigert, E. "Soren Kierkegaard's Mood-Swings." *International Journal of Psycho-Analysis* 16 (1960): 521-5.
320. Strachey, J. "Papers on Technique: Editor's Introduction." *The Standard Edition of the Complete Psychological Works of Sigmund Freud,* Volume 12. London: Hogarth Press, 1958, 85-8.
321. Hartmann, H. "Technical Implications of Ego Psychology." *Psychoanalytic Quarterly* 20 (1951): 31-43.
322. Rapaport, D. "The Structure of Psychoanalytic Theory: A. Systematizing Attempt." *Psychological Issues,* Volume 2, edited by G. S. Klein. International Universities Press, 1960.
323. Alexander, F. Review of *Theory of Psychoanalytic Technique. Science* 129 (1959): 1732-3.
324. Eckstein, R. "Psychoanalytic Techniques." In *Progress in Clinical Psychology,* edited by P. Brower and S. E. Abt. New York: Grune & Stratton, 1956, 79.
324a. Eckstein, R. "A Historical Survey on the Technique of Teaching Psychoanalytic Technique." *Journal of the American Psychoanalytic Association* 8 (1960): 500-17.
324b. Eckstein, R. "Concerning Teaching and Learning of Psychoanalysis." *Journal of American Psychoanalytic Association* 17 (1969): 312-32.

325. Freud, S. *Beyond the Pleasure Principle.* London: International Psychoanalytic Press, 1922.
326. Bentham, J. *An Introduction to the Principles of Morals and Legislation.* London: Pickering, 1882, 1; in Northrop, F.S.C. *The Meeting of East and West.* New York: The Macmillan Co., 1949, 131.
327. Whittaker, E., Sir. "Eddington's Principle in the Philosophy of Science." *American Scientist* 40 (1952): 46.
328. Gould, R. A. "The Marginally Asocial Personality: The Beatnik-Hippie Alienation." In *The World Biennial of Psychiatry and Psychotherapy,* Volume 1, edited by S. Arieti. New York: Basic Books, 1971, 284.
329. Holt, R. H. "Clinical Judgment as a Disciplined Inquiry." *Journal of Nervous and Mental Disease* 133 (1961): 369-82.
330. Rapaport, A. "Psychoanalysis as Science." *Bulletin of the Menninger Clinic* 31 (1968): 1-20.
331. Simpson, G. "Biology and the Nature of Science." *Science* 139 (1963): 81-8; "Evolution's Two Components: Biological and Cultural." *Science* 136 (1962): 142-3.
332. Bunge, M. "Causality, Chance and Law." *American Scientist* 49 (1961): 432-48.
333. Hook, S. *Psychoanalysis: Scientific Method and Philosophy.* New York: Grove Press, 1960, 214.
334. Kuhn, T. S. *The Structure of Scientific Revolutions.* Chicago: University of Chicago Press, 1964, 109.
335. von Weizäcker, C. F. *The Relevance of Science: Creation and Cosmogony.* New York: Harper & Row, 1964.
336. Ehrenwald, J. *Psychotherapy: Myth and Method.* New York: Grune & Stratton, 1966, 192.
337. Ford, D. H. and Urban, H. B. *Systems of Psychotherapy.* New York: J. Wiley & Sons, 1964, 4.
338. Cohen, D. "Magneto-encephalography: Evidence of Magnetic Fields Produced by Alpha-Rhythm Currents." *Science* 161 (1968): 784-6.
339. Northrop, F. S. C. *The Logic of the Sciences and the Humanities.* New York: The Macmillan Co., 1949.
340. Heuscher, J. S. "Spontaneity versus Technique." *American Journal of Psychoanalysis* 28 (1967): 61-74.
341. Herrigel, E. *Zen in the Art of Archery.* New York: Pantheon, 1953.
342. Buber, M. *Tales of the Hasidim, The Early Masters.* Translated by Olga Marx. New York: Shocken Books, 1957; *Tales of the Hasidim, The Later Masters.* Translated by Olga Marx. New York: Shocken Books, 1948.

Being)." In *Kairos: The Auspicious Moment,* edited by H. Kelman. Unpublished manuscript.

Arieti, S. *The Intrapsychic Self.* New York: Basic Books, 1967.

—— "The Meeting of the Inner and the External World: In Schizophrenia, Everyday Life, and Creativity." *American Journal of Psychoanalysis,* 29 (1969): 115-30.

Azorin, L. A. "The Analyst's Personal Equation." *American Journal of Psychoanalysis* 27 (1957): 34-8.

Balint, M. *The Basic Fault: Therapeutic Aspects of Regression.* London: Tavistock Publications, 1967.

Bally, G. "Psychoanalysis and Social Change." *American Journal of Psychoanalysis* 24 (1964): 145-52.

—— "Sociological Aspects of Psychoanalysis." *American Journal of Psychoanalysis* 26 (1966): 5-19.

Bentham, J. *An Introduction to the Principles of Morals and Legislation.* London: Pickering, 1882.

Bettelheim, B. "Personality Formation in the Kibbutz." *American Journal of Psychoanalysis* 29 (1969): 3-9.

Bibring, E. "Symposium on the Theory of Therapeutic Results of Psychoanalysis." *International Journal of Psycho-Analysis* 18 (1937): 170-89.

Binger, C. A. L., Ackerman, N. W., Cohen, A. E., Schroeder, H. A., and Steele, J. M. *Personality in Arterial Hypertension.* New York: The American Society for Research in Psychosomatic Problems, 1945.

Bird, B. "On Candidate Selection and Its Relation to Analysis." *International Journal of Psycho-Analysis* 49 (1968): 513-26.

Bjerre, P. *Das Träumen als Heilungsweg der Seele.* Zurich: Rascher, 1936.

Bleuler, E. *Acute Psychische Begleiterscheinungen Koerperlicher Krankheiten.* [Acute Psychic Symptomatology Associated with Somatic Illness]. Stuttgart, Germany: Georg Thieme Verlag, 1966.

Blitzen, L. and Fleming, J. "What Is a Supervisory Analysis?" *Bulletin of the Menninger Clinic* 17 (1953): 117-29.

Bose, G. "Bose-Freud Correspondence." *Samiksa* 10 (1956): 155-66. Bose's letter of April 11, 1939.

Boss, M. *Psychoanalysis and Daseinsanalysis.* New York: Basic Books, 1963.

—— *The Analysis of Dreams.* London: Rider, 1957.

Boss, M. and Condrau, G. "Existential Psychoanalysis." In *Psychoanalytic Technique,* edited by B. B. Wolman. New York: Basic Books, 1967.

Brés, Y. *Freud et la psychoanalyse américaine Karen Horney.* Paris:

Librairie Philosophique J. Vrin., 1970.

Brodsky, B. "Working Through: Its Widening Scope and Some Aspects of its Metapsychology." *Psychoanalytic Quarterly* 36 (1967): 485-96.

Brody, N. and Oppenheim, A. "Tensions in Psychology Between Methods of Behaviorism and Phenomenology." *Psychological Review* 3 (1966): 295-305.

—— "Methodologic Differences Between Behaviorism and Phenomenology in Psychology." *Psychological Review* 74 (1967): 330-4.

Bruch, H. "Perceptual and Conceptual Disturbances in Anorexia Nervosa." *Psychosomatic Medicine* 24 (1962): 187.

—— "Transformation of Oral Impulses in Eating Disorders." *Psychiatric Quarterly* 35 (1961): 458-81.

Bruns, B. D. *The Uncertain Nervous System.* Baltimore: William & Wilkins, 1969. Reviewed in *Medical Opinion and Review* 5 (1969): 92-6.

Buber, M. *Tales of the Hasidim: The Early Masters.* Translated by Olga Marx. New York: Shocken Books, 1957.

—— *Tales of the Hasidim: The Later Masters.* Translated by Olga Marx. New York: Shocken Books, 1948.

Bunge, M. "Causality, Chance and Law." *American Scientist* 49 (1961): 432-48.

Burnshaw, S. *The Seamless Web.* New York: George Braziller, 1970.

Burrow, T. *Preconscious Foundations of Human Experience.* Edited by W. E. Galt. New York: Basic Books, 1964.

Burtt, E. A. "The Value Presuppositions of Science." *Bulletin of the Atomic Scientists* 13 (1957): 99-106.

Bychowski, G. "The Archaic Object and Alienation." *International Journal of Psycho-Analysis* 48 (1967): 384-93.

Cameron, E. D. "Karen Horney: A Pioneer in the Science of Human Relations." *American Journal of Psychoanalysis* 14 (1954): 19-29.

Cantor, M. B. "Mobilizing Constructive Forces." *American Journal of Psychoanalysis* 27 (1967): 188-99.

—— "Problems in Diagnosing and Prognosing Occult Schizophrenic Patients." *American Journal of Psychoanalysis* 29 (1969): 36-46.

—— "The Initial Interview." *American Journal of Psychoanalysis* 27 (1957): 39-44, 121-6.

—— "The Quality of the Analyst's Attention." *American Journal of Psychoanalysis* 19 (1959): 28-32.

Cassirer, E. *Essay on Man.* New York: Doubleday & Co., 1953.

Caws, P. "The Structure of Discovery." *Science* 166 (1969): 1375-80.

Ciardi, J. "Internal Man and External World." *Saturday Review* (June 11, 1960): 15.

594

Cohen, D. "Magneto-encephalography: Evidence of Magnetic Fields Produced by Alpha-Rhythm Currents." *Science* 161 (1968): 784-6.

Delling, G. *Theological Dictionary of the New Testament.* 3 Volumes. Edited by G. Kittel and G. W. Bramley. Translated by G. W. Bramley. Grand Rapids, Michigan: W. B. Erdman, 1964, 1965, 1967.

Downie, R. A. *Frazer and the Golden Bough.* London: Gollancz, 1970.

Downing, A. B. *Euthanasia and the Right to Die: The case for Voluntary Euthanasia.* New York: Humanities Press, 1970.

Draper, G., Dupertuis, C. W., and Caughey, J. L. *Human Constitution in Clinical Medicine.* New York: Paul B. Hoeber, 1944.

Dunbar, F. *Emotions and Bodily Changes.* New York: Columbia University Press, 1935.

Eckstein, R. "A Historical Survey on the Technique of Teaching Psychoanalytic Technique." *Journal of the American Psychoanalytic Association* 8 (1960): 500-17.

—— "Concerning Teaching and Learning of Psychoanalysis." *Journal of the American Psychoanalytic Association* 17 (1969): 312-32.

—— "Psychoanalytic Techniques." In *Progress in Clinical Psychology,* edited by P. Brower and S. E. Abt. New York: Grune & Stratton, 1956.

Ehrenwald, J. *Psychotherapy: Myth and Method.* New York: Grune & Stratton, 1966.

Eisenberg, L. "Student Unrest: Sources and Consequences." *Science* 167 (1970): 1688-92.

Eliade, M. *Myths, Dreams, Mysteries.* New York: Harper & Bros., 1960.

Elkind, D. "Erik Erikson's Eight Ages of Man." *New York Times Magazine.* (April 12, 1970): 25-119.

Engel, G. L. Review of *Psychosomatic Specificity. Science* 164 (1969): 689-90.

—— "The Psychoanalytic Approach to Psychoanalytic Medicine." In *Modern Psychoanalysis,* edited by J. Marmor. New York: Basic Books, 1968.

Erikson, E. H. *Childhood and Society.* New York: W. W. Norton & Co., 1963.

—— *Gandhi's Truth: On the Origins of Militant Nonviolence.* New York: W. W. Norton & Co., 1969.

—— *Identity: Youth and Crisis.* New York: W. W. Norton, 1968.

—— *Young Man Luther, a Study of Psychoanalysis and History.* New York: W. W. Norton & Co., 1958.

595

Fairbum, W. R. D. *An Object-Relations Theory of the Personality.*
New York: Basic Books, 1954.

Feinstein, A. R. *Clinical Judgment.* Baltimore: Williams & Wilkins,
1967. Reviewed in the *Journal of the American Medical Association* 201 (1967): 985.

Fenichel, O. Review of *New Ways in Psychoanalysis. Psychoanalytic
Quarterly* 9 (1940): 114-21.

—— *Problems of Psychoanalytic Technique.* New York: The Psychoanalytic Quarterly Inc., 1941.

—— *The Psychoanalytic Theory of Neurosis.* New York: W. W.
Norton & Co., 1945.

Ferreira, A. J. *Prenatal Environment.* Springfield, Illinois: Charles
C. Thomas, 1969.

Fleming, J. and Benedek, T. *Psychoanalytic Supervision.* New York:
Grune & Stratton, 1966.

Ford, D. H. and Urban, H. B. *Systems of Psychotherapy.* New York:
J. Wiley & Sons, 1964.

Freud, A. *Difficulties of Psychoanalysis.* New York: International
Universities Press, 1969.

—— "Problems of Technique in Adult Analysis." *Bulletin of the
Philadelphia Association of Psychoanalysis* 2 (1954): 607-20.

—— *The Ego and the Mechanisms of Defense.* New York: International Universities Press, 1946.

—— "The Theory of the Parent-Child Relationship." *International
Journal of Psycho-Analysis* 42 (1962): 240-2.

Freud, S. "Analysis Terminable and Interminable." In *Collected
Papers,* Volume 5. London: Hogarth Press, 1956.

—— *An Outline of Psychoanalysis.* New York: W. W. Norton &
Co., 1949.

—— *Beyond the Pleasure Principle.* London: International Psychoanalytic Press, 1922.

—— "Female Sexuality (1931)." In *Collected Papers,* Volume 5.
London: Hogarth Press, 1956.

—— "Further Recommendations in the Technique of Psycho-Analysis
(1913)." *Collected Papers,* Volume 2. London: Hogarth Press,
1933.

—— *On the History of the Psychoanalytic Movement.* London:
Hogarth Press, 1957.

—— "Recommendations for Physicians on the Psycho-Analytic
Method of Treatment (1912)." *Collected Papers,* Volume 2.
London: Hogarth Press, 1933.

—— "Some Psychological Consequences of the Anatomical Distinction Between the Sexes (1925)." *Collected Papers,* Volume 5. London: Hogarth Press, 1956.

―― *The Complete Introductory Lectures on Psychoanalysis*. New York: W. W. Norton, 1966.

―― *The Ego and the Id*. London: Hogarth Press, 1923.

―― *The Interpretation of Dreams*. New York: The Macmillan Co., 1945.

Fromm, E. *Man for Himself*. New York: Rinehart & Co., 1947.

Fromm-Reichmann, F. *Principles of Intensive Psychotherapy*. Chicago: University of Chicago Press, 1950.

―― *Psychoanalysis and Psychotherapy: Selected Papers*. Edited by D. M. Bullard. Chicago: University of Chicago Press, 1959.

Gendlin, E. "A Theory of Personality Change." In *Personality Change*, edited by P. Worchel and D. Byrne. New York, John Wiley, 1964.

―― *Experiencing and the Creation of Meaning*. New York: The Free Press of Glencoe, 1962.

―― "Values and the Process of Experiencing." In *The Goals of Psychotherapy*, edited by A. H. Mahrer. New York: Appleton-Century-Crofts, 1967.

Gergen, K. J. "Self-Theory and the Process of Self-Observation." *Journal of Nervous and Mental Disease* 148 (1969): 437-48.

Gershman, H. "Homosexuality and Some Aspects of Creativity." *American Journal of Psychoanalysis* 24 (1964): 29-35.

―― "Reflections on the Nature of Homosexuality." *American Journal of Psychoanalysis* 26 (1966): 46-9.

―― "The Role of Gender Identity in the Genesis of Perversions." *American Journal of Psychoanalysis* 30 (1970): 58-67.

Gifford, S. and Gunderson, J. G. "Cushing's Disease as a Psychosomatic Disorder." *Perspectives in Biology and Medicine* 13 (1970): 169-221.

Gittelson, M. "Curative Factors in Psychoanalysis." *International Journal of Psycho-Analysis* 43 (1962): 194-205.

―― Review of *Psychoanalytic Education in the United States*. *Psychoanalytic Quarterly* 29 (1960): 559-67.

Glover, E. *The Technique of Psychoanalysis*. New York: International Universities Press, 1953.

Goldstein, K. *Human Nature in the Light of Psychopathology*. Cambridge, Massachusetts: Harvard University Press, 1946.

―― "The Concept of Transference in Treatment of Organic and Functional Nervous Disease." *Acta Psychotherepeutica Psychosomatica et Orthopaedagogica* 2 (1954): 334-53.

―― *The Organism*. New York: American Book Co., 1939.

―― "The Smiling of the Infant and the Problem of Understanding the Other." *Journal of Psychology,* 44 (1957): 175-91.

Gould, R. A. "The Marginally Asocial Personality: The Beatnik-

Hippie Alienation." In *The World Biennial of Psychiatry and Psychotherapy*, Volume 1, edited by S. Arieti. New York: Basic Books, 1971.

Greenacre, P. "A Critical Digest of the Literature on Selection of Candidates for Psychoanalytic Training." *Psychoanalytic Quarterly* 30 (1961): 38-55.

Greenson, R. R. and Wexler, M. "The Non-Transference Relationship in the Psychoanalytic Situation." *International Journal of Psycho-Analysis* 50 (1969): 27-39.

Grinker, R. R., Sr. " 'Open-System' Psychiatry." *American Journal of Psychoanalysis* 26 (1966): 115-28.

—— "Transactional Model for Psychotherapy." *Archives of General Psychiatry* 1 (1959): 132-48.

Grinker, R. R., Sr., Werble, B., and Drye, R. C. *The Borderline Syndrome.* New York: Basic Books, 1968.

Grotjahn, M. "Problems and Techniques of Supervision." *Psychiatry* 18 (1955): 9-15. "Growing Old in America. The Unwanted Generation." *Time* 96 (1970): 43-8.

Guttman, S. A. "Criteria for Analyzability." *Journal of the American Psychoanalytic Association* 8 (1960): 141-51.

Haas, W. S. *The Destiny of the Mind: East and West.* New York: Macmillan Co., 1956.

Hartmann, H. *Ego Psychology and the Problem of Adaptation.* New York: International Universities Press, 1958.

—— "Technical Implications of Ego Psychology." *Psychoanalytic Quarterly* 20 (1951): 31-43.

Heinemann, F. H. *Existentialism and the Modern Predicament.* New York: Harper & Bros., 1958.

Herrigel, E. *Zen in the Art of Archery.* New York: Pantheon, 1953.

Heuscher, J. S. "Spontaneity versus Technique." *American Journal of Psychoanalysis* 28 (1967): 61-74.

Hill, L. B. "Psychotherapy of a Schizophrenic." *American Journal of Psychoanalysis* 27 (1957): 99-109.

Hippocrates. "De Affectionibus." In *Oeuvres Complètes d'Hippocrate*, Volume 6, edited by E. Littré. Paris: J. B. Baillière, 1849. 270-71.

Hoch, E. "Desakalajnana: An Indian Contribution to the Discussion on Kairos." In *Kairos: The Auspicious Moment*, edited by H. Kelman. Unpublished manuscript.

Hohlenberg, J. *Soren Kierkegaard.* Translated by T. H. Croxall. New York: Pantheon, 1954.

Hollender, M. H. *The Practice of Psychoanalytic Psychotherapy.* New York: Grune & Stratton, 1965.

Holt, R. H. "Clinical Judgment as a Disciplined Inquiry." *Journal of Nervous and Mental Disease* 133 (1961): 369-82.

Hook, S. *Psychoanalysis: Scientific Method and Philosophy.* New York: Grove Press, 1960.

Horney, Karen, ed. *Are You Considering Psychoanalysis?* New York: W. W. Norton & Co., 1946.

—— Autobiographical Material. Found in her files; possibly prepared for organizations and press releases, 1932.

—— "Can You Take a Stand?" *Journal of Adult Education* 11 (1932): 129-32.

—— "Conceptions and Misconceptions of the Analytical Method." *Journal of Nervous and Mental Disease* 81 (1935): 339-410.

—— "Concepts and Misconcepts of the Analytic Method." *Archives of Neurology and Psychiatry* 32 (1934): 880-3.

—— "Culture and Neurosis." *American Sociological Review* 1 (1936): 221-34.

—— "Das Misstrauen zwischen den Geschlechtern" [The Distrust Between the Sexes]. *Die Ärztin* 7 (1931): 5-12.

—— "Das Misstrauen zwischen den Geschlechtern" [The Distrust Between the Sexes]. *Psychoanalytische Bewegung* 2 (1930): 521-37.

—— "Das neurotische Liebesbedürfnis." [The Neurotic Need for Love]. *Zentralblatt für Psychotherapie* 10 (1937): 69-82.

—— "Der Kampf in der Kultur, Einige Gedanken und Bedenken zu Freud's Todestrieb und Destruktionstrieb" [The Role of Aggression in Civilization. Some Thoughts and Objections Regarding Freud's Death Instinct and Drive for Destruction]. In *Das Problem der Kultur und die ärztliche Psychologie* [The Problem of Civilization and Medical Psychology]. Vorträge der Institut für Geschichte der Medizin, Universität Leipzig. [Lectures of the Institute for the History of Medicine at Leipzig University] 4 (1931): 105-18. Leipzig, Germany: Thieme-Verlag; *American Journal of Psychoanalysis* 20 (1960): 130-8.

—— "Der Männlichtkeitskomplex der Frau" [The Masculinity Complex of Women]. *Archiv für Frauenkunde* 13 (1927): 141-54.

—— "Die Angst vor der Frau. Uber einen spezifischen Unterschied in der männlichen und weiblichen Angst vor dem anderen Geschlecht" [The Dread of Woman. Observations on a Specific Difference in the Dread Felt by Men and by Women Respectively for the Opposite Sex]. *Internationale Zeitschrift für Psychoanalyse* 18 (1932): 5-18; *International Journal of Psycho-Analysis* 13 (1932): 348-60.

—— "Die monogame Forderung" [The Demand for Monogamy]. *Internationale Zeitschrift für Psychoanalyse* 13 (1927): 397-409; *Psychoanalytische Almanach* 3 (1928): 38-54.

—— "Die prämenstruellen Verstimmungen" [The Premenstrual

Emotional Disturbances]. *Zeitschrift für psychoanalytische Pädagogik* 5 (1931): 1-7.

—— "Die spezifische Problematik der Zwangsneurose im Lichte der Psychoanalyse" [The Specific Problems of Compulsion Neurosis in the Light of Psychoanalysis]. *Archiv für Psychiatrie* 91 (1930): 597-601.

—— "Die Technik der psychoanalytischen Therapie" [The Technique of Psychoanalytic Therapy]. *Zeitschrift für Sexualwissenschaft* 4 (1917): 185-91; In *Bericht über die Fortschritte der Psychoanalyse* 1914-1919. Vienna: Internationaler Psychoanalytischer Verlag, 1921; *American Journal of Psychoanalysis* 28 (1968): 3-12.

—— "Die Verleugnung der Vagina. Ein Beitrag zur Frage der spezifisch weiblichen Genitalängst" [The Denial of the Vagina. Contribution to Problem of Genital Anxieties Specific to Women]. *Internationale Zeitschrift für Psychoanalyse* 19 (1933): 372-84; *International Journal of Psycho-Analysis* 14 (1933): 57-70.

—— "Diskussion der Laienanalyse" [Discussion: Symposium on Lay Analysis]. *Internationale Zeitschrift für Psychoanalyse* 13 (1927): 101-7; *International Journal of Psycho-Analysis* 8 (1927): 255-9.

—— *Ein kasuistischer Beitrag zur Frage der traumatischen Psychosen.* [A Casuistic Contribution to the Question of Traumatic Psychoses]. Berlin: H. Bode, 1915.

—— "Erhohung und Erniedergung der Frau" [Adoration and Degradation of Women]. Unpublished lecture before Berlin General Medical Society for Psychotherapy, 1932.

—— "Finding the Real Self." Foreword to a Letter. *American Journal of Psychoanalysis* 10 (1950): 64-5.

—— "Flucht aus der Weiblichkeit" [The Flight from Womanhood]. *Internationale Zeitschrift für Psychoanalyse* 12 (1926): 360-74; *International Journal of Psycho-Analysis* 7 (1926): 324-39.

—— "Gehemmte Weiblichkeit. Psychoanalytischer Beitrag zum Problem der Frigidität" [Inhibited Femininity: A Psychoanalytic Contribution to the Problem of Frigidity]. *Zeitschrift für Sexualwissenschaft* 13 (1926): 67-77.

—— "Human Nature Can Change." Contribution to a Symposium. *American Journal of Psychoanalysis* 12 (1952): 67-8.

—— "Inhibitions in Work." *American Journal of Psychoanalysis* 7 (1947): 18-25; *Psyché* 3 (1947): 481-92; *Psyché* 4 (1949): 581-95.

—— Letter to the Members of the American Psychoanalytic Association by Five Resigning Members of the New York Psychoanalytic Society, Signed by Harmon S. Ephron, Karen Horney, Sarah R. Kelman, Bernard S. Robbins, Clara Thompson. Reprinted in

American Journal of Psychoanalysis 1 (1941): 9-10.

—— "Maturity and the Individual." Contribution to a Symposium. (1933): 455-63.

—— "Maternal Conflicts." *American Journal of Orthopsychiatry* 3 *American Journal of Psychoanalysis* 7 (1947): 85-7.

—— *Neurosis and Human Growth.* New York: W. W. Norton & Co., 1950.

—— *New Ways in Psychoanalysis.* New York: W. W. Norton & Co., 1939.

—— "On Difficulties in Dealing with the Transference." *News-Letter of American Association of Psychiatric Social Workers* 5 (1935): 1-12.

—— "On Feeling Abused." *American Journal of Psychoanalysis* 11 (1951): 5-12.

—— *Our Inner Conflicts.* New York: W. W. Norton & Co., 1945.

—— "Personality Changes in Female Adolescents." *American Journal of Orthopsychiatry* 5 (1935): 19-26.

—— "Psychiatrist-Social Worker Interrelationship." *American Journal of Psychiatry* 98 (1942): 504-8.

—— "Psychische Eignung und Nichteignung zur Ehe" [Psychological Suitability and Unsuitability for Marriage]. In *Ein biologisches Ehebuch,* edited by Max Marcuse. Berlin und Köln: A. Marcus und E. Weber Verlag, 1927.

—— "Psychoanalysis and Moral Values." Contribution to Symposium. *American Journal of Psychoanalysis* 10 (1950): 64-5.

—— "Psychogenic Factors in Functional Female Disorders." *American Journal of Obstetrics and Gynecology* 25 (1933): 694-703; *Medical and Professional Woman's Journal* 40 (1933): 319-24.

—— "Restricted Applications of Psychoanalysis to Social Work." *The Family* 15 (1934): 169-72.

—— *Self-Analysis.* New York: W. W. Norton & Co., 1942.

—— Tenth Anniversary Address at the Association for the Advance of Psychoanalysis. *American Journal of Psychoanalysis* 11 (1951): 3-4.

—— "The Future of Psychoanalysis." Contribution to a Symposium. *American Journal of Psychoanalysis* 6 (1946): 66-7.

—— "The Individual and Therapy." Contribution to Symposium. *American Journal of Psychoanalysis* 11 (1951): 54-5.

—— *The Neurotic Personality of Our Time.* New York: W. W. Norton & Co., 1937.

—— "The Overevaluation of Love. A Study of a Common Present-Day Feminine Type." *Psychoanalytic Quarterly* 3 (1934): 605-38.

—— "The Paucity of Inner Experiences." *American Journal of Psychoanalysis* 12 (1952): 3-9.

—— "The Problem of the Monogamic Statute." *Psychoanalytic Review* 15 (1928): 92-3.

—— "The Problem of the Monogamous Ideal." *International Journal of Psycho-Analysis* 9 (1928): 318-31.

—— "The Problem of the Negative Therapeutic Reaction." *Psychoanalytic Quarterly* 5 (1966): 29-44.

—— "The Search for Glory." *Pastoral Psychology* 1 (1950): 13-20.

—— "The Value of Vindictiveness." *American Journal of Psychoanalysis* 8 (1948): 3-12; *Psyché* 6 (1951): 159, 230-50.

—— "Uber die psychischen Bestimmungen der Gattenwahl" [On the Psychological Conditions of the Choice of a Marriage Partner]. In *Ein biologisches Ehebuch,* edited by Max Marcuse. Berlin und Köln: A. Marcus und E. Weber Verlag, 1927.

—— "Uber die psychischen Wurzeln einiger typischen Ehekonflikte" [On the Psychological Roots of Some Typical Marriage Conflicts]. In *Ein Biologisches Ehebuch,* edited by Max Marcuse. Berlin und Köln: A. Marcus und E. Weber Verlag, 1927.

—— "Values and Problems of Group Analysis." Contribution to Symposium. *American Journal of Psychoanalysis* 12 (1952): 80-1.

—— "Was tut eigentlich der Psychoanalytiker?" [What Does the Analyst Do?]. *Psyché* 4 (1950): 1-10.

—— "Ziele der Analytischen Therapie" [Goals of Analytic Therapy]. *Psyché* 6 (1957): 463-72.

—— "Zur Genese des weiblichen Kastrationskomplexes" [On the Genesis of the Castration Complex in Women]. *Internationale Zeitschrift für Psychoanalyse* 9 (1923): 12-26; *International Journal of Psycho-Analysis* 5 (1924): 50-65.

—— "Zur Problematik der Ehe" [Problems of Marriage]. *Psychoanalytische Bewegung* 4 (1932): 212-23.

Hulbeck, C. R. "Three Creative Phases in Psychoanalysis: The Encounter, The Dialogue and the Process of Articulation." *American Journal of Psychoanalysis* 23 (1963): 157-62.

Huxley, A. *The Perennial Philosophy.* New York: Harper & Bros., 1945.

Ivimey, M. "Negative Therapeutic Reaction." *American Journal of Psychoanalysis* 9 (1948): 24-33.

Jones, E. "A Valedictory Address." *International Journal of Psycho-Analysis* 27 (1946): 7-11.

—— Review of *Neurotic Personality of Our Time. International Journal of Psycho-Analysis* 20 (1940): 240-1.

—— "The Early Development of Female Sexuality." *International Journal of Psycho-Analysis* 8 (1927): 459.

—— *The Life and Work of Sigmund Freud.* 2 Volumes. New York: Basic Books, 1953, 1955.

Kanner, L. "Centripetal Forces in Personality Development." *American Journal of Psychoanalysis* 19 (1959): 123-32.

Kanzer, M. and Blum, H. P. "Classical Psychoanalysis Since 1939." In *Psychoanalytic Techniques,* edited by B. B. Wolman. New York: Basic Books, 1967.

Kardiner, A. "New Horizons and Responsibilities of Psychoanalysis." *American Journal of Psychoanalysis* 18 (1958): 115-6.

Karen Horney's Biography. In *Current Biography.* Volume 2. New York: H. W. Wilson Co., 1941.

Karen Horney Memorial Issue. *American Journal of Psychoanalysis* 14 (1954).

Karen Horney Seventy-fifth Anniversary Issue. "Alienation and the Search for Identity." *American Journal of Psychoanalysis* 21 (1961).

Karush, A. "Working Through." *Psychoanalytic Quarterly* 36 (1967): 497-531.

Kelman, H. "A New Approach to Dream Interpretation." *American Journal of Psychoanalysis* 4 (1944): 89-107.

—— "A Phenomenologic Approach to Dream Interpretation." *American Journal of Psychoanalysis* 25 (1965): 188-202, 27 (1967): 75-94.

—— "A Unitary Theory of Anxiety." *American Journal of Psychoanalysis* 16 (1956): 127-52.

—— "Character and the Traumatic Syndrome." *Journal of Nervous and Mental Disease* 102 (1945): 125-52.

—— "Communing and Relating." *American Journal of Psychoanalysis* 18 (1958): 77-98, 158-70, 19 (1959): 73-105, 188-215.

—— "Communing and Relating." *American Journal of Psychotherapy* 16 (1960): 70-96.

—— "Communing and Relating." Unpublished manuscript.

—— "Communion et la conscience — Témoin" [Communing as Witness Consciousness]. In *Roger Godel — De L'Humanisme à L'Humaine,* edited by S. Nacht. Paris: Les Belles-Lettres (Association Guillaume Budé), 1963.

—— "Creative Talent and Creative Passion as Therapy." *American Journal of Psychoanalysis* 22 (1963): 133-41.

—— "Diagnosing and Prognosing in Psychoanalysis." *American Journal of Psychoanalysis* 15 (1955): 49-70.

—— "Freer Associating: Its Phenomenology and Inherent Paradoxes." *American Journal of Psychoanalysis* 22 (1962): 176-200.

—— "How Does Psychoanalysis Fit into the Total Concept of Care?" Read before New York District Branch, Biannual Meeting, November 15, 1969.

—— "Indonesian Psychiatric Services." *Transcultural Psychiatric*

Report and Newsletter 5 (1968): 206-7.
—— "Indonesia: Some Psychiatric Impressions." *Indonesian Quarterly of Psychiatry* 1 (1969): 65-79.
—— "Intervention in Psychotherapy." A Round Table Discussion. *American Journal of Psychoanalysis* 22 (1962): 43-83.
—— "Kairos and the Therapeutic Process." *Journal of Existential Psychiatry* 1 (1960): 233-69.
—— "Kairos: The Auspicious Moment." *American Journal of Psychoanalysis* 29 (1969): 59-83.
—— " 'Kairos': The Auspicious Moment." Unpublished manuscript.
—— "Karen Horney." In *Major Contributors to Modern Psychotherapy*. Nutley, N.J.: Roche Laboratories, 1971.
—— "Life History as Therapy." *American Journal of Psychoanalysis* 16 (1956): 145-69.
—— "Masochism and Self-Realization." In *Science and Psychoanalysis*. Volume 2, edited by J. Masserman. New York: Grune & Stratton, 1959.
—— "Medical Problems in Psychoanalysis." *American Journal of Psychoanalysis* 9 (1949): 56-66.
—— "Neurotic Pessimism." *Psychoanalytic Review* 32 (1945): 419-48.
—— "Oriental Psychological Processes and Creativity." *American Journal of Psychoanalysis* 23 (1963): 67-84.
—— "Prognosis in Psychotherapy." *Samiksa* 12 (1958): 29-48; *Psychiatria, Neurologia, Neurochirurgia* 63 (1960): 81-92.
—— "Psychoanalysis and the Study of Etiology: A Definition of Terms." In *The Etiology of Neuroses*, edited by J. H. Merin. Palo Alto, California: Science and Behavior Books, 1966.
—— "Psychoanalysis in Cosmology." *Comprehensive Psychiatry* 9 (1968): 581-607.
—— "Psychoanalytic Education: A Twenty-five Year Experience." Unpublished manuscript.
—— "Psychoanalytic Thought and Eastern Wisdom." In *Science and Psychoanalysis*, Volume 3, edited by J. H. Masserman. New York: Grune & Stratton, 1960.
—— "Psychotherapy in the Far East." In *Progress in Psychotherapy*, Volume 4, edited by J. Masserman and J. C. Moreno. New York: Grune & Stratton, 1959.
—— "Techniques of Dream Interpretation." *American Journal of Psychoanalysis* 25 (1965): 3-20.
—— "Tension Is Not Stress." *Advances in Psychosomatic Medicine*, Volume 3. New York: Karger, Basel, 1963.
—— "The Changing Image of Psychoanalysis." *American Journal of Psychoanalysis* 26 (1966): 169-77.

—— "The Chronic Analyst." In *Science and Psychoanalysis,* Volume 16, edited by J. H. Masserman. New York: Grune & Stratton, 1970.

—— "The Clinical Tradition and Clinical Research." *Newsletter, American Academy of Psychoanalysis* 13 (1969): 1-3.

—— "The Doctor-Patient Relationship." A Round Table Discussion. *American Journal of Psychoanalysis* 15 (1955): 16-19.

—— "The Holistic Approach (Horney)." In *American Handbook of Psychiatry,* Volume 2, edited by S. Arieti. New York: Basic Books, 1959.

—— *The Process in Psychoanalysis.* New York: Postgratudate Center for Mental Health, 1969.

—— "The Psychopathic Process." Unpublished manuscript.

—— "The Role of Psychoanalysis in Psychiatry: Present and Future." *Bulletin of the New York State District Branches.* American Psychiatric Association 11 (1968): 1-3.

—— "The Therapy of Essential Hypertension." In *Modern Psychotherapeutic Practice,* edited by A. Burton. Palo Alto, California: Science and Behavior Books, 1965.

—— "The Traumatic Syndrome." *American Journal of Psychoanalysis* 6 (1946): 12-19.

—— "The Uses of the Analytic Couch." *American Journal of Psychoanalysis* 14 (1954): 65-82.

—— "Toward a Definition of Mind." In *Theories of the Mind,* edited by J. M. Scher. New York: The Free Press of Glencoe, 1962.

—— "Training Analysis: Past, Present and Future." *American Journal of Psychoanalysis* 22 (1963): 205-17.

—— "What Are Your Doubts About Analysis?" In *Are You Considering Psychoanalysis?,* edited by K. Horney. New York: W. W. Norton, 1946.

—— "Who Should Your Analyst Be?" In *Are You Considering Psychoanalysis?,* edited by K. Horney. New York: W. W. Norton, 1946.

—— "Women with Troubles." *Journal of Societal Issues* 2 (1969): 8.

Kelman, H., ed. *Advances in Psychoanalysis. Contributions to Karen Horney's Holistic Approach.* New York: W. W. Norton & Co., 1964.

—— *Feminine Psychology.* New York: W. W. Norton & Co., 1966.

—— *New Perspectives in Psychoanalysis. Contributions to Karen Horney's Holistic Approach.* New York: W. W. Norton & Co., 1965.

Kelman, H. and Field, H. "Psychosomatic Relationships in Pruriginous Lesions." *Journal of Nervous and Mental Disease* 88 (1938): 627-43.

Kelman, H. and Vollmerhausen, J. W. "On Horney's Psychoanalytic Techniques: Developments and Perspectives." In *Psychoanalytic Techniques*, edited by B. B. Wolman. New York: Basic Books, 1967.

Kelman, N. "Clinical Aspects of Externalized Living." *American Journal of Psychoanalysis* 12 (1952): 15-23.

Keniston, K. "Youth as a 'New' Stage of Life." *American Journal of Psychoanalysis* 31 (1971): 115-31.

Khan, M. M. R. "Vicissitudes of Being, Knowing, and Experiencing in the Therapeutic Situation." *British Journal of Medical Psychology* 42 (1969): 383-93.

Kielholz, A. *"Von Kairos — Zum Problem der Kurpfuscherei"* [Concerning *Kairos* and the Problem of Quackery]. *Schweizerische Medizinische Wochenschrift* 86 (1956): 982-94.

Kierkegaard, S. *The Diary of Soren Kierkegaard*. New York: Philosophical Library, 1960.

King, L. S. "Cecil-Loeb Textbook of Medicine." *Journal of the American Medical Association* 202 (1967): 151-2.

Knapp, P. H. "Image, Symbol and Person." *Archives of General Psychiatry* 21 (1969): 392-406.

Knapp, P. H., Levin, S., McCarter, R. H., Werner, H. and Zetzel, E. "Suitability for Psychoanalysis." *Psychoanalytic Quarterly* 29 (1961): 459-77.

Knight, R. P. "The Present Status of Organized Psychoanalysis in the United States." *Journal of the American Psychoanalytic Association* 1 (1953): 197-221.

Koestler, A. "Beyond Atomism and Holism — the Concept of the Holon." *Perspectives in Biology and Medicine* 13 (1970): 131-54.

Kondo, A. "Kairos Experience in Japanese Culture." In *Kairos: The Auspicious Moment*, edited by H. Kelman. Unpublished manuscript.

Kretschmer, E. *Physique and Character*. London: Kegan Paul, Trench, Trubner, 1925.

Krishnamurti, J. *The First and Last Freedom*. New York: Harper & Bros., 1954.

Kübler-Ross, E. *On Death and Dying*. New York: The Macmillan Co., 1969.

Kuhn, T. S. *The Structure of Scientific Revolutions*. Chicago: University of Chicago Press, 1964.

Lennard, H. L. and Bernstein, A. *The Anatomy of Psychotherapy*. New York: Columbia University Press, 1960.

Lewin, B. D. and Ross, H. *Psychoanalytic Education in the United States*. New York: W. W. Norton & Co., 1960.

Lidz, T. "Psychoanalytic Theories of Development and Maldevelopment: Some Reconceptualizations." *American Journal of Psychoanalysis* 17 (1967): 115-26.

Lifton, R. J. "On Spiritual Innovators: Erikson and Gandhi." *Psychiatry and Social Science Review* 4 (1970): 3-8.

—— "Protean Man." *Yale Alumni Magazine* 22 (1969): 14-21.

Little, M. "On Basic Unity." *International Journal of Psycho-Analysis* 41 (1960): 377-84.

—— "On Delusional Transference (Transference Psychosis)." *International Journal of Psycho-Analysis* 39 (1958): 105-9.

Lomas, P. "Passivity and Failure of Identity Development." *International Journal of Psycho-Analysis* 46 (1965): 438-54.

Lorand, S. and Console, W. A. "Therapeutic Results in Psychoanalytic Treatment Without Fee." *International Journal of Psycho-Analysis* 39 (1958): 59-64.

Manuel, F. E. *Shapes of Philosophical History.* Palo Alto, California: Stanford University Press, 1964.

Marmor, J. "Origins of the Institute." *W.A.W.* [William Alanson White] *Newsletter* 3 (1968): 6-7.

—— "The Pre-History and the Founding of the Comprehensive Course in Psychoanalysis." *Newsletter, Society of Medical Psychoanalysts* 5 (1964): 1-3.

Martin, A. R. "Idle Hands and Giddy Minds." *American Journal of Psychoanalysis* 29 (1969): 147-56.

—— "Psychoanalytic Contribution to the Study of Effort." *American Journal of Psychoanalysis* 10 (1944): 108-21.

—— "Reassurance in Therapy." *American Journal of Psychoanalysis* 9 (1949): 17-29.

—— "Self-Alienation and the Loss of Leisure." *American Journal of Psychoanalysis* 21 (1961): 156-65.

—— "The Body's Participation in Anxiety and Dilemma Phenomena." *American Journal of Psychoanalysis* 15 (1945): 28-48.

—— "The Dynamics of Insight." *American Journal of Psychoanalysis* 12 (1952): 24-38.

—— "The Fear of Relaxation and Leisure." *American Journal of Psychoanalysis* 11 (1951): 42-50.

—— "The Whole Patient in Therapy." In *Progress in Psychotherapy,* Volume 1, edited by F. Fromm-Reichmann and J. L. Moreno. New York: Grune & Stratton, 1956.

Maslow, A. "Fusions of Facts and Values." *American Journal of Psychoanalysis* 23 (1963): 117-31.

—— *Toward a Psychology of Being.* New York: D. Van Nostrand, 1962.

Masserman, J. H. "Anxiety Revisited." *American Journal of Psychoanalysis* 25 (1965): 115-28.

May, R. *Psychology and the Human Dilemma.* Princeton, New Jersey: D. Van Nostrand, 1967.

May, R., Angel, E. and Ellenberger, H. F. *Existence.* New York: Basic Books, 1958.

Mayr, E. "Cause and Effect in Biology." *Science* 134 (1961): 1501-6.

McAlpine, I. "The Development of Transference." *Psychoanalytic Quarterly* 19 (1950): 501-53.

Meissner, W. W. "Dreaming as Process." *International Journal of Psycho-Analysis* 49 (1968): 63-79.

Menninger, K. *Theory of Psychoanalytic Technique.* New York: Basic Books, 1958.

Metzgar, E. A. "Understanding the Patient As the Basis of All Technique." *American Journal of Psychoanalysis* 16 (1956): 26-31.

Middelman, F. "Linguistic Relativity in Psychotherapy." *Comprehensive Psychiatry* 10 (1969): 31-43.

Miller, N. E. "Learning of Visceral and Glandular Responses." *Science* 163 (1969): 434-45.

Mullahy, P. *Oedipus, Myth and Complex.* New York: Hermitage Press, 1948.

Munroe, R. L. *Schools of Psychoanalytic Thought.* New York: Dryden Press, 1955.

Natterson, J. M. "Karen Horney — The Cultural Emphasis." In *Psychoanalytic Pioneers,* edited by F. Alexander, S. Eisenstein, and M. Grotjahn. New York: Basic Books, 1966.

Needleman, J. trans. *Being-in-the-World. Selected Papers of Ludwig Binswanger.* New York: Basic Books, 1963.

Neki, J. S. *Ausar* [Kairos: And Its Place in Creative Psychotherapy]. In *Kairos: The Auspicious Moment,* edited by H. Kelman. Unpublished manuscript.

Newsletter. Society of Medical Psychoanalysts, Volume 9, Number 3 (September 1969).

Northrop, F. S. C. *The Logic of the Sciences and the Humanities.* New York: The Macmillan Co., 1949.

—— *The Meeting of East and West.* New York: The Macmillan Co., 1949.

Oberndorf, C. P. Obituary on Karen Horney. *International Journal of Psycho-Analysis* 34 (1953): 154-5.

Palazzoli, M. S. "Anorexia Nervosa." In *The World Biennial of Psychiatry and Psychotherapy,* Volume 1, edited by S. Arieti. New York: Basic Books, 1970.

Pappenheim, F. *The Alienation of Modern Man.* New York: Monthly Review Press, 1959.

Piaget, J. *Six Psychological Studies*. New York: Random House. 1968.

Pleune, F. G. "All Dis-Ease is Not Disease: A Consideration of Psycho-Analysis, Psychotherapy and Psycho-Social Engineering." *International Journal of Psycho-Analysis* 46 (1965): 358-66.

Pollock, G. H. "Historical Perspectives in the Selection of Candidates for Psychoanalytic Training." *Psychoanalytic Quarterly* 30 (1961): 481-96.

Portnoy, I. "Anxiety States." In *American Handbook of Psychiatry, Volume 1*, edited by S. Arieti. New York: Basic Books, 1959.

Ramo, S. *Cure for Chaos*. New York: David McKay, 1969; *Medical Opinion and Review* 5 (1969): 96-133 (September), 100-61 (October), 98-145 (November).

Rapaport, A. *Operational Philosophy*. New York: Harper & Bros., 1954.

—— "Psychoanalysis as Science." *Bulletin of the Menninger Clinic* 31 (1968): 1-20.

Rapaport, D. "The Structure of Psychoanalytic Theory: A Systematizing Attempt." *Psychological Issues* 2 (1960): 126.

Reuben, D. *Everything You Always Wanted to Know About Sex*. New York: David McKay, 1969.

Riese, W. "Phenomenology and Existentialism in Psychiatry: An Historical Analysis." *Journal of Nervous and Mental Disease* 132 (1961): 469-84.

Rioch, D. McK. "Recent Contributions of Neuropsychiatric Research to the Theory and Practice of Psychotherapy." *American Journal of Psychoanalysis* 20 (1960): 115-29.

Rioch, J. "Origins of the Institute." *W.A.W.* [William Alanson White] *Newsletter* 3 (1969): 3.

Roazen, P. *Brother Animal: The Story of Freud and Tausk*. New York: A. A. Knopf, 1969.

Rubins, J. L. "A Holistic (Horney) Approach to the Psychoses: The Schizophrenias." *American Journal of Psychoanalysis* 29 (1969): 131-46, 30 (1970): 30-50, 31 (1971): 136-51.

—— "On the Early Development of the Self: Its Role in Neuroses." *American Journal of Psychoanalysis* 22 (1962): 122-37.

—— "Sexual Perversions: Some Psychodynamic Considerations." *American Journal of Psychoanalysis* 29 (1969): 94-105.

Ruesch, J. "Declining Clinical Tradition." *Journal of the American Medical Association* 182 (1962): 110-5.

—— *Therapeutic Communication*. New York: W. W. Norton & Co., 1961.

Rümke, H. C. "Contradictions in the Concepts of Schizophrenia." *Comprehensive Psychiatry* 1 (1960): 331-7.

Sackett, W. W., Jr. "Death with Dignity." *Medical Opinion and* *Review* 5 (1969): 25-31.

Salzman, L. "Socio-Psychological Theories in Psychoanalysis." In *Science and Psychoanalysis,* Volume 7, edited by J. H. Masserman. New York: Grune & Stratton, 1964.

Sandifer, M. G., Hordern, A., and Green, M. "The Psychiatric Interview: The Impact of the First Three Minutes." *American Journal of Psychiatry* 126 (1970): 968-73; Pittinger, R. E., Hockett, C. F. and Danehy, J. J. *The First Five Minutes.* Ithaca, New York: Paul Martineau, 1960.

Schachtel, E. G. *Metamorphosis.* New York: Basic Books, 1959.

Schilder, P. F. *The Image and Appearance of the Human Body.* New York: International Universities Press, 1950.

Scott, J. P. "Critical Periods in Behavioral Development." *Science* 138 (1962): 949-58.

Scott, J. P. and Fuller, J. L. *Genetics and the Social Behavior of the Dog.* Chicago: University of Chicago Press, 1965.

Sheiner, S. "Free Association." *American Journal of Psychoanalysis* 27 (1967): 200-8.

—— "Investigation of a Learning Block in a Schizophrenic." *American Journal of Psychoanalysis* 30 (1969): 205-11.

—— "On the Therapy of Schizophrenia." *American Journal of Psychoanalysis* 24 (1964): 167-83.

—— "Schizophrenia." *American Journal of Psychoanalysis* 22 (1957): 110-4.

—— "The Communications of Psychotics." *American Journal of Psychoanalysis* 29 (1969): 11-16.

—— "The Importance of Emotional Experiences in the Analytic Process." *American Journal of Psychoanalysis* 26 (1966): 88-90.

—— "The Intensity of Casual Relationships in Schizophrenia." *American Journal of Psychoanalysis* 28 (1968): 156-61.

—— "The Psychoanalytic Approach to the Psychoses." *American Journal of Psychoanalysis* 26 (1956): 76-80.

Sherfey, M. J. "The Evolution and Nature of Female Sexuality in Relation to Psychoanalytic Theory." *Journal of the American Psychoanalytic Association* 14 (1966): 28-128.

Simpson, G. "Biology and the Nature of Science." *Science* 139 (1963): 81-8.

—— "Evolution's Two Components: Biological and Cultural." *Science* 136 (1962): 142-3.

Slater, R. "Aims of Psychoanalytic Therapy." *American Journal of Psychoanalysis* 16 (1956): 24-5.

—— "Evaluation of Change." *American Journal of Psychoanalysis* 20 (1960): 3-7.

—— "Interpretation." *American Journal of Psychoanalysis* 26 (1956): 118-24.

Sorokin, P. "The Factor of Creativity in Human History." *Main Currents in Modern Thought* 18 (1962): 99-104.

Spiegel, J. P. "Anatomy of Student Revolt." *Roche Report: Frontiers of Clinical Psychiatry* 7 (1970): 5-11.

Spitz, R. "Hospitalism." In *Psychoanalytic Study of the Child I.* New York: International Universities Press, 1945.

Stern, A. Review of *New Ways in Psychoanalysis. International Journal of Psycho-Analysis* 21 (1940): 360-3.

Stoller, R. J. *Sex and Gender.* New York: Science House, 1968.

Strachey, J. "Papers on Technique." *The Standard Edition of the Complete Psychological Works of Sigmund Freud,* Volume 12, edited by J. Strachey. London: Hogarth Press, 1958.

Strupp, H. "Psychoanalytic Therapy of the Individual." In *Modern Psychoanalysis,* edited by J. Marmor. New York: Basic Books, 1968.

Sullivan, H. S. "Conceptions of Modern Psychiatry." *Psychiatry* 111 (1940): 1-117.

—— *The Interpersonal Theory of Psychiatry.* New York: W. W. Norton & Co., 1953.

Suzuki, D. T. *The Zen Doctrine of No-Mind.* London: Rider & Co., 1949.

Tarachow, S. "Discussion." In *Current Approaches to Psychoanalysis,* edited by P. H. Hoch and J. Zubin. New York: Grune & Stratton, 1960.

—— "The Limitations of Technique." *Israel Annals of Psychiatry and Related Disciplines* 3 (1965): 197-212.

Tarachow, S. and Stein, A. "Psychoanalytic Psychotherapy." In *Psychoanalytic Techniques,* edited by B. B. Wolman. New York: Basic Books, 1967.

Tauber, E. S. and Green, M. R. *Prelogical Experience: An Inquiry into Dreams and Other Creative Processes.* New York: Basic Books, 1959.

Thompson, C. "History of the William Alanson White Institute of Psychiatry, Psychoanalysis and Psychology." *W.A.W.* [William Alanson White] *Newsletter* 3 (1968): 406.

—— *Interpersonal Psychoanalysis.* Edited by M. Green. New York: Basic Books, 1964.

Tillich, P. "Kairos." In *A Handbook of Christian Theology.* New York: Meridian Books, 1958.

—— Funeral Services for Karen Horney. Dec. 7, 1952. Unpublished.

—— "Toward a New Image of Man." *Main Currents in Modern Thought* 16 (1960): 114-6.

—— "What Is Basic in Human Nature?" *American Journal of Psychoanalysis* 22 (1962): 115-21.

Tolstoy, L. *The Death of Ivan Illych and Other Stories.* [First Printing.] New York: The New American Library, 1959.

Turner, V. W. *The Ritual Process, Structure and Anti-Structure.* Chicago: Aldine Publishing Co., 1969.

Tymieniecka, A. T. *Phenomenology and Science in Contemporary European Thought.* New York: Noonday Press, 1962.

Ullman, M. and Krippner, S. "An Experimental Approach to Dreams and Telepathy: II." *American Journal of Psychiatry* 126 (1970): 1282-9.

Van Bark, B. "What is Effective in the Therapeutic Process?" A Round Table Discussion. *American Journal of Psychoanalysis* 17 (1957): 3-33.

van der Post, L. *The Lost World of the Kalahari.* New York: Pyramid Books, 1966.

Van Leewen, K. "Pregnancy-Envy in the Male: Case History." *International Journal of Psycho-Analysis* 47 (1966): 319-24.

Vico, G. *Autobiography of Giambattista Vico.* Translated by M. H. Fisch and T. G. Bergen. Ithaca, New York: Cornell University Press, 1963.

von Bertalanffy, L. *Problems of Life.* New York: John Wiley and Sons, 1952.

von Weizäcker, X. F. *The Relevance of Science: Creation and Cosmogony.* New York: Harper & Row, 1964.

Waldhorn, H. F. "Assessment of Analyzability: Technical and Theoretical Observations." *Psychoanalytic Quarterly* 29 (1961): 478-506.

—— "The Silent Patient." Panel Report. *Journal of the American Psychoanalytic Association* 7 (1959): 548-60.

Watts, A. *The Wisdom of Insecurity.* New York: Pantheon Books, 1951.

Weigert, E. "Søren Kierkegaard's Mood Swings." *International Journal of Psycho-Analysis* 16 (1960): 521-5.

—— "The Function of Sympathy in the Psychotherapeutic Process." *American Journal of Psychoanalysis* 22 (1962): 3-14.

Weisman, A. D. "Misgivings and Misconceptions in the Psychiatric Care of Terminal Patients." *Psychiatry* 33 (1970): 67-81.

—— *The Existential Core of Psychoanalysis: Reality, Sense and Responsibility.* Boston: Little, Brown & Co., 1965.

—— "The Right Way to Die." *Psychiatry and Social Science Review* 2 (1968): 2-7.

Weiss, F. A. "Constructive Forces in Dreams." *American Journal of Psychoanalysis* 9 (1949): 30-7.

—— "Dreaming: A Creative Process." *American Journal of Psychoanalysis* 24 (1964): 17-27.

—— "Karen Horney — A Bibliography." *American Journal of Psychoanalysis* 14 (1954): 15-18.

—— "Karen Horney — Her Early Papers." *American Journal of Psychoanalysis* 14 (1954): 55-64.

—— "Some Aspects of Sex in Neuroses." *American Journal of Psychoanalysis* 10 (1950): 27-37.

Weiss, P. "Beauty and the Beast. Life and the Rule of Order." *Scientific Monthly* 81 (1955): 286-99.

Wenkart, A. "Creativity and Freedom." *American Journal of Psychoanalysis* 23 (1963): 195-201.

—— "Self-Acceptance." *American Journal of Psychoanalysis* 25 (1955): 135-43.

Werble, B. "Second Follow-Up Studies of Borderline Patients." *Archives of General Psychiatry* 23 (1970): 3-7.

Whitehorn, J. C. "The Scope of Motivation in Psychopathology and Psychotherapy." *American Journal of Psychoanalysis* 14 (1954): 30-9.

Whittaker, E., Sir. "Eddington's Principle in the Philosophy of Science." *American Scientist* 40 (1952): 46.

Whorf, B. L. *Language, Thought and Reality*. New York: Wiley & Sons, 1958.

Whyte, L. L. *Accent on Form*. New York: Harper & Bros., 1954.

—— *Aspects of Form*. Bloomington: Indiana University Press, 1961.

—— *The Next Development in Man*. New York: New American Library, 1950.

—— *The Unconscious Before Freud*. New York: Basic Books, 1960.

Whyte, L. L., Wilson, A. G., and Wilson, D. *Hierarchical Structures*. New York: American Elsevier Publishing Co., 1969.

Willig, W. "Dreams." *American Journal of Psychoanalysis* 28 (1958): 127-37.

Willner, G. "Duerckheim's Existential Philosophy." *American Journal of Psychoanalysis* 18 (1958): 38-51.

—— "The Role of Anxiety in Obsessive-Compulsive Disorders." *American Journal of Psychoanalysis* 27 (1968): 201-11.

—— "The Role of Anxiety in Schizophrenia." *American Journal of Psychoanalysis* 25 (1965): 171-80.

Wittkower, E. D. and Aufreiter, J. "Education in Psychosomatic Concepts." In *Science and Psychoanalysis*, Volume 5, edited by J. H. Masserman. New York: Grune & Stratton, 1962.

Wynne, L. C. "Variations Within and Between Families of Schizophrenics: Implications for Etiology and Treatment." *American Journal of Psychoanalysis* 30 (1970): 100-14.

Zelmanovits, J. Review of *The Collected Papers of David Rapaport*. *Psychiatry* 31 (1968): 292-99.

Zetzel, E. R. "The Theory of Therapy." *International Journal of Psycho-Analysis* 46 (1965): 39-45.

Zilboorg, G. "Male and Female." *Psychiatry* 7 (1944): 275-96.

Zimmerman, J. "Blockages in Therapy." *American Journal of Psychoanalysis* 16 (1956): 112-7.

Zuckmayer, C. *A Part of Myself.* New York: Harcourt Brace Jovanovich, 1970.

Index

Bunge, M., 456
Burnshaw, S., 192
Bychowski, G., 47

Camus, Albert, 47
Cassirer, E., 203
Chance factors, 406
Chicago Institute for Psychoanalysis, 9, 16
Childhood and Society, (Erikson), 429
Classical Psychoanalysis, (Kanzer and Blum), 42
Clinical Judgement, (Feinstein), 168, 353
Communion, 184, 186, 192, 199, 201
Communitas, 422
Compartmentalization, 280
Conflict, 121, 122, 409
  basic, 44
Countertransference, 39, 474, 475
"Creative reality", (Watts), 159
Creativity, in psychoanalysis, 454
Curative process in dreaming, (Bjerre), 274
Cynicism, 280, 282

Daniels, G., 540
Danielssen, Bernt Henrik Wackels, 1
Davis, J. M., 214
Death instinct, 35
Death of Ivan Ilyich, The, (Tolstoy), 444
Decathexis, 444, 445
Defensive mechanism, 212, 213
de Groot, Jeanne Lampl, 7
Delayed interpretations, 387
"Delusional Transference (Transference Psychosis)", (Little), 265
Descartes, René, 123
Deutsch, Helene, 7, 8
Diary of the Seducer, (Kierkegaard), 44
Diatrophic functions, 395, 399
Discontinuity, 381
Disillusioning process, 211, 270, 409
Doctor-patient relationship, 169
Doctrinal compliance, 106
Draper, G., 535
Dreams, 99, 258, 270, 433
  approach to, 246
  attitudes toward, 312-332
  crucial, 333-345
  curative process in, 274
  fear and anxiety, 287
  feeling in, 314
  recurrent, 316, 317
  symbols in, 335
  termination, 333-346
  writing of, 376
Dunbar, Flanders, 539
Duerckheim, 433

Eckardt, Marianne Horney, 33
Eckstein, R., 448, 449, 475
Ego, 36, 120
  analysis of, 37
Ego and the Mechanisms of Defense, The, (Anna Freud), 37, 129
Ego Psychology and the Problem of Adaptation, (Hartmann), 37, 129
Egocentricity, 50
Ehrenwald, J., 456
Eisenberg, L., 430
Elkind, D., 429
Elusiveness, 282
Emotions and Bodily Changes, (Dunbar), 539
Empirical self, 121
Encounter, 425
End of phase analysis, 414, 418
Engel, G. L., 534, 538, 540, 545, 546, 561
Environmental assets, 140
Ephron, Harmon S., 17, 18
Erikson, Erik, 56, 203, 211, 266, 381, 422, 428, 429, 431, 505
Etiology, 424
Existential neurosis, 425, 430
Existentialism, 201, 227, 421-446, 452
Externalization, 280, 282
"Externalized living", 47, 49

False reassurance, 171
Fantasies, 233, 251
Feelings, 379
  in dreams, 278
Fees, 359
Feinchel, O., 14, 39, 41, 448
Feinstein, A. R., 168, 353
Feminine Psychology, (Horney), 6, 9, 11, 28, 44, 70
Ferenczi, Sandor, 8, 179
Fleming, J., 229, 411, 412, 413, 474, 475, 476, 477, 491
Ford, D. H., 457
Formative tendency, 253
Free association, 101, 397, 408
French, T., 397, 539
Freud, Anna, 37, 129, 131, 176, 179, 206, 266, 463
Freud, Sigmund, 4, 6, 7, 8, 10, 13, 35, 37, 38, 39, 40, 41, 42, 52, 70, 81, 128, 130, 133, 134, 147, 155, 160, 211, 256, 287, 398, 411, 424, 447, 449, 451, 453, 461, 462, 474, 482
Freudian concept, 133
Fromm, Erich, 16, 18, 19, 27
Fromm-Reichman, Freida, 48, 136, 166, 187, 266, 385, 398

Gandhi, 422
Gandhi's Truth, (Erikson), 429

617

Gendlin, E., 398
Gergen, K. J., 56
Gershman, H., 55, 56, 93
Gesellschaft, 422-423
Gifford, S., 563
Gitelson, M., 179, 180, 182, 206
Glover, Edward, 6, 382
Glover, James, 6
Goals, 403
Goethe, Johann Wolfgang von, 397
Goldstein, K., 123, 125, 132, 177, 184, 287, 293, 455
Greenson, Ralph, 14, 175
Grendlin, E., 149
Grinker, R. R., 139, 430, 540, 563
Grotjahn, M., 183, 475
Growing pains, 410
Guilt feelings, 36
Gunderson, J. G., 563

Harrigel, E., 459
Hartmann, H., 129, 130, 131, 253, 265, 266, 399, 448
Heidegger, Martin, 423
Heraclitus, 123
Heuscher, J. S., 459
Hippocrates, 426
Holism, 36, 266
Holistic
  psychoanalysis, 38
  technique, defined, 458
  therapy, attitudes of, 151
Hollender, M. H., 411, 412, 414, 415, 416, 451, 454
Homosexuality, 56, 66
Horkheimer, Max, 22, 27
Horney, Heinrich Wilhelm Oscar, 3
Horney, Karen Clementine Theodore, 1
  on change, 504-505
  children of, 3
  divorce of, 25
  education of, 2
  friendships of, 16, 27
  marriage of, 3
  painting and, 26
  on sex, 421
Hostility, basic, 43
Hulbeck, C. R., 99
Husserl, E., 153, 423
Huxley, Aldous, 99, 427
Hypertension, 556, 559

Id, the, 207
"Idealized Image," (Horney), 44, 45, 111, 137, 139, 263, 409
Illuminators, 397, 402
"Image, Symbol and Person," (Knapp), 56

Independence, inner, 410
Infantile anxiety, 11
Insight, 386-401
"Inspired spontaneity," (Krishnamurti), 159
Insurance coverage, 359
International Training Committee, 15
Interpersonal Theory of Psychiatry, The, (Sullivan), 48
Interpretation, 386-401, 402
Intervention, 389, 391
Interview, initial, 347-374
Intrapsychic self, the, 48
Ivimey, Muriel, 32

Jewett, Stephen P., 18
Johnson, Alvin, 11
Jones, E., 7, 12, 15, 41
Jung, C. G., 256

Kahn, Masud, 183
Kairos, 355, 409, 424-430, 432, 436, 439, 443, 455, 459
Kant, Immanuel, 123, 153
Kanzer, M., 388, 389, 390, 399
Kardiner, Abram, 16, 17, 19, 21, 462
Karen Horney Clinic, 359, 469, 470, 478
Karush, A., 175, 228
Kelman, Sarah R., 17
Kielholz, A., 426
Kierkegaard, S., 12, 44, 423, 445, 446
Klee, Paul, 102
Klein, Melanie, 6, 328
Knapp, P. H., 56
Knight, R. P., 462
Koblentz, A. E., 108
Koestler, Arthur, 476
Krishnamurti, J., 152, 159, 160
Kübler-Ross, E., 444, 445
Kuhn, T. S., 123

Lao Tzu, 367
Lasswell, Harold, 27
Lebensneid, (Nietzsche), 44
Lennard, H. L., 477
Lewin, B. D., 467, 478, 490
Liabilities in the individual, 141, 142
Libido theory, 130, 133
Life form, 433
Lifton, Robert J., 381, 429, 430, 431
Liminality, 422
Little, M., 265, 266, 492
Lomas, 37, 138
Love and sex, 50

McAlpine, I., 181, 363, 395, 454
"Magic-mirror symbiosis," 56

618

343. Jones, E. *The Life and Work of Sigmund Freud,* Volume 1 and 2. New York: Basic Books, 1953, 244; 1955, 31, 32.
344. Freud, S. *On the History of the Psychoanalytic Movement.* London: Hogarth Press, 1957, 7-66.
345. Lewin, B. D. and Ross, H. *Psychoanalytic Education in the United States.* New York: W. W. Norton & Co., 1960, 146, 28.
346. Knight, R. P. "The Present Status of Organized Psychoanalysis in the United States." *Journal of the American Psychoanalytic Association* 1 (1953): 197-221.
347. Bird, B. "On Candidate Selection and Its Relation to Analysis." *International Journal of Psycho-Analysis* 49 (1968): 513-26.
348. Freud, A. "Difficulties in the Path of Psychoanalysis." Eighteenth Freud Anniversary Lecture, Hunter College, New York, April 16, 1968. International Universities Press, 1969.
349. Waldhorn, H. F. "Assessment of Analyzability: Technical and Theoretical Observations." *Psychoanalytic Quarterly* 29 (1961): 478-506.
350. Pollock, G. H. "Historical Perspectives in the Selection of Candidates for Psychoanalytic Training." *Psychoanalytic Quarterly* 30 (1961): 481-96.
351. Kelman, H. "Psychoanalytic Education: A Twenty-five Year Experience." Unpublished manuscript.
352. Blitzen, L. and Fleming, J. "What Is a Supervisory Analysis?" *Bulletin of the Menninger Clinic* 17 (1953): 117-29.
353. Grotjahn, M. "Problems and Techniques of Supervision." *Psychiatry* 18 (1955): 9-15.
354. Whyte, L. L. *The Unconscious Before Freud.* New York: Basic Books, 1960.
355. Lennard, H. L. and Bernstein, A. *The Anatomy of Psychotherapy,* New York: Columbia University Press, 1960.
356. Gittelson, M. Review of *Psychoanalytic Education in the United States. Psychoanalytic Quarterly* 29 (1960): 559-67.
357. Greenacre, P. "A Critical Digest of the Literature on Selection of Candidates for Psychoanalytic Training." *Psychoanalytic Quarterly* 30 (1961): 38-55.
358. Guttman, S. A. "Criteria for Analyzability." *Journal of the American Psychoanalytic Association* 8 (1960): 141-51.
359. Knapp, P. H., Levin, S., McCarter, R. H., Werner, H. and Zetzel, E. "Suitability for Psychoanalysis." *Psychoanalytic Quarterly* 29 (1961): 459-77.
360. Little, M. "On Delusional Transference (Transference Psychosis)." *International Journal of Psycho-Analysis* 39 (1958): 105.
361. Reuben, D. *Everything You Always Wanted to Know About Sex.* New York: David McKay, 1969.

362. Rümke, H. C. "Contradiction in the Concepts of Schizophrenia." *Comprehensive Psychiatry* 1 (1960): 331-7.
363. "Growing Old in America. The Unwanted Generation." *Time* 96 (1970): 43-8.
364. Werble, B. "Second Follow-up Studies of Borderline Patients." *Archives of General Psychiatry* 23 (1970); 3-7.
365. Kelman, H. "Medical Problems in Psychoanalysis." *American Journal of Psychoanalysis* 9 (1949): 56-66.
366. Kelman, H. "Women With Troubles." *Journal of Societal Issues* 2 (1969): 8-33.
367. Palazzoli, M. S. "Anorexia Nervosa." In *The World Biennial of Psychiatry and Psychotherapy,* Volume 1, edited by S. Arieti. New York: Basic Books, 1970, 201.
368. Engel, G. L. "The Psychoanalytic Approach to Psychoanalytic Medicine." In *Modern Psychoanalysis,* edited by J. Marmor. New York: Basic Books, 1968.
369. Draper, G., Dupertuis, C. W., and Caughey, J. L. *Human Constitution in Clinical Medicine.* New York: Paul B. Hoeber, 1944.
370. Engel, G. L. Review of *Psychosomatic Specificity. Science* 164 (1969): 689-90.
371. Wittkower, E. D. and Aufreiter, J. "Education in Psychosomatic Concepts." In *Science and Psychoanalysis,* Volume 5, edited by J. H. Masserman. New York: Grune & Stratton, 1962, 118-28.
372. Dunbar, F. *Emotions and Bodily Changes.* New York: Columbia University Press, 1935.
373. Kelman, H. and Field, H. "Psychosomatic Relationships in Pruriginous Lesions." *Journal of Nervous and Mental Disease* 88 (1938): 627-43.
374. Kelman, H. "Tension Is Not Stress." *Advances in Psychosomatic Medicine,* Volume 3. New York: Karger, Basel, 1963.
375. Binger, C. A. L., Ackerman, N. W., Cohen, A. E., Schroeder, H. A., and Steele, J. M. *Personality in Arterial Hypertension.* New York: The American Society for Research in Psychosomatic Problems, 1945.
376. Kelman, H. "The Therapy of Essential Hypertension." In *Modern Psychotherapeutic Practice,* edited by A. Burton, Palo Alto, California: Science and Behavior Books, 1965.
377. Gifford, S. and Gunderson, J. G. "Cushing's Disease as a Psychosomatic Disorder." *Perspectives in Biology and Medicine* 13 (1970): 169-221.
378. Downie, R. A. *Frazer and the Golden Bough.* London: Gollancz, 1970.

379. Downing, A. B. *Euthanasia and the Right to Die: The case for Voluntary Euthanasia.* New York: Humanities Press, 1970.
380. Sackett, W. W., Jr. "Death with Dignity." *Medical Opinion and Review,* Volume 4, (1969): 25-31.
381. Bruch, H. "Transformation of Oral Impulses in Eating Disorders." *Psychiatric Quarterly* 35 (1961): 458-81; Perceptual and Conceptual Disturbances in Anorexia Nervosa." *Psychosomatic Medicine* 24 (1962): 187.

Bibliography

Alexander, F. "Neurosis and Creativity," *American Journal of Psychoanalysis* 24 (1964): 116-30.
—— Review of *Neurotic Personality of Our Time. Psychoanalytic Quarterly* 7 (1937): 536-50.
—— Review of *Theory of Psychoanalytic Technique* by K. Menninger. *Science* 129 (1959): 1732-3.
Alexander, F. and French, T. *Fundamentals of Psychoanalysis.* New York: W. W. Norton & Co., 1948.
—— *Psychoanalytic Therapy.* New York: The Ronald Press, 1946.
Allen, F. H. "Horney's Conception of the Basic Conflict Applied to Child Psychiatry," *American Journal of Psychoanalysis* 16 (1956): 99-111.
Angyal, A. *Foundations for a Science of Personality.* New York: Commonwealth Fund, 1941.
—— *Neurosis and Treatment: A Holistic Theory.* New York: John Wiley & Sons, 1965.
Apfelbaum, B. "Ego Psychology: Critique of the Structural Approach to Psychoanalytic Theory." *International Journal of Psycho-Analysis* 47 (1966): 451-75.
Appel, K. E. "Principles and Practice of Psychotherapy," *American Journal of Psychoanalysis* 15 (1955): 99-106.
Applegarth, A. Review of *Feminine Psychology* by K. Horney, edited by H. Kelman. *Archives of General Psychiatry* 18 (1968): 124-5.
Arasteh, A. R. "Greek *Kairos* and Persian *An* (The Climax of